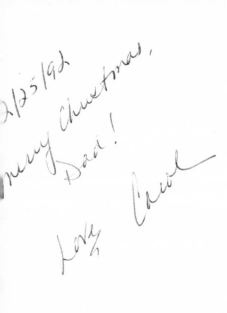

2/25/92
Merry Christmas,
Dad !

Love, Carol

THE CUBAN MISSILE CRISIS, 1962

The Cuban Missile Crisis, 1962

NATIONAL SECURITY ARCHIVE
DOCUMENTS READER

EDITED BY
LAURENCE CHANG
AND
PETER KORNBLUH

THE NEW PRESS, NEW YORK 1992

Buildup in Cuba" (DOCUMENT 12) appears under the heading "National Security Action Memorandum No. 181" (DOCUMENT 13), on pages 63–65. "National Security Action Memorandum No. 181" appears under the heading "The Military Buildup in Cuba," on pages 61–62.

PUBLISHED IN THE UNITED STATES BY THE NEW PRESS, NEW YORK
DISTRIBUTED BY W.W. NORTON AND COMPANY INC.
500 FIFITH AVENUE, NEW YORK, NY 10110

LIBRARY OF CONGRESS CATALOGING-IN-PUBLICATION DATA

Cuban Missile Crisis, 1962 : a documents reader /
editors, Laurence Chang, Peter Kornbluh.
p.   cm.
Includes bibliographical references.
ISBN 1-56584-019-4 : $25.00. — ISBN 1-56584-044-5 (pbk.)
1. Cuban Missile Crisis, 1962—Sources.   I. Chang, Laurence.   II. Kornbluh, Peter.
E841.C845   1992
973.922—dc20   92-53734
                                                              CIP

First Edition

ESTABLISHED IN 1990 AS A MAJOR ALTERNATIVE TO THE LARGE, COMMERCIAL PUB-
LISHING HOUSES, THE NEW PRESS IS INTENDED TO BE THE FIRST FULL-SCALE
NONPROFIT AMERICAN BOOK PUBLISHER OUTSIDE OF THE UNIVERSITY PRESSES.
THE PRESS IS OPERATED EDITORIALLY IN THE PUBLIC INTEREST, RATHER THAN
FOR PRIVATE GAIN; IT IS COMMITTED TO PUBLISHING IN INNOVATIVE WAYS WORKS
OF EDUCATIONAL, CULTURAL, AND COMMUNITY VALUE, WHICH, DESPITE THEIR
INTELLECTUAL MERITS, MIGHT NOT NORMALLY BE "COMMERCIALLY VIABLE."

ACKNOWLEDGEMENTS

This book evolved from a six-year project by the National Security Archive to obtain, organize, and disseminate the declassified records of the Cuban missile crisis of 1962. Success required an enormous research effort, a labor-intensive series of systematic Freedom of Information Act (FOIA) requests, a lawsuit against the State Department, and the cooperation of literally dozens of individuals and organizations.

The Cuban missile crisis project owes its genesis to the prodigious energy and creativity of journalist Scott Armstrong, who founded the Archive in 1985 and served as its first Executive Director, until 1989. Armstrong's long-standing interest in the crisis led him to file FOIA requests on the subject as early as 1982, when he worked at the *Washington Post*; he continues to serve as a major advocate for openness in government in general and on the missile crisis in particular.

A number of Archive staffmembers deserve special credit for turning the idea of the project into reality. Archive senior analyst Peter Kornbluh performed much of the early investigative work to identify pertinent government files. He located the vital mini-archive of documents at the State Department, and drafted the first series of Freedom of Information Act requests for those documents. Analysts Laurence Chang and Donna Rich followed up the FOIA requests with appeals and further requests, while compiling a comprehensive chronology, glossary, and bibliography on the missile crisis. After Ms. Rich's departure for graduate school at the Johns Hopkins University School of Advanced International Studies, Mr. Chang edited the collection for publication on microfiche, and wrote the final versions of the reference materials that have been adapted for this reader.

To produce this book, the editors drew on the talents of a gifted Archive staff. Lynda Davis tracked the FOIA requests and provided invaluable editorial assistance, as did Mary Burroughs with her transcriptions of the more lengthy and less legible documents. Director of Analysis Malcolm Byrne offered extraordinary copyediting and proofreading skills. David Wallace's knowledge of computers saved the editors hours of lost work. Various interns also volunteered their time and energy; in particular, Brian Lowinger proved indispensible in organizing and preparing the documents for publication, along with Karin Edlund who provided an irreplaceable and meticulous service in helping to copyedit and finalize the manuscript.

The documents reproduced in this book could not have been obtained without the legal talents of Archive general counsel Sheryl Walter, who coordinated a successful Freedom of Information Act lawsuit against the State Department. Originally drafted and filed by former Archive counsel David Sobel, the suit was litigated by the pro bono legal team from the Washington, D.C., law firm of Crowell and Moring.

We would like to thank Lead counsel Stuart Newberger who set a high standard for pro bono performance, with able assistance from associates Melissa McKenney, Robert Deyling, Michael Hodge, and Allison Barr, and much encouragement from Philip Fleming.

Professor Philip Brenner of American University, a Cuban scholar and member of the Archive advisory board, graciously served as pro bono plaintiff in the FOIA lawsuit, provided the Archive with expert analysis and advice on the development of the collection, and took an initiative with Soviet officials that significantly contributed to the eventual release of the Kennedy-Khrushchev letters.

James Blight, David Welch, Bruce Allyn, Janet Lang, David Lewis, and their colleagues at Harvard's

Center for Science and International Affairs and Brown University's Center for Foreign Policy Development deserve special thanks for their pioneering scholarship, as well as their conference-organizing skills. They immediately grasped the value of the Archive's declassified documentation for their "critical oral history" project, and welcomed the Archive's participation in a five-year series of extraordinary conferences on the missile crisis that began in Hawks Cay, Florida, in 1987 and finished in Havana, Cuba, in 1992. These conferences produced a wealth of information and also led to the release of several important documents in Cuba. David Lewis deserves additional thanks for the translations of several of the documents in this book.

Through this project and additional outreach, the Archive recruited a superlative editorial board for the missile crisis document collection, including a number of eminent scholars as well as members of President Kennedy's ExComm (Executive Committee of the National Security Council). Members of the editorial board are Graham Allison, George Ball, Barton J. Bernstein, James Blight, Philip Brenner, C. Douglas Dillon, Raymond Garthoff, Richard Ned Lebow, Robert S. McNamara, Theodore C. Sorensen, Arthur Schlesinger, Jr., and William Taubman. Ambassador Garthoff in particular provided detailed advice and guidance for the Archive's efforts; and Mr. McNamara graciously contributed the Foreword to this volume.

The Archive also thanks the John F. Kennedy Presidential library and national security librarian Suzanne Forbes for years of guidance and assistance on the missile crisis project.

Generous special project funding to support Archive staff participation in the Moscow and Havana conferences, as well as the intensive Freedom of Information Act work involved, came from the Arca Foundation, headed by Smith Bagley and ably directed by Margery Tabankin and Janet Shenk. Sustaining grants for this work came from the Archive's general support funding from the Ford Foundation, the Carnegie Corporation of New York, and the John D. and Catherine T. MacArthur Foundation, for which Gary Sick, Frederic A. Mosher, and Ruth Adams, respectively, were responsible. The W. Alton Jones Foundation and then–Program Officer Jane Wales also generously supported the Archive's efforts to document nuclear weapons policy, including the Cuban missile crisis. The J. Roderick MacArthur Foundation and its president, Lance Lindblom, supported the Archive's Freedom of Information Litigation Project over the many years necessary to win the FOIA lawsuit for these documents.

The National Security Archive's Malcolm Byrne led the effort to produce prototypes of documents readers such as this one. Peter Kornbluh made the contacts, at W. W. Norton and then at The New Press, that ultimately led to the publication of the first in a series of documents readers. André Schiffrin and his expert staff at The New Press have been the most congenial of colleagues in this effort; as not-for-profit publishers they are kindred spirits indeed. We thank Ted Byfield for applying his vast copyediting talents to these pages, and Charles Nix for the design. And Editor extraordinaire David Sternbach deserves special notice for his patient work on this volume; we look forward to many more to come.

Thomas S. Blanton
Executive Director
The National Security Archive

CONTENTS

FOREWORD

The actions of the Soviet Union, Cuba, and the United States in October 1962 brought these nations to the verge of military conflict and the world to the brink of nuclear disaster. None of these nations intended, by its actions, to create such risks. In order to understand what caused the crisis and how to avoid such events in the future, some of the actors involved in it have met together in a series of conferences, of which the meeting in Havana, Cuba, in January 1992, was the fifth.°

By the conclusion of the third meeting, in Moscow in January 1989, it had become clear that the decisions of each of the three nations, immediately before and during the crisis, had been distorted by misinformation, miscalculation, and misjudgment. I shall cite only four of many examples:

First: Before Soviet missiles were introduced into Cuba in the summer of 1962, the Soviet Union and Cuba believed the United States intended to invade the island in order to overthrow President Castro and remove his government. As I shall discuss more fully, we had no such intention.

Second: The United States believed the Soviets would not move nuclear warheads outside the Soviet Union—they never had—but in fact they did. In Moscow, we were told that by October 24, 1962, twenty Soviet nuclear warheads had been delivered to Cuba, and that their missiles were to be targeted on cities in the United States.

Third: The Soviets believed the missiles could be introduced into Cuba secretly, without detection, and that when their presence was disclosed, the United States would not respond. Here, too, they were in error.

Fourth: Those who urged President Kennedy to destroy the missiles by a U.S. air attack, which in all likelihood would have been followed by a sea and land invasion, were almost certainly mistaken in their belief that the Soviets would not respond with military action. At the time, the CIA had reported 10,000 Soviet troops in Cuba. At the Moscow conference, participants were told there were in fact 43,000 along with 270,000 well-armed Cuban troops. Both forces, in the words of their commanders, were determined to "fight to the death." The Cuban officials estimated they would have suffered 100,000 casualties. The Soviets expressed disbelief that we would have thought that, in the face of such a catastrophic defeat, they would not have responded militarily somewhere in the world. The result would very probably have been uncontrollable escalation.

By the end of our meeting in Moscow, I believe we had agreed we could draw two major lessons from our discussions: First, that in this age of high-technology weapons, crisis management is dangerous, difficult, and uncertain. Due to the misjudgment, misinformation, and miscalculation of the kind I have referred to, it is not possible to predict with confidence the consequences of military action between the Great Powers and their allies.

Second, therefore, we must direct our attention to crisis avoidance. At a minimum, crisis avoidance will require that potential adversaries take great care to try to understand how their actions will be interpreted by the other party. In this respect, we all performed poorly during the missile crisis. Let me illustrate my point

---

°The process of reconstructing the events of October 1962 was supported by the participation of the National Security Archive, a public-interest research library. The Archive provided documentation—including classified documents obtained through the Freedom of Information Act—as well as a comprehensive chronology of events. Many of those documents, as well as an abridged version of the chronology, are presented in this reader, making this information available to the general public for the first time.

by referring to an exchange at the opening of the Moscow meeting.

Gorbachev's aide, Georgi Shaknazarov, was the chair. He asked me, as one of the U.S. participants present who had been a member of President Kennedy's Executive Committee during the crisis, to ask the first question. I said: "My question is a very obvious one from our point of view: What was the purpose of the deployment of the nuclear-tipped missiles into Cuba by the Soviet Union?"

Shaknazarov asked, "Who wants to answer?"

Andrei Gromyko, the Soviet foreign minister in 1962, responded, "I can answer that question with a few words. Their action was intended to strengthen the defensive stability of Cuba. To avert the threats against it. I repeat, to strengthen the defensive capability of Cuba. That is all."

I then replied, "Mr. Chairman, that leads me to make two comments. My first comment is stimulated by the implication of Mr. Gromyko's answer—the implication being that the U.S. intended, prior to the emplacement of missiles, to invade Cuba. I want to make two points with respect to that implication. The first is that if I had been a Cuban, I think I might have thought that. I want to be very frank in saying that. One of the most important lessons of this event is that we must look at ourselves from the point of view of others. And I want to state quite frankly with hindsight, if I had been a Cuban leader, I think I might have expected a U.S. invasion. We had authorized the Bay of Pigs invasion…We did not support it militarily—and I think this should be recognized and emphasized, as it was specifically the decision of President Kennedy not to support the operation with the use of U.S. military force—but in any event, we had assisted in carrying it out. And after the debacle, there were many voices in the United States that said the error was not in approving the Bay of Pigs operation but in the failure to support it with military force, the implication being that at some point in the future, force would be applied. Secondly, there were U.S. covert operations extending over a long period of time. The

Cubans knew that. My recollection is that the operations began in the late 1950s and extended into the period we're discussing, the summer and fall of 1962. And thirdly, there were important voices in the United States—important leaders of our Senate, important leaders of our House—who were calling for the invasion of Cuba. So I state quite frankly again that if I had been a Cuban leader at that time, I might well have concluded that there was a great risk of U.S. invasion. And I should say, as well, if I had been a Soviet leader at the time, I might have come to the same conclusion.

"The second point I want to make—and I think it shows the degree of misperception that can exist and can influence both parties to a dispute—is that I can state unequivocally we had absolutely no intention of invading Cuba. No, I don't want to suggest there were not contingency plans; all of you—certainly our Cuban friends and our Soviet friends—are familiar with contingency plans. All of our militaries—Soviet, Cuban, and the U.S.—have contingency plans covering a wide range of contingencies. Obviously, there were contingency plans. But I state again, we had absolutely no intention of invading Cuba, and therefore the Soviet action to install missiles with that as its objective was, I think, based on a misconception—a clearly understandable one, and one that we, in part were responsible for. I accept that."

Some of us believed that the United States faced great danger during the missile crisis. During the Havana conference, though, we learned that we had greatly underestimated that danger.

While in Havana, we were told by the Russians that the Soviet forces in Cuba in October 1962—numbering forty-two thousand men instead of the ten thousand reported by the CIA—possessed thirty-six nuclear warheads for the twenty-four intermediate-range missiles that were capable of striking in the United States. At the time, the CIA had stated they did not believe there were any nuclear warheads on the island. We were also told that there were six dual-purpose tactical launchers—designated "Luna launchers" by the Soviets, we called them "FROGs"—supported by nine tactical missiles with nuclear warheads to be used against a U.S. invasion force. We were further informed that the authority to use those nuclear warheads had been delegated to the Soviet field commanders in Cuba—in other words, that no further authorization from Moscow was needed.

We need not speculate about what would have happened had a U.S. attack been launched, as many in the U.S. government—military and civilian alike—were recommending to the president on October 27 and 28. We can predict the results with certainty.

Although the U.S. forces would not have been accompanied by tactical nuclear warheads, no one should believe that had U.S. troops been attacked with tactical nuclear warheads, the United States would have refrained from responding with nuclear warheads. And where would it have ended? In utter disaster.

Human beings are fallible. We all make mistakes. The record of the missile crisis is replete with examples of misinformation, misjudgment, miscalculation. Such errors are costly in conventional war. When they affect decisions relating to nuclear forces, they can result in the destruction of nations. Surely this must lead to the conclusion that drastic reductions are required in nuclear forces—which now total over fifty thousand warheads—across the globe.

Robert S. McNamara

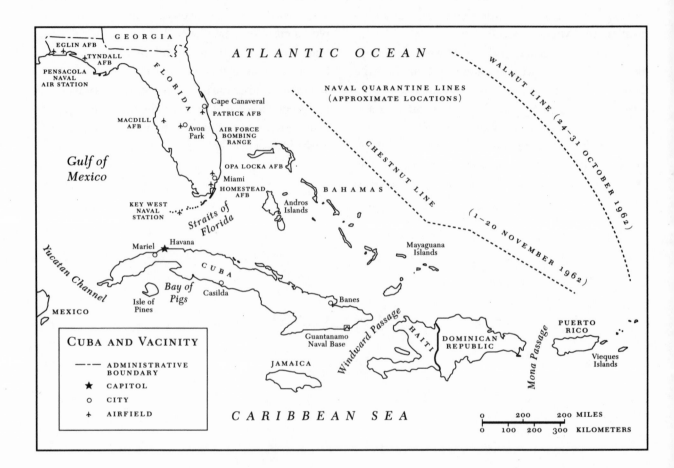

ATLANTIC OCEAN

GEORGIA

EGLIN AFB
TYNDALL AFB
PENSACOLA
NAVAL
AIR STATION

FLORIDA

Cape Canaveral
PATRICK AFB

MACDILL
AFB

Avon
Park

AIR FORCE
BOMBING
RANGE

Gulf of
Mexico

OPA LOCKA AFB

Miami
HOMESTEAD
AFB

KEY WEST
NAVAL
STATION

Straits of
Florida

NAVAL QUARANTINE LINES
(APPROXIMATE LOCATIONS)

WALNUT LINE (24–31 OCTOBER 1962)

CHESTNUT LINE

BAHAMAS

Andros
Islands

Mayaguana
Islands

(1–20 NOVEMBER 1962)

Yucatan Channel

Mariel
Havana

CUBA

Isle of
Pines

Bay of
Pigs

Casilda

Banes

MEXICO

Guantanamo
Naval Base

Windward Passage

HAITI

DOMINICAN
REPUBLIC

PUERTO
RICO

Vieques
Islands

Mona Passage

JAMAICA

CARIBBEAN SEA

CUBA AND VACINITY

–·–· ADMINISTRATIVE
BOUNDARY

★ CAPITOL

○ CITY

✈ AIRFIELD

0   200   200 MILES
0 100 200 300 KILOMETERS

INTRODUCTION

At midday, and again in the early evening of October 16, 1962, John F. Kennedy called together a group of his closest advisers at the White House. Late the night before, the CIA had produced detailed photo intelligence identifying Soviet nuclear missile installations under construction on the island of Cuba, some ninety miles off the Florida coast; now the president and his men confronted the dangerous decision of how the United States should respond.

Secretary of Defense Robert McNamara outlined three possible courses of action for the president: "the political course of action" of openly approaching Castro, Khrushchev, and U.S. allies in a gambit to resolve the crisis diplomatically, an option that McNamara and others considered unlikely to succeed; "a course of action that would involve declaration of open surveillance" coupled with "a blockade against offensive weapons entering Cuba"; and "military action directed against Cuba, starting with an air attack against the missiles." Much of the conversation that day centered on the military option and the hazardous unknowns of Soviet retaliation, including the possibility of nuclear escalation. "I don't believe we have considered the consequences," McNamara told the president. "I don't know quite what kind of a world we live in after we've struck Cuba, and we, we've started it.... How, how do we stop at that point?"[1]

Thankfully, the Kennedy administration never had to answer that extraordinary question. Ultimately, President Kennedy chose to initiate a naval blockade against Soviet ships carrying missile equipment. His strategy proved successful; the Soviets withdrew the missiles and nuclear war was averted.

Three decades later, however, Soviets, Cubans, and Americans learned how close the world had come to a nuclear conflagration. At a unique conference held in Havana, Cuba, in January 1992—attended by former Kennedy administration members, Soviet participants in the crisis, and a Cuban delegation led by President Fidel Castro—Soviet General Anatoly Gribkov informed participants that, in addition to their intermediate-range ballistic missiles, the Soviets had deployed nine tactical missiles in Cuba to be used against any U.S. invasion force. Even more significant, General Gribkov stated that Soviet field commanders in Cuba had the authority to fire those tactical nuclear weapons without further direction from the Kremlin![2]

What might have happened had the United States invaded Cuba, as some advisers had recommended to President Kennedy throughout the missile crisis? "We can predict the results with certainty," former secretary of defense McNamara answers in his Foreword to this book: "no one should believe that had United States troops been attacked with tactical nuclear warheads, the United States would have refrained from responding with nuclear warheads. And where would it have ended? In utter disaster."

LEARNING ABOUT THE MISSILE CRISIS

Thirty years after the respective actions of the United States, the Soviet Union, and Cuba brought the world to the brink of the unthinkable, new and important information about the Cuban missile crisis continues to emerge. No event during the Cold War has generated more popular and scholarly attention; indeed, with hundreds of articles, books, and essays already written on this episode, it has become perhaps the most studied international confrontation of the twentieth century. And so it should be, for the missile crisis represents the one time that world leaders and the international community stared down what Kennedy speechwriter Theodore Sorensen called "the gun barrel of nuclear war," the death of history as we know it. Despite the end of the Cold War, the process of exploration and discovery remains necessary to understand more fully what caused this crisis and, more important, to learn how to avoid such potentially cataclysmic events in the future. "Having come so close to the edge," observes Kennedy's national security adviser, McGeorge Bundy, "we must make it our business not to pass this way again."[3]

Toward that goal, the National Security Archive began a concerted campaign in 1987 to advance the historical record on the missile crisis. The objective was to build a major collection of declassified U.S. government documents, through the systematic use of the Freedom of Information Act (FOIA), and to make them available to scholars, students, journalists, and concerned citizens in order to enhance the public discussion over what actually happened in 1962 and why. In the early 1970s, many key internal documents had been made public at the John F. Kennedy Presidential Library. But thousands of other secret documents remained beyond the access of the public at large. Despite the passage of time, the U.S. government refused to declassify these documents, citing reasons of national security.

In the aftermath of the missile crisis, the papers from all the national security agencies involved were scattered throughout the executive branch. Some important records, for example, were found in a shopping cart in the basement of the State Department. Other documents, however, were gathered together and centralized. Researchers at the National Security Archive discovered, through interviews with former U.S. officials, that in 1965 the Johnson administration had retrieved some seventy-five files from various agencies and stored them in Room 7512 on the seventh floor of the State Department. This mini-archive of approximately three thousand records, totalling ten thousand pages in all, included contingency plans, military scenarios, minutes of Kennedy's Executive Committee, intelligence reports, analyses, chronologies, cables, and a wide variety of other highly sensitive State Department, Defense Department, National Security Council, and Central Intelligence Agency documents on the missile crisis.

In April 1987, the National Security Archive filed a series of FOIA requests for these files.[4] When the State Department proved unresponsive, the Archive filed a FOIA lawsuit nine months later seeking to compel the release of all requested documents. Pursuant to that suit, by mid 1989 the State Department had declassified two thousand documents in full or in part. These documents, supplemented by hundreds of additional declassified records obtained through other FOIA requests by Archive analysts and other scholars of the missile crisis, or from presidential and military libraries, were published in the National Security Archive's microfiche documents collection, *The Cuban Missile Crisis, 1962: The Making of U.S. Policy*. Since the publication of that collection in 1990, the Archive has continued to pursue and obtain the declassification of hundreds of important State, Defense, CIA, and NSC documents relating to the Cuban missile crisis.

REVISING THE HISTORY OF THE CRISIS

The availability of previously classified material has enabled scholars both to challenge the conventional wisdom and to revise long-standing historical interpretations of the events that took place before, during, and after October 1962. Despite the wealth of books and articles published on this subject, until only a few years ago the historiography of the crisis was built around the memoirs of former Kennedy administration officials, in particular Robert Kennedy's *Thirteen Days: A Memoir of the Cuban Missile Crisis*. Similarly, scholarly works on the crisis were dominated by Graham Allison's seminal book, *Essence of Decision*, which drew heavily on the official memoirs to cast the episode as the "classic" model of crisis management.

The declassified U.S. records have allowed scholars to highlight the inevitable distortions, limitations, and inaccuracies in the narratives of former Kennedy administration officials, and to augment and supplement these officials' memories. The most striking example of this dynamic occurred between 1987 and 1992, during a series of retrospective conferences sponsored by Harvard and Brown universities and organized by professor James G. Blight, which brought together former policymakers and scholars from the United States, the Soviet Union, and Cuba to reconstruct the perilous events of 1962 and to reevaluate why they happened.[5] Applying a research technique that he calls "critical oral history," Blight used the documents to supply facts and details that the former policymakers had distorted or forgotten while the participants supplied the missing context of the documents.[6] The result was a new body of information that provides a much fuller picture of events and fundamentally alters how the scope and meaning of the missile crisis has been and will be considered.

The very definition of the missile crisis has changed. Rather than a sudden episode, the crisis now emerges as the culmination of deteriorating relations between the United States and the Soviet Union, and between the United States and Cuba. Moreover, no longer can the confrontation be understood as confined to Robert Kennedy's "thirteen days," beginning with the discovery of Soviet missiles in Cuba on October 16 and ending with Khrushchev's decision to withdraw the missiles on October 28. A series of letters between Kennedy and Khrushchev, declassified and released to the National Security Archive in January 1992, demonstrates that the crisis lasted through late November of 1962, at the very least.

New revelations about the missile crisis have also undermined its image as a paradigm of successful crisis management. For years Arthur Schlesinger, Jr.'s description of President Kennedy's decision-making as "so brilliantly controlled, so matchlessly calibrated" reflected a mythology that the successful outcome of the missile crisis derived from Kennedy's masterful management of both the making and implementation of U.S. policy.[7] In reality, as Robert McNamara notes, the decision-making process in Washington, as well as in Moscow and Havana, was characterized by "misin-formation, miscalculation, and misjudgment." Despite management efforts, according to Theodore Sorensen, the crisis "came close to spinning out of control before it was ended."[8]

For example, during the crisis, U.S. officials mistook a number of Soviet political and military actions as deliberate "signals" from the Kremlin when, in fact, they had not been cleared by Khrushchev. Unbeknownst to the White House, officials of the CIA and the U.S. military undertook, in the midst of tense negotiations, a number of threatening operations—among them the dispatch of covert sabotage teams into Cuba—which were similarly misunderstood by the Soviets and Cubans. There were also dangerous accidents, such as the straying of a U.S. aircraft into Soviet airspace at the height of the crisis. This combination of unauthorized military and covert actions, misinterpreted military and political signals, and significant failures in intelligence—all of which threatened to set a war in motion—not only challenges earlier depictions of this event as a model of a "controlled crisis" but calls into question the fundamental assumption that severe international crises can, in fact, be "managed" at all.

The new documentation, combined with recent testimony by Soviet and Cuban officials, also sheds light on what is perhaps the most important puzzle of the missile crisis, namely, what motivated the Soviets to deploy nuclear weapons in Cuba. The declassified record shows that U.S. officials were well aware that their deployment of Jupiter missiles near Soviet borders in Turkey and Italy in 1959 would be deeply resented by Soviet officials; even President Eisenhower noted that it would be a "provocative" step analogous to the deployment of Soviet missiles in "Mexico or Cuba."[9] A declassified military history of the Jupiter system reveals that the rockets became operational in April 1962—an event that may have contributed to Khrushchev's proposal, made the very same month, to deploy similar weapons in Cuba.[10]

In addition, the documents lend credence to Khrushchev's claim that a primary Soviet motivation was the defense of Cuba against a U.S. invasion. For years, U.S. analysts have dismissed this as a face-saving, after-the-fact rationale that enabled the Soviets to declare victory in the confrontation rather than admit defeat. But formerly top-secret documents, released to the National Security Archive in January 1989, provide a detailed description of a 1962 U.S. covert action program known as OPERATION MONGOOSE, which combined sabotage, infiltration, and psychological warfare activities with military exercises and contingency operations for a possible invasion to overthrow the Castro government. Guidelines for OPERATION MONGOOSE, tacitly approved by President Kennedy in March 1962, noted that the "final success" of the program would "require decisive U.S. military intervention." Although Kennedy never formally authorized an invasion, former administration officials acknowledge that Cuban intelligence had infiltrated the CIA's exile groups and learned of plans for a potential invasion—which, ironically, was scheduled for October 1962.

If the new documents illuminate how the crisis began, they also clarify how it ended. For years, conservative analysts have alleged that, in return for the Soviet withdrawal of the missiles, Kennedy made a secret deal with Khrushchev not to invade Cuba. The recently declassified Kennedy-Khrushchev correspondence, published here, reveals that no such U.S. commitment was made. Khrushchev repeatedly urged Kennedy to "formalize through the U.N." a noninvasion pledge to end the crisis. The letters show Kennedy repeatedly refused, citing the Soviets' inability to meet U.S. inspection and verification demands. Highly classified State Department memoranda, released in April 1992 to the National Security Archive, reveal the Kennedy administration's internal arguments against finalizing an agreement on the crisis: a settlement would limit the United States in its ongoing efforts to overthrow Fidel Castro. In the end, U.S. officials preferred free rein to intervene in Cuba over an international accord that would settle the Cuban missile crisis.

USING THIS DOCUMENTS READER

This book is an effort to tell the story of the Cuban missile crisis through a selection from the many documents that were generated by these extraordinary events. Not every interested person has the time or resources to sift through the vast quantity of secondary and primary materials available; this book is designed, then, to provide access to some of the most important declassified documentation, thereby permitting the broader public to explore, understand, and discuss this critical episode. Those who want to study the crisis further are urged to consult the comprehensive bibliography included in this volume, and to make use of the National Security Archive's holdings of over four thousand documents, totalling some eighteen thousand pages.

The records in this documents reader are drawn from the Archive's indexed microfiche collection, *The Cuban Missile Crisis, 1962: The Making of U.S. Policy*, and from hundreds of other documents subsequently obtained through the Freedom of Information Act. Most of these documents are original photoreproductions; a few have been transcribed—for example, Khrushchev's letters to Kennedy—for reasons of legibility or length. Almost all of the selected documents were once highly classified internal U.S. government records; however, important public communiqués or speeches have been included to render as complete an account of events as possible. Important documents generated by the Soviet and Cuban governments are also included.

The documents are divided into four sections, each of which is prefaced by a contextual introduction, in which the documents are cited by number. Generally, the records are organized chronologically, although in a few cases, materials on one specific aspect of the missile crisis have been gathered together for continuity. Those readers who prefer to start with a comprehensive overview of events are urged to read the chronology at the back of the book in order to place the individual documents in the broader context of events.

INTRODUCTION

Admittedly, the documents reproduced here do not present a complete picture of the extraordinary events surrounding the missile crisis. For reasons of space limitations, we were forced to select records that, in our judgment, represented important aspects of the crisis, and in some cases to edit them for length. Even more important, the vast majority of these documents are U.S. government records that reflect only the view from Washington. The recent conferences in Moscow and Havana have contributed critically needed Soviet and Cuban information and perspectives to the history of the crisis. To date, though, few Soviet or Cuban documents have been released. Until these nations' archives are opened to the public, U.S., Soviet, and Cuban historians will be unable to present anything approximating a full account of the crisis, and books on the crisis will necessarily remain incomplete.

Public discourse on the Cuban missile crisis, however, need not wait, for there is more than enough accessible information to advance our collective education and sustain an ongoing discussion on how to prevent similar confrontations in the future. In his memoir, *Thirteen Days*, Robert Kennedy ascribed the successful outcome of the crisis to the ability of the president and his aides to discuss, consider, and reconsider the most prudent U.S. approach: "The fact that we were able to talk, debate, argue, disagree, and then debate some more was essential in choosing our ultimate course."[11] A broader public discussion of issues such as intervention, nuclear weapons, and the use of military power is similarly essential to chart the future foreign policy course of the nation. We hope this volume will contribute to just such a debate.

Peter Kornbluh
Laurence Chang
July 14, 1992

NOTES

1. Transcript of the ExComm meeting on the evening of October 16, 1962 (see Document 16).

2. "Small Missiles Heightened Peril in 1962 Cuban Crisis," *Washington Post*, Jan. 14, 1992.

3. McGeorge Bundy, *Danger and Survival: Choices about the Bomb in the First Fifty Years* (New York: Random House, 1989), p. 462.

4. The requests were filed in the name of Professor Philip Brenner, a Cuba specialist and member of the Archive advisory board.

5. These conferences have resulted in three major books and numerous articles by Blight and his colleagues. See James G. Blight and David A. Welch, *On the Brink: Americans and Soviets Reexamine the Cuban Missile Crisis* (New York: Hill and Wang, 1989); James G. Blight, *The Shattered Crystal Ball: Fear and Learning in the Cuban Missile Crisis* (Savage, Md.: Rowman and Littlefield, 1990); Bruce J. Allyn, James G. Blight, and David A. Welch, *Back to the Brink: The Moscow Conference on the Cuban Missile Crisis* (Lanham, Md.: University Press of America, 1991), and *Cuba On the Brink: Fidel Castro, the Missile Crisis and the Collapse of Communism* (New York: Pantheon; 1993). Among

their many articles, see Allyn, Blight, and Welch, "Essence of Revision: Moscow, Havana and the Cuban Missile Crisis," *International Security* 14, no.3 (1989/1990), pp. 136–172.

6. For a discussion of using the documents and critical oral history, see Blight and Welch, *On the Brink*, pp. 5, 6.

7. Arthur Schlesinger, Jr., *A Thousand Days: JFK in the White House* (Boston: Houghton Mifflin, 1965), p. 841.

8. Quoted in Blight, *On the Brink*, p. 315.

9. "Memorandum of Conference with the President," June 6, 1959. Available in the National Security Archive's microfiche collection, *The Cuban Missile Crisis, 1962: The Making of U.S. Policy*.

10. James N. Grimwood and Francis Strowd, "History of the Jupiter Missile System," July 27, 1962. Available in the National Security Archive's microfiche collection, *The Cuban Missile Crisis, 1962: The Making of U.S. Policy*.

11. Robert Kennedy, *Thirteen Days: A Memoir of the Cuban Missile Crisis* (New York: W. W. Norton, 1969), p. 111.

SELECTED GLOSSARY

This glossary is divided into three sections: principal actors, organizations, and military and technical terms.

PRINCIPAL ACTORS

Acheson, Dean G.
Secretary of State, United States, Jan. 21, 1949–Jan. 20, 1953. Although not formally part of the administration, Acheson served President Kennedy as an unofficial foreign policy adviser, attending Executive Committee meetings and advocating a hard-line position against the Soviet Union.

Alekseyev, Aleksandr
Soviet Ambassador to Cuba, May 31, 1962–1968. A personal friend of Fidel and Raúl Castro, Alekseyev was chosen to broach to the Cuban government the idea of deploying nuclear missiles; during the missile crisis, he stayed in close contact with the Cuban leadership.

Ball, George W.
Under Secretary of State, Dec. 4, 1961–Sept. 30, 1966. Ball was active at the State Department in implementing the U.S. trade embargo against Cuba; as a member of the Executive Committee, he argued for a naval blockade during the missile crisis.

Bundy, McGeorge
Assistant to the President for National Security Affairs, Oct. 20, 1961–Feb. 1966. A member of the Executive Committee, Bundy took minutes for the meetings. After expressing concern that a decision might be made without adequate discussion and consideration of possible Soviet countermeasures against Berlin, Bundy unsuccessfully argued for a massive airstrike on Cuba.

Castro Ruz, Fidel
Prime Minister, President, and Commander-in-Chief of Armed Forces, Cuba, Jan. 1, 1959–Present. Following the 1961 invasion by U.S.-backed Cuban exiles at the Bay of Pigs, Castro and other Cuban officials believed a new U.S. invasion was imminent, so the Soviet offer of missiles was quickly accepted. Toward the end of the crisis, Castro was infuriated by Khrushchev's unilateral decision to remove the missiles from Cuba, as well as by U.S. demands (and Soviet pressure) for Cuban agreement to on-site inspection and the removal of IL-28 bombers; relations between Cuba and the Soviet Union were strained for the next several years.

Dillon, C. Douglas
Secretary of the Treasury, United States, Jan. 21, 1961–March 1965. A staunch anticommunist leader of the Republican party and a member of the Executive Committee, Dillon argued for an airstrike in early Executive Committee sessions; he was persuaded to support the blockade option, but he continued to recommend military action if needed to resolve the crisis.

Dobrynin, Anatoly F.
Soviet Ambassador to the United States, March 30, 1962–1986. Uninformed of the missile deployment by his superiors, Dobrynin offered his assurances in September and early October of 1962 that only "defensive" Soviet military equipment was being provided to Cuba. He was aware of negotiations between Aleksandr Fomin and John Scali, and began his own secret talks with Robert Kennedy, during which Kennedy suggested that the removal of the U.S. Jupiter missiles in Turkey might be part of a settlement to the crisis.

Finletter, Thomas K.

United States Ambassador to NATO, March 2, 1961–Sept. 2, 1965. Responsible for informing NATO allies of crisis developments, Finletter warned the Executive Committee that the unilateral removal of Jupiter missiles from Turkey would damage relations with Turkey and divide the NATO alliance.

Fomin, Aleksandr S.

KGB Station Chief, Soviet embassy, Washington. Apparently acting without the knowledge of the Kremlin, Fomin opened a negotiating channel with ABC News correspondent John Scali, passing on a proposal to end the crisis by withdrawing the missiles in return for a pledge that the U.S. would not invade Cuba.

Garthoff, Raymond L.

Analyst, Bureau of Politico-Military Affairs, State Department. During his tenure as a State Department analyst, Garthoff authored several memoranda for the Executive Committee on the missiles and on recommendations for defining "offensive weapons" in negotiations with Soviet representatives in November 1962. He is the author of *Reflections on the Cuban Missile Crisis* and other influential histories of the crisis and of U.S.-Soviet relations.

Gromyko, Andrei A.

Foreign Minister, Soviet Union 1957–1986. Gromyko was among the first to discuss with Khrushchev and object to the idea of deploying medium- and long-range missiles in Cuba with Khrushchev in early May 1962. Particularly concerned over the probable U.S. reaction when the deployment was discovered or became public, Gromyko met with President Kennedy at the White House on October 18, 1962; unaware that Kennedy already knew of the Soviet medium-range ballistic missiles, Gromyko carefully offered assurances that the Soviet arms shipped to Cuba were "defensive."

Hare, Raymond A.

United States Ambassador to Turkey, April 4, 1961– Aug. 27, 1965. Responsible for discussing with Turk-ish officials the possible dismantling of Jupiter bases, Hare reported on October 26 that the Turkish government objected to a trade but not to the gradual removal of the missiles, even through a secret agreement.

Harvey, William K.

Chief, Task Force W, OPERATION MONGOOSE, CIA. A veteran clandestine operator, Harvey sent several CIA teams into Cuba during the missile crisis without the knowledge of the Executive Committee or CIA Director John McCone, an action that brought strong criticism from Robert Kennedy and Harvey's subsequent reassignment to Rome.

Hilsman, Roger, Jr.

Assistant Secretary for Intelligence and Research, State Department Feb. 19, 1961–April, 25, 1963. Hilsman was responsible for the production of numerous intelligence analyses before and during the missile crisis, and also served as liaison with ABC News correspondent John Scali during his meetings with Aleksandr Fomin.

Johnson, U. Alexis

Deputy Under Secretary for Political Affairs, State Department of State, May 2, 1961–July 12, 1964. Present at most of the Executive Committee sessions and armed with his extensive experience in intelligence work, Johnson initially favored a surgical airstrike on the missile bases but later supported the blockade. His important staffwork for the group included drafting, with Paul Nitze, a scenario that formed the basis for the timing and execution of military and political actions prior to President Kennedy's October 22 speech.

Kennedy, John F.

President, United States, Jan. 20, 1961–Nov. 22, 1963. Preoccupied by tensions with the Soviet Union and dissatisfaction with the Cuban government, President Kennedy quickly established a select committee of advisers known as the Executive Committee (Ex-Comm) to decide on U.S. actions in response to the presence of Soviet missiles in Cuba. By enacting a blockade and taking various steps to avoid further escalation of the conflict, Kennedy was able to avoid general war and to reach a peaceful settlement that included with the removal of the missiles.

Kennedy, Robert F.

Attorney General, United States; Member of the Executive Committee, National Security Council, Jan. 21, 1961–Sept. 1964. Robert Kennedy was possibly President Kennedy's most intimate and influential adviser. He met secretly with Soviet Ambassador Dobrynin in an attempt to end the crisis.

Khrushchev, Nikita S.

First Secretary, Communist Party of the Soviet Union, Sept. 1953–Oct. 14, 1964; Premier, Soviet Union, March 1958–Oct. 14, 1964. As U.S.-Soviet relations rapidly deteriorated, Khrushchev, according to Soviet sources, developed the idea of secretly stationing medium-range nuclear missiles in Cuba. After the U.S. blockade was established, Khrushchev asked Kennedy to negotiate a settlement to the crisis; on October 28 he promptly agreed to Kennedy's proposal and withdrew the missiles, thus ending the crisis.

Kuznetsov, Vasily V.

First Deputy Minister of Foreign Affairs, Soviet Union, 1955–1977. Kuznetsov briefed Soviet Bloc ambassadors in Moscow on the Soviet Union's reaction to the U.S. blockade, and was assigned by Premier Khrushchev on October 28 to negotiate an end to the crisis at the United Nations with Adlai Stevenson and John McCloy.

Lansdale, Edward G.

Operations Chief, OPERATION MONGOOSE, CIA. A renowned counterinsurgency specialist, Lansdale designed an ambitious six-phase covert program under MONGOOSE designed to foment an uprising against the Cuban government by October 1962.

Lundahl, Arthur C.

Chief, National Photographic Interpretation Center, CIA. On October 15, Lundahl notified Ray Cline, the CIA deputy director of intelligence, of the discovery of missile equipment in Cuba; the following day, he personally briefed President Kennedy and the Executive Committee on the photographic evidence that the Soviet Union was constructing missile sites there.

Martin, Edwin M.

Assistant Secretary for Inter-American Affairs, State Department, May 18, 1962–Jan. 2, 1964. Martin attended several Executive Committee meetings and was responsible for a key briefing of Organization of American States (OAS) ambassadors prior to OAS introduction of the resolutions supporting U.S. action against the missiles.

McCloy, John J.

Coordinator for United States Disarmament Activities, Jan. 1961–Oct. 1961. The first adviser to be contacted by President Kennedy for advice, McCloy recommended firm action, including, if necessary, an airstrike and invasion to remove the missiles; his tough stance encouraged Kennedy to send him to meet with Soviet and U.N. officials in New York to resolve outstanding missile crisis issues.

McCone, John A.

Director, Central Intelligence Agency, United States, Nov. 29, 1961–April 28, 1965. Although McCone was convinced by early August 1962 that the large number of Soviet ships in transit to Cuba were carrying nuclear missiles, he lacked hard evidence to persuade President Kennedy until the U-2 photographs revealed construction of missile sites in October. During the crisis, McCone began each Executive Committee meeting with an update on the status of the missile bases and any other significant intelligence items, and he advocated a hard-line stance toward the Soviet Union throughout the crisis.

McNamara, Robert S.

Secretary of Defense, Jan. 21, 1961–Feb. 29, 1968. As a member of the Executive Committee, McNamara was initially a forceful opponent of an air attack on

Cuba, but he pressed for a blockade as a way to keep options open and to control the pace of events. He supported the idea of assuring the Soviets of the later removal of Jupiter missiles from Turkey in order to negotiate a settlement.

Mikoyan, Anastas I.
First Deputy Prime Minister, Soviet Union, 1955–1964. A close friend and primary adviser to Nikita Khrushchev, Mikoyan was sent to Cuba for the delicate task of persuading Castro to allow the missiles and IL-28 bombers to be removed as well as to smooth over strained Cuban-Soviet relations.

Nitze, Paul H.
Assistant Secretary for International Security Affairs, Department of Defense, Jan. 29, 1961–Jan. 23, 1963. As chairman of the Executive Committee's Berlin Subcommittee, Nitze urged immediate military action against the missile sites in Cuba, arguing that the missiles in Cuba significantly altered the strategic nuclear balance (a view rejected by many on the committee), and that U.S nuclear and conventional superiority in the region would prevent the Soviet Union from responding to a U.S. attack on Cuba.

Rostow, Walt W.
Director, Policy Planning Staff Department of State, United States, Nov. 1961–March 1966; Chairman, Planning Subcommittee, Executive Committee, National Security Council, United States, Oct, 23, 1962–Jan. 1963. As chairman of the Executive Committee's Planning Subcommittee, Rostow was asked by President Kennedy to assess the Cuban military buildup, and recommended a strong hard-line position against the Soviet Union.

Rusk, Dean
Secretary of State, Jan. 21, 1961–Jan. 20, 1969. As a member of the Executive Committee, Rusk advocated early in the missile crisis a surgical strike on Cuba with prior political warning to Castro or Khrushchev; later in the crisis he suggested that Robert Kennedy offer Ambassador Dobrynin oral assurances on the

U.S. intention to withdraw Jupiter missiles from Turkey.

Scali, John A.
Correspondent, ABC News. Scali was contacted by Soviet embassy official (and KGB Station Chief) Aleksandr Fomin about a proposed settlement to the crisis, and subsequently he acted as a contact between Fomin and the Executive Committee; however, it was without government direction that Scali responded to new Soviet conditions with a warning that a U.S. invasion was only hours away, prompting the Soviets to settle the crisis quickly.

Schlesinger, Arthur M., Jr.
Special Assistant to the President, Jan. 30, 1961–Jan. 1964. As a White House aide and personal confidant of President Kennedy, Schlesinger did not play a large role during the missile crisis beyond helping to draft Adlai Stevenson's statements for the United Nations. A historian by training, Schlesinger later authored two comprehensive accounts of the Kennedy administration, *A Thousand Days* and *Robert Kennedy and His Times,* which included detailed descriptions of events inside the White House during the missile crisis.

Smith, Bromley
Executive Secretary, National Security Council. Responsible for the coordination and distribution of internal papers in the National Security Council, Smith took official notes on most of the Executive Committee meetings after October 24.

Sorensen, Theodore C.
Special Counsel to the President, Jan. 1960–Feb. 1964. After receiving assurances in September from Soviet Ambassador Dobrynin on the defensive nature of the military buildup in Cuba, Sorensen advocated the blockade as an initial step in the crisis and wrote Kennedy's speech announcing the presence of the missiles. Sorensen also wrote *Kennedy,* one of the standard accounts of the Kennedy presidency, and edited Robert Kennedy's account of the crisis, *Thirteen Days.*

Stevenson, Adlai E.

United States Ambassador to the United Nations, Jan 23, 1961–July 14, 1965. Stevenson, John Kennedy's political rival, consistently argued for a diplomatic settlement, with the Jupiter missiles in Turkey and the U.S. naval base at Guantánamo as items for negotiation, proposals that were rejected by the Executive Committee. As Ambassador to the U.N., Stevenson also played a role in negotiations in New York during and after the crisis.

Sweeney, Walter C., Jr.

Commander, Tactical Air Command (TAC), United States Air Force. As chief of TAC, the command that would have carried out airstrikes against Cuba, in the fall of 1962 General Sweeney oversaw the development of military plans for such attacks. He personally briefed President Kennedy on TAC's proposal and planning for strikes on Cuba.

Taylor, Maxwell D.

Military Advisor to the President, United States, July 1961–Sept. 30, 1962; Chairman, Joint Chiefs of Staff, United States, Oct. 1, 1962–July 1, 1964. A member of the Executive Committee and a self-described "two-fold hawk from start to finish," General Taylor personally argued for military action against Cuba and also pressed for a full invasion of Cuba, believing that the maintenance of U.S. military superiority in both nuclear and conventional forces around Cuba required the United States to take an uncompromising position.

Thant, U

Acting Secretary General of the United Nations. Although apparently informed about the existence of a crisis involving Cuba on October 21, 1962, U Thant made no direct attempt to mediate until October 24; however, most of his offers to negotiate during and after the crisis were essentially rejected and had little effect on the final outcome.

Thompson, Llewellyn E.

United States Ambassador to the Soviet Union, July 16, 1957–July 27, 1962; United States Ambassador-at-Large, Oct. 3, 1962–Dec. 26, 1966. As the only Soviet expert on the Executive Committee, Thompson presented assessments of Soviet thinking and, based on his assessments, took positions supporting the blockade and against negotiating with the Turkish Jupiter missiles. Thompson's analysis was essential in President Kennedy's decision to accept Khrushchev's October 26 proposal and to ignore his October 27 proposal involving the Jupiter missiles.

SELECTED ORGANIZATIONS

Atlantic Command, Commander-in-Chief (CINCLANT)

The commander-in-chief of the Atlantic Command headed the unified military command responsible for coordinating U.S. military activities and plans relating to Cuba. Admiral Robert L. Dennison served as CINCLANT in 1962.

Executive Committee (ExComm)

A group of advisers known as the Executive Committee of the U.S. National Security Council was created by President Kennedy on October 16, the first day of the crisis; the group was officially constituted only on October 22. The committee was the key decision-making body governing U.S. responses and actions during the crisis period. Statutory members included Vice President Lyndon Johnson; Secretary of State Dean Rusk; Secretary of Defense Robert McNamara; Joint Chiefs of Staff Chairman General Maxwell Taylor; Special Assistant to the President for National Security Affairs McGeorge Bundy; Secretary of the Treasury Douglas Dillon; CIA Director John McCone; Attorney General Robert Kennedy; Under Secretary of State George Ball; Deputy Secretary of Defense Roswell Gilpatric; and Ambassador-at-Large Llewellyn Thompson. In addition, the ExComm unofficially included Deputy Under Secretary of State for Political Affairs U. Alexis Johnson; Assistant Secretary of Defense for International Security Paul Nitze;

former Secretary of State Dean Acheson; private advisers John McCloy and Robert Lovett; U.S. Ambassador to the U.N. Adlai Stevenson; Deputy Director of the USIA Donald Wilson; Assistant Secretary of State for Inter-American Affairs Edwin Martin; and, on the first day of the crisis, former U.S. Ambassador to the Soviet Union Charles Bohlen. President Kennedy chaired the Executive Committee.

Executive Committee. Berlin Subcommittee

Chaired by Assistant Secretary of Defense for International Security Paul Nitze, the Berlin Subcommittee of the Executive Committee conducted contingency planning on Berlin in the event that the Cuban missile crisis escalated into a Soviet move against West Berlin. In addition, the interagency group sent recommendations to the Executive Committee on other issues, including the Turkey-for-Cuba missile trade.

Special Group Augmented (SGA)

President Kennedy created the Special Group Augmented in late November 1961 to oversee OPERATION MONGOOSE, the covert action operation designed to overthrow Fidel Castro. The SGA included the members of the Special Group task force that oversaw most unconventional warfare operations, but it was "augmented" by the presence of Attorney General Robert Kennedy and the Joint Chiefs of Staff Chairman General Maxwell Taylor. Although Taylor chaired the SGA, Kennedy, because he was the president's brother, was the dominant member.

Task Force W (of OPERATION MONGOOSE)

Task Force W was the entity within the CIA responsible for activities conducted against Cuba under OPERATION MONGOOSE, including sabotage and paramilitary operations by anti-Castro guerrilla units infiltrated into Cuba. During the missile crisis, several CIA teams were sent into Cuba without the knowledge or authorization of the Executive Committee; one was caught by Cuban authorities on October 25. Despite Robert Kennedy's efforts to terminate Task Force W operations on October 30, 1962, another sabotage team destroyed a Cuban industrial facility on November 8, adding tension to the final days of the crisis.

MILITARY AND TECHNICAL TERMS

DEFCON

Defense Condition levels, or DEFCONs, establish the readiness status of U.S. military forces; they range from DEFCON 1, a state of war, to DEFCON 5, the most relaxed military posture. During the missile crisis, the U.S. Strategic Air Command was placed on DEFCON 2 for the first time in history, while the rest of U.S. military commands (with the exception of the U.S. Air Forces in Europe) went on DEFCON 3.

FROG Missiles

Free Rocket Over Ground (FROG) missiles were Soviet ground-to-ground rockets capable of carrying a nuclear warhead, with a range of about twenty-five miles. Former Soviet military officials have said that six such missiles were deployed in Cuba, along with larger ballistic missiles.

IL-28 Aircraft

An aging Soviet light bomber aircraft capable of carrying nuclear weapons, forty-two Ilyushin (IL) 28 planes were delivered to Cuba before and during the missile crisis, although only seven planes were actually assembled. The planes were militarily obsolete in 1962, yet the United States nevertheless demanded that they be withdrawn as part of a settlement of the missile crisis. Khrushchev acceded to Washington's demand, but Castro's refusal to release the planes extended the crisis into late November 1962.

IRBMs

Intermediate-range ballistic missiles are surface-to-surface weapons with a range of between fifteen hundred and three thousand nautical miles.

Jupiter Missiles

A class of intermediate-range ballistic missiles known as the Jupiter were developed by the U.S. Army in the mid 1950s. Under agreements signed in 1959, thirty Jupiters were deployed in Italy and fifteen in Turkey near the Soviet border. The Kennedy administration's quiet agreement to withdraw the Jupiters from Turkey in return for the Soviet withdrawal of missiles from Cuba helped to end the Cuban missile crisis.

MRBMs

Medium-range ballistic missiles are surface-to-surface missiles with a range of approximately six hundred to fifteen hundred miles.

POL

POL stands for petroleum, oil, and lubricants. At several points during the missile crisis, U.S. decision makers considered increasing pressure on the Soviet Union and Cuba by extending the naval blockade on offensive weapons to include POL.

SAMs

Twenty four Soviet SA-2 surface-to-air missile (SAM) sites were constructed in Cuba in the fall of 1962. At that time, the SA-2 or "Guideline" missile system was the most advanced air defense system available to the Soviet Union.

PART I

PRELUDE TO THE CRISIS

In April 1962, Soviet Premier Nikita Khrushchev first considered the idea of deploying nuclear missiles on the Caribbean island of Cuba. Over the next few weeks, Khrushchev would discuss this dangerous proposition with key advisers, and in May he dispatched the head of Soviet Strategic Rocket Forces, Marshal Sergei Biryuzov—traveling incognito as a member of an agricultural delegation—to confer with Cuban leader Fidel Castro and determine whether the missiles could be installed without detection by U.S. intelligence. When in early June Biryuzov reported back that Castro had responded positively to the Soviet proposal, and that clandestine installation was possible, Khrushchev ordered the project to proceed. By early September, shipments of equipment, materials, and weapon parts for deploying some forty-two SS-4 medium-range ballistic missiles (MRBMs) and thirty-two SS-5 intermediate-range ballistic missiles (IRBMs) began arriving in Cuba.

What caused the Cuban missile crisis? Only a partial answer to this question can be found in the series of extraordinary decisions made by Soviet and Cuban leaders in the spring and summer of 1962; for Khrushchev's decision to deploy the missiles, and Castro's decision to accept them, did not take place in a vacuum. While their plan to secretly¹ install nuclear missiles in Cuba was a bold and reckless *initiative*, it also represented a *response* to the underlying military and political tensions that characterized relations be-

tween Washington, Moscow, and Havana at the beginning of the 1960s. The origins of the missile crisis, therefore, can be found in the Cold War dynamic between the United States and the Soviet Union, and in the United States' hostile policy toward the Cuban revolution.

THE UNITED STATES AND THE SOVIET UNION

U.S.-Soviet relations in the period preceding the missile crisis were characterized by recurring conflict. Many issues, including the accelerating nuclear arms race, U.S. deployment of nuclear weapons along the Soviet periphery, Soviet support for revolution in the Third World, and most important, the unresolved status of Berlin, inflamed superpower tensions and sustained fears on both sides that the Cold War might escalate into some form of open military conflict.

Nuclear weapons rendered such conflict exceedingly dangerous. The Soviets had launched Sputnik in 1957 and Khrushchev began to rattle his atomic sabers, referring publicly to the Soviets' ability to "deliver a crushing blow" against an aggressor on any part of the globe, and raising concerns in Washington that the Soviet Union was developing a dangerous nuclear advantage. Perceptions of a "missile gap" became a key theme in John F. Kennedy's 1960 campaign for the presidency, and prompted a series of crash Pentagon programs to increase the United States' nuclear capability.

A missile gap did in fact exist—but it favored the United States rather than the Soviet Union. On the basis of new satellite photography, U.S. intelligence concluded in mid 1961 that previous estimates of Soviet nuclear strength had been vastly overstated. Indeed, by the time of the missile crisis, the Soviet Union had only some twenty to forty intercontinental ballistic missiles (ICBMs), compared to over 170 U.S. long-range missiles. The disparity in strategic bombers and submarine-launched ballistic missiles (SLBMs) was even greater. In total, the United States had some three thousand nuclear warheads ready to fire, compared to about 250 on the Soviet side.[2]

The Kennedy administration showed no hesitation in exploiting this advantage. U.S. officials underscored America's nuclear prowess both in public speeches and in private meetings with Soviet representatives. As the disparity in power continued to widen, Soviet leaders no doubt feared that the United States might gain the ability for a preemptive nuclear strike or use its nuclear superiority to compel political concessions from the Soviets on major international disputes such as Berlin.

The military, ideological, and geopolitical struggle between East and West converged in Berlin. Since the end of World War II, Berlin had existed as a single city, with British, French, American, and Soviet troops controlling different sectors. The presence of an armed Western enclave in the midst of communist East Germany was, as Khrushchev complained, a "bone in the throat" of Soviet leaders. In 1958, Khrushchev threatened to expel the Western powers and make Berlin a "free city" under exclusive Soviet control. Before, during, and even after August 1961, when the East Germans closed the border and constructed the infamous wall between the east and west sides of the city, Berlin's status continued to threaten a major U.S.-Soviet crisis. As Kennedy prepared for his first superpower summit in the summer of 1961, U.S. Ambassador to Moscow Llewllyn Thompson cabled Washington that Khrushchev had "so deeply committed his personal prestige and that of Soviet Union to

some action on Berlin and German problems that if we take [a] completely negative stand [on] Berlin, this would probably lead to developments in which [the] chances of war or ignominious western retreat are close to 50-50."[3]

Disagreement over Berlin dominated the summit, which was held in Vienna on June 3 and 4, 1961. At the final session, Khrushchev informed Kennedy that the United States had until December to accept Soviet demands on Berlin, to which Kennedy replied that "it would be a cold winter." After the meeting, the president gravely told reporters that the prospect of war was now "very real."[4]

At Vienna, Kennedy and Khrushchev also discussed other world issues, including their divergent views on, and policies toward, revolution in the Third World. Their conversation regarding Cuba foreshadowed the coming missile crisis. President Kennedy told Khrushchev that his authorization of the Bay of Pigs invasion was "a misjudgment," and that such misjudgments in the nuclear era should be avoided. According to Document 1, a memorandum of the conversation, Kennedy "emphasized that the purpose of this meeting was to introduce greater precision in these judgments so that our two countries could survive this period of competition without endangering their national security." Khrushchev agreed, but he nevertheless took the opportunity to berate Kennedy for trying to overthrow Castro. If Washington believed it had the right to intervene in Cuba because Castro followed a Soviet line, Khrushchev argued, "what about Turkey and Iran?"

> These two countries are U.S. followers, they march in its wake, and they have U.S. bases and rockets. If the U.S. believes that it is free to act, then what should the USSR do? The U.S. has set a precedent for intervention in internal affairs of other countries. The USSR is stronger than Turkey and Iran, just as the U.S. is stronger than Cuba. This situation may cause miscalculation, to use the President's term.

As Khrushchev's remarks attest, the presence of U.S. nuclear installations and military bases close to, and even along the borders of, the Soviet Union clearly galled Soviet leaders and was an object of extreme resentment in Moscow's relations with the United States. As a result of NATO agreements signed in 1959, the United States had deployed some thirty Jupiter IRBMs in Italy and fifteen in Turkey. Even as the Jupiters were being installed, however, U.S. analysts had concluded that the liquid-fueled weapons were technologically obsolete; and early in his administration Kennedy began to consider the pros and cons of canceling their deployment. As Document 2, a memorandum on "Turkish IRBM's," indicates, exploration of this possibility was met coolly by Turkish (as well as Italian) officials.

According to recent Soviet accounts, the Jupiters in Turkey provided both an impetus and a justification for Khrushchev's decision to deploy missiles in Cuba. Khrushchev's initial conversation with defense minister Rodion Malinovsky took place at a retreat in the Crimea, overlooking the Black Sea, at about the same time that the Jupiter missiles in Turkey became operational. Malinovsky called the premier's attention to the U.S. missiles just over the horizon in Turkey and informed him that they could strike the Soviet Union in ten minutes. As Raymond Garthoff relates the story, "Khrushchev then mused on whether the Soviet Union shouldn't do the same thing in Cuba, just over the horizon from the United States."[5]

By that time Cuba had become the Soviet Union's first major ally in the western hemisphere. The expansion of their political, economic, and military relationship paralleled mounting U.S. hostility toward Castro's regime; the more the U.S. tried to roll back the Cuban revolution, the more the Cubans turned to the Soviet Union for support, including weapons to defend Cuba against a potential U.S. invasion.

Most Western analysts have argued that Khrushchev and his aides decided to deploy the missiles in order to offset the U.S. strategic advantage. But several Soviets close to the decision-making circle have recently suggested that the decision was driven in part, if not predominently, by the desire to prevent an expected U.S. attack on Cuba. When Khrushchev discussed sending nuclear missiles to Cuba with First Deputy Prime Minister Anastas Mikoyan and then with a select group of advisers at the end of April 1962, according to Mikoyan's son, Sergo, "the main idea was the defense of Fidel":

> Khrushchev had some reasons to think the United States would repeat the Bay of Pigs, but not make mistakes anymore.... In 1962, at Punta del Este, Cuba was excluded from the Organization of American States. Khrushchev regarded this exclusion as a diplomatic isolation and a preparation for an invasion. And then the propagandistic preparation was the accusation of exporting revolution. So he thought an invasion was inevitable, that it would be massive, and that it would use all American force.[6]

In early May, yet another meeting took place, this one attended by Alexandr Alekseyev, a Soviet diplomat close to Fidel Castro. According to Alekseyev's account, Khrushchev offered two rationales for sending the missiles: first, he favored deployment "to repay the Americans in kind" for encircling the Soviet Union with nuclear weapons; and second, Khrushchev saw the missiles as an "effective means of deterrence" for the inevitable the U.S. invasion of Cuba.[7]

THE UNITED STATES AND CUBA

The United States had an established history of invading Cuba: U.S. Marines landed on Cuban shores in 1898, 1906, 1912, and 1917. Dating all the way back to the 1820s when John Quincy Adams declared that Cuba had "an importance in the sum of our national interests, with which that of no other foreign territory can be compared," the tropical island had been an object of empire for the United States. In 1859, Congress considered legislation to annex the island as a potential slave state. In 1898, the United States helped to liberate Cuba from Spanish colonial rule, only to assert aggressively its own dominion over Cuba's internal political and economic affairs.[8] The island became known as "the pearl of the Antilles," a favorite spot for American tourists, U.S. corporations, and the mafia—with social stability maintained, between 1933 and 1958, by the corrupt pro-American military government of Fulgencio Batista. For most of his reign, General Batista could count on U.S. support and largess. Washington withdrew its military assistance just before the revolution led by Fidel Castro came to fruition in January 1959.

Washington's efforts to undermine Castro's nationalist revolution began well before his government turned hostile toward U.S. corporate holdings and then established diplomatic relations with the Soviet Union in May of 1960. Less than three months after the January 1959 revolution, President Eisenhower's National Security Council first evaluated the prospects of bringing "another government to power in Cuba."[9] A few weeks later, in April 1959, Vice President Nixon met with Castro and immediately became, in his own words, "the strongest and most persistant advocate for setting up and supporting" covert operations to overthrow the revolutionary leader.[10]

The CIA initiated planning for such operations in January 1960, and, by the time John F. Kennedy was elected, had already recruited and trained hundreds of Cuban exiles for a major invasion of the island. President-elect Kennedy was informed of the plan on November 18, 1960; he received a full briefing after his inauguration, and subsequently agreed to let the operation go forward with the proviso that the CIA should come up with "a quiet landing…without the appearance of a WW II type amphibious assault," in order to preserve the plausible denial of U.S. participation in the operation.[11] Under no circumstances did he want to commit U.S. military personnel to a war in Cuba: "I'm not going to risk an American Hungary," he told aides.[12] When the U.S.-sponsored landing faltered on April 16, 1962, Kennedy refused to authorize U.S. air cover—which could not have been plausibly denied—for the exile force trapped by Castro's

army at Playa Girón. The result was the U.S. foreign policy disaster known as the Bay of Pigs.

Although chastened by the Bay of Pigs—"How could I have been so stupid?" Kennedy remarked to his speechwriter, Theodore Sorensen—with its failure the president and his advisers became all the more obsessed with overthrowing Castro. "We were hysterical about Castro at the time of the Bay of Pigs and thereafter," former Secretary of Defense Robert McNamara later told Senate investigators.[13] For U.S. officials, the Cuban leader—now an avowed Marxist—embodied a variety of national security challenges. A week after the debacle, Walt Rostow outlined "five threats to us represented by the Castro regime" (see Document 6): the possibility that the Soviet Union would establish an offensive air or missile base; an ideology that constituted "a moral and political offense to us"; Cuba's conventional arms buildup and its threat to other Latin American nations; revolutionary subversion; and the threat of Cuba as a successful revolutionary model. A presidential task force, headed by Assistant Secretary of Defense Paul Nitze, similarly highlighted Castro's threat as a revolutionary example:

He has provided a working example of a communist state in the Americas, successfully defying the United States. Thus he has appealed to widespread anti-American feeling, a feeling often shared by non-communists. His survival, in the face of persistant U.S. efforts to unseat him, has unquestionably lowered the prestige of the United States…. As long as Castro thrives, his major threat—the example and stimulus of a working communist revolution—will persist.[14]

OPERATION MONGOOSE

On November 30, 1961, President Kennedy authorized a covert program known as OPERATION MONGOOSE, to "use our available assets…to help Cuba overthrow the Communist regime."[15] The CIA program subsequently developed under MONGOOSE would become the largest ever undertaken by the agency, involving some four hundred agents, a budget of $50 million and a variety of covert, economic, and psychological operations—including assassination attempts against Fidel Castro. After the Bay of Pigs debacle, rather than turn the operation to oust Castro over to the CIA, which the president had come to distrust, oversight was given to the so-called Special Group of covert operations overseers, "augmented" by Attorney General Robert Kennedy and General Maxwell Taylor. According to Document 4, a summary of the attorney general's meeting with the members of the Special Group Augmented (SGA) on December 1, he told them that a "higher authority"—that is, the president—had decided that "higher priority should be given to Cuba." The military's foremost specialist in counterinsurgency, Brigadier General Edward Lansdale, would be designated as "Chief of Operations" and tasked with fomenting "eventual revolution within Cuba."

On January 18, 1962, General Lansdale laid out the scope of "the Cuba Project."[16] The objective would be "to help the Cubans overthrow the Communist regime from within Cuba and institute a new government with which the United States can live in peace." The coordinated means to accomplish that goal included hostile diplomacy, economic warfare, paramilitary sabotage activities, and the creation of cells of Cuban "political action agents" who could organize an internal revolt in the midst of economic and social upheaval fostered by the MONGOOSE operations. Once the anticommunist insurrection began, it was to be aided by direct U.S. military intervention. "The United States…will then give open support to the Cuban peoples' revolt," stated Lansdale's program review. "Such support will include military force, as necessary."

Throughout the spring of 1962, planning for overthrowing Castro became more refined. In February, Landsdale laid out a six-phase "specific plan" for the covert war to come to fruition. Document 5 reveals that intelligence, political, economic, psychological, sabotage, and military operations were supposed to culminate in an internal anti-Castro revolt in October 1962—ironically the same month the missile crisis took place—and result in a new, pro-American government by the end of that month. In his report to the SGA, Lansdale urged that the "vital decision" be made "on the use of open U.S. force to aid the Cuban people in winning their liberty." In March, the "Guidelines for OPERATION MONGOOSE" (Document 6) acknowledged that "final success will require decisive U.S. military intervention," but the SGA deferred that decision, limiting its authorization to intelligence work and sabotage operations. While the Pentagon prepared contingency plans for such intervention, MONGOOSE operations concentrated on acquiring intelligence in Cuba and conducting political, economic, and covert operations that would set the stage for a counterrevolution.

Phase One of operations took place between March and July 1962. During those months, the CIA acquired "hard intelligence" and established the Caribbean Admission Center at Opa-Locka, Florida, to train recruited exiles for operations inside Cuba. By the end of July, Lansdale wrote in his review of operations, the CIA would have infiltrated eleven teams and "guerrilla warfare could be activated with a good chance of success, if assisted properly." While sabotage had been planned, however, none had taken place (see Document 7).

Lansdale also reported that the objective of "intervention planning" had been met "fully." As part of OPERATION MONGOOSE, Pentagon strategists drafted several contingency plans for an invasion and military occupation (see Document 8). Throughout the spring, summer, and fall of 1962, the U.S. military conducted a series of highly visible and intimidating military exercises simulating an invasion of Cuba. In April, the military conducted LANTPHIBEX 1-62, a mock assault on the Puerto Rican island of Vieques. From April through May, the U.S. Navy carried out OPERATION QUICK KICK—maneuvers involving seventy-nine ships and forty thousand troops off the southeastern coast of the United States. SWIFT STRIKE II was conducted in August in the Carolinas.

Also in August, the Defense Department announced plans for PHILBRIGLEX-62, which involved another mock military assault on the island of Vieques and the simulated overthrow of a leader named "Ortsac"— Castro spelled backward.

Preparations for PHILBRIGLEX corresponded to a significant escalation of covert sabotage and psychological operations under OPERATION MONGOOSE. In early October, as Soviet construction of the missile sites continued unbeknownst to U.S. officials, President Kennedy brought pressure on the SGA to step up Phase Two of MONGOOSE with "more dynamic action." On October 11, Lansdale recommended a series of new action proposals, "with sabotage given priority attention" (see Document 9). These operations included actions to bomb and "destroy" Cuban-owned ships, and a Voice of America Russian propaganda program aimed at inciting hostilities between Soviet technicians in Cuba and the Cuban public. At a planning meeting held on October 14, just one day before the missiles were discovered, the SGA agreed that "all efforts should be made to develop new and imaginative approaches with the possibility of getting rid of the Castro regime."[17]

From the Soviet and Cuban perspective, the military maneuvers and covert operations, combined with the implentation of a full economic embargo in February 1962 and a U.S.-led diplomatic initiative to expel Cuba from the Organization of American States and isolate Castro, added up to preparations for an invasion. Cuban intelligence had infiltrated exile groups recruited for MONGOOSE and, according to Kennedy's press secretary, Pierre Salinger, had obtained internal memoranda that discussed the timetable for an invasion.[18] Former Kennedy administration officials have since stated categorically, and repeatedly, that while there were contingency plans, at no time following the Bay of Pigs had the president authorized an invasion.[19] The Soviet-Cuban perception was, however, understandable. "I state quite frankly," former secretary of defense Robert McNamara declared at the Havana conference, "that if I had been a Cuban leader at that time, I might well have concluded that there was a great risk of U.S. invasion. And I should say, as well, if I had been a Soviet leader at the time, I might have come to the same conclusion."[20]

In preparation for that invasion, high-level Soviet and Cuban officials secretly negotiated the deployment of the missiles, as well as vast amounts of other military armaments and a large contingent of conventionally armed Soviet troops. In July, Raúl Castro traveled to Moscow and, with Marshal Malinovsky, drew up and initialed a draft military cooperation agreement to "take the necessary steps to jointly defend [the] legitimate rights of the people of Cuba…in the face of possible aggression" (Document 10). Che Guevara carried a revised draft back to Moscow at the end of August. Although Khrushchev never signed the pact, by midsummer the Soviets had begun the transfer of advanced air defense equipment, MiG-21 interceptors, coastal defense forces, and combat personnel eventually totalling forty-two thousand troops.[21]

Kennedy administration officials and the intelligence community monitored this massive deployment with growing concern. On August 22, the CIA released an intelligence assessment on "Recent Soviet Military Aid to Cuba" (Document 11). The study cited an "unprecedented" level of military activities and observed that "clearly something new and different is taking place." A CIA National Intelligence Estimate (NIE), dated in mid September, noted the possibility that the Soviets were moving nuclear arms into Cuba. Nonetheless, the NIE concluded that the deployment of nuclear missiles "would be incompatible with Soviet practice to date and with Soviet policy as we presently estimate it" (Document 12).

Unconvinced that the Soviets would deploy nuclear missiles, but alarmed enough to prepare for that contingency, President Kennedy's National Security Advisor McGeorge Bundy issued National Security Action Memorandum 181 on August 23 (Document 13). The presidential directive called for upgrading analysis of Soviet shipments, military contingency planning for eliminating nuclear installations in Cuba, development "with all possible speed" of new OPERATION MONGOOSE activities, and, presciently, an assessment of actions "to get Jupiter missiles out of Turkey." Kennedy's advisers also recommended that he publicly "draw the line," as Walt Rostow suggested on September 3, "at the installation in Cuba or in Cuban waters of nuclear weapons or delivery vehicles, sea or land based" (Document 14).

On September 4, President Kennedy issued a public statement to address a growing cacaphony of rumors and allegations on Capitol Hill. There was no ev-idence "offensive ground-to-ground missiles" in Cuba, he stated. "Were it to be otherwise, the gravest issues would arise." Even as Soviet diplomats assured U.S. officials that all weapons going to Cuba were defensive, Kennedy reiterated the U.S. position again during a press conference on September 13. If Cuba should ever "become an offensive military base of significant capacity for the Soviet Union," he declared, the United States would "do whatever must be done to protect its own security...."[22]

NOTES

1. At the January 1992 Havana conference, Castro made it clear that he had forcefully disagreed with Khrushchev's decision to deploy the missiles surreptitiously and had argued that, because the deployment was legal under international law, it should have been done openly. "Why do it secretly—as if we had no right to do it? I warned Nikita that secrecy would give the imperialists the advantage." Castro is quoted in Arthur Schlesinger, Jr., "Four Days with Fidel: A Havana Diary," in *The New York Review of Books* (March 16, 1992), p.24.

2. See Raymond L. Garthoff, *Reflections on the Cuban Missile Crisis* (2d ed., Washington, D.C.: Brookings Institution, 1989), p. 208.

3. See Moscow cable 2939, May 27, 1961, from Thompson to the State Department. This cable has been published as part of the National Security Archive's microfiche collection, *The Berlin Crisis, 1958–1962: The Making of U.S. Policy* (Washington, D.C.: National Security Archive/Chadwyck Healey, 1992)

4. Sorensen, *Kennedy* (New York: Harper and Row, 1965), p. 549.

5. Garthoff, *Reflections*, p. 12.

6. James G. Blight and David A. Welch, *On the Brink: Americans and Soviets Reexamine the Cuban Missile Crisis* (New York: Hill and Wang, 1989), p. 238

7. Garthoff, *Reflections*, p. 15.

8. The U.S. military occupied Cuba in the aftermath of the Spanish-American war, and in 1903 the new Cuban constitution, drafted under the occupation, contained an amendment giving the United States the "right to intervene for the preservation of Cuban independence, [and] the maintenance of a government adequate for the protection of life, property and individual liberty." The constitution also gave the United States the right to build and maintain a naval base at Guantánamo Bay. The United States' withdrawal from Guantánamo later became one of Castro's demands for settling the missile crisis. See George Black, *The Good Neighbor* (New York: Pantheon, 1989), pp. 22, 23.

9. Peter Wyden, *Bay of Pigs* (New York: Simon and Schuster, 1979), p 25.

10. Nixon is quoted in ibid, pp. 28, 29

11. Report to the President (the Taylor Commission Report), "Narrative of the Anti-Castro Cuban Operation Zapata," June 13, 1961, pp. 4–6, 9, in the National Security Archive, *The Cuban Missile Crisis, 1962: The Making of U.S. Policy.*

12. Michael R. Beschloss, *The Crisis Years: Kennedy and Khrushchev, 1960–1963*, (New York: HarperCollins, 1991) p. 114.

13. See U.S. Senate, Select Committee to Study Governmental Operations with Respect to Intelligence Activities, *Alleged Assassination Plots Involving Foreign Leaders*, 94th Congress, 1st sess. (Nov. 18, 1975), p. 142 (hereafter referred to as the Church Committee report).

14. Ibid, p. 8.

15. Ibid, p. 139.

16. See Lansdale to Special Group, "The Cuba Project," Jan. 18, 1962, in the National Security Archive, *The Cuban Missile Crisis, 1962: The Making of U.S. Policy.*

17. Church Committee report, p. 147.

18. See Garthoff, *Reflections*, p. 8; Salinger was interviewed by a Florida TV station WPLG following the Havana conference in January 1992. He stated, "actually, OPERATION MONGOOSE contributed to the decision of Nikita Khrushchev to deploy the missiles in Cuba. We found out that Cuban intelligence managed to penetrate the CIA and get some of the papers on OPERATION

MONGOOSE, and they discovered in those papers that we had set a date in October 1962 that if Castro had not been overthrown by then, we would have to move up our operation to get rid of him."

19. For a full treatment of the invasion issue see James Hershberg, "Before 'The Missiles of October': Did Kennedy Plan a Military Strike Against Cuba?" *Diplomatic History* 14, no. 12 (Spring 1990): pp. 163–199.

20. McNamara initially made this statement during his Opening Remarks at the Tripartite Conference on the October Crisis of 1962 in Havana, Jan. 9, 1992.

21. Garthoff, *Reflections*, p. 18. According to Garthoff, U.S. intelligence wrongly assumed that the Soviet arms buildup was intended for the Cuban armed forces. CIA estimates that ten thousand Soviet troops were in Cuba at the time of the crisis turned out to be far less than the actual number.

22. "News Conference at the White House with Pierre Salinger," Sept. 4, 1962, and "The President's News Conference of Sept. 13, 1962," can be found in the National Security Archive's collection, *The Cuban Missile Crisis, 1962: The Making of U.S. Policy.*

D/P:AAkalovsky:rh　　　　　　　　　SECRET

SANITIZED COPY

DEPARTMENT OF STATE

Memorandum of Conversation

DATE: June 3, 1961
3:00 P.M.
Residence of the
American Ambassador
Vienna

SUBJECT: Vienna Meeting Between The President
and Chairman Khrushchev.

US	USSR
PARTICIPANTS:	
The President	Chairman Khrushchev
D - Mr. Akalovsky,	Mr. Sukhodrev, Interpreter,
(Interpreting)	USSR Ministry of Foreign Affairs

COPIES TO:　　The White House
　　　　　　　The Secretary
　　　　　　　Mr. Kohler
　　　　　　　Permanent record copy for the
　　　　　　　Executive Secretariat's conference file.

After lunch the President invited Mr. Khrushchev for a short walk in the garden. While in the garden, the President asked Mr. Khrushchev how he managed to make himself available for such prolonged conversations as, for example, he had had with Senator Humphrey and Walter Lippmann. The President said he understood that no one had interrupted the Chairman during those meetings. As far as he was concerned, the President continued, his schedule was very crowded and he was constantly wanted on the telephone, so that it was very difficult for him to have time for lengthy uninterrupted meetings.

Mr. Khrushchev replied that it was true that he had indeed had prolonged uninterrupted meetings with Senator Humphrey and Lippmann. The reason why he had time for such meetings was that the Soviet Government had been decentralized to the extent that administrative functions had been transferred to the governments of the individual republics, while the government of the Union retained the responsibility for over-all planning.

The President remarked that our system of several branches of government involved contacts and consultations between the President and the various branches, and that this was a time consuming process.

To this, ——

E.O. 12356, Sec. 3.4
NLK-86-138 APPEAL
SEF　NARA, Date 9/9=

SECRET

SANITIZED COPY

DOCUMENT 1: Memorandum of conversation between President Kennedy and Premier Nikita Khrushchev, at the Vienna Summit, June 3, 1961 (pages not relevant to Cuba have not been included).

PAGE 2 OF 6

To this, Mr. Khrushchev replied: "Well, why don't you switch to our system?"

The President then invited Mr. Khrushchev for a private talk inside.

The President referred to the conversation before lunch and said that some of the problems faced by the two countries had been discussed. Now he wanted to come back to the general thesis. While Laos was one problem now under discussion, others might come up in the future. Thus, it would be useful to discuss the general problem underlying the situation and consider the specifics perhaps later. In addition to Laos, which had already been discussed, such specifics might include Germany and nuclear tests. The President then recalled Mr. Khrushchev's earlier reference to the death of feudalism. He said he understood this to mean that capitalism was to be succeeded by Communism. This was a disturbing situation because the French Revolution, as the Chairman well knew, had caused great disturbances and upheavals throughout Europe. Even earlier the struggle between Catholics and Protestants had caused the Hundred Year War. Thus it is obvious that when systems are in transition we should be careful, particularly today when modern weapons are at hand. Whatever the result of the present competition -- and no one can be sure what it will be -- both sides should act in such a way as to prevent them from coming into direct contact and thus prejudicing the establishment of lasting peace, which, the President said, was his ambition.

Mr. Khrushchev interjected that he fully understood this.

Even the Russian Revolution had produced convulsions, even intervention by other countries, the President continued. He then said that he wanted to explain what he meant by "miscalculation". In Washington, he has to attempt to make judgments of events, judgments which may be accurate or not; he made a misjudgment with regard to the Cuban situation. He has to attempt to make judgments as to what the USSR will do next, just as he is sure that Mr. Khrushchev has to make judgments as to the moves of the US. The President emphasized that the purpose of this meeting was to introduce greater precision in these judgments so that our two countries could survive this period of competition without endangering their national security.

Mr. Khrushchev responded by saying that this was a good idea and that this was what he called demonstration of patience and understanding. However, judging by some of the President's statements, the Soviet Union understood the situation differently.

The US

-3-

The US believes that when people want to improve their lot, this is a machination by others. Mr. Khrushchev said that he liked the President's statement in his message to Congress to the effect that it was difficult to defend ideas not supporting better standards of living. However, the President drew the wrong conclusion. He believes that when people rise against tyrants, that is a result of Moscow's activities. This is not so. Failure by the US to understand this generates danger. The USSR does not foment revolution but the United States always looks for outside forces whenever certain upheavals occur.

The Soviet Union does not sympathize with dictators or tyranny. This is the crux of the matter. No agreement seems to be possible on this point, but this fact should be taken into account. Mr. Khrushchev reiterated that the President's views were correct but that he drew the wrong conclusion. Another example of this situation is Cuba. A mere handful of people, headed by Fidel Castro, overthrew the Batista regime because of its oppressive nature. During Castro's fight against Batista, US capitalist circles, as they are called in the USSR, supported Batista and this is why the anger of the Cuban people turned against the United States. The President's decision to launch a landing in Cuba only strengthened the revolutionary forces and Castro's own position, because the people of Cuba were afraid that they would get another Batista and lose the achievements of the revolution. Castro is not a Communist but US policy can make him one. US policy is grist on the mill of Communists, because US actions prove that Communists are right. Mr. Khrushchev said that he himself had not been born a Communist and that it was capitalists who had made him a Communist. He continued by saying that the President's concept was a dangerous one. The President had said that the US had attacked Cuba because it was a threat to American security. Can six million people really be a threat to the mighty US? The United States has stated that it is free to act, but what about Turkey and Iran? These two countries are US followers, they march in its wake, and they have US bases and rockets. If the US believes that it is free to act, then what should the USSR do? The US has set a precedent for intervention in internal affairs of other

countries

[11]

DOCUMENT 1: Memorandum of conversation between President Kennedy and Premier Nikita Khrushchev, at the Vienna Summit, June 3, 1961 (pages not relevant to Cuba have not been included).

PAGE 4 OF 6

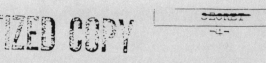

SECRET

-4-

countries. The USSR is stronger than Turkey and Iran, just as the US is stronger than Cuba. This situation may cause miscalculation, to use the President's term. Both sides should agree to rule out miscalculation. This is why, Mr. Khrushchev said, he was happy that the President had said that Cuba was a mistake.

The President said that he agreed with Mr. Khrushchev ▇▇▇▇▇▇▇▇▇▇▇▇▇▇▇▇▇▇▇▇▇▇▇▇▇▇▇▇▇▇▇▇▇▇▇▇ The second point he wanted to make, the President said, was that he held no brief for Batista. The disagreement between the United States and Castro is not over monopolies; this question could be subject to discussion. The main point is that Castro has announced his intention to act in that general area, using Cuba as a base. This could eventually create a peril to the United States. A further point is, the President said, that the United States recognizes that it has bases in Turkey and Iran. However, these two countries are so weak that they could be no threat to the USSR, no more than Cuba to the US. The President reminded Mr. Khrushchev of the announced policy of the USSR that it would not tolerate governments hostile to it in areas which it regards as being of national interest to it. He inquired what the USSR's reaction would be if a government associated with the West were established in Poland. The United States stands for the right of free choice for all peoples and if Castro had acted in that spirit, he might have obtained endorsement. The United States has never taken any action with regard to such countries as ▇▇▇▇▇▇▇▇▇ because the governments in those countries were freely elected and their policies are regarded by the United States as the judgment of their leadership. The President concluded by saying that it was critical to have the changes occurring in the world and affecting the balance of power take place in a way that would not involve the prestige or the treaty commitments of our two countries. The changes should be peaceful. Finally, the President said, if certain governments should fail to produce better living for their people, if they failed to give better education, higher standard of living, etc., to their people, and if they worked in the interest of only a small group, their days would be doomed. But in all these developments, the President reiterated, we should avoid direct contact between our two countries so as not to prejudice the interests of their national security.

Mr. Khrushchev said he agreed with the President's conclusion. Likewise, there were some points of agreement between him and the President with regard to Cuba, although there was still considerable disagreement. For instance, Mr. Khrushchev said, he agreed

that

SECRET

DOCUMENT 1: Memorandum of conversation between President Kennedy and Premier Nikita Khrushchev, at the Vienna Summit, June 3, 1961 (pages not relevant to Cuba have not been included).

PAGE 5 OF 6

SECRET

-5-

that the right of free choice should be ensured to all peoples but the question of choice should be solely up to the people themselves. If Castro has not held any elections, this is an internal affair and it grants no one the right to intervene. If Castro fails to give freedom to his people he will detach himself from them and he will be removed just as Batista was. It would be a different situation if our two countries took it upon themselves to decide this question. Mr. Khrushchev then said that he had noted some inconsistency in US policy. He specified that he did not mean the policy of the President personally, because he had been in the White House only since quite recently, but rather US policy in general. He said that the United States places great emphasis on democracy.

The United States supports the most reactionary regimes and this is how the people see US policy. This weakens US policy. The United States knows that Soviet policy is more popular than US policy in many areas where there is no Communism today. The USSR supports the aspirations of the people but it believes that the main thing is to be tolerant and not to interfere. People should be left to decide for themselves which form of government they desire. As to Fidel Castro, he was no Communist but when the US put pressure on him and applied sanctions against him, the USSR came to his assistance, in the form of trade and technical support. Under the influence of this aid he may turn Communist but, Mr. Khrushchev said, he as a Communist could not see which way Castro would go. Mr. Khrushchev then expressed the hope that the relations between the US and Cuba would improve in such fields as trade, etc. Such a statement, Mr. Khrushchev observed, might sound strange to the United States, but the USSR believes that such a development would improve relations not only in the Western Hemisphere, but also throughout the world. Mr. Khrushchev then referred to Turkey and said that in the recent change that had occurred in that country, the USSR had remained neutral because it regarded the change as an internal affair of that country. Likewise, there had been a second change in Korea within a relatively short time. Neither the USSR nor North Korea had interfered. One can say, however, that the present government will not last very long because it

cannot

SECRET

-6-

cannot give anything to the people. Of course, if South Korea did something in North Korea, the latter will act and the USSR will support it. However, the USSR's position is that of non-interference and of not creating new points of friction. It is a policy directed at bringing about a stable situation throughout the world. Mr. Khrushchev then addressed himself to the Laotian situation and said that the President knew very well that it had been the US Government which had overthrown Souvanna Phouma. One should be frank and recognize that both the United States and the USSR are supplying arms in Laos. The sides supported by the USSR will be more successful because the arms supplied by the United States are directed against the people and the people do not want to take them. In China, the arms supplied by the United States to Chiang Kai Shek went to Mao Tse Tung. Chiang Kai Shek became sort of a transfer point for American arms to Mao Tse Tung. The reason for that was/Chiang's troops simply would not fight against the people. At that point Mao Tse Tung was weaker militarily than Chiang Kai Shek, but he won because his ideas won. In general, the history of revolutions is very instructive. During the Russian Revolution, the revolutionaries were weak and a counter-revolution occurred. The revolutionaries had to fight against the counter-revolutionaries, the British, the Japanese, the French, and others. Even the United States intervened. Mr. Khrushchev recalled in this connection that he had read a book by an American Colonel entitled "U.S. Adventure in Siberia". Notwithstanding all this, the revolution was victorious because the people were on its side. Mr. Khrushchev then said that we must be patient. If the United States supports old, moribund, reactionary regimes, then a precedent of internal intervention will be set, which might cause a clash between our two countries. The USSR certainly does not desire such a development.

The President rejoined by saying that he wished to explain the logic of what Mr. Khrushchev considered to be the illogical point in US position. He said that he wanted to do this not in order to defend any of our actions, but simply to explain things as we saw them. The President stated that we regard the present balance of power between Sino-Soviet forces and the forces of the United States and Western Europe as being more or less in balance. The President said that he did not wish to discuss the details of the respective military postures, but that generally this was how we saw the situation.

Mr. Khrushchev interjected that he agreed with this.

[14]

C-O-P-Y

~~SECRET~~   June 22, 1961

MEMORANDUM FOR MR. McGEORGE BUNDY
THE WHITE HOUSE

Subject: Turkish IRBM's

1. This memorandum is intended to discharge the
obligation which the President laid upon me when he   asked
that I study and report on the matter of Turkish IRBM's.

2. It has been concluded that action should not be
taken to cancel projected deployment of IRBM's to Turkey.

3. This conclusion is based primarily on the view
that, in the aftermath of Khrushchev's hard posture at   Vienna,
cancellation of the IRBM deployment might seem a sign of
weakness. Moreover:

>   (a) When the Secretary of State raised
>   this matter with the Turkish Foreign Minister
>   at CENTO, the Turkish reaction was strongly
>   adverse.

>   (b) When the Turkish Foreign Minister
>   discussed the problem with SACEUR, General
>   Norstad underlined the military importance
>   of sending IRBM's to Turkey. This made it
>   unlikely that any attempt to persuade the
>   Turkish military that they should abandon
>   this project would succeed.

4. The Secretary of State has discussed this
conclusion with General Norstad, who concurs.

/s/

George C. McGhee

DECLASSIFIED
E.O. 11652, Sec. 3(E) and 5(D) or (E)
NLK 75-122 State Letter 6/5/75
~~SECRET~~ By _DLD_ NARS, Date 8/8/75

[15]

DOCUMENT 3: W. W. Rostow, a post–Bay of Pigs strategy paper on Cuba, "Notes on Cuba Policy," April 24, 1961.

PAGE 1 OF 4

THE WHITE HOUSE

Washington

~~TOP SECRET~~   April 24, 1961

MEMORANDUM TO: The Secretary of State
                 The Secretary of Defense
                 Director of Central Intelligence

FROM: W. W. Rostow

SUBJECT: Notes on Cuba Policy.

        Herewith, as promised, some notes on a possible approach to the problem of Cuba. You may wish to consider these tentative notions as you develop your own views in coming days.

        1.   The Approach. The line of approach suggested has these two characteristics:

              a.   it would deal separately with each of the five separate threatening dimensions of the problem represented by Castro.

              b.   it would deal with these problems in ways consistent with -- and, if possible -- reinforcing to our world-wide commitments and, especially, to our relations with other Latin American states.

        2.   The Five Threats. The argument begins by identifying these five threats to us represented by the Castro regime.

              a.   it might join with the USSR in setting up an offensive air or missile base.

              b.   it might build up sufficient conventional military strength to trigger an arms race in the hemisphere and threaten the independence of other Latin American nations.

              c.   it might develop its covert subversive network in ways which would threaten other Latin American nations from within.

              d.   its ideological contours are a/moral and political offense to us; and we are committed, by one means or another, to remove that offense, including our commitment to the Cuban refugees among us.

                              ~~TOP SECRET~~

6

TOP SECRET   -2-

        e.   its ideological contours and success may tend to
inflame disruptive forces in the rest of Latin America, accentuating
existing economic, social, and political tensions which we, in any
case, confront.

     Notes on possible lines of action towards each follow.

    3.   The Threat of an Offensive Base. Following the opening in
Khrushchev's latest note, Thompson should be instructed, at an early
but cooler moment, to tell Gromyko: we note with satisfaction the
Soviet commitment to forego an offensive base in Cuba; that, in line
with the President's speech to the newspaper publishers, this is one
of the minimum conditions for world stability. A further action on
this threat is noted in paragraph 4, below.

    4.   The Threat of an Arms Build-up. An OAS meeting should
be called soon, but after careful diplomatic preparation. The objective
would be to achieve common assertion of the following propositions:

        a.   The constructive tasks of this Hemisphere --
symbolized by the Alliance for Progress -- are such that we cannot
afford to divert excessive resources to arms, picking up here from
the proposal of Alessandri for hemispheric arms limitation.

        b.   We are not prepared to see extra-hemispheric
military forces emplaced in the Western Hemisphere.

    On the basis of such declarations, the OAS would immediately
mount arrangements for: hemispheric arms limitation; cooperative
military arrangements to cope with any military extension of Castro's
power; a demand that Castro accept arms limitation appropriate to the
size of his country, under the common rules of the game; an assertion
that the hemisphere will jointly act to prevent the creation of a foreign
military base or other form of intrusion into the hemisphere.

    If Castro failed to play, we would move towards a selective OAS
blockade of Cuba, designed to prevent arms shipments to him by sea,
if not by air.

TOP SECRET

DOCUMENT 3: W. W. Rostow, a post–Bay of Pigs strategy paper on Cuba, "Notes on Cuba Policy," April 24, 1961.

PAGE 3 OF 4

TOP [SECRET]

-3-

6

5.   The Threat of the Castro and Other Communist Networks. Quite independent of the OAS actions suggested under 4, above, we should begin/ _____   _____ to build up knowledge of the Communist network and to develop common counter-measures. _____   will be able to work with us seriously to the extent that the effort is not made an overt political issue. Moreover, this is mainly a professional, not a political, job.

6.   The Ideological Threat of the Castro Regime Itself.   Here the first step is to make a fresh analysis, on the basis of all the rich intelligence available to us, of the vulnerabilities of the Castro regime. This involves two things. First, a detailed assessment of the Cuban order of battle; located of Castro's control mechanism; of attitudes of key individuals/at strategic points in the regime; of class and regional attitudes towards the regime and recent and foreseeable trends in those attitudes. We need a map of the cohesive forces and tensions within the Castro system. Second, we require a systematic analysis of various alternative means of exploiting in our interest the weaknesses of the regime that lie within our present capabilities or capabilities that might be developed.

_____ In any case, it is essential that we think again before acting in the old grooves.

7.   The Threat of Castroism in Other Latin American States. The roots of Castroism lie in Latin American poverty, social inequality, and that form of zenophobic nationalism which goes with a prior history of inferiority on the world scene. The vulnerability of the Latin American populations to this form of appeal will depend on the pace of economic growth; the pace at which social inequality is reduced; and the pace at which the other Latin American nations move towards what they regard as dignified partnership with the U.S.   What is required here is a radical acceleration and raising of sights in the programs being launched within the Alliance for Progress.

8.   A Contingency Plan.   We do not know what Castro's policy towards the U.S. will be; nor do we know what Soviet policy towards Cuba will be.

A fully developed contingency plan is evidently required.

TOP SECRET

-4-   6

9.   The Ottawa Speech. If we can develop and agree a new line of approach to the Cuban problem in coming days, one possible occasion for suggesting some of its elements might be the President's address in Ottawa, scheduled (I believe) for 17 May. This would be particularly appropriate if we propose to induce Canada to join in the OAS. Other occasions, however, could easily be found; and it is, of course, essential that we make various soundings in the Hemisphere before committing ourselves to this course, notably those outlined under paragraphs 4 and 5.

10.   A Final Point. In two of the four areas where we inherited Communist enclaves of power in the Free World on January 20, we have, initially, not done terribly well. Laos, at best, will yield in the short run a muddy and weak Free World position; in Cuba our first effort at a solution failed. There is building up a sense of frustration and a perception that we are up against a game we can't handle. This frustration and simple anger could lead us to do unwise things or exert scarce national effort and resources in directions which would yield no significant results, while diverting us from our real problems. There is one area where success against Communist techniques is conceivable and where success is desperately required in the Free World interest. That area is Viet-Nam. A maximum effort -- military, economic, political, and diplomatic -- is required there; and it is required urgently.

It is not simple or automatic that we can divert anxieties, frustrations, and anger focussed on a place 90 miles off our shores to a place 7,000 miles away. On the other hand, I believe that the acute domestic tension over Cuba can be eased in the short run if we can get the OAS to move with us along the lines suggested here; and a clean-cut success in Viet-Nam would do much to hold the line in Asia while permitting us -- and the world -- to learn how to deal with indirect aggression.

In the end -- given our kind of society -- we must learn to deal overtly with major forms of covert Communist aggression. And we must teach the Free World how to do it. The combination of the suggested approaches to Cuba and Viet-Nam could help.

DOCUMENT 4: Minutes of first OPERATION MONGOOSE meeting with Attorney General
Robert Kennedy, December 1, 1961.

PAGE 1 OF 3

DRAFT - 12/1/61

Cuba

The Attorney General told the Group about a series of meetings which had been held recently with higher authority. Out of these had come a decision that higher priority should be given to Cuba. General Lansdale had been designated as "Chief of Operations," with authority to call on all appropriate Government agencies for assistance, including the assignment of senior representatives from State, Defense and CIA. General Lansdale is to keep the Special Group informed of his progress, but is authorized to take actions now which are clearly desirable to strengthen operations and facilities now in being. In making this appointment, the need for General Lansdale in the Far East had been recognized but it had been decided that for the time being his responsibility would be Cuba.

After some discussion, it was agreed that General Lansdale should develop a long-range program which would be reviewed by the Special Group and then presented for approval to higher authority. At that time, formal language would be proposed to record the decision to pursue a new or revised Cuba policy. General Lansdale will meet with the Special Group next week to report progress and actions required.

General Lansdale then gave his appreciation of the situation. He said that, bearing in mind the objective [of] eventual revolution within Cuba,] he had surveyed all resources available. He had concluded that there are a sizeable number of latent as well

Moskowitz. 3/18/88

CONFIDENTIAL -OADR

DOCUMENT 4: Minutes of first OPERATION MONGOOSE meeting with Attorney General Robert Kennedy, December 1, 1961.

PAGE 2 OF 3

~~CONFIDENTIAL~~ OADR

- 2 -

as active resources, but that there is a very difficult job ahead. He stressed also the necessity of coming to an agreement at some early date as to the future of Cuba after the Castro government is overthrown, so that appeals to potential resistance elements can be geared to a positive long-range program. General Lansdale also thought it important to obtain cooperation and assistance from selected Latin American countries, preferably those not previously involved with U.S. anti-Castro activities.

.b)(1) ⁼
(d) ⁼
c (4)

DOCUMENT 4: Minutes of first OPERATION MONGOOSE meeting with Attorney General
Robert Kennedy, December 1, 1961.

PAGE 3 OF 3

- 3 -

Finally, in answer to the Chairman's question as to the
significance of the two weeks review which had been elsewhere alluded
to, the Attorney General said that this was intended to mean a review
by the Special Group, with subsequent reference to higher authority.

DOCUMENT 5: Brig. Gen. Edward Lansdale, "The Cuba Project," February 20, 1962 (progam review and basic action plan for OPERATION MONGOOSE).

PAGE 1 OF 15

SENSITIVE   20 February 1962

Program Review
by Brig. Gen. Lansdale

THE CUBA PROJECT

The Goal. In keeping with the spirit of the Presidential memorandum of 30 November 1961, the United States will help the people of Cuba overthrow the Communist regime from within Cuba and institute a new government with which the United States can live in peace.

The Situation. We still know too little about the real situation inside Cuba, although we are taking energetic steps to learn more. However, some salient facts are known. It is known that the Communist regime is an active Sino-Soviet spearhead in our Hemisphere and that Communist controls inside Cuba are severe. Also, there is evidence that the repressive measures of the Communists, together with disappointments in Castro's economic dependency on the Communist formula, have resulted in an anti-regime atmosphere among the Cuban people which makes a resistance program a distinct and present possibility.

Time is running against us. The Cuban people feel helpless and are losing hope fast. They need symbols of inside resistance and of outside interest soon. They need something they can join with the hope of starting to work surely towards overthrowing the regime. Since late November, we have been working hard to re-orient the operational concepts within the U.S. government and to develop the hard intelligence and operational assets required for success in our task.

The next National Intelligence Estimate on Cuba (NIE 85-62) promises to be a useful document dealing with our practical needs and with due recognition of the sparsity of hard facts. The needs of the Cuba project, as it goes into operation, plus the increasing U.S. capability for intelligence collection, should permit more frequent estimates for our guidance. These will be prepared on a periodic basis.

Premise of Action. Americans once ran a successful revolution. It was run from within, and succeeded because there was timely and strong political, economic, and military help by nations outside who supported our cause. Using this same concept of revolution from within, we must now help the Cuban people to stamp out tyranny and gain their liberty.

On 18 January, the Chief of Operations assigned thirty-two tasks to Departments and Agencies of the U.S. government, in order to provide a realistic assessment and preparation of U.S. capabilities. The Attorney General and the Special Group were apprised of this action. The answers received on 15 February provided the basis for planning a realistic course of action. The answers also revealed that the course of action must contain continuing coordination and firm overall guidance.

The course of action set forth herein is realistic within present operational estimates and intelligence. Actually, it represents the maximum target timing which the operational people jointly considered feasible. It aims for a revolt which can take place in Cuba by October 1962. It is a

Excluded from
automatic regrading:
DoD Dir 5200.10
does not apply.

SENSITIVE
UNCLASSIFIED
TOP SECRET

This document contains ____ pg
Copy No. 4 of 12 copie

DOCUMENT 5: Brig. Gen. Edward Lansdale, "The Cuba Project," February 20, 1962 (progam review and basic action plan for OPERATION MONGOOSE).

PAGE 2 OF 15

series of target actions and dates, not a rigid time-table. The target dates are timed as follows:

Phase I, <u>Action</u>, March 1962. Start moving in.

Phase II, <u>Build-up</u>, April-July 1962. Activating the necessary operations inside Cuba for revolution and concurrently applying the vital political, economic, and military-type support from outside Cuba.

Phase III, <u>Readiness</u>, 1 August 1962, check for final policy decision.

Phase IV, <u>Resistance</u>, August-September 1962, move into guerrilla operations.

Phase V, <u>Revolt</u>, first two weeks of October 1962. Open revolt and overthrow of the Communist regime.

Phase VI, <u>Final</u>, during month of October 1962. Establishment of new government.

<u>Plan of Action</u>. Attached is an operational plan for the overthrow of the Communist regime in Cuba, by Cubans from within Cuba, with outside help from the U.S. and elsewhere. Since this is an operation to prompt and support a revolt by the people in a Communist police state, flexibility is a must for success. Decisions on operational flexibility rest with the Chief of Operations, with consultation in the Special Group when policy matters are involved. Target actions and dates are detailed in the attached operational plans, which cover:

        A. Basic Action Plan Inside Cuba

        B. Political Support Plan

        C. Economic Support Plan

        D. Psychological Support Plan

        E. Military Support Plan

        F. Sabotage Support Plan

        G. Intelligence Support Plan

<u>Early Policy Decisions</u>. The operational plan for clandestine U.S. support of a Cuban movement inside Cuba to overthrow the Communist regime is within policy limits already set by the President. A vital decision, still to be made, is on the use of open U.S. force to aid the Cuban people in winning their liberty. If conditions and assets permitting a revolt are achieved in Cuba, and if U.S. help is required to sustain this condition, will the U.S. respond promptly with military force to aid the Cuban revolt? The contingencies under which such military deployment would be needed, and recommended U.S. responses, are detailed in a memorandum being prepared by the Secretaries of State and of Defense. An early decision is required, prior to deep involvement of the Cubans in this program.

DOCUMENT 5: Brig. Gen. Edward Lansdale, "The Cuba Project," February 20, 1962 (progam review and basic action plan for OPERATION MONGOOSE).

PAGE 3 OF 15

Distribution:

Copy No.

1.	The President
2.	The Attorney General
3.	General Taylor
4.	The Secretary of State (through Deputy Under Secretary Johnson)
5.	The Secretary of Defense (through Deputy Secretary Gilpatric)
6.	The Director, Central Intelligence Agency
7.	The Director, U. S. Information Agency (through Deputy Director Wilson)
8.	State (Mr. Goodwin)
9.	Defense (Brig. Gen. Craig)
10.	CIA (Mr. Harvey)
11.-12.	Chief of Operations (Brig. Gen. Lansdale)

DOCUMENT 5: Brig. Gen. Edward Lansdale, "The Cuba Project," February 20, 1962 (program review and basic action plan for OPERATION MONGOOSE).

PAGE 4 OF 15

UNCLASSIFIED ~~SITIVE~~

OFFICE OF THE SECRETARY OF DEFENSE
WASHINGTON 25, D.C.

⑨

20 February 1962

EYES ONLY

EYES ONLY OF ADDRESSEES

FROM: Brig. Gen. Lansdale SIGNED

SUBJECT: The Cuba Project

Transmitted herewith is the projection of actions to help Cubans recapture their freedom. This total plan is EYES ONLY. The lives of many brave people depend on the security of this paper entrusted to you. Any inference that this plan exists could place the President of the United States in a most damaging position.

This is a specific plan, with time phases. It responds to the request of the Special Group (5412) for such a paper. I urge that this paper _not_ be made known, in this complete form, beyond yourself and those named as addressees.

The Attorney General
Special Group: General Taylor
State: Secretary Rusk, Alexis Johnson, Richard Goodwin
Defense: Secretary McNamara, Deputy Secretary Gilpatric,
        Brig. Gen. Craig   Gen. Lemnitzer
CIA: John McCone, Richard Helms, William Harvey
USIA: Ed Murrow, Don Wilson

UNCLASSIFIED ~~SENSITIVE~~

DOCUMENT 5: Brig. Gen. Edward Lansdale, "The Cuba Project," February 20, 1962 (progam review and basic action plan for OPERATION MONGOOSE).

PAGE 5 OF 15

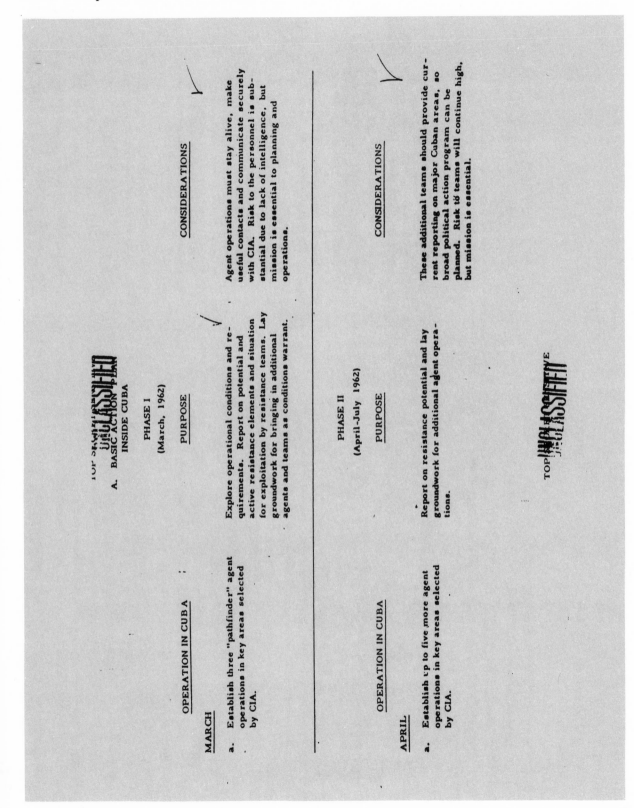

TOP SECRET — UNCLASSIFIED

A. BASIC ACTION PLAN
INSIDE CUBA

PHASE I
(March, 1962)

PURPOSE	OPERATION IN CUBA	CONSIDERATIONS
Explore operational conditions and requirements. Report on potential and active resistance elements and situation for exploitation by resistance teams. Lay groundwork for bringing in additional agents and teams as conditions warrant.	**MARCH** a. Establish three "pathfinder" agent operations in key areas selected by CIA.	Agent operations must stay alive, make useful contacts and communicate securely with CIA. Risk to the personnel is substantial due to lack of intelligence, but mission is essential to planning and operations.

PHASE II
(April-July 1962)

PURPOSE	OPERATION IN CUBA	CONSIDERATIONS
Report on resistance potential and lay groundwork for additional agent operations.	**APRIL** a. Establish up to five more agent operations in key areas selected by CIA.	These additional teams should provide current reporting on major Cuban areas, so broad political action program can be planned. Risk to teams will continue high, but mission is essential.

TOP SECRET — UNCLASSIFIED

DOCUMENT 5: Brig. Gen. Edward Lansdale, "The Cuba Project," February 20, 1962 (progam review and basic action plan for OPERATION MONGOOSE).

PAGE 6 OF 15

UNCLASSIFIED

A. BASIC ACTION PLAN

PHASE II (cont.)

OPERATION IN CUBA	PURPOSE	CONSIDERATIONS
APRIL (cont.) b. "Voice" of Cuban movement goes on the air.	Establishes vital psychological assurance to people that a movement exists to overthrow the regime.	Preferably, the "voice" should be from mobile transmitter inside Cuba. Broadcasts can be brief ones at first: identifying music, slogan, and short news. News to include reports on "resistance" acts, taking credit for all sabotage. As daily broadcasts are established, "criminals against people" should be named and promised swift justice, two names per broadcast. If operational judgment dictates, [redacted] It is vital to take risks by having it inside Cuba; a second transmitter and crew should be moved in if the first is lost.
MAY c. Re-supply agent operations as necessary.	Deliver supplies to satisfy needs developed by agent operations, if valid.	The agents will have to prove to local partisans that outside support is a reality. Thus, as arms, ammunition, and equipment, etc., are needed to equip resistance groups, we must be able to respond effectively to these needs. Maritime and, as feasible, air re-supply will be used. This capability will have to expand as resistance is developed.

UNCLASSIFIED

TOP SECRET

DOCUMENT 5: Brig. Gen. Edward Lansdale, "The Cuba Project," February 20, 1962 (progam review and basic action plan for OPERATION MONGOOSE).

PAGE 7 OF 15

UNCLASSIFIED

A. BASIC ACTION PLAN

PHASE II (cont.)

	PURPOSE	CONSIDERATIONS
OPERATION IN CUBA		
d. By June establish 12 more agent operations in key areas selected by CIA.	Mission is the same as for previous "pathfinder" operations.	These will be the last agent operations infiltrated into key areas from the outside. Further expansion by "pathfinders," after these teams are in, can be done from groups inside. It is likely that some of these last "pathfinders" will be replacing casualties.
JUNE		
e. By June, introduce three resistance teams in areas under initial "pathfinder" surveillance, if situation is favorable.	This will test acceptance and use of the more highly trained teams that must guide development of the popular revolution within Cuba. This also will check emphasis and timing of program from viewpoint of Cuban situation.	Very minor resistance actions by important population elements such as labor must be tried and groundwork laid for broader anti-regime program leading toward firm uprising program. Realism of political platform can be tested.
f. Establish bases for guerrilla operations.	To have focal points, with some viability to stockpile for defensive needs and for future attack operations.	These bases are to be selected after on-the-ground surveys by the teams inside Cuba. Some may exist already. These will also be logistical bases, for caches and stockpiling of arms and equipment to be used by the resistance. The p. a. teams will need not only supplies for active resistance, but also should be able to provide some welfare aid (such as to families of resistance members, families affected by plants shut-down by sabotage, etc.).

TOP SECRET UNCLASSIFIED

DOCUMENT 5: Brig. Gen. Edward Lansdale, "The Cuba Project," February 20, 1962 (progam review and basic action plan for OPERATION MONGOOSE).

PAGE 8 OF 15

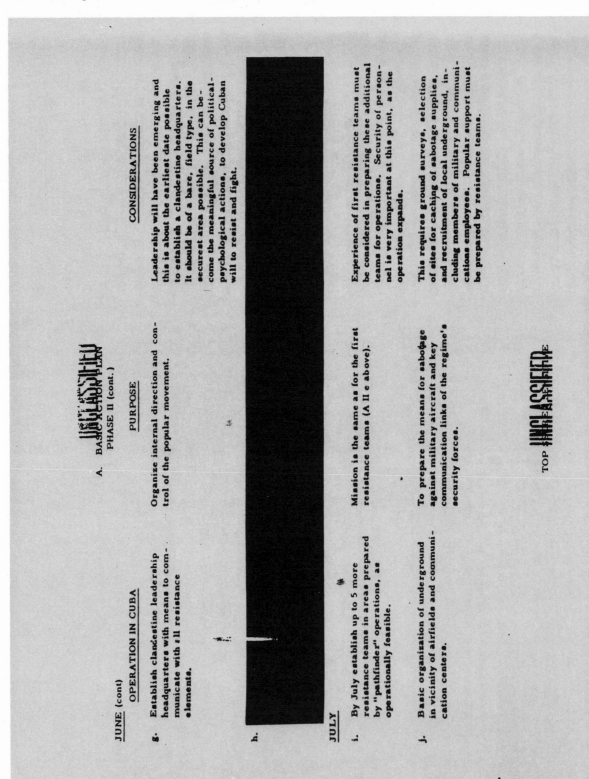

UNCLASSIFIED

A. BASIC ACTION PLAN

PHASE II (cont.)

OPERATION IN CUBA	PURPOSE	CONSIDERATIONS
JUNE (cont)		
g. Establish clandestine leadership headquarters with means to communicate with all resistance elements.	Organize internal direction and control of the popular movement.	Leadership will have been emerging and this is about the earliest date possible to establish a clandestine headquarters. It should be of a bare, field type, in the securest area possible. This can become the meaningful source of political-psychological actions, to develop Cuban will to resist and fight.
h.		
JULY		
i. By July establish up to 5 more resistance teams in areas prepared by "pathfinder" operations, as operationally feasible.	Mission is the same as for the first resistance teams (A II e above).	Experience of first resistance teams must be considered in preparing these additional teams for operations. Security of personnel is very important at this point, as the operation expands.
j. Basic organization of underground in vicinity of airfields and communication centers.	To prepare the means for sabotage against military aircraft and key communication links of the regime's security forces.	This requires ground surveys, selection of sites for caching of sabotage supplies, and recruitment of local underground, including members of military and communications employees. Popular support must be prepared by resistance teams.

TOP SECRET UNCLASSIFIED

DOCUMENT 5: Brig. Gen. Edward Lansdale, "The Cuba Project," February 20, 1962 (progam review and basic action plan for OPERATION MONGOOSE).

PAGE 9 OF 15

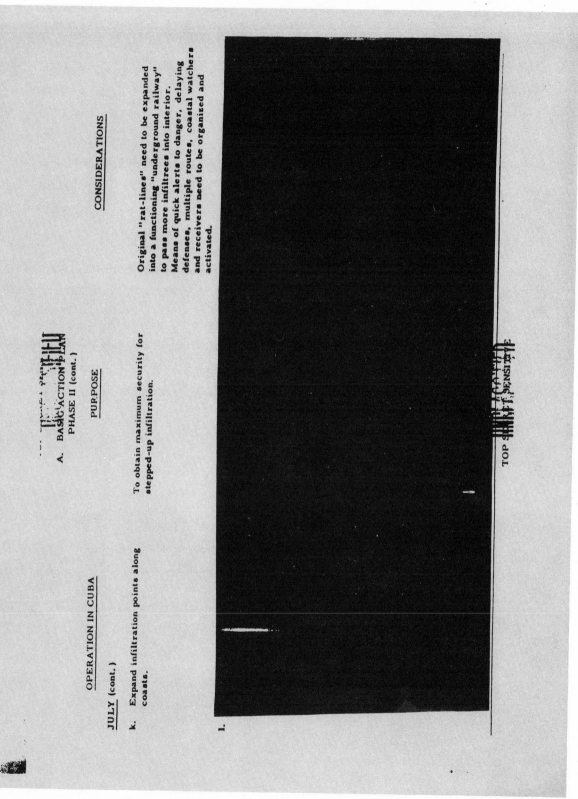

BASIC ACTION PLAN

A. BASIC ACTION PLAN
PHASE II (cont.)

PURPOSE

To obtain maximum security for
stepped-up infiltration.

CONSIDERATIONS

Original "rat-lines" need to be expanded
into a functioning "underground railway"
to pass more infiltrees into interior.
Means of quick alerts to danger, delaying
defenses, multiple routes, coastal watchers
and receivers need to be organized and
activated.

OPERATION IN CUBA

JULY (cont.)

k. Expand infiltration points along
coasts.

l.

TOP SECRET SENSITIVE

DOCUMENT 5: Brig. Gen. Edward Lansdale, "The Cuba Project," February 20, 1962 (progam review and basic action plan for OPERATION MONGOOSE).

PAGE 10 OF 15

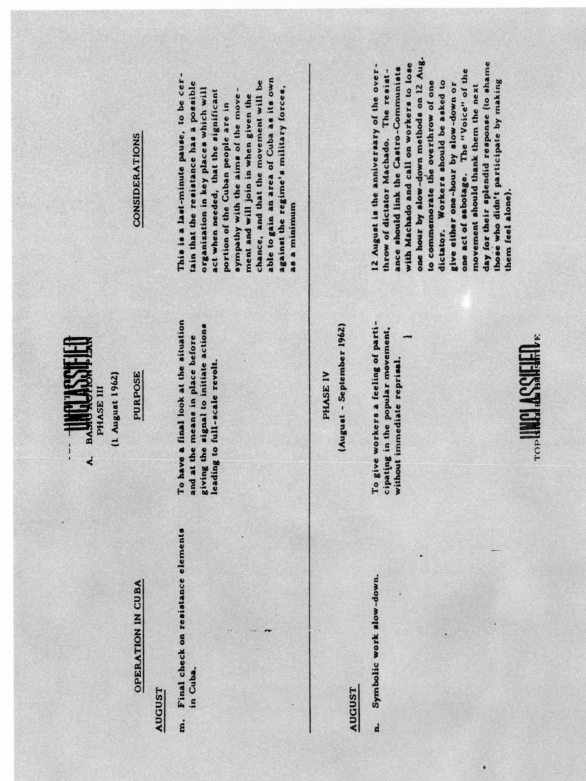

UNCLASSIFIED

A. BASIC ACTION PLAN
PHASE III
(1 August 1962)

OPERATION IN CUBA	PURPOSE	CONSIDERATIONS
AUGUST m. Final check on resistance elements in Cuba.	To have a final look at the situation and at the means in place before giving the signal to initiate actions leading to full-scale revolt.	This is a last-minute pause, to be certain that the resistance has a possible organization in key places which will act when needed, that the significant portion of the Cuban people are in sympathy with the aims of the movement and will join in when given the chance, and that the movement will be able to gain an area of Cuba as its own against the regime's military forces, as a minimum

PHASE IV
(August - September 1962)

	PURPOSE	CONSIDERATIONS
AUGUST n. Symbolic work slow-down.	To give workers a feeling of participating in the popular movement, without immediate reprisal.	12 August is the anniversary of the overthrow of dictator Machado. The resistance should link the Castro-Communists with Machado and call on workers to lose one hour by slow-down methods on 12 Aug. to commemorate the overthrow of one dictator. Workers should be asked to give either one-hour by slow-down or one act of sabotage. The "Voice" of the movement should thank them the next day for their splendid response (to shame those who didn't participate by making them feel alone).

UNCLASSIFIED

DOCUMENT 5: Brig. Gen. Edward Lansdale, "The Cuba Project," February 20, 1962 (progam review and basic action plan for OPERATION MONGOOSE).

PAGE 11 OF 15

UNCLASSIFIED

A. BASIC ACTION PLAN
PHASE IV (cont.)

OPERATION IN CUBA	PURPOSE	CONSIDERATIONS
AUGUST (cont.)		
o. Symbolic signs painted on walls: "Machado One"	To commemorate the downfall of one remembered dictator and give a symbolic pace to the resistance.	Timed with the symbolic work slowdown (A IV n above). Spaced a few days apart, the signs should have lines added to them to read: "Machado One Batista Two Castro Three."
p. By August, have actions to penetrate and subvert the regime.	To weaken and frustrate organized actions against the popular movement.	These are actions on officials of the regime, including the military and the police. Some should be defected in place. Others should be defected and helped to escape to the outside world to tell the inside story of the regime's tyranny, to evoke world sympathy with the freedom fighters.
q. Cuban paramilitary teams infiltrated to bases in the hills.	To provide a trained guerrilla cadre upon which to form guerrilla units.	The paramilitary teams must be capable of initiating minor harassment and reprisal actions, as well as organizing and training guerrilla units. Popular support is essential.
r. Guerrilla bands activated in key areas.	To build a military striking force for the popular movement inside Cuba.	Recruits will be coming in after the symbolic harassment and reprisal actions. They will be screened, organized, and trained for guerrilla action. The regime's security forces can be expected to be very active. Anti-tank and anti-aircraft tactics are necessary. Increased popular support is a must in this phase.

UNCLASSIFIED

DOCUMENT 5: Brig. Gen. Edward Lansdale, "The Cuba Project," February 20, 1962 (progam review and basic action plan for OPERATION MONGOOSE).

PAGE 12 OF 15

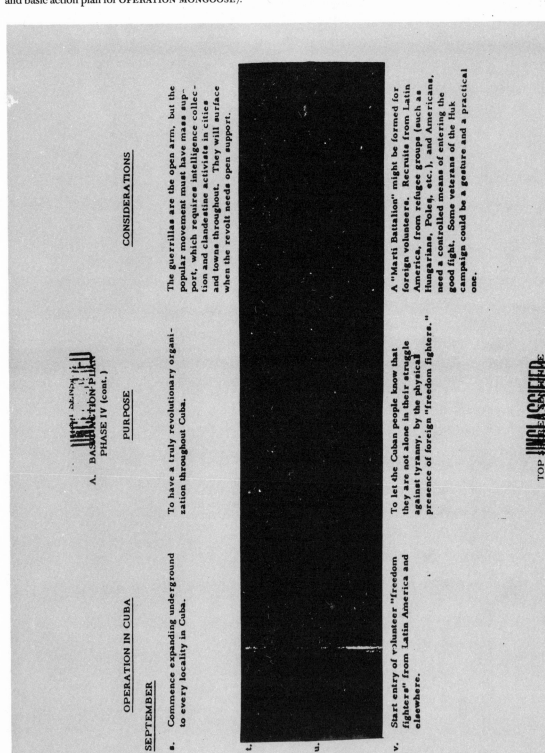

A. BASIC ACTION PLAN (cont.)

PHASE IV (cont.)

OPERATION IN CUBA

SEPTEMBER

s. Commence expanding underground to every locality in Cuba.

t.

u.

v. Start entry of volunteer "freedom fighters" from Latin America and elsewhere.

PURPOSE

To have a truly revolutionary organization throughout Cuba.

To let the Cuban people know that they are not alone in their struggle against tyranny, by the physical presence of foreign "freedom fighters."

CONSIDERATIONS

The guerrillas are the open arm, but the popular movement must have mass support, which requires intelligence collection and clandestine activists in cities and towns throughout. They will surface when the revolt needs open support.

A "Marti Battalion" might be formed for foreign volunteers. Recruits from Latin America, from refugee groups (such as Hungarians, Poles, etc.), and Americans, need a controlled means of entering the good fight. Some veterans of the Huk campaign could be a gesture and a practical one.

TOP SECRET

DOCUMENT 5: Brig. Gen. Edward Lansdale, "The Cuba Project," February 20, 1962 (progam review and basic action plan for OPERATION MONGOOSE).

PAGE 13 OF 15

DOCUMENT 5: Brig. Gen. Edward Lansdale, "The Cuba Project," February 20, 1962 (progam review and basic action plan for OPERATION MONGOOSE).

PAGE 14 OF 15

UNCLASSIFIED

A. BASIC ACTION PLAN

OPERATION IN CUBA	PURPOSE	CONSIDERATIONS

PHASE IV (cont.)

SEPTEMBER (cont.)

z.

PHASE V

(FIRST TWO WEEKS, OCTOBER 1962)

OCTOBER

OPERATION IN CUBA	PURPOSE	CONSIDERATIONS
a. General strike by the Cuban workers.	To make public the popular support of the militant revolt, signifying the passing from underground to open rebellion.	Strike must tie-up transportation and communications. The resistance teams must have set the readiness of the workers for this defiance of the regime. Arms must be available. Military cells will be activated. Funds will be needed to help the workers hold on and to bait defections of groups.
b. Anti-regime demonstrations.	Same purpose as noted above (A V a) for the general strike.	The resistance teams must have set the readiness of all population elements (youth, farmers, Church, etc.), to openly defy the regime. Arms must be available, including anti-tank weapons. Military cells will be activated.
c. Declaration of the revolt.	To initiate the hour of decision by calling on all Cubans for open support.	Since the aims of the liberation will have been publicized previously, this is the "go" signal. All Cubans and the world need to hear it.

UNCLASSIFIED

DOCUMENT 5: Brig. Gen. Edward Lansdale, "The Cuba Project," February 20, 1962 (progam review and basic action plan for OPERATION MONGOOSE).

PAGE 15 OF 15

A. BASIC ACTION PLAN (cont.)

PHASE V (cont.)

OPERATION IN CUBA	PURPOSE	CONSIDERATIONS
OCTOBER (cont.)		
d. Open revolt by the Cuban people.	To overthrow the Communist regime.	This is the combat phase, fighting to take and hold ground.
e. Return of Cuban refugees who are qualified and want to help liberate their homeland.	To start a more open movement back to Cuba of those Cuban refugees who are able and willing to risk their lives in overthrowing the Communist regime.	Cuban refugee organizations will be tested with a "put up or shut up" proposition. Those who have ability to contribute to the popular movement inside Cuba should be given a chance to go home and act. Their screening and infiltration will have to be controlled. It must be a joining-in, not a taking-over of the inside movement.

PHASE VI

(DURING OCTOBER 1962)

a. Establish a new Cuban government, which can be recognized by the U.S.	To give legality to the moral right of the Cuban revolt.	When the popular movement is holding meaningful territory in Cuba, it should form a provisional government. This should permit open Latin American and U.S. help, if requested and necessary. A military government situation will exist for the initial period and we must insist upon realism in this interim period preceding reasonable civilian control.

17

UNCLASSIFIED   14 March 1962

Guidelines for Operation Mongoose

1.   Operation Mongoose will be developed on the following
assumptions:

   a.   In undertaking to cause the overthrow of the target
government, the U.S. will make maximum use of indigenous resources, internal and external, but recognizes that final
success will require decisive U.S. military intervention.

   b.   Such indigenous resources as are developed will be
used to prepare for and justify this intervention, and thereafter to facilitate and support it.

2.   The immediate priority objective of U.S. efforts during
the coming months will be the acquisition of hard intelligence on
the target area. Concurrently, all other political, economic and
covert actions will be undertaken short of those reasonably calculated to inspire a revolt within the target area, or other development
which would require U.S. armed intervention. These actions, insofar
as possible, will be consistent with overt policies of isolating the
▓▓▓▓ ▓▓▓▓▓ ▓▓▓ of neutralizing his influence in the Western
▓▓▓▓▓▓▓▓▓▓

███

                                                 The JCS will
continue the planning ████████████████████████████

Cy __2__ of 10 Copies

UNCLASSIFIED

UNCLASSIFIED

- 2 -

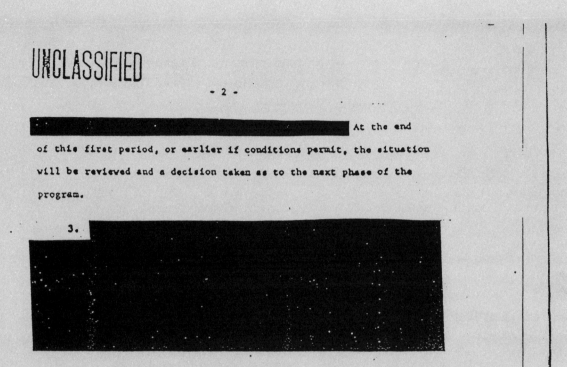

At the end of this first period, or earlier if conditions permit, the situation will be reviewed and a decision taken as to the next phase of the program.

3.

4.   During this period, General Lansdale will continue as chief of operations, calling directly on the participating departments and agencies for support and implementation of agreed tasks. The heads of these departments and agencies are responsible for performance through normal command channels to higher authority. General Lansdale is responsible for coordinating combined planning and execution, reporting to higher authority through the Special Group (5412), augmented by the Attorney General and the Chairman, JCS. The Special Group (5412 augmented) is responsible for providing policy guidance to the project, for approving important operations and for monitoring progress.

Lansdale
-- chief of
Op Mongoose
and report to
Special Group

DOCUMENT 7: Brig. Gen. Edward Lansdale, "Review of OPERATION MONGOOSE,"
Phase One, July 25, 1962.

PAGE 1 OF 8

UNCLASSIFIED ~~TOP SECRET~~ **MONGOOSE**

OFFICE OF THE SECRETARY OF DEFENSE
WASHINGTON 25, D. C.

(40)

SENSITIVE   25 July 1962

MEMORANDUM FOR THE SPECIAL GROUP (AUGMENTED)

From: Brig. Gen. Lansdale

Subject: Review of Operation Mongoose

     This is the Operations report at the end of Phase I. It has
been compiled to assist you in reviewing Operation Mongoose thus
far and in determining the best course of U.S. action for the future.

     This Operations report contains the contribution of each major
participant, on objectives, on the planning and operational activity
to win these objectives, and on future possibilities to be governed by
the policy framework. A National Intelligence Estimate (NIE 85-2-62)
is being submitted separately for consideration in connection with
this report.

     As Chief of Operations, I am indicating in this covering
memorandum what I consider to be the most significant aspects of
our policy and program picture. The full report of each major participant is appended, to ensure that you have access to the exact reporting
as submitted.

OBJECTIVES

     As desired by higher authority on 30 November 1961, the U.S.
undertook a special effort "in order to help Cuba overthrow the Communist
regime." After a review of operational planning and programming concepts, the Special Group (Augmented) provided guidelines on 14 March
1962 for Phase I, Operation Mongoose (roughly until the end of July 1962).
The main objectives were seen as:

     a. The acquisition of hard intelligence on the target area.

Excluded from automatic
regrading: DoD Dir 5200.10
does not apply.

UNCLASSIFIED ~~TOP SECRET~~

DOCUMENT 7: Brig. Gen. Edward Lansdale, "Review of OPERATION MONGOOSE,"
Phase One, July 25, 1962.

PAGE 2 OF 8

UNCLASSIFIED

b. Undertaking all other political, economic, and covert actions, short of inspiring a revolt in Cuba or developing the need for U.S. armed intervention.

c. Be consistent with U.S. overt policy, and remain in position to disengage with minimum loss in assets and U.S. prestige.

d. Continue JCS planning and essential preliminary actions for a decisive U.S. capability for intervention.

ACCOMPLISHMENT

Elements of the U.S. government were organized to reach the goals set for Phase I. My assessment of where we are on each objective is noted under appropriate sub-headings below. In general, this has been a remarkably quiet operation, well within the "noise" and "visibility" limits imposed.

Higher authority has been kept informed of progress through the Special Group (Augmented), by frequent reports. The Special Group has provided policy guidance, as required, in Phase I.

The Chief of Operations has coordinated the efforts of participating departments and agencies, through meetings of the Operational Representatives and by constant review of progress. The Operational Representative of each major U.S. participant in Operation Mongoose are William Harvey (CIA), Robert Hurwitch (State), Brig. Gen. Benjamin Harris (Defense), and Don Wilson (USIA).

My assessment of the organization, planning, and actions to reach the goals in Phase I:

Intelligence. CIA had the main assignment to acquire the "hard-intelligence" desired. The headquarters and field staff of CIA are now well organized for a major effort for this aspect of Operation Mongoose, being strengthened by a number of CIA officers experienced in "denied area" operations elsewhere in the world. Planning and actions rate superior, in a professional sense of intelligence collection.

CIA established the Caribbean Admission Center at Opa-Locka, Florida, ███████████████████████████████

2

UNCLASSIFIED

40:

TO **UNCLASSIFIED**

████████████████████████████

However, the effort in more remote provincial areas of Cuba,
where guerrilla resistance was expected to be spotted, recruited,
and organized, was short of the hoped-for goal; this was due to the
regime's security precautions and, to some degree, to policy limitations on the risks to be assumed.

Defense contributed the majority of personnel to staff the
Caribbean Admission Center, ████████████████████
despite changes and improved sophistication of Cuban communication
procedures, and brought into play the available assets of Service intelligence organizations, in coordination with CIA. State stepped up its
information collection from diplomatic and refugee organization sources.
Justice (FBI and INS) and USIA provided significant support to the
Caribbean Admission Center.

Political. State appointed a representative to devote full-time
to Operation Mongoose and to develop the required political actions.
During Phase I, the Punta del Este conference was a major U.S. political
action to isolate Castro and neutralize his influence in the Hemisphere,
but was not developed within the context of Operation Mongoose. The
successful visit of President Kennedy to Mexico was another major U.S.
political action, with a potential impact upon our special goals, but was
not developed within the context of Operation Mongoose. Two Operation
Mongoose efforts in political action were attempted in Phase I: to
counter Castro-Communist propaganda exploitation of May Day and to
arouse strong Hemisphere reaction to Cuban military suppression of the
hunger demonstration at Cardenas, in June. Ambassadors in Latin America
were asked to undertake a special effort, as possible, with the help of their
Country Teams; political action results in both instances were mostly
negative, due to lack of capability and the local attitude in Latin American
countries.

State is responsible for refugee political policy matters, assisted
by CIA in daily liaison. This is an area of major interest to Operation
Mongoose, since the Cuban refugees have an open objective of overthrowing the Communist regime in Havana and recapturing their homeland.

3

TO **UNCLASSIFIED**

DOCUMENT 7: Brig. Gen. Edward Lansdale, "Review of OPERATION MONGOOSE,"
Phase One, July 25, 1962.

PAGE 4 OF 8

TO~~UNCLASSIFIED~~

They are given open U.S. assistance to remain in this country, yet
are participating in covert actions in a limited way. Only a fractional
opening has been made to release the frustrated energy of these refugees
in freeing their homeland and in creating a favorable political climate in
Latin America for the liberation of Cuba. Policy limitations of "audibility"
and "visibility" apply directly in considering the handling and use of this
dynamic refugee potential.

As a working document for U.S. operational guidance, State
developed a definition of a political program for a free Cuba, with the
understanding that any real political program must be developed by the
Cubans themselves.

Psychological. Psychological activities for Operation Mongoose
make use of existing assignments of responsibilities within the U. S.
government: State, having the policy role, chairs an inter-agency Cuba
Psychological Operations Group which meets weekly; USIA disseminates
any U.S. government information (VOA and Press Service) ████████████

██

Conditions and events in Cuba have provided many effective themes,
which have been promptly and sharply exploited by available means in the
Western Hemisphere. However, the U.S. still lacks the capability of
effectively getting information to the majority of the Cuban people. Our
short-wave broadcasts are highly regarded by the Cuban people, but short-
wave receiver sets are limited inside Cuba. Our medium-wave broadcasts
compete against stronger Cuban signals; it was felt that greater U.S.
competition in medium-wave broadcasts could lead to Cuban interference
of U.S. commercial broadcasts over a fairly wide area of the U.S.
Clandestine broadcasts ████████████ (appearing as broadcasts by
Cuban guerrillas inside Cuba) have been initiated; they are in their infancy,
and have a long way to develop before their messages are believed and
get passed among Cubans by word-of-mouth. Dissemination of leaflets
and propaganda inside Cuba ████████████ has not received policy
approval.

Economic. State has the main responsibility for developing economic
actions. State has chaired an inter-agency working group, which generated

4

TO~~UNCLASSIFIED~~

DOCUMENT 7: Brig. Gen. Edward Lansdale, "Review of OPERATION MONGOOSE,"
Phase One, July 25, 1962.

PAGE 5 OF 8

~~UNCLASSIFIED~~

the U.S. trade embargo, denial of bunkering facilities, increased port
security, and control procedures on transhipment, technical data, and
customs inspection. Diplomatic means were used to frustrate Cuban
trade negotiations in Israel, Jordan, Iran, Greece, and possibly Japan.
Under Resolution VIII adopted at Punta del Este, the OAS has established
a special committee to study "the feasibility and desirability of extending
the suspension of trade with Cuba to other items (than arms)," State has
prepared a program to be submitted to this OAS committee in the future.

The evidence in that Cuba's economy is suffering. Trade with the
Communist Bloc and others has kept it limping along, despite scarcity
of U.S. goods, the bad drought limiting agrarian crops, increased worker
non-cooperation and the regime's bungling of economic control measures.
Critical spare parts still arrive in Cuba, including shipments from British
and Canadian firms. Chartered shipping from Free World sources still
plays a major role in Cuba's trade, and the U.S. has little hope of cutting
this life-line to Castro.

CIA reports that 11 teams will have been infiltrated by
the end of July and that 19 maritime operations have aborted. Of the
teams in, the most successful is the one in Pinar del Rio in western Cuba;
its success was helped greatly by a maritime re-supply of arms and
equipment; the fact that it is a "going concern" and receives help from
outside has attracted recruits. Its potential has been estimated at about
250, which is a sizeable guerrilla force. With equally large guerrilla
forces in other Cuban provinces, guerrilla warfare could be activated
with a good chance of success, if assisted properly. However, the teams
in other provinces have not been so successful; our best hope is that we
will have viable teams in all the potential resistance areas by early October.
Bad weather, high seas, and increased security patrols will make the
infiltration of teams and their re-supply from small boats a hard task.

5

~~UNCLASSIFIED~~

DOCUMENT 7: Brig. Gen. Edward Lansdale, "Review of OPERATION MONGOOSE,"
Phase One, July 25, 1962.

PAGE 6 OF 8

UNCLASSIFIED

Sabotage has not taken place, on a U.S.-sponsored basis. Planning for such action by CIA has been thorough, including detailed study of the structures and vulnerabilities of key targets. Commando type raids would take maritime means which now have priority use in support of CIA teams being infiltrated inside to survey and create a guerrilla potential. CIA has reported that there is now some capability inside Cuba for sabotage action, that target selection has been under further careful review, and that a proposal is forthcoming to be submitted for policy approval.

Intervention Planning. The JCS were given the responsibility for planning and undertaking essential preliminary actions for a decisive U.S. capability for intervention in Cuba. This "Guidelines" objective has been met, fully. Also, U.S. military readiness for intervention in Cuba has been under continuing review within Defense, being improved wherever feasible. In addition, rumors during June of a possible uprising inside Cuba led to further planning for a contingency where a non-U.S. inspired revolt might start inside Cuba; inter-agency staffing of U.S. planning for such a Cuban contingency is being completed, under Defense leadership.

Assets. Whatever we decide to do in the future depends, to a large degree, on the assets available to us. Our own U.S. assets in organization, personnel, and equipment are sufficient to liberate Cuba, given the decision to do so. Assets among the Cubans, to liberate themselves, are capable of a greater effectiveness once a firm decision is made by the U.S. to provide maximum support of Cubans to liberate Cuba, and the Cubans start being helped towards that goal by the U.S. There are enough able-bodied and properly motivated Cubans inside Cuba and in exile to do the job. There is wide-spread disaffection in Cuba, with strong indications that economic distress and demoralization of population is causing real concern and strain for the regime's control officials. Firm U.S. intention to help free Cuba is the key factor in assessing the Cubans themselves as an operational asset for Operation Mongoose.

At the close of Phase I, my concern is strong that time is running out for the U.S. to make a free choice on Cuba, based largely on what is happening to the will of the Cuban people. Rightly or wrongly, the Cubans have looked and are looking to the U.S. for guidance on what to aspire to and do next. They wonder if we are not merely watching Cuba closely, as

6

UNCLASSIFIED

DOCUMENT 7: Brig. Gen. Edward Lansdale, "Review of OPERATION MONGOOSE,"
Phase One, July 25, 1962.

PAGE 7 OF 8

UNCLASSIFIED

a matter of our own security, undertaking some economic proscription, and isolating the Castro/Communist gang from contaminating the Hemisphere. Along with recognition of our humanitarian sympathies, this seems to be the fear among Cuban refugees, although they are still hopeful. .

If Cubans become convinced that the U.S. is not going to do more than watch and talk, I believe they will make other plans for the future. The bulk of Cuban refugees in the U.S. are most likely to start getting serious about settling down for life in the U.S., dulling their desire to return home with personal risk involved. The bulk of disaffected people inside Cuba will lose hope and incentive for futile protests against the regime and start accepting their status as captives of the Communists. Some Cuban activists will not accept the loss of their homeland so easily and may seek release from frustration by liberation operations outside U.S. territory and control. The recent wildcat Cuban scheme to bomb Habana from Central America is an example.

Our probes of the guerrilla potential inside Cuba have been hampered by similar morale factors. Cubans sent to risk their lives on missions inside Cuba feel very much alone, except for their communications link back to the U.S. They are unable to recruit freedom fighters aggressively by the time-proven method of starting an active resistance and thus attracting recruits; U.S. guidelines to keep this short of a revolt have made the intention behind the operation suspect to local Cubans. The evidence of some intent is seen in the recent maritime re-supply of the team in Pinar del Rio. We brought in extra weapons, for which there were immediate recruits; if we were to exploit the evident guerrilla potential in this province, it appears likely that we would have to furnish supplies by air and probably open the U.S. to strong charges of furnishing such support to Cuban resistance elements.

Therefore, we have been unable to surface the Cuban resistance potential to a point where we can measure it realistically. The only way this can be done, accurately, is when resistance actually has a rallying point of freedom fighters who appear to the Cuban people to have some chance of winning, and that means at least an implication that the U.S. is in support. Word-of-mouth information that such a freedom movement is afoot could cause the majority of the Cuban people to choose sides. It would be the first real opportunity for them to do so since Castro and the Communists came to power. There was little opportunity for the Cuban people to join an active resistance in April 1961; there is less opportunity today. If the Cuban people are to feel they have a real opportunity, they must have something which they can join with some belief in its success.

7

UNCLASSIFIED

DOCUMENT 7: Brig. Gen. Edward Lansdale, "Review of OPERATION MONGOOSE,"
Phase One, July 25, 1962.

PAGE 8 OF 8

TO~~UNCLASSIFIED~~

PROJECTION (PHASE II).

As a help towards the making of a U.S. decision on a future course of action, the Operational Representatives developed working statements of four possibilities; at my request they have commented on the positive and negative factors worth considering for each possible course, and it is suggested that these thoughtful statements are worth reading in full. The working statements of the choices open to the U.S. are as follows:

a. Cancel operational plans; treat Cuba as a Bloc nation; protect Hemisphere from it, or

b. Exert all possible diplomatic, economic, psychological, and other pressures to overthrow the Castro-Communist regime without overt employment of U.S. military, or

c. Commit U.S. to help Cubans overthrow the Castro-Communist regime, with a step-by-step phasing to ensure success, including the use of U.S. military force if required at the end, or

d. Use a provocation and overthrow the Castro-Communist regime by U.S. military force.

RECOMMENDATION.

It is recommended that this review of Phase I be considered by the Special Group as providing the operational basis for guidelines and objectives for Phase II. It is a matter of urgency that these be arrived at by the Special Group, to permit developing specific plans and schedules for Phase II.

4 Attachments

"Eyes Only" copies to:

Special Group (Augmented)

1. General Taylor
2. Mr. Alexis Johnson
3. Mr. Roswell Gilpatric
4. Mr. John McCone
5. Mr. Robert Kennedy
6. General Lemnitzer

Operational Representatives

7. Mr. William Harvey (CIA)
8. Mr. Robert Hurwitch (State)
9. General Harris (Defense)
10. Mr. Don Wilson (USIA)
11. Chief of Operations

8

DOCUMENT 8: Defense Department/Joint Chiefs of Staff, projection of "Consequences of U.S. Military Intervention in Cuba" (prepared for Special Group Augmented), August 8, 1962.

PAGE 1 OF 4

UNCLASSIFIED   SPECIAL HANDLING   NOFORN

(58)

8 AUG 1962

MEMORANDUM FOR THE SPECIAL GROUP (AUGMENTED)

Subject: Consequences of US Military Intervention
in Cuba (TS)

1. On 2 August 1962 the Chief of Operations, Operation
MONGOOSE, requested the DOD/JCS Representative, Operation
MONGOOSE, to prepare a paper for distribution to the Special
Group (Augmented) on 8 August 1962. The specific requirement
is to set forth "Consequences of (US) Military Intervention
(in Cuba) to include cost (personnel, units and equipment),
effect on world-wide ability to react, possibility of a requirement for sustained occupation, the level of national mobilization required, and Cuban counteraction." Pursuant to
this request, the requirement has been divided into its
separate parts.

2. <u>Requirements (personnel, units and equipment)</u>

c. Major units involved in the initial assault include:

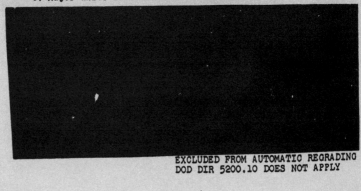

EXCLUDED FROM AUTOMATIC REGRADING
DOD DIR 5200.10 DOES NOT APPLY

DOCUMENT 8: Defense Department/Joint Chiefs of Staff, projection of "Consequences of U.S. Military Intervention in Cuba" (prepared for Special Group Augmented), August 8, 1962.

PAGE 2 OF 4

TOP SECRET SPECIAL HANDLING NOFORN

d. For approximately ten days, CONUS MATS airlift would be fully committed.

TOP SECRET ~~UNCLASSIFIED~~ SPECIAL HANDLING NOFORN

e. CONAD air defense capabilities in southeast United States will be augmented by the additional Naval and Air Force forces brought into the area for this operation. Therefore, no redeployment of CONAD forces from other areas is anticipated.

5. <u>Castro-Cuban Counteraction</u>.

a. The military reaction will be determined in large measure by the will of the Cuban armed forces to resist, as well as by the weapons available to them and their proficiency in their use, at the time of US military intervention.

b. The military capabilities of Cuba are oriented primarily toward defensive activities. Cuban plans are believed to contemplate a strong initial resistance, followed by a determined defense of preselected keypoints, and finally by protracted guerrilla warfare.

c. Cuba has about 50 MIG fighters, some of which may be configured for carrying light bombs. Any of these that survive the US air strikes could be used offensively against targets in Florida. Also they have 11 B-26 aircraft some of which, if they survive the air strikes by US forces, could attempt to attack targets in the southeastern United States. All forces engaged in the operation, as well as the Continental Air Defense forces, however, would be alert to guard against any such attempts at retaliation.

d. In the future the Castro-Cuban capability for counteraction will improve if Soviet's continue to provide the Cubans with additional military equipment and training. Thus, the urgency of the requirement to remove the Communist government from Cuba is made apparent by Castro's constantly increasing capabilities.

UNCLASSIFIED　SPECIAL HANDLING　NOFORN

6. Possibility of a Requirement for a Sustained Occupation.

a. The duration of a US military presence in Cuba is contingent upon such factors as the will of Castro-Cuban forces to resist invasion, the degree of popular support a defeated Castro might receive for the conduct of residual guerrilla operations, and time required to reconstitute an effective friendly Cuban government.

b. Following the establishment of essential military control of the island, a substantial US military commitment may be required in Cuba for a significant period of time. Post assault tasks will include restoration of law and order and the conduct of counterguerrilla operations.

c. To achieve the objectives of subparagraph b above, it is planned that the post assault military presence initially will consist of substantial Army follow-on forces with such other sea and air support as may be required. This will be reduced gradually in size as the effectiveness of the now Cuban government increases. Thereafter, a lengthy period of providing military assistance is anticipated.

DOCUMENT 9: Brig. Gen. Edward Lansdale, "Action Proposals, [OPERATION] MONGOOSE," October 11, 1962.

PAGE 1 OF 2

OFFICE OF THE SECRETARY OF DEFENSE
WASHINGTON 25, D.C.

11 October 1962

MEMORANDUM FOR THE SPECIAL GROUP (AUGMENTED)

From: Brig. Gen. Lansdale

Subject: Action Proposals, Mongoose

At your 4 October meeting, it was your desire that Mongoose be stepped up. The Operational Representatives were so tasked, promptly, and we can expect a series of proposals in the near future (with sabotage given priority attention).

The Operational Representatives have discussed the three attached proposals thoroughly and they reflect a consensus of our operational views. I believe the proposals are realistic and do-able, and thus recommend early approval.

Comments on each proposal:

Sabotage of Cuban-Owned Ships.

23 Cuban-owned ships are known, ranging from 6500 tons down to 500 tons. Several make frequent voyages to Europe, including visits to both Bloc and NATO-country ports. The Operational Representatives and I agree that actions to destroy these ships (with time delay fuses) should aim to have actual destruction take place on the following priority:

A.

B.

Broadcasting in Russian to Cuba.

It is noted that many of the Bloc technicians now in Cuba are young, in their early 20's, and that the proposed VOA programs will be specifically tailored for them, as well as being consistent with open U.S. policy. It is believed that advantages far outweigh the disadvantages listed.

DOCUMENT 9: Brig. Gen. Edward Lansdale, "Action Proposals, [OPERATION] MONGOOSE,"
October 11, 1962.

PAGE 2 OF 2

(b)(1)
(a)(4)
(5)

3 Attachments

"Eyes Only" copies to:

Mr. Kennedy   Mr. McCone
Mr. Bundy   General Taylor
Mr. Johnson   Mr. Murrow
Mr. Gilpatric   Chief of Operations

DOCUMENT 10: Draft Agreement between Cuba and the USSR on Military Cooperation and Mutual Defense, August 1962 (Translation from Spanish)

PAGE 1 OF 3

Agreement between the Government of the Republic of Cuba and the Government of the Union of Socialist Soviet Republics on military cooperation for the defense of the national territory of Cuba in the event of aggression.

Agreement between the Government of the Republic of Cuba and the Government of the Union of Socialist Soviet Republics on military cooperation and mutual defense.

Agreement between the Government of the Republic of Cuba and the Government of the Union of Socialist Soviet Republics on military support of the Soviet Armed Forces in defending the national territory of Cuba in the event of aggression.

(Any of the previous three titles is suggested)

The Government of the Republic of Cuba and the Government of the Union of Socialist Soviet Republics,

Guiding themselves by the principles and objectives of the United Nations Organization Charter.

Reiterating their desire to live in peace with all states and peoples.

Determined to make all possible efforts to contribute to the preservation and strengthening of world peace.

Anxious to establish and develop mutual friendship, collaboration and mutual help between all peoples on the basis of the principle of respecting the sovereignty and independence of states and of that of non-intervention in their internal affairs.

Faithful to a policy of principle based on friendship and solidarity between peoples defending a common cause, of which the fundamental pillars are the peaceful coexistence between states with different social systems, the legitimate defense in the face of aggression, the right of every people to give itself the form of government it deems appropriate to its aspirations of well-being and progress and to live in peace without being perturbed or attacked from abroad and the recognition of the historic prerogative of every nation, when it so desires, to break the binds that tie it to any form of dominion or economic exploitation.

Decided to take the necessary steps to jointly defend such legitimate rights of the people of Cuba (if it is preferred this could read the peoples of Cuba and of the Soviet Union.)

Also taking into account the urgency of taking measures to assure mutual defense in the face of possible aggression against the Republic of Cuba and the USSR.

Desiring to agree on all questions relating to the support which the Soviet Armed Forces will provide in the defense of the national territory of Cuba in the event of agression,

have agreed to subscribe to the present agreement.

Article 1

The Soviet Union will send to the Republic of Cuba armed forces to reinforce its defenses in the face of the danger of an external aggression and to contribute to the preservation of world peace.

The type of Soviet troops and the areas of their basing on the territory of the Republic of Cuba will be set by the representatives named in accordance with Article 11 of this agreement.

Article 2

In the event of aggression against the republic of Cuba or against the Soviet Armed Forces on the territory of the Republic of Cuba, the Government of the Union of Socialist Soviet Republics and the Government of the Republic of Cuba, making use of

DOCUMENT 10: Draft Agreement between Cuba and the USSR on Military Cooperation and Mutual Defense, August 1962 (Translation from Spanish)

PAGE 2 OF 3

the right to individual or collective defense, provided for in Article 51 of the United Nations Organization Charter, will take all necessary measures to repel the aggression.

Any information regarding any act of aggression and the actions taken in fulfillment of this article will be presented to the Security Council in accordance with the rules of the United Nations Charter.

The above mentioned actions will be suspended once the Security Council takes the measures necessary to reestablish and preserve world peace.

Article 3

The Soviet Armed Forces based in the Republic of Cuba will fully respect its sovereignty.

All personnel attached to the Soviet Armed Forces and their family members will observe the laws of the Republic of Cuba.

Article 4

The Government of the Union of Socialist Soviet Republics will assume the upkeep costs of the Soviet Armed Forces based on the territory of the Republic of Cuba by virtue of this agreement.

Article 5

So as not to affect supplies to the Cuban population, consumer goods, various materials, machinery, equipment and other goods destined to the Soviet Armed Forces will be supplied by the Soviet Union. Such supplies, the equipment and munitions destined to the Soviet Armed Forces, along with the ships assigned for their transportation will have free entry into the territory of Cuba.

Article 6

The Government of the Republic of Cuba agrees with the Government of the Union of Socialist Soviet Republics, to provide its Armed Forces with all the services necessary for their installation, basing, communication and mobility.

The transportation of personnel of the Soviet Armed Forces, the use of electric energy and communications, along with other public services, provided to the Soviet Armed Forces will be paid by them, in accordance with the rates applicable to the Armed Forces of the Republic of Cuba.

The sites and land for the installation and basing will be provided, free of charge, by the Republic of Cuba. Their adaptation and repair will be done by the Soviet Armed Forces.

Article 7

In areas assigned to the Soviet Armed Forces, the construction of buildings, airfields, roads, bridges, permanent radio-communication facilities and other types, will be undertaken using means and materials of the Soviet Armed Forces and with prior coordination with the competent organ of the Republic of Cuba charged with such matters.

Article 8

In the event that the Soviet Armed Forces abandon them, the military barracks, airfields and other constructions, along with permanent installations will be turned over to the Government of the Republic of Cuba without any compensation.

Article 9

Matters of jurisdiction relating to the presence of Soviet Armed Forces personnel on the territory of the Republic of Cuba will be governed by separate agreements based on the principles enunciated in

DOCUMENT 10: Draft Agreement between Cuba and the USSR on Military Cooperation and Mutual Defense, August 1962 (Translation from Spanish)

PAGE 3 OF 3

Article 3 of this agreement.

Article 10

Both parties agree that the military units of each state will be under the command of their respective governments who will, in coordination, determine the use of their respective forces to repel external aggression and restore the peace.

Article 11

So as to adequately regulate daily matters deriving from the presence of Soviet Armed Forces on the territory of the Republic of Cuba, the Government of the Republic of Cuba and the Government of the USSR will name their respective representatives.

Article 12

This agreement will be submitted for ratification by the respective governments and will enter into force on the day of the exchange of letters of ratification, which will be on

Article 13

This agreement is valid for a five year term. Either party may annul the agreement, notifying the other party within one year before the expiration date of this agreement.

In the event that the five year term is concluded without either party requesting its annulment, this agreement will be in force for five more years.

Article 14

After the conclusion of this agreement's validity, the Soviet Armed Forces will abandon the territory of the Republic of Cuba.

The Soviet party reserves the right to evacuate from the territory of the Republic of Cuba materials, munitions, equipment, machinery, mechanisms and all war materiel and other goods that are the property of the Soviet Armed Forces.

The Government of the Republic of Cuba will furnish all the aid necessary for the evacuation of the Soviet Armed Forces from the territory of the Republic of Cuba.

This agreement has been drafted on the ___ of 1962, in two copies, one in the Spanish language and the other in the Russian language, each of equal value.

Certifying the above mentioned, the heads of Government of both states sealed and signed this agreement.

Prime Minister of the Republic of Cuba	President of the Council of Ministers of the Union of Socialist Soviet Republics
Fidel Castro Ruz	Khrushchev N.S.

SECRET   NLK-77-970   #1

CENTRAL INTELLIGENCE AGENCY
OFFICE OF CURRENT INTELLIGENCE
22 August 1962

OSI No. ~~~~~~~~~~~~~   Copy No. 10

CURRENT INTELLIGENCE MEMORANDUM

SUBJECT: Recent Soviet Military Aid to Cuba

1.   Intelligence on recent Soviet military
assistance to Cuba indicates that an unusually large
number of Soviet ships have delivered military cargoes
to Cuba since late July and that some form of military
construction is underway at several locations in Cuba
by Soviet bloc personnel who arrived on some of these
ships and are utilizing material delivered by the
vessels.   During the period at least 1,500 passengers
have debarked from four ships under security conditions
suggesting that their mission is related to the construction and military activity; another 1,500 arrived
during the period and were greeted with considerable
publicity as economic specialists and students.   Some
still unconfirmed reports suggest that recently arrived
Soviet bloc personnel number as many as 5,000.   The
speed and magnitude of this influx of bloc personnel
and equipment into a non-bloc country is unprecedented
in Soviet military aid activities; clearly something
new and different is taking place.   As yet limited
evidence suggests that present activities may include
the augmentation of Cuba's air defense system, possibly
including the establishment of surface-to-air missile
sites or the setting up of facilities for electronic
and communications intelligence.

2.   As many as 20 Soviet vessels may have already
arrived in Cuba since late July with military cargoes.
Five more Soviet vessels have left Black Sea ports under
conditions suggesting that they are en route to Cuba
with additional military equipment.   Most reports on
these shipments have referred to large quantities of
transportation, electronic, and construction equipment,
such as communications and radar vans, trucks of many

Declassified by 056375
date   26 OCT 1977

SECRET

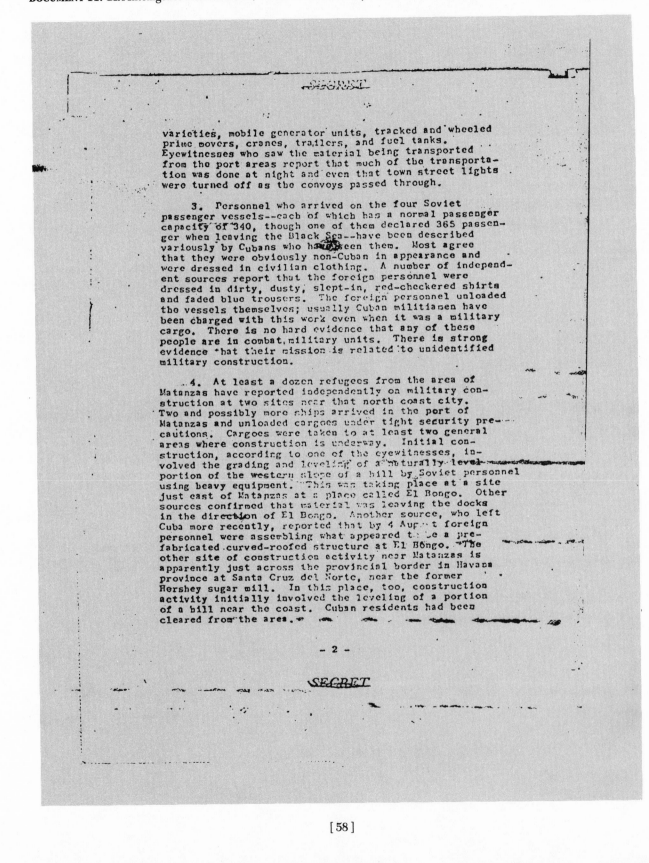

SECRET

varieties, mobile generator units, tracked and wheeled
prime movers, cranes, trailers, and fuel tanks.
Eyewitnesses who saw the material being transported
from the port areas report that much of the transportation was done at night and even that town street lights
were turned off as the convoys passed through.

3. Personnel who arrived on the four Soviet
passenger vessels--each of which has a normal passenger
capacity of 340, though one of them declared 365 passenger when leaving the Black Sea--have been described
variously by Cubans who have seen them. Most agree
that they were obviously non-Cuban in appearance and
were dressed in civilian clothing. A number of independent sources report that the foreign personnel were
dressed in dirty, dusty, slept-in, red-checkered shirts
and faded blue trousers. The foreign personnel unloaded
the vessels themselves; usually Cuban militiamen have
been charged with this work even when it was a military
cargo. There is no hard evidence that any of these
people are in combat military units. There is strong
evidence that their mission is related to unidentified
military construction.

4. At least a dozen refugees from the area of
Matanzas have reported independently on military construction at two sites near that north coast city.
Two and possibly more ships arrived in the port of
Matanzas and unloaded cargoes under tight security precautions. Cargoes were taken to at least two general
areas where construction is underway. Initial construction, according to one of the eyewitnesses, involved the grading and leveling of a naturally level
portion of the western slope of a hill by Soviet personnel
using heavy equipment. This was taking place at a site
just east of Matanzas at a place called El Bongo. Other
sources confirmed that material was leaving the docks
in the direction of El Bongo. Another source, who left
Cuba more recently, reported that by 4 August foreign
personnel were assembling what appeared to be a pre-
fabricated curved-roofed structure at El Bongo. The
other site of construction activity near Matanzas is
apparently just across the provincial border in Havana
province at Santa Cruz del Norte, near the former
Hershey sugar mill. In this place, too, construction
activity initially involved the leveling of a portion
of a hill near the coast. Cuban residents had been
cleared from the area.

- 2 -

SECRET

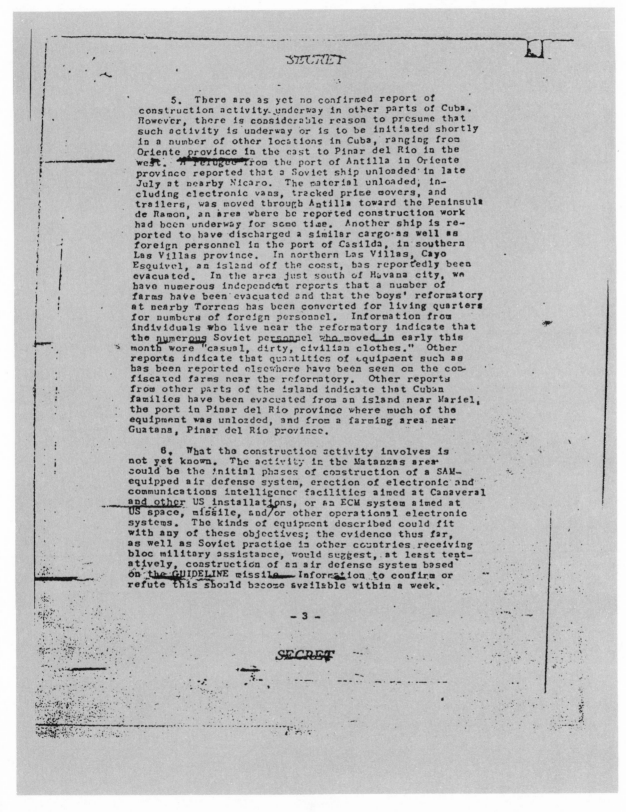

SECRET

5. There are as yet no confirmed report of construction activity underway in other parts of Cuba. However, there is considerable reason to presume that such activity is underway or is to be initiated shortly in a number of other locations in Cuba, ranging from Oriente province in the east to Pinar del Rio in the west. A refugee from the port of Antilla in Oriente province reported that a Soviet ship unloaded in late July at nearby Nicaro. The material unloaded, including electronic vans, tracked prime movers, and trailers, was moved through Antilla toward the Peninsula de Ramon, an area where be reported construction work had been underway for some time. Another ship is reported to have discharged a similar cargo as well as foreign personnel in the port of Casilda, in southern Las Villas province. In northern Las Villas, Cayo Esquivel, an island off the coast, has reportedly been evacuated. In the area just south of Havana city, we have numerous independent reports that a number of farms have been evacuated and that the boys' reformatory at nearby Torrens has been converted for living quarters for numbers of foreign personnel. Information from individuals who live near the reformatory indicate that the numerous Soviet personnel who moved in early this month wore "casual, dirty, civilian clothes." Other reports indicate that quantities of equipment such as has been reported elsewhere have been seen in the confiscated farms near the reformatory. Other reports from other parts of the island indicate that Cuban families have been evacuated from an island near Mariel, the port in Pinar del Rio province where much of the equipment was unloaded, and from a farming area near Guatana, Pinar del Rio province.

6. What the construction activity involves is not yet known. The activity in the Matanzas area could be the initial phases of construction of a SAM-equipped air defense system, erection of electronic and communications intelligence facilities aimed at Canaveral and other US installations, or an ECM system aimed at US space, missile, and/or other operational electronic systems. The kinds of equipment described could fit with any of these objectives; the evidence thus far, as well as Soviet practice in other countries receiving bloc military assistance, would suggest, at least tentatively, construction of an air defense system based on the GUIDELINE missile. Information to confirm or refute this should become available within a week.

– 3 –

SECRET

DOCUMENT 11: CIA Intelligence Memorandum, "Recent Soviet Military Aid to Cuba," August 22, 1962.

PAGE 4 OF 4

SECRET

7. The step-up in military shipments and the
construction activity once again provide strong evidence
of the magnitude of the USSR's support for the Castro
regime. Together with the extraordinary Soviet bloc
economic commitments made to Cuba in recent months,
these developments amount to the most extensive campaign
to bolster a non-bloc country ever undertaken by the
USSR.

SECRET

DOCUMENT 12: CIA Special National Intelligence Estimate, "The Military Buildup in Cuba," September 19, 1962 (summary pages only).

PAGE 1 OF 2

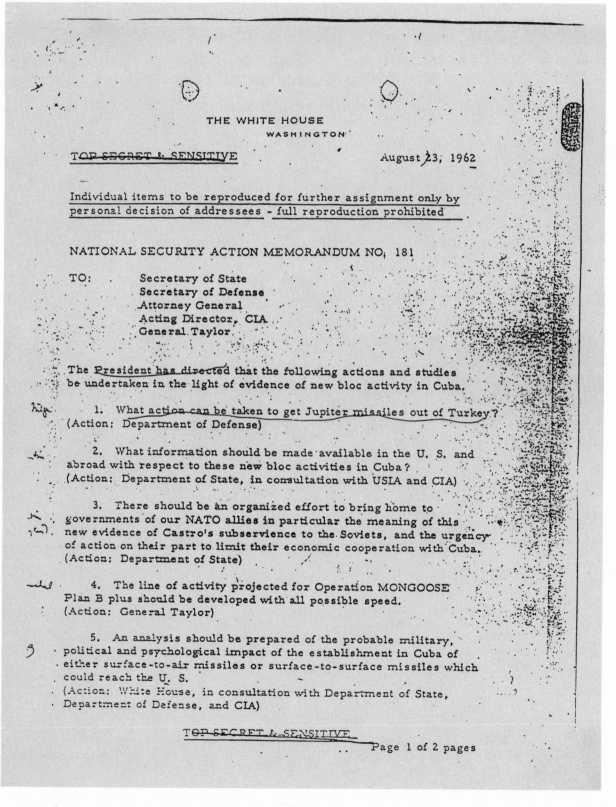

THE WHITE HOUSE
WASHINGTON

TOP SECRET & SENSITIVE   August 23, 1962

Individual items to be reproduced for further assignment only by personal decision of addressees - full reproduction prohibited

NATIONAL SECURITY ACTION MEMORANDUM NO. 181

TO: Secretary of State
           Secretary of Defense
           Attorney General
           Acting Director, CIA
           General Taylor

The President has directed that the following actions and studies be undertaken in the light of evidence of new bloc activity in Cuba.

   1. What action can be taken to get Jupiter missiles out of Turkey?
(Action: Department of Defense)

   2. What information should be made available in the U. S. and abroad with respect to these new bloc activities in Cuba?
(Action: Department of State, in consultation with USIA and CIA)

   3. There should be an organized effort to bring home to governments of our NATO allies in particular the meaning of this new evidence of Castro's subservience to the Soviets, and the urgency of action on their part to limit their economic cooperation with Cuba.
(Action: Department of State)

   4. The line of activity projected for Operation MONGOOSE Plan B plus should be developed with all possible speed.
(Action: General Taylor)

   5. An analysis should be prepared of the probable military, political and psychological impact of the establishment in Cuba of either surface-to-air missiles or surface-to-surface missiles which could reach the U. S.
(Action: White House, in consultation with Department of State, Department of Defense, and CIA)

TOP SECRET & SENSITIVE

Page 1 of 2 pages

TOP SECRET & SENSITIVE   -2-   August 23, 1962

6. A study should be made of the advantages and disadvantages of making a statement that the U. S. would not tolerate the establishment of military forces (missile or air, or both?) which might launch a nuclear attack from Cuba against the U. S.
(Action: Department of State, in consultation with Department of Defense with respect to the study in item 7 below)

7. A study should be made of the various military alternatives which might be adopted in executing a decision to eliminate any installations in Cuba capable of launching nuclear attack on the U. S. What would be the pros and cons, for example, of pinpoint attack, general counter-force attack, and outright invasion?
(Action: Department of Defense)

To facilitate coordination of these efforts, I should like to receive an immediate report from action Departments indicating which officer of the Department will be directly responsible for items in which action is assigned to that Department. Insofar as practicable, except for item 1, item 3, and item 5, these assignments should be made from among senior officers already informed of MONGOOSE.

There will be a further meeting with the President about September 1 to review progress on all these items. In the event of important new information, an earlier meeting will be called.

The President emphasizes again the sensitive character of these instructions.

McGeorge Bundy

TOP SECRET & SENSITIVE

DOCUMENT 13: "National Security Action Memorandum No. 181," Presidential Directive on actions and studies in response to new Soviet Bloc activity in Cuba, August 23, 1962.

PAGE 1 OF 3

· SPECIAL

NATIONAL INTELLIGENCE ESTIMATE

NUMBER 85–3–62

The Military Buildup in Cuba

SANITIZED COPY

Approved for Release
Date *15 April 1975.*

DOCUMENT 13: "National Security Action Memorandum No. 181," Presidential Directive on actions and studies in response to new Soviet Bloc activity in Cuba, August 23, 1962.

PAGE 2 OF 3

THE MILITARY
BUILDUP IN CUBA

THE PROBLEM

To assess the strategic and political significance of the recent military buildup in Cuba and of the possible future development of additional military capabilities there.

CONCLUSIONS

A. We believe that the USSR values its position in Cuba primarily for the political advantages to be derived from it, and consequently that the main purpose of the present military buildup in Cuba is to strengthen the Communist regime there against what the Cubans and the Soviets conceive to be a danger that the US may attempt by one means or another to overthrow it. The Soviets evidently hope to deter any such attempt by enhancing Castro's defensive capabilities and by threatening Soviet military retaliation. At the same time, they evidently recognize that the development of an offensive military base in Cuba might provoke US military intervention and thus defeat their present purpose. (Paras. 1–11)

B. In terms of military significance, the current Soviet deliveries are substantially improving air defense and coastal defense capabilities in Cuba. Their political significance is that, in conjunction with the Soviet statement of 11 September, they are likely to be regarded as ensuring the continuation of the Castro regime in power, with consequent discouragement to the opposition at home and in exile. The threat inherent in these developments is that, to the extent that the Castro regime thereby gains a sense of security at home,

1

DOCUMENT 13: "National Security Action Memorandum No. 181," Presidential Directive on actions and studies in response to new Soviet Bloc activity in Cuba, August 23, 1962.

PAGE 3 OF 3

it will be emboldened to become more aggressive in fomenting revolutionary activity in Latin America. *(Paras. 18–21)*

C. As the buildup continues, the USSR may be tempted to establish in Cuba other weapons represented to be defensive in purpose, but of a more "offensive" character: e.g., light bombers, submarines, and additional types of short-range surface-to-surface missiles (SSMs). A decision to provide such weapons will continue to depend heavily on the Soviet estimate as to whether they could be introduced without provoking a US military reaction. *(Paras. 22–28)*

D. The USSR could derive considerable military advantage from the establishment of Soviet medium and intermediate range ballistic missiles in Cuba, or from the establishment of a Soviet submarine base there. As between these two, the establishment of a submarine base would be the more likely. Either development, however, would be incompatible with Soviet practice to date and with Soviet policy as we presently estimate it. It would indicate a far greater willingness to increase the level of risk in US-Soviet relations than the USSR has displayed thus far, and consequently would have important policy implications with respect to other areas and other problems in East-West relations. *(Paras. 29–33)*

E. The Latin American reaction will be to the evidence of an increased Soviet commitment to Cuba, rather than to the technical implications of the military buildup. Many Latin Americans will fear and resent a Soviet military intrusion into the Hemisphere, but will regard the problem as one to be met by the US and not their responsibility. We estimate the chances are better now than they were at Punta del Este to obtain the necessary two-thirds OAS majority for sanctions and other steps short of direct military action aimed at Cuba. If it became clear that the USSR was establishing an "offensive" base in Cuba, most Latin American governments would expect the US to eliminate it, by whatever means were necessary, but many of them would still seek to avoid direct involvement. *(Paras. 34–37)*

2

DOCUMENT 14: W. W. Rostow, "Memorandum to the President," assessing Soviet military aid to Cuba, September 3, 1962.

PAGE 1 OF 10

~~TOP SECRET and SENSITIVE~~

OADR

September 3, 1962

MEMORANDUM TO THE PRESIDENT

At your request, I have reviewed the Cuban position over the week end. Herewith my reflections. You will understand, of course, that I have not been following the matter closely over recent months.

W.W.R.

~~Attachment~~

~~TOP SECRET and SENSITIVE~~

DEPARTMENT OF STATE A/CDC/MR

REVIEWED by *J.W. Cool* DATE *01/10/90*

( ) RELEASE ( ) DECLASSIFY
( ) EXCISE ( ) DECLASSIFY in PART
( ) DENY ( ) Non-responsive Info
( ) FPC/PA exemptions _____
_____
_____

OADR

DOCUMENT 14: W. W. Rostow, "Memorandum to the President," assessing Soviet military aid to Cuba, September 3, 1962.

PAGE 2 OF 10

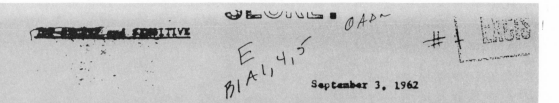

September 3, 1962

Situation and Problem.

On the basis of existing intelligence the Soviet military deliveries to Cuba do not constitute a substantial threat to U.S. security. They do constitute a deterrent to certain types of surveillance and a means for improving certain types of Soviet intelligence. They also constitute evidence that Moscow, having been frustrated in certain directions, is in a mood to double its bet rather than cut its losses, at least on a selective basis. In this case, Moscow has moved strongly but defensively to meet Castro's anxieties about overflights and other intrusions, and to shore up his flagrantly weak economy.

These deliveries constitute, further:

1. A psychological move of some power in the Caribbean (where the fear of Cuba is authentic) and in the rest of Latin America (where the move could be regarded as the extension of a challenge to U.S. military hegemony in the Hemisphere).

2. A psychological move likely to heighten U.S. domestic anxiety with respect to Cuba.

3. A testing thrust by Moscow, which, at considerable financial cost and further commitment of prestige, places before us the question of where and how we should draw the line with respect to unacceptable action and behavior by the Communists in Cuba and the Hemisphere.

We face, therefore, a problem of both formulating a reaction and articulating it in ways designed to: diminish the political costs under 1 and 2, above; minimize the likelihood of any further extension of Cuban capabilities or Soviet capabilities emplaced in Cuba; and provide the legal and policy basis, under certain contingent circumstances, for the liquidation of communism in Cuba by force.

The following memorandum outlines the possible elements of both policy and exposition designed to meet the circumstances.

Policy

A. Drawing the line. The ambiguities in the public mind, here and abroad, about the military meaning of the Soviet deliveries require not merely that we explain what they are and why -- up to a point -- we are prepared to regard them as acceptable, but that we also clarify the

DOCUMENT 14: W. W. Rostow, "Memorandum to the President," assessing Soviet military aid to Cuba, September 3, 1962.

PAGE 3 OF 10

~~TOP SECRET and SENSITIVE~~

-2-

kinds of installations and capabilities emplaced in Cuba which we would regard as unacceptable. The President must consider going beyond his statement of April 20, 1961: "I want it clearly understood that this Government will not hesitate in meeting its primary obligations which are to the security of our Nation!" These deliveries, rightly or wrongly, raise the question in the public mind of the security of the Nation; and it may, therefore, be appropriate to indicate what we would not be prepared to accept without direct military <u>riposte</u>. In general, that line should be drawn at the installation in Cuba or in Cuban waters of nuclear weapons or delivery vehicles, sea or land based. There may be other types of aggressive instruments that we would wish to include in this definition. In addition, this may be an appropriate occasion to underline our willingness to act with others in the Hemisphere against Cuba should Castro undertake direct or indirect aggression against other Latin American nations.

B. <u>Legal basis for the line</u>. If we are to put ourselves in a position at home and abroad to back this line effectively with the full weight of U.S. force and commitment, the line should be carefully grounded in law. Although the Monroe Doctrine is emotionally acceptable to most Americans as a legal basis for U.S. military action, it is not acceptable to our allies, either in the Hemisphere or abroad. On the other hand, various Hemispheric documents recognize the special status in this Hemisphere of "extra-continental" intervention (including the Rio Treaty of 1947); and Resolution II of the Punta del Este conference of January 1962 includes as paragraph 3 the following: "To urge the member states to take those steps that they may consider appropriate for their individual or collective self-defense, and to cooperate, as may be necessary or desirable, to strengthen their capacity to counteract threats or acts of aggression, subversion, or other dangers to peace and security resulting from the continued intervention in this hemisphere o Sino-Soviet powers, in accordance with the obligations established in treaties and agreements such as the Charter of the Organization of American States and the Inter-American Treaty of Reciprocal Assistance."

I am not an expert on Latin American law and agreement; but I believe it is possible and essential for us to establish our position in terms of our interpretation of those commitments. Having had a direct hand in drafting and negotiating the paragraph quoted above, I can attest that it was designed to provide two types of flexibility: with respect to various types of aggressive threats from Havana; and with respect to various possible groupings of Latin American states which might be prepared, under varying circumstances, to operate with us.

~~TOP SECRET and SENSITIVE~~

QADR

DOCUMENT 14: W. W. Rostow, "Memorandum to the President," assessing Soviet military aid to Cuba, September 3, 1962.

PAGE 4 OF 10

TOP SECRET and SENSITIVE

-3-

OADC

The Communist position will, undoubtedly, be that we have established on the Eurasian land mass military installations proximate to their borders, including nuclear delivery capabilities. Our reply must be and can be that by regional security action, provided for under the Charter of the United Nations, this Hemisphere operates under a different set of rules than the Eurasian land mass. In this context it should be noted that we would be playing directly into Moscow's hands to use the occasion of pressure on us in Cuba to withdraw IBORS from Turkey. There is no clear stopping place for Communist activities based in Cuba unless we hold fast to the special status in Hemispheric law and agreement of "extra-continental" intervention.

C. _Heightening deterrence to indirect aggression._ In association with those Latin American states willing to work with us on a bilateral or other basis, we should examine much more intensively than we have thus far the exact nature of the subversive activities operating out of Havana into Latin America. I understand that these are probably now at a relatively low level, involving the training and infiltration of agents; the passage of funds; and various forms of propaganda. We should heighten our efforts to interfere with these activities for two reasons: to strengthen the sense of confidence of the Caribbean countries; and to try to surface some firm evidence of this activity so that we have, in legal reserve, the right to invoke the collective security provisions of the Punta del Este conference of 1962. We need to prepare a "Jorden Report" on the Communist operation in Latin America. I am fully conscious of the difficulties of accumulating hard evidence. But I am not convinced a determined and professional effort has been made.

D. _Increased economic pressure._ These new Soviet deliveries give us the occasion to increase somewhat the economic pressure on Cuba and the cost to the Communist bloc of maintaining Cuba by diminishing Cuban trade with the Free World. That trade is not large and is not, at its present level, a major strategic variable in the fate of Cuba. We should not, therefore, expend an excessive amount of diplomatic capital trying to reduce it drastically. On the other hand, it is essential that our allies understand that we take seriously this new Soviet commitment to Cuba; that we are committing ourselves to the drawing of a line; and that they would be well advised to contract their trade with Cuba. This should be a quiet, determined, sustained campaign, not a one-shot effort at the level of the North Atlantic Council. Our NATO allies must come to understand that we are not prepared to accept symmetry between the Allied position on the Eurasian land mass and the Communist presence in this Hemisphere; and that a condition for understanding with Washington is their recognition of the seriousness of this matter to us.

TOP SECRET and SENSITIVE

OADR

DOCUMENT 14: W. W. Rostow, "Memorandum to the President," assessing Soviet military aid to Cuba, September 3, 1962.

PAGE 5 OF 10

█████████████████████

-4-

OADR

E. <u>Communications with</u> Moscow. In addition to explaining diplomatically to the Soviet Union the character and seriousness of the line we have drawn, we might consider suggesting that, given our world responsibilities, stretching from Berlin to Viet Nam, we would have to consider whether we were prepared to accept the continued existence of a Communist state in Cuba should Communist initiatives elsewhere lead to a heightening of tension. If they argue they are only doing in Cuba what we do in Turkey, West Germany, etc., we must underline very hard with them these two points: first, the security arrangements of the Hemisphere have a long history which, by common agreement, places the intrusion of extra-continental military power outside the law; second, the crises in the world -- for example, in West Berlin and in South Viet Nam -- derive from Communist expansionist initiatives, beyond the legal limits of Communist power. We are now bearing a unique responsibility for meeting those aggressive thrusts throughout the Free World; and we have the right and duty to calculate whether we are prepared to accept the Cuban annoyance on our flank, if their aggressive ventures continue or expand, in Berlin, Viet Nam, or elsewhere.

F. <u>Collective action: Hemispheric or Caribbean?</u> We should consider carefully whether we shall wish to organize in the next several months either a Hemispheric or Caribbean meeting (or both) to consider collectively the problems posed by the present situation in Cuba. We do not wish to have a Hemispheric meeting which results in extended conflict and debate between those who are worried and those who are not particularly worried about the Cuban threat. On a Hemispheric basis it may emerge, however, that the line proposed here would be accepted; that is, the development of an offensive Communist capability in the Hemisphere would be judged unacceptable. In that case the area of security understanding in the Hemisphere would have been clarified and the bases for possible subsequent action would be strengthened. If we should find that no useful Hemispheric meeting can be held -- or, perhaps, in any case -- it may well be helpful for us to meet with the Caribbean nations who share our ██████████████████, as a sub-regional grouping of the OAS. The language of ███████████ lution II of the Punta del Este conference of January 19██ ███████████ (paragraph B), provides a flexibility which might ██████████████ OAS a meeting of interested members. This involves ████████████ litting the OAS; but these might be mitigated if such a ██████████████ its findings to the Council. In any case, the heightened situation in Cuba dramatizes further the split between the Caribbean nations and the rest. A great deal of OAS maneuvering has been designed to limit the possibility of unilateral U.S. intervention in other Latin American countries. We must make clear that, while we are prepared to accept that inhibition, we are a Caribbean as well as a Hemisphere nation; there are others who share our anxiety about the

<u>TOP SECRET</u> and SENSITIVE

OADR

DOCUMENT 14: W. W. Rostow, "Memorandum to the President," assessing Soviet military aid to Cuba, September 3, 1962.

PAGE 6 OF 10

-5-

Cuban situation; and we cannot permit the less interested members of the OAS preventing the more interested nations from protecting their vital interests centered in the Caribbean.

In facing this issue we should be conscious of the following possibility: the whole Hemisphere may agree with the line we draw with respect to offensive and defensive arms in Cuba; only the Caribbean nations (plus a few others) may be willing to act with respect to indirect aggression or cooperate with us in covert operations against Cuba. This distinction could pull the Hemisphere apart; or, with skillful diplomacy, it might be turned to our advantage.

(1)
) of (5)

we should consider the possibility of a Two-Track

would consist of a heightened effort to move along the present Mongoose lines. The minimum objective here would be harassment: the maximum objective would be the triggering of a situation where there might be conflict at the top of the Cuban regime leading, hopefully, to its change or overthrow by some group within Cuba commanding arms.

DOCUMENT 14: W. W. Rostow, "Memorandum to the President," assessing Soviet military aid to Cuba, September 3, 1962.

PAGE 7 OF 10

TOP SECRET and SENSITIVE

-6-

OADR

Track Two would consist of an effort to engage Cubans more deeply, both within Cuba and abroad, in efforts for their own liberation. This requires an operation with the following characteristics:

a. Authentic Cuban leadership with a considerable range of freedom to implement ideas and to assume risk.

b. Minimal U.S. direct participation: ideally, one truly wise U.S. adviser -- available, but laying back; equipped to provide finance, but not monitoring every move; capable of earning their respect rather than commanding it by his control over money or equipment.

c. Basing outside the United States.

d. A link-up with the scattered and sporadic groups and operations now going forward of their own momentum in Cuba.

e. A plan of operation which aims at the overthrow of Castro primarily from within rather than by invasion from without.

f. A long enough time horizon to build the operation carefully and soundly.

In suggesting that Track Two be studied -- and sharply distinguished from Track One -- I am, of course, wholly conscious of our failure of last year. But, as I read that failure in retrospect, its root lay in: U.S. bureaucratic domination; the lack of a Cuban political and organizational base; and a plan of operation that hinged on a type of overt invasion by a fixed date rather than the patient build-up of a true movement of national liberation. I'm sure it would be easy to argue that such a movement could not be generated against a Communist control system; that the Cuban refugees lack the capacity to play their part in such an enterprise with skill and minimal security; etc. And I am in no position to reply with confidence to such argument. On the other hand, Cuba is not located in Eastern Europe; and, presumably, we and the Cubans learned something from last year's failure, too.

In balance, I am prepared to recommend that Track Two be sympathetically studied and that General Lansdale be asked to formulate a design for it.

H. Contingencies. Evidently the contingencies suggested for planning in NSAM 181 deserve urgent attention. Among the tactical possibilities not listed in that memorandum might be included, under circumstances of heightened tension (but short of justification for blockade, invasion, or counterforce air strike), [

D PAD

*(b)(1)
(a)(1)(4)*

TOP SECRET and SENSITIVE

DOCUMENT 14: W. W. Rostow, "Memorandum to the President," assessing Soviet military aid to Cuba, September 3, 1962.

PAGE 8 OF 10

TOP SECRET and SENSITIVE

-7-

OADR

These should now be prepared and the contingent military operations should be related, in each case, to the relevant rationale.

    I.   **Policy conclusions.** To sum up, I propose that you consider that we:

        -- expose the reasons why the recent shipments do not constitute a threat to national security sufficient to justify our destroying communism in Cuba with our own arms;

        -- draw the line on the basis of Hemispheric agreements on which we would go to war;

        -- use the occasion to underline the illegitimacy of indirect aggression in the Hemisphere, on the basis of Hemispheric agreements, and heighten our efforts to develop hard evidence which might be the basis for later collective action against Cuba on such grounds;

        -- use the occasion to move our NATO allies towards a deeper understanding of our concern and gradually press them towards a reduction of their trade with Cuba;

        -- communicate to Moscow the possible unacceptability of _____ under protracted or increased tension initiated by _____ into the Free World;

        -- consider whether Hemispheric, Caribbean, or two-level collaboration is feasible or desirable in reinforcing our position;

        -- press forward with Mongoose, but consider Track Two;

        -- prepare and relate intimately military and political contingency plans for the full spectrum of possible occasions when the direct application of U.S. force may be appropriate.

TOP SECRET and SENSITIVE

DOCUMENT 14: W. W. Rostow, "Memorandum to the President," assessing Soviet military aid to Cuba, September 3, 1962.

PAGE 9 OF 10

TOP SECRET and SENSITIVE

-8-

OADR

J.   Articulation.

1.   The public articulation of our reaction -- if policy should assume something like the form suggested here -- might well involve two major statements: one by the President; the other, a substantial speech by Secretary Rusk. Since we do not propose to bring U.S. force to bear now, it would be inappropriate for the President to go to the country with a major address. But, since we may wish to draw a line, with rather complex contingent consequences, underlining its relation to Hemispheric agreements, a more spacious exposition by the Secretary of State may well be appropriate.

2.   What follows is an outline for a speech by Mr. Rusk. Some of its major themes might constitute also the substance of a prior statement by the President at, say, a Press conference.

3.   Outline of speech by the Secretary of State.

Note: The general tone of the speech should be low key, factual, somewhat legalistic, confident, with its warning to Moscow and Havana and its seriousness for our allies and our own people unmistakable.

a.   Recall Castro history and takeover as part of 1957-61 Communist offensive embracing Southeast Asia, Berlin, Congo, as well as Cuba. Describe what has happened to that offensive.

b.   Describe degeneration of Cuba and relate to degeneration in East Germany, China, etc.

c.   Describe Soviet moves in some detail, emphasizing their character as a shoring up operation on the economic side. Comment on bleak prospects for Cuban agriculture under collectivization.

d.   On military side, emphasize the defensive character of new installations and equipment. Recall President's April 20, 1961 reservation with respect to national security; and characterize new installations as not now constituting a threat to national security. Reference Indonesia, Iraq, U.S. ability to cope should a crisis come.

e.   Draw the line, with extensive references to mutual commitments in the Hemisphere going back at least to 1947.

f.   Recall Castro's earlier activities against Caribbean nations; recall Punta del Este Resolutions; issue sharper warning than ever before on indirect aggression, perhaps in context of Castro's December 2, 1961 references to guerrilla warfare being "the match thrown into the haystack." Describe our efforts with Latin American states to deter and deal with such efforts.

TOP SECRET and SENSITIVE

DOCUMENT 14: W. W. Rostow, "Memorandum to the President," assessing Soviet military aid to Cuba, September 3, 1962.

PAGE 10 OF 10

TOP SECRET and SENSITIVE

-9-

O_ADR

       g.   Reaffirm our intent to hold the frontiers of freedom on a world basis, from Berlin to Viet Nam, adding, perhaps: "We do not intend to permit communism in Cuba to distract us or to interfere with us in the conduct of this mission."

       h.   Express confidence that Cubans, in old Latin American tradition, will find ways to rid themselves of this dictatorship.

       i.   Close with references to Alliance for Progress; beginnings of serious movement forward (first DAC meeting on Colombia scheduled for second week in September); confidence that Latin America will carry through Alliance for Progress successfully; and assert that we shall not only contribute to Alliance for Progress but, if necessary, assure, by our combined action in the Hemisphere, backed by total U.S. capabilities, that communism shall not disrupt this decade of constructive effort.

TOP SECRET and SENSITIVE

PART II

THE MISSILE CRISIS

In the early morning hours of October 14, 1962, a U.S. U-2 reconnaissance aircraft flew over Cuba, taking nearly one thousand photographs of the western half of the island. By the following afternoon, photographic interpreters would notify top CIA officials that the mission had obtained definitive photographic evidence of Soviet medium-range ballistic missile (MRBMs) bases under construction near San Cristóbal, Cuba. After making sure that the missile sites were clearly marked on the photographs, Deputy CIA Director Ray Cline, passed them on to the White House. At 8:45 A.M. on October 16, National Security Advisor McGeorge Bundy alerted President Kennedy that a major international crisis was at hand.

The new intelligence provided the first conclusive proof that Soviet missile sites were indeed being constructed on the island. During the summer of 1962, President Kennedy and his advisers had watched the accelerated movement into Cuba of an array of Soviet weapons—including jet bombers, cruise missile boats, and advanced MiG fighters, and antiaircraft missiles—with growing consternation. But the consensus among officials in Washington at the time (with the notable exception of CIA Director John McCone) was that the Soviets would not recklessly cross the line of provocation by deploying nuclear-capable surface-to-surface missiles. In meetings with Soviet officials throughout September and early October, the United States sought and received public and private assur-

ances that "offensive" missiles were not being installed in Cuba. Now, Kennedy officials discovered, the United States had been flagrantly deceived.

THE U.S. REACTION

One of President Kennedy's first decisions upon learning of the missiles in Cuba was to select a core group of individuals to serve as his advisers during the crisis. Among those chosen were his brother Robert, Secretary of Defense Robert McNamara, Secretary of State Dean Rusk, National Security Advisor McGeorge Bundy, the President's Special Counsel Theodore Sorensen, Joint Chiefs of Staff Chairman Maxwell Taylor, Under Secretary of State George Ball, Secretary of the Treasury Douglas Dillon, CIA Director John McCone, and the State Department's Soviet specialist, Llewellyn Thompson. In addition, Kennedy would request the counsel of several prominent individuals outside of his administration, such as Dean Acheson, John McCloy, and Robert Lovett.

The president's advisory group, formally constituted through National Security Action Memorandum 196 as the Executive Committee of the National Security Council, known as the "ExComm," gathered at the White House for its first meeting shortly before noon on October 16. Unknown to Kennedy's advisers, the ExComm meetings, like a number of other meetings at the White House during the Kennedy era, were tape-recorded by the president. As the transcription of ExComm's first meeting indicates, no serious consideration was given to permitting the missiles to stay in Cuba; the question foremost in the minds of President Kennedy and his advisers was how to secure their removal. "I do think we have to set in motion a chain of events that will eliminate this base," stated Secretary of State Dean Rusk. "I don't think we can sit still" (Document 15).

The consensus among the key U.S. decision-makers, that the Soviet missiles could not be allowed to remain in Cuba, did not stem entirely, indeed if at all, from concerns about the strategic military threat posed by the MRBMs. Although the members of the CIA, JCS chief Taylor, and State Department analyst Raymond Garthoff believed that the strategic significance of the deployment could be substantial, Theodore Sorensen's notes from the initial ExComm sessions indicate that Kennedy's advisers "generally agreed that these missiles, even when fully operational, do not significantly alter the balance of power—i.e., they do not significantly increase the potential megatonnage capable of being unleashed on American soil" (Document 17). The Soviet missile deployment was seen as unacceptable because of the political challenge it represented. As Douglas Dillon's October 17 memorandum to President Kennedy argued, the deployment represented a "public test of our intentions" (Document 18). Since Kennedy had clearly articulated in public statements on September 4 and 13 the U.S. position that Soviet missiles in Cuba would not be tolerated, the surreptitious Soviet move was seen as a political threat to U.S. credibility, which, if unmet, could lead to further challenges over Berlin and in other parts of the world.

THE BLOCKADE DECISION

President Kennedy's initial reaction, shared by many of his advisers, was to view some form of air attack on the missile sites as the most appropriate U.S. response. Transcripts of the first Excomm meeting record him as stating: "we're going to take out these, uh, missiles.... At least we're going to do [that], so it

seems to me that we don't have to wait very long. We ought to be making *those* preparations." But as the ExComm discussions continued at the State Department and the White House over the next several days, it became increasingly apparent that the United States had a range of plausible options regarding the Cuban missiles. General Taylor later characterized the choices: the U.S. could "take them out" through a military strike, "squeeze them out" through coercive pressure, or "buy them out" through a negotiated settlement.[1]

U.N. Ambassador Adlai Stevenson's recommendation that diplomatic negotiations be tried first (a suggestion also made by Charles Bohlen, the former ambassador to the Soviet Union) failed to garner support among U.S. decision-makers (Document 19). A diplomatic demarche was seen as unlikely to persuade the Soviets to remove the missiles while alerting the Soviets and Cubans that the United States had discovered the missiles in Cuba, thereby allowing Khrushchev and Castro to take the initiative in the crisis. On the other hand, the option of "taking out" the missiles by means of some form of military attack had vociferous supporters in Dean Acheson and General Taylor, who argued that an airstrike would be the surest means of eliminating the threat (Document 21). A draft option plan called for "a surprise strike aimed at medium range missiles, surface to air missiles, and high performance aircraft and nuclear storage sites in Cuba" (Document 22). Counterpoised against this military option were Robert McNamara, Robert Kennedy, George Ball, Theodore Sorensen, and former Secretary of Defense Robert Lovett, who became increasingly convinced that coercive pressure, in the form of a naval blockade of Cuba, constituted the more prudent, less dangerous, initial course of action.

Both the eventual consensus reached by ExComm members and President Kennedy's ultimate decision to exercise the blockade option rested largely on two objections to the air attack. First, an airstrike, as Robert Kennedy repeatedly argued during crisis deliberations, would represent a "sneak attack" on a small nation "with all the memory of Pearl Harbor" (Document 21). Under Secretary of State George Ball summed up this argument:

> [W]e cannot launch a surprise attack against Cuba without destroying our moral position and alienating our friends and allies. If we were to do so we would wake up the following morning to find that we had brought down in ruins the structure of alliances and arrangements and that our whole post-war effort of trying to organize the combined strength of the Free World was in shards and tatters. (Document 20)

Perhaps more significantly, the airstrike was clearly the more drastic and irrevocable action, while the blockade option was, as Sorensen wrote, "the step least likely to precipitate general war" (Document 23)—an assessment bolstered by the CIA's Special National Intelligence Estimate, "Major Consequences of Certain U.S. Courses of Action on Cuba" (Document 24). If the quarantine failed, further U.S. actions, including a military strike, could be taken. The blockade, in other words, represented what McGeorge Bundy later noted was "only a first step, not a last."[2]

The airstrike option, moreover, was rendered considerably less palatable by the air force's insistence on the need for a massive airstrike against Cuba, rather than a "surgical" one, and its estimate that even a full-scale attack involving several hundred sorties would at best eliminate only 90 percent of the known missiles in Cuba (Document 25). In reality, a report by General Walter Sweeney, the commander-in-chief of the Tactical Air Command, which stated that the airstrike could not ensure the elimination of all the missile sites, was the final nail in the coffin for the airstrike option. By the time Sweeney made his presentation on October 21, President Kennedy had all but decided to enact a limited blockade, or what U.S. policymakers would call a naval "quarantine."[3]

With President Kennedy's decision to exercise the blockade option, political and military preparations quickly followed. The ExComm set October 22 as the date for the president to publicly announce the discovery of the Cuban missiles and the U.S. response. On the day of the speech, U.S. diplomats briefed key world allies, White House staff informed congressional leaders of the quarantine action, and the White House moved to persuade newspaper editors to delay publication of the story in the interests of national security. One hour prior to President Kennedy's nationally televised speech, Secretary of State Rusk presented Soviet Ambassador Anatoly Dobrynin with an advance copy of the speech and a letter (Documents 26, 27, 28). Reporters later wrote that the Soviet ambassador—who had not been informed of the missile deployment by his own government—emerged from the meeting looking "ashen."

At 7:00 P.M., Kennedy addressed the nation. "Within the past week, unmistakable evidence has established the fact that a series of offensive missile sites is now in preparation" on Cuba, the president began. "The purpose of these bases can be none other than to provide a nuclear strike capability against the Western Hemisphere." The seventeen-minute speech, drafted by Theodore Sorensen, announced "a strict quarantine on all offensive military equipment under shipment to Cuba." Should any missiles be launched from Cuba against any nation, Kennedy warned, the United States would regard it "as an attack by the Soviet Union on the United States, requiring a full retaliatory response upon the Soviet Union" (Document 28).

At the same hour, nearly all U.S. military forces worldwide increased their alert status to Defense Condition (DEFCON) 3 (Document 29). U.S. nuclear forces were placed on an even higher alert footing, DEFCON 2, only one step away from DEFCON 1—war. On his own initiative, General Thomas Power, the commander-in-chief of the Strategic Air Command, chose to raise SAC's alert posture using nonencrypted messages so that Soviet intelligence would not mistake the seriousness of the U.S. military preparations to wage nuclear war.[4]

THE CRISIS BUILDS

President Kennedy's announcement and the imposition of the quarantine caught Khrushchev and other Soviet leaders by surprise. The initial Soviet response was a statement by Khrushchev, transmitted by the Soviet news agency TASS, denouncing the U.S. action and claiming that the Soviet weapons in Cuba were intended "solely for defensive purposes" (Document 30). While the initial political reaction by Khrushchev appeared to be relatively restrained, U.S. officials worried about possible Soviet and Cuban military reactions. In particular, on October 23 the ExComm discussed the possibility that the Soviet Union would take some counteraction in Berlin, as well as the possibility that U.S. reconnaissance planes flying over Cuba would be shot down by the advanced SA-2 surface-to-air missile sites that Soviet technicians were rapidly constructing on the island (Document 31).

An even greater specter was the possibility that Soviet ships would challenge the U.S. blockade of Cuba, which was scheduled to go into effect at 10:00 A.M. on October 24. Not only did Soviet ships appear to continue their advance toward the quarantine line, but U.S. intelligence reported to Kennedy and the ExComm that Soviet submarines had been spotted moving into the Caribbean. President Kennedy feared that if the Soviet ships refused to halt and if Soviet submarines attempted to escort them, U.S. Navy vessels would be forced to fire on the vessels, possibly igniting war between the superpowers.

As Robert Kennedy would later write in his posthumously published memoir of the Cuban missile crisis, the ExComm meeting on the morning of October 24 (summarized in Document 35) seemed "the most trying, the most difficult, and the most filled with tension."[5] As U.S. Navy ships along the quarantine line stood ready to intercept any oncoming Soviet vessels, the ExComm members nervously waited in Washington for the latest report on the events in the Caribbean. At 10:25 A.M., an intelligence report was finally rushed in indicating that Soviet ships had stopped short of the quarantine line, occasioning

Dean Rusk's famous comment, "We're eyeball to eyeball and I think the other fellow just blinked."

The success of the quarantine line, however, did not resolve the problem of inducing Khrushchev to withdraw the missiles from Cuba. By this time, U.S. intelligence had found signs of rapid and unremitting construction at two complexes for the Soviet SS-4 MRBMs, as well as two complexes for longer range SS-5 IRBMs. Drawing on further intelligence gathered by U-2 and low-level reconnaissance planes, on October 25, the CIA notified the ExComm that some of the missiles in Cuba had become "operational."

Despite the possibility that the missiles in Cuba might be ready to fire, direct military action against Cuba remained very much a live option. Records from the ExComm's meetings on October 25, 26, and 27, indicate that the president and his men continued to consider an airstrike/invasion scenario. Using military force, proponents argued, would demonstrate that the U.S. had "the will to fight and to protect vital interests" (Document 37). A military fact sheet prepared for President Kennedy on October 27 reflected the preparations of U.S. military forces during the crisis (and indeed, for several weeks before the crisis) to dramatically increase their capabilities to carry out military action against Cuba (Document 46).

By then, military planners had developed three separate contingency plans: Operation Plan (Oplan) 312, Oplan 314, and Oplan 316. Whereas Oplan 312 set out plans for launching an air attack on Cuba, the latter contingency plans involved a full invasion of the island. Eventually, Oplan 316 was designated as the primary invasion plan: it called for a full U.S. airstrike—over one thousand air sorties on the first day—followed by an airborne assault by U.S. forces, and finally an amphibious landing. While the air attacks could be carried out on short notice, JCS Chairman Taylor noted, the logistics involved in deploying the 140,000 U.S. troops massing for a Cuban invasion necessitated a full seven day's notice in advance of an invasion (Document 40).

Even as tensions subsided on October 29, U.S. military planners "proposed to have tactical nuclear weapons readily available" for an invasion force, for fear that Soviet troops on the island had nuclear warheads for their short-range FROG missiles (Document 41). In part because U.S. intelligence was never able to ascertain whether any nuclear warheads were on the island, Secretary of Defense McNamara declined to authorize the invasion fleet to carry tactical nuclear weapons. Soviet sources have recently suggested, however, that nine warheads for FROGs had indeed reached the island, and likely would have been employed against invading U.S. forces.[6]

THE ELEVENTH HOUR OF THE CRISIS

The continuing work on the missile sites seemed to cast doubt on the likelihood that the Soviets would withdraw their offensive weapons from Cuba. Indeed, on the morning of October 26, President Kennedy offered his view to the ExComm that the quarantine by itself was unlikely to induce the Soviets to remove the missiles: "we will get the Soviet strategic missiles out of Cuba only by invading Cuba or by trading," he concluded (Document 42). But by the end of the day, glimmers of hope had emerged in Washington that some type of diplomatic solution might be within reach. The cause for optimism was two Soviet diplomatic initiatives undertaken during the day. The first initiative came from the KGB's Washington station chief, Aleksandr Fomin. Fomin asked John Scali, a correspondent for ABC News who was well connected with several State Department officials, to meet for lunch. According to notes taken by Scali during the meeting, Fomin proposed a settlement to the crisis involving the removal of the Soviet missiles under U.N. inspection in return for a U.S. pledge not to invade Cuba (Document 43).

Some five hours after Fomin made his proposal, a new, private message from Premier Khrushchev to President Kennedy was received by the State Department. The long, emotional missive vividly captures the tension of the moment. "You and I should not now pull on the ends of the rope in which you have tied a knot of war, because the harder you and I pull, the tighter the knot will become," Khrushchev warned Kennedy. "And a time may come when this knot is tied so tight that the person who tied it is no longer capable of cutting it" (Document 44).

Though rambling in places, the letter also appeared to hint at a possible basis for a crisis settlement. If Kennedy would agree to offer a guarantee not to invade or support the invasion of Cuba, Khrushchev suggested, the "necessity for the presence of our military specialists in Cuba will be obviated." The ExComm, believing that the Khrushchev letter and the Fomin approach together formed a coherent negotiating position, chose to read Khrushchev's unstructured proposal in light of the more concrete formula offered by Fomin. Soviet sources have only recently revealed that, contrary to the assumptions of U.S. decision-makers at the time, the Kremlin neither had authorized nor even had any foreknowledge of Fomin's diplomatic approach.[7]

If October 26 gave rise to growing optimism in Washington, similar sentiments were not shared by Fidel Castro and other Cuban leaders. For Castro, the continuing U.S. military buildup rendered the possibility of a U.S. airstrike or invasion very real. Writing from the bomb shelter in the Soviet embassy in Havana on the night of October 26, Castro relayed his fears to Khrushchev in a letter translated and transmitted by the Soviet ambassador to Cuba, Alexander Alekseyev—who has since stated that his grasp of Spanish was less than perfect, and that his translation may have misrepresented Castro's intent. The letter appeared to suggest that a preemptive strike should be launched against U.S. forces if they invaded Cuba. "If...the imperialists invade Cuba with the goal of occupying it," Castro wrote, "the danger that that aggressive policy poses for humanity is so great that following that event the Soviet Union should never allow the circumstances in which the imperialists could launch the first nuclear strike against it" (Document 45). Almost thirty years later, at the 1992 Havana conference, Castro explained his thinking:

I remembered how Stalin had refused to believe that the Nazis were planning to attack in 1941. I did not want Nikita to make the same mistake. I wanted to be sure that the Soviet forces were ready for anything. I was convinced that an invasion of Cuba would lead on to nuclear war against the Soviet Union. My recommendation for a preventative strike was not in case of an American air attack but in case of invasion and occupation.[8]

On October 27, the cautious but growing optimism in Washington gave way to the "blackest hour" of the crisis. Early in the morning, U.S. intelligence reported that five missile sites in Cuba "appear to be fully operational" (Document 47). Another unsettling report came from the FBI, which informed Robert Kennedy that Soviet personnel in New York were preparing to destroy their diplomatic documents.[9] Finally, around 9:00 A.M., a new message from Khrushchev was broadcast over Radio Moscow. In contrast to the private letter received the day before, the new Soviet letter was formal in tone. Alarmingly, Khrushchev was now raising the stakes by agreeing to withdraw the missiles in Cuba only if "the United States, for its part, considering the uneasiness and anxiety of the Soviet State, will remove its analogous means from Turkey" i.e., the Jupiter Missiles (Document 48).

The ExComm, which was meeting to consider a positive response to Khrushchev's October 26 proposal, found the new letter deeply troubling (Document 49). Administration officials had worried from the beginning of the crisis that the Jupiter issue might get entangled in negotiations over Cuba with the Soviets. Indeed, even before the crisis, U.S. officials had linked the Turkish IRBMs to the Cuban situation. In the August 23 National Security Action Memorandum (181) requesting several studies in light of Soviet activity in Cuba, President Kennedy ordered the Pentagon to examine "what actions can be taken to get Jupiter missiles out of Turkey" (Document 12). On October 25, the possibility of trade involving the Jupiter missiles was publicly aired in a column by Wal-

ter Lippmann, a prominent U.S. journalist, as well as in a statement by Austrian Foreign Minister Bruno Kreisky. But the public attempt on the part of the Soviets to make the Jupiter missiles part of a crisis settlement pinned the U.S. on the horns of a dilemma.

On the one hand, a public trade of the Jupiters for the Cuban missiles seemed diplomatically impossible, selling out a NATO ally in a moment of crisis. Raymond Hare, the U.S. ambassador to Turkey, cabled Washington on October 27, expressing concern that any missile trade "would present major problem[s] not only in terms of bilateral Turkish-American relationship but also NATO association" (Document 50). The ExComm had received similar arguments against a Turkey-Cuba trade from Lauris Norstad, the commander of NATO forces, and the U.S. ambassador to NATO, Thomas Finletter. On the other hand, as President Kennedy argued, "to any...rational man it [the Turkey-Cuba missile deal] will look like a very fair trade"—particularly if the alternative to accepting it became a nuclear holocaust (Document 49).

As the October 27 transcript records, the ExComm spent much of the morning finding an acceptable response to the new Soviet initiative. Eventually, several advisers, including Sorensen, Bundy, and Robert Kennedy, developed the idea of sending a new letter to Khrushchev in which the Jupiter proposal would simply be ignored. In the proposed response, the president would just "accept" Khrushchev's October 26 "proposal" for a Soviet withdrawal in exchange for a U.S. pledge not to invade Cuba. Although President Kennedy initially expressed skepticism toward this negotiating ploy, his advisers argued that Khrushchev might be willing to accept an end to the crisis on such a basis. As Llewellyn Thompson, the Soviet specialist on the ExComm, argued, "The important thing for Khrushchev...it seems to me, is to be able to say, I saved Cuba, I stopped an invasion..." (Document 49). Ultimately, Kennedy agreed to send the new letter, and directed Robert Kennedy to relay the U.S. position in a meeting with Soviet Ambassador Dobrynin that evening.

Around midday, however, more bad news reached

Washington. The ExComm received a report that a U-2 reconnaissance plane was missing over eastern Cuba. Within hours, U.S. intelligence confirmed the officials' worst fears: the aircraft had been downed by a Soviet SA-2 SAM battery and the American pilot killed (Document 49). As if to underscore the extent to which the crisis appeared to be spinning out of control, the ExComm subsequently learned that another U-2 aircraft on a routine air sampling mission off the coast of Alaska had accidently flown into Soviet airspace, alerting Soviet interceptor forces.

The alarm and despair felt in Washington on October 27 was mirrored in Moscow. The U-2 flight over Soviet territory may have been seen not as the accident that it was but as a deliberate military reconnaissance mission prior to the onset of hostilities. Soviet leaders must also have been alarmed by the information coming through the Scali-Fomin back channel. At the request of the Secretary of State Rusk, Scali had asked Aleksandr Fomin to meet again on the afternoon of October 27. At the meeting, Scali expressed outrage that the Soviet negotiating position had hardened, and he exclaimed that a Cuban invasion was "only a matter of hours away." (Fomin apparently relayed the invasion warning to Moscow even though Scali's comments regarding the invasion were not authorized by U.S. officials.) Finally, the U-2 downing over Cuba must have caused concern to Soviet leaders in Moscow, primarily because they had not ordered the action! Instead, as historians recently learned, the plane was shot down on the orders of local Soviet commanders in Cuba.

Kennedy and the ExComm understandably—but incorrectly—perceived the U-2 downing as a deliberate escalatory act by the Kremlin. While the ExComm had earlier agreed to respond to interference with U.S. reconnaissance with an immediate air attack on the offending SAM sites, President Kennedy now exercised caution. In order to give diplomacy another chance to end the crisis, the president decided not to authorize an airstrike—a decision reportedly met with disbelief by officials in the Pentagon.[10]

A DEAL TO WITHDRAW THE MISSILES

At 7:45 P.M. on October 27, Robert Kennedy met with Soviet Ambassador Anatoly Dobrynin at the attorney general's office. Unknown to any U.S. official except the president—and until very recently, unknown to historians—the two had also met on the previous evening. In the October 26 meeting at the Soviet embassy, according to Dobrynin, Robert Kennedy himself suggested making the missiles in Turkey a part of a crisis settlement. The attorney general, Dobrynin has recently revealed, went so far as to phone his brother in order to confirm that the United States intended to remove the missiles from Turkey after the crisis had ended.[11] Thus, it is possible that Khrushchev's public demand for a Turkey-Cuba missile trade—made on the morning of the 27th—may have been based on Robert Kennedy's remarks, relayed through Dobrynin.

In their October 27 meeting, Robert Kennedy warned Dobrynin that time was running out for a diplomatic solution to the crisis. The United States had to have a commitment by the following day that the missile bases would be removed by the Soviet Union, he stated, or else "we [the United States] would remove them." At the same time, the attorney general passed on a message regarding the Jupiter missiles which President Kennedy had authorized in a meeting with a small group of advisers that afternoon. Robert Kennedy remarked that while no explicit quid pro quo involving the missiles in Turkey and Cuba could be made part of any crisis settlement, "it was our judgement that, within a short time after the crisis was over, those missiles would be gone."[12]

Later that night, President Kennedy took further steps to enhance the missile swap option should it prove necessary to end the crisis. Kennedy asked Dean Rusk to secretly contact Andrew Cordier, a former U.N. official, and provide him with a statement calling for the removal of the Jupiters in Turkey and the Soviet missiles in Cuba. Rusk instructed Cordier that if he received a further signal he was to have U.N. Secretary General U Thant issue the statement so that

President Kennedy would be in a position to agree to a U.N., rather than a Soviet, proposal involving the Turkish missiles.[13] While the Cordier maneuver was clearly a contingency plan, the instructions to Rusk, together with Kennedy's remarks at the October 27 ExComm meeting and the messages to Dobrynin, indicate that President Kennedy was extremely reluctant to allow obsolete missiles in Turkey to stand in the way of a negotiated settlement to avert nuclear war.

In Moscow, Khrushchev scrambled to find a new course of action. Soviet and Cuban intelligence on the U.S. military buildup, and probably reports from Fomin and Dobrynin, supported the contention that a U.S. military strike against the missiles would take place soon if he ordered work on the missile sites to continue. A decision to back down, on the other hand, would be compensated by a face-saving U.S. noninvasion guarantee and by private U.S. assurances that the IRBMs in Turkey would be removed. No doubt adding to Khrushchev's calculations were the uncertain events in Cuba. The Soviet command-and-control failure that led to the U-2 downing as well as the Cuban decision to fire on low-altitude U.S. reconnais-

sance planes created a sense of urgency in the Kremlin, as in the White House. With the help of his closest aides, a new message to Kennedy was rapidly drafted at Khrushchev's dacha. To avoid any possible communication delay, the letter was rushed to a radio station for public broadcast.

At 9:00 A.M. on October 28, Khrushchev's message was broadcast from Moscow. "In order to complete with greater speed the liquidation of the conflict dangerous to the cause of peace," Khrushchev wrote, "the Soviet government, in addition to previously issued instructions on the cessation of further work at building sites for the weapons, has issued a new order on the dismantling of the weapons which you describe as 'offensive,' and their crating and return to the Soviet Union" (Document 52). With the news of the Soviet decision, President Kennedy released a statement hailing Khrushchev's decision and calling it "an important contribution to peace" (Document 53). Abruptly, the shadow of nuclear warfare hanging over the United States, the Soviet Union, Cuba, and the rest of the world had lifted.

NOTES

1. Taylor is quoted in Raymond Garthoff, *Reflections on the Cuban Missile Crisis* (2d ed., Washington, D.C.: Brookings Institution, 1980), pp. 44, 45.

2. McGeorge Bundy, *Danger and Survival: Choices About the Bomb in the First Fifty Years* (New York: Random House, 1988), p. 398.

3. Ibid. p. 400–401.

4. Garthoff, *Reflections*, p. 62.

5. Robert Kennedy, *Thirteen Days: A Memoir of the Cuban Missile Crisis* (New York: W. W. Norton, 1969), p. 68.

6. Arthur Schlesinger, Jr., "Four Days with Fidel: A Havana Diary," *The New York Review of Books* (March 16, 1992), p. 23.

7. Garthoff, *Reflections*, p. 73.

8. Schlesinger, "Four Days with Fidel," p. 24.

9. Robert Kennedy, *Thirteen Days*, p. 93.

10. Graham Allison, *Essence of Decision* (Boston: Little, Brown, 1971), p. 225.

11. Garthoff, *Reflections*, p. 87.

12. Robert Kennedy, *Thirteen Days*, pp. 108, 109.

13. James G. Blight and David A. Welch, *On the Brink: Americans and Soviets Reexamine the Cuban Missile Crisis* (New York: Hill and Wang, 1989), pp. 83, 84.

DOCUMENT 15: Transcript of the first Executive Committee Meeting, October 16, 1962, 11:50 A.M.–12:57 P.M. (from the John F. Kennedy Library; edited for length).

PAGE 1 OF 12

PAPERS OF JOHN F. KENNEDY
PRESIDENTIAL PAPERS
PRESIDENT'S OFFICE FILES

Presidential Recordings

Transcripts

Cuban Missile Crisis Meetings
October 16, 1962

THE JOHN F. KENNEDY LIBRARY
Columbia Point
Boston, MA 02125
(617) 929-4500

DOCUMENT 15: Transcript of the first Executive Committee Meeting, October 16, 1962, 11:50 A.M.–12:57 P.M. (from the John F. Kennedy Library; edited for length).

PAGE 2 OF 12

Off-the-Record Meeting on Cuba
October 16, 1962
11:50 A.M.–12:57 P.M.

SPEAKERS (in order of appearance)

CAROLINE: Caroline Kennedy, President Kennedy's daughter.

JFK: John F. Kennedy, President

LUNDAHL: Arthur C. Lundahl, Director, National Photographic Interpretation Center

GRAYBEAL: Sidney Graybeal, Chief, Guided Missile Division, Office of Scientific Intelligence, CIA

McNAMARA: Robert McNamara, Secretary of Defense

TAYLOR: Maxwell Taylor, Chairman, Joint Chiefs of Staff

RUSK: Dean Rusk, Secretary of State

BUNDY: McGeorge Bundy, Special Assistant to the President

DILLON: Douglas Dillon, Secretary of the Treasury

JOHNSON: Lyndon Baines Johnson, Vice President

RFK: Robert F. Kennedy, Attorney General

SPEAKER?: Speaker unknown or identity uncertain

A NOTE ON THE TRANSCRIPT

Punctuation, with some exceptions, remains as in the original. The following codes are used as follows:

(remarks)
Remarks in parentheses reflect comments of the original tape transcriber.

[remarks]
Remarks in brackets reflect comments by editors of this volume.

—
Dashes reflect that a speaker has paused or been interrupted, or that a short comment of the transcriber has been eliminated for continuity.

…
Ellipses between sections of text indicate that material has been deleted due to space limitations.

CAROLINE: The text

JFK: in this portion has

CAROLINE: been closed

JFK: in accordance with

CAROLINE: the donor's deed

JFK: of gift.

(Laughter)

SPEAKER?: (Words unintelligible)

JFK: Okay.

LUNDAHL: This is a result of the photography taken Sunday, sir.

JFK: Yeah.

LUNDAHL: There's a medium-range ballistic missile launch site and two new military encampments on the southern edge of Sierra del Rosario in west central Cuba.

JFK: Where would that be?

LUNDAHL: Uh, west central, sir. That—

…

JFK: How do you know this is a medium-range ballistic missile?

LUNDAHL: The length, sir.

JFK: The what? The length?

LUNDAHL: The length of it. Yes.

DOCUMENT 15: Transcript of the first Executive Committee Meeting, October 16, 1962, 11:50 A.M.–12:57 P.M. (from the John F. Kennedy Library; edited for length).

PAGE 3 OF 12

...

JFK: Is this ready to be fired?

GRAYBEAL: No, sir.

JFK: How long have we got—We can't tell, I take it—

GRAYBEAL: No, sir.

JFK: —how long before it can be fired?

GRAYBEAL: That depends on how ready the (GSC?) (how or hours?)

JFK: But, what does it have to be fired from?

GRAYBEAL: It would have to be fired from a stable hard surface. This could be packed dirt; it could be concrete or, or asphalt. The surface has to be hard, then you put a flame deflect—, a deflector plate on there to direct the missile.

McNAMARA: Would you care to comment on the position of nuclear warheads—this is in relation to the question from the president—explain when these can be fired?

GRAYBEAL?: Sir, we've looked very hard. We can find nothing that would spell nuclear warhead in term of any isolated area or unique security in this particular area. The mating of the nuclear warhead to the missile from some of the other short-range missiles there would take about, uh, a couple of hours to do this.

McNAMARA: This is not defensed, I believe, at the moment?

LUNDAHL: Not yet, sir.

McNAMARA: This is important as it relates to whether these, today, are ready to fire, Mr. President. It seems almost impossible to me that they would be ready to fire with nuclear warheads on the site without even a fence around it. It may not take long to k—, to place them there, to erect a fence, but at least at the moment there is some reason to believe the warheads aren't present and hence they are not ready to fire.

GRAYBEAL: Yes, sir, we do not believe they are ready to fire—

TAYLOR?: However, there is no feeling that they can't fire from this kind of field position very quickly, isn't that true? It's not a question of waiting for extensive concrete, uh, pads and that sort of thing?

GRAYBEAL?: The unknown factor here, sir, is the degree to which the equipment has been checked out after it's been shipped from the Soviet Union here. It's the readiness of the equipment. If the equipment is checked out, the site has to be accurately surveyed, the position as is known. Once this is known, then you're talking a matter of hours.

...

McNAMARA: There's no question about that. The question is one of readiness of the, to fire and—and this is highly critical in forming our plans—that the time between today and the time when the readiness to fire capability develops is a very important thing. To estimate that we need to know where these warheads are, and we have not yet found any probable storage of warheads and hence it seems extremely unlikely that they are now ready to fire or may be ready to fire within a matter of hours or even a day or two.

...

JFK: Secretary Rusk?

RUSK: Yes, (Well?), Mr. President, this is a, of course, a (widely?) serious development. It's one that we, all of us, had not really believed the Soviets could, uh, carry this far. Uh, they, uh, seemed to be denying that they were going to establish bases of their own (in the same?) (words unintelligible) with a Soviet base, thus making it (essential to or essentially?) Cuban point of view. The Cubans couldn't (word unintelligible) with it anyhow, so—now, um, I do think we have to set in motion a chain of events that will eliminate this base. I don't think we (can?) sit still. The questioning becomes whether we do it by sudden, unannounced strike of some sort, or we, uh, build up the crisis to the point where the other side has to consider very seriously about giving in, or, or even the Cubans themselves, uh, take some, take some action on this. The thing that I'm, of course, very conscious of is that there is no such thing, I think, as unilateral action by the United States. It's so (eminently or heavily?) involved with forty-two allies and confrontation in many places, that any action that we take, uh, will greatly increase the risks of direct action involving, uh, our other alliances and our other forces in other parts of the world. Uhm, so I think we, we have to think very hard about two major, uh, courses of action as alternatives. One is the quick strike. The point where we (make or think?), that is the, uh, overwhelming, overriding necessity to take all the risks that are involved [in] doing that. I don't think this in itself would require an invasion of Cuba. I think that with or without such an invasion, in other words if we make it clear that, uh, what we're doing is eliminating this particular base or any other such base that is established. We ourselves are not moved to general war, we're simply doing what we said we would do if they took certain action. Uh, or we're going to decide that this is the time to eliminate the Cuban problem by actually eliminating the island.

The other would be, if we have a few days—from the military point of view, if we have the whole time, uh, then I would think, that, uh there would be another course of action, a combination of things that, uh, we might wish to consider. Uhm, first, uh, that we, uh, stimulate the OAS [Organization of American States] procedure immediately for prompt action to make it quite clear that the entire hemisphere considers that the Rio Pact has been violated (and actually?) what acts should (we take or be taken?) in, under the terms of the Rio Pact. The OAS could constitute itself an organ of consultation promptly, although maybe, it may take two or three days to get, uh, instructions from governments and things of that sort. The OAS could, I suppose, at any moment, uh, take action to insist to the Cubans that an OAS inspection, uh, team be permitted to come and, itself, look directly at these sites, provide assurance(s?) to the hemisphere. That will undoubtedly be turned down, but it will be another step in building up the, uh, building a position.

I think also that we ought to consider getting some word to Castro, perhaps through the Canadian ambassador in Havana or through, uh, his representative at the U.N. Uh, I think perhaps the Canadian ambassador would be the best, the better channel to get to Castro (apart?) privately and tell him that, uh, this is no longer support for Cuba, that Cuba is being victimized here, and that, uh, the Soviets are

DOCUMENT 15: Transcript of the first Executive Committee Meeting, October 16, 1962, 11:50 A.M.–12:57 P.M. (from the John F. Kennedy Library; edited for length).

PAGE 5 OF 12

preparing Cuba for destruction or betrayal.

You saw the *[New York] Times* story yesterday morning that high Soviet officials were saying, "We'll trade Cuba for Berlin." This ought to be brought to Castro's attention. It ought to be said to Castro that, uh, uh, this kind of a base is intolerable and not acceptable. The time has now come when he must take the interests of the Cuban people, must now break clearly with the Soviet Union, prevent this missile base from becoming operational.

And I think there are certain military, um, uh, actions that we could, we might well want to take straight away. First, to, uh, to call up, uh, highly selective units (no more than?) 150,000. Unless we feel that it's better, more desirable to go to a general national emergency so that we have complete freedom of action. If we announce, at the time that we announce this development—and I think we do have to announce this development some time this week— uh, we announce that, uh, we are conducting a surveillance of Cuba, over Cuba, and we will enforce our right to do so. We reject the mission of secrecy in this hemisphere in any matters of this sort. We, we reinforce our forces in Guantánamo. We reinforce our forces in the southeastern part of the United States—whatever is necessary from the military point of view to be able to give, to deliver an overwhelming strike at any of these installations, including the SAM sites. And, uh, also, to take care of any, uh, MiGs or bombers that might make a pass at Miami or at the United States. Build up heavy forces, uh, if those are not already in position.

[15 lines excised]

I think also that we need a few days, um, to alert our other allies, for consultation with NATO. I'll assume that we can move on this line at the same time to interrupt all air traffic from free world countries going into Cuba, insist to the Mexicans, the Dutch, that they stop their planes from coming in. Tell the British, who, and anyone else who's involved at this point, that, uh, if they're interested in peace, they've got to stop their ships from Cuban trade at this point. Uh, in other words, isolate Cuba completely without at this particular moment a, uh, a forceful blockade. I think it would be important to use the, uh, consider, uh, calling in General [Dwight] Eisenhower, giving him a full briefing before a public announcement is made as to the situation and the (forcible?) action which you might determine upon.

But I think that, by and large, there are, there are these two broad alternatives: one, the quick strike; the other, to alert our allies *and* Mr. Khrushchev that there is utterly serious crisis in the making here, and that, uh—Mr. Khrushchev may not himself really understand that or believe that at this point. I think we'll be facing a situation that could well lead to general war; that we have an obligation to do what has to be done but do it in a way that gives, uh, everybody a chance to, uh, put the (word unintelligible) down before it gets too hard. Those are my, my reactions of this morning, Mr. President. I naturally need to think about this very hard for the next several hours, uh, what I and what my colleagues at the State Department can do about it.

MCNAMARA: Mr. President, there are a number of

DOCUMENT 15: Transcript of the first Executive Committee Meeting, October 16, 1962, 11:50 A.M.–12:57 P.M. (from the John F. Kennedy Library; edited for length).

PAGE 6 OF 12

unknowns in this situation I want to comment upon, and, in relation to them, I would like to outline very briefly some possible military alternatives and ask General Taylor to expand upon them. But before commenting on either the unknowns or outlining some military alternatives, there are two propositions I would suggest that we ought to accept as, uh, foundations for our further thinking. My first is that if we are to conduct an airstrike against these installations, or against any part of Cuba, we must agree now that we will schedule that prior to the time these missile sites become operational. I'm not prepared to say when that will be, but I think it is extremely important that our talk and our discussion be founded on this premise: that any airstrike will be planned to take place prior to the time they become operational. Because, if they become operational before the airstrike, I do not believe we can state we can knock them out before they can be launched; and if they're launched there is almost certain to be, uh, chaos in part of the east coast or the area, uh, in a radius of six hundred to a thousand miles from Cuba.

Uh, secondly, I, I would submit the proposition that any airstrike must be directed not solely against the missile sites, but against the missile sites plus the airfields plus the aircraft which may not be on the airfields but hidden by that time plus all potential nuclear storage sites. Now, this is a fairly extensive airstrike. It is not just a strike against the missile sites; and there would be associated with it potential casualties of Cubans, not of U.S. citizens, but potential casualties of Cubans in, at least in the hundreds, more likely in the low thousands, say two or three thousand. It seems to me these two propositions, uh, should underline our, our discussion.

Now, what kinds of military action are we capable of carrying out and what may be some of the consequences? Uh, we could carry out an airstrike within a matter of days. We would be ready for the start of such an airstrike within, within a matter of days. If it were absolutely essential, it could be done almost literally within a matter of hours. I believe the chiefs would prefer that it be deferred for a matter of days, but, we are prepared for that quickly. The airstrike could continue for a matter of days following the initial day, if necessary. Uh, presumably there would be some political discussions taking place within, just before the airstrike or both before and during. In any event, we would be prepared, following the airstrike, for an air, invasion, both by air and by sea. [Words excised] —after the start of the airstrike, that would be possible if the political environment made it desirable or necessary at that time. (Fine?) Associated with this airstrike undoubtedly should be some degree of mobilization. Uh, I would think of the mobilization coming not before the airstrike but either concurrently with or somewhat following, say possibly five days afterwards, depending upon the possible invasion requirements. The character of the mobilization would be such that it could be carried out in its first phase at least within the limits of the authority granted by Congress. There might have to be a second phase, and then it would require a declaration of a national emergency.

Now, this is very sketchily the military, uh, capabilities, and I think you may wish to hear General Taylor, uh, outline his choice.

SPEAKER?: Almost too (words unintelligible) to Cuba.

SPEAKER?: Yes.

TAYLOR: Uh, we're impressed, Mr. President, with the great importance of getting a, a strike with all the benefit of surprise, uh, which would mean *ideally* that we would have all the missiles that are in Cuba above ground where we can take them out. Uh, that, that desire runs counter to the strong point the secretary made if the other optimum would be to get every missile before it could, becomes operational. Uh, practically, I think the, our knowledge of the timing of the readiness is going to be so, so, uh, difficult that we'll never have the, the exact permanent, uh, the perfect timing. What we'd like to do is to look at this new photography, I think—and take any additional— and try to get the, the layout of the targets in as near an optimum, uh, position as possible and then take 'em out without any warning whatsoever. That does not preclude, I don't think, Mr. Secretary, some of the things you've been talking about. It's a little hard to say in terms of time how much I'm discussing. But we must do a good job the first time we go in there, uh, pushing a 100 percent just as far, as closely as we can with our, with our strike. I'm having all the responsible planners in this afternoon, Mr. President, at four o'clock, to talk this out with 'em and get their best judgment.

I would also mention among the, the military actions we should take that once we have destroyed as many of these offensive weapons as possible, we should, should prevent any more coming in, which means a naval blockade. So I suppose that all—and also a reinforcement of Guantánamo and evacuation of dependents. So, really, the, in point of time, I'm, I'm thinking in terms of three phases.

One, a, an initial pause of some sort while we get completely ready and get, get the right posture on the part of the target, so we can do the best job. Then, virtually concurrently, an airstrike against, as the secretary said, missiles, airfields, uh, nuclear sites that we know of. At the same time, naval blockade. At the same time, reinforce Guantánamo and evacuate the dependents. I'd then start this continuous reconnaissance, the list that you had, continue over Cuba.

Then, then the decision can be made as we, as we're mobilizing, uh, with the airstrike as to whether we invade or not. I think that's the hardest question militarily in the whole business—one which we should look at very closely before we get our feet in that deep mud in Cuba.

RUSK: There are st—, one or two things, Mr. President, uh. [Andrei] Gromyko asked to see you Thursday. Uh, it may be of some interest to know what he says about this, if he says anything. He may be bringing a message on this subject. Uh, but that—I just want to remind you that you are seeing him and that may be relevant to this (topic?). I might say incidentally, sir, that you delay anything else you have to do at this point.

Secondly, I don't believe, myself, that the critical question is whether you get a particular missile before *it* goes off because if they shoot *those* missiles we are in general nuclear war. In other words, the Soviet Union

DOCUMENT 15: Transcript of the first Executive Committee Meeting, October 16, 1962, 11:50 A.M.–12:57 P.M. (from the John F. Kennedy Library; edited for length).

PAGE 8 OF 12

has got quite a different decision to make. If they, if they shoot those missiles, want to shoot 'em off before they get knocked out by aircraft—So, I'm not sure that this is, uh, necessarily the precise (critical?) element, Bob.

MCNAMARA: Well, I would strongly emphasize that I think our time should be based on the assumption it is, Dean. We don't know what kinds of communications the Soviets have with those sites. We don't know what kinds of control they have over the warheads.

RUSK: Yes, (words unintelligible).

MCNAMARA: If we saw a warhead on the site and we knew that launcher was capable of launching that warhead, I would—frankly, I would strongly urge against the air attack, to be quite frank about it, because I think the danger to this country in relation to the gain that would accrue with the excessive (time?)—this is why I suggest that if we're talking about an air attack, I believe we should consider it *only* on the assumption that we can carry it off before these become operational.

JFK: What is the, uh, advant—Must be some major reason for the Russians to, uh, set this up as a—must be that they're not satisfied with their ICBMs. What'd be the reason that they would, uh—

TAYLOR: What it'd give 'em is primary, it makes the launching base, uh, for short-range missiles against the United States to supplement their rather [defective?] ICBM system, for example. There's one reason.

JFK: Of course, I don't see how we could prevent further ones from coming in by submarine.

TAYLOR: Well, I think that thing is all over—

JFK: I mean if we let 'em blockade the thing, they come in by submarine.

MCNAMARA: Well, I think the only way to prevent them coming in, quite frankly, is to say you'll take them out the moment they come in. You'll take them out and you'll carry on open surveillance and you'll have a policy to take them out if they come in. [Words excised]

[3 lines excised]

BUNDY: Are you absolutely clear of your premise that an airstrike must go to the whole air complex?

MCNAMARA: Well, we are, Mac—because we are fearful of these MiG 21s. We don't know where they are. We don't know what they're capable of. If there are nuclear warheads associated with the launchers, you must assume there will be nuclear warheads associated with aircraft. Even if there are not nuclear warheads associated with aircraft, you must assume that those aircraft have high explosive potential.

[8 lines excised]

RUSK: Still, about why the Soviets are doing this, uhm, Mr. McCone suggested some weeks ago that one thing Mr. Khrushchev may have in mind is that, uh, uh, he knows that we have a substantial nuclear superiority, but he also knows that we don't really live under fear of his nuclear weapons to the extent that, uh, he has to live under fear of ours. Also we have nuclear weapons nearby, in Turkey and places like that. Um—

JFK: How many weapons do we have in Turkey?

TAYLOR?: We have Jupiter missiles—

BUNDY?: Yeah. We have how many?

MCNAMARA: About fifteen, I believe it is.

Bundy?: I think that's right. I think that's right.

SPEAKER?: (Words unintelligible)

RUSK: But then there are also delivery vehicles that are, could easily—

McNAMARA: Aircraft.

RUSK: —be moved through the air, aircraft and so forth.

SPEAKER?: Route 'em through Turkey.

RUSK: Um, and that Mr. McCone expresses the view that Khrushchev may feel that it's important for us to learn about living under medium-range missiles, and he's doing that sort of balance that, uh, that political, psychological (plank?). I think also that, uh, Berlin is, uh, very much involved in this. Uhm, for the first time, I'm beginning really to wonder whether maybe Mr. Khrushchev is entirely rational about Berlin. We've (hardly?) talked about his obsession with it. And I think we have to, uh, keep our eye on that element. But, uh, they may be thinking that they can either bargain Berlin and Cuba against each other, or that they could provoke us into a kind of action in Cuba which would give an umbrella for them to take action with respect to Berlin. In other words, like the Suez-Hungary combination. If they could provoke us into taking the first overt action, then the world would be confused and they would have, uh, what they would consider to be justification for making a move somewhere else. But, uh, I must say I don't really see the rationality of, uh, the Soviets' pushing it this far unless they grossly misunderstand the importance of Cuba to this country.

BUNDY: It's important, I think, to recognize that they did make this decision, as far as our estimates now go, in early summer, and this has been happening since August. The TASS statement of September 12, which the experts, I think, attribute very strongly to Khrushchev himself, is all mixed up on this point. It has a rather explicit statement, "The harmless military equipment sent to Cuba designed exclusively for defense, defensive purposes. The president of the United States and the American military, the military of any country know what means of defense are. How can these means threaten (the) United States?"

Now there, it's very hard to reconcile *that* with what has happened. The rest, as the secretary says, has many comparisons between Cuba and Italy, Turkey, and Japan. We have other evidence that Khrushchev is, honestly believes, or, or at least affects to believe that we have nuclear weapons in, in Japan, that combination, (word unintelligible)—

…

JFK: Doug, do you have any—

DILLON: No. The only thing I'd, would say is that, uh, this alternative course of, of warning, getting, uh, public opinion, uh, OAS action and telling people in NATO and everything like that, would appear to me to have the danger of, uh, getting us wide out in the open and forcing the Russians to, uh, Soviets to take a, a position that if anything was done, uh, they would, uh, have to retaliate. Whereas, uh, a, a quick action, uh, with a statement at the same time saying this is all there is to it, might give them a chance to, uh, back off and not do anything. Meanwhile, I think that the chance of getting through this thing without a Russian reaction is greater under a

DOCUMENT 15: Transcript of the first Executive Committee Meeting, October 16, 1962, 11:50 A.M.–12:57 P.M. (from the John F. Kennedy Library; edited for length).

PAGE 10 OF 12

quick, uh, strike than, uh, building the whole thing up to a, a climax then going through—(It will be a lot of debate on it?)

RUSK: That is, of course, a possibility, but uh—

BUNDY: The difficulties—I, I share the Secretary of the Treasury's feeling a little bit—the difficulties of organizing the OAS and NATO; the amount of noise we would get from our allies saying that, uh, they can live with Soviet MRBMs, why can't we; uh, the division in the alliance; the certainty that the Germans would feel that we *were* jeopardizing Berlin because of our concern over Cuba. The prospect of that pattern is not an appetizing one—

RUSK: Yes, but you see—

BUNDY: (words unintelligible)

RUSK: —uh, uh, everything turns crucially on what *happens*.

BUNDY: I agree, Mr. Secretary.

RUSK: And if we go with the quick strike, then, in fact, they *do* back it up, then you've exposed all of your allies (words unintelligible), ourselves to all these great dangers without—

BUNDY: You get all these noises again.

RUSK: —without, uh, the slightest consultation or, or warning or preparation.

JFK: But, of course, warning them, uh, it seems to me, is warning everybody. And I, I, obviously you can't sort of announce that in four days from now you're going to take them out. They may announce within three days they're going to fire them. Then what'll, what'll we do? Then we don't take 'em out. Of course, we then announce, well, if they do that, then

we're going to attack with nuclear weapons.

DILLON: Yes, sir, that's the question that nobody, I didn't understand, nobody had mentioned, is whether this s—, uh, "take-out," this mission, uh, was (word unintelligible) to deal with—

SPEAKER?: I don't know.

DILLON: —high explosives?

SPEAKER?: High explosives, yes.

JFK: How effective can the take-out be, do they think?

TAYLOR?: It'll never be a 100 percent, Mr. President, we know. Uh, we hope to take out a vast majority in the first strike, but this is not just one thing, one strike, one day, but continuous air attack for whenever necessary, whenever we di—, discover a target.

. . .

JFK: How long will, do we estimate this will remain secure, this, uh, information, uh, people have it?

BUNDY: In terms of the tightness of our intelligence control, Mr. President, I think we are in [an] unusually and fortunately good position. We set up a, uh, new security classification governing precisely the field of offensive capability in Cuba just five days ago, four days ago, under General Carter. That, uh, limits this, uh, to people who have an immediate, operational necessity in intelligence terms to work on the data and the people who have—

JFK: How many would that be, about?

BUNDY: Oh, that will be a very *large* number, but that's not generally where leaks come from. Uh, the more (important?) limitation is that only officers with the policy responsibility for advice directly to you'll receive this—

JFK: How many would get it over in the Defense Department, General, with your meeting this afternoon?

TAYLOR: Well, I was going to mention that. We'd have to ask for relaxation of the ground rules, uh, that, that Mac has just enunciated, so that I can, uh, give it to the senior commanders who are involved in the plans.

JFK: Would that be about fifty?

TAYLOR: By then—No, sir. I would say that, uh, within, at this stage *ten* more.

McNAMARA: Well, Mr. President, I, I think, to be realistic, we should assume that this will become fairly widely known, if not in the newspapers, at least by political representatives of both parties within—I would, I'm just picking a figure—I'd say a week.

                    . . .

JFK: You have any thoughts, Mr. Vice President?

JOHNSON: —I think that, uh, we're committed at any time that we feel that there's a buildup that in any way endangers (us) to take whatever action we must take to assure our security. I would think the secretary's evaluation of this being around all over the lot is a pretty accurate one, I would think it would take a week to do it. Maybe a little before then.

        I would, uh, like to hear what the responsible commanders have to say this afternoon. I think the question with the base is whether we take it out or whether we talk about it, and, uh, both, either alternative is a very distressing one, but of the two, I would take it out.

JFK: Well, uh, the, uh—

JOHNSON: Assuming these commanders felt that way—I spent the weekend with the ambassadors of the Organization of American States. I think this organization is fine, but I don't think, I don't rely on 'em much for any strength in anything like this. People are really concerned about this, in my opinion. Uh, I think we have to be prudent and cautious, talk to the commanders and see what they say, what they're—(I'm) not much for circularizing it over the Hill or our allies, even though I realize it's a breach of faith. It's the one not to confer with them. We're not going to get much help out of them.

                    . . .

JFK: Uh, eh, well, this, which—What you're really talking about are two or three different, uh, (tense?) operations. One is the strike just on this, these three bases. One, the second, is the broader one that Secretary McNamara was talking about, which is on the airfields and on the SAM sites and on anything else connected with, uh, missiles. Third is doing both of those things and also at the same time launching a blockade, which requires really the, uh, the, uh, third, and which is a larger step. And then, as I take it, the fourth question is the, uh, degree of consultation—

[3 lines excised]

SPEAKER?:   Uhm.

JFK: Just have to (words unintelligible) and do it. Probably ought to tell them, though, the night before.

RFK: Mr. President.

JFK: Yes.

RFK: We have the fifth one, really, which is the invasion. I would say that, uh, you're dropping bombs all over Cuba

DOCUMENT 15: Transcript of the first Executive Committee Meeting, October 16, 1962, 11:50 A.M.–12:57 P.M. (from the John F. Kennedy Library; edited for length).

PAGE 12 OF 12

if you do the second, uh, air, the airports, knocking out their planes, dropping it on all their missiles. You're covering most of Cuba. You're going to kill an awful lot of people, and, uh, we're going to take an awful lot of heat on it—

SPEAKER?: Yeah.

RFK: —and, uh, and then, uh, you know, the heat, you're going to announce the reason that you're doing it is because, uh, they're sending in these kind of missiles. Well, I would think it's almost incumbent upon the Russians, then, to say, Well, we're going to send them in again, and if you do it again, we're going to do, we're going to do the same thing to Turkey, or we're going to do the same thing to Iran.

...

JFK: I think we ought to, what we ought to do is, is, uh, after this meeting this afternoon we ought to meet tonight again at six, consider these various, uh, proposals. In the meanwhile, we'll go ahead with this maximum, whatever is needed from the flights, and, in addition, we will—I don't think we got much time on these missiles. They may be—so it may be that we just have to, we can't wait two weeks while we're getting ready to, to roll. Maybe just have to just take *them out*, and continue our other preparations if we decided to do that. That may be where we end up. I think we ought to, beginning right now, be preparing to—because that's what we're going to do *anyway*. We're certainly going to do number one; we're going to take out these, uh, missiles. Uh, the questions will be whether, which, what I would describe as number two, which would be a general airstrike. That we're not ready to say, but we should be in preparation for it. The third is the, is the, uh, the general invasion. At least we're going to do number one, so it seems to me that we don't have to wait very long. We ought to be making *those* preparations.

...

DOCUMENT 16: Transcript of the second Executive Committee meeting, October 16, 1962, 6:30 P.M.–7:55 P.M. (from the John F. Kennedy Library; edited for length).

PAGE 1 OF 17

Off-the-Record Meeting on Cuba
October 16, 1962
6:30 P.M.–7:55 P.M.

SPEAKERS (in order of appearance)

JFK John F. Kennedy, President

CARTER: Marshall Carter, Deputy Director, Central Intelligence Agency

RUSK: Dean Rusk, Secretary of State

BUNDY: McGeorge Bundy, Special Assistant to the President

MARTIN: Edwin Martin, Assistant Secretary of State for Inter-American Affairs

McNAMARA: Robert McNamara, Secretary of Defense

TAYLOR: Maxwell Taylor, Chairman, Joint Chiefs of Staff

RFK: Robert F. Kennedy, Attorney General

Ball: George Ball, Undersecretary of State

U.A.JOHNSON: U. Alexis Johnson, Deputy Undersecretary of State for Political Affairs

DILLON: Douglas Dillon, Secretary of the Treasury

GILPATRIC: Roswell Gilpatric, Deputy Secretary of Defense

SPEAKER?: Speaker unknown or identity uncertain

A NOTE ON THE TRANSCRIPT

Punctuation, with some exceptions, remains as in the original. The following codes are used as follows:

(remarks)
Remarks in parentheses reflect comments of the original tape transcriber.

[remarks]
Remarks in brackets reflect comments by editors of this volume.

—

Dashes reflect that a speaker has paused or been interrupted, or that a short comment of the transcriber has been eliminated for continuity.

…

Ellipses between sections of text indicate that material has been deleted due to space limitations.

JFK: Uh, anything in 'em?

CARTER: Nothing on the additional film, sir. We have a much better read-out on what we had initially. There's good evidence of their back-up missiles for each of the four launchers at each of the three sites, so that there would be twice the number for a total of eight which could eventually be erected. This would mean a capability of from sixteen or possibly twenty-four missiles. We feel, on the basis of information that we presently have, that these are solid propellant, inertial guidance missiles with eleven-hundred-mile range rather than the oxygen propellant, uh, radar-controlled. Primarily because we have no indication of any radar or indication of any oxygen equipment. And it would appear to be logical from an intelligence estimate viewpoint that if they are going to this much trouble that they would go ahead and put in threat coverage. Let me see that (words unintelligible).

…

JFK: Uh, General, how long would you say

DOCUMENT 16: Transcript of the second Executive Committee meeting, October 16, 1962, 6:30 P.M.–7:55 P.M. (from the John F. Kennedy Library; edited for length).

PAGE 2 OF 17

we had, uh, before these—at least to the best of your ability for the ones we know—will be ready to fire?

CARTER: Well, our people estimate that these could be fully operational within two weeks. Uh, this would be the total complex. If they're the oxygen type, uh, we have no—it would be considerably longer since we don't have any indication of, uh, oxygen refueling there nor any radars.

SPEAKER?: This wouldn't rule out the possibility that one of them might be operational very much sooner.

CARTER: (Well, or No?), one of 'em, uh, one of them could be operational much sooner. Our people feel that this has been, being put in since probably early September. We have had two visits of a Soviet ship that has an eight-foot-hold capacity sideways. And this about, so far, is the only delivery vehicle that we would have any suspicion that they came in on. And that came in late August, and one in early September.

...

JFK: There isn't any question in your mind however, uh, that it is an intermediate-range missile?

CARTER: No, there's no question in our minds at all. These are—

JFK: Just (word unintelligible)

CARTER: —all the characteristics that we have seen, (live ones?).

RUSK: You've seen actual missiles themselves and not just the boxes have you?

CARTER: No, we've seen—In the picture there is an actual missile.

RUSK: Yeah. Sure there is.

CARTER: Yes. There's no question in our mind,

sir. And they are genuine. They are not, uh, a camouflage or covert attempt to fool us.

BUNDY: How much do we know, uh, (Pat)? I don't mean to go behind your judgment here, except that there's one thing that would be really catastrophic would be to make a judgment here on, on a bad guess as to whether these things are. We must'nt do that.

CARTER: Well

BUNDY: How do we really know what these missiles are and what their range is?

[4 lines excised]

...

JFK: Have you finished, General?

CARTER: Yes, sir. That, I think that's at, uh, (word unintelligible)

RUSK: (Because?) we've had some further discussion meetings this afternoon and we'll be working on it (presently?) this evening, but, um, I might mention certain points that are, some of us are concerned about. The one is, um, the chance that, uh, this might be the issue on which, uh, Castro would elect to break with Moscow if he knew that he were in deadly jeopardy. Now, this is one chance in a hundred, possibly. But, in any event, um, we, we're very much, uh, interested in the possibility of a direct message to Castro, uh, as well as Khrushchev, might make some sense [words excised]. Uh, Mr. [Edwin] Martin will present you with outline, uh, the kind of, uh, message to Castro that, uh, we had in mind.

MARTIN: This would be an oral note, message through a third party. Uh, first, uh, describing just what we know about

DOCUMENT 16: Transcript of the second Executive Committee meeting, October 16, 1962, 6:30 P.M.–7:55 P.M. (from the John F. Kennedy Library; edited for length).

PAGE 3 OF 17

what exists in th—, the missile sites, so that he knows that we are informed about what's going on. Uh, second, to point out that the issues this raises as far as the U.S. security is concerned, it's a breach of two of the points that you have made public. Uh, first, the ground-to-ground missiles, and, second, obviously, it's Soviet-operated bases in Cuba. Uh, thirdly, this raises the greatest problems for Castro, as we see it. In the first place, uh, by this action the Soviets have, uh, threatened him with attack from the United States, and, uh, therefore the overthrow of his regime; used his territory to, uh make this, uh, to put him in this jeopardy. And, secondly, the Soviets are talking to other people about the possibility of bargaining this support and these missiles, uh, against concessions in Berlin and elsewhere, and therefore are threatening to, to bargain him away. Uh, in these circumstances, we wonder whether he, uh, realizes the, the position that, uh, he's been put in and the way the Soviets are using him.

Then go on to say that, uh, we will have to inform our people of the threat that exists here, and we mean to take action about it in the next day or so. And we'll have to do this unless we receive word from him that he is prepared to take action to get the Soviets out of the site. Uh, he will have to show us that not only by statements, privately or publicly, but, uh, by action; that we intend to, uh, keep close surveillance by overflights of the site to make su—to know what is being done. But we will have to know that he is doing something to remove this threat, uh, in order to withhold the action that we intend to, we will be compelled to take.

Uh, if, uh, Castro feels that an attempt by him to take the kind of action that we're suggesting to him, uh, would result in serious difficulties for him within Cuba, we at least want him to know that, uh, er, to, and to convey to him and remind him of the statement that you, Mr. President, made a year and a half ago, in effect that there are two points that are non-negotiable. One is the Soviet tie and presence, and the second is aggression in Latin America. This is a, a hint, but no more than that, that, uh, we might have sympathy and help for him in case he ran into trouble trying to throw the old-line Communists and the Soviets out.

RUSK: Yes.

MARTIN: We'll give him twenty-four hours to respond.

RUSK: The disadvantage in that is, of course, the, uh, the advance notice if he judges that we, we would not in this, in such approach here say exactly what we would do, but, uh, it might, of course, lead him to bring up mobile antiaircraft weapons around these, uh, missiles themselves, uh, or, uh, take some other action that will make the strike that more difficult. Um, but there is that, there is that (move that?).

There are two other problems that we are concerned about. Uh, if we strike these missiles, we would expect, I think, uh, maximum communist reaction in Latin America. In the case of about six of those governments, unless the heads of government had some intimation, uh, requiring some preparatory steps from the security point of view, uh, one or another of those governments could easi—, uh, could easily be overthrown—[words excised]—uh, and therefore, uh, uh, the question

DOCUMENT 16: Transcript of the second Executive Committee meeting, October 16, 1962, 6:30 P.M.–7:55 P.M. (from the John F. Kennedy Library; edited for length).

PAGE 4 OF 17

will arise as to whether we should not somehow, uh, indicate to them in some way the seriousness of the situation so they can take precautionary steps, whether we tell them exactly what we have in mind or, or not.

The other is the NATO problem. Um, we, uh, we would estimate that the Soviets, uh, would almost certainly take, uh, some kind of action somewhere. Um, for us to, to take an action of this sort without letting, uh, our closer allies know of a matter which could subject them to very great, uh, danger, uh, is a very, uh, far-reaching decision to make. And, uh, we could find ourselves, uh, isolated and the alliance crumbling, very much as it did for a period during the Suez affair, but at a moment of much greater danger over an issue of much greater danger than the Suez affair, for the alliance. I think that these are matters that we'll be working on very hard this evening, but I think I ought to mention them because it's, uh, necessarily a part of this problem.

JFK: Can we get a little idea about what the military thing is? Well, of course, one, would you suggest taking these out?

…

JFK: Of course, all you'd really get there would be—What would you get there? You'd get the, probably you'd get the missiles themselves that are, have to be on the—

McNamara: You'd get the launchers—

JFK: (Wwords unintelligible).

McNamara: —the launchers and the missiles on the (words unintelligible).

JFK: The launchers are just what? They,

they're not much are they?

McNamara: No, they're simply a mobile launchers, uh, device.

Taylor: This is a point target, Mr., uh, President. You're never sure of having, absolutely of getting everything down there. We intend to do a great deal of damage because we can (words unintelligible). But, as the secretary says here, there was unanimity among all the commanders involved in the Joint Chiefs, uh, that in our judgement, it would be a mistake to take this very narrow, selective target because it invited reprisal attacks and it may be detrimental. Now if the, uh, Soviets have been willing to give, uh, nuclear warheads to these missiles, there is every, just as good reason for them to nuclear capability to these bases. We don't think we'd ever have a chance to take 'em again, so that we lose this, the first-strike surprise capability. Our recommendation would be to get complete intelligence, get all the photography we need the next two or three days, no, no hurry in our book. Then look at this target system. If it really threatens the United States, then take it right out with one hard crack.

…

McNamara: Mr. President, could I outline three courses—

JFK?: (Yes?)

McNamara: —of action we have considered and speak very briefly on each one? The first is what I would call the political course of action, in which we, uh, follow some of the possibilities that Secretary Rusk mentioned this morning by approaching Castro, by approaching Khrushchev, by discussing with our allies. An overt

DOCUMENT 16: Transcript of the second Executive Committee meeting, October 16, 1962, 6:30 P.M.–7:55 P.M. (from the John F. Kennedy Library; edited for length).

PAGE 5 OF 17

and open approach politically to the problem (attempting, or in order?) to solve it. This seemed to me likely to lead to no satisfactory result, and it almost stops subsequent military action.

[4 lines excised]

A second course of action we haven't discussed but lies in between the military course we began discussing a moment ago and the political course of action is a course of action that we would immediately impose an, uh, a blockade against offensive weapons entering Cuba in the future; and an indication that with our open-surveillance reconnaissance which we would plan to maintain indefinitely for the future—

[2 lines excised]

...

MCNAMARA: But the third course of action is any one of these variants of military action directed against Cuba, starting with an air attack against the missiles. The chiefs are strongly opposed to so limited an air attack. But even so limited an air attack is a very extensive air attack. It's not twenty sorties or fifty sorties or a hundred sorties, but probably several hundred sorties. Uh, we haven't worked out the details. It's very difficult to do so when we lack certain intelligence that we hope to have tomorrow or the next day. But it's a substantial air attack.

[words excised, 3 lines excised]

This is the very, very rough plan that the chiefs have outlined, and it is their judgment that that is the type of air attack that should be carried out.

[2 lines and words excised]

It seems to me almost certain that any one of these forms of direct military action will lead to a Soviet military response of some type some place in the world. It may well be worth the price. Perhaps we should pay that. But I think we should recognize that possibility, and, moreover, we must recognize it in a variety of ways. We must recognize it by trying to deter it, which means we probably should alert SAC, probably put on an airborne alert, perhaps take other s—, alert measures. These bring risks of their own, associated with them. It means we should recognize that by mobilization. Almost certainly, we should accompany the initial air strike with at least a partial mobilization. We should accompany an, an invasion following an air strike with a large-scale mobilization, a very large-scale mobilization, certainly exceeding the limits of the authority we have from Congress requiring a declaration therefore of a national emergency. We should be prepared, in the event of even a small air, for the possibility of a Cuban uprising, which would force our hand in some way. Either force u—, us to accept a, a, uh, an unsatisfactory uprising, with all of the adverse comment that result; or would, would, force an invasion to support the uprising.

RUSK: Mr. President, may I make a very brief comment on that? I think that, um, uh, any course of action involves heavy political involvement. Um, it's going to affect all sorts of policies, positions, uh, as well as the strategic situation. So I don't think there's any such thing as a nonpolitical course of action. I think also that, um, uh, we have to consider what political preparation, if any, is to occur before

[101]

DOCUMENT 16: Transcript of the second Executive Committee meeting, October 16, 1962, 6:30 P.M.–7:55 P.M. (from the John F. Kennedy Library; edited for length).

PAGE 6 OF 17

an air strike or in connection with any military action. And when I was talking this morning, I was talking about some steps which would put us in the best position to attack the—

JFK: I think the difficulty—

RUSK: —the strength of Cuba.

JFK: —it seems to me, is—I completely agree that there isn't any doubt that if we announced that there were MRBM sites going up that that would change uh, the fact that we indicated our desire to restrain, this really would put the burden on the Soviets. On the other hand, the very fact of doing that makes the military—We lose all the advantages of our strike. Because if we announce that it's there, then it's quite obvious to them that we're gonna probably do something about it. I would assume. Now, I don't know, that, it seems to me what we ought to be thinking about tonight is if we made an announcement that the intelligence has revealed that there are, and if we (did the note?) message to Khrushchev—I don't think, uh, that Castro has to know we've been paying much attention to it any more than—Over a period of time, it might have some effect, (have settled?) back down, change. I don't think he plays it that way. So (have?) a note to Khrushchev—I don't—It seems to me, uh, my press statement was so clear about how we wouldn't do anything under these conditions and under the conditions that we would. He must know that we're going to find out, so it seems to me he just, uh—

BUNDY: That's, of course, why he's been very, very explicit with us in communications to us about how dangerous this is, and—

JFK: That's right, but he's—

BUNDY: —the TASS statement and his other messages.

JFK: He's initiated the danger really, hasn't he? He's the one that's playing (his card, or God?), not us. So we could, uh—

RUSK: And his statement to [U.S. Ambassador to the Soviet Union Foy] Kohler on the subject of his visit and so forth, completely hypocritical.

…

RUSK: I would not think that they would use a nuclear weapon unless they're prepared to (join?) a nuclear war, I don't think. I just don't s—, don't, see that possibility.

SPEAKER?: I would agree.

BUNDY?: I agree.

RUSK: That would mean that, uh, we could be just utterly wrong, but, uh, we've never really believed that, that Khrushchev would take on a general nuclear war over Cuba.

BUNDY: May I ask a question in that context?

JFK: We certainly have been wrong about what he's trying to do in Cuba. There isn't any doubt about that (possibly a word unintelligible)

BUNDY: (Words unintelligible) that we've been wrong.

JFK: —many of us thought that he was going to put MRBMs on Cuba.

BUNDY: Yeah. Except John McCone.

Carter: Mr. McCone.

JFK: Yeah.

BUNDY: But, the, uh, question that I would like to ask is, quite aside from what we've said—and we're very hard-locked onto it, I know—What is the

DOCUMENT 16: Transcript of the second Executive Committee meeting, October 16, 1962, 6:30 P.M.–7:55 P.M. (from the John F. Kennedy Library; edited for length).

PAGE 7 OF 17

strategic impact on the position of the United States of MRBMs in Cuba? How gravely does this change the strategic balance?

MCNAMARA: Mac, I asked the chiefs that this afternoon, in effect. And they said, substantially. My own personal view is, not at all.

BUNDY: Not so much.

...

TAYLOR: —point of view, Mr. President. You're quite right in saying that these, these are just a few more missiles, uh, targeted on the United States. Uh, however, they can become a, a very, a rather important adjunct and reinforcement to the, to the strike capability of the Soviet Union. We have no idea how far they will go. But more than that, these are, uh, uh, to our nation means, it means a great deal more. You all are aware of that, in Cuba and not over in the Soviet Union.

...

JFK: —let's just say that, uh, they get these in there and then you can't, uh, they get sufficient capacity so we can't uh, with warheads. Then you don't want to knock 'em out ('cause?), uh, there's too much of a gamble. Then they just begin to build up those air bases there and then put more and more. I suppose they really—Then they start getting ready to squeeze us in Berlin, doesn't that—you may say it doesn't make any difference if you get blown up by an ICBM flying from the Soviet Union or one that was ninety miles away. Geography doesn't mean that much.

...

JFK: Last month I should have said we're—

SPEAKER?: Well—

JFK: —that we don't care. But when we said we're not going to and then they go ahead and do it, and then we do nothing, then—

SPEAKER?: That's right.

JFK: —I would think that our risks increase. Uh, I agree. What difference does it make? They've got enough to blow us up now anyway. I think it's just a question of—after all, this is a political struggle as much as military. Well, uh, so where are we now? Where is the—don't think the message to Castro's got much in it. Uh, let's just, uh, let's try to get an answer to this question. How much—it's quite obviously to our advantage to surface this thing to a degree before—first to inform these governments in Latin America, as the secretary suggests; secondly to, uh, the rest of NATO [words excised and notes excised] Uh, how much does this diminish—Not that we're going to do anything, but the existence of them, without any say about what we're gonna do. Let's say we, twenty-four hours ahead of our doing something about it [words excised] we make a public statement that these have been found on the island. That would, that would be notification in a sense that, uh, of their existence, and everybody could draw whatever conclusion they wanted to.

...

BALL?: So you would say that, uh, the strike should precede any public discussion?

MCNAMARA: I believe so, yes, if you're going to strike. I think before you make any

DOCUMENT 16: Transcript of the second Executive Committee meeting, October 16, 1962, 6:30 P.M.–7:55 P.M. (from the John F. Kennedy Library; edited for length).

PAGE 8 OF 17

announcements, you should decide whether you're going to strike. If you are going to strike, you shouldn't make an announcement.

…

JFK: I'm not completely, uh, I don't think we ought to abandon just knocking out these missile bases as opposed to, that's much more, uh, defensible, explicable, politically or satisfactory-in-every-way action than the general strike which takes us—

SPEAKER?: Move down—

JFK: —us into the city of Havana—

SPEAKER?: —those two.

JFK: —and (it is plain to me?) takes us into much more—

SPEAKER?: (words unintelligible)

JFK: —hazardous, shot down. Now I know the chiefs say, Well, that means their bombers can take off against us, uh, but, uh—

BUNDY: Their bombers take off against us, then they have made a general war against Cuba of it, which is a, it then becomes much more their decision. We move this way—the political advantages are, are very strong, it seems to me, of the small strike. Uh, it corresponds to the, the punishment fits the crime in political terms, the we are doing only what we warned repeatedly and publicly we would have to do. Uh, we are not generalizing the attack. The things that we've already recognized and said that we have not found it necessary to attack and said we would not find it necessary to attack—

JFK: Well, here's—let's, look, let's, let's, tonight, it seems to me we ought to go on the assumption that we're going to have the general—number

two we've called it—

BUNDY: Uh-huh.

JFK: —course number two, which would be a general strike—that you ought to be in position to do that—

BUNDY: I agree.

JFK: —then if you decide you'd like to do number one.

RFK: How does that in—

JFK: What?

RFK: Does that encompass, uh, an invasion?

JFK: Uh, no, I'd say that's the third course. Let's first start with—I'd have to say first find out, uh, the air, so that I would think that we ought to be in position to do one and two. Which would be—one would be just taking out these missiles, if there were others we'd find in the next twenty-four hours. Number two would be to take out all the airplanes, and number three is invade (here?).

…

McNAMARA: Mr. President, we need to do two things, it seems to me. First, we need to develop a specific strike plan limited to the missiles and the nuclear storage sites, which we have not done. This would be a part of the broader plan—

JFK: Yeah.

McNAMARA: —but I think we ought to estimate the minimum number of sorties. Since you've indicated some interest in that possibility, we ought to provide you that option. We haven't done this.

JFK: Okay.

McNAMARA: But that's an easy job to do. The second thing we ought to do, it seems

DOCUMENT 16: Transcript of the second Executive Committee meeting, October 16, 1962, 6:30 P.M.–7:55 P.M. (from the John F. Kennedy Library; edited for length).

PAGE 9 OF 17

to me as a government, is to consider the consequences—

SPEAKER?: (Words unintelligible)

McNAMARA: And you'll miss some. That's right. Now after we've launched [words excised] sorties, what kind of a world do we live in? How, how do we stop at that point? I don't know the answer to this. I think tonight State and we ought to work on the consequences of any one of these courses of actions, consequences which I don't believe are entirely clear—

        …

RFK: Mr. President, while we're considering this problem tonight, I think that we should also consider what, uh, Cuba's going to be a year from now, or two years from now. Assume that we go in and knock these sites out, uh, I don't know what's gonna stop them from saying, we're gonna build the sites six months from now, bring 'em in—

TAYLOR: Noth—nothing permanent about it.

RFK: Uh, the, what, where are we six months from now? Or that we're in any better position or aren't we in worse position if we go in and knock 'em out and say, uh—

SPEAKER?: (We sure are?)

RFK: —Don't do it. Uh, I mean, obviously they're gonna have to do it then.

McNAMARA: You have to put a blockade in following any—

SPEAKER?: Sure.

McNAMARA: —limited action.

RFK: Then we're gonna have to sink Russian ships.

McNAMARA?: Right.

RFK: Then we're gonna have to sink—

McNAMARA: Right.

RFK: —Russian submarines. Now whether it wouldn't be, uh, the, argument, if you're going to get into it at all, uh, whether we should just get into it and get it over with and say that, uh, take our losses, and if we're gonna—if he wants to get into a war over this, uh—hell, if it's war that's gonna come on this thing, or if he sticks those kinds of missiles in, it's after the warning, and he's gonna, and he's gonna get into a war for, six months from now, so—

McNAMARA: Mr. President, this is why I think tonight we ought to put on paper the alternative plans and the probable, possible consequences thereof in a way that State and Defense could agree on, even if we, uh, disagree and put in both views. Because the consequences of these actions have not been thought through clearly. The one that the attorney general just mentioned is illustrative of that.

JFK: If the, uh, it doesn't increase very much their strategic, uh, strength, why is it, uh, can any Russian expert tell us why they—After all Khrushchev demonstrated a sense of caution (thousands?)

SPEAKER?: Well, there are several, several possible—

JFK: —Berlin, he's been cautious, I mean, he hasn't been, uh—

BALL?: Several possibilities, Mr. President. One of them is that he has given us word now that he's coming over in November to, to the UN. If, he may be proceeding on the assumption, and this lack of a sense of apparent urgency would seem to, to support this, that this isn't going to be discovered at the moment and that, uh, when he comes over this is

DOCUMENT 16: Transcript of the second Executive Committee meeting, October 16, 1962, 6:30 P.M.–7:55 P.M. (from the John F. Kennedy Library; edited for length).

PAGE 10 OF 17

something he can do, a ploy. That here is Cuba armed against the United States, or possibly use it to try to trade something in Berlin, saying he'll disarm Cuba if, uh, if we'll, uh, yield some of our interests in Berlin and some arrangement for it. I mean, that this is a, it's a trading ploy.

BUNDY: I would think one thing that I would still cling to is that he's not likely to give Fidel Castro nuclear warheads. I don't believe that has happened or is likely to happen.

JFK: Why does he put these in there though?

BUNDY: Soviet-controlled nuclear warheads (of the kind?)

JFK: That's right, but what is the advantage of that? It's just as if we suddenly began to put a major number of MRBMs in Turkey. Now that'd be goddam dangerous, I would think.

BUNDY?: Well, we did, Mr. President.

U. A. JOHNSON?:

We did it. We—

JFK: Yeah, but that was five years ago.

U. A. Johnson?:

—did it in England; that's why we were short.

JFK: What?

U. A. JOHNSON?:

We gave England two when we were short of ICBMs.

JFK: Yeah, but that's, uh—

U. A. JOHNSON?:

(Testing?)

JFK: —that was during a different period then.

U. A. JOHNSON?:

But doesn't he realize he has a

deficiency of ICBMs, needs a PR capacity perhaps, in view of—He's got lots of MRBMs and this is a way to balance it out a bit?

BUNDY?: I'm sure his generals have been telling him for a year and a half that he had, was missing a golden opportunity to add to his strategic capability.

BALL?: Yes, I think, I think you, you look at this possibility that this is an attempt to, to add to his strategic capabilities. A second consideration is that it is simply a trading ploy, that he, he wants this in so that he could, he could (words unintelligible)

...

U. A. JOHNSON?:

—offensive capability.

TAYLOR?: You have to consider them Soviet missiles.

U. A. JOHNSON?:

It seems to me if we go in there, lock-stock-and-barrel, we can consider them entirely Cuban.

BUNDY: Ah, well, what we say for political purposes and what we think are not identical here.

SPEAKER?: But, I mean, any, any rational approach to this must be that they are Soviet missiles, because I think—

SPEAKER?: You mean—

SPEAKER?: —Khrushchev himself would never, would never risk a major war on, on a fellow as obviously erratic, uh, and foolish as, as Castro.

SPEAKER?: (A sub-lieutenant?)

JFK: Well, now let's say—

RFK: Let me say, of course—

JFK: Yeah.

DOCUMENT 16: Transcript of the second Executive Committee meeting, October 16, 1962, 6:30 P.M.–7:55 P.M. (from the John F. Kennedy Library; edited for length).

PAGE 11 OF 17

RFK: —one other thing is whether, uh, we should also think of, uh, uh, whether there is some other way we can get involved in this through, uh, Guantánamo Bay, or something, er, or whether there's some ship that, you know, sink the Maine again or something.

TAYLOR: We think, Mr. President, that under any of these plans we will probably get an attack on, on Guantánamo, at least by, by fire. They have artillery and mortars in the, easily within range, and, uh, any of these actions we take we'll have to give our support to Guantánamo and probably reinforce the garrison.

JFK: Well, that's why, uh, it seems to me that, uh, this, if we decide that we are going to be in a position to do this, either one and two Saturday or Sunday, then I would think we would also want to be in a position, depending on (really?) what happens, either because of an invasion, attack on Guantánamo or some other reason to do the inva—, uh, to, do the eviction.

TAYLOR: Mr. President, I personally would just urge you not to set a schedule such as Saturday or Sunday—

JFK: No, I haven't.

TAYLOR: —until all the intelligence that could be—

JFK: That's right. I just wanted, I just wanted, I thought we ought to be moving, I don't want to waste any time though if we decide that, uh, time is not particularly with us. I just think we ought to be ready to do something, even if we decide not to do it.

. . .

JFK: Uh, Mr. Secretary, is there anything

that, or any of these contingencies if we go ahead that, uh, the next twenty-four hours—we're going to meet again tomorrow (for this?) in the afternoon—is there anything (words unintelligible)

McNAMARA: No, sir, I believe that the military planning has been carried on for a considerable period of time, is well under way. And I believe that all the preparation that we could take without the risk of preparations causing discussion and knowledge of this, either among our public or in Cuba, have been taken and are authorized; all the necessary reconnaissance measures are being taken and are authorized. The only thing we haven't done, really, is to consider fully these alternatives.

BUNDY: Our principal problem is to try and imaginatively to think—

McNAMARA: Yes.

BUNDY: —what the world would be like if we do this—

McNAMARA: That's exactly right.

BUNDY: —if we fail if we do.

McNAMARA: We ought to work on that tonight.

. . .

BUNDY: It would be a great improvement not to have any more intense White House meetings—trouble with all the (words unintelligible) if we could meet at the State Department tomorrow.

(Several speakers speak at once and none of the words are intelligible.)

JFK: All right, then I could meet you, Mac, when I get back tomorrow and just as well, whatever the thing is and then we can meet Thursday morning. I don't—the question is whether, uh—

I'm going to see [Andrei] Gromyko Thursday and I think the question that I'd really like to have is some sort of a judgement on, is whether we ought to do anything with Gromyko. Whether we ought to say anything to him; whether we ought to, uh, indirectly give him sort of a, give him an ultimatum on this matter, or whether we just ought to go ahead without him. It seems to me that—

SPEAKER?: In other words—

JFK: —he said we'd be—the attorney general, the ambassador told the attorney general, as he told [Charles] Bohlen the other day that they were not going to put these weapons there. Now either he's lying or doesn't know. Whether the attorney general saw Dobrynin—not acting as if we had any information about 'em—said that, of course, that they must realize that if this ever does happen. Now I don't know what would come out of that, I—possibly nothing. Possibly, uh, this'd alert them. Possibly they would reconsider their decision, but I don't think we've had any clear evidence of that, and it would give them—We'd lose a week.

BALL?: You mean tell them that—

JFK: Well, not tell them that we know that they've got it, but merely in the course of a conversation Dobrynin, having said that they would never do it, the attorney general, who sees Dobrynin once in a while, would—

. . .

BUNDY: My, I wouldn't bet a cookie that Dobrynin doesn't know a bean about—

DILLON?: Uh-huh.

BUNDY: —this.

JFK: You think he does know?

RFK: He didn't know.

BUNDY: I, I would (words unintelligible)

RFK: He didn't even know that (words unintelligible) in my judgment.

SPEAKER?: (Words unintelligible)

TAYLOR: Why it's, I mean there's evidence of sightings in late August, I think, and early September of, of some sort.

SPEAKER?: It seems to me, Mr. President, there's, in your public presentation simultaneous or subsequent to an action, your hand is strengthened somewhat if the Soviets have, uh, lied to you, either privately or in public.

BUNDY?: I'll agree to that.

SPEAKER?: And then if, or if you, uh, without knowing, if you ask Gromyko, or if Bobby asks Dobrynin again, or if some other country could get the Soviets to say publicly in the U.N., No, we have no offensive—

. . .

JFK: I don't know enough about the Soviet Union, but if anybody can tell me any other time since the Berlin blockade where the Russians have given us so clear provocation, I don't know when it's been, because they've been awfully cautious really. The Russians, I never—Now, maybe our mistake was in not saying some time before this summer that if they do this we're (word unintelligible) to act. Maybe they'd gone in so far (that?) it's—

. . .

BUNDY: What I would suggest is that someone be deputed to, to do a piece of paper which really is what happens. I think the margin is between whether we take out the (missile zone?, or missiles on?) strike or take a lot of air bases. This is tactical within a decision to take military action. Now, doesn't overwhelmingly, it may substantially if it doesn't overwhelmingly change the world. I think any military action does change the world. And I think not taking action changes the world. And I think these are the two worlds that we need to look at.

McNAMARA: I'm very much inclined to agree, but I think we have to make that point—

BUNDY: I agree.

McNAMARA: —within the military action—

BUNDY: I agree.

McNAMARA: —a gradation—

BUNDY: Oh, many graduations and they have major, it can have major effects.

McNAMARA: Yeah.

BUNDY: I mean, I don't need to exaggerate that now. The question is how to get ahead with that, and whether, uh, I would think, myself, that it, it, if the appropriate place to make this preliminary analysis is at the Department of State. I think the rest of us ought to spend the evening really to some advantage separately trying to have our own views of this. And I think we should meet in order, at least, to trade pieces of paper, before two o'clock, uh, tomorrow morning if that's agreeable.

...

BUNDY: I think there's an enormous political advantage, myself, within these options, granting that all the chiefs didn't fully agree, taking out the thing that gives the trouble and not the thing that doesn't give the trouble.

McNAMARA?: This, as opposed to, uh, is it an air attack on—

BUNDY: Supplementary to an air attack. I mean, how're you gonna know that you've got 'em? And if you haven't got 'em, what've you done?

TAYLOR: Well, this, this, of course, raises the question of having gotten this set, what happens to the set that arrives next week?

McNAMARA: Oh, I, I think the ans—

TAYLOR: Yeah.

McNAMARA: —I, let me answer Mac's question first. How do we know we've got them? We will have photo recon (militarily?) with the strike. Sweeney specifically plans this, and—

BUNDY: Proving a negative is a hell of a job.

McNAMARA: Pardon me?

BUNDY: Proving a negative is a hell of a job.

TAYLOR: [1 line excised]

BUNDY: That's true.

McNAMARA: Terrible risk to put them in there, uh—

BUNDY: I ag—, I think the (words unintelligible) is probably a bad idea, but it—

McNAMARA: I think the risk troubles me, it's too great in relation to the risk of not knowing whether we get them.

BUNDY: Well—

McNAMARA: But, in any case, this is a small variant of one—

BUNDY: That's right, it's a minor—

McNAMARA: —of the plans.

BUNDY: —variant of one plan.

McNAMARA: It seems to me that there are some major alternatives here that I don't think we discussed them fully enough today, and I'd like to see them laid on the paper, if State agrees. The first is

DOCUMENT 16: Transcript of the second Executive Committee meeting, October 16, 1962, 6:30 P.M.–7:55 P.M. (from the John F. Kennedy Library; edited for length).

PAGE 14 OF 17

what I, I still call it the political approach. Uh, let me say it, a nonmilitary action.

(Laughter)

MCNAMARA: It doesn't start with one and it isn't gonna end with one.

SPEAKER?: Yeah.

MCNAMARA: And I, for that reason I call it a political approach.

SPEAKER?: Right—

MCNAMARA: And I say it isn't gonna end with one because once you start this political approach, I don't think you're gonna have any opportunity for a military operation.

SPEAKER?: I agree.

TAYLOR: It becomes very difficult.

MCNAMARA: But at least I think we ought to put it down there, uh.

TAYLOR: Right.

BUNDY: And it should be worked out. I mean what, what is the maximum—

SPEAKER?: Your ride is waiting downstairs (words unintelligible).

SPEAKER?: Very good, thank you (words unintelligible)

MCNAMARA: Yeah, it should, should definitely be worked out. What, exactly what does it in—, involve, and what are the chances of success of it? They're not zero. They're plus I think.

TAYLOR?: We did an outline this morning along these lines.

MCNAMARA: All right. That, that's (word unintelligible) anyway—

BUNDY: Um, but, do you see, it's, it's not just the chances of success, it's the, it ought to be examined in terms of the pluses and minuses of, of non-

success—

MCNAMARA: Yes. Yes.

BUNDY: —because there is such a thing as making this thing pay off in ways that are—

MCNAMARA: Yeah. Yeah.

BUNDY: —are of some significance, even though we don't act—

MCNAMARA: Yeah. I completely agree.

BUNDY: —or go with that.

MCNAMARA: And, and this is my second alternative in—

BUNDY: Yeah.

MCNAMARA: —particular and I want to come to that in a moment. But the first one I—

BUNDY: Yeah.

MCNAMARA: —I completely agree it isn't. I, I phrased it improperly. Not the chances of success. It's the results—

SPEAKER?: (words unintelligible)

MCNAMARA: —that (we're calling? or causing?)

BUNDY: Yep.

MCNAMARA: —for mankind.

BUNDY: Yep.

MCNAMARA: Now, the second alternative, I, I'd like to discuss just a second, because we haven't discussed it fully today, and I alluded it to, to it a moment ago. I, I I'll be quite frank. I don't think there is a military problem here. This is my answer to Mac's question—

BUNDY: That's my honest (judgment?)

MCNAMARA: —and therefore, and I've gone through this today, and I asked myself, Well, what is it then if it isn't a military problem? Well, it's just

[110]

exactly this problem, that, that, uh, if Cuba should possess a capacity to carry out offensive actions against the U.S., the U.S. would act.

SPEAKER?: That's right.

SPEAKER?: That's right.

MCNAMARA: Now, it's that problem, this—

SPEAKER?: You can't get around that one.

MCNAMARA: —this, this is a domestic, political problem. The announcement- we didn't say we'd go in and not, and kill them, we said we'd act. Well, how will we act? Well, we want to act to prevent their use, and it's really the—

BUNDY: Yeah.

MCNAMARA: —the act. Now, how do we pre—, act to prevent their use? Well, first place, we carry our open surveillance, so we know what they're doing. All times. Twenty-four hours a day from now and forever, in a sense indefinitely. What else do we do? We prevent any further offensive weapons coming in. In other words, we blockade offensive weapons.

BUNDY: How do we do that?

MCNAMARA: We search every ship.

TAYLOR: There're two kinds of, of blockade: a blockade which stops ships from coming in and, and simply a seizure, I mean a, simply a search.

MCNAMARA: A search, that's right—

TAYLOR: Yeah.

MCNAMARA: —and—

SPEAKER?: Well, it would be a search and removal if found.

BUNDY: You have to make the guy stop to search him, and if he won't stop, you have to shoot, right?

SPEAKER?: All (word unintelligible) up—

SPEAKER?: And you have to remove what you're looking for if you find it.

SPEAKER?: That's right.

MCNAMARA: Absolutely. And then an ul—, I call it an ultimatum associated with these two actions is a statement to the world, particularly to Khrushchev, that we have located these offensive weapons; we're maintaining a constant surveillance over them; if there is ever any indication that they're to be launched against this country, we will respond not only against Cuba, but we will respond directly against the Soviet Union with, with a full nuclear strike. Now this alternative doesn't seem to be a very acceptable one, but wait until you work on the others.

BUNDY: That's right

(Laughter)

. . .

MCNAMARA: Well, we have a blockade. Search and, uh—removal of, of offensive weapons entering Cuba. Uh, (word unintelligible) again, I don't want to argue for this.

BALL: No, no, I—

MCNAMARA: —because I, I don't think it's—

BALL: —I think it's an alternative.

MCNAMARA: —a perfect solution by any means. I just want to—

BUNDY: Which one are we (still on?) would you say?

MCNAMARA: Still on the second one, uh—

BALL: Now, one of the things we look at is whether any, the actual operation of a blockade doesn't, isn't a greater involvement almost than a—

MCNAMARA: Might well be, George.

DOCUMENT 16: Transcript of the second Executive Committee meeting, October 16, 1962, 6:30 P.M.–7:55 P.M. (from the John F. Kennedy Library; edited for length).

PAGE 16 OF 17

BALL: —military action.

SPEAKER?: I think so.

McNAMARA: It's, it's a search, not a not an embargo, uh—

SPEAKER?: Yeah.

BALL: It's a series of single, unrelated acts, not by surprise. This, uh, come in there on Pearl Harbor just frightens the hell out of me as to what's going beyond. (Yeah, well, anyway?) the Board of National Estimates have been working on this ever since—

BUNDY: What, what goes, what goes beyond what?

BALL: What happens beyond that. You go in there with a surprise attack. You put out all the missiles. This isn't the end. This is the beginning, I think. There's a whole hell of a lot of things—

BUNDY: Are they all working on powerful reaction in your (word unintelligible)?

CARTER: Yes, sir.

BUNDY: Good.

BALL: —point of, to connect—

(Two conversations are going on at once. Only these fragments are intelligible.)

McNAMARA: Well, that, that takes me into the third category of action. I'd lump them all in the third category. I call it over military action of varying degrees of intensity, ranging—and, if you feel there's any difference in them, in the kind of a world we have after the varying degrees of intensity—

SPEAKER?: Right.

McNAMARA: —you have to divide category three into subcategories by intensity and probable effect on the world thereafter. And I think there is, at least in the sense of the Cuban uprising, which I happen to believe is a most important element of category three, but not all. But, in any event, what, what kind of a world do we live in? In Cuba what action do we take? What do we expect Castro will be doing after, uh, you attack these missiles? Does he survive as a, as a political leader? Is he overthrown? Uh, is he stronger, weaker? Uh, how will he react? How will the Soviets react? What can—how, how could Khrushchev afford to accept this action without some kind of rebuttal? I don't think, he can't accept it without some rebuttal. It may not be a substantial rebuttal, but it's, it's gonna have to be some. Where? How do we react in relation to it? What happens when we do mobilize? How does this affect our allies' support of us in relation to Berlin? Well, you know far better than I the problems, uh, but it would seem to me if we could lay this out tonight and then meet a reasonable time in the morning to go over a tentative draft, discuss it, and then have another draft for some time in the afternoon—

GILPATRIC?: One kind of planning, Bob, that, uh, that, uh, we didn't explicitly talk about today, uh, which is to look at the points of vulnerability around the world, not only in Berlin—

McNAMARA: Sure.

GILPATRIC?: —not only in Turkey—

McNAMARA: Sure. Iran.

GILPATRIC?: Iran and all of them—

McNAMARA: And Korea.

GILPATRIC?: Well, these, this, these are, these are both military and political—

MCNAMARA: Exactly. Well, uh, and we call it a worldwide alert—

SPEAKER?: (Yeah?)

MCNAMARA: —under that heading we've got a whole series of precautionary measures that we, we think, uh should be taken. All of our forces should be put on alert, but beyond that, mobilization, redeployment, movement, and so on—if you think of anything we can do. We'll, we'll go to work tonight and get these numbers of sorties by target systems laid out. I'll, Reilly's up in Mac's office and I'll go down there now and get them started on it.

...

(Recording ends.)

DOCUMENT 17: Theodore Sorensen, Summary of Agreed Facts and Premises, Possible Courses of Action and Unanswered Questions, October 17, 1962.

PAGE 1 OF 2

TCS-10/17/62

1. It is generally agreed that Soviet MRBM's—offensive weapons—are now in Cuba. While only one complex of three sites and no nuclear warheads have been spotted, it must be assumed that this is the beginning of a larger build-up.

2. It is generally agreed that these missiles, even when fully operational, do not significantly alter the balance of power—i.e., they do not significantly increase the potential megatonnage capable of being unleashed on American soil, even after a surprise American nuclear strike. The Soviet purpose in making this move is not understood—whether it is for purposes of diversion, harassment, provocation or bargaining.

3. Nevertheless it is generally agreed that the United States cannot tolerate the known presence of offensive nuclear weapons in a country 90 miles from our shore, if our courage and our commitments are ever to be believed by either allies or adversaries. Retorts from either our European allies or the Soviets that we can become as accustomed as they to accepting the nearby presence of MRBM's have some logic but little weight in this situation.

4. It is also agreed that certain of our NATO allies would be notified but not consulted immediately prior to any action by the United States; that certain Latin nations would at least be notified; and that, if there is to be military action, the President would hold announcing the existence of the missiles and the justification of our action until after that action had been completed.

5. The following possible tracks or courses of action have each been considered. Each has obvious diplomatic and military disadvantages, but none others as yet occur.

Track A–Political action, pressure and warning, followed by a military strike if satisfaction is not received.

Track B–A military strike without prior warning, pressure or action, accompanied by messages making clear the limited nature of this action.

Track C–Political actions, pressure and warning, followed by a total naval blockade, under the authority of the Rio Pact and either a Congressional Declaration of War on Cuba or the Cuban Resolution of the 87th Congress.

Track D–Full-scale invasion, to "take Cuba away from Castro".

Obviously any one of these could lead to one of the others—but each represents a distinguishable approach to the problem.

6. Within Tracks A and C, the political actions, pressures and warnings could include one or more of the following:

(a) Letter to Khrushchev

—Stating if ever offensive bases exist, they will be struck; or

—Warning that we know they exist, and must be dismantled or they will be struck; or

—Summoning him to a Summit, offering to withdraw our MRBM's from Turkey, etc.

(b) Letter to Castro

—Warning him of action if bases not dismantled; and/or

—Seeking to separate him from Soviets on grounds that they are willing to see him destroyed

(c) Take this threat to the peace before the UN, requesting inspection team, etc.

(d) Take this threat to the Hemisphere to the OAS and obtain authorization for action

7. Within Tracks A and B, the most likely military alternatives aside from blockade and invasion include the following:

(a) A 50 sortie, 1 swoop air strike limited to the

DOCUMENT 17: Theodore Sorensen, Summary of Agreed Facts and Premises, Possible Courses of Action and Unanswered Questions, October 17, 1962.

PAGE 2 OF 2

missile complex, followed by open surveillance and announcement that future missile sites would be similarly struck.

(b) Broadened air strikes to eliminate all Cuban air power or other retaliatory capacity, up to 200 sortie (one day's activities).

(c) Not yet considered: Commando raid, under air cover, by helicopter or otherwise, to take out missiles with bullets, destroy launches, and leave.

(d) Note: It is generally agreed that we must also be prepared to take further action to protect Guantánamo, from which dependents will have to be evacuated in advance.

8. Other questions or points of disagreement

(a) Whether Soviet reaction would be more intense to Tracks A, B, C or D

(b) Whether Moscow would be either able or willing to prevent Soviet missile commanders from firing on United States when attacked, or Castro and/or his Air Force or any part of it attacking U.S. mainland. This includes the further question of whether, if a military strike is to take place, it must take place before these missiles become operational in the next 2 weeks or so.

(c) Whether Soviets would make, or threaten in response to any note, an equivalent attack on U.S. missiles in Turkey or Italy—or attack Berlin or somewhere else—or confine themselves to stirring up UN and world opinion.

(d) What our response would be to such a Soviet attack—or a Soviet defiance of blockade—and what their response would be to our response

(e) Whether Castro would risk total destruction by sending planes to U.S. mainland—or be able to control all his planes

(f) Whether any Congressmen should be consulted, whether war need be declared, whether the President should cancel all remaining speeches

(g) Whether NATO allies should be briefed at highest level by high-level spokesman

(h) Fate of the 1100 prisoners under any alternative

(i) Whether it would be helpful to obtain a public (UN) and private (Gromyko) denial

(j) To what extent any advance notice—through political notes or pressure, etc.—makes more difficult the military's task, if in the meantime

—the missiles are concealed; or

—the missiles become operational

(k) Whether, if missiles are taken out, the Soviets would bring in additional missiles—or, if aware of continued surveillance, would find "their bayonets had struck steel instead of mush" and therefore desist

(l) Whether reservists call-up, National Emergency, or Declaration of War by a reconvened Congress are necessary

(m) How successful we would be in justifying to world military action against Cuba

(n) Whether the effect on our allies would be worse if we do strike or if we do not

DOCUMENT 18: Secretary of the Treasury Douglas Dillon's opinions favoring an airstrike against Cuba, ca. October 17, 1962.

PAGE 1 OF 3

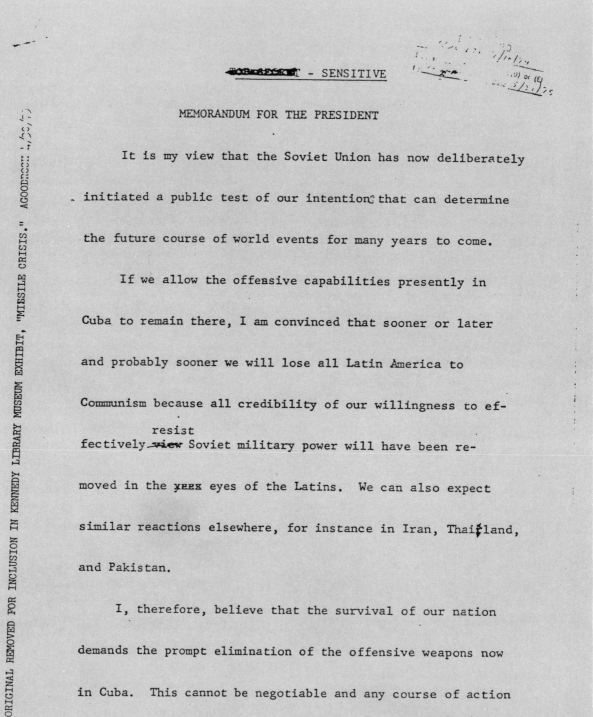

~~TOP SECRET~~ - SENSITIVE

MEMORANDUM FOR THE PRESIDENT

It is my view that the Soviet Union has now deliberately

initiated a public test of our intention that can determine

the future course of world events for many years to come.

If we allow the offensive capabilities presently in

Cuba to remain there, I am convinced that sooner or later

and probably sooner we will lose all Latin America to

Communism because all credibility of our willingness to ef-

fectively ~~view~~ resist Soviet military power will have been re-

moved in the ~~xxxx~~ eyes of the Latins. We can also expect

similar reactions elsewhere, for instance in Iran, Thailand,

and Pakistan.

I, therefore, believe that the survival of our nation

demands the prompt elimination of the offensive weapons now

in Cuba. This cannot be negotiable and any course of action

leading

DOCUMENT 18: Secretary of the Treasury Douglas Dillon's opinions favoring an airstrike against Cuba, ca. October 17, 1962.

PAGE 2 OF 3

~~TOP SECRET~~ - SENSITIVE

-2-

leading to negotiation on this issue, which inevitably

would be prolonged, would have the results outlined

above.

The question remains how best to achieve the prompt

elimination of these weapons from Cuba. I recognize fully

the public opinion difficulties involved in a surprise

attack but believe that, if no other effective course is

available, they must be accepted rather than run the grave

risk to our national security involved in allowing the

weapons to remain in Cuba.

Accordingly, I would reject the blockade course insofar

as it is designed to lead to negotiations either in the UN

or direct with Khrushchev.

If militarily acceptable, I would prefer to initiate

action with a blockade and intensive ~~low-level~~ low-level surveillance,

coupled

DOCUMENT 18: Secretary of the Treasury Douglas Dillon's opinions favoring an airstrike against Cuba, ca. October 17, 1962.

PAGE 3 OF 3

TOP SECRET - SENSITIVE

-3-

coupled with an element a demand on Cuba to immediately re-

move at the weapons and to accept international inspection

beginning within 24 hours. In the event of Cuban re-

fusal, the air strike would follow immediately, no later

than 72 hours after the initial public statement.

If this is not militarily acceptable or if such delay

would involve inacceptable risks of the use of nuclear

weapons from Cuba against the US, I would favor an early

     in

strike/accordance with the air strike course of action.

In such a situation, I believe that, in the interests

of the survival of the entire free world fabric, we must

be prepared to accept the public opinion results of a

surprise attack strike, placing the full blame on Cuba for

ignoring our clear and repeated warnings as well as the

strong views of the other American states.

Douglas Dillon

DOCUMENT 19: U.N. Ambassador Adlai Stevenson's opinions against an airstrike on Cuba, October 17, 1962.

PAGE 1 OF 2

DECLASSIFIED
E.O. 11652, Sec 3(E) and 5(D) or (E)
~/te Dept Ltr. 8 7-14
By 77 h. A   HARS. Date 9-17-74

~~SECRET~~ - EYES ONLY

Dear Mr. President:

I have reviewed the planning thus far and have the following comments for you:

As I have said I think your _personal_ emissaries should deliver your messages to C and K.   There is no disagreement as to C.   As to K an emissary could better supplement the gravity of the situation you have communicated to Gromyko.   And _talking_ with K would afford a chance of uncovering his motives and objectives far better than correspondence thru the "usual channels."

As to your announcement, assuming it becomes imperative to say something soon, I think it would be a mistake at this time to disclose that an attack was imminent and that merely reciting the facts, emphasizing the gravity of the situation and that further steps were in process would be enough for the _first_ announcement.

Because an attack would very likely result in Soviet reprisals somewhere-- Turkey, Berlin, etc. -- it is most important that we have as much of the world with us as possible.   To start or risk starting a nuclear war is bound to be divisive at best and the judgments of history seldom coincide with the tempers of the moment.

If war comes, in the long run our case must rest on stopping while there was still time the Soviet drive to world domination, our obligations under the Inter-American system, etc.   We must be prepared for the widespread reaction that if we have a missile base in Turkey and other places around the Soviet Union surely they have a right to one in Cuba.   If we attack Cuba, an ally of the USSR, isn't an attack on NATO bases equally justified.   One could go on and on.   While the explanation of our action may be clear to us it won't be clear to many others.   Moreover, if war is the consequence, the Latin American republics may well divide and some say that the U.S. is not acting with their approval and consent.   Likewise unless the issue is very clear there may be sharp differences with our Western Allies who have lived so long under the same threat of Soviet attack from bases in the satellite countries by the same IRBMs.

But all these considerations and obstacles to clear and universal understanding that we are neither rash, impetuous or indifferent to the fate of others are, I realize, only too familiar to you.

~~SECRET~~ - EYES ONLY

DOCUMENT 19: U.N. Ambassador Adlai Stevenson's opinions against an airstrike on Cuba, October 17, 1962.

PAGE 2 OF 2

DECLASSIFIED
E.O. 11652, Sec. 3(E) and 5(D) or (E)

By_____ NARS, Date _____

~~SECRET~~ - EYES ONLY   -2-

I know your dilemma is to strike before the Cuban sites are
operational or to risk waiting until a proper groundwork of
justification can be prepared.   The national security must come
first.   But the means adopted have such incalculable consequences
that I feel you should have made it clear that the existence of nuclear
missile bases anywhere is negotiable before we start anything.

Our position, then, is that we can't negotiate with a gun at our head,
a gun that imperils the innocent, helpless Cuban people as much as
it does the U. S., and that if they won't remove the missiles and
restore the status quo ante we will have to do it ourselves -- and
then we will be ready to discuss bases in the context of a disarmament
treaty or anything else with them.   In short it is they, not the U.S.,
that have upset the balance and created this situation of such peril
to the whole world.

I confess I have many misgivings about the proposed course of action,
but to discuss them further would add little to what you already have
in mind.   So I will only repeat that it should be clear as a pikestaff
that the U. S. was, is and will be ready to negotiate the elimination
of bases and anything else; that it is they who have upset the
precarious balance in the world in arrogant disregard of your
warnings -- by threats against Berlin and now from Cuba -- and
that we have no choice except to restore that balance, i.e.,
blackmail and intimidation never,   negotiation and sanity always.

Yours,

/s/ Adlai S. Stevenson

Wednesday morning, Oct. 17

P. S.   I'm returning to New York and can return, of course, at
your convenience.

~~SECRET~~ - EYES ONLY

DOCUMENT 20: "Position of [Under Secretary of State] George W. Ball," in support of blockade option against Cuba, ca. October 18, 1962.

PAGE 1 OF 2

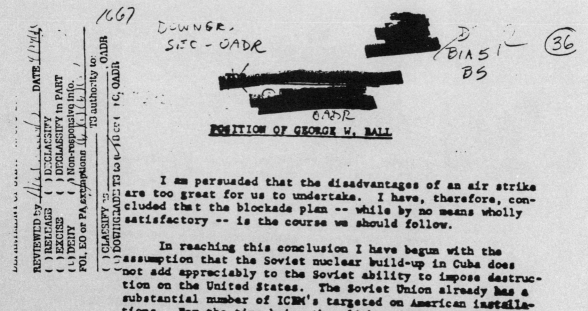

POSITION OF GEORGE W. BALL

I am persuaded that the disadvantages of an air strike are too great for us to undertake. I have, therefore, concluded that the blockade plan -- while by no means wholly satisfactory -- is the course we should follow.

In reaching this conclusion I have begun with the assumption that the Soviet nuclear build-up in Cuba does not add appreciably to the Soviet ability to impose destruction on the United States. The Soviet Union already has a substantial number of ICBM's targeted on American installations. For the time being the slight additional increment of destructive capacity provided by the MRBM's and IRBM's in Cuba might have some marginal significance. As the Soviet Union accumulates additional numbers of ICBM's even this transitory advantage will tend to disappear.

If this assumption be valid -- and I have heard no compelling arguments against it -- then the menace we face is not the addition of new Soviet military capabilities so much as their moral and propaganda advantage. As I understand it, the proponents of the strike plan insist that what we are facing is a test of will that will be witnessed by all the world. Unless the United States is prepared to use decisive military power, the world will lose confidence in our strength and determination.

But I think that -- far from establishing our moral strength -- we would, in fact, alienate a great part of the civilized world by behaving in a manner wholly contrary to our traditions, by pursuing a course of action that would cut directly athwart everything we have stood for during our national history, and condemn us as hypocrites in the opinion of the world.

We tried Japanese as war criminals because of the sneak attack on Pearl Harbor. We condemned the Soviet action in Hungary. We took a strong moral line against the use of force by the French and British at Suez when they felt their vital interests were threatened. We have taken a strong line in the United Nations and in other world councils against the dangers of a surprise attack with nuclear weapons.

DOCUMENT 20: "Position of [Under Secretary of State] George W. Ball," in support of blockade option against Cuba, ca. October 18, 1962.

PAGE 2 OF 2

- 2 -

It is my strongly held view that we cannot launch a surprise attack against Cuba without destroying our moral position and alienating our friends and allies. If we were to do so we would wake up the following morning to find that we had brought down in ruins the structure of alliances and arrangements and that our whole post-war effort of trying to organize the combined strength of the Free World was in shards and tatters.

I find the blockade plan unsatisfactory -- primarily because it does not provide a way to prevent the Soviet missiles from becoming operational. But, on the assumption I have stated above, I do not believe that this is a con- clusive argument against it. While the blockade may create some stickiness with other Free World nations, it will be generally accepted as a legal and and consistent with our traditions. Particularly if the blockade includes POL is can, within a relatively short time, bring the Cuban economy to a screeching halt. Meanwhile, the Soviet Union will have the choice either of running the blockade or of accepting it with the intention of creating a counter- thrust elsewhere. If it accepts the blockade the Cubans will feel isolated and deserted and I think the days of the Castro regime will be numbered.

DOCUMENT 21: Minutes of the October 19, 1962, Executive Committee Meeting, 11:00 A.M. (taken by State Department legal adviser Leonard Meeker).

PAGE 1 OF 5

11 O'CLOCK   19 OCTOBER 1962

CONFERENCE ROOM OF THE
UNDER SECRETARY OF STATE (MR. BALL)

PARTICIPANTS:

Secretary Rusk

Assistant Secretary Nitze

Under Secretary Ball

General Taylor

Ambassador Thompson

Attorney General Kennedy

Deputy Under Secretary Johnson

Deputy Attorney General Assistant Secretary Martin Katzenbach

Leonard C. Meeker

John A. McCone

Secretary Dillon Ray

S. Cline

Secretary McNamara

McGeorge Bundy

Deputy Secretary Gilpatric

Theodore Sorensen

Dean Acheson

Secretary Rusk opened the meeting by asking Mr. Johnson if he was ready to lay a program before the group. Mr. Johnson said that he was not.

Then ensued a military photographic intelligence briefing on installations in Cuba, presented by a CIA representative (Arthur Lundall). Following this, Mr. McCone called on Mr. Cline to give the most recent intelligence estimate conclusions of the United States Intelligence Board. Mr. Cline did so on the basis of three papers which were distributed to the group. (As he started, Mr. Cline spoke of China by inadvertence instead of Cuba; a few *moments* later this was called to his attention and corrected.)

Secretary Rusk then said he thought there should be an exposition of the legal framework surrounding possible military measures by the United States, turned to me, and seemed about to call on me, when the Attorney General signalled and said "Mr. Katzenbach". Secretary Rusk then called on the latter. Mr. Katzenbach said he believed the President had ample constitutional and statutory authority to take any needed military measures. He considered a declaration of war unnecessary. From the standpoint of international law, Mr. Katzenbach thought the United States action could be justified on the principle of self-defense.

I said that my analysis ran along much the same lines. I did not think a declaration of war would improve our position, but indeed would impair it. I said that a defensive quarantine of Cuba would involve a use of force, and this had to be considered in relation to the United Nations Charter. The Charter contained a general prohibition against the use of force except in certain limited kinds of situation. One of these was "armed attack", but the situation in Cuba did not constitute armed attack on any country. Another exception was collective action voted by the competent United Nations organ to deal with a situation under Chapter VII of the Charter. Obviously, no resolution could be obtained from the Security Council. And it seemed quite problematical whether we could obtain a recommendation from the [U.N.] General Assembly.

The Charter also contained Chapter VIII on regional arrangements. Article 52 provided that regional arrangements could deal with "such matters relating to the maintenance of international peace and security as are appropriate for regional action". Thus a case could be made under the

DOCUMENT 21: Minutes of the October 19, 1962, Executive Committee Meeting, 11:00 A.M. (taken by State Department legal adviser Leonard Meeker).

PAGE 2 OF 5

Charter for the use of force if it were sanctioned by the American Republics acting under the Rio Treaty. The Organ of Consultation, pursuant to Article 6 and 8 of that Treaty, could recommend measures, including the use of armed force, to meet a situation endangering the peace of America. As to the prospects for securing the necessary two-thirds vote in the Organ of Consultation, Mr. Martin would have something to say about that.

If the contention were advanced that a defensive quarantine voted under the Rio Treaty constituted "enforcement action" under Article 53 of the United Nations Charter, and therefore required the authorization of the Security Council, we would be able to make a reasonably good argument to the contrary. While our ability to persuade seven members of the Security Council to vote with us on this issue might be uncertain, we would in any event be able to prevent a vote going against our [text missing].

Mr. Martin then gave as his estimate that the United States could secure immediately a vote of 14 in the OAS. He thought the majority could be increased within 24 hours to 17 or perhaps even 18 or 19. He was hopeful in regard to Ecuador and Chile, and believed there was a good chance of getting Mexico. The Attorney General said the President would be placed in an impossible position if we went to the OAS and then failed to get the necessary votes, or if there were a delay. He asked if we could be perfectly sure of the outcome before seeking OAS concurrence. Mr. Martin said he hated to guarantee anything, but he had a lot of confidence about this. You couldn't go to the American Republics in advance without the loss of security, but he felt that a last-minute approach to heads of state, laying the situation on the line, would produce the votes. The Attorney General again expressed his great concern at the possibility of a slip.

There followed a discussion covering the meeting held the night before with the President. One participant looked back on the meeting as having arrived at a tentative conclusion to institute a blockade, and thought the President had been satisfied at the consensus by then arrived at among his advisers. General Taylor quickly indicated that he had not concurred and that the Joint Chiefs had reserved their position.

Mr. Bundy then said that he had reflected a good deal upon the situation in the course of a sleepless night, and he doubted whether the strategy group was serving the President as well as it might, if it merely recommended a blockade. He had spoken with the President this morning, and he felt there was further work to be done. A blockade would not remove the missiles. Its effects were uncertain and in any event would be slow to be felt. Something more would be made more difficult by the prior publicity of a blockade and the consequent pressures from the United Nations for a negotiated settlement. An air strike would be quick and would take out the bases in a clean surgical operation. He favored decisive action with its advantages of surprise and confronting the world with a fait accompli.

Secretary Rusk asked Mr. Acheson for his views. Mr. Acheson said that Khrushchev had presented the United States with a direct challenge, we were involved in a test of wills, and that sooner we got to a showdown the better. He favored cleaning the missile bases out decisively with an air strike. There was something else to remember. This wasn't just another instance of Soviet missiles aimed at the United States. Here they were in the hands of a madman whose actions would be perfectly irresponsible; the usual restraints operating on the Soviets would not apply. We had better act, and act quickly. So far as questions of international law might be involved, Mr. Acheson agreed with Mr. Katzenbach's position that self-defense was and entirely sufficient justification. But if there were to be imported a qualification or requirement of

DOCUMENT 21: Minutes of the October 19, 1962, Executive Committee Meeting, 11:00 A.M.
(taken by State Department legal adviser Leonard Meeker).

PAGE 3 OF 5

approval by the OAS, as apparently suggested by Mr. Meeker, he could not go along with that.

Secretary Dillon said he agreed there should be a quick air strike. Mr. McCone was of the same opinion.

General Taylor said that a decision now to impose a blockade was a decision to abandon the possibility of an air strike. A strike would be feasible for only a few more days; after that the missiles would be operational. Thus it was now or never for an air strike. He favored a strike. If it were to take place Sunday morning, a decision would have to be made at once so that the necessary preparations could be ordered. For a Monday morning strike, a decision would have to be reached tomorrow. Forty-eight hours notice was required.

Secretary McNamara said that he would give orders for the necessary military dispositions, so that if the decision were for a strike the Air Force would be ready. He did not, however, advocate an air strike, and favored the alternative of blockade.

Under Secretary Ball said that he was a waverer between the two courses of actions.

The Attorney General said with a grin that he too had had a talk with the President, indeed very recently this morning. There seemed to be three main possibilities as the Attorney General analyzed the situation: one was to do nothing, and that would be unthinkable; another was an air strike; the third was a blockade. he thought it would be very, very difficult indeed for the President if the decision were to be for an air strike, with all the memory of Pearl Harbor and with all the implications this would have for us in whatever world there would be afterward. For 175 years we had not been that kind of country. A sneak attack was not in our traditions. Thousands of Cubans would be killed without warning, and a lot of Russians too. He favored *action*, to make known unmistakably the seriousness of United States determination to get the missiles out of Cuba, but he thought the action should allow the Soviets some room for maneuver to pull back from their over-extended position in Cuba.

Mr. Bundy, addressing himself to the Attorney General, said this was very well but a blockade would not eliminate the bases; an air strike would.

I asked at this point: who would be expected to be the government of Cuba after an air strike? Would it be anyone other than Castro? If not, would anything be solved, and would we not be in a worse situation than before? After a pause, Mr. Martin replied that, of course, a good deal might be different after a strike, and Castro might be toppled in the aftermath. Others expressed the view that we might have to proceed with invasion following a strike. Still another suggestion was that US armed forces seize the base areas alone in order to eliminate the missiles. Secretary McNamara thought this a very unattractive kind of undertaking from the military point of view.

Toward one o'clock Secretary Rusk said he thought this group could not make the decision as to what was to be done; that was for the President in consultation with his constitutional advisers. The Secretary thought the group's duty was to present to the President, for his consideration, fully staffed-out alternatives. Accordingly, two working groups should be formed, one to work up the blockade alternative and the other to work up air strike. Mr. Johnson was designated to head the former, and Mr. Bundy the latter. Mr. Johnson was to have with him Ambassador Thompson, Deputy Secretary Gilpatric, Mr. Martin, Mr. Nitze, and Mr. Meeker. Mr. Bundy was to have Secretary Dillon, Mr. Acheson, and General Taylor. Mr. McCone, when asked to serve with the air strike group, begged off on the ground that his position and duties on the US Intelligence Board made it undesirable for him to participate in the working group. Mr. Katzenbach was detailed to the Johnson group, later visiting the Bundy group to observe and possibly serve as a devil's advocate.

DOCUMENT 21: Minutes of the October 19, 1962, Executive Committee Meeting, 11:00 A.M. (taken by State Department legal adviser Leonard Meeker).

PAGE 4 OF 5

Mr. Sorensen commented that he thought he had absorbed enough to start on the draft of a speech for the President. There was some inconclusive discussion on the timing of such a speech, on the danger of leaks before then, and on the proper time for meeting with the President once more, in view of his current Western campaign trip.

Before the whole group dispersed, Ambassador Thompson said the Soviets attached importance to questions of legality and we should be able to present a strong legal case. The Attorney General, as he was about to leave the room, said he thought there was ample legal basis for a blockade. I said: yes, that is so provided the Organ of Consultation under the Rio Treaty adopted an appropriate resolution. The Attorney General said: "That's all political; it's not legal." On leaving the room, he said to Mr. Katzenbach, half humorously: "Remember now, you're working for me."

The two groups met separately until four o'clock. They then reconvened and were joined once more by the cabinet officers who had been away in the earlier afternoon.

The Johnson group scenario, which was more nearly complete and was ready earlier, was discussed first. Numerous criticisms were advanced. Some were answered; others led to changes. There was again a discussion of timing, now in relation to a Presidential radio address. Mr. Martin thought Sunday might be too early, as it would be virtually impossible to get to the Latin American heads of state on Sunday. Ambassador Thompson made the point that 24 hours must be allowed to elapse between announcement of the blockade and enforcement, so as to give the Soviet Government time to get instructions to their ship captains.

Approximately two hours were spent on the Johnson scenario. About 6 o'clock the Bundy approach was taken up, its author saying, "It's been much more fun for us up to this point, since we've had a chance to poke holes in the blockade plan;

now the roles will be reversed." Not much more than half an hour was spent on the Bundy scenario.

More than once during the afternoon Secretary McNamara voiced the opinion that the US would have to pay a price to get the Soviet missiles out of Cuba. He thought we would at least have to give up our missile bases in Italy and Turkey and would probably have to pay more besides. At different times the possibility of nuclear conflict breaking out was referred to. The point was made that once the Cuban missile installations were complete and operational, a new strategic situation would exist, with the United States more directly and immediately under the gun than ever before. A striking Soviet military push into the Western Hemisphere would have succeeded and become effective. The clock could not be turned back, and things would never be the same again. During this discussion, the Attorney General said that in looking forward into the future it would be better for our children and grandchildren if we decided to face the Soviet threat, stand up to it, and eliminate it, now. The circumstances for doing so at some future time were bound to be more unfavorable, the risks would be greater, the chances of success less good.

Secretary Rusk, toward the end of the afternoon, stated his approach to the problem as follows: the US needed to move in a way such that a planned action would be followed by a pause in which the great powers could step back from the brink and have time to consider and work out a solution rather than be drawn inexorably from one action to another and escalate into general nuclear war. The implication of his statement was that he favored blockade rather than strike.

In the course of the afternoon discussion, the military representatives, especially Secretary McNamara, came to expressing the view that an airstrike could be made some time after Sunday if a blockade did not produce results as to the missile bases in Cuba. The

Attorney General took particular note of this shift, and toward the end of the day made clear that he firmly favored blockade as the first step; other steps subsequently were not precluded and could be considered; he thought it was now pretty clear what the decision should be.

At about six-thirty Governor Stevenson came into the room. After a few minutes, Secretary Rusk asked him if he had some views on the question of what to do. He replied: "Yes, most emphatic views." When queried as to them, he said that in view of the course the discussion was taking he didn't think it was necessary to express them then. When asked: "But you are in favor of blockade, aren't you?", he answered affirmatively. He went on to say he thought we must look beyond the particular immediate action of blockade; we need to develop a plan for solution of the problem — elements for negotiation designed to settle the current crisis in a stable and satisfactory way and enable us to move forward on wider problems; he was working on some ideas for a settlement. One possibility would be the demilitarization of Cuba under effective international supervision, perhaps accompanied by neutralization of the island under international guaranties [*sic*] and with UN observers to monitor compliance.

Once again there was discussion of when another meeting with the President should be held. It was generally agreed that the President should continue on his trip until Sunday morning. He would be reachable by telephone prior to that time.

The meeting broke up about seven o'clock.

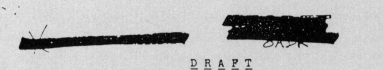

D R A F T

I - AIR STRIKE SCENARIO, OCTOBER 19, 1962

The Military Program

This plan would call for a surprise strike aimed at medium range missiles, surface to air missiles, and high performance aircraft and nuclear storage sites in Cuba. The object would be to ensure by conventional means the most rapid and complete removal of any operational capability in these fields. This operation should be followed by continual close surveillance and very promptly by a blockade in which all Bloc shipping would be turned back and imports of fuel prohibited. The alternative of omitting the blockade is not recommended, because of the danger of a recreated threat. The alternative of a strike limited to known missile sites is no longer recommended even by those who first proposed it because of the dangers presented by a surviving and substantial air capability. This build-up should be hit as a whole complex, or not at all.

Schedule of Public Statements

Intelligence estimates put a high premium on maximum tactical surprise, but political considerations at home and abroad dictate some minimum announcement that medium range missiles are being installed in Cuba. The current recommendation is that there should be a White House announcement of the estimates of the introduction of such missiles early Monday evening. This statement would also announce that the

oADR

President was recalling the Congress to a special session to
meet on Thursday morning. This announcement would be followed
by a brief Presidential statement on all networks Tuesday
morning at the time the strike begins and the announcement
presently would be completed by a Presidential TV address
by mid-morning Tuesday.

<u>Notice to Khrushchev and Castro - Alternative 1</u>

It is recommended that no advance notice be given to
Khrushchev. The principal point here is that there is no
notice to which he cannot make a politically damaging reply,
and no serious advantage ingiving him any precise advance
indication of a course which is inevitable. We have been
unable to draft any advance warning which would carry
conviction either in the following days of crises or in
history.

There should, however, be a carefully drafted statement
to Khrushchev delivered approximately simultaneously with the
air strike. This message would carry much of the President's
argument in his later public speech. It would carefully
define and delimit the grounds and the extent of the
military operation with special emphasis on its conventional
character. It would renew and reemphasize the depth and
intensity of the United States commitment to defend Berlin
by <u>all</u> necessary means. It would include an urgent invitation
to a Summit meeting. It might also include a statement that

2

while we are currently treating these as Cuban missiles, any nuclear use of them would have to be regarded as an act of the Soviet Government.

The problem of notice to Castro is different. It is his country which will come under attack, and it is best from our point of view to focus responsibility on him. At some time between the White House statement of Monday evening and the air strike a message should be delivered to the Cuban representative in the UN which would indicate plainly that what we now know is completely inconsistent with Cuban assurances, Soviet statements, and our own clearly announced position; thus it will now be necessary for us to take appropriate steps. The military preference is that warning to Cuba should be given nor more than 2 hours before attack if tactical surprise is not to be jeopardized.

Notice to Khrushchev and Castro - Alternative 2

On the political side there is a strong feeling that a real advance communication to Khrushchev and Castro is needed, if the United States is not to be marked as a reckless aggressor and this Administration cursed forever as the force which opened the door to a world of catch-as-catch-can violence. In spite of the difficulty of saying anything that could not be turned against us, this group has urged that advance warning be given. If this is done, the military operation is degraded in the ways argued in Annex _____, depending on whether 6 or 24 hours of notice is given.

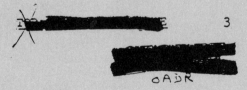

3

DOCUMENT 22: Theodore Sorensen, draft "Air Strike Scenario for October 19, 1962."

PAGE 4 OF 5

~~TOP SECRET~~

Such a warning could not be precise in its threat. Its basic sentence might be something saying that "unless the Soviet (Cuban) Government can give immediate and unequivocable assurance that these offensive weapons (missiles and IL-28s; MIGs?) will be removed immediately, the United States Government will have to meet its own responsibilities." The rest of the message would be, in essence, a preview of the President's speech.

If this sort of warning were given, it should be given simultaneously with or shortly after initial public statement. In that case the timing of the statement from the White House should be changed accordingly.

Notice to Friends

It appears to us essential that advance notice of this action be given to the heads of Governments of the following countries: The United Kingdom, France, Germany, Italy, Japan and Turkey. The timing of such advance notice is complex. If it is early Tuesday morning in Europe it is almost dawn over Cuba. If it is late evening in Europe, it is twelve hours before dawn in Cuba. On balance the following is recommended:

A message to MacMillan, DeGaulle and Adenauer late Monday evening and to Fanfani and the Turks early Tuesday morning, and to the Japanese Tuesday afternoon local time. The

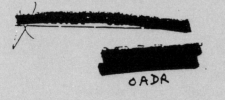

4

OADR

DOCUMENT 22: Theodore Sorensen, draft "Air Strike Scenario for October 19, 1962."

PAGE 5 OF 5

OADR

messages to our principal Allies should rehearse basic evidence and argumentation and the messages to Italy, Japan and Turkey, and also to Great Britain, should direct attention to the particular problem of ▓▓▓▓▓ which may become a hazard. The United States should not indicate any fear on its own part, but should indicate a readiness to take account of the desires of its Allies in this grave situation. (If warning is given to Khrushchev, the content of these messages should be revised, and their timing advanced)

Early on Tuesday the United States would call a meeting of the Consultative Organ of the OAS and in that Organ it would press for a two-thirds majority endorsing this remedial action.

The United States would brief the North Atlantic Council on Tuesday, perhaps through a special emissary who may also be dispatched to DeGaulle. This briefing would emphasize the great provocation of the Soviet action, the increased determination of the United States, and the real balance of strategic power.

OADR

5

DOCUMENT 23: Theodore Sorensen, summary of objections to airstrike option and advantages of blockade option, October 20, 1962.

PAGE 1 OF 1

1´14

TCS - 10/20/62

I. There are 2 fundamental objections to air strike which have never

been answered:

1) Inasmuch as no one has been able to devise a satisfactory
    message to Khrushchev to which his reply could not
    outmaneuver us, an air strike means an U. S. -initiated
    "Pearl Harbor" on a small nation which history could neither
    understand nor forget

2) Inasmuch as the concept of a clean, swift strike has been
    abandoned as militarily impractical, it is generally
    agreed that the more widespread air attack will inevitably
    lead to an invasion with all of its consequences.

II. There are 2 fundamental advantages to a blockade which have never

been answered:

1) It is a more prudent and flexible step which enables us to
    move to an air strike, invasion or any other step at any
    time it proves necessary, without the "Pearl Harbor"
    posture.

2) It is the step least likely to precipitate general war while
    still causing the Soviets -- unwilling to engage our Navy
    in our waters -- to back down and abandon Castro.

DOCUMENT 24: CIA Special National Intelligence Estimate, "Major Consequences of Certain U.S. Courses of Action on Cuba," October 20, 1962.

PAGE 1 OF 10

CENTRAL INTELLIGENCE AGENCY

20 October 1962

SUBJECT: SNIE 11-19-62: MAJOR CONSEQUENCES OF CERTAIN US COURSES OF
ACTION ON CUBA

THE PROBLEM

To estimate the major consequences of certain US courses of action
with respect to Cuba

THE ESTIMATE

STATUS OF SOVIET MILITARY BUILDUP IN CUBA

1. Firm evidence indicates the presence in Cuba of four MRBM and
two IRBM launch sites in various stages of construction and organized
into at least three regiments. Of these, two regiments of eight
launchers each are mobile and designed to launch MRBMs with a range of
about 1,100 n.m., while one regiment of eight fixed launchers may be
designed for IRBMs with a range of about 2,200 n.m.

CERTIFIED COPY

Approved for Release
Date *15 April 1975*

DOCUMENT 24: CIA Special National Intelligence Estimate, "Major Consequences of Certain U.S. Courses of Action on Cuba," October 20, 1962.

PAGE 2 OF 10

2. The 16 launchers for 1,100 n.m. MRBMs must be considered operational now. Four of the fixed launchers for the 2,200 n.m. IRBMs could
probably become operational within the next six weeks. The other four
would become operational in 8 to 10 weeks.

the construction of
at least one probable nuclear storage facility is a strong indication
of the Soviet intent to provide nuclear warheads. In any case, it is
prudent to assume that when the missiles are otherwise operational,
nuclear warheads will be available. These could be brought in by air,
submarine, or surface ship.

3. We estimate that operational MRBM missiles can be fired in
eight hours or less after a decision to launch, depending on the condition of readiness. After the IRBM sites are completed and missiles
are on launcher, a state of readiness of five hours may be maintained.
Both systems are believed to be provided with two missiles per launcher,
providing a refire capability from each launcher after about four to
six additional hours for the MRBMs and six to eight hours for the IRBMs.

4. It is possible that further evidence will uncover additional
launch sites which are presently undetected, but the extent of our
coverage leads us to believe that such evidence would not drastically

- 2 -

DOCUMENT 24: CIA Special National Intelligence Estimate, "Major Consequences of Certain U.S. Courses of Action on Cuba," October 20, 1962.

PAGE 3 OF 10

increase the total now deployed. On the other hand, new deployments could be started at any time.

5. The inventory of other major Soviet weapons now identified in Cuba includes:

a. 22 IL-28 jet light bombers, of which one is assembled and three others have been uncrated;

b. 39 MIG-21 jet fighters, of which 35 are assembled and four are still crates, and 62 other jet fighters of less advanced types;

c. 24 SA-2 sites, of which 16 are believed to be individually operational with some missiles on launcher;

d. 3 cruise missile sites for coastal defense, of which 2 are now operational;

e. 12 Komar cruise missile patrol boats, all probably operational or nearly so.

6. Cuban-based MRBMs and IRBMs with nuclear warheads would augment the present limited Soviet ICBM capability by virtue of their ability to strike at similar types of targets with warheads of generally similar yields. In the near future, therefore, Soviet gross capabilities for initial attack on US military and civilian targets can be increased considerably by Cuban-based missiles. However, the deployment of these missiles in Cuba will probably not, in the Soviet judgment, insure destruction of the US second strike capability to a degree which would

- 3 -

eliminate an unacceptably heavy retaliatory attack on the USSR. If the
missile buildup in Cuba continues, the Soviet capability to blunt a retaliatory attack will be progressively enhanced.

PURPOSE OF SOVIET BUILDUP

7. A major Soviet objective in their military buildup in Cuba is
to demonstrate that the world balance of forces has shifted so far in
their favor that the US can no longer prevent the advance of Soviet offensive power even into its own hemisphere. In this connection they
assume, of course, that these deployments sooner or later will become
publicly known. At the same time, they expect their missile forces in
Cuba to make an important contribution to their total strategic capability vis-a-vis the US.

8. Consequently, it is unlikely that the USSR is installing these
missiles primarily in order to use them in bargaining for US concessions
elsewhere. Moreover, the public withdrawal of Soviet missiles from Cuba
would create serious problems in the USSR's relations with Castro; it
would cast doubt on the firmness of the Soviet intention to protect the
Castro regime and perhaps on their commitments elsewhere.

- 4 -

DOCUMENT 24: CIA Special National Intelligence Estimate, "Major Consequences of Certain U.S. Courses of Action on Cuba," October 20, 1962.

PAGE 5 OF 10

US ACQUIESCENCE IN THE BUILDUP

9. If the US acquiesces to the presence of strategic missiles in Cuba, we believe that the Soviets will continue the buildup. We have no basis for estimating the force level which they would wish to reach, but it seems entirely clear now that they are going well beyond a token capability.

10. This course of US action would provide strong encouragement to Communists, pro-Communists, and the more anti-American sectors of opinion in Latin America. We believe that, especially over the long run, there would be loss of confidence in US power and determination and a serious decline of US influence, particularly in Latin America. Should any additional Latin American government fall to the Communists the Soviets would feel free to establish bases in the country in question if they chose. A major immediate consequence would be that the Soviets would probably estimate lower risks in pressing the US hard in other confrontations, such as Berlin.

EFFECT OF WARNING

11. If the US confronts Khrushchev with its knowledge of the MRBM deployment and presses for a withdrawal, we do not believe the Soviets would halt the deployment. Instead, they would propose negotiations on the general question of foreign bases, claiming equal right to establish Soviet bases and assuring the US of tight control over the missiles.

- 5 -

DOCUMENT 24: CIA Special National Intelligence Estimate, "Major Consequences of Certain
U.S. Courses of Action on Cuba," October 20, 1962.

PAGE 6 OF 10

They would probably link Cuba with the Berlin situation and emphasize
their patience and preference for negotiations, implying that Berlin was
held hostage to US actions in Cuba.

12. There is some slight chance that a warning to Castro might make
a difference, since the Soviets could regard this as a chance to stand
aside, but it also would give time for offers to negotiate, continued
buildup, and counterpressures, and we think the result in the end would
be the same.

13. Any warning would of course degrade the element of surprise in
a subsequent US attack.

A US BLOCKADE

14. Two basic modes of blockade could be considered: total and
selective. We believe that even under a total blockade individual aircraft and submarines might get through to deliver vital military items,
e.g., nuclear warheads. Even the most severe blockade would not deprive
the Soviets of the use of missiles already in Cuba for a nuclear strike
on the US.

15. Under any form of blockade, the Soviets would concentrate on
political exploitation, especially in the UN. They might risk violent
encounters in attempts to penetrate the blockade, but they would not resort to major force in the area of Cuba or forceful retaliation elsewhere,

- 6 -

DOCUMENT 24: CIA Special National Intelligence Estimate, "Major Consequences of Certain U.S. Courses of Action on Cuba," October 20, 1962.

PAGE 7 OF 10

at least initially. If US enforcement of the blockade involved use of force by the US, the Soviets might respond on an equivalent level, but would seek to avoid escalation.

16. Thus any blockade situation would place the Soviets under no immediate pressure to choose a response with force. They could rely on political means to compel the US to desist, and reserve a resort to force until the US had actually used force. They would estimate that the inherent difficulties of enforcing the blockade and the generally adverse reactions, including those of US allies to it, would result in enormous pressures on the US to desist. They could heighten these pressures by threatening retaliation in Berlin or actually undertaking major harassments on the access routes, which could become tantamount to a blockade, and would probably do so at some stage.

17. We do not believe that even a severe blockade, of itself, would bring down the Cuban regime. Castro would tighten internal security and, unless action against the regime subsequently developed on Cuban soil, the Cuban population would be increasingly reluctant to oppose the regime. Direct action would still be required to bring down the Castro regime.

SOVIET REACTION TO USE OF MILITARY FORCE

18. In the case of US use of force against Cuban territory, the likelihood of a Soviet response by force, either locally or for retaliation elsewhere, would be greater than in the case of blockade. The

DOCUMENT 24: CIA Special National Intelligence Estimate, "Major Consequences of Certain U.S. Courses of Action on Cuba," October 20, 1962.

PAGE 8 OF 10

Soviets would be placed automatically under great pressure to respond in ways which, if they could not save Cuba, would inflict an offsetting injury to US interests. This would be true whether the action was limited to an effort to neutralize the strategic missiles, or these missiles plus airfields, surface-to-air missile sites, or cruise missile sites, or in fact an outright invasion designed to destroy the Castro regime.

19. In reaction to any of the various forms of US action, the Soviets would be surprised and probably alarmed, since they appear to have estimated that the US would probably not take military action in the face of Soviet warnings of the danger of nuclear war. They would recognize that US military action posed a major challenge to the prestige of the USSR. We must of course recognize the possibility that the Soviets, under pressure to respond, would again miscalculate and respond in a way which, through a series of actions and reactions, could escalate to general war.

20. On the other hand, the Soviets have no public treaty with Cuba and have not acknowledged that Soviet bases are on the island. This situation provides them with a pretext for treating US military action against Cuba as an affair which does not directly involve them, and thereby avoiding the risks of a strong response. We do not believe that the USSR would attack the US, either from Soviet bases or with its missiles in Cuba, even if the latter were operational and not put out of action before they could be readied for firing.

- 8 -

DOCUMENT 24: CIA Special National Intelligence Estimate, "Major Consequences of Certain U.S. Courses of Action on Cuba," October 20, 1962.

PAGE 9 OF 10

21. Since the USSR would almost certainly not resort to general war and could not hope to prevail locally, we believe that the Soviets would consider retaliatory actions outside Cuba. The timing and selection of such moves would depend heavily upon the immediate context of events and the USSR's appreciation of US attitudes. The most likely location for broad retaliation outside Cuba appears to be Berlin. They would probably react here with major harassments, interruptions of access to the city or even a blockade, with or without the signing of a separate peace treaty. Retaliation against some US installation overseas is possible but in our view unlikely.

22. We believe that there would probably be a difference between Soviet reaction to all-out invasion and Soviet reaction to more limited US use of force against selected objectives in Cuba. We believe that the Soviets would be somewhat less likely to retaliate with military force in areas outside Cuba in response to speedy, effective invasion than in response to more limited forms of military action against Cuba. We recognize that such an estimate cannot be made with very great assurance and do not rule out the possibility of Soviet retaliation outside Cuba in case of invasion. But we believe that a rapid occupation of Cuba would be more likely to make the Soviets pause in opening new theaters of conflict than limited action or action which drags out.

23. Finally, we believe that, whatever course of retaliation the USSR elected, the Soviet leaders would not deliberately initiate general

- 9 -

DOCUMENT 24: CIA Special National Intelligence Estimate, "Major Consequences of Certain U.S. Courses of Action on Cuba," October 20, 1962.

PAGE 10 OF 10

war or take military measures, which in their calculation, would run grave risks of general war.

DOCUMENT 25: Secretary of Defense Robert McNamara, military briefing, "Notes on October 21, 1962 Meeting with the President."

PAGE 1 OF 2

TOP SECRET

8

NOTES ON OCTOBER 21, 1962 MEETING WITH THE PRESIDENT

1. The meeting was held in the Oval Room at the White House and lasted from 11:30 a.m. to approximately 12:30 p.m. In attendance were the Attorney General, General Taylor, General Sweeney and the Secretary of Defense.

2. The Secretary of Defense stated that following the start of an air attack, the initial units of the landing force could invade Cuba within 7 days. The movement of troops in preparation for such an invasion will start at the time of the President's speech. No mobilization of Reserve forces is required for such an invasion until the start of the air strike. General LeMay had stated that the transport aircraft, from Reserve and Guard units, which would be required for participation in such an invasion, can be fully operational within 24 to 48 hours after the call to active duty.

3. The Secretary of Defense reported that, based on information which became available during the night, it now appears that there is equipment in Cuba for approximately 40 MRBM or IRBM launchers. (Mr. McCone, who joined the group 15 or 20 minutes after the start of the discussion, confirmed this report.) The location of the sites for 36 of these launchers is known. 32 of the 36 known sites appear to have sufficient equipment on them to be included in any air strike directed against Cuba's missile capability.

4. We believe that 40 launchers would normally be equipped with 80 missiles. John McCone reported yesterday that a Soviet ship believed to be the vessel in which the Soviets have been sending missiles to Cuba has made a sufficient number of trips to that island, within recent weeks, to offload approximately 48 missiles. Therefore, we assume there are approximately that number on the Island today, although we have only located approximately 30 of these.

5. General Sweeney outlined the following plan of air attack, the object of which would be the destruction of the known Cuban missile capability.

   a. The 5 surface-to-air missile installations, in the vicinity of the known missile sites, would each be attacked by approximately 8 aircraft; the 3 MIG airfields defending the missile sites would be covered by 12 U.S. aircraft per field. In total, the defense supression operations, including the necessary replacement aircraft, would require approximately 100 sorties.

   b. Each of the launchers at the 8 or 9 known sites (a total of approximately 32 to 36 launchers) would be attacked by 6 aircraft. For the purpose, a total of approximately 250 sorties would be flown.

   c. The U.S. aircraft covering the 3 MIG airfields would attack the MIG's if they became airborne. General Sweeney strongly recommended attacks on each of the airfields to destroy the MIG aircraft.

1

TOP SECRET

DOCUMENT 25: Secretary of Defense Robert McNamara, military briefing, "Notes on October 21, 1962 Meeting with the President."

PAGE 2 OF 2

TOP SECRET

8

6. General Sweeney stated that he was certain the air strike would be "successful"; however, even under optimum conditions, it was not likely that all of the known missiles would be destroyed. (As noted in 4 above, the known missiles are probably no more than 60% of the total missiles on the Island.) General Taylor stated, "The best we can offer you is to destroy 90% of the known missiles." General Taylor, General Sweeney and the Secretary of Defense all strongly emphasized that in their opinion the initial air strike must be followed by strikes on subsequent days and that these in turn would lead inevitably to an invasion.

7. CIA representatives, who joined the discussion at this point, stated that it is probable the missiles which are operational (it is estimated there are now between 8 and 12 operational missiles on the Island) can hold indefinitely a capability for firing with from 2-1/2 to 4 hours notice. Included in the notice period is a countdown requiring 20 to 40 minutes. In relation to the countdown period, the first wave of our attacking aircraft would give 10 minutes of warning; the second wave, 40 minutes of warning; and the third wave a proportionately greater warning.

8. As noted above, General Sweeney strongly recommended that any air strike include attacks on the MIG aircraft and, in addition, the IL28s. To accomplish the destruction of these aircraft, the total number of sorties of such an air strike should be increased to 500. The President agreed that if an air strike is ordered, it should probably include in its objective the destruction of the MIG aircraft and the IL28s.

9. The President directed that we be prepared to carry out the air strike Monday morning or any time thereafter during the remainder of the week. The President recognized that the Secretary of Defense was opposed to the air strike Monday morning, and that General Sweeney favored it. He asked the Attorney General and Mr. McCone for their opinions:

    a. The Attorney General stated he was opposed to such a strike because:
       (1) "It would be a Pearl Harbor type of attack."
       (2) It would lead to unpredictable military responses by the
           Soviet Union which could be so serious as to lead to general
           nuclear war.
       He stated we should start with the initiation of the blockade and
       thereafter "play for the breaks."

    b. Mr. McCone agreed with the Attorney General, but emphasized he
       believed we should be prepared for an air strike and thereafter
       an invasion.

Robert S. McNamara,
Robert S. McNamara

10/21/62

TOP SECRET

DOCUMENT 26: State Department cable on Secretary of State Dean Rusk Meeting with Soviet Ambassador Dobrynin to give Kennedy letter to Premier Khrushchev, announcing discovery of the Missiles, October 22, 1962.

PAGE 1 OF 2

OUTGOING TELEGRAM Department of State

INDICATE: ☐ COLLECT
☐ CHARGE TO

CONFIDENTIAL

52
Origin

ACTION: Amembassy MOSCOW 970 PRIORITY Oc: 22 8 14 PM '62

SS

INFO: Amembassy LONDON 2275
Amembassy PARIS 2318
Amembassy ROME 856   USMISSION BERLIN
Amembassy BONN 1053   PARIS FOR USRO
AMembassy OTTAWA 500

ELITE - EYES ONLY

Following is based on uncleared memcon. Secretary

called in Soviet Ambassador this afternoon. Secretary

stated that at direction of President he had been instructed

to hand Ambassador letter from President to Khrushchev and

copy of speech which President would make at 7:00 p.m. tonight.

Dobrynin read both texts very carefully and was told US

Government had no intention publishing letter but would

inform Soviets if this decision changed. Secretary confirmed that

President's speech will refer to letter but would give no

substance of it.

Secretary said he not instructed to add comments but

wished to say informally that it was incomprehensible to

him how leaders in Moscow could make such gross error of

judgment

Drafted by:
EUR:SOV:JCGuthrie:AMR 10/22

Telegraphic transmission and
classification approved by: EUR - William R. Tyler

Clearances:
S/S

CONFIDENTIAL

FORM DS-322

DOCUMENT 26: State Department cable on Secretary of State Dean Rusk Meeting with Soviet
Ambassador Dobrynin to give Kennedy letter to Premier Khrushchev, announcing discovery of the Missiles,
October 22, 1962.

PAGE 2 OF 2

Page _____ of telegram to _____ Amembassy MOSCOW

CONFIDENTIAL

judgment as to what US can accept. He expressed hope Soviet

Union would make major effort to reverse situation.

Dobrynin commented "all of this" unjustifiable and will

very strongly aggravate international situation. He said he

would report conversation and messages promptly.

EMD

CONFIDENTIAL

THE WHITE HOUSE

WASHINGTON

October 22, 1962

Sir:

A copy of the statement I am making tonight concerning
developments in Cuba and the reaction of my Government thereto has been handed to your Ambassador in
Washington. In view of the gravity of the developments
to which I refer, I want you to know immediately and
accurately the position of my Government in this matter.

In our discussions and exchanges on Berlin and other
international questions, the one thing that has most concerned me has been the possibility that your Government
would not correctly understand the will and determination
of the United States in any given situation, since I have
not assumed that you or any other sane man would, in
this nuclear age, deliberately plunge the world into war
which it is crystal clear no country could win and which
could only result in catastrophic consequences to the
whole world, including the aggressor.

At our meeting in Vienna and subsequently, I expressed
our readiness and desire to find, through peaceful negotiation, a solution to any and all problems that divide us.
At the same time, I made clear that in view of the objectives of the ideology to which you adhere, the United
States could not tolerate any action on your part which
in a major way disturbed the existing over-all balance
of power in the world. I stated that an attempt to force
abandonment of our responsibilities and commitments in
Berlin would constitute such an action and that the United
States would resist with all the power at its command.

It was in order to avoid any incorrect assessment on the
part of your Government with respect to Cuba that I
publicly stated that if certain developments in Cuba took
place, the United States would do whatever must be done
to protect its own security and that of its allies.

- 2 -

Moreover, the Congress adopted a resolution expressing
its support of this declared policy. Despite this, the
rapid development of long-range missile bases and other
offensive weapons systems in Cuba has proceeded. I
must tell you that the United States is determined that
this threat to the security of this hemisphere be removed. At the same time, I wish to point out that the
action we are taking is the minimum necessary to remove the threat to the security of the nations of this
hemisphere. The fact of this minimum response should
not be taken as a basis, however, for any misjudgement
on your part.

I hope that your Government will refrain from any action
which would widen or deepen this already grave crisis
and that we can agree to resume the path of peaceful
negotiation.

> Sincerely,

His Excellency
Nikita S. Khrushchev
Chairman of the Council of Ministers
    of the Union of Soviet Socialist Republics
MOSCOW

DOCUMENT 28: "Radio-TV Address of the President to the Nation from the White House," October 22, 1962.

PAGE 1 OF 5

FOR IMMEDIATE RELEASE, OCTOBER 22, 1962

OFFICE OF THE WHITE HOUSE PRESS SECRETARY

THE WHITE HOUSE

RADIO-TV ADDRESS OF THE PRESIDENT
TO THE NATION
FROM THE WHITE HOUSE
OCTOBER 22, 1962

(AS ACTUALLY DELIVERED)

Good evening, my fellow citizens:

This government, as promised, has maintained the closest surveillance of the Soviet military build-up on the island of Cuba. Within the past week, unmistakable evidence has established the fact that a series of offensive missile sites is now in preparation on that imprisoned island. The purpose of these bases can be none other than to provide a nuclear strike capability against the Western Hemisphere.

Upon receiving the first preliminary hard information of this nature last Tuesday morning at 9:00 a.m., I directed that our surveillance be stepped up. And having now confirmed and completed our evaluation of the evidence and our decision on a course of action, this government feels obliged to report this new crisis to you in fullest detail.

The characteristics of these new missile sites indicate two distinct types of installations. Several of them include Medium Range Ballistic Missiles, capable of carrying a nuclear warhead for a distance of more than 1000 nautical miles. Each of these missiles, in short, is capable of striking Washington, D. C., the Panama Canal, Cape Canaveral, Mexico City, or any other city in the Southeastern part of the United States, in Central America, or in the Caribbean area.

Additional sites not yet completed appear to be designed for intermediate range ballistic missiles -- capable of traveling more than twice as far -- and thus capable of striking most of the major cities in the Western Hemisphere, ranging as far North as Hudson's Bay, Canada, and as far South as Lima, Peru. In addition, jet bombers, capable of carrying nuclear weapons, are now being uncrated and assembled in Cuba, while the necessary air bases are being prepared.

This urgent transformation of Cuba into an important strategic base -- by the presence of these large, long-range, and clearly offensive weapons of sudden mass destruction -- constitutes an explicit threat to the peace and security of all the Americas, in flagrant and deliberate defiance of the Rio Pact of 1947, the traditions of this Nation and Hemisphere, the Joint Resolution of the 87th Congress, the Charter of the United Nations, and my own public warnings to the Soviets on September 4 and 13. This action also contradicts the repeated assurances of Soviet spokesmen, both publicly and privately delivered, that the arms build-up in Cuba would retain its original defensive character, and that the Soviet Union had no need or desire to station strategic missiles on the territory of any other nation.

MORE

(OVER)

DOCUMENT 28: "Radio-TV Address of the President to the Nation from the White House,"
October 22, 1962.

PAGE 2 OF 5

Page 2

The size of this undertaking makes clear that it has been planned for some months. Yet only last month, after I had made clear the distinction between any introduction of ground-to-ground missiles and the existence of defensive anti-aircraft missiles, the Soviet Government publicly stated on September 11 that, and I quote, "The armaments and military equipment sent to Cuba are designed exclusively for defensive purposes," and, and I quote the Soviet Government, "There is no need for the Soviet Government to shift its weapons for a retaliatory blow to any other country, for instance Cuba," and that, and I quote the government, "The Soviet Union has so powerful rockets to carry these nuclear warheads that there is no need to search for sites for them beyond the boundaries of the Soviet Union." That statement was false.

Only last Thursday, as evidence of this rapid offensive build-up was already in my hand, Soviet Foreign Minister Gromyko told me in my office that he was instructed to make it clear once again, as he said his government had already done, that Soviet assistance to Cuba, and I quote, "pursued solely the purpose of contributing to the defense capabilities of Cuba," that and I quote him, "training by Soviet specialists of Cuban nationals in handling defensive armaments was by no means offensive," and that "if it were otherwise," Mr. Gromyko went on, "the Soviet Government would never become involved in rendering such assistance." That statement also was false.

Neither the United States of America nor the world community of nations can tolerate deliberate deception and offensive threats on the part of any nation, large or small. We no longer live in a world where only the actual firing of weapons represents a sufficient challenge to a nation's security to constitute maximum peril. Nuclear weapons are so destructive and ballistic missiles are so swift, that any substantially increased possibility of their use or any sudden change in their deployment may well be regarded as a definite threat to peace.

For many years, both the Soviet Union and the United States, recognizing this fact, have deployed strategic nuclear weapons with great care, never upsetting the precarious status quo which insured that these weapons would not be used in the absence of some vital challenge. Our own strategic missiles have never been transferred to the territory of any other nation, under a cloak of secrecy and deception; and our history, unlike that of the Soviets since the end of World War II, demonstrates that we have no desire to dominate or conquer any other nation or impose our system upon its people. Nevertheless, American citizens have become adjusted to living daily on the bull's eye of Soviet missiles located inside the USSR or in submarines.

MORE

DOCUMENT 28: "Radio-TV Address of the President to the Nation from the White House,"
October 22, 1962.

PAGE 3 OF 5

Page 3

In that sense, missiles in Cuba add to an already clear and present danger -- although it should be noted the nations of Latin America have never previously been subjected to a potential nuclear threat.

But this secret, swift and extraordinary build-up of Communist missiles -- in an area well known to have a special and historical relationship to the United States and the nations of the Western Hemisphere, in violation of Soviet assurances, and in defiance of American and Hemispheric policy -- this sudden, clandestine decision to station strategic weapons for the first time outside of Soviet soil -- is a deliberately provocative and unjustified change in the status quo which cannot be accepted by this country, if our courage and our commitments are ever to be trusted again by either friend or foe.

The 1930's taught us a clear lesson: aggressive conduct, if allowed to grow unchecked and unchallenged, ultimately leads to war. This nation is opposed to war. We are also true to our word. Our unswerving objective, therefore, must be to prevent the use of these missiles against this or any other country, and to secure their withdrawal or elimination from the Western Hemisphere.

Our policy has been one of patience and restraint, as befits a peaceful and powerful nation, which leads a worldwide alliance. We have been determined not to be diverted from our central concerns by mere irritants and fanatics. But now further action is required -- and it is underway; and these actions may only be the beginning. We will not prematurely or unnecessarily risk the costs of worldwide nuclear war in which even the fruits of victory would be ashes in our mouth -- but neither will we shrink from that risk at any time it must be faced.

Acting, therefore, in the defense of our own security and of the entire Western Hemisphere, and under the authority entrusted to me by the Constitution as endorsed by the Resolution of the Congress, I have directed that the following initial steps be taken immediately:

1) <u>First</u>: To halt this offensive build-up, a strict quarantine on all offensive military equipment under shipment to Cuba is being initiated. All ships of any kind bound for Cuba from whatever nation or port will, if found to contain cargoes of offensive weapons, be turned back. This quarantine will be extended, if needed, to other types of cargo and carriers. We are not at this time, however, denying the necessities of life as the Soviets attempted to do in their Berlin blockade of 1948.

2) <u>Second</u>: I have directed the continued and increased close surveillance of Cuba and its military build-up. The Foreign Ministers of the OAS, in their communique of October 6, rejected secrecy on such matters in this Hemisphere. Should these offensive military preparations continue, thus increasing the threat to the Hemisphere, further action will be justified. I have directed the Armed Forces to prepare for any eventualities; and I trust that in the interest of both the Cuban people and the Soviet technicians at the sites, the hazards to all concerned of continuing this threat will be recognized.

MORE   (MORE)

DOCUMENT 28: "Radio-TV Address of the President to the Nation from the White House,"
October 22, 1962.

PAGE 4 OF 5

Page 4

3) Third: It shall be the policy of this Nation to regard any
nuclear missile launched from Cuba against any nation in the
Western Hemisphere as an attack by the Soviet Union on the United
States, requiring a full retaliatory response upon the Soviet
Union.

4) Fourth: As a necessary military precaution, I have reinforced
our base at Guantanamo, evacuated today the dependents of our
personnel there, and ordered additional military units to be on
a standby alert basis.

5) Fifth: We are calling tonight for an immediate meeting of
the Organ of Consultation under the Organization of American
States, to consider this threat to hemispheric security and to
invoke Articles 6 and 8 of the Rio Treaty in support of all
necessary action. The United Nations Charter allows for regional
security arrangements -- and the nations of this Hemisphere
decided long ago against the military presence of outside powers.
Our other allies around the world have also been alerted.

6) Sixth: Under the Charter of the United Nations, we are asking
tonight that an emergency meeting of the Security Council be con-
voked without delay to take action against this latest Soviet
threat to world peace. Our resolution will call for the prompt
dismantling and withdrawal of all offensive weapons in Cuba, under
the supervision of UN observers, before the quarantine can be
lifted.

7) Seventh and finally: I call upon Chairman Khrushchev to halt
and eliminate this clandestine, reckless and provocative threat
to world peace and to stable relations between our two nations.
I call upon him further to abandon this course of world domination,
and to join in an historic effort to end the perilous arms race
and transform the history of man. He has an opportunity now to
move the world back from the abyss of destruction -- by returning
to his government's own words that it had no need to station missiles outside its own territory, and withdrawing these weapons
from Cuba -- by refraining from any action which will widen or
deepen the present crisis -- and then by participating in a search
for peaceful and permanent solutions.

        This Nation is prepared to present its case against
the Soviet threat to peace, and our own proposals for a peaceful
world, at any time and in any forum -- in the OAS, in the United
Nations, or in any other meeting that could be useful -- without
limiting our freedom of action. We have in the past made strenuous
efforts to limit the spread of nuclear weapons. We have proposed
the elimination of all arms and military bases in a fair and
effective disarmament treaty. We are prepared to discuss new
proposals for the removal of tensions on both sides -- including
the possibilities of a genuinely independent Cuba, free to determine its own destiny. We have no wish to war with the Soviet
Union -- for we are a peaceful people who desire to live in peace
with all other peoples.

        But it is difficult to settle or even discuss these
problems in an atmosphere of intimidation. That is why this latest
Soviet threat -- or any other threat which is made either
independently or in response to our actions this week -- must and
will be met with determination. Any hostile move anywhere in the

MORE

DOCUMENT 28: "Radio-TV Address of the President to the Nation from the White House," October 22, 1962.

PAGE 5 OF 5

Page 5

world against the safety and freedom of peoples to whom we are committed -- including in particular the brave people of West Berlin -- will be met by whatever action is needed.

Finally, I want to say a few words to the captive people of Cuba, to whom this speech is being directly carried by special radio facilities. I speak to you as a friend, as one who knows of your deep attachment to your fatherland, as one who shares your aspirations for liberty and justice for all. And I have watched and the American people have watched with deep sorrow how your nationalist revolution was betrayed -- and how your fatherland fell under foreign domination. Now your leaders are no longer Cuban leaders inspired by Cuban ideals. They are puppets and agents of an international conspiracy which has turned Cuba against your friends and neighbors in the Americas -- and turned it into the first Latin American country to become a target for nuclear war -- the first Latin American country to have these weapons on its soil.

These new weapons are not in your interest. They contribute nothing to your peace and well being. They can only undermine it. But this country has no wish to cause you to suffer or to impose any system upon you. We know that your lives and land are being used as pawns by those who deny you freedom.

Many times in the past, the Cuban people have risen to throw out tyrants who destroyed their liberty. And I have no doubt that most Cubans today look forward to the time when they will be truly free -- free from foreign domination, free to choose their own leaders, free to select their own system, free to own their own land, free to speak, and write, and worship without fear or degradation. And then shall Cuba be welcomed back to the society of free nations and to the associations of this Hemisphere.

My fellow citizens: Let no one doubt that this is a difficult and dangerous effort on which we have set out. No one can foresee precisely what course it will take or what costs or casualties will be incurred. Many months of sacrifice and self-discipline lie ahead -- months in which both our patience and our will will be tested -- months in which many threats and denunciations will keep us aware of our dangers. But the greatest danger of all would be to do nothing.

The path we have chosen for the present is full of hazards, as all paths are -- but it is the one most consistent with our character and courage as a nation and our commitments around the world. The cost of freedom is always high -- but Americans have always paid it. And one path we shall never choose, and that is the path of surrender or submission.

Our goal is not the victory of might, but the vindication of right -- not peace at the expense of freedom, but both peace and freedom, here in this Hemisphere, and, we hope, around the world. God willing, that goal will be achieved.

Thank you and good night.

END

DOCUMENT 29: Cable from Joint Chiefs of Staff, announcing DEFCON 3 military alert, October 23, 1962.

PAGE 1 OF 1

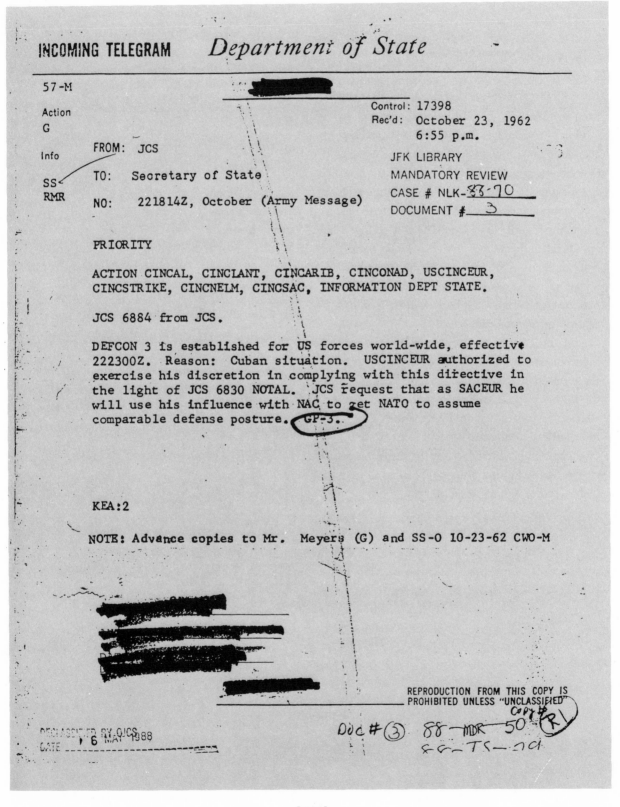

INCOMING TELEGRAM   *Department of State*

57-M

Action
G

Info

SS

RMR

FROM: JCS

TO: Secretary of State

NO: 221814Z, October (Army Message)

Control: 17398
Rec'd: October 23, 1962
          6:55 p.m.

JFK LIBRARY
MANDATORY REVIEW
CASE # NLK-88-70
DOCUMENT # 3

PRIORITY

ACTION CINCAL, CINCLANT, CINCARIB, CINCONAD, USCINCEUR,
CINCSTRIKE, CINCNELM, CINCSAC, INFORMATION DEPT STATE.

JCS 6884 from JCS.

DEFCON 3 is established for US forces world-wide, effective
222300Z. Reason: Cuban situation. USCINCEUR authorized to
exercise his discretion in complying with this directive in
the light of JCS 6830 NOTAL. JCS request that as SACEUR he
will use his influence with NAC to get NATO to assume
comparable defense posture. GP-3.

KEA:2

NOTE: Advance copies to Mr. Meyers (G) and SS-O 10-23-62 CWO-M

DECLASSIFIED BY OJCS
DATE   16 MAY 1988

Doc# ③ 88-MDR 50 R1

~~SECRET~~

[Embossed Seal of the USSR]

Moscow, October 23, 1962

Mr. President:

I have just received your letter, and have also acquainted myself with the text of your speech of October 22 regarding Cuba.

I must say frankly that the measures indicated in your statement constitute a serious threat to peace and to the security of nations. The United States has openly taken the path of grossly violating the United Nations Charter, the path of violating international norms of freedom of navigation on the high seas, the path of aggressive actions both against Cuba and against the Soviet Union.

The statement by the Government of the United States of America can only be regarded as undisguised interference in the internal affairs of the Republic of Cuba, The Soviet Union and other states. The United Nations Charter and international norms give no right to any state to institute in international waters the inspection of vessels bound for the shores of the Republic of Cuba.

And naturally, neither can we recognize the right of the United States to establish control over armaments which are necessary for the Republic of Cuba to strengthen its defense capability.

We reaffirm that the armaments which are in Cuba, regardless of the classification to which they may belong, are intended solely for defensive purposes in order to secure the Republic of Cuba against the attack of an aggressor.

His Excellency
    John Kennedy,
        President of the United States of America

I hope that the United States Government will display wisdom and renounce the actions pursued by you, which may lead to catastrophic consequances for world peace.

The viewpoint of the Soviet Government with regard to your statement of October 22 is set forth in a Statement of the Soviet Government, which is being transmitted to you through your Ambassador at Moscow.

[s] N. Khrushchev
N. Khrushchev

UNCLASSIFIED

THE WHITE HOUSE

WASHINGTON

TOP SECRET - SENSITIVE

October 23, 1962

Executive Committee Minutes, October 23, 1962, 10:00 am

1. Intelligence

The meeting began with a briefing by Mr. McCone in which, in addition to written material, he emphasized the strength of ~~efforts~~ evidence substantiating the non-participation of Cubans in Soviet missile installations in Cuba.

2. Unity on the Home Front

There was general discussion of the problem of adequate briefing of Members of the Congress and of the press on the way in which the crisis had developed and on the reasons for the decisions which had been taken. A number of assignments were given to individual members of the Committee for further work on this problem.

3. Blockade Effects Estimates

The President asked the Director of Central Intelligence for an analysis of effects of the blockade on Cuba, not to include food and medicine, and for comparable analysis of the effects of a comparable blockade on Berlin.

4. Items presented by the Department of Defense

a. The President approved plans for the issue of the Proclamation of Interdiction of ship delivery of offensive weapons to Cuba. The Proclamation was to be issued at 6:00 pm and the Interdiction to become effective at dawn October 24.

b. The President approved and later signed an Executive Order authorizing the extension of tours of duty of certain members of the Armed Forces.

c. The President approved the following contingency plan for action in the event of an incident affecting U-2 overflights. The President will be informed through SAC/DOD channels, and it is expected that if there is clear indication that the incident is the result of hostile action, the recommendation will be for immediate retaliation upon the most likely surface-to-air site involved in this action. The President delegated authority for decision on this point to the Secretary of Defense under the following conditions:

TOP SECRET - SENSITIVE

UNCLASSIFIED

(76 F 110)

11652

M. Hornblow

87

DOSO 1667 PB

UNCLASSIFIED

TOP SECRET - SENSITIVE   -2-   10/23/62

    (1) that the President himself should be unavailable

    (2) that evidence of hostile Cuban action should be very clear

    d. It was expected, but not definitely decided, that if hostile actions should continue after such a single incident and single retaliation, it would become necessary to take action to eliminate the effectiveness of surface-to-air missiles in Cuba.

    e. The Secretary reported that he was not ready to make a recommendation on air intercept of Soviet flights to Cuba, that he was maintaining aircraft on alert for prompt reaction against known missile sites, that preparationsfor invasion were proceeding at full speed, that the quarantine would initially exclude POL, though this decision should be reexamined continuously.

    f. The Attorney General was delegated to check the problem of the legal possibility of permitting foreign flag ships to participate in U. S. coastwise trade, in order to prevent shipping requirements for an invasion from disrupting U. S. commerce.

    g. The Secretary of Defense recommended, and the President approved, about six low-level reconnaissance flights for the purpose of obtaining still more persuasive photography of Soviet missile sites.

    h. The President, on hearing these reports, asked whether U. S. air forces in Southeastern United States were properly deployed against possible hostile reaction, and after discussion he directed that photographs be taken of U. S. airfields to show their current condition.

5. State Department business

    a. Secretary Ball reported the urgent need for persuasive evidence in New York as described by Ambassador Stevenson and Mr. McCloy, and the President directed Secretary Ball and Mr. McCone to work together to meet this requirement as well as possible.

    b. There was a brief discussion of possible reactions in Berlin, and the President indicated that he would wish to consider whether additional Soviet inspection of convoys would be acceptable. After the meeting, the President designated Assistant Secretary Nitze to be Chairman of a Subcommittee of the Executive Committee for Berlin Contingencies.

TOP SECRET - SENSITIVE   UNCLASSIFIED

BTF-Hillenbrand

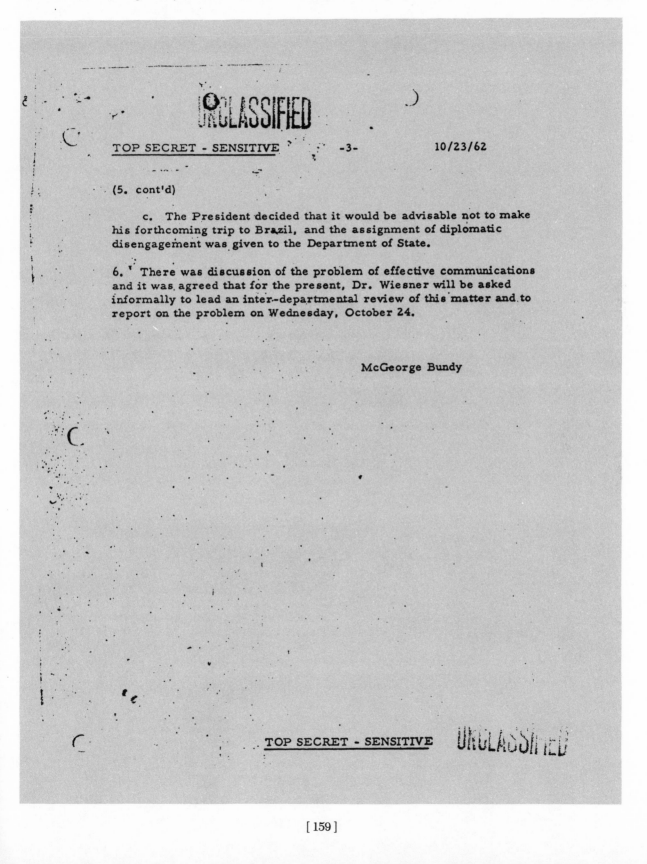

UNCLASSIFIED

TOP SECRET - SENSITIVE   -3-   10/23/62

(5. cont'd)

    c. The President decided that it would be advisable not to make his forthcoming trip to Brazil, and the assignment of diplomatic disengagement was given to the Department of State.

6. There was discussion of the problem of effective communications and it was agreed that for the present, Dr. Wiesner will be asked informally to lead an inter-departmental review of this matter and to report on the problem on Wednesday, October 24.

                              McGeorge Bundy

TOP SECRET - SENSITIVE   UNCLASSIFIED

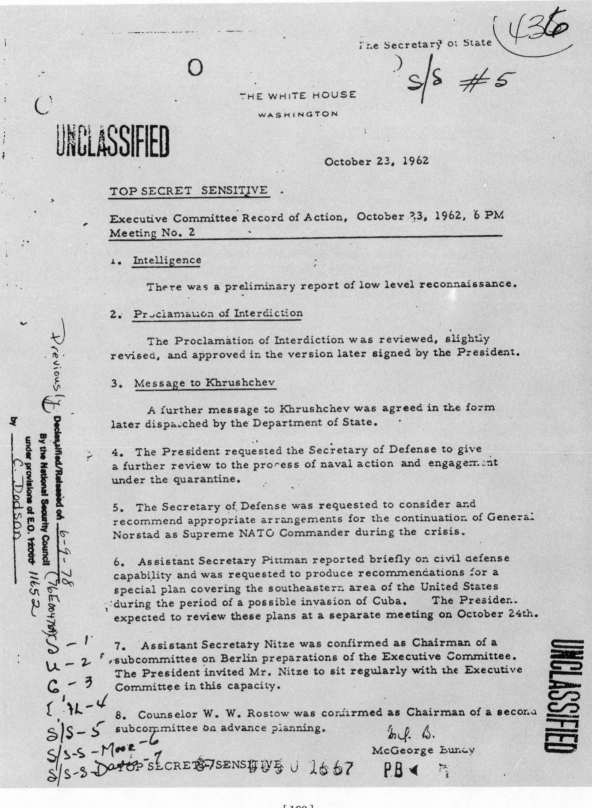

THE WHITE HOUSE

WASHINGTON

UNCLASSIFIED

The Secretary of State

S/S #5

October 23, 1962

TOP SECRET SENSITIVE .

Executive Committee Record of Action, October 23, 1962, 6 PM
Meeting No. 2

1. Intelligence

    There was a preliminary report of low level reconnaissance.

2. Proclamation of Interdiction

    The Proclamation of Interdiction was reviewed, slightly revised, and approved in the version later signed by the President.

3. Message to Khrushchev

    A further message to Khrushchev was agreed in the form later dispatched by the Department of State.

4. The President requested the Secretary of Defense to give a further review to the process of naval action and engagement under the quarantine.

5. The Secretary of Defense was requested to consider and recommend appropriate arrangements for the continuation of General Norstad as Supreme NATO Commander during the crisis.

6. Assistant Secretary Pittman reported briefly on civil defense capability and was requested to produce recommendations for a special plan covering the southeastern area of the United States during the period of a possible invasion of Cuba. The President expected to review these plans at a separate meeting on October 24th.

7. Assistant Secretary Nitze was confirmed as Chairman of a subcommittee on Berlin preparations of the Executive Committee. The President invited Mr. Nitze to sit regularly with the Executive Committee in this capacity.

8. Counselor W. W. Rostow was confirmed as Chairman of a second subcommittee on advance planning.

McGeorge Bundy

TOP SECRET SENSITIVE

UNCLASSIFIED

DOCUMENT 33: President Kennedy's Letter to Premier Khrushchev, October 23, 1962.

PAGE 1 OF 2

OUTGOING TELEGRAM Department of State

INDICATE: ☐ COLLECT
☐ CHARGE TO

~~CONFIDENTIAL~~

M

SS

ACTION: Amembassy MOSCOW 985   NIACT

EYES ONLY

OCT 23 ~~6 51 PM~~ '62

You should deliver following letter addressed by the President to Chairman Khrushchev immediately. This replaces message contained Deptel 982.

QUOTE

Dear Mr. Chairman:

I have received your letter of October twenty-third. I think you will recognize that the steps which started the current chain of events was the action of your Government in secretly furnishing offensive weapons to Cuba. We will be discussing this matter in the Security Council. In the meantime, I am concerned that we both show prudence and do nothing to allow events to make the situation more difficult to control than it already is.

I hope

Drafted by: U:GWBall:bc   10/23/62

White House - Mr. Bundy
S/S - Mr. Brubeck

Telegraphic transmission and classification approved by:

George W. Ball

DECLASSIFIED

~~CONFIDENTIAL~~

REPRODUCTION FROM TH
COPY IS PROHIBITED
UNLESS "UNCLASSIFIED"

FORM
8-61 DS-322   E.O. 11652, Sec. 3(E) and 5(D) or (E)
B) NARS, Date 2/25/74

Page 2 of telegram to American Embassy MOSCOW

CONFIDENTIAL

I hope that you will issue immediately the necessary instructions to your ships to observe the terms of the quarantine, the
basis of which was established by the vote of the Organization of
American States this afternoon, and which will go into effect at
1400 hours Greenwich time October twenty-four.

Sincerely,

JFK

UNQUOTE

RUSK

CONFIDENTIAL

~~SECRET~~
46234
T-94/T-24
Russian

[Embossed Seal of the USSR]
Ministry of Foreign Affairs of the USSR
Moscow, October 24, 1962

Mr. Ambassador:

Enclosed herewith is a letter from N.S. Khrushchev, Chairman of the Council of Ministers of the Union of Soviet Socialist Republics, to John F. Kennedy, President of the United States of America,

It is requested that this letter be transmitted to the President without delay.

Sincerely yours
[s] Smirnovski

Officer in Charge of
USA Bureau
Ministry of Foreign
Affairs, USSR

Enclosure: Letter from the Chairman of the Council of Ministers of USSR to the President of the United States.

Mr. Foy D. Kohler,
Ambassador of the United States of America,
Moscow.

[Embossed Seal of the USSR]

Dear Mr. President:

I have received your letter of October 23, have studied it, and am answering you.

Just imagine, Mr. President, that we had presented you with the the conditions of an ultimatum which you have presented us by your action. How would you have reacted to this? I think that you would have been indignant at such a step on our part. And this would have been understandable to us.

In presenting us with these conditions, you, Mr. President, have flung a challenge at us. Who asked you to do this? By what right did you do this? Our ties with the Republic of Cuba, like our relations with other states, regardless of what kind of states they may be, concern only the two countries between which these relations exist. And if we now speak of the quarantine to which your letter refers, a quarantine may be established, according to accepted international practice, only by agreement of states between themselves, and not by some third party. Quarantines exist, for example, on agricultural goods and products. But in this case the question is in no way one of quarantine, but rather of far more serious things, and you yourself understand this.

You, Mr. President, are not declaring a quarantine, but rather are setting forth an ultimatum and threatening that if we do not give in to your demands you will use force. Consider what you are saying! And you want to persuade me to agree to this! What would it mean to agree to these demands? It would mean guiding oneself in one's relations with other countries not by reason, but by submitting to arbitrariness. You are no longer appealing to reason, but wish to intimidate us.

No, Mr. President, I cannot agree to this, and I think that in your own heart you recognize that I am correct. I am convinced that in my place you would act the same way.

Reference to the decision of the Organization of American States cannot in any way substantiate the demands now advanced by the United States. This Organization has absolutely no authority or basis for adopting decisions such as the one you speak of in your letter. Therefore, we do not recognize these decisions. International law exists and universally recognized norms of conduct exist. We firmly adhere to the principles of international law and observe strictly the norms which regulate navigation on the high seas, in international waters. We observe these norms and enjoy the rights recognized by all states.

You wish to compel us to renounce the rights that every sovereign state enjoys, you are trying to legislate in questions of international law, and you are violating the universally accepted norms of that law. And you are doing all this not only out of hatred for the Cuban people and its government, but also because of considerations of the election campaign in the United States. What morality, what law can justify such an approach by the American Government to international affairs? No such morality or law can be found, because the actions of the United States with regard to Cuba constitute outright banditry or, if you like, the folly of degenerate imperialism. Unfortunately, such folly can bring grave suffering to the peoples of all countries, and to no lesser degree to the American people themselves, since the United States has completely lost its former isolation with the advent of modern types of armament.

Therefore, Mr. President, if you coolly weigh the situation which has developed, not giving way to passions, you will understand that the Soviet Union cannot fail to reject the arbitrary demands of the United States. When you confront us with such conditions, try to put yourself in our place and consider how the United States would react to these conditions. I do not doubt that if someone attempted to dictate similar conditions to you—the United States—you would reject such an attempt. And we also say—no.

The Soviet government considers that the violation of the freedom to use international waters and international air space is an act of aggression which pushes mankind toward the abyss of a world nuclear-missile war. Therefore, the Soviet Government cannot instruct the captains of Soviet vessels recognized by all states.

You wish to compel us to renounce the rights that every sovereign state enjoys, you are trying to legislate in questions of international law, and you are violating the universally accepted norms of that law. And you are doing all this not only out of hatred for the Cuban people and its government, but also because of considerations of the election campaign in the United States. What morality, what law can justify such an approach by the American Government to international affairs? No such morality or law can be found, because the actions of the United States with regard to Cuba constitute outright banditry or, if you like, the folly of degenerate imperialism. Unfortunately, such folly can bring grave suffering to the peoples of all countries, and to no lesser degree to the American people themselves, since the United States has completely lost its former isolation with the advent of modern types of armament.

Therefore, Mr. President, if you coolly weigh the situation which has developed, not giving way to passions, you will understand that the Soviet Union cannot fail to reject the arbitrary demands of the United States. When you confront us with such conditions, try to put yourself in our place and consider how the United States would react to these conditions. I do not doubt that if someone attempted to dictate similar conditions to you—the United States—you would reject such an attempt. And we also say—no.

The Soviet government considers that the violation of the freedom to use international waters and international air space is an act of aggression which pushes mankind toward the abyss of a world nuclear-missile war. Therefore, the Soviet Government cannot instruct the captains of Soviet vessels bound for Cuba to observe the orders of American naval forces blockading that Island. Our instructions to Soviet mariners are to observe strictly the universally accepted norms of navigation in international waters and not to retreat one step from them. And if the American side violates these rules, it must realize what responsibility will rest upon it in that case. Naturally we will not simply be bystanders with regard to piratical acts by American ships on the high seas. We will then be forced on our part to take the measures we consider necessary and adequate in order to protect our rights. We have everything necessary to do so.

Respectfully,
[s] N. Khrushchev
N. Khrushchev

Moscow
October 24, 1962

F780011-070

THE WHITE HOUSE
WASHINGTON

October 24, 1962

UNCLASSIFIED

TOP SECRET - SENSITIVE

Executive Committee Record of Action, October 24, 1962, 10:00 A.M.,
Meeting No. 3

1. Intelligence

The Director of Central Intelligence summarized the intelligence briefing. The President directed that the Secretary of the Treasury and the Director of Central Intelligence take immediate action to obtain more "black boxes.

2. Defense Operations

a. The Secretary of Defense presented photographs of dispersal of existing U. S. planes in the southeast U. S., and the Chairman of the Joint Chiefs of Staff reported that modifications of readiness were being considered to permit improvement of the situation.

b. The Secretary of Defense reported the plans for naval interception, noted the presence of a submarine near the more interesting ships, and warned that radio silence might be imposed. There was discussion of the problem █████████████████████████

3. In the middle of the meeting there were reports that certain Soviet ships had appeared to have stopped or turned back, and the President directed that there be no interception of any target for at least another hour while clarifying information was sought.

4. Dr. Wiesner presented an initial briefing on the communications situation and the President directed that most urgent action be taken by State, Defense and CIA to improve communications worldwide,

UNCLASSIFIED TOP SECRET SENSITIVE

Partially Declassified/Released on 8-18-88
under provisions of E.O. 12356 (F88-822)
by N. Menan, National Security Council

87- D0S0 1667 PB

F780011-0706

- 2 -

TOP SECRET SENSITIVE

but particularly in the Caribbean area. After the meeting, the
President, in discussion with the Secretary of State and the
Secretary of Defense, directed that special responsibilities
should be assigned to designated individuals and a plan for this
purpose will be presented for approval by State, Defense and
White House officers at the next meeting of the Committee.

5. The President directed that State and USIA should give
immediate attention to increasing understanding in Europe of the
fact that any Berlin crisis would be fundamentally the result of
Soviet ambition and pressure, and that inaction by the United
States in the face of the challenge in Cuba would have been more
and not less dangerous for Berlin.

6. The President directed that a senior representative of USIA
should regularly be present at meetings of the Executive Committee.

McGeorge Bundy

TOP SECRET SENSITIVE

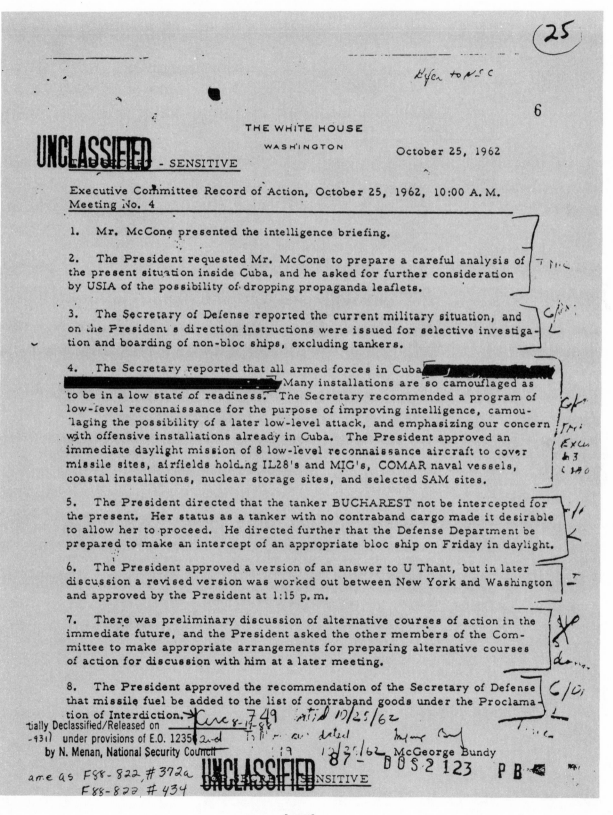

(25)

Refer to NSC

6

THE WHITE HOUSE

WASHINGTON   October 25, 1962

UNCLASSIFIED - SENSITIVE

Executive Committee Record of Action, October 25, 1962, 10:00 A. M.
Meeting No. 4

1.   Mr. McCone presented the intelligence briefing.

2.   The President requested Mr. McCone to prepare a careful analysis of
the present situation inside Cuba, and he asked for further consideration
by USIA of the possibility of dropping propaganda leaflets.

3.   The Secretary of Defense reported the current military situation, and
on the President's direction instructions were issued for selective investigation and boarding of non-bloc ships, excluding tankers.

4.   The Secretary reported that all armed forces in Cuba ▮▮▮▮▮▮▮▮▮▮
▮▮▮▮▮▮▮▮▮▮▮▮▮▮▮▮▮▮▮▮▮ Many installations are so camouflaged as
to be in a low state of readiness. The Secretary recommended a program of
low-level reconnaissance for the purpose of improving intelligence, camou-
flaging the possibility of a later low-level attack, and emphasizing our concern
with offensive installations already in Cuba. The President approved an
immediate daylight mission of 8 low-level reconnaissance aircraft to cover
missile sites, airfields holding IL28's and MIG's, COMAR naval vessels,
coastal installations, nuclear storage sites, and selected SAM sites.

5.   The President directed that the tanker BUCHAREST not be intercepted for
the present. Her status as a tanker with no contraband cargo made it desirable
to allow her to proceed. He directed further that the Defense Department be
prepared to make an intercept of an appropriate bloc ship on Friday in daylight.

6.   The President approved a version of an answer to U Thant, but in later
discussion a revised version was worked out between New York and Washington
and approved by the President at 1:15 p. m.

7.   There was preliminary discussion of alternative courses of action in the
immediate future, and the President asked the other members of the Committee to make appropriate arrangements for preparing alternative courses
of action for discussion with him at a later meeting.

8.   The President approved the recommendation of the Secretary of Defense
that missile fuel be added to the list of contraband goods under the Proclamation of Interdiction.

McGeorge Bundy

UNCLASSIFIED SENSITIVE

same as F88-822 #372a
F88-822 #434

DOCUMENT 37: Dillon group discussion paper, "Scenario for Airstrike Against Offensive Missile Bases and Bombers in Cuba," October 25, 1962.

PAGE 1 OF 4

[handwritten at top] ...y ...retary Dillon's group at Bundy request. For possible
discussion 5:00 meeting 10 25 62.

[handwritten] 32

TOP SECRET -- SENSITIVE   *[handwritten]* SEC...

[handwritten] DILLON PAPER

Final Draft

—Scenario for Airstrike against offensive
missile bases and bombers in Cuba.

[handwritten] In response to
Meeting 10/25 am
para 7 Minute 4

ADVANTAGES

1. Carries out President's pledge to eliminate offensive
threat to U.S. and Hemisphere from Cuba and avoids any erosion
of U.S. momentum and position. The pledge carried out shows
that U.S. has will to fight and to protect vital interests
(of great importance vis-a-vis Berlin).

2. Since directed at offensive weapons, keeps issue
focused on Soviet nuclear presence in Cuba in defiance of OAS
and majority of Security Council.

3. Sharp, possible one time action, may carry smaller
risks of further escalation than a series of confrontations
over a period of time. Soviet decision to risk major war
unlikely to be decisively affected by this action in an area
non-vital to the Soviets.

4. Prompt action will avoid danger of a growth of hands-
off Cuba movement throughout Latin America which might make it
increasingly difficult to strike at offensive weapons. Present
willingness of Latin Americans to support strong action probably
cannot be maintained indefinitely.

5. Signals clearly that U.S. not prepared to bargain bases
in Cuba for positions in Berlin, NATO and elsewhere.

6. It could demonstrate to Cubans, Castro and others, the
weakness of Soviet position in Cuba. In the absence of a strong
Soviet reaction in defense of Cuba, we would start the process
of disenchantment and disaffection requisite to undermining
Castro and Cuban reliance on the Soviet Union. We would also
weaken any tendencies to rely on Soviets elsewhere in world.

7. Removes a military threat to U.S. from Cuban territory.

8. Denies Khrushchev a possible cheap victory through
successful maintenance of offensive weapons in Cuba.

[handwritten/stamped] DEPARTMENT OF STATE 19 DEC ...

[handwritten] DIST.
S, u, G, S/AL, S/S, S/S-s—Davis Mo
—G/PM----

DOCUMENT 37: Dillon group discussion paper, "Scenario for Airstrike Against Offensive Missile Bases and Bombers in Cuba," October 25, 1962.

PAGE 2 OF 4

Final Draft

—

TOP SECRET - SENSITIVE

DISADVANTAGES

1. This action may force Khrushchev to react strongly and could result in some type of war. Khrushchev will not order launch of a missile from Cuba unless he is ready for war essentially on other grounds. There is greater likelihood of a riposte in kind. However, it is unlikely that the risks of major war are greater than through escalation of blockade.

2. There is remote possibility that some local Soviet commander in Cuba may order firing of a missile.

3. Adverse effect on U. S. image of initiation of use of force against a small country. This can be minimized by making attack selective and focused on Soviet offensive weapons. At same time there would be positive increments to our image from demonstration of clear willingness to take on the Soviets in protection of our vital interests.

4. Unless carefully handled could damage long-range U.S.-Cuban relations.

5. May not totally eliminate offensive weapons thus calling for follow up attacks and/or invasion, unless full and unlimited international inspection is agreed to.

DOCUMENT 37: Dillon group discussion paper, "Scenario for Airstrike Against Offensive Missile Bases and Bombers in Cuba," October 25, 1962.

PAGE 3 OF 4

Final Draft

TOP SECRET -- SENSITIVE

PREREQUISITES FOR DECISION

    1. Veto of U.S. resolution in Security Council.

    2. Evidence that Soviets have continued build-up of existing offensive capability in Cuba in defiance of Presidential warning and OAS resolution.

ACTIONS PRIOR OR SIMULTANEOUS TO STRIKE

    1. White House statement that offensive build-up is continuing, a dangerous and provocative act, which increases gravity of situation. Repeats warning for those engaged in this work.

    2. Delivery of copy of White House statement to Cuban representative at UN.

    3. Evacuation warning (as long as militarily feasible) to personnel in strike areas by leaflet drop. A strike plan designed to accomplish mission with minimum damage to non-military targets.

    4. Inform OAS (Chairman) shortly in advance of strike.

    5. Arrange for Ambassadors to notify Latin American heads of state at zero hour.

    6. Inform NATO Allies and others at appropriate time.

    7. Letter to K delivered at zero hour, describing action and indicating regret that continuation of work at offensive sites had forced action, limited nature of operation, our effort to limit personnel losses, and calling for immediate consultations to reduce world-wide tensions.

DOCUMENT 37: Dillon group discussion paper, "Scenario for Airstrike Against Offensive Missile Bases and Bombers in Cuba," October 25, 1962.

PAGE 4 OF 4

TOP SECRET -- SENSITIVE

Final Draft

FOLLOW UP ACTIONS

    1. Continuation of close air surveillance.

    2. Be prepared to hit SAM sites and airfields if reconnaissance planes attacked.

    3. Immediate report to Organ of Consultation (OAS) and adoption of resolution requesting Soviets to evacuate offensive forces from Cuba under international inspection.

    4. Report to UN Security Council explaining limited nature of operation and requesting immediate despatch of UN observer team to Cuba.

    5. Maintenance of blockade extended to include POL until clear evidence is available that offensive bases have been eliminated.

    6. Major Presidential address including special message to Cuban people.

    7. Appropriate leaflet drops over Cuba.

REF NSC
R

(433)

A °

UNCLASSIFIED

THE WHITE HOUSE

WASHINGTON

TOP SECRET - SENSITIVE   October 25, 1962

Executive Committee Record of Action, October 25, 1962, 5:00 PM
Meeting No. 5

1. Mr. McCone presented the intelligence briefing which contained no major new information.

2. The Secretary of Defense reported on the current military situation. The Lebanese ship which was to be boarded turned back and therefore no ship so far had been boarded.

3. The Secretary of State reported on the political situation, calling attention to one suggestion, namely, the denuclearization of Latin America, which he thought would be supported by a large number of UN members. He referred to preliminary discussions which are to take place during the next two or three days between U Thant and Zorin on the one side and Stevenson and U Thant on the other. He felt that any talks could not go on very long because the missiles in Cuba were becoming operational and the IL-28s would soon be dangerous.

4. The Secretary of Defense recommended, and the President approved:

    a. A low-level air reconnaissance tomorrow.
       Planning for
    b. /a low-level reconnaissance tomorrow night which would be achieved by dropping flares to obtain photographs as well as to produce a psychological effect.

    c. Permitting the East German passenger ship Volker Freundschaft to enter Cuban waters.

5. Three draft analyses of the next major move were discussed in a preliminary way -- a military path, a political path, and an intensified economic path.

6. The President, referring to the second message which he has just sent to U Thant, said any incident should be avoided until after we heard, probably tomorrow afternoon, whether Khrushchev had accepted or rejected U Thant's latest proposal. A decision as to whether to stop the tanker Grazny, if it continues on its course toward Cuba, can be made at that time.

S
U
S/A:
SIP

excerpts to
Io G/PM, INR
ARA

McGeorge Bundy

TOP SECRET - SENSITIVE   UNCLASSIFIED

87- 00S0 1667   PB

October 25, 1962

Dear Mr. Chairman:

I have received your letter of October 24, and I regret very much that you still do not appear to understand what it is that has moved us in this matter.

The sequence of events is clear. In August there were reports of important shipments of military equipment and technicians from the Soviet Union to Cuba. In early September I indicated very plainly that the United States would regard any shipment of offensive weapons as presenting the gravest issues. After that time, this Government received the most explicit assurances from your Government and its representatives, both publicly and privately, that no offensive weapons were being sent to Cuba. If you will review the statement issued by Tass in September, you will see how clearly this assurance was given.

In reliance on these solemn assurances I urged restraint upon those in this country who were urging action in this matter at that time. And then I learned beyond doubt what you have not denied -- namely, that all these public assurances were false and that your military people had set out recently to establish a set of missile bases in Cuba. I ask you to recognize clearly, Mr. Chairman, that it was not I who issued the first challenge in this case, and that in the light of this record these activities in Cuba required the responses I have announced.

I repeat my regret that these events should cause a deterioration in our relations. I hope that your Government will take the necessary action to permit a restoration of the earlier situation.

Sincerely yours,

John F. Kennedy

N. S. Khrushchev
Chairman of the Council of Ministers of the
Union of Soviet Socialist Republics
Moscow USSR

DOCUMENT 40: General Maxwell Taylor, "Timing Factors" for implementing military attacks and invasion of Cuba, October 25, 1962.

PAGE 1 OF 1

TOP SECRET

OFF SECY OF THE JOINT CHIEFS OF STAFF
WASHINGTON 25, D. C.

JCSM-821-62

OCT 25 1962

MEMORANDUM FOR THE SECRETARY OF DEFENSE

Subject: Timing Factors

1. In order to assure understanding of the timing factors which govern the implementation of military actions related to Cuba, the following list shows the time from the receipt of the implementation order to initiation of action on or over Cuba.

 a. Low-level reconnaissance of selected targets. Reaction Time - 2 hours.

 b. Reprisal strike to hit a single SA-2 site. Reaction Time - 2 hours.

 c. Air strike against all SA-2 sites. Reaction Time - 2 hours (contingent on maintenance of present posture).

 d. Full air strike. Reaction Time - 12 hours. (CINCLANT OPLAN 312).

 e. Implement CINCLANT OPLAN 316. Reaction Time - Initial assault, Decision Day + 7 days. All assault and essential support forces ashore by Decision Day + 18 days, perhaps somewhat earlier.

2. Invasion planning is being concentrated on OPLAN 316 and measures to make a coordinated assault on Strike Day + 7 with the remainder of landing and essential support forces being put ashore in the shortest possible time. Because of the vulnerability of airborne forces while in flight to ground and aircraft fire, all or most of the 7 day interval between Strike Day and D-Day will be necessary to neutralize or eliminate the hostile air and ground capability.

For the Joint Chiefs of Staff:

MAXWELL D. TAYLOR
Chairman
Joint Chiefs of Staff

Copy 1 of 9 Copies each

of 1 13 es series "A"

Reproduction of this document in whole or in part is prohibited except with permission of the issuing office.

DOWNGRADED AT 3 YEAR INTERVALS;
DECLASSIFIED AFTER 12 YEARS.
DOD DIR 5200.10

TOP SECRET

Secret Control No. 6856

DOCUMENT 41: CINCLANT's request to have tactical nuclear weapons available for U.S. invasion force, December 29, 1962.

PAGE 1 OF 2

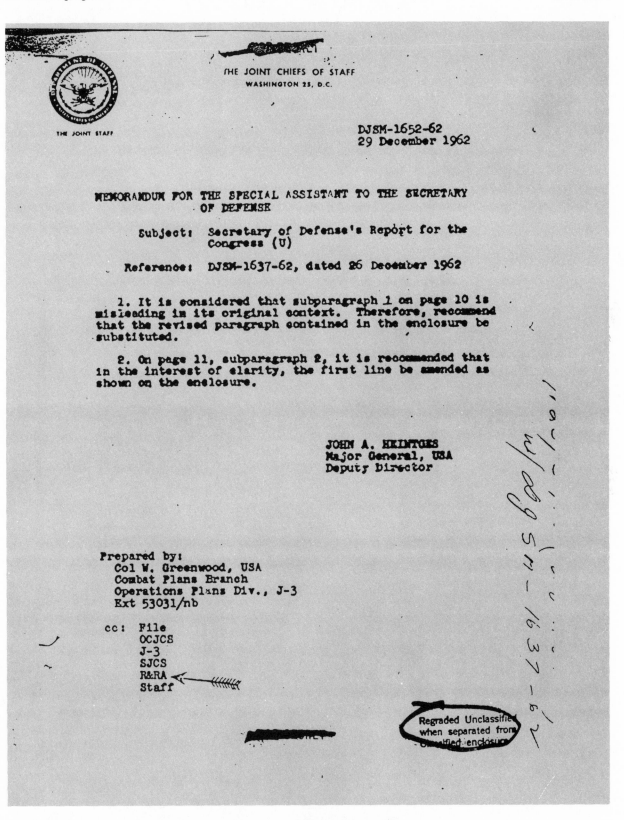

THE JOINT CHIEFS OF STAFF
WASHINGTON 25, D.C.

THE JOINT STAFF

DJSM-1652-62
29 December 1962

MEMORANDUM FOR THE SPECIAL ASSISTANT TO THE SECRETARY
OF DEFENSE

Subject: Secretary of Defense's Report for the
Congress (U)

Reference: DJSM-1637-62, dated 26 December 1962

1. It is considered that subparagraph 1 on page 10 is
misleading in its original context. Therefore, recommend
that the revised paragraph contained in the enclosure be
substituted.

2. On page 11, subparagraph 2, it is recommended that
in the interest of clarity, the first line be amended as
shown on the enclosure.

JOHN A. HEINTGES
Major General, USA
Deputy Director

Prepared by:
Col W. Greenwood, USA
Combat Plans Branch
Operations Plans Div., J-3
Ext 53031/nb

cc: File
OCJCS
J-3
SJCS
R&RA
Staff

Regraded Unclassified
when separated from
classified enclosure

[175]

DOCUMENT 41: CINCLANT's request to have tactical nuclear weapons available for U.S. invasion force, December 29, 1962.

PAGE 2 OF 2

ENCLOSURE

CHANGES TO ENCLOSURE TO DJSM-1637-62, 26 December 1962 (U)

1. Page 10, subparagraph 1. Delete and substitute the following:

"1. CINCLANT's original plan did not contemplate the use of nuclear weapons in any Cuban operation. However, when a determination was made that nuclear capable FROG (Free Rocket Over Ground) missiles were present in Cuba, CINCLANT expressed his concern, and proposed to have tactical nuclear weapons readily available in his invasion force. These weapons would be used only in retaliation for the employment of nuclear weapons against US forces. The Joint Chiefs of Staff approved only so much of CINCLANT's proposal that authorized him to take nuclear capable delivery systems (e. g., 8 inch howitzers and Honest John rockets) into Cuba, but did not authorize the introduction into Cuba of nuclear weapons themselves without further JCS approval."

2. Page 11, subparagraph 2. First line, modify as follows:

"2. Secondly, although not originally included in the plan, the 5th Infantry Division . . . ."

DOCUMENT 42: Bromley Smith, "Summary Record of NSC Executive Committee Meeting
October 26, 1962, 10:00 A.M."

PAGE 1 OF 7

SANITIZED COPY

Summary Record of NSC Executive Committee Meeting No. 6,
October 26, 1962, 10:00 AM

Director McCone summarized the attached intelligence memorandum,
including a statement on the current status of Soviet air readiness.

Mr. McCone described the celebration which took place in Havana
following the arrival of the tanker Bucharest which had been allowed
to pass the quarantine line because it was carrying only oil, which
is not now contraband. He said non-Bloc ships could be used to carry
military materials if they had been chartered on a bare boat basis by
the Russians.

Mr. Bundy reported that three subcommittees are at work -- one on
Berlin, chaired by Paul Nitze, one on forward planning, chaired by
Walt Rostow, and one on worldwide communications problems, chaired
by William Orrick, who is working closely with the Defense Communications Agency.

Mr. Bundy called attention to the civil defense problem and obtained
agreement that no crash program would be undertaken now, although

TOP SECRET SENSITIVE

DOCUMENT 42: Bromley Smith, "Summary Record of NSC Executive Committee Meeting
October 26, 1962, 10:00 A.M."

PAGE 2 OF 7

TOP SECRET SENSITIVE — 2 — FI, 4

preliminary measures are to be initiated. He referred to the amount
of sensitive information which has been leaking to the press and urged
that information about future actions must be more carefully guarded.

Secretary McNamara reported on the status of the quarantine. The
Defense Department was authorized to release information on the
boarding of the Lebanese ship, the Marucla, the first dry cargo ship
which had been loaded in a Soviet port. In the event that comparisons
were made between stopping the Lebanese ship and permitting an East
German ship to go through the quarantine line, the point will be made
that the East German ship carried only passengers.

Secretary McNamara read a list of Bloc ships and their locations and noted that there would be no intercepts at sea today. The
tanker Graznyy is apparently moving but will not cross the line today.
He suggested that shortly we should embargo fuel used by bombers
and substances from which airplane fuel is made, i.e. petroleum
products.

The President suggested that if we decide to embargo bomber fuel,
we should also mention the fact that we were embargoeing fuel which
was contributing to the operational capability of the strategic missiles.

Secretary Rusk asked that POL not be embargoed for at least twenty-
four hours in order to avoid upsetting the U Thant talks now under way
in New York.

Under Secretary Ball asked for agreement on the embargo of petroleum
as the next step in the effort to increase pressures -- the timing of the
embargo to be decided later in relation to the New York talks.

Secretary Dillon stated his reservations concerning this course of
action. He said it ended up in stopping Soviet ships. Thus, a confrontation with the Russians would not be over the missiles, but over
Soviet ships. He believed we should go for the missiles rather than
force a confrontation with the USSR at sea.

A decision on adding petroleum to the embargo list was delayed until the
political path was decided upon.

Secretary McNamara pointed out that construction on the strategic missile
sites in Cuba was continuing. He asked that public announcement be made

TOP SECRET SENSITIVE

DOCUMENT 42: Bromley Smith, "Summary Record of NSC Executive Committee Meeting October 26, 1962, 10:00 A.M."

PAGE 3 OF 7

F1.5

- 3 -

of our continuation of air surveillance. He recommended that daylight reconnaissance measures be flown today and a night mission tonight, including the dropping of flares.

Secretary Rusk asked that the night mission not be flown because of the unfortunate effect which it might have on the U Thant negotiations in New York.

Secretary McNamara thought that one way of avoiding reaction to night reconnaissance was to inform the Cubans and the Russians in advance that we were initiating such flights.

Ambassador Stevenson opposed any public announcement of our surveillance activities.

The President directed that we dramatize the fact that the missile buildup in Cuba is continuing. He authorized daylight reconnaissance measures but decided to delay night flights.

Secretary Rusk praised Ambassador Stevenson's UN performance. He urged that USIA keep the pressure on the Cuban people and mentioned the dropping of leaflets over Cuba.

Acting Director Wilson requested that better aerial pictures be made available to USIA for distribution. The President authorized the use of any reconnaissance pictures, including those used by Ambassador Stevenson in his UN speech.

- Secretary Rusk summarized political actions now under way. He said the object of the talks with U Thant today was to set up some form of negotiations with the Russians in New York. The objective would be to obtain a commitment from the Russians that there would be no further construction at the missile sites in Cuba, no further Soviet military shipments, the defuzing of existing weapons in Cuba, UN inspection of all nuclear-capable missiles, and an observer corps on the ground in Cuba of 350 technically able inspectors. The U.S. quarantine would continue until a UN quarantine is in place. UN teams would be put into specified Cuban ports. U.S. Navy ships would stay close to all Cuban ports to ensure that there were no landings unknown to the UN inspectors and no cargoes landed anywhere which UN inspectors did not see.

Mr. McCloy stated that our quarantine was vital and should be kept in place until the Russians had accepted all of our conditions.

TOP SECRET - SENSITIVE

DOCUMENT 42: Bromley Smith, "Summary Record of NSC Executive Committee Meeting October 26, 1962, 10:00 A.M."

PAGE 4 OF 7

- 4 -

Secretary Rusk pointed out that we must make clear to U Thant that the quarantine is related to the Soviet missiles rather than to Soviet military shipments to Cuba.

(5)(2) + (3)

Secretary Rusk felt that it was better for us not to participate in such action as would be necessary if it were done by an organization, i. e. the OAS, to which we belong.

The President noted that the plan proposed by Brazil not only calls for an atomic-free zone in Latin America, but it also encompasses a guarantee of the territorial integrity on all Latin American States. He asked whether we could commit ourselves not to invade Cuba. Secretary Rusk commented that we are committed not to invade Cuba, having signed the UN Charter and the Rio Treaty.

TOP SECRET SENSITIVE

DOCUMENT 42: Bromley Smith, "Summary Record of NSC Executive Committee Meeting October 26, 1962, 10:00 A.M."

PAGE 5 OF 7

~~TOP SECRET SENSITIVE~~ - 5 - F1, 7

S(a)(b)* (b)

Secretary Rusk read a draft cable [   ] In commenting on the draft cable, Mr. Nitze called attention to the importance of getting Soviet missiles out urgently.

Mr. McCone expressed his dislike of a situation involving continued control of Cuba by Castro. Even if the Soviet missiles are removed, Castro, if he is left in control, will be in an excellent position to undertake the Communization of Latin America.

Secretary Rusk said the present position is that Cuba ties to the USSR are not negotiable. Mr. Bundy pointed out, and the President agreed, that our objective was to get the Soviet missiles out of Cuba.

The President said work on the missile sites has to cease and we have to verify what is going on at the sites every day during the talks in New York. As to the message to Castro, he agreed in general, but wanted to have another look at it. He doubted that it would do any good, but it might be undertaken if done now with the greatest urgency.

Ambassador Stevenson discussed the immediate negotiations now under way with U Thant and the longer talks which would follow if agreement can be reached with the Russians in New York. He said the immediate talks were aimed at getting a 24-48-hour standstill on the missile buildup in Cuba. He acknowledged that in these talks it would be impossible to obtain an agreement to make the weapons inoperable. He wanted to know whether he should seek a standstill on all Soviet arms or only offensive weapons. He would seek to get a commitment that there be no further construction, but it would not be possible to set up a system to ensure that the weapons were made inoperable and kept inoperable. In addition, he needed to know whether in return we would be prepared to suspend the quarantine.

Ambassador Stevenson said the aim of the longer term talks would be the withdrawal from this hemisphere of the strategic missiles and the dismantlement of existing sites. He predicted that the Russians would ask us for a new guarantee of the territorial integrity of Cuba and the dismantlement of U.S. strategic missiles in Turkey.

Mr. McCone disagreed with Ambassador Stevenson's linking of Soviet missiles in Cuba to U.S. missiles in Turkey. He said the Soviet weapons

~~TOP SECRET SENSITIVE~~

DOCUMENT 42: Bromley Smith, "Summary Record of NSC Executive Committee Meeting October 26, 1962, 10:00 A.M."

PAGE 6 OF 7

- 6 -

F1, 8

in Cuba were pointed at our heart and put us under great handicap in continuing to carry out our commitments to the free world. He urged that we do not drop the quarantine until the Soviet missiles are out of Cuba. He believed that we must keep up the momentum so far achieved by the quarantine.

The President said we will get the Soviet strategic missiles out of Cuba only by invading Cuba or by trading. He doubted that the quarantine alone would produce a withdrawal of the weapons. He said our objective should be to prevent further military shipments, further construction at missile sites, and to get some means of inspection.

Mr. McCone urged that any inspectors sent to Cuba be U.S. inspectors knowledgeable about strategic missiles.

The President said he understood Ambassador Stevenson to be asking for time during which he would try to negotiate the withdrawal of the missiles.

Secretary Rusk doubted that we could get any pre-conditions to negotiation.

Secretary Dillon agreed that the Soviets could not back down merely in return for dropping the quarantine.

Mr. Nitze called attention to the importance of obtaining a guarantee that the nuclear missiles would be disassembled from their launchers.

Mr. Bundy said negotiations for a standstill or a standdown were not enough for our security because we must press, in addition, for guaranteed inspection of Cuba.

Secretary Dillon said we could not negotiate for two weeks under the missile threat which now exists in Cuba.

The President noted that there appeared to be little support for Ambassador Stevenson's plan. If the quarantine would not result in the Soviets withdrawing the missiles, what will we do if negotiations break down?

Mr. Bundy said when the interim 24-48-hour talks fail, then our choice would be to expand the blockade or remove the missiles by air attack.

DOCUMENT 42: Bromley Smith, "Summary Record of NSC Executive Committee Meeting October 26, 1962, 10:00 A.M."

PAGE 7 OF 7

- 7 - F, 9

General Taylor urged that we increase our reconnaissance activity in order to keep informed as to what was happening in Cuba.

The President decided to delay night reconnaissance missions, at least until the Soviets turn down U Thant's proposal. He also agreed that we should announce publicly that construction work at the missile sites in Cuba was going on and that, therefore, we will continue our aerial reconnaissance flights. The President also wanted attention called by a White House spokesman to his earlier speech which insisted that work at the missile sites in Cuba cease. The President decided that a presentation of the current situation should be made to the Congressional Leaders.

Bromley Smith

DOCUMENT 43: John Scali's notes of first meeting with Soviet embassy counselor and KGB officer Alexandr Fomin, October 26, 1962.

PAGE 1 OF 1

From John Scali to Hilsman:
(Secretary has in hand)

O—Master

act. 27 (3

alexandr s. fomin, sov emby counselor, at lunch
which he sought urgently, asks if state would be
interested in settlement of cuban crisis along
these lines:

> bases would be dismantled under united nations
> supervision and castro would pledge not to
> accept offensive weapons of any kind, ever,
> in return for us. pledge not to invade cuba.

I said I didn't know but that pershaps
this is something that could be talked about he
said if stevenson pursued this line, zorin would
be interested. asked that i check with state and
let him know. he gave me his home telephone number
so I could call him tonight, if necessary.

formin claimed that cuban delegate to un
during secrurity council debate asked for such no-
invasion assurances in return for dismantling
but that he got no reply. i told him I'd followed
the un debate very carefully but could not recall
any such remarks on cuban's part.

fomin also said russia had been forced
"to make some concessions" to communist china
in order to convince them to stop the fighting
against india. he declined to say what under
my my questioning. but he recalled they
hadn't helped the chicoms with nuclear weapons
or conventional weapons in the past, even tanks,
and hinted it might be aid in the conventional
field.

scali

Mc M # 4

cc. Mr Ball # 5
Bundy # 3

Mr Johnson —
Smith # 2

Amb. Thompson —

INR —

DEPARTMENT OF STATE
DIVISION OF LANGUAGE SERVICES
(TRANSLATION)

LS NO. 46118
T-85/T-94
Russian

[Embossed Seal of the USSR]
Ministry of Foreign Affairs

Moscow, October 26, 1962

Mr. Ambassador:

I transmit herewith a letter from N.S. Khrushchev, Chairman of the Council of Ministers of the Union of Soviet Socialist Republics, to J.F. Kennedy, President of the United States of America.

Respectfully,
[s] A. Gromyko
A. Gromyko
Minister of Foreign Affairs, USSR

Enclosure: Letter for transmittal to J. F. Kennedy, President of the United States

His Excellency
Foy D. Kohler,
Ambassador of the United States of America,
Moscow

DEPARTMENT OF STATE
DIVISION OF LANGUAGE SERVICES
(TRANSLATION)

LS NO. 46118
T-85/T-94
Russian

[Embossed Seal of the USSR]

Dear Mr. President:

I have received your letter of October 25. From your letter I got the feeling that you have some understanding of the situation which has developed and a sense of responsibility. I appreciate this.

By now we have already publicly exchanged our assessments of the events around Cuba and each of us has set forth his explanation and his interpretation of these events. Therefore, I would think that, evidently, continuing to exchange opinions at such a distance, even in the form of secret letters, would probably not add anything to what one side has already said to the other.

I think you will understand me correctly if you are really concerned for the welfare of the world. Everyone needs peace: both capitalists, if they have not lost their reason, and all the more, communists—people who know how to value not only their own lives but, above all else, the life of nations. We communists are against any wars between states at all, and have been defending the cause of peace ever since we came into the world. We have always regarded war as a calamity, not as a game or a means for achieving particular purposes, much less as a goal in itself. Our goals are clear, and the means of achieving them is work. War is our enemy and a calamity for all nations.

This is how we Soviet people, and together with us, other peoples as well, interpret questions of war and peace. I can say this with assurance at least for the peoples of the Socialist countries, as well as for all progressive people who want peace, happiness, and friendship among nations.

His Excellency
John Kennedy
President of the United States of America

I can see, Mr. President, that you also are not without a sense of anxiety for the fate of the world, not without an understanding and correct assessment of the nature of modern warfare and what war entails. What good would a war do you? You threaten us with war. But you well know that the very least you would get in response would be what you had given us; you would suffer the same consequences. And that must be clear to us—people invested with authority, trust and responsibility. We must not succumb to light-headedness and petty passions, regardless of whether elections are forthcoming in one country or another. These are all transitory things, but should war indeed break out, it would not be in our power to contain or stop it, for such is the logic of war. I have taken part in two wars, and I know that war ends only when it has rolled through cities and villages, sowing death and destruction everywhere.

I assure you on behalf of the Soviet Government and the Soviet people that your arguments regarding offensive weapons in Cuba are utterly unfounded. From what you have written me it is obvious that our interpretations on this point are different, or rather that we have different definitions for one type of military means or another. And indeed, the same types of armaments may in actuality have different interpretations.

You are a military man, and I hope you will understand me. Let us take a simple cannon for instance. What kind of a weapon is it—offensive or defensive? A cannon is a defensive weapon if it is set up to defend boundaries or a fortified area. But when artillery is concentrated and supplemented by an appropriate number of troops, then the same cannon will have become an offensive weapon, since they prepare and clear the way for infantry to advance. The same is true for nuclear missile weapons, for any type of these weapons.

You are mistaken if you think that any of our armaments in Cuba are offensive. However, let us not argue at this point. Evidently, I shall not be able to convince you. But I tell you: You, Mr. President, are a military man and you must understand: How can you possibly launch an offensive even if you have an enormous number of missiles of various ranges and power on your territory, using these weapons alone? These missiles are a means of annihilation and destruction. But it is impossible to launch an offensive by means of these missiles, even nuclear missiles of 100 megaton yield, because it is only people—troops—who can advance. Without people any weapons, whatever their power, cannot be offensive.

How can you, therefore, give this completely wrong interpretation, which you are now giving, that some weapons in Cuba are offensive, as you say? All weapons there—and I assure you of this—are of a defensive nature; they are in Cuba solely for purposes of defense, and we have sent them to Cuba at the request of the Cuban Government. And you say that they are offensive weapons.

But, Mr. President, do you really seriously think that Cuba could launch an offensive upon the United States and that even we, together with Cuba, could advance against you from Cuban territory? Do you really think so? How can that be? We do not understand. Surely, there has not been any such new development in military strategy that would lead one to believe that it is possible to advance that way. And I mean advance, not destroy; for those who destroy are barbarians, people who have lost their sanity.

I hold that you have no grounds to think so. You may regard us with distrust, but you can at any rate rest assured that we are of sound mind and understand perfectly well that if we launch an offensive against you, you will respond in kind. But you too will get in response whatever you throw at us. And I think you understand that too. It is our discussion in Vienna that gives me the right to speak this way.

This indicates that we are sane people, that we understand and assess the situation correctly. How could we, then, allow [ourselves] the wrong actions which you ascribe to us? Only lunatics or suicides, who themselves want to perish and before they die destroy the world, could do this. But we want to live and by no means do we want to destroy your country. We want something quite different: to compete with your country in a peaceful endeavor. We argue with you; we have differences on ideological questions. But our concept of the world is that questions of ideology, as well as economic problems, should be settled by other than military means; they must be solved in peaceful contest, or as this is interpreted in capitalist society—by competition. Our premise has been and remains that peaceful coexistence, of two different sociopolitical systems—a reality of our world—is essential, and that it is essential to ensure lasting peace. These are the principles to which we adhere.

You have now declared piratical measures, the kind that were practiced in the Middle Ages when ships passing through international waters were attacked, and you have called this a "quarantine" around Cuba. Our vessels will probably soon enter the zone patrolled by your Navy. I assure you that the vessels which are now headed for Cuba are carrying the most innocuous peaceful cargoes. Do you really think that all we spend our time on is transporting so-called offensive weapons, atomic and hydrogen bombs? Even though your military people may possibly imagine that these are some special kind of weapons, I assure you that they are the most ordinary kind of peaceful goods.

Therefore, Mr. President, let us show good sense. I assure you that the ships bound for Cuba are carrying no armaments at all. The armaments needed for the defense of Cuba are already there. I do not mean to say that there have been no shipments of armaments at all. No, there were such shipments. But now Cuba has already obtained the necessary weapons for defense.

I do not know whether you can understand me and believe me. But I wish you would believe yourself and agree that one should not give way to one's passions; that one should be master of them. And what direction are events taking now? If you begin stopping vessels it would be piracy, as you yourself know. If we should start doing this to your ship you would be just as indignant as we and the whole world are now indignant. Such actions cannot be interpreted otherwise, because lawlessness cannot be legalized. Were this allowed to happen then there would be no peace; nor would there be peaceful coexistence. Then we would be forced to take the necessary measures of a defensive nature which would protect our interests in accordance with international law. Why do this? What would it all lead to?

Let us normalize relations. We have received an appeal from U Thant, Acting Secretary General of the U.N., containing his proposals. I have already answered him. His proposals are to the effect that our side not ship any armaments to Cuba for a certain period of time while negotiations are being conducted—and we are prepared to enter into such negotiations—and the other side not undertake any piratical actions against vessels navigating on the high seas. I consider these proposals reasonable. This would be a way out of the situation which has evolved that would give nations a chance to breathe easily.

You asked what happened, what prompted weapons to be supplied to Cuba? You spoke of this to our Minister of Foreign Affairs. I will tell you frankly, Mr. President, what prompted it.

We were very grieved by the fact—I spoke of this in Vienna—that a landing was effected and an attack made on Cuba, as a result of which many Cubans were killed. You yourself told me then that this had been a mistake. I regarded that explanation with respect. You repeated it to me several times, hinting that not everyone occupying a high position would acknowledge his mistakes as you did. I appreciate such frankness. For my part I told you that we too possess no less courage; we have also acknowledged the mistakes which have been made in the history of our state, and have not only acknowledged them but have sharply condemned them.

While you really are concerned for peace and for the welfare of your people—and this is your duty as President—I, as Chairman of the Council of Ministers, am concerned for my people. Furthermore, the preservation of universal peace should be our joint concern, since if war broke out under modern conditions, it would not be just a war between the Soviet Union and the United States, which actually have no contentions between them, but a world-wide war, cruel and destructive.

Why have we undertaken to render such military and economic aid to Cuba? The answer is: we have done so only out of humanitarian considerations. At one time our people accomplished its own revolution, when Russia was still a backward country. Then we were attacked. We were the target of attack by many countries. The United States took part in that affair. This has been documented by the participants in aggression against our country. An entire book has been written on this by General Graves, who commanded the American Expeditionary Force at that time. Graves entitled it *American Adventure in Siberia*.

We know how difficult it is to accomplish a revolution and how difficult it is to rebuild a country on new principles. We sincerely sympathize with Cuba and the Cuban people. But we do not interfere in questions of internal organization; we are not interfering in their affairs. The Soviet Union wants to help the Cubans build their life, as they themselves desire, so that others would leave them alone.

You said once that the United States is not preparing an invasion. But you have also declared that you sympathize with the Cuban counterrevolutionary emigrants, support them, and will help them in carrying out their plans against the present government of Cuba. Nor is it any secret to anyone that the constant threat of armed attack and aggression has hung and continues to hang over Cuba. It is only this that has prompted us to respond to the request of the Cuban Government to extend it our aid in strengthening the defense capability of that country.

If the President and Government of the United States would give their assurances that the United States would itself not take part in an attack upon Cuba and would restrain others from such action; if you recall your Navy—this would immediately change everything. I do not speak for Fidel Castro, but I think that he and the Government of Cuba would, probably, announce a demobilization and would call upon the people to commence peaceful work. Then the question of armaments would also be obviated, because when there is no threat, armaments are only a burden for any people. This would also change the approach to the question of destroying not only the armaments which you call offensive, but of every other kind of armament.

I have spoken on behalf of the Soviet Government at the United Nations and introduced a proposal to disband all armies and to destroy all weapons. How then can I stake my claims on these weapons now?

Armaments bring only disasters. Accumulating them damages the economy, and putting them to use would destroy people on both sides. Therefore, only a madman can believe that armaments are the principal means in the life of society. No, they are a forced waste of human energy, spent, moreover, on the destruction of man himself. If people do not display wisdom, they will eventually reach the point where they will clash, like blind moles, and then mutual annihilation will commence.

Let us therefore display statesmanlike wisdom. I propose: we, for our part, will declare that our ships bound for Cuba are not carrying any armaments. You will declare that the United States will not invade Cuba with its tropps and will not support any other forces which might intend to invade Cuba. Then the necessity for the presence of our military specialists in Cuba will be obviated.

Mr. President, I appeal to you to weigh carefully what the aggressive, piratical actions which you have announced the United States intends to carry out in international waters would lead to. You yourself know that a sensible person simply cannot agree to this, cannot recognize your right to such action.

If you have done this as the first step towards unleashing war—well then—evidently nothing remains for us to do but to accept this challenge of yours. If you have not lost command of yourself and realize clearly what this could lead to, then, Mr. President, you and I should not now pull on the ends of the rope in which you have tied a knot of war, because the harder you and I pull, the tighter the knot will become. And a time may come when this knot is tied so tight that the person who tied it is no longer capable of untying it, and then the knot will have to be cut. What that would mean I need not explain to you, because you yourself understand perfectly what dread forces our two countries possess.

Therefore, if there is no intention of tightening this knot, thereby dooming the world to the catastrophe of thermonuclear war, let us not only relax the forces straining on the ends of the rope, let us take measures for untying this knot. We are agreeable to this.

We welcome all forces which take the position of peace. Therefore, I both expressed gratitude to Mr. Bertrand Russell, who shows alarm and concern for the fate of the world, and readily responded to the appeal of the Acting Secretary General of the U.N., U Thant.

These, Mr. President, are my thoughts, which, if you should agree with them, could put an end to the tense situation which is disturbing all peoples.

These thoughts are governed by a sincere desire to alleviate the situation and remove the threat of war.

Respectfully,
[s] N. Khrushchev
N. Khrushchev

October 26, 1962

DOCUMENT 45: Prime Minister Fidel Castro's letter to Premier Khrushchev, October 26, 1962 (reproduced from the international edition of Granma).

PAGE 1 OF 1

Havana, October 26, 1962

Dear Comrade Khrushchev:

From an analysis of the situation and the reports in our possession, I consider that the aggression is almost imminent within the next 24 or 72 hours.

There are two possible variants: the first and likeliest one is an air attack against certain targets with the limited objective of destroying them; the second, less probable although possible, is invasion. I understand that this variant would call for a large number of forces and it is, in addition, the most repulsive form of aggression, which might inhibit them.

You can rest assured that we will firmly and resolutely resist attack, whatever it may be.

The morale of the Cuban people is extremely high and the aggressor will be confronted heroically.

At this time I want to convey to you briefly my personal opinion.

If the second variant is implemented and the imperialists invade Cuba with the goal of occupying it, the danger that that aggressive policy poses for humanity is so great that following that event the Soviet Union must never allow the circumstances in which the imperialists could launch the first nuclear strike against it.

I tell you this because I believe that the imperialists' aggressiveness is extremely dangerous and if they actually carry out the brutal act of invading Cuba in violation of international law and morality, that would be the moment to eliminate such danger forever through an act of clear legitimate defense, however harsh and terrible the solution would be, for there is no other.

It has influenced my opinion to see how this aggressive policy is developing, how the imperialists, disregarding world public opinion and ignoring principles and the law, are blockading the seas, violating our airspace and preparing an invasion, while at the same time frustrating every possibility for talks, even though they are aware of the seriousness of the problem.

You have been and continue to be a tireless defender of peace and I realize how bitter these hours must be, when the outcome of your superhuman efforts is so seriously threatened. However, up to the last moment we will maintain the hope that peace will be safeguarded and we are willing to contribute to this as much as we can. But at the same time, we are ready to calmly confront a situation which we view as quite real and quite close.

Once more I convey to you the infinite gratitude and recognition of our people to the Soviet people who have been so generous and fraternal with us, as well as our profound gratitude and admiration for you, and wish you success in the huge task and serious responsibilities ahead of you.

Fraternally,

Fidel Castro

DOCUMENT 46: "Cuba Fact Sheet," U.S. military preparedness information provided to
President Kennedy, October 27, 1962.

PAGE 1 OF 4

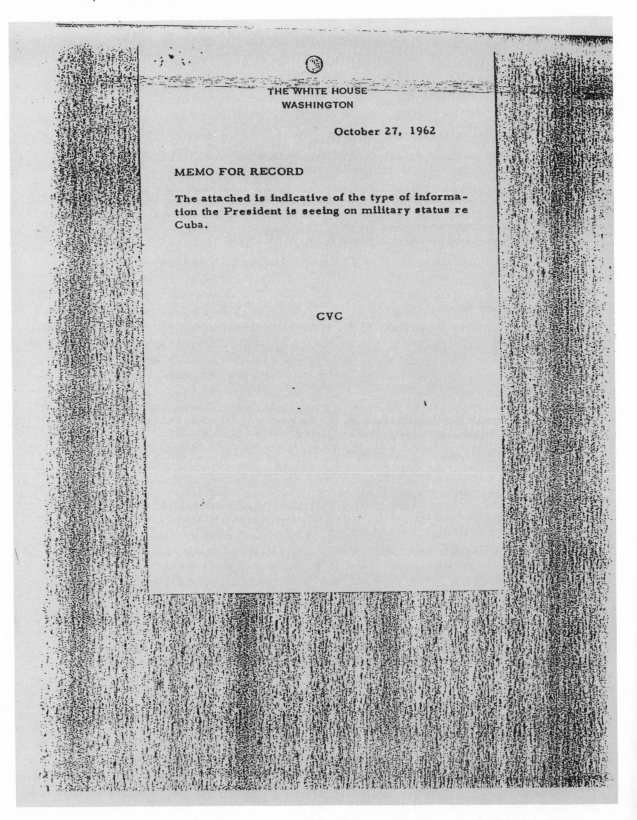

THE WHITE HOUSE
WASHINGTON

October 27, 1962

MEMO FOR RECORD

The attached is indicative of the type of information the President is seeing on military status re
Cuba.

CVC

DOCUMENT 46: "Cuba Fact Sheet," U.S. military preparedness information provided to
President Kennedy, October 27, 1962.

PAGE 2 OF 4

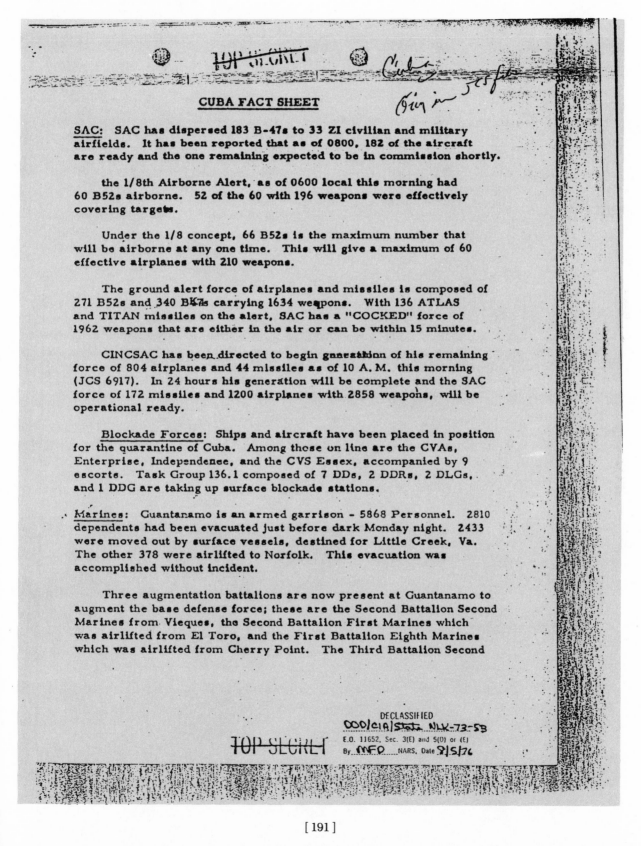

~~TOP SECRET~~

CUBA FACT SHEET

<u>SAC</u>: SAC has dispersed 183 B-47s to 33 ZI civilian and military
airfields. It has been reported that as of 0800, 182 of the aircraft
are ready and the one remaining expected to be in commission shortly.

the 1/8th Airborne Alert, as of 0600 local this morning had
60 B52s airborne. 52 of the 60 with 196 weapons were effectively
covering targets.

Under the 1/8 concept, 66 B52s is the maximum number that
will be airborne at any one time. This will give a maximum of 60
effective airplanes with 210 weapons.

The ground alert force of airplanes and missiles is composed of
271 B52s and 340 B47s carrying 1634 weapons. With 136 ATLAS
and TITAN missiles on the alert, SAC has a "COCKED" force of
1962 weapons that are either in the air or can be within 15 minutes.

CINCSAC has been directed to begin generation of his remaining
force of 804 airplanes and 44 missiles as of 10 A.M. this morning
(JCS 6917). In 24 hours his generation will be complete and the SAC
force of 172 missiles and 1200 airplanes with 2858 weapons, will be
operational ready.

<u>Blockade Forces</u>: Ships and aircraft have been placed in position
for the quarantine of Cuba. Among those on line are the CVAs,
Enterprise, Independence, and the CVS Essex, accompanied by 9
escorts. Task Group 136.1 composed of 7 DDs, 2 DDRs, 2 DLGs,
and 1 DDG are taking up surface blockade stations.

<u>Marines</u>: Guantanamo is an armed garrison - 5868 Personnel. 2810
dependents had been evacuated just before dark Monday night. 2433
were moved out by surface vessels, destined for Little Creek, Va.
The other 378 were airlifted to Norfolk. This evacuation was
accomplished without incident.

Three augmentation battalions are now present at Guantanamo to
augment the base defense force; these are the Second Battalion Second
Marines from Vieques, the Second Battalion First Marines which
was airlifted from El Toro, and the First Battalion Eighth Marines
which was airlifted from Cherry Point. The Third Battalion Second

~~TOP SECRET~~

DOCUMENT 46: "Cuba Fact Sheet," U.S. military preparedness information provided to
President Kennedy, October 27, 1962.

PAGE 3 OF 4

TOP S.

A5-3

Marines is afloat near Cuba and will take station 150 miles Northeast of the island. The First Battalion, Sixth Marines aboard two JPH's will be positioned 50 miles South of Guantanamo. The Second Battalion, Sixth Marines is proceeding from Norfolk aboard an amphibious squadron to take up position 140 miles Northeast of Cuba. A third HAWK Battalion has prepared to depart 29 Palms, California, to stage through Cherry Point en route to Guantanamo. MATS had completed 60% of this deployment as of 0800 24 October. This places the deployment ahead of their schedule.

Marine Air Group 14 from Cherry Point has arrived at Key West, except for its sorting equipment, which is awaiting airlift. On the West Coast, the 5th MEB is now outloading for the move through the Panama Canal.

CONAD: To meet his air defense responsibilities, CINCONAD has an interceptor force of 183 interceptors under the operational control of the Montgomery Air Defense Sector. These interceptors are in the Florida Peninsula below a line Panama City - Jacksonville. 22 are standing a five minute alert, 72 on 15 minutes and 43 are on a one to three hour alert.

At all times CONAD has four interceptors on airborne alert. They patrol on a line generally from just West of Key West to a point just Southeast of Miami.

This regular airborne alert is augmented daily, one hour before first light until one hour after, by five airplanes. These airplanes are positioned:

        a. One over MacDill
        b. One 40 miles East of Patrick
        c. One 85 miles East of Miami
        d. One 85 miles Southwest of Tampa
        e. One 65 miles Northwest of Key West

Should conditions of tension warrant, CINCONAD will have two additional aircraft on airborne alert over Homestead and Patrick.

TAC: The infiltration of TAC airplanes into the Florida bases has ended. This infiltration accomplished over the last few days has brought 850 airplanes into these bases. The greater majority of the airplanes are primarily for the tactical air role but many (62) will augment CONAD forces in the air defense role.

TOP ~~C~~

A5-4

ALERT WORLD-WIDE: Alert condition of US forces world-wide
has been increased to DefCon 3.

Army: The following strike forces have been assigned to CINCLANT
for Operational Control as of 220430Z.

　　　101 ABN Div Ft Campbell Ky
　　　54 FA Gp (Hdq) Ft Bragg N. C.
　　　Hq XVIII ABN Corps Ft Bragg N. C.
　　　XVIII ABN Corps Arty Ft Bragg N. C.
　　　13 AD Gp (Hq) Ft Stewart
　　　82 ABN Div Ft Bragg
　　　1st Inf Div (1/5 BG, 1/28 BG, 2/8 BG) Ft Riley
　　　2nd Inf Div (1/87 BG, 2/1 BG, 2/9 BG, 1/26 BG) Ft Benning

Task Force Charlie in transit to ports of embarkation.

UNIT	INCREMENT	STRENGTH	MOVE TO	PORT
1st Brig/1st Armd Div	1st	809	Ft Stewart	Lauderdale
1st Bn 31st Armor Co C, 13th Armor				
1st Bn, 52d Inf Co A, 6th Inf	2d	1268	Ft Stewart	Lauderdale
1st Bn, 6th Arty	3d	471	--	New Orleans
3d Bn, 6th Arty Btry D, 732 Arty	4th	574	--	New Orleans
Co A, 16th Engr	5th	360	Ft Stewart	Lauderdale
Five Support Div Arty	6th	317	Ft Stewart	Lauderdale
Other support elements		207		
		4006		

Personnel Mobilization: The JCS has identified the order of magnitude
of forces to be mobilized under the 150,000 ceiling and made recommendations now under consideration of SecDef.

TOP ~~SE~~

DOCUMENT 47: CIA daily report, "The Crisis USSR/Cuba," October 27, 1962. (summary page and map only).

PAGE 1 OF 3

CENTRAL INTELLIGENCE AGENCY

Memorandum

THE CRISIS
USSR/CUBA

Information as of 0500

27 October 1962

DOCUMENT 47: CIA daily report, "The Crisis USSR/Cuba," October 27, 1962.
(summary page and map only).

PAGE 2 OF 3

27 October 1962

SC No. 08184/62

SUMMARY CONTENTS

I. Based on the latest low-level reconnaissance mission, three of the four MRBM sites at San Cristobal and the two sites at Sagua La Grande appear to be fully operational. No further sites or missiles have been identified.

The mobilization of Cuban military forces continues at a high rate. However, they remain under orders not to take any hostile action unless attacked.

Steps toward establishing an integrated air defense system are under way. On the diplomatic front, Cuban representatives are trying to plant the idea that Havana would be receptive to UN mediation. They indicate, however, that a prerequisite must be "proof" that the US does not intend to attack Cuba.

II. Despite Khrushchev's declaration to U Thant that Soviet ships would temporarily avoid the quarantine area, we have no information as yet that the six Soviet and three satellite ships en route have changed course. A Swedish vessel, believed to be under charter to the USSR, refused to stop yesterday when intercepted by a US destroyer and was allowed to continue to Havana.

III. No significant redeployment of Soviet ground, air or naval forces have been noted. Three F-class submarines have been identified on the surface inside or near the quarantine line.

IV. There has been no distinct shift in the pattern of reaction. In Western Europe, further support for the US has come from several quarters and unfavorable reactions are decidedly in the minority.

Official London seems intent on checking premature optimism which is showing up in widely scattered parts of the world, particularly among the neutrals. French support for the US is hardening.

There are reports that anti-US demonstrations have broke out in several Latin American capitals, including Buenos Aire Caracas, and La Paz.

DOCUMENT 47: CIA daily report, "The Crisis USSR/Cuba," October 27, 1962. (summary page and map only).

PAGE 3 OF 3

LOCATIONS OF OFFENSIVE MISSILE SITES IN CUBA

SAN CRISTOBAL MRBM COMPLEX

GUANAJAY IRBM COMPLEX

SAGUA LA GRANDE MRBM COMPLEX

REMEDIOS IRBM

DOCUMENT 48: Khrushchev Communiqué to Kennedy, October 27, 1962. (Calling for Trading Cuban
Missiles for Turkish Missiles)(State Department Translation)

PAGE 1 OF 3

DEPARTMENT OF STATE

DIVISION OF LANGUAGE SERVICES

(TRANSLATION)

LS NO.46236
T-94/T-24
Russian

[Embossed Seal of the USSR]
J. Kennedy, President of the United States
Copy to U Thant, Acting Secretary General of the
U.N.

Dear Mr. President,

I have studied with great satisfaction your reply to
Mr. Thant concerning measures that should be
taken to avoid contact between our vessels and
thereby avoid irreparable and fatal consequences.
This reasonable step on your part strengthens my
belief that you are showing concern for the
preservation of peace, which I note with satisfaction.

I have already said that our people, our
Government, and I personally, as Chairman of the
Council of Ministers, are concerned solely with
having our country develop and occupy a worthy
place among all peoples of the world in economic
competition, in the development of culture and the
arts, and in raising the living standard of the people.
This is the most noble and necessary field for
competition, and both the victor and the vanquished
will derive only benefit from it, because it means
peace and an increase in the means by which man
lives and finds enjoyment.

In your statement you expressed the opinion that
the main aim was not simply to come to an
agreement and take measures to prevent contact
between our vessels and consequently a deepening
of the crisis which could, as a result of such contacts,
spark a military conflict, after which all negotiations
would be superfluous because other forces and
other laws would then come into play—the laws of
war. I agree with you that this is only the first step.
The main thing that must be done is to normalize
and stabilize the state of peace among states and
among peoples.

I understand your concern for the security of the
United States, Mr. President, because this is the
primary duty of a President. But we too are

disturbed about these same questions; I bear these
same obligations as Chairman of the Council of
Ministers of the U.S.S.R. You have been alarmed by
the fact that we have aided Cuba with weapons, in
order to strengthen its defense capability—precisely
defense capability—because whatever weapons it
may possess, Cuba cannot be equated with you since
the difference in magnitude is so great, particularly
in view of modern means of destruction. Our aim
has been and is to help Cuba, and no one can
dispute the humanity of our motives, which are
oriented toward enabling Cuba to live peacefully
and develop in the way its people desire.

You wish to ensure the security of your country,
and this is understandable. But Cuba, too, wants the
same thing; all countries want to maintain their
security. But how are we, the Soviet Union, our
Government, to assess your actions which are
expressed in the fact that you have surrounded the
Soviet Union with military bases; surrounded our
allies with military bases; placed military bases
literally around our country; and stationed your
missile armaments there? This is no secret.
Responsible American personages openly declare
that it is so. Your missiles are located in Britain, are
located in Italy, and are aimed against us. Your
missiles are located in Turkey.

You are disturbed over Cuba. You say that this
disturbs you because it is 90 miles by sea from the
coast of the United States of America. But Turkey
adjoins us; our sentries patrol back and forth and see
each other. Do you consider, then, that you have the
right to demand security for your own country and
the removal of the weapons you call offensive, but
do not accord the same right to us? You have placed
destructive missile weapons, which you call
offensive, in Turkey, literally next to us. How then
can recognition of our equal military capacities be
reconciled with such unequal relations between our
great states? This is irreconcilable.

It is good Mr. President, that you have agreed to
have our represntatives meet and begin talks,
apparently through the mediation of U Thant,
Acting Secretary General of the United Nations.
Consequently, he to some degree has assumed the
role of a mediator and we consider that he will be
able to cope with this responsible mission, provided,

of course, that each party drawn into this controversy displays good will.

I think it would be possible to end the controversy quickly and, normalize the situation, and then the people could breathe
more easily, considering that statesmen charged with responsibility are of sober mind and have an awareness of their responsibility combined with the ability to solve complex questions and not bring things to a military catastrophe.

I therefore make this proposal: We are willing to remove from Cuba the means which you regard as offensive. We are willing to carry this out and to make this pledge in the United Nations. Your representatives will make a declaration to the effect that the United States, for its part, considering the uneasiness and anxiety of the Soviet State, will remove its analogous means from Turkey. Let us reach agreement as to the period of time needed by you and by us to bring this about. And, after that, persons entrusted by the United Nations Security Council could inspect on the spot the fulfillment of the pledges made. Of course, the permission of the Governments of Cuba and of Turkey is necessary for the entry into those countries of these representatives and for the inspection of the fulfillment of the pledge made by each side. Of course it would be best these representatives enjoyed the confidence of the Security Council, as well as yours and mine—both the United States and the Soviet Union—and also that of Turkey and Cuba. I do not think it would be difficult to select people who would enjoy the trust and respect of all parties concerned.

We, in making this pledge, in order to give satisfaction and hope of the peoples of Cuba and Turkey and to strengthen their confidence in their security, will make a statement within the framework of the Security Council to the effect that the Soviet Government gives a solemn promise to respect the inviolability of the borders and sovereignty of Turkey, not to interfere in its internal affairs, not to invade Turkey, not to make available our territory as a bridgehead for such an invasion, and that it would also restrain those who contemplate committing aggression against Turkey, either from the territory of the Soviet Union or from the territory of Turkey's other neighboring states.

The United States Government will make a similar statement within the framework of the Security Council regarding Cuba. It will declare that the United States will respect the inviolability of Cuba's borders and its sovereignty, will pledge not to interfere in its internal affairs, not to invade Cuba itself or make its territory available as a bridgehead for such an invasion, and will also restrain those who might contemplate committing aggression against Cuba, either from the territory of the United States or from the territory of Cuba's other neighboring states.

Of course, for this we would have to come to an agreement with you and specify a certain time limit. Let us agree to some period of time, but without unnecessary delay—say within two or three weeks, not longer than a month.

The means situated in Cuba, of which you speak and which disturb you, as you have stated, are in the hands of Soviet officers. Therefore, any accidental use of them to the detriment of the United States is excluded. These means are situated in Cuba at the request of the Cuban Government and are only for defense purposes. Therefore, if there is no invasion of Cuba, or attack on the Soviet Union or any of our other allies, then of course these means are not and will not be a threat to anyone. For they are not for purposes of attack.

If you are agreeable to my proposal, Mr. President, then we would send our representatives to New York, to the United Nations, and would give them comprehensive instructions in order that an agreement may be reached more quickly. If you also select your people and give them the corresponding instructions, then this question can be quickly resolved.

Why would I like to do this? Because the whole world is now apprehensive and expects sensible actions of us. The greatest joy for all peoples would be the announcement of our agreement and of the eradication of the controversy that has arisen. I attach great importance to this agreement in so far as it could serve as a good beginning and could in particular make it easier to reach agreement on banning nuclear weapons tests. The question of the tests could be solved in parallel fashion, without

DOCUMENT 48: Khrushchev Communiqué to Kennedy, October 27, 1962. (Calling for Trading Cuban
Missiles for Turkish Missiles)(State Department Translation)

PAGE 3 OF 3

connecting one with the other, because these are different issues. However, it is important that agreement be reached on both these issues so as to present humanity with a fine gift, and also to gladden it with the news that agreement has been reached on the cessation of nuclear tests and that consequently the atmosphere will no longer be poisoned. Our position and yours on this issue are very close together.

All of this could possibly serve as a good impetus toward the finding of mutually acceptable agreements on other controversial issues on which you and I have been exchanging views. These issues have so far not been resolved, but they are awaiting urgent solution, which would clear up the international atmosphere. We are prepared for this.

These are my proposals, Mr. President.

Respectfully yours,
[s] N. Khrushchev
N. Khrushchev

October 27, 1962

DOCUMENT 49: Transcript of the Executive Committee meeting, October 27, 1962
(from the John F. Kennedy Library; edited for length).*

PAGE 1 OF 21

Off-the-Record Executive Committee Meetings on Cuba
October 27, 1962

SPEAKERS (in order of appearance)

JFK: John F. Kennedy, President

SALINGER: Pierre Salinger, Presidential Press Secretary

RUSK: Dean Rusk, Secretary of State

NITZE: Paul H. Nitze, Assistant Secretary of Defense

BALL: George W. Ball, Undersecretary of State

BUNDY: McGeorge Bundy, Special Assistant to the President

SORENSEN: Theodore C. Sorensen, Presidential Counsel

McCONE: John McCone, Director of the Central Intelligence Agency

McNAMARA: Robert S. McNamara, Secretary of Defense

RFK: Robert F. Kennedy, Attorney General

DILLON: Douglas Dillon, Secretary of the Treasury

THOMPSON: Llewellyn Thompson, Special Advisor for Soviet Affairs

TAYLOR: Maxwell D. Taylor, Chairman, Joint Chiefs of Staff

GILPATRIC: Roswell Gilpatric, Deputy Secretary of Defense

U.A.JOHNSON: U. Alexis Johnson, Deputy Undersecretary of State for Political Affairs

LBJ: Lyndon Baines Johnson, Vice President

MARTIN: Edwin Martin, Assistant Secretary of State for Inter-American Affairs

SPEAKER?: Speaker unknown or identity uncertain

A NOTE ON THE TRANSCRIPT

Punctuation, with some exceptions, remains as in the original transcript. The following codes are used as follows:

(remarks)

Remarks in parentheses reflect comments of the original tape transcriber, McGeorge Bundy.

[remarks]

Remarks in brackets reflect editors' comments.

—

Dashes reflect that the speaker has paused or been interrupted, or that a short comment has been eliminated for continuity.

...

Ellipses between sections of text indicate that material has been deleted due to space limitations.

[The tape begins with a discussion of plans to interdict the Soviet ship *Grozny* and proposals for surveillance missions. This discussion is interrupted as the president reads a news story coming over the wire.

JFK: "Premier Khrushchev told President
(Reading) Kennedy yesterday he would withdraw offensive missiles from Cuba if the United States withdrew its rockets from Turkey."

(Voices unclear)

SPEAKER?: He didn't really say that, did he?

JFK: That may not be—he may be putting out another letter.

(Mixed voices. Calls for Pierre [Salinger])

*This transcript is drawn from audio tapes of the October 27, 1962 meeting, transcribed by McGeorge Bundy, September 1987. See also David A. Welch and James G. Blight "October 27, 1962: Transcripts of the Meetings of the ExComm," *International Security* 12, no. 3 (Winter 1987–1988), pp. 30–92.

DOCUMENT 49: Transcript of the Executive Committee meeting, October 27, 1962 (from the John F. Kennedy Library; edited for length).

PAGE 2 OF 21

JFK: That wasn't in the letter we received, was it?

SPEAKER?: No.

(Voices unclear)

JFK: Is he supposed to be putting out a letter he's written me or putting out a statement?

SALINGER: Putting out a letter he wrote to you.

JFK: Let's just—uh—keep on going (words unclear).

SPEAKER?: It's in a different statement.

RUSK: Well, I think we better get—uh—(words unclear). Will you check and be sure that the letter that's coming in on the ticker is the letter that we were seeing last night.

(Mixed voices)

...

JFK: I ought to have—In case this *is* an accurate statement, where are we with our conversations with the Turks about the withdrawal of these—

NITZE: [U.S. Ambassador to Turkey Raymond] Hare says this is absolutely anathema, and as a matter of prestige and politics. George is ready with a report from [U.S. Ambassador to NATO Thomas] Finletter.

BALL: Yeah, we have a report from Finletter, and we've also got a report from Rome on the Italians which indicates that would be relatively easy. Turkey creates more of a problem. We would have to work it out with the Turks on the basis of putting a Polaris in the waters, and even that might not be enough according to the judgment that we've had on the spot. We've got a—we've got one paper on it already, and we're having more work done right now. It is a complicated problem, because

these were put in under a NATO decision, and (words unclear).

NITZE: The NATO requirement involves the whole question as to whether we are going to denuclearize NATO, and I would suggest that what you do is to say that we're prepared only to discuss *Cuba* at this time. After the Cuban thing is settled we can thereafter be prepared to discuss anything—

JFK: —I don't think we can—if this is an accurate—and this is the whole deal—we just have to wait—I don't think we can take the position—

BUNDY: —It's very odd, Mr. President, if he's changed his terms from a long letter to you and an urgent appeal from the counselor [Aleksandr Fomin] only last night, set in a purely Cuban context, it seems to me we're well within our—there's nothing wrong with our posture in sticking to that line.

JFK: But let's wait and let's assume that this is an accurate report of what he's now proposing this morning—there may have been changes over there—

BUNDY: He—uh—I still think he's in a difficult position to change it overnight, having sent you a personal communication—

JFK: —Well now let's say he has changed it. This is his latest position.

BUNDY: I would answer back saying I would prefer to deal with your—with your interesting proposals of last night.

JFK: Well now that's just what we ought to be thinking about. We're going to be in an insupportable position on this matter if this becomes his proposal. In the first place, we last year tried to get the missiles out of there because they're not militarily useful, number

DOCUMENT 49: Transcript of the Executive Committee meeting, October 27, 1962
(from the John F. Kennedy Library; edited for length).

PAGE 3 OF 21

NITZE: one. Number two, it's going to—to any man at the United Nations or any other rational man it will look like a very fair trade.

NITZE: I don't think so. I don't think—I think you would get support from the United Nations on the proposition, "Deal with this Cuban thing." We'll talk about other things later, but I think everybody else is worried that they'll be included in this great big trade, and it goes beyond Cuba—

...

JFK: (Reading) "A special message appeared to call for negotiations and both nations, Cuba and Turkey, should give their consent to the United Nations to visit their territories. Khrushchev said the Security Council of the Soviet Union was solemnly pledged not to use its territory as a bridgehead for an attack on Turkey, called for a similar pledge from the United States not to let its territory be used as a bridgehead for an attack on Cuba—" Now we've known this was coming for a week— uh—we can't—it's going to be hung up here now (words unclear).

(Mixed voices)

JFK: How much negotiation have we had with the Turks?

RUSK: We haven't talked with the Turks. The Turks have talked with us—the Turks have talked with us in—uh— NATO.

JFK: Well, have we gone to the Turkish government before this came out this week? I've talked about it now for a week. Have we had any conversation in Turkey, with the Turks?

RUSK: We've asked Finletter and Hare to give us their judgments on it. We've not actually talked to the Turks.

BALL: We did it on a basis where if we talked to the Turks, I mean this would be an extremely unsettling business.

JFK: Well *this* is unsettling *now*, George, because he's got us in a pretty good spot here, because most people will regard this as not an unreasonable proposal, I'll just tell you that. In fact, in many ways—

BUNDY: But what most people, Mr. President?

JFK: I think you're going to find it very difficult to explain why we are going to take hostile military action in Cuba, against these sites—what we've been thinking about—the thing that he's saying is, if you'll get yours out of Turkey, we'll get ours out of Cuba. I think we've got a very tough one here.

BUNDY: I don't see why we pick that track when he's offered us the other track, within the last twenty-four hours. You think the public one is serious? (words unclear)

JFK: Yeah. I think you have to assume that this is their new and latest position and it's a public one.

RUSK: What would you think of releasing the letter of yesterday?

(Pause)

BUNDY: I think it has a good deal of virtue.

JFK: Yes, but I think we have to be now thinking about what our position's going to be on this one, because this is the one that's before us, and before the world.

(Short pause)

SORENSEN: As between the two I think it clear that practically everyone here would favor the private proposal.

RUSK: We're not being offered the choice—

We may not be offered the choice.

JFK: But seriously, there are disadvantages also in the private one, which is a guarantee of Cuba. But in any case this is now his official [*sic*] and we can release his other one, and it's different, but this is the one that the Soviet government obviously is going on.

...

[The tape stops here and begins again with Secretary Rusk reading highlights of Khrushchev's letter. The president has left the room.]

...

BUNDY: This should be knocked down publicly. A private—let me suggest this scenario—we knock this down publicly in the way we've just described, separating the issues, keeping attention on Cuba, and the four-point reply that Bob has framed. Privately we say to Khrushchev, "Look, uh, your public statement is a very dangerous one because—uh—it makes impossible immediate discussion of your private proposals and requires us to proceed urgently with the things that we have in mind. You'd better get straightened out."

SPEAKER?: This is exactly what I'd say.

MCCONE: I think that's exactly right.

SPEAKER?: And we release the fact that there was the other letter?

BUNDY: No, we don't. I guess we say we are reluctant to release this letter which would display the inconsistency in your position, but we don't have very much time.

MCNAMARA: The point, Bobby, is he's changed the deal (words unclear). Before we even got the first letter translated, he added a completely new deal and he released it publicly, and under these circumstances (words unclear).

(Voices)

...

RFK: —I think that we're going to have to, in the next three or four hours, not just put the ball completely in—uh—in his hands and allow him to do whatever he wants. We have an exchange with him and say he's double-crossed us, and we don't know which deal to accept, and then he writes back, and in the meantime he's got all the play throughout the world, and the fact that he (word unclear).

MCNAMARA: Just turn it down publicly.

RFK: Yeah, but I think that's awful tough—

(Voices overlap)

MCCONE: I don't think you can turn that down publicly without—uh—referring publicly to his letter of yesterday.

RFK: I'd like to have the consideration of my thoughts (words unclear). He's offered this deal—uh—(words unclear) that he will withdraw the bases in Cuba for assurances that we don't intend to invade. We've *always* given those assurances. We will be glad to give them again. He said, in his letter to me, he said that we were to permit inspection. Obviously that entails inspection not only of Cuba but entails inspection of the United States to ensure that we're not—by United Nations observers to ensure that we're not getting ready to—uh—invade. Now this is one of the things U Thant—the bases in Cuba—uh—involve—uh—the security of the western hemisphere. This is not just a question of the United States. This is a question of all the Latin American countries, which have all joined together in this effort. Time is

DOCUMENT 49: Transcript of the Executive Committee meeting, October 27, 1962 (from the John F. Kennedy Library; edited for length).

PAGE 5 OF 21

running out on us. This must be brought to fruition—uh—The question of the Turkish bases, we think that's excellent, that you brought that up, and that—uh—that—uh—there should be disarmament of the Turkish bases, but that has nothing to do with the security of the western hemisphere. It does have to do with the security of Turkey, and we would be happy, and we're sure the Turks would be, of making a similar arrangement in Turkey. We will withdraw the bases from Turkey if—uh—and allow (word unclear) inspection of Turkey to make sure we've done that, and you withdraw your invasion bases of—uh—of the Soviet Union and permit inspection there.

SPEAKER?: I think it's too complicated, Bobby.

RFK: Well, I don't think it is.

JFK: Wait, just, it seems to me the first thing we ought to try to do is not let the Turks issue some statement that's wholly unacceptable. So that before we've even had a chance to get our own diplomacy the first thing it seems to me we ought to emphasize is that (noises). But they've given us several different proposals in twenty-four hours. And work's got to stop today, before we talk about *anything*. At least then we're in a defensible position. The other thing is to not have the Turks making statements, so that this thing—Khrushchev puts it out and the next thing the Turks say they won't accept it. Then whatever we do in Turkey—in Cuba—it seems to me he has set the groundwork to do something in Turkey. So I think we ought to have the Turks—we ought to have a talk with the Turks because I think they've got to understand the peril that they're going to move in the next week. When we take some action in Cuba, the chances are that he'll take some action in Turkey, and they ought to understand that. And in fact he may even come out and say that (words unclear) he's tried to be fair and if we do any more about Cuba then he's going to do it to Turkey. So I think the Turks ought to think a little (noise). We ought to try to get them not to respond to this till we've had a chance to consider what action we'll take. Now how long will it take to get in touch with the Turks?

(Voices overlapping: "it's going to be awfully hard," "the NATO problem.")

RUSK: I think this is the thing the Turks ought to say that—uh—the security of Turkey, and the military arrangement in Turkey are part of the NATO problem or NATO.

BUNDY: Part of the Atlantic—part of the Western Alliance—and have no other and they have nothing to do with (word unclear, possibly NATO). They ought to—they can certainly make a statement disassociating themselves.

SPEAKERS?: Yes.

BUNDY: It seems to me it's important that they should. If anyone pulls them in, it'll be us, and they *can't* be expected to do that.

JFK: Well, but—uh—we want to give them some guidance. These are American missiles, not Turkish missiles; they're under American control, not Turkish control.

RUSK: The missiles—don't they own the missiles?

McNAMARA: They belong to Turkey and are manned by Turks, but the warheads are in U.S. custody.

SPEAKER?: It seems to me that—

DOCUMENT 49: Transcript of the Executive Committee meeting, October 27, 1962
(from the John F. Kennedy Library; edited for length).

PAGE 6 OF 21

RUSK: And they're committed to NATO.

JFK: In other words, we couldn't withdraw the missiles anyway (words unclear).

...

BUNDY: The work's going on. While you were out of the room Mr. President, we reached an informal consensus—I don't know whether Tommy agrees—that this—last night's message was Khrushchev and this one is his own hard-nosed people overruling him—the public one—that they didn't like what he said to you last night. Nor would I, if I were a Soviet hard-nose.

...

[Executive Committee turns again to the Turkish missile problem.]

SPEAKER?: The only question I'd like to raise about that is that while really it sets Turkey as a quid pro quo—

SPEAKER?: That's my worry about it.

JFK: Well, the negotiations. The point is—the point is that we're not in a position today to make the trade. That's number one. And we won't be—maybe—maybe in three or four days, I don't know, we have to wait and see what the Turks say. We don't want to be—we don't want the Soviet Union or the United Nations to be able to say that the United States rejected it. So I think we're better off to stick on the question; freeze, and then we'll discuss it—

BUNDY: Well there are two (words unclear) different audiences here, Mr. President, there re·lly are, and I think that if we sound as if we wanted to make this trade, to our NATO people and to all the people who are tied to us by alliance, we are in real trouble. I think that—we'll all join in doing this if it's the decision, but I

think we should tell you that that's the universal assessment of everyone in the government that's connected with these alliance problems.

RFK: Well now what reports did you get from Chip [Charles] Bohlen, saying that?

BUNDY: That the knockdown in this White House statement this morning was well received. Finletter's report is in. Hare's long telegram is in. They all make the same proposition, that if we appear to be trading our—the defense of Turkey for the threat to Cuba we—we will—we just have to face a radical decline in the—

JFK: Yes, but I should say that also, as the situation is moving, Mac, if we don't for the next twenty-four or forty-eight hours, this trade has appeal. Now if we reject it out of hand and then have to take military action against Cuba, then we also face a decline. Now the only thing we've got for which I would think we'd be able to hold general support would be—well let's try to word it so that we don't harm NATO—but the thing that I think everybody would agree to—while these matters, which are complicated, are discussed, there should be a cessation of work. Then I think we can hold general support for that. If they don't agree to that, the Soviet Union, then we retain the initiative—

...

JFK: I don't think the alternative's been explained to them. You see, they just think it's a continuation of the quarantine. They don't have any notion that we're about to *do* something. That's got to be on them. You see that hasn't been explained to NATO. I'm not going to get into *that*

DOCUMENT 49: Transcript of the Executive Committee meeting, October 27, 1962 (from the John F. Kennedy Library; edited for length).

PAGE 7 OF 21

before they do something.

DILLON: If you have a council meeting you'll probably get a strong reaction from a great many of the members of NATO against our taking any action in Cuba. They say, Don't trade, but they also say, Don't do anything in Cuba.

SPEAKER?: Exactly.

(Low voices)

McNAMARA: Mr. President, I wonder if we should not take certain actions with respect to the Jupiters in Turkey and Italy *before* we act in Cuba. If we decided to take that action with respect to the Jupiters in Turkey and Italy before we acted in Cuba, then we could *tell* NATO that at the time we talked to them about this proposal from Khrushchev and our response to it. If we act in Cuba, the only way we can act now is with a full attack. I don't think we can make any limited attacks when they're shooting at our reconnaissance aircraft because we would—we would not dare to go in with the kind of limited attack that we've been thinking about the last twenty-four hours without taking out their SAM sites. The moment we take out the SAM sites and the MiG airfields we're up to the [excised] sortie program. If we send [excised] sorties in against Cuba, we must be prepared to follow up with an invasion in about [excised] days. If we start out on that kind of a program, it seems to me the Soviets are very likely to feel forced to reply with military action someplace, particularly if these missiles—Jupiter missiles—are still in Turkey. We might be able to either shift the area in which they would apply their military force or give them no excuse to apply military force by taking out the Turkish Jupiters and the Italian

Jupiters before we attack Cuba. One way to take them out would be to simply develop a program of bilateral negotiations between Turkey, Italy, and the U.S., saying that we are today defusing the Jupiters in those two countries and replacing them with Polaris submarines stationed off the shores of those nations to carry the same targets the Jupiters were directed to in order to reduce the risk to those two nations but maintain the full defense of NATO. Now if we were willing to undertake—First place, I think that kind of action is desirable prior to invasion of Cuba. In the second place, if we're willing to decide to do that, we're in a much better position to present this whole thing to NATO.

...

JFK: It's going to be—You see, they haven't had the alternatives presented to them. They'll say, Well God, we don't want to trade them off. They don't realize that in two or three days we may have a military strike which could bring perhaps the seizure of Berlin or a strike on Turkey, and then they'll say, By God we should have taken it. So when the time—the crucial time comes, obviously we want it, now the question is whether it's tomorrow morning or Monday morning.

(Voices unclear)

McNAMARA: I think the point is related to the strike. If tomorrow we don't have a favorable answer from U Thant or Khrushchev to this message that's going out now, is it important to strike tomorrow or do we have some more time? If we have some more time, then you can still have the NATO meeting. It would seem to me the NATO meeting ought to be held

DOCUMENT 49: Transcript of the Executive Committee meeting, October 27, 1962 (from the John F. Kennedy Library; edited for length).

PAGE 8 OF 21

before the strike. If it's necessary to strike tomorrow, there ought to be a NATO meeting tomorrow morning.

…

SPEAKER?: Take them out.

JFK: I think that—uh—the real problem is what we do with the Turks first.

SPEAKER?: Yeah.

JFK: If we follow Secretary McNamara, what we're going to do is say to the Turks—which they're bound to think is—uh—under Soviet pressure, we want to get your missiles out of there.

McNAMARA: Well what I'd say—what I'd say to the Turks: "Look here, we're going to have to invade Cuba. You're in mortal danger. We want to reduce your danger while at the same time maintaining your defense. We propose that you defuse those missiles tonight. We're putting Polaris submarines along your coast. We'll cover the same targets that your Jupiter missiles did, and we'll announce this to the world before we invade Cuba and thereby would reduce the pressure on the Soviet Union to attack you, Turkey, as a response to our invasion of Cuba." Now this is what I would say to the Turks.

RFK: Now, then they say—uh—what if the Soviet Union attacks us anyway. Will you use the missiles on the nuclear submarines?

McNAMARA: Then, I think, before we attack Cuba I think we've got to decide how we'll respond to Soviet military pressure on NATO, and I'm not prepared to answer the question.

…

THOMPSON: Mr. President, if we go on the basis of a trade which I gather is—somewhat

in your mind, we end up, it seems to me, with the Soviets still in Cuba with planes and technicians and so on even though the missiles are out, and that would surely be unacceptable and put you in a worse position—

JFK: Yeah, but our technicians and planes and guarantees would still exist for Turkey. I'm just thinking about what—what we're going to have to do in a day or so, which is [excised] sorties and [excised] days, and possibly an invasion, all because we wouldn't take missiles out of Turkey, and we all know how quickly everybody's courage goes when the blood starts to flow, and that's what's going to happen in NATO, when they—we start these things, and they grab Berlin, and everybody's going to say, Well that was a pretty good proposition. Let's not kid ourselves that we've got—that's the difficulty. Today it sounds great to reject it, but it's not going to, after we do something.

NITZE: There are alternatives. One of them is to tell (words unclear) that this is going to result in an attack by them some place—The other alternative is to make a blockade, total—

(Mixed voices)

…

JFK: [Strategic Air Command, Europe's General Lauris] Norstad just feels that no matter what we do, there's going to be—we've got to have NATO have a hand on this thing or otherwise we'll find no matter—if we take no action or if we take action—they're all going to be saying we should have done the reverse—and we've got to get them with us. Now the question really if two or three—two questions—first, whether we go

DOCUMENT 49: Transcript of the Executive Committee meeting, October 27, 1962 (from the John F. Kennedy Library; edited for length).

PAGE 9 OF 21

immediately to the Turks and see if we can work out some—see if they're receptive to the kind of deal which the secretary talked about. If they're not receptive then we ought to go to the general NATO meeting because the NATO meeting may put enough pressure on them (pause). I just tell you I think we're better off to get those missiles out of Turkey and out of Cuba, because I think the way of getting them out of Turkey and out of Cuba is going to be very grave (words unclear), and very bloody, one place or another.

...

SORENSEN: I wonder, Mr. President, inasmuch as your statement this morning does give some answer to the public statement of the Soviets, whether we can't defer this for twenty-four or forty-eight hours while we try the private letter route in answer to his private letter of last night. There's always a chance that he'll accept that (words unclear). We meanwhile would have broken up NATO over something that never would have come to NATO.

...

JFK: It seems to me what we ought to—to be reasonable. We're not going to get these weapons out of Cuba, probably, anyway. But I mean—by negotiation—we're going to have to take our weapons out of Turkey. I don't think there's any doubt he's not going to (word unclear) now that he made that public, Tommy, he's not going to take them out of Cuba if we—

THOMPSON: I don't agree, Mr. President, I think there's still a chance that we can get this line going.

JFK: He'll back down?

THOMPSON: Well, because he's already got this other proposal which he put forward—

JFK: Now this other public one, it seems to me, has become their public position, isn't it?

THOMPSON: This is, maybe, just pressure on us, I mean, to accept the other, I mean so far—

(Mixed voices)

THOMPSON: The important thing for Khrushchev, it seems to me, is to be able to say, I saved Cuba, I stopped an invasion—and he can get away with this, if he wants to, and he's had a go at this Turkey thing, and that we'll discuss later. And then, and that discussion will probably take—

JFK: All right, what about at the end of this, we use this letter and say, "will be a grave risk to peace. I urge—urge you to join us in a rapid settlement of the Cuban crisis as your letter (word unclear) suggests, and (words unclear). The first ingredient, let me emphasize, for any solution is a cessation of the uh—work and the possibility (word unclear) under reasonable standards"—I mean, I want to just come back to that. Otherwise time uh—slips away on us.

(Pause. Words unclear and mixed voices.)

SORENSEN: In other words, Mr. President, your position is that once he meets this condition of the—uh—halting of the work and the inoperability [sic], you're then prepared to go ahead on either the specific Cuban track or what we call the general détente track.

JFK: Yeah, now it all comes down—I think it's a substantive question, because it really depends on whether we believe

DOCUMENT 49: Transcript of the Executive Committee meeting, October 27, 1962 (from the John F. Kennedy Library; edited for length).

PAGE 10 OF 21

that we can get a deal on just the Cuban—or whether we have to agree to his position of tying. Tommy doesn't think we do. I think that having made it public how can he take these missiles out of Cuba—if we just do nothing about Turkey.

...

BUNDY: I think that Bobby's notion of a concrete acceptance on our part of how we read last night's telegram is very important.

TAYLOR: Mr. Kennedy—

JFK: In other words, you want to—you have to say we accept your proposal.

RFK: (Words unclear) accept it and then say you—I just the last paragraph of the other letter and however you phrase it.

TAYLOR: Mr. President, the chiefs [the Joint Chiefs of Staff] have been in session during the afternoon on—really the same basis as we have over here. This if the recommendation they give is as follows: that the big strike OP Plan 3-12—be executed no later than Monday morning the 29th unless there is irrefutable evidence in the meantime that offensive weapons are being dismantled and rendered inoperable; that the execution of the Strike Plan be part of the execution of 3-16, the Invasion Plan, [excised] days later.

(Pause)

RFK: That was a surprise.

(Laughter, mixed voices)

TAYLOR: It does look now from a military point of view—They just feel that the longer we wait now.

DILLON: Well, also we're getting shot at—

(Mixed voices)

...

McNAMARA: Let's put it this way. We had fire on the surveillance. Now the first question we have to face tomorrow morning is, are we going to send surveillance flights in? And I think we have basically two alternative[s]. Either we decide not to send them in at all or we decide to send them in with proper cover. If we send them in with proper cover and they're attacked, we must attack back, either the SAMs and/or MiG aircraft that come against them, or the ground fire that comes up. We have another problem tomorrow, the [Soviet ship] *Grozny* approaching the zone—we sent out a message today outlining the interception zone which was publicly released (words unclear). Well, we sent it to U Thant and it's released publicly. The *Grozny* will be coming into the zone. Khrushchev has said he is ordering his ships to stay out of the zone. If a Russian ship moves into the zone after he's said that publicly, we have two choices: stop it and board it, or don't. Now when you—

SPEAKER?: Stop it.

McNAMARA: When you put the two of these together—the question of—you know stopping surveillance and not stopping the ship—it seems to me we're too weak—

SPEAKER?: Yeah, yeah.

TAYLOR: I'd say we must continue surveillance. That's far more important than the ship.

McNAMARA: Well—uh—my main point is I don't think at this particular point we should—uh—show a weakness to Khrushchev, and I think we would show a weakness if we—if we failed on both of these actions.

DOCUMENT 49: Transcript of the Executive Committee meeting, October 27, 1962 (from the John F. Kennedy Library; edited for length).

PAGE 11 OF 21

...

JFK: I'm rather inclined to think that the more general response—-However, why don't we wait. Let's be prepared for either one tomorrow—let's wait and see whether they fire on us tomorrow. Meanwhile we've got this message to U Thant and we're—so let's be well prepared.

DILLON: We've got to be very clear then that—uh—if we're doing this tomorrow, and they do shoot weapons, and then we do need to have the general response, there's no time to do what you're talking about with Turkey, and then we—

JFK: That's why I think we ought to get to that. I think what we ought to do is not worry so much about the cover, do the reconnaissance tomorrow. If we get fired on, then we meet here, and we decide whether we do a much more general (words unclear) announce that the work is going ahead, announce that we haven't got an answer from the Soviets, and then we decide that we're going to do a much more general one than just shooting up some gun down there.

...

SPEAKER: The U-2.

McNAMARA: The U-2 is shot down—the fire against our low-altitude surveillance

RFK: U-2 shot down?

McNAMARA: Yes, (words unclear) it was found shot down.

RFK: Pilot killed?

TAYLOR: It was shot down near Banes which is right near a U-2 [sic] site in Eastern Cuba.

SPEAKER?: A SAM site.

TAYLOR: The pilot's body is in the plane. Apparently this was a SAM site that

had actually had the energy (words unclear). It all ties in in a very plausible way.

(Voice unclear)

JFK: This is much of an escalation by them, isn't it?

McNAMARA: Yes, exactly, and this relates to the timing. I think we can defer an air attack on Cuba until Wednesday or Thursday, but only if we continue our surveillance and—and—uh—fire against anything that fires against the surveillance aircraft, and only if we maintain a tight blockade in this interim period. If we're willing to do these two things, I think we can defer the air attack until Wednesday or Thursday and take time to go to NATO—

JFK: How do we explain the effect—uh—this Khrushchev message of last night and their decision, in view of their previous orders, the change of orders? We've both had flak and a SAM site operation. How do we I mean, that's a—

McNAMARA: How do we interpret this? I know—I don't know how to interpret—

(Voice unclear)

TAYLOR: They feel they must respond now. The whole world knows where we're flying. That raises the question of retaliation against the SAM sites. We think we—we have various other reasons to believe that we know the SAM sites. A few days ago—

JFK: How can we put a U-2 fellow over there tomorrow unless we take out all the SAM sites?

McNAMARA: That's just exactly—in fact, I don't think we can.

(Voices unclear)

DOCUMENT 49: Transcript of the Executive Committee meeting, October 27, 1962 (from the John F. Kennedy Library; edited for length).

PAGE 12 OF 21

SPEAKER?: They've fired the first shot.

McCONE: If there's any continuation of this, we just take those SAM sites out of there.

(Voices over each other)

SPEAKER?: Isn't this what we told the NATO people we'd do?

SPEAKER?: Yes we told (words unclear).

BUNDY: You can go against one. Can you, now, tonight?

McNAMARA: No, it's too late. This is why it gets into tomorrow, and I—without thinking about retaliation today, what are we going to do if we want to defer the air attack to Wednesday or Thursday?

(Voices unclear)

TAYLOR: It would be very dangerous, I would say, Mr. Secretary, unless we can reconnoiter—reconnoiter each day (words unclear).

McNAMARA: And if we're going to reconnaissance, carry out surveillance, each day, we must be prepared to fire each day.

JFK: We can't very well send a U-2 over there, can we, now? And have a guy killed again tomorrow?

TAYLOR: We certainly shouldn't do it until we retaliate and say that if they fire again on one of our planes, that we'll come back with great force.

SPEAKER?: I think you've just got to take out that SAM site, you can't (word unclear) with them

JFK: Well, except that we've still got the problem of even if you take out *this* SAM site—the fellow still is going to be awfully vulnerable tomorrow from all the others, isn't he?

(Voices unclear)

SPEAKER?: If you take *one* out—

(Voices unclear)

McNAMARA: I think we can forget the U-2 for the moment—

(Mixed voices)

RUSK: It builds up, though, on a somewhat different plane than the all-out attack plan.

McNAMARA: We can carry out low-altitude surveillance tomorrow, take out this SAM site, and take out more SAM sites tomorrow and make aircraft (words unclear).

...

JFK: I think we ought to announce that—uh—that—uh—action is being taken—action will be taken to protect our fliers.

McNAMARA: Exactly. Then we ought to go in at dawn and take out that SAM site, and we ought to send the surveillance aircraft in tomorrow with the regular flights early in the morning, and we ought to be prepared to take out more SAM sites and knock out the—

JFK: Well what we ought to do then is get this announcement written (word unclear). Ros, why don't you write this out, plus this thing about what we're going to do, and then we'll get back to what we're going to do about the Turks (words unclear).

(Voices unclear)

...

McNAMARA: This is a change of pattern, now—why it's a change of pattern, we don't know.

RFK: Yeah.

SPEAKER?: The important thing to find out if we possibly can is whether this was a SAM site.

DOCUMENT 49: Transcript of the Executive Committee meeting, October 27, 1962 (from the John F. Kennedy Library; edited for length).

PAGE 13 OF 21

MCNAMARA: There's no way to find out. What we know is that that particular SAM was the one that had the Fruit-set radar—

SPEAKER?: In operation.

MCNAMARA: Which was required for control of the missiles.

SPEAKER?: Would we know whether it's in operation?

MCNAMARA: And it was in operation, we believe, at the same time that the U-2 was over. We checked it this morning (words unclear).

U. A. JOHNSON: It's a very different thing. You could have an undisciplined antiaircraft—Cuban antiaircraft outfit fire, but to have a SAM site and a Russian crew fire is not any accident.

…

JFK: I think we ought to—why don't we send an instruction to Hare to have a conversation, but also have the NATO meeting? And say to them what's happening over here. Otherwise we're going to be carrying a hell of a bag.

DILLON: I think we're going to have such pressure internally in the United States too, to act quickly—

JFK: That's why I think we'd better have a NATO meeting tomorrow—Explain the thing, where we are—uh—I'm just afraid of what's going to happen in NATO, to Europe, when we get into this thing more and more, and I think they ought to feel that they've a part of it. Even if we don't do anything about the Turks, they ought to feel that they know what—

MCNAMARA: I would agree, but I think we ought to know what we want NATO to do tomorrow, which means that we have to have a proposition. NATO itself won't initiate anything.

…

[The Executive Committee discusses what to tell the NATO allies. A discussion ensues of a possible scenario in which Khrushchev fails to respond positively to Kennedy's new letter. The president appears to be absent from most of the meeting.]

MCNAMARA: Let me start my proposition over again. We must be in a position to attack, quickly. We've been fired on today. We're going to send surveillance aircraft in tomorrow. Those are going to be fired on without question. We're going to respond. You can't do this very long. We're going to lose airplanes, and we'll be shooting up Cuba quite a bit, but we're going to lose airplanes every day. So you just can't maintain this position very long. So we must be prepared to attack Cuba—quickly. That's the first proposition. Now the second proposition. When we attack Cuba we're going to have to attack with an all-out attack, and that means [excised] sorties at a minimum the first day, and it means sorties every day thereafter, and I personally believe that this is almost certain to lead to an invasion, I won't say certain to, but almost certain to lead to an invasion—

DILLON: Unless you get a cease-fire around the world—

MCNAMARA: That's the second proposition.

BUNDY: Or a general war.

MCNAMARA: The third proposition is that if we do this, and leave those missiles in Turkey the Soviet Union *may*, and I think probably will, attack the Turkish missiles. Now the fourth

DOCUMENT 49: Transcript of the Executive Committee meeting, October 27, 1962 (from the John F. Kennedy Library; edited for length).

PAGE 14 OF 21

proposition is, *if* the Soviet Union attacks the Turkish missiles, we *must* respond. We *cannot* allow a Soviet attack on the—on the Jupiter missiles in Turkey without a military response by NATO.

THOMPSON: Somewhere.

McNAMARA: Somewhere, that's right. Now, that's the next proposition.

(Mixed voices)

SPEAKER?: Frankly, I don't—

McNAMARA: Well, I've got a—why don't I get through—then let's go back and attack each one of my propositions. Now the minimum military response by NATO to a Soviet attack on the Turkish Jupiter missiles would be a response with conventional weapons by NATO forces in Turkey, that is to say Turkish and U.S. aircraft, against Soviet warships and/or naval bases in the Black Sea area. Now that to me is the absolute minimum, and I would say that it is *damned dangerous* to— have had a Soviet attack on Turkey and a NATO response on the Soviet Union. This is extremely dangerous. Now I'm not sure we can avoid anything like that, if we attack Cuba, but I think we should make every effort to avoid it, and one way to avoid it is to defuse the Turkish missiles *before* we attack Cuba. Now this (words unclear) this is the sequence of thought—

(Voices mixed and unclear)

SPEAKER?: Why you don't make the trade then?

BALL: I would say that in the assumption that if you defuse the Turkish missiles that saves you from a reprisal, it may—may mean a reprisal *elsewhere*.

McNAMARA: Oh, I think it doesn't save you from a reprisal.

(Mixed voices)

BALL: I think you're in a position where you've gotten rid of your missiles for *nothing*.

McNAMARA: Well, wait a minute. I didn't say it saved you from a reprisal. I simply said it reduced the chances of military action against Turkey.

BALL: Well, but what good does that do you (unclear) action against Berlin, or somewhere else?

(Mixed voices)

McNAMARA: You have to go back in my proposition and say if there aren't Jupiter missiles in Turkey to attack, they're going to employ military force elsewhere. I'm not—I'm not at all certain of that.

BALL: Oh, I am.

LBJ: Bob, if you're willing to give up your missiles in Turkey, you think you ought to (words unclear) why don't you say that to him and say we're cutting a trade—make the trade there? (mixed voices) save all the invasion, lives and—

(Mixed voices)

SPEAKER?: The State Department, they invite them—we talked about this, and they said they'd be *delighted* to trade those missiles in Turkey for the things in Cuba.

McNAMARA: I said I thought it was the realistic solution to the problem.

LBJ: Sure. What we were afraid of was he'd never offer this, but what he'd want to do was trade (mixed voices) *Berlin.*

SPEAKER?: This was just the kind of thing.

(Mixed voices)

McNAMARA: I'm not opposed to it, now, all I'm

DOCUMENT 49: Transcript of the Executive Committee meeting, October 27, 1962
(from the John F. Kennedy Library; edited for length).

PAGE 15 OF 21

suggesting is, don't push us into a position where we *haven't* traded it and we are forced to attack Cuba, and the missiles remain in Turkey. That's all I'm suggesting. Let's avoid that position. We're fast moving into that.

BALL: Well, but I—

BUNDY: We were going to let him have his strike in Turkey, as I understood it last week—at one point at least that was the way we talked about it.

McNAMARA: Yeah, that's right. That was one alternative.

BALL: What—actually, what we were thinking last week was that what he was doing was (words unclear). We thought that if we could trade it out for Turkey this would be an easy trade and a very advantageous deal. Now, we've—uh—made that offer to him—(unclear). And then we don't want it, and we're talking about a course of action which involves military action with enormous casualties and a great—a great risk of escalation. Now I—I really don't think this is—we ought to shift this one.

McNAMARA: Well, why don't we look at two courses of action?

SPEAKER?: Let's see what consequence George draws.

BALL: Well. I would far rather if we're going to get the damned missiles out of Turkey *anyway*, say, We'll trade you the missiles, we're going to put Jupiters—I mean we're going to put Polaris in there, you're not going to benefit by this but *we will*, if this is a matter of *real* concern to you, to have these on your borders, all right, we'll get rid of them, you get rid of them in Turkey—in, in Cuba. These things are obsolete anyway—-I mean (word

unclear) you're not going to reduce the retaliatory power of the NATO Alliance.

SPEAKER?: You put Polaris in there, it's going to be a lot bigger.

BALL: Yeah.

McNAMARA: Well, I think you have two alternatives.

(Mixed voices)

BUNDY: I missed your statement: I have to ask you to say it again.

BALL: I'd say, sure, we'll accept your offer. If this is a matter of grave concern to you, and you equate these things, which we don't but if you do, OK, we can work it out. We're going to put Polaris in the Mediterranean because you've got the whole seas to range in, and we can't keep you out of the ocean—

BUNDY: And what's left of NATO?

BALL: I don't think NATO is going to be wrecked, and if NATO isn't any better than that, it isn't that good to us.

...

McNAMARA: We probably ought to think about the course of action in the next two or three days, what we're going to (words unclear). Max[well Taylor] is going back to work out the surveillance problem for tomorrow with the chiefs and see how much cover we need and so on. So we're just going to get shot up sure as hell. There's no question about it. We're going to have to go in and shoot. We can carry this on I would think a couple of days, maybe three days, possibly even four. But we're going to lose planes. We had eight planes going out today. Two aborted for mechanical reasons. Two went

DOCUMENT 49: Transcript of the Executive Committee meeting, October 27, 1962 (from the John F. Kennedy Library; edited for length).

PAGE 16 OF 21

through safely and returned, and four ran into fire.

MCCONE: You know, it seems to me we're missing a bet here. I think that we ought to take this case to—send directly to Khrushchev by fast wire the most violent protest, and demand that he stop this business and stop it right away, or we're gong to take those SAM sites out *immediately*. That's what I'd tell him. I'd tell him this is a—I'd just use one of the (mixed voices) messages *he* sends *us*, and I'd send it right off, and if he won't—and I'd trade these Turkish things out right now. I wouldn't even talk to anybody about it. We sat for a week, and everybody was in favor of doing it, and I'd make that part of the message. I'd tell him we're going to conduct surveillance, as announced by the president, and *one shot* and in we come, and he can expect it. If he wants to sit down and talk about this thing, he can call off his gunfire and do it right away.

MCNAMARA: Well, I think that we can assume that that kind of an approach will be made—ex the—I think we can assume an approach to trade the missiles will be made one way or another. He'll know that. But now let's assume that that's made and time goes by and nothing happens and we're losing airplanes. What—what do we do there?

DILLON: Well, I mean this is a job for the—

(Mixed voices)

MCNAMARA: Let's assume that the approach is made—

SPEAKER?: And he doesn't do it.

MCNAMARA: Either he doesn't do it or he comes back—let me go back a second. When I read that message of last night this morning, I thought, *my God* I'd never sell—I'd never base a transaction on *that contract*. Hell, that's no offer. There's not a damned thing in it that's an offer. You read that message carefully. He didn't propose to take the missiles out. Not once there isn't a single word in it that proposes to take the missiles out. It's twelve pages of—of fluff.

SPEAKER: Well his message this morning wasn't—

(Mixed voices)

MCNAMARA: Well, no, I'm speaking of the last-night message. The last-night message was twelve pages of fluff. That's no contract. You couldn't sign that and say we know what we signed. And *before* we got the damned thing read the whole deal changed—completely changed. All of which leads me to conclude that the *probabilities* are that nothing's going to be signed quickly. Now my question is, *assuming* nothing is signed quickly, what do we do. (Pause) Well, I don't think attack is the only answer. I think we ought to be *prepared* for attack, all-out attack, but I think we ought to know how far we can postpone that. But I *don't* think that's the only answer, and we ought to think of some other answers here. Now John's suggestion, I think, is obviously one—to try to negotiate a deal.

MCCONE: I wouldn't try to negotiate a deal—I'd send him a threatening letter. I'd say, You've made public an offer. We'll accept that offer. But you shot down a plane today before we even had a chance to send you a letter, despite the fact that *you knew* that we were sending unarmed planes on a publicly announced surveillance. Now we're telling you, Mr.

[215]

DOCUMENT 49: Transcript of the Executive Committee meeting, October 27, 1962 (from the John F. Kennedy Library; edited for length).

PAGE 17 OF 21

Khrushchev, this just one thing, that we're sending unarmed planes over Cuba. If one of them is shot at, we're going to take the installations out, and you can expect it. And therefore, you issue an order *immediately*.

SPEAKER?: Right.

McCONE: And I'd be prepared to follow that up.

...

THOMPSON: These boys are beginning to give way. Let's push harder. I think they'll change their minds when we take continued forceful action, stopping their ship or—or taking out a SAM site. That kills some Russians (words unclear). But if we are not going to shoot any planes that come up or shoot (words unclear).

DILLON: Well, would you rather send them a thing like this which says if they shoot at all you're going to take them all out, or would you rather just go in and take *one* SAM site out.

THOMPSON: I'm inclined to take one because I don't think giving an ultimatum is recommended.

LBJ: You warhawks ought to get together.

...

LBJ: You just ask yourself what made the greatest impression on you today, whether it was his letter last night or whether it was his letter this morning. Or whether it was his (words unclear) U-2 boys?

THOMPSON: The U-2.

LBJ: That's exactly right. That's what everybody (words unclear), and that's what's going to make an impression on him.

[President Kennedy returns to the meeting]

JFK: I'm sorry to keep you. I think we ought to go—essentially go back to this problem and then when we get these messages to the Turks, the British, and the NATO messages.

BUNDY: We have to go back to—we have to instruct Finletter, we have really to agree on the track, you see, Mr. President and I think there's a very substantial difference of opinion—

LBJ: McNamara is drafting that message.

...

JFK: Well, I think we ought to—just a second—I'll just say, of *course* we ought to try to go the first route which you suggest. Get him back—that's what our letter's doing—that's what we're going to do by one means or another. But it seems to me we *ought* to have this discussion with NATO about these Turkish missiles, but more generally about sort of an up-to-date briefing about where we're going.

...

JFK: We can't very well invade Cuba with all its toil, and long as it's going to be, when we could have gotten them out by making a deal on the same missiles in Turkey. If that's part of the record I don't see how we'll have a very good war.

...

JFK: Let me say, I think we ought to wait till tomorrow afternoon, to see whether we get any answer—if U Thant goes down there—we're rapidly approaching a real—I don't think that firing back at a twenty millimeter coming off the ground is good. I think we ought to figure that Monday—if tomorrow they fire at us, and we don't have any answer from the Russians, then Monday, it seems

DOCUMENT 49: Transcript of the Executive Committee meeting, October 27, 1962 (from the John F. Kennedy Library; edited for length).

PAGE 18 OF 21

to me, we ought to—we can consider making a statement tomorrow about the fire and that we're going to take action now any place in Cuba, on those areas which can fire, and then go in and take all the SAM sites out. I'd rather take—I don't think that it does any good to take out—to try to fire at a twenty millimeter on the ground. You just hazard our planes, and the people on the ground have the advantage. On the other hand, I don't want to—I don't think we do any good to begin to sort of *half* do it. I think we ought to keep tomorrow clean, do the best we can with the surveillance. If they still fire, and we haven't got a satisfactory answer back from the Russians then I think we ought to put a statement out tomorrow that we were fired upon, and we are therefore considering the island of Cuba as an open territory, and then take out all these SAM sites. Otherwise what we're going to do is find this build-up of the—of the protection for the SAM sites, low, and the SAM sites high—and we'll find ourselves without—our requirement will be so limited, that we'll find ourselves with all the disadvantages. I think we ought to, tomorrow—let's get U Thant our messages—if they fire on us, tell them we'll take them all out and if we don't get some satisfaction from the Russians or U Thant or Cuba tomorrow night, figure that Monday we're going to do something about the SAM sites. What do you think?

McNAMARA: (Words unclear) I would say only that we ought to keep some kind of pressure on (words unclear) tomorrow night, that indicates we're (words unclear). Now if we call up these air squadrons tonight, I think that settles (words unclear). I have a paper here (words unclear). I believe we should issue an order tonight calling up the twenty-four air reserve squadrons, roughly three hundred troop carrier transports, which are required for an invasion, and this would both be a preparatory move, and also a strong indication of what lies ahead—

JFK: I think we ought to do it.

[The Executive Committee now discusses what to do about Soviet ships approaching the quarantine line. A decision on whether to intercept the vessel is put off for the following day.]

...

RUSK: Mr. President, just to remind us of seven things that have happened today. He, by the way, is telling us the pressure's on Khrushchev (words unclear). One was the statement this morning on the broadcast. Second, was this business on the intercept (word unclear) U Thant. Third, was an announcement on enforced surveillance. Fourth, was our short message to U Thant (words unclear). Five was our answer to K[rushchev]'s letter of October 2. Six, was a call-up of air squadrons. Seven will be a warning to U Thant of an approaching ship. Now, in general I think that's—uh—for one day, that's building up. Tomorrow, we'll need to be sure that the pressures continue to build up.

JFK: Well, we've got two things. First place we've got the POL. Secondly, we've got the announcement about these—whatever happens—if we don't *take* the ship, we announce that the (words unclear) been broken, and from now on, it's POL, all ships, and—uh—so on (words unclear).

DOCUMENT 49: Transcript of the Executive Committee meeting, October 27, 1962
(from the John F. Kennedy Library; edited for length).

PAGE 19 OF 21

Nine ships (words unclear) in addition [to] our own ships. So it seems to me we've got two or three things tomorrow—

...

JFK: Well now, will the introduction of Turkey, we think that if we take an action which we may have to take, I don't think we ought to say—which we may well have to take the way it's escalating, if they hit Turkey and they hit Berlin, we want them—If they want to get off, now's the time to speak up.

McNAMARA: Mr. President, do we believe that we'll be able to settle Cuba more easily with or without the Jupiters in Turkey? I think we ought to decide this point before we open the door to NATO.

RFK: That's what—can't we wait? Isn't it possible to get through tomorrow at three or four o'clock without even getting into NATO with the Turkey business? And then figuring, I mean if we lose the gamble with—and I think that—if once they find, playing around and figuring on Turkey, we're willing to make some deal—if I were they I'd push on that, and then I'd push on Italy, figuring that well if they're going to go on that they can carry it one step further. But if we are hard on this thing—the gains that we have—we know that we've got some respite—that (words unclear) see some way in Moscow—the way that they made the offer initially. Why don't we just wait another eighteen hours, see if that's been eased at all. We're hard and tough on this. We called up the planes tonight, and we wait. We find out if U Thant is successful, then we find that he's not successful—the whole thing looks like it's collapsing, and we're going to

have to go in there. So then we call them together, and we say what the problem is.

JFK: Have we called the meeting yet?

SPEAKER?: Yes, we have.

(Mixed voices)

BUNDY: I think it says in Norstad's message ten o'clock (words unclear). Three o'clock our time. No, other way around, morning our time.

RFK: I think you could say it tomorrow, if you had the information. State the facts, and say we think that this should be based—based completely in the western hemisphere. This is what we had

BUNDY: We have an obligation to talk with you, and more of an obligation and we'll meet with you again raising this irrelevance [*sic*], at ten o'clock tomorrow morning.

RFK: Then if the thing blows tomorrow, then we go at ten o'clock the next morning and say that—Well, I think you've got to figure that's another twenty-four hours. You could do it— OK. Well—uh—one day, I can't believe it's going to make that much difference.

(Voices unclear)

RFK: I think—I think you've got to give them a chance. But I think if we indicate to them tomorrow that we're willing to make a deal on Turkey if they're willing to make a deal, that half of them are going to be willing to make it, half aren't—I think then you'd be in a—

JFK: Well, but the only thing is have we lost anything (words unclear).

SPEAKER?: You shouldn't discuss the Turkey deal.

DOCUMENT 49: Transcript of the Executive Committee meeting, October 27, 1962 (from the John F. Kennedy Library; edited for length).

PAGE 20 OF 21

RFK: No, I think you just keep silent. Tell them what has happened today. Go through the whole thing. This is just to report to them what we've done, and what steps we're taking, and then they're—that we called up the air, and we're thinking of calling up the ships (words unclear) calling up the ships. This is what happened: we sent the U-2 over—it looks like it got shot down—we got some of these—and this is the offer that they've made to us, with the messages that came through Scali and through the other people we've accepted this—the president (words unclear) when they suddenly came in with the Turkey business—we haven't considered that because we think it should be restricted to the western hemisphere—uh, we made that—we said that we would accept that. We haven't heard yet. We will report to them when we hear and we suggest that we meet at ten o'clock tomorrow morning, and then the Russians come back and say we're only going to do it if you can get the bases out of Turkey, and then we come in and we talk to them and say, "Now this is what our suggestion is, what do *you* want to do," and they say, "We want to hold fast," and then on Tuesday we go in. I think if we indicate tomorrow (words unclear).

THOMPSON: It'll become public.

JFK: All right, does anybody—uh—Mr. Secretary, what do you think of that?

RUSK: No, I think that's all right.

JFK: Mac, you can draw the—

BUNDY: Yes, sir.

JFK: You and Ted [Sorensen] draw the instructions based on what Bobby said.

...

JFK: Let's just say, it seems to me that on Hare if we don't want to—we try to get the Russians off the Turkish trade—then we probably don't want to do anything with Hare for twenty-four hours till we get some sort of an answer.

THOMPSON: This is Hare's telegram. I don't know if you saw it or not.

(Mixed voices)

JFK: Well, let's see—uh—let's give him an explanation of what we're trying to do. We're trying to get it back on the original proposition of last night, and—because we don't want to get into this trade. If we're unsuccessful, then we—it's *possible* that we may have to get back on the Jupiter thing. If we do, then we would of course want it to come from the Turks themselves and NATO, rather than just the United States. We're hopeful, however, that that won't come. If he does, his judgment on how should it be handled (words unclear) we're prepared to do the Polaris and others, does he think this thing can be made? We'll be in touch with him in twenty-four hours when we find out if we're successful in putting the Russians back on the original track (words unclear).

THOMPSON: All right, we'll get that.

...

SPEAKER?: What time did we decide on tomorrow morning?

(Mixed voices and laughter and more mixed voices.)

RFK: How are you doing, Bob?

McNAMARA: Well, hard to tell. You have any doubts?

RFK: Well, I think we're doing the only

DOCUMENT 49: Transcript of the Executive Committee meeting, October 27, 1962
(from the John F. Kennedy Library; edited for length).

PAGE 21 OF 21

thing we can do and well, you know.

MCNAMARA: I think the one thing, Bobby we ought to seriously (words unclear) we need to have two things ready, a government for Cuba, because we're going to need one (words unclear) and secondly, plans for how to respond to the Soviet Union in Europe, because sure as hell they're going to do something there.

(Mixed voices)

SPEAKER?: Suppose we make Bobby mayor of Havana.

(Mixed voices, tape ends)

DOCUMENT 50: Cable received from U.S. Ambassador to Turkey Raymond Hare to State Department, regarding Turkish Missiles, October 27, 1962 (section one only).

PAGE 1 OF 2

F770005-1470

INCO'G TELEGRAM   *Department of State*

ACTION COPY
PERMANENT RECORD

W
Action

SS
Info

SECRET

EYES ONLY

Control: 19238
Rec'd: October 27, 1962
1:18 p.m.

FROM: Ankara

TO: Secretary of State

NO: 587, October 26, 6 p.m. (SECTION ONE OF THREE)

PRIORITY

ACTION DEPARTMENT 587, INFORMATION PARIS TOPOL PRIORITY 21, ROME 57

EYES ONLY SECRETARY AND AMBASSADORS FINLETTER AND REINHARDT

Reference: Department telegram 445

As recognized reference telegram removal Jupiters from Turkey in context Cuban situation would present major problem not only in terms of bilateral Turkish-American relationship but also NATO association. Problem would be partly psycho-political, partly substantive; psycho-political, in sense that Turks are proud courageous people who do not understand concept or process of compromise. It is this quality of steadfast, even stolid, courage in both spirit and policy, together with traditional Turkish military skill which is actually their greatest asset to US and to West generally and by same token it is here that we would have most to lose if in process of Jupiter removal Turks should get the impression that their interests as an ally were being sacrificed in order to appease an enemy. Furthermore, as brought out in conversation with Foreign Minister Erkin yesterday, Turks deeply resent any coupling of Turkey and Cuba on ground that situations completely different and that suggestions to that effect,   especially when coming from Western sources, are both inexcusable and seriously damaging; and all the more so when associated with idea that Turkish relationship with US can be equated with stooge status of Cuba with USSR.

● This copy must be returned to RM/R central files with notation of action taken ●

| ACTION ASSIGNED TO | ACTION TAKEN | REPRODUCTION FROM THIS COPY IS PROHIBITED UNLESS "UNCLASSIFIED" |
| NAME OF OFFICER & OFFICE SYMBOL | DATE OF ACTION | DIRECTIONS TO RM/R |

EYES ONLY

GPO 930 500

DOCUMENT 50: Cable received from U.S. Ambassador to Turkey Raymond Hare to State Department, regarding Turkish Missiles, October 27, 1962 (section one only).

PAGE 2 OF 2

F770005-1471

SECRET

-2-587, October 26, 6 p.m. (SECTION ONE OF THREE), from Ankara

(#) Turks, as we well know, set great store on arms which they feel necessary meet their needs and were adamant in refusing our suggestion last year that Jupiter project not be implemented. No indication in meantime that their position has changed and can therefore be assumed that, rhirhihdftst* to contrary, demand for arms to fill vacuum would be specific and sizeable.

In so briefly outlining Turkish side of matter, I am of course mindful of significant non-Turkish considerations and that ihrs chkif ncipf bnda* of being able to use what some regard as a dubious and waning asset in the fe m jc* Turkish Jupiters as a negotiating counter to effect removal of immediately dangerous Soviet missiles in Cuba has strong attractions In bolstering this point of view I would also venture to suggest that, as a bargaining asset, Turkish Jupiters might be a more potent factor in Soviet eyes than they are in fact for simple reason that propinquity tends to magnify as we have repeatedly seen in Soviet reaction to military installations on their periphery irrespective of their defensive purpose. It is also recognized that timing is an important element since assets of terminal value must be exploited, if at all, sufficiently in advance of expiration of usefulness, either real or imagined.

HARE

MCA

*As received. Will be serviced upon request.

(#) Omission. Correction to follow.

SECRET

DOCUMENT 51: President Kennedy's letter to Premier Khrushchev, responding to proposal to end the crisis, October 27, 1962.

PAGE 1 OF 3

OUTGOING TELEGRAM Department of State

3 69

UNCLASSIFIED
Classification

ACTION: Amembassy MOSCOW C/S NIACT

OCT 27 8 05 PM '62

Following message from President to Khrushchev should be delivered as soon as possible to highest available Soviet official. Text has been handed Soviet Embassy in Washington and has been released to press.

QUOTE

Dear Mr. Chairman:

I have read your letter of October 26 with great care and welcomed the statement of your desire to seek a prompt solution to the problem. The first thing that needs to be done, however, is for work to cease on offensive missile bases in Cuba and for all weapons systems in Cuba capable of offensive use to be rendered inoperable, under effective United Nations arrangements.

Assuming this is done promptly, I have given my representatives in New York instructions that will permit them to work out this week and -- in cooperation with the

Acting Secretary

S/S - Mr. Allbeck   S/S - Mr. Ball

UNCLASSIFIED
Classification

DS-322

DOCUMENT 51: President Kennedy's letter to Premier Khrushchev, responding to proposal to end the crisis, October 27. 1962.

PAGE 2 OF 3

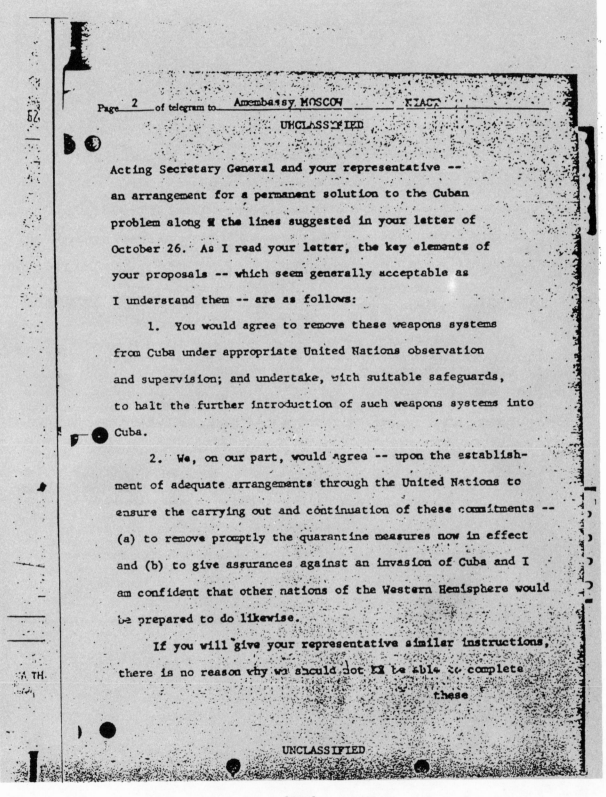

Page 2 of telegram to Amembassy MOSCOW KIACT

UNCLASSIFIED

Acting Secretary General and your representative --

an arrangement for a permanent solution to the Cuban

problem along the lines suggested in your letter of

October 26. As I read your letter, the key elements of

your proposals -- which seem generally acceptable as

I understand them -- are as follows:

1. You would agree to remove these weapons systems

from Cuba under appropriate United Nations observation

and supervision; and undertake, with suitable safeguards,

to halt the further introduction of such weapons systems into

Cuba.

2. We, on our part, would agree -- upon the establish-

ment of adequate arrangements through the United Nations to

ensure the carrying out and continuation of these commitments --

(a) to remove promptly the quarantine measures now in effect

and (b) to give assurances against an invasion of Cuba and I

am confident that other nations of the Western Hemisphere would

be prepared to do likewise.

If you will give your representative similar instructions,

there is no reason why we should not be able to complete

these

UNCLASSIFIED

DOCUMENT 51: President Kennedy's letter to Premier Khrushchev, responding to proposal to end the crisis, October 27. 1962.

PAGE 3 OF 3

Page 3 of telegram to Amembassy MOSCOW

UNCLASSIFIED

these arrangements and announce them to the world within a couple of days. The effect of such a settlement on easing world tensions would enable us to work toward a more general arrangement regarding "other armaments", as proposed in your second letter which you made public. I would like to say again that the United States is very much interested in reducing tensions and halting the arms race; and if your letter signifies that you are prepared to discuss a detente affecting NATO and the Warsaw Pact, we are quite prepared to consider with our allies any useful proposals.

But the first ingredient, let me emphasize, is the cessation of work on missile sites in Cuba and measures to render such weapons inoperable, under effective inter-national guarantees. The continuation of this threat, or a prolonging of this discussion concerning Cuba by linking these problems to the broader questions of European and world security, would surely lead to an intensification of the Cuban crisis and a grave risk to the peace of the world. For this reason I hope we can quickly agree along the lines outlined in this letter and in your letter of October 26.

/S/ John F. Kennedy

END

UNCLASSIFIED   RUSK

DOCUMENT 52: Premier Khrushchev's communiqué to President Kennedy, accepting an end to the missile crisis, October 28, 1962.

PAGE 1 OF 4

TEXT OF KHRUSHCHEV MESSAGE

MOSCOW DOMESTIC SERVICE IN RUSSIAN 1425 28 OCT 62 L

(TEXT) ESTEEMED MR. PRESIDENT: I HAVE RECEIVED YOUR MESSAGE OF OCTOBER 27, 1962. I EXPRESS MY SATISFACTION AND GRATITUDE FOR THE SENSE OF PROPORTION AND UNDERSTANDING OF THE RESPONSIBILITY BORNE BY YOU AT PRESENT FOR THE PRESERVATION OF PEACE THROUGHOUT THE WORLD WHICH YOU HAVE SHOWN. I VERY WELL UNDERSTAND YOUR ANXIETY AND THE ANXIETY OF THE UNITED STATES PEOPLE IN CONNECTION WITH THE FACT THAT THE WEAPONS WHICH YOU DESCRIBE AS "OFFENSIVE" ARE, IN FACT, GRIM WEAPONS. BOTH YOU AND I UNDERSTAND WHAT KIND OF WEAPON THEY ARE.

IN ORDER TO COMPLETE WITH GREATER SPEED THE LIQUIDATION OF THE CONFLICT DANGEROUS TO THE CAUSE OF PEACE, TO GIVE CONFIDENCE TO ALL PEOPLE LONGING FOR PEACE, AND TO CALM THE AMERICAN PEOPLE, WHO, I AM CERTAIN, WANT PEACE AS MUCH AS THE PEOPLE OF THE SOVIET UNION, THE SOVIET GOVERNMENT, IN ADDITION TO PREVIOUSLY ISSUED INSTRUCTIONS ON THE CESSATION OF FURTHER WORK AT BUILDING SITES FOR THE WEAPONS, HAS ISSUED A NEW ORDER ON THE DISMANTLING OF THE WEAPONS WHICH YOU DESCRIBE AS "OFFENSIVE," AND THEIR CRATING AND RETURN TO THE SOVIET UNION.

MR. PRESIDENT, I WOULD LIKE TO REPEAT ONCE MORE WHAT I HAD ALREADY WRITTEN TO YOU IN MY PRECEDING LETTERS--THAT THE SOVIET GOVERNMENT HAS PLACED AT THE DISPOSAL OF THE CUBAN GOVERNMENT ECONOMIC AID, AS WELL AS ARMS, INASMUCH AS CUBA AND THE CUBAN PEOPLE HAVE CONSTANTLY BEEN UNDER THE CONTINUOUS DANGER OF AN INVASION.

THE SHELLING OF HAVANA TOOK PLACE FROM A PIRATIC SHIP. IT IS SAID THAT IRRESPONSIBLE CUBAN EMIGRES DID THE SHOOTING. THIS IS POSSIBLY THE CASE. HOWEVER, THE QUESTION ARISES: FROM WHERE DID THEY FIRE? AFTER ALL, THEY, THESE CUBANS, HAVE NO TERRITORY, THEY HAVE NO PRIVATE MEANS, AND THEY HAVE NO MEANS TO WAGE MILITARY ACTION. THUS SOMEBODY PUT THE ARMS NEEDED TO SHELL HAVANA AND CARRY OUT THEIR PIRATIC ACTIONS IN THE CARIBBEAN--IN CUBAN TERRITORIAL WATERS--IN THEIR HANDS!

IT IS UNTHINKABLE IN OUR TIME NOT TO NOTICE A PIRATE SHIP, PARTICULARLY IF ONE TAKES INTO ACCOUNT SUCH A SATURATION OF AMERICAN SHIPS IN THE CARIBBEAN FROM WHICH ACTUALLY ALL THIS IS WATCHED AND OBSERVED. IN SUCH CIRCUMSTANCES, PIRATIC SHIPS ARE FREELY MOVING AROUND CUBA, SHELLING CUBA, AND CARRYING OUT PIRATIC ATTACKS UPON PEACEFUL TRANSPORT VESSELS! IT IS, AFTER ALL, KNOWN THAT THEY EVEN SHELLED A BRITISH FREIGHTER!

IN SHORT, CUBA HAS BEEN UNDER THE CONSTANT THREAT OF AGGRESSIVE FORCES WHICH DID NOT CONCEAL THEIR INTENTIONS TO INVADE CUBAN TERRITORY.

THE CUBAN PEOPLE WANT TO BUILD THEIR LIFE IN THEIR OWN INTEREST WITHOUT INTERFERENCE FROM WITHOUT. YOU ARE RIGHT IN THIS, AND ONE CANNOT BLAME THEM BECAUSE THEY WANT TO BE MASTERS OF THEIR OWN COUNTRY AND DISPOSE OF THE FRUITS OF THEIR LABOR. THE THREAT OF CUBA'S INVASION AND ALL THE OTHER VENTURES AIMED AT BRINGING ABOUT TENSION AROUND CUBA ARE DESIGNED TO ENGENDER UNCERTAINTY IN THE CUBAN PEOPLE, INTIMIDATE THEM, AND HINDER THEM IN BUILDING THEIR NEW LIFE UNDISTURBED.

MR. PRESIDENT, I WANT TO SAY CLEARLY AGAIN THAT WE COULD NOT BE INDIFFERENT TO THIS. THE SOVIET GOVERNMENT DECIDED TO HELP CUBA WITH MEANS OF DEFENSE AGAINST AGGRESSION--AND ONLY WITH MEANS FOR PURPOSES OF DEFENSE.

(MORE)

DOCUMENT 52: Premier Khrushchev's communiqué to President Kennedy, accepting an end to the missile crisis, October 28, 1962.

PAGE 2 OF 4

FIRST ADD 53 (KHRUSHCHEV TEXT)

X X X PURPOSES OF DEFENSE

(CONTINUING TEXT) WE STATIONED DEFENSE MEANS THERE WHICH YOU CALL OFFENSIVE. WE STATIONED THEM THERE IN ORDER THAT NO ATTACK SHOULD BE MADE AGAINST CUBA AND THAT NO RASH ACTION SHOULD BE PERMITTED TO TAKE PLACE.

I REGARD WITH RESPECT AND TRUST YOUR STATEMENT IN YOUR MESSAGE OF OCTOBER 27, 1962 THAT NO ATTACK WILL BE MADE ON CUBA--THAT NO INVASION WILL TAKE PLACE--NOT ONLY BY THE UNITED STATES, BUT ALSO BY OTHER COUNTRIES OF THE WESTERN HEMISPHERE, AS YOUR MESSAGE POINTED OUT. THEN THE MOTIVES WHICH PROMPTED US TO GIVE AID OF THIS NATURE TO CUBA CEASE. THEY ARE NO LONGER APPLICABLE. HENCE WE HAVE INSTRUCTED OUR OFFICERS--AND THESE MEANS, AS I HAVE ALREADY STATED, ARE IN THE HANDS OF SOVIET OFFICERS--TO TAKE NECESSARY MEASURES FOR STOPPING THE BUILDING OF THE SAID PROJECTS AND THEIR DISMANTLING AND RETURN TO THE SOVIET UNION.

AS I ALREADY TOLD YOU IN MY LETTER OF OCTOBER 27, WE BOTH AGREE TO COME TO AN AGREEMENT THAT UNITED NATIONS RAPRESENTATIVE COULD VERIFY THE DISMANTLING OF THESE MEANS.

IN THIS WAY, IF ONE IS TO RELY ON YOUR ASSURANCES WHICH YOU HAVE MADE AND ON OUR ORDERS TO DISMANTLE, THEN ALL NECESSARY CONDITIONS FOR LIQUIDATION OF THE CONFLICT WHICH HAS ARISEN APPEAR TO EXIST.

I NOTE WITH SATISFACTION THAT YOU HAVE RESPONDED TO MY WISH THAT THE SAID DANGEROUS SITUATION SHOULD BE LIQUIDATED AND ALSO THAT CONDITIONS SHOULD BE CREATED FOR A MORE THOUGHTFUL APPRAISAL OF THE INTERNATIONAL SITUATION WHICH IS FRAUGHT WITH GREAT DANGERS IN OUR AGE OF THERMONUCLEAR WEAPONS, ROCKET TECHNOLOGY, SPACESHIPS, GLOBAL ROCKETS, AND OTHER LETHAL WEAPONS. ALL PEOPLE ARE INTERESTED IN INSURING PEACE. THEREFORE, WE WHO ARE INVESTED WITH TRUST AND GREAT RESPONSIBILITY MUST NOT PERMIT AN EXACERBATION OF THE SITUATION AND MUST LIQUIDATE THE BREEDING GROUNDS WHERE A DANGEROUS SITUATION HAS BEEN CREATED FRAUGHT WITH SERIOUS CONSEQUENCES FOR THE CAUSE OF PEACE. IF WE SUCCEED ALONG WITH YOU AND WITH THE AID OF OTHER PEOPLE OF GOOD WILL IN LIQUIDATING THIS TENSE SITUATION, WE MUST ALSO CONCERN OURSELVES TO SEE THAT OTHER DANGEROUS CONFLICTS DO NOT ARISE WHICH MIGHT LEAD TO A WORLD THERMONUCLEAR CATASTROPHE.

IN CONCLUSION, I WISH TO SPEAK OF THE REGULATION OF RELATION BETWEEN NATO AND STATES OF THE WARSAW TREATY, WHICH YOU MENTION. WE HAVE LONG AGO SPOKEN OF THIS AND ARE READY TO CONTINUE AN EXCHANGE OF OPINIONS WITH YOU ON THIS QUESTION AND FIND A REASONABLE SOLUTION. I ALSO WISH TO CONTINUE AN EXCHANGE OF OPINIONS ON THE PROHIBITION OF ATOMIC AND THERMONUCLEAR WEAPONS, GENERAL DISARMAMENT, AND OTHER QUESTIONS CONCERNING THE LESSENING OF INTERNATIONAL TENSION.

MR. PRESIDENT, I TRUST YOUR STATEMENT. HOWEVER, ON THE OTHER HAND, THERE ARE RESPONSIBLE PEOPLE WHO WOULD LIKE TO CARRY OUT AN INVASION OF CUBA AT THIS TIME, AND IN SUCH A WAY TO SPARK OFF A WAR. IF WE TAKE PRACTICAL STEPS AND ANNOUNCE THE DISMANTLING AND EVACUATION OF THE APPROPRIATE MEANS FROM CUBA, THEN, DOING THAT, WE WISH TO ESTABLISH AT THE SAME TIME THE CONFIDENCE OF THE CUBAN PEOPLE THAT WE ARE WITH THEM AND ARE NOT DIVESTING OURSELVES OF THE RESPONSIBILITY OF GRANTING HELP TO THEM.

WE ARE CONVINCED THAT THE PEOPLE OF ALL COUNTRIES, LIKE YOURSELF, MR. PRESIDENT, WILL UNDERSTAND ME CORRECTLY. WE DO NOT ISSUE THREATS. WE DESIRE ONLY PEACE. OUR COUNTRY IS NOW ON THE UPSURGE. OUR PEOPLE ARE ENJOYING THE FRUITS OF THEIR PEACEFUL LABOR. THEY HAVE ACHIEVED TREMENDOUS SUCCESSES SINCE THE OCTOBER REVOLUTION AND CREATED SUPREME MATERIAL AND SPIRITUAL-CULTURAL TREASURES. OUR COUNTRY IS MAKING USE OF THESE TREASURES AND WANTS TO DEVELOP ITS SUCCESSES FURTHER AND INSURE FURTHER DEVELOPMENT ON THE ROAD OF PEACE AND SOCIAL PROGRESS BY ITS STEADFAST LABOR.

DOCUMENT 52: Premier Khrushchev's communiqué to President Kennedy, accepting an end to the missile crisis, October 28, 1962.

PAGE 3 OF 4

FSIS 55

SECOND AND LAST ADD 53 (KHRUSHCHEV TEXT)

X X X ITS STEADFAST LABOR

(CONCLUDING TEXT) I SHOULD LIKE, MR. PRESIDENT, TO REMIND YOU
THAT MILITARY AIRCRAFT OF A RECONNAISSANCE CHARACTER HAVE
VIOLATED THE FRONTIER OF THE SOVIET UNION IN CONNECTION WITH WH CH
WE HAD CONFLICTS WITH YOU. AN EXCHANGE OF NOTES TOOK PLACE.

IN 1960, WE SHOT DOWN YOUR U-2 AIRCRAFT, THE RECONNAISSANCE
FLIGHT OF WHICH OVER THE USSR LED TO THE WRECKING OF THE MEET NG
OF THE POWERS IN PARIS. YOU THEN TOOK A CORRECT POSITION IN
CONDEMNING THAT CRIMINAL ACTION BY THE FORMER UNITED STATES
GOVERNMENT. HOWEVER, DURING THE PERIOD OF YOUR TENURE OF OFFICE
AS PRESIDENT, A SECOND INSTANCE OF THE VIOLATION OF OUR FRONTIER
BY AN AMERICAN U-2 AIRCRAFT TOOK PLACE IN THE SAKHALIN AREA.
WE WROTE YOU ABOUT THIS VIOLATION ON AUGUST 30. YOU REPLIED
THAT THIS VIOLATION HAD TAKEN PLACE AS THE RESULT OF BAD WEATHER
AND GAVE AN ASSURANCE THAT IT WOULD NOT BE REPEATED. WE GAVE
CREDENCE TO YOUR ASSURANCE BECAUSE THERE WAS INDEED BAD WEATHER
IN THAT AREA AT THAT TIME. HOWEVER, IF YOUR AIRCRAFT DID NOT
HAVE THE TASK OF FLYING NEAR OUR TERRITORY, THEN EVEN BAD WEATHER
COULD NOT CAUSE AN AMERICAN AIRCRAFT TO ENTER OUR AIRSPACE.

THE CONCLUSION FOLLOWS FROM THIS THAT IT IS DONE WITH THE
KNOWLEDGE OF THE PENTAGON, WHICH TRAMPLES ON INTERNATIONAL
PRACTICES AND VIOLATES THE FRONTIERS OF OTHER STATES.

AN EVEN MORE DANGEROUS CASE OCCURRED ON OCTOBER 28 WHEN
YOUR RECONNAISSANCE AIRCRAFT INTRUDED INTO THE TERRITORY OF THE
SOVIET UNION IN THE NORTH, IN THE AREA OF THE CHUKOTKA PENINSULA,
AND FLEW OVER OUR TERRITORY.

ONE ASKS, MR. PRESIDENT, HOW SHOULD WE REGARD THIS? WHAT S T?
A PROVOCATION? YOUR AIRCRAFT VIOLATES OUR FRONTIER AND AT TIMES
AS ANXIOUS AS THOSE WHICH WE ARE NOW EXPERIENCING WHEN EVERYTHING
HAS BEEN PLACED IN A STATE OF COMBAT READINESS. FOR AN INTRUDING
AMERICAN AIRCRAFT CAN EASILY BE TAKEN FOR A BOMBER WITH NUCLEAR
WEAPONS, AND THIS COULD PUSH US TOWARD A FATAL STEP--ALL THE MORE
SO BECAUSE BOTH THE UNITED STATES GOVERNMENT AND PENTAGON HAVE
LONG BEEN SAYING THAT BOMBERS WITH ATOMIC BOMBS ARE CONSTANTLY ON
DUTY IN YOUR COUNTRY.

DOCUMENT 52: Premier Khrushchev's communiqué to President Kennedy, accepting an end to the missile crisis, October 28, 1962.

PAGE 4 OF 4

THEREFORE, YOU CAN IMAGINE WHAT KIND OF RESPONSIBILITY YOU ASSUME, ESPECIALLY NOW DURING THE ANXIOUS TIMES WE ARE NOW EXPERIENCING.

I WOULD LIKE TO ASK YOU TO ASSESS THIS CORRECTLY AND TAKE STEPS ACCORDINGLY IN ORDER THAT IT WOULD NOT SERVE AS A PROVOCATION FOR UNLEASHING WAR.

I WOULD ALSO LIKE TO EXPRESS THE FOLLOWING WISH. OF COURSE, IT IS A MATTER FOR THE CUBAN PEOPLE. YOU DO NOT AT PRESENT MAINTAIN ANY DIPLOMATIC RELATIONS BUT THROUGH MY OFFICERS ON CUBA I HAVE REPORTS THAT FLIGHTS OF AMERICAN AIRCRAFT OVER CUBA ARE BEING CARRIED OUT. WE ARE INTERESTED THAT THERE SHOULD NOT BE ANY WAR AT ALL IN THE WORLD, AND THAT THE CUBAN PEOPLE SHOULD LIVE QUIETLY. HOWEVER, MR. PRESIDENT, IT IS NO SECRET THAT WE HAVE OUR PEOPLE ON CUBA. ACCORDING TO THE TREATY WITH THE CUBAN GOVERNMENT, WE HAVE OFFICERS AND INSTRUCTORS THERE WHO ARE TRAINING THE CUBANS. THEY ARE MAINLY ORDINARY PEOPLE--EXPERTS, AGRONOMISTS, ZOOTECHNICIANS, IRRIGATION AND SOIL IMPROVEMENT EXPERTS, ORDINARY WORKERS, TRACTOR DRIVERS, AND OTHERS. WE ARE CONCERNED ABOUT THEM.

I WOULD LIKE TO ASK YOU, MR. PRESIDENT, TO BEAR IN MIND THAT A VIOLATION OF CUBAN AIRSPACE BY AMERICAN AIRCRAFT MAY ALSO HAVE DANGEROUS CONSEQUENCES. IF YOU DO NOT WANT THIS, THEN NO PRETEXT SHOULD BE GIVEN FOR THE CREATION OF A DANGEROUS SITUATION.

WE MUST BE NOW VERY CAUTIOUS AND NOT TAKE SUCH STEPS WHICH WILL BE OF NO USE FOR THE DEFENSE OF THE STATES INVOLVED IN THE CONFLICT, BUT WHICH ARE LIKELY TO AROUSE ONLY IRRITATION AND EVEN PROVE A PROVOCATION LEADING TO THE BANEFUL STEP. WE MUST, THEREFORE, DISPLAY SOBRIETY AND WISDOM AND REFRAIN FROM STEPS OF THIS SORT.

WE VALUE PEACE, PERHAPS EVEN MORE THAN OTHER PEOPLE, BECAUSE WE EXPERIENCED THE TERRIBLE WAR AGAINST HITLER. HOWEVER, OUR PEOPLE WILL NOT FLINCH IN THE FACE OF ANY ORDEAL. OUR PEOPLE TRUST THEIR GOVERNMENT, AND WE ASSURE OUR PEOPLE AND THE WORLD PUBLIC THAT THE SOVIET GOVERNMENT WILL NOT ALLOW ITSELF TO BE PROVOKED.

SHOULD THE PROVOCATEURS UNLEASH A WAR, THEY WOULD NOT ESCAPE THE GRAVE CONSEQUENCES OF SUCH A WAR. HOWEVER, WE ARE CONFIDENT THAT REASON WILL TRIUMPH. WAR WILL NOT BE UNLEASHED AND THE PEACE AND SECURITY OF PEOPLE WILL BE INSURED.

IN CONNECTION WITH NEGOTIATIONS IN PROGRESS BETWEEN U.N. ACTING SECRETARY GENERAL U THANT AND RDPRESENTATIVES OF THE SOVIET UNION, THE UNITED STATES, AND THE CUBAN REPUBLIC, THE SOVIET GOVERNMENT HAS SENT TO NEW YORK USSR FIRST DEPUTY MINISTER OF FOREIGN AFFAIRS KUZNETSOV WITH A VIEW TO ASSISTING U THANT IN HIS NOBLE EFFORTS AIMED AT LIQUIDATION OF THE PRESENT DANGEROUS SITUATION.

WITH RESPECT FOR YOU, KHRUSHCHEV. OCTOBER 28, 1962.

(ENDALL)

28 OCT 1043A HML/HM

DOCUMENT 53: President Kennedy's letter to Premier Khrushchev, confirming terms to settle the missile crisis, October 28, 1962.

PAGE 1 OF 3

OUTGOING TELEGRAM Department of State 3649

DUPLICATE □ COLLECT
CHARGE TO

130

UNCLASSIFIED
Classification

Oct 28 5 03 PM '62

SS

ACTION: AMEmbassy MOSCOW 1320 NIACT

Rpt Info: AMEmbassy PARIS 2387 PRIORITY
AMEmbassy LONDON 2353 Priority
USUN NEW YORK 1129 PRIORITY

R

Following is text President's reply to Khrushchev letter of October 28 for delivery to highest available Soviet official Text has been handed to Soviet Embassy and released by White House at 4:35 PM

Begin text

Dear Mr. Chairman:

I am replying at once to your broadcast message of October twenty-eight even though the official text has not yet reached me because of the great importance I attach to moving forward promptly to the settlement of the Cuban crisis. I think that you and I, with our heavy responsibilities for the maintenance of peace, were aware that developments were approaching a point where events could have become unmanageable So I welcome this message and consider it an important contribution to peace.

The distinguished efforts of Acting Secretary General U Thant have greatly facilitated both our tasks. I consider my letter

Drafted by: S/AL-L. Thompson
U: George W. Ball

The Secretary

White House - Mr. Bundy

S/S - M. Davis

UNCLASSIFIED
Classification

DS-322

DOCUMENT 53: President Kennedy's letter to Premier Khrushchev, confirming terms to settle the missile crisis, October 28, 1962.

PAGE 2 OF 3

Page ___2___ of telegram to   MOSCOW, repreated PARIS, LONDON, US. I_____

my letter to you of October twenty-seventh and your reply of today as firm undertakings on the part of both our governments which should be promptly carried out. I hope that the necessary measures can at once be taken through the United Nations as your message says, so that the United States in turn can remove the quarantine measures now in effect. I have already made arrangements to report all these matters to the Organization of American States, whose memebers share a deep interest in a genuine peace in the Caribbean area.

You referred in your letter to a violation of your frontier by an American aircraft in the area of the Chukotsk Peninsula. I have learned that this plane, without arms or photographic equipment, was engaged in an air sampling mission in connection with your nuclear tests. Its course was direct from Eielson Air Force Base in Alaska to the North Pole and return. In turning south, the pilot made a serious navigational error which carried him over Soviet territory. He immediately made an emergency call on open radio for navigational assistance and was guided back to his home base by the most direct route. I regret this incident and will see to it that every precaution is taken to prevent recurrence.   Mr. Chairman

DOCUMENT 53: President Kennedy's letter to Premier Khrushchev, confirming terms to settle the missile crisis, October 28, 1962.

PAGE 3 OF 3

Page 3 of telegram to MOSCOW repeated PARIS LONDON USUN

UNCLASSIFIED
Classification

Mr. Chairman, both of our countries have great unfinished tasks and I know that your people as well as those of the United States can ask for nothing better than to pursue them free from the fear of war. Modern science and technology have given us the possibility of making labor fruitful beyond anything that could have been dreamed of a few decades ago.

I agree with you that we must devote urgent attention to the problem of disarmament, as it relates to the whole world and also to critical areas. Perhaps now, as we step back from danger, we can together make real progress in this vital field. I think we should give priority to questions relating to the proliferation of nuclear weapons, on earth and in outer space, and to the great effort for a nuclear test ban. But we should also work hard to see if wider measures of disarmament can be agreed and put into operation at an early date. The United States Government will be prepared to discuss these questions urgently, and in a constructive spirit, at Geneva or elsewhere.

/s/ John F. Kennedy

End Text

RUSK

UNCLASSIFIED
Classification

PART III

THE NOVEMBER EXTENSION

With Khrushchev's decision on October 28 to withdraw the missiles from Cuba the crisis abated, but it did not end. Tensions between the United States and the Soviet Union quickly mounted again over several residual issues, including: the withdrawal of other Soviet weapons that the Kennedy administration defined as offensive, particularly Ilyushin-28 (IL-28) bombers; inspection and verification of the withdrawal; and formalization of the U.S. noninvasion pledge, which the Soviets wanted to codify at the United Nations. The Cubans, who were left out of the U.S.-Soviet negotiations to end the Cuban missile crisis, also asserted their interests with a settlement that differed substantially from those of the superpowers (Document 55). Angry that Khrushchev had not consulted, let alone informed, him before cutting a deal with Kennedy, Fidel Castro issued his own "five points" for settlement, which included ending the U.S. trade embargo, terminating covert operations against Cuba and support for anti-Castro Cuban exiles, and U.S. withdrawal from Guantánamo (Document 56). Subsequently, Castro refused to allow the Soviets to remove forty-two IL-28 jet bombers from Cuba, and he forbade the on-site inspection and verification that Khrushchev had agreed upon with Kennedy. "Whoever tries to inspect Cuba must come in battle array," Castro warned.[1]

In the midst of this tense situation, negotiations for a final settlement continued between U.S. Ambas-sador Adlai Stevenson, John McCloy, and Soviet Deputy Foreign Minister Vasily Kuznetzov in New York, and between First Deputy Prime Minister Anastas Mikoyan and Fidel Castro in Havana. Until November 20, when Khrushchev assured Washington that the IL-28s would be expeditiously removed, the possibility of escalating overt hostilities between the superpowers continued to hang over the world.

THE IL-28 BOMBERS

On October 28, the Executive Committee met and discussed, among other things, the removal of the Soviet IL-28 bombers (Document 59). President Kennedy indicated that he did not want to get "hung up" over these planes, which were twelve years old, and obsolete as strategic weapons. Nevertheless, the IL-28s topped the list of arms that U.S. officials believed could be defined as "offensive." State Department intelligence analyst Raymond Garthoff recommended in an October 29 memorandum that "in addition to the MRBMs and IRBMs, the IL-28s should definitively be included" in the list of weapons the U.S. wanted the Soviets to remove (Document 60). Since Kennedy had, in his October 22 speech, publicly included the IL-28s among the offensive weapons systems that the United States was committed to removing from Cuba, the ExComm chose to adopt these recommendations. On November 2, the White House transmitted a list of weapons to U.S. negotiators in New York that included not only the Soviet missiles and warheads but also the bomber planes and Komar-class torpedo boats. In a set of negotiating points cabled to Stevenson and McCloy on November 3, Kennedy instructed them to give the list to Mikoyan who was stopping over in New York on his way to Cuba. "In this situation," the president's instructions read,

> the Soviet Government has a clear choice between verified removal of all offensive weapons systems and renewed action by the United States. It has no middle choice, and we believe its own interests should lead it to accept the honest and full execution of the Kennedy-Khrushchev agreement, and to see to it that Castro provides the necessary cooperation.[2]

These demands caused extreme consternation in Moscow and Havana. Khrushchev complained to Kennedy in a November 4 letter that "it is hard for us to understand what aim is being pursued by the introduction of that list...at a moment when we have already agreed with you on the main questions and when we on our part have already fulfilled what we agreed upon" (Document 66). In his November 11 letter, the Soviet premier again rejected Kennedy's "incomprehensible argument" about the planes (Document 69). Nevertheless, without informing Castro, and without requesting anything in return, Khrushchev agreed to remove the bombers at such time when the Soviets had mended relations with the Cubans: "we give a gentleman's word that we will remove the IL-28 planes with all the personnel and equipment related to those planes, although not now but later. We would like to do that some time later when we determine that the conditions are ripe to remove them" (Document 69). Later that evening, the president directed his brother to tell Ambassador Dobrynin that the United States would accept Khrushchev's word on the withdrawal and "lift all quarantine" with the expectation that the planes would be withdrawn within thirty days (Document 70).

Yet tension continued to mount over the IL-28s for another week because Khrushchev would not agree to a specific time frame to withdraw the planes. On November 14, he wrote Kennedy that thirty days was insufficient but "it can be done in 2–3 months" (Document 71). Kennedy responded that "as soon as you give the order for the removal of the IL-28's and their men and equipment, to be completed within thirty days...we will announce the lifting of the quarantine" (Document 72). Within the ExComm, there was mounting pressure to take a harder stance toward what was perceived as Soviet stalling. A Pentagon briefing paper prepared for a November 16 meeting between JCS Chairman General Maxwell Taylor and the president argued that the United States should pressure not only for the IL-28s to be removed but all other Soviet weapons and Soviet military personnel as well. In addition, the JCS urged that the blockade should be expanded and the IL-28s removed "if need be, by military action" (Document 73). A State Department contingency paper prepared for the ExComm went further and proposed "harassing surveillance" over Cuba, and as a last resort, that aerial reconnaissance might be used "as a means of provoking attack on our planes, which would in turn justify retaliation from the air on Cuban targets (including the IL-28's on the ground)."[3]

On November 19, President Kennedy sent personal messages to Charles de Gaulle, Konrad Adenauer, and Harold Macmillan, stating that the United States might have to use "renewed action" to get the bombers out of Cuba. That same day, however, Fidel Castro conceded to pressure and notified the United Nations that Cuba would "not object" if the Soviets withdrew the planes (Document 75). Khrushchev wrote to Kennedy late on the 19th that "we intend to remove [the IL-28s] within a month term and may be even sooner" (Document 76). The ExComm met the next day and agreed to set aside further concerns about other Soviet military equipment and personnel in Cuba and to end the crisis. At a press conference on the evening of November 20, President Kennedy informed the public that the missiles had been dismantled, and the Soviets were withdrawing IL-28s; consequently, the U.S. naval quarantine around Cuba was being lifted and the crisis was finally over. On the eve of the Thanksgiving holiday, Kennedy observed, the United States had "much for which we can be grateful, as we look back to where we stood only four weeks ago."[4]

INSPECTION AND VERIFICATION

Although the Soviets ultimately persuaded Fidel Castro to allow the IL-28s to be removed, Mikoyan proved unable to force him to accept any kind of international on-site inspection to verify removal of all offensive weapons systems. U.N. Secretary General U Thant reported on November 1 that he had found Castro in an "impossible and intractable mood" and "extremely bitter at [the] Soviets." Castro was "furious with Khrushchev for making verification commitment and made it clear he would not permit even inspection of what is left behind after [the] sites [are] dismantled and evacuated" (Document 61). The only way he would allow U.N. inspection was if the United States also agreed to allow its territory to be inspected for evidence of paramilitary anti-Castro activities. In a letter to Khrushchev dated November 3, Kennedy warned that if Castro "maintains this position this would raise very serious problems" (Document 64).

Through most of November, the ExComm debated how to pressure the Soviets and Cubans to obtain an inspection and verification agreement. On November 5, Kennedy and the ExComm considered the issue of trading U.N. inspection of Cuba for U.N. inspection of paramilitary Cuban exile camps in Florida, but rejected the idea (Document 65). The possibility of having the International Red Cross inspect ships going in and out of Cuban ports was also discussed. Two days later, the ExComm weighed U Thant's proposal to use a team of Latin American ambassadors as on-site inspectors. According to minutes of the meeting, "the President said these Ambassadors could look at caves and inspect possible Soviet submarine base sites" (Document 68).

The Soviets, it turned out, were open to almost any proposal; the Cubans were not. Despite heavy Soviet pressure, and the constant threat of attack by the United States, Fidel Castro stuck to his position that Cuba's sovereignty would not permit outside inspectors on its national territory. Ultimately, neither the Soviets nor the United States proved capable of fully untying what both Kennedy and Khrushchev called "the Cuban knot."

THE U.S. NONINVASION PLEDGE

President Kennedy's pledge not to invade Cuba—in return for which Khrushchev agreed to withdraw the nuclear missiles on October 28—was conditioned on the implementation of adequate inspection and verification procedures. In his letter to Khrushchev affirming a deal on evening of October 27, Kennedy wrote that "we, on our part, would agree—upon the establishment of adequate arrangements through the United Nations to ensure the carrying out and continuation of these commitments—...to give assurances against an invasion of Cuba and I am confident that other nations of the Western Hemisphere would be prepared to do likewise" (Document 51).

Although Cuba did not allow on-site inspection, Khrushchev did agree to a procedure whereby Soviet ships carrying the missile parts would allow U.S. ships and aircraft to photograph that equipment on their decks in order to verify that the missiles were, in fact, being withdrawn. Yet, despite verification by U.S. intelligence of the complete removal of the missiles, and later of the IL-28 bombers, and despite pleas from Stevenson and McCloy in New York that the U.S. demand for on-site inspection be dropped and a settlement reached at the United Nations, Kennedy administration officials refused to resolve the issue diplomatically.

For almost thirty years after the Cuban missile crisis the myth persisted that Kennedy had struck a secret deal with Khrushchev binding the U.S. to a commitment not to invade Cuba. But the recent declassification of the remaining correspondence between

Kennedy and Khrushchev, and of internal State Department memoranda, reveal that no such deal was ever made and why it was not.

Initially, President Kennedy seemed predisposed to formalize his noninvasion pledge. Minutes of a November 7 ExComm meeting record him as stating that "we might make a formal commitment not to invade when the Soviets comply fully by removing the IL-28 bombers and we have assurances that there will be no reintroduction of strategic missiles" (Document 68). By November 20, however, Kennedy had clearly retreated from that position.

Internal State Department memoranda declassified in April 1992 reveal that U.S. officials who saw the missile crisis as a great opportunity to overthrow Castro lobbied hard against any pledge that would inhibit future U.S. policy toward Cuba. Even before the crisis ended, the ExComm began weighing U.S. strategy for a post-crisis Cuba. On November 7, the State Department's Policy Planning Council submitted a long-term strategy paper, which called for "a maximal U.S. strategy...directed at the elimination...of the Castro regime."[5] Leaving the missile crisis diplomatically unresolved favored such a strategy, according to the State Department's Bureau of Intelligence and Research. In a November 17 report, analyst Roger Hilsman concluded that "a stalemate in the Cuban talks might actually be more beneficial to U.S. interests in Latin America [and] Cuba...than a settlement." A settlement, according to Hilsman's argument, meant that "the Castro regime would be substantially safeguarded from invasion, and by implication, at least, from other U.S. actions against it." In a stalemate, on the other hand, the United States would not

> commit itself to the preservation of the Castro regime and the Soviet presence in Cuba. In effect, the present crisis with the possibility of further U.S. action against Cuba would be perpetuated. The talks in New York would soon be obviously futile and would probably be allowed to peter out. (Document 74)

The latitude to overthrow Castro, this argument implied, was more important than a concrete resolution to the most dangerous international crisis of the twentieth century. "Our interest lies in...avoiding the kind of commitment that unduly ties our hands in dealing with the Castro regime while it lasts," Secretary of State Rusk informed McCloy.[6]

The impact of this position on Kennedy helps to explain his evasiveness in his correspondence with Khrushchev. The letters show Khrushchev repeatedly pressuring Kennedy to formalize the U.S. noninvasion commitment. On November 11, the Soviet premier suggested that the pledges of both sides "be registered in the appropriate documents in the United Nations Organization; non-invasion of Cuba and strict observance of her sovereignty guaranteed" (Document 69). Three days later, Khrushchev again suggested that the two sides "write down the mutual commitments ensuing from the messages of the President and mine of October 27 and 28 to which end your representatives and ours have to prepare with the participation of the UN acting Secretary General U Thant an appropriate document" (Document 71). And on November 19, the day before the crisis ended, Khrushchev complained to Kennedy that "proper consideration through the UN of the commitment not to invade Cuba...so far is being delayed" (Document 76).

In his responses, Kennedy either ignored Khrushchev's entreaties or deflected them on the grounds that the Soviets and Cubans had not met U.S. conditions: "we want nothing better than to be able to give our assurances," Kennedy wrote on November 15, "just as we said we would, when the necessary conditions exist" (Document 72). In his November 20 press conference, Kennedy made it clear that "important parts of the understanding of October 27th and 28th still remain to be carried out" and substantially reconditioned the U.S. commitment not to invade. "If Cuba is not used for the export of aggressive Communist purposes," he stated, "there will be peace in the Caribbean."[7]

Although the Soviets presented draft protocols for

negotiation, in the end there was no formal resolution of the missile crisis, and the United States "never made an unadorned commitment not to invade Cuba," as Dean Rusk told an executive session of the Senate Foreign Relations Committee.[8] Instead, the United States and the Soviet Union simply agreed to disagree. On January 7, 1963, Ambassador Stevenson and Deputy Minister Kuznetzov jointly asked U Thant to remove the missile crisis issue from the agenda of the United Nations: "While it has not been possible for our Governments to resolve all the problems that have arisen in connection with this affair...it is not necessary for this item to occupy further the attention of the Security Council at this time" (Document 79).

NOTES

1 Castro is quoted in Kai Bird, *The Chairman: John J. McCloy and the Making of the American Establishment* (New York: Simon and Schuster, 1992), p. 532.

2. Kennedy's November 3 instructions can be found in the National Security Archive, *The Cuban Missile Crisis, 1962: The Making of U.S. Policy*.

3. During a November 15 meeting between Chester Bowles and Soviet Ambassador Anatoly Dobrynin, Bowles offered this curious rationale for getting the IL-28s out of Cuba. Castro, he argued, was "emotionally unstable, and it was not at all inconceivable that he might load these antiquated planes with bombs and drop them on New Orleans, Mobile, or Miami. He might then maneuver the situation to make it appear that the attacks had been sponsored by the Soviet Union and thus attempt to draw the Soviet Union and the U.S. into a conflict which neither of us wanted." The memorandum of conversation of their meeting, and the State Department contingency paper are reproduced in ibid.

4. The text of Kennedy's November 20, 1962 statement can be found in ibid.

5. Pursuant to a Freedom of Information Act lawsuit, this document was released to the National Security Archive in April 1992.

6. See Rusk's instructions to McCloy and Stevenson, "Next Steps in New York Negotiations," November 21, 1962, in the National Security Archive, *The Cuban Missile Crisis, 1962: The Making of U.S. Policy*.

7. See Kennedy's November 20, 1962 statement in ibid.

8. See Rusk's "Briefing of the World Situation," January 11, 1963, reproduced in ibid.

DOCUMENT 54: Premier Khrushchev's letter to Prime Minister Castro, informing him of a deal to withdraw the missiles, October 28, 1962 (reprinted from the international edition of *Granma*).

PAGE 1 OF 1

Dear Comrade Fidel Castro:

Our October 27 message to President Kennedy allows for the question to be settled in your favor, to defend Cuba from an invasion and prevent war from breaking out. Kennedy's reply, which you apparently also know, offers assurances that the United States will not invade Cuba with its own forces, nor will it permit its allies to carry out an invasion. In this way the president of the United States has positively answered my messages of October 26 and 27, 1962.

We have now finished drafting our reply to the president's message. I am not going to convey it here, for you surely know the text, which is now being broadcast over the radio.

With this motive I would like to recommend to you now, at this moment of change in the crisis, not to be carried away by sentiment and to show firmness. I must say that I understand your feelings of indignation toward the aggressive actions and violations of elementary norms of International law on the part of the United States.

But now, rather than law, what prevails is the senselessness of the militarists at the Pentagon. Now that an agreement is within sight, the Pentagon is searching for a pretext to frustrate this agreement. This is why it is organizing the provocative flights. Yesterday you shot down one of these, while earlier you didn't shoot them down when they overflew your territory. The aggressors will take advantage of such a step for their own purposes.

Therefore, I would like to advise you in a friendly manner to show patience, firmness and even more firmness. Naturally, if there's an invasion it will be necessary to repulse it by every means. But we mustn't allow ourselves to be carried away by provocations, because the Pentagon's unbridled militarists, now that the solution to the conflict is in sight and apparently in your favor, creating a guarantee against the invasion of Cuba, are trying to frustrate the agreement and provoke you into actions that could be used against you. I ask you not to give them the pretext for doing that.

On our part, we will do everything possible to stabilize the situation in Cuba, defend Cuba against invasion and assure you the possibilities for peacefully building a socialist society.

I send you greetings, extensive to all your leadership group.

N. Khrushchev

October 28, 1962

DOCUMENT 55: Prime Minister Castro's letter to Premier Khrushchev, October 28, 1962 (reprinted from the international edition of *Granma*).

PAGE 1 OF 1

Havana
October 28, 1962

Mr. Nikita Khrushchev
Prime Minister of the Union
of Soviet Socialist Republics
USSR

Dear Comrade Khrushchev:

I have just received your letter.

The position of our government concerning your communication to us is embodied in the statement formulated today, whose text you surely know.

I wish to clear up something concerning the antiaircraft measures we adopted. You say: "Yesterday you shot down one of these [planes], while earlier you didn't shoot them down when they overflew your territory."

Earlier isolated violations were committed without a determined military purpose or without a real danger stemming from those flights.

This time that wasn't the case. There was the danger of a surprise attack on certain military installations. We decided not to sit back and wait for a surprise attack, with our detection radar turned off, when the potentially aggressive planes flying with impunity over the targets could destroy them totally. We didn't think we should allow that after all the efforts and expenses incurred in and, in addition, because it would weaken us greatly, militarily and morally. For that reason, on October 24 the Cuban forces mobilized 50 antiaircraft batteries, our entire reserve then, to provide support to the Soviet forces' positions. If we sought to avoid the risks of a surprise attack, it was necessary for Cuban artillerymen to have orders to shoot. The Soviet command can furnish you with additional reports of what happened to the plane that was shot down.

Earlier, airspace violations were carried out de facto and furtively. Yesterday the American government tried to make official the privilege of violating our airspace at any hour of the day and night. We cannot accept that, as it would be tantamount to giving up a sovereign prerogative. However, we agree that we must avoid an incident at this precise moment that could seriously harm the negotiations, so we will instruct the Cuban batteries not to open fire, but only for as long as the negotiations last and without revoking the declaration published yesterday about the decision to defend our airspace. It should also be taken into account that under the current tense conditions incidents can take place accidentally.

I also wish to inform you that we are in principle opposed to an inspection of our territory.

I appreciate extraordinarily the efforts you have made to keep the peace and we are absolutely in agreement with the need for struggling for that goal. If this is accomplished in a just, solid and definitive manner, it will be an inestimable service to humanity.

Fraternally,

Fidel Castro

DOCUMENT 56: Prime Minister Castro's "five points" letter to U.N. Secretary General U Thant, October 29, 1962.

PAGE 1 OF 2

UNITED NATIONS

GENERAL

ASSEMBLY

Distr.
GENERAL

A/5271
29 October 1962
ENGLISH
ORIGINAL: SPANISH

Seventeenth session

LETTER DATED 28 OCTOBER 1962 FROM THE PERMANENT REPRESENTATIVE OF CUBA
TO THE UNITED NATIONS, ADDRESSED TO THE SECRETARY-GENERAL

No. 492

Sir,

On the instructions of the Revolutionary Government of Cuba, I have the honour to convey to you the following message:

"U Thant,
"Acting Secretary-General of the United Nations

"With reference to the statement made by Mr. John F. Kennedy, President of the United States, in a letter addressed to Mr. Nikita Khrushchev, Chairman of the Council of Ministers of the USSR, to the effect that the United States would agree, after suitable arrangements had been made through the United Nations, to remove the blockade now in effect and to give guarantees against an invasion of Cuba, and with reference to the decision, announced by Mr. Nikita Khrushchev, to withdraw strategic defence weapons facilities from Cuban territory, the Revolutionary Government of Cuba wishes to make the following statement:

"The guarantees mentioned by President Kennedy that there will be no aggression against Cuba will be ineffective unless, in addition to the removal of the naval blockade which he promises, the following measures, inter alia, are adopted:

"1. Cessation of the economic blockade and of all the measures of commercial and economic pressure being carried out by the United States against our country throughout the world.

"2. Cessation of all subversive activities, of the dropping and landing of weapons and explosives by air and sea, of the organization of invasions by mercenaries, and of the infiltration of spies and saboteurs - all of which activities are being carried on from the territory of the United States and certain accomplice countries.

"3. Cessation of the piratical attacks being carried out from bases in the United States and Puerto Rico.

62-23702

/...

[241]

DOCUMENT 56: Prime Minister Castro's "five points" letter to U.N. Secretary General U Thant, October 29, 1962.

PAGE 2 OF 2

English
Page 2

"4. Cessation of all violations of our air space and territorial waters by United States aircraft and warships.

"5. Withdrawal of the naval base of Guantánamo and return of the Cuban territory occupied by the United States.

"Accept, Sir, the assurance of my highest consideration.

"Major Fidel Castro Ruz
"Prime Minister of the Revolutionary Government of Cuba."

I request you to have the text of this note circulated as an official document of the General Assembly.

Accept, Sir, etc.

(Signed) Mario García Incháustegui
Ambassador
Permanent Representative of Cuba to the
United Nations

DOCUMENT 57: Premier Khrushchev's letter to Prime Minister Castro, October 30, 1962 (reprinted from the international edition of *Granma*).

PAGE 1 OF 1

Dear Comrade Fidel Castro:

We have received your letter of October 28 and the reports on the talks that you as well as President Dorticós have had with our ambassador.

We understand your situation and take into account the difficulties you now have during the first transitional stage after the liquidation of maximum tension that arose due to the threat of attack on the part of the U.S. imperialists, which you expected would occur at any moment.

We understand that certain difficulties have been created for you as a result of our having promised the U.S. government to withdraw the missile base from Cuba, since it is viewed as an offensive weapon, in exchange for the U.S. commitment to abandon plans for an invasion of Cuba by U.S. troops or those of its allies in the western hemisphere, and lift the so-called "quarantine," that is, bring the blockade of Cuba to an end. This led to the liquidation of the conflict in the Caribbean zone which, as you well realize, was characterized by the clash of two superpowers and the possibility of it being transformed into a thermonuclear world war using missiles.

As we learned from our ambassador, some Cubans have the opinion that the Cuban people want a declaration of another nature rather than the declaration of the withdrawal of the missiles. It's possible that this kind of feeling exists among the people. But we, political and government figures, are leaders of a people who doesn't know everything and can't readily comprehend all that we leaders must deal with. Therefore, we should march at the head of the people and then the people will follow us and respect us.

Had we, yielding to the sentiments prevailing among the people, allowed ourselves to be carried away by certain passionate sectors of the population and refused to come to a reasonable agreement with the U.S. government, then a war could have broken out, in the course of which millions of people would have died and the survivors would have pinned the blame on the leaders for not having taken all the necessary measures to prevent that war of annihilation.

Preventing the war and an attack on Cuba depended not just on the measures adopted by our governments but also on an estimate of the actions of the enemy forces deployed near you. Accordingly, the overall situation had to be considered.

In addition, there are opinions that you and we, as they say, failed to engage in consultations concerning these questions before adopting the decision known to you.

For this reason we believe that we consulted with you, dear Comrade Fidel Castro, receiving the cables, each one more alarming than the next, and finally your cable of October 27, saying you were nearly certain that an attack on Cuba would be launched. You believed it was merely a question of time, that the attack would take place within the next 24 or 72 hours. Upon receiving this alarming cable from you and aware of your courage, we viewed it as a very well-founded alarm.

Wasn't this consultation on your part with us? I have viewed this cable as a signal of extreme alarm. Under the conditions created, also bearing in mind the information that the unabated warmongering group of U.S. militarists wanted to take advantage of the situation that had been created and launch an attack on Cuba, if we had continued our consultations, we would have wasted time and this attack would have been carried out.

We came to the conclusion that our strategic missiles in Cuba became an ominous force for the imperialists: they were frightened and because of their fear that our rockets could be launched, they could have dared to liquidate them by bombing them or launching an invasion of Cuba. And it must be said that they could have knocked them all out. Therefore, I repeat, your alarm was absolutely well-founded.

In your cable of October 27 you proposed that we be the first to launch a nuclear strike against the territory of the enemy. You, of course, realize where that would have led. Rather than a simple strike, it would have been the start of a thermonuclear world war.

Dear Comrade Fidel Castro, I consider this proposal of yours incorrect, although I understand your motivation.

We have lived through the most serious moment when a nuclear world war could have broken out. Obviously, in that case, the United States would have sustained huge losses, but the Soviet Union and the whole socialist camp would have also suffered greatly. As far as Cuba is concerned, it would be difficult to say even in general terms what this would have meant for them. In the first place, Cuba would have been burned in the fire of war. There is no doubt that the Cuban people would have fought courageously or that they would have died heroically. But we are not struggling against imperialism in order to die, but to take advantage of all our possibilities, to lose less in the struggle and win more to overcome and achieve the victory of communism.

Now, as a result of the measures taken, we reached the goal sought when we agreed with you to send the missiles to Cuba. We have wrested from the United States the commitment not to invade Cuba and not to permit their Latin American allies to do so. We have wrested all this from them without a nuclear strike.

We consider that we must take advantage of all the possibilities to defend Cuba, strengthen its independence and sovereignty, defeat military aggression and prevent a nuclear world war in our time.

And we have accomplished that.

Of course, we made concessions, accepted a commitment, acting according to the principle that a concession on one side is answered by a concession on the other side. The United States also made a concession. It made the commitment before all the world not to attack Cuba.

That's why when we compare aggression on the part of the United States and thermonuclear war with the commitment of a concession in exchange for a concession, the upholding of the inviolability of the Republic of Cuba and the prevention of a world war, I think that the total outcome of this reckoning, of this comparison is perfectly clear.

Naturally, in defending Cuba as well as the other socialist countries, we can't rely on a U.S. government veto. We have adopted and will continue to adopt in the future all the measures necessary to strengthen our defense and build up our forces, so that we can strike back if needed. At present, as a result of our weapons supplies, Cuba is stronger than ever. Even after the dismantling of the missile installations you will have powerful weapons to throw back the enemy, on land, in the air and on the sea, in the approaches to the island. At the same time, as you will recall, we have said in our message to the president of the United States dated October 28, that at the same time we want to assure the Cuban people that we stand at their side and we will not forget our responsibility to help the Cuban people. It is clear to everyone that this is an extremely serious warning to the enemy on our part.

You also stated during the rallies that the United States can't be trusted. That, of course, is correct. We also view your statements on the conditions of the talks with the United States as correct. The shooting down of a U.S. plane over Cuba turned out to be a useful measure because this operation ended without complications. Let it be a lesson for the imperialists.

Needless to say, our enemies will interpret the events in their own way. The Cuban counterrevolution will also try to raise its head. But we think you will completely dominate your domestic enemies without our assistance. The main thing we have secured is preventing aggression on the part of your foreign enemy at present.

We feel that the aggressor came out the loser. He made preparations to attack Cuba but we stopped him and forced him to recognize before world public opinion that he won't do it at the current stage. We view this as a great victory. The imperialists, of course, will not stop their struggle against communism. But we also have our plans and we are going to adopt our measures. This process of struggle will continue as long as there are two political and social systems in the world, until one of these — and we know it will be our communist system — wins and triumphs throughout the world.

Comrade Fidel Castro, I have decided to send this reply to you as soon as possible. A more detailed analysis of everything that has happened will be made in the letter I'll send you shortly. In that letter I will make the broadest analysis of the situation and give you my evaluation of the outcome of the end of the conflict.

Now, as the talks to settle the conflict get underway, I ask you to send me your considerations. For our part, we will continue to report to you on the development of these talks and make all necessary consultations.

I wish you success, Comrade Fidel Castro. You will no doubt have success. There will still be machinations against you, but together with you, we will adopt all the measures necessary to paralyze them and contribute to the strengthening and development of the Cuban Revolution.

October 30, 1962

DOCUMENT 58: Prime Minister Castro's letter to Premier Khrushchev, October 31, 1962
(reprinted from the international edition of *Granma*).

PAGE 1 OF 1

Havana
October 31, 1962
Mr. Nikita S Khrushchev
Prime Minister of the Soviet Union
USSR
Dear Comrade Khrushchev:

I received your letter of October 30. You understand that we indeed were consulted before you adopted the decision to withdraw the strategic missiles. You base yourself on the alarming news that you say reached you from Cuba and, finally, my cable of October 27. I don't know what news you received; I can only respond for the message that I sent you the evening of October 26, which reached you the 27th.

What we did in the face of the events, Comrade Khrushchev, was to prepare ourselves and get ready to fight. In Cuba there was only one kind of alarm, that of battle stations.

When in our opinion the imperialist attack became imminent I deemed it appropriate to so advise you and alert both the Soviet government and command — since there were Soviet forces committed to fight at our side to defend the Republic of Cuba from foreign aggression — about the possibility of an attack which we could not prevent but could resist.

I told you that the morale of our people was very high and that the aggression would be heroically resisted. At the end of the message I reiterated to you that we awaited the events calmly.

Danger couldn't impress us, for danger has been hanging over our country for a long time now and in a certain way we have grown used to it.

The Soviet troops which have been at our side know how admirable the stand of our people was throughout this crisis and the profound brotherhood that was created among the troops from both peoples during the decisive hours. Countless eyes of Cuban and Soviet men who were willing to die with supreme dignity shed tears upon learning about the surprising, sudden and practically unconditional decision to withdraw the weapons.

Perhaps you don't know the degree to which the Cuban people was ready to do its duty toward the nation and humanity.

I realized when I wrote them that the words contained in my letter could be misinterpreted by you and that was what happened, perhaps because you didn't read them carefully, perhaps because of the translation, perhaps because I meant to say so much in too few lines. However, I didn't hesitate to do it. Do you believe, Comrade Khrushchev, that we were selfishly thinking of ourselves, of our generous people willing to sacrifice themselves, and not at all in an unconscious manner but fully assured of the risk they ran?

No, Comrade Khrushchev. Few times in history, and it could even be said that never before, because no people had ever faced such a tremendous danger, was a people so willing to fight and die with such a universal sense of duty.

We knew, and do not presume that we ignored it, that we would have been annihilated, as you insinuate in your letter, in the event of nuclear war. However, that didn't prompt us to ask you to withdraw the missiles, that didn't prompt us to ask you to yield. Do you believe that we wanted that war? But how could we prevent it if the invasion finally took place? The fact is that this event was possible, that imperialism was obstructing every solution and that its demands were, from our point of view, impossible for the USSR and Cuba to accept.

And if war had broken out . . . .

with the insane people who unleashed the war? You yourself have said that under current conditions such a war would inevitably have escalated quickly into a nuclear war.

I understand that once aggression is unleashed, one shouldn't concede to the aggressor the privilege of deciding, moreover, when to use nuclear weapons. The destructive power of this weaponry is so great and the speed of its delivery so great that the aggressor would have a considerable initial advantage.

And I did not suggest to you, Comrade Khrushchev, that the USSR should be the aggressor, because that would be more than incorrect, it would be immoral and contemptible on my part. But from the instant the imperialists attack Cuba and while there are Soviet armed forces stationed in Cuba to help in our defense in case of an attack from abroad, the imperialists would by this act become aggressors against Cuba and against the USSR, and we would respond with a strike that would annihilate them.

Everyone has his own opinions and I maintain mine about the dangerousness of the aggressive circles in the Pentagon and their preference for a preventive strike. I did not suggest, Comrade Khrushchev, that in the midst of this crisis the Soviet Union should attack, which is what your letter seems to say; rather, that following an imperialist attack, the USSR should act without vacillation and should never make the mistake of allowing circumstances to develop in which the enemy makes the first nuclear strike against the USSR. And in this sense, Comrade Khrushchev, I maintain my point of view, because I understand it to be a true and just evaluation of a specific situation. You may be able to convince me that I am wrong, but you can't tell me that I am wrong without convincing me.

I know that this is a delicate issue that can only be broached in circumstances such as these and in a very personal message.

You may wonder what right I have to broach this topic. I do so without worrying about how thorny it is, following the dictates of my conscience as a revolutionary duty and inspired by the most unselfish sentiments of admiration and affection for the USSR, for what she represents for the future of humanity and by the concern that she should never again be the victim of the perfidy and betrayal of aggressors, as she was in 1941, and which cost so many lives and so much destruction. Moreover, I spoke not as a troublemaker but as a combatant from the most endangered trenches.

I do not see how you can state that we were consulted in the decision you took.

I would like nothing more than to be proved wrong at this moment. I only wish that you were right.

There are not just a few Cubans, as has been reported to you, but in fact many Cubans who are experiencing at this moment unspeakable bitterness and sadness.

The imperialists are talking once again of invading our country, which is proof of how ephemeral and untrustworthy their promises are. Our people, however, maintain their indestructible will to resist the aggressors and perhaps more than ever need to trust in themselves and in that will to struggle.

We will struggle against adverse circumstances, we will overcome the current difficulties and we will come out ahead, and nothing can destroy the ties of friendship and the eternal gratitude we feel toward the USSR.

Fraternally

DOCUMENT 59: Bromley Smith, "Summary Record of NSC Executive Committee Meeting,"
October 28, 1962.

PAGE 1 OF 2

SANITIZED COPY

Summary Record of NSC Executive Committee Meeting No. 10
October 28, 1962, 11:10 AM

The full Tass text of the Khrushchev reply to the President offering to withdraw
Soviet offensive weapons from Cuba under UN supervision had been read by
all prior to the opening of the meeting. (It had been received over the FBIS
ticker beginning about 9:00 AM -- copy attached.)

Secretary Rusk began by making general comments to the effect that everyone
present had helped to bring about the highly advantageous resolution of the
Cuban missile crisis. Mr. Bundy interrupted to say that everyone knew
who were hawks and who were doves, but that today was the doves' day.

Secretary McNamara said we would not have to face a decision on halting
a Bloc ship today because the Soviet tanker Graznyy was lying dead in the
water outside the quarantine zone and no other Bloc ships, if they continued
toward Cuba, would be reaching the barrier.

Secretary McNamara and Secretary Rusk recommended, and the President
agreed, that no air reconnaissance missions be flown today.

The President asked what we would substitute for our air surveillance of Cuba.

Secretary McNamara said this surveillance might be by the UN or a joint
inspection of U.S./UN inspectors in a neutral plane, flown by Brazilians or
Canadians. He said our objective should be to have reconnaissance carried
out by the UN tomorrow. Technically, this could be arranged, but we do
not know whether the UN would undertake the task.

The President suggested that we tell the UN they must carry out reconnaissance
or else we will. He authorized the release to UN officials of classified information on Cuba, including photographs and refugee reports,[   ]
The purpose of the release of this information on Soviet armaments in Cuba was t
facilitate the inspection task which we expected the UN to promptly undertake.

Secretary Rusk, in commenting in Khrushchev's reply, called attention to the
text which said the Russians would "come to an agreement." He said Kuznetsov
was coming to New York to conduct the negotiations. He suggested that we pick
up and accept Khrushchev's description of what he was prepared to withdraw
from Cuba, i.e. "offensive weapons."

TOP SECRET SENSITIVE

[245]

DOCUMENT 59: Bromley Smith, "Summary Record of NSC Executive Committee Meeting," October 28, 1962.

PAGE 2 OF 2

~~TOP SECRET SENSITIVE~~   - 2 -

The President called attention to the IL-28 bombers which he said we should ask the Russians to withdraw by making a private approach to Khrushchev. He said we should not get "hung up" on the IL-28 bombers, but we should seek to include them in the Soviet definition of "offensive weapons" or "weapons we call offensive."

General Taylor said our objective should be the status quo ante.

The President agreed, but added that he did not want to get into a position where we would appear to be going back on our part of the deal. The IL-28 bombers were less important than the strategic missiles. Admittedly, we would face the problem of Soviet armaments in Cuba if the Russians continued to build up their defensive capability there.

At this point the Attorney General arrived.

The President agreed to a statement to be made public, as revised in the meeting. He asked that a draft reply to Khrushchev's statement be prepared for him to consider. He directed that comments by everyone on the Soviet statement be reserved. Our posture is to be one of welcoming the Soviet offer to take out the offensive weapons under UN inspection, but attention should be called to the many problems we would encounter in the implementation of Khrushchev's offer. We should point out that we were under no illusion that the problem of Soviet weapons in Cuba is solved. In addition, he said we should make clear that we can draw no general conclusions about how the Russians will act in the future in areas other than Cuba. He made specific mention of the problem of Communist subversion in Latin America and asked that we refer to this problem either in our letter to Khrushchev or in U Thant's letter to Khrushchev. He directed that Ambassador Stevenson be asked to talk to UN officials about this aspect of the Cuban problem.

Bromley Smith

~~TOP SECRET SENSITIVE~~

DOCUMENT 60: State Department memorandum, "Considerations in Defining Weapons Which Must be Removed from Cuba," October 29, 1962.

PAGE 1 OF 2

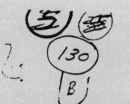

DEPARTMENT OF STATE
DEPUTY UNDERSECRETARY
G/PM

October 29, 1962

MEMORANDUM

SUBJECT: Considerations in Defining Weapons
Which Must be Removed from Cuba

The United States objective has been the removal of offensive weapons from Cuba. There is, of course, no generally accepted definition of "offensive weapons." We would like to see maximum military withdrawal from Cuba, but we must balance against this a reasonable interpretation of what is intolerable to us. On September 4, the President clearly indicated that weapons then in Cuba--including fighter aircraft, coastal defense cruise-type missiles, missile armed patrol boats, and surface-to-air missiles--were not at that time regarded as "offensive weapons." On the other hand, the list of weapons entry of which was prohibited under the quarantine proclamation included all surface-to-surface missiles, bomber and fighter-bomber aircraft, bombs, and other support equipment for the above systems.

It is clear that the weapons systems which must be removed are the 1,000 n.m. and 2,200 n.m. surface-to-surface missiles, IL-28 jet light bombers, and the warheads and support equipment for these systems.

We cannot reasonably insist that the MIG fighters, surface-to-air missiles, or non-missile ground force weapons should be removed. Similarly, it would not be reasonable to demand that the planned fishing port not be built. The items on which there may be a legitimate difference of opinion are: short range (about 35 n.m.) coastal defense missiles, short range (about 15-25 n.m.) artillery rockets, and the short range (about 25 n.m.) missiles carried on patrol craft. Of these, the missile carrying patrol boats are most susceptible of offensive employment. None of these three systems, incidentally, has a nuclear delivery capability.

We would recommend that the United States initially propose that "surface-to-surface missiles" be removed, and that on the actual implementation a low-key effort be made to secure the return to the USSR of the patrol craft and coastal defense missiles, but that if challenged we should fall back to exclude the three short range systems. In addition to the MRBMs and IRBMs, the IL28s should definitely be included, but the MIG fighters should not be.

DEPARTMENT OF STATE A/CDC/MR

REVIEWED BY *J. L. Smith* DATE APR 2 1984

RESTor KOSTEXT. DATE _____
TO AUTH.   REASON(S) _____
RETAIN EXISTING MARKINGS ☐
DECLASSIFIED RELEASABLE ☑
RELEASE DENIED ☐
PA or FOI EXEMPTIONS _____

DOCUMENT 60: State Department memorandum, "Considerations in Defining Weapons Which Must be Removed from Cuba," October 29, 1962.

PAGE 2 OF 2

- 2 -

The question of excluding visits of Soviet submarines or bombers should best be handled by appropriate unilateral US declaration at some appropriate time that any new attempt to create Soviet offensive bases in Cuba, including submarines as well as missiles and bombers, would be an even more serious infringement of the security of the Western Hemisphere than had been the present Soviet attempt to build such bases, and would of course require us to take the necessary measures to secure their removal.

Khrushchev's message of October 28 flatly stated that, in view of US assurances against an invasion, "the motives which induced us to render assistance of such a kind to Cuba disappeared." In view of the fact that Khrushchev was referring to what he termed means of defense--and which would seem to cover all Soviet military assistance to Cuba--there is some foundation for a US demand that all Soviet military advisers return to the Soviet Union. While this would not be a sine qua non of our position, it would seem to be a useful line to pursue. The departure of Soviet military specialists would, in the judgment of the Intelligence Community, initially render inoperable the surface-to-air missile sites, coastal defense missile sites, and most of the MIG-21 force. The JCS-proposed procedures for rendering offensive systems to Cuba inoperable, and creating suitable guidelines for the UN inspection, seem satisfactory.

G/PM:RLGarthoff

DOCUMENT 61: State Department cable on U.N. Secretary General U Thant's meetings with
Prime Minister Castro, November 1, 1962.

PAGE 1 OF 3

INCOMING TELEGRAM   *Department of State*

~~UNCLASSIFIED~~

48   ~~CONFIDENTIAL~~

Action   Control: 10,
IO   Rec'd: November 1, 1962
                                                     1:35 a.m.

Info   FROM: New York

SS   TO: Secretary of State
G
SP   NO: 1585, November 1, 1 a.m.
L
SAL
ARA
EUR   PRIORITY
DAC
P   DEPARTMENT PASS TO WHITE HOUSE
IOP
SCA   CUBA
SCS
INR   LIMIT DISTRIBUTION

RMR   FOLLOWING IS SUMMARY OF SYG'S PRELIMINARY REPORT OF CUBAN
          VISIT GIVEN THIS EVENING TO STEVENSON, MCCLOY AND YOST AND
          ALREADY TELEPHONED TO SECRETARY.

          AT FIRST MEETING YESTERDAY SYG FOUND CASTRO IN IMPOSSIBLE
          AND INTRACTABLE MOOD. HE WAS EXTREMELY BITTER AT SOVIETS,
          PARTICULARLY BECAUSE KHRUSHCHEV HAD NOT CONSULTED HIM BEFORE
          DESPATCHING HIS LETTER TO PRESIDENT SUNDAY MORNING. CASTRO
          MADE HIS FIVE-POINT DECLARATION THREE HOURS LATER IN ORDER
          TO COMPLICATE SITUATION FOR SOVIETS. SYG FORESEES SHOWDOWN
          WHEN MIKOYAN ARRIVES. CASTRO DECLARED CATEGORICALLY THAT
          THERE COULD BE NO INSPECTION OF ANY KIND OR ANY OUTSIDE AGENCY
          ON CUBAN SOIL. IT WAS ALSO CLEAR THERE ARE NOT AND HAVE NOT
          BEEN ANY CUBANS ON MISSILE SITES FROM WHICH THEY HAVE BEEN
          RIGIDLY EXCLUDED. CASTRO SAID UN COULD INSPECT ON HIGH
          SEAS, BUT NOT IN CUBAN TERRITORY AND WAS FURIOUS WITH
          KHRUSHCHEV FOR MAKING VERIFICATION COMMITMENT AND MADE IT
          CLEAR HE WOULD NOT PERMIT EVEN INSPECTION OF WHAT IS LEFT
          BEHIND AFTER SITES DISMANTLED AND EVACUATED. HE WAS VERY
          STRONGLY OPPOSED TO AERIAL RECONNAISSANCE, EVEN BY UN, AS
          VIOLATION CUBAN SOVEREIGNTY.

          YESTERDAY SYG ASKED SOVIET AMB WHEN DISMANTLING STARTED AND
          HOW LONG IT WOULD TAKE. AMB REPLIED HE WOULD SEEK ANSWERS
          FROM MILITARY. HE AND SOVIET GENERAL CALLED ON U THANT THIS
          AFTERNOON AND REPLIED AS FOLLOWS: INSTRUCTIONS WERE

          ~~CONFIDENTIAL~~ UNCLASSIFIED

DOCUMENT 61: State Department cable on U.N. Secretary General U Thant's meetings with
Prime Minister Castro, November 1, 1962.

PAGE 2 OF 3

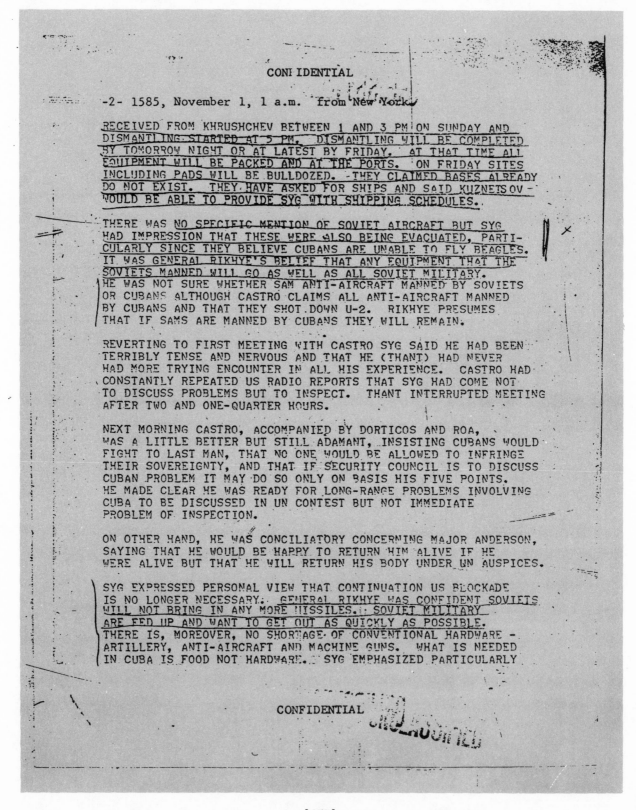

CONFIDENTIAL

-2- 1585, November 1, 1 a.m. from New York

RECEIVED FROM KHRUSHCHEV BETWEEN 1 AND 3 PM ON SUNDAY AND
DISMANTLING STARTED AT 5 PM. DISMANTLING WILL BE COMPLETED
BY TOMORROW NIGHT OR AT LATEST BY FRIDAY. AT THAT TIME ALL
EQUIPMENT WILL BE PACKED AND AT THE PORTS. ON FRIDAY SITES
INCLUDING PADS WILL BE BULLDOZED. -THEY CLAIMED BASES ALREADY
DO NOT EXIST. THEY HAVE ASKED FOR SHIPS AND SAID KUZNETSOV
WOULD BE ABLE TO PROVIDE SYG WITH SHIPPING SCHEDULES.

THERE WAS NO SPECIFIC MENTION OF SOVIET AIRCRAFT BUT SYG
HAD IMPRESSION THAT THESE WERE ALSO BEING EVACUATED, PARTI-
CULARLY SINCE THEY BELIEVE CUBANS ARE UNABLE TO FLY BEAGLES.
IT WAS GENERAL RIKHYE'S BELIEF THAT ANY EQUIPMENT THAT THE
SOVIETS MANNED WILL GO AS WELL AS ALL SOVIET MILITARY.
HE WAS NOT SURE WHETHER SAM ANTI-AIRCRAFT MANNED BY SOVIETS
OR CUBANS ALTHOUGH CASTRO CLAIMS ALL ANTI-AIRCRAFT MANNED
BY CUBANS AND THAT THEY SHOT DOWN U-2. RIKHYE PRESUMES
THAT IF SAMS ARE MANNED BY CUBANS THEY WILL REMAIN.

REVERTING TO FIRST MEETING WITH CASTRO SYG SAID HE HAD BEEN
TERRIBLY TENSE AND NERVOUS AND THAT HE (THANT) HAD NEVER
HAD MORE TRYING ENCOUNTER IN ALL HIS EXPERIENCE. CASTRO HAD
CONSTANTLY REPEATED US RADIO REPORTS THAT SYG HAD COME NOT
TO DISCUSS PROBLEMS BUT TO INSPECT. THANT INTERRUPTED MEETING
AFTER TWO AND ONE-QUARTER HOURS.

NEXT MORNING CASTRO, ACCOMPANIED BY DORTICOS AND ROA,
WAS A LITTLE BETTER BUT STILL ADAMANT, INSISTING CUBANS WOULD
FIGHT TO LAST MAN, THAT NO ONE WOULD BE ALLOWED TO INFRINGE
THEIR SOVEREIGNTY, AND THAT IF SECURITY COUNCIL IS TO DISCUSS
CUBAN PROBLEM IT MAY DO SO ONLY ON BASIS HIS FIVE POINTS.
HE MADE CLEAR HE WAS READY FOR LONG-RANGE PROBLEMS INVOLVING
CUBA TO BE DISCUSSED IN UN CONTEST BUT NOT IMMEDIATE
PROBLEM OF INSPECTION.

ON OTHER HAND, HE WAS CONCILIATORY CONCERNING MAJOR ANDERSON,
SAYING THAT HE WOULD BE HAPPY TO RETURN HIM ALIVE IF HE
WERE ALIVE BUT THAT HE WILL RETURN HIS BODY UNDER UN AUSPICES.

SYG EXPRESSED PERSONAL VIEW THAT CONTINUATION US BLOCKADE
IS NO LONGER NECESSARY. GENERAL RIKHYE WAS CONFIDENT SOVIETS
WILL NOT BRING IN ANY MORE MISSILES. SOVIET MILITARY
ARE FED UP AND WANT TO GET OUT AS QUICKLY AS POSSIBLE.
THERE IS, MOREOVER, NO SHORTAGE OF CONVENTIONAL HARDWARE -
ARTILLERY, ANTI-AIRCRAFT AND MACHINE GUNS. WHAT IS NEEDED
IN CUBA IS FOOD NOT HARDWARE. SYG EMPHASIZED PARTICULARLY

CONFIDENTIAL

DOCUMENT 61: State Department cable on U.N. Secretary General U Thant's meetings with
Prime Minister Castro, November 1, 1962.

PAGE 3 OF 3

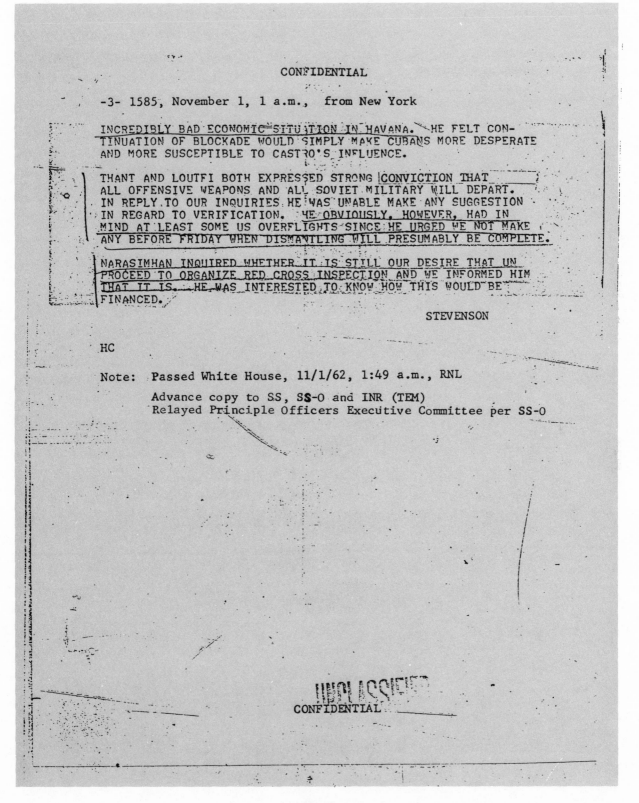

CONFIDENTIAL

-3- 1585, November 1, 1 a.m., from New York

INCREDIBLY BAD ECONOMIC SITUATION IN HAVANA. HE FELT CON-
TINUATION OF BLOCKADE WOULD SIMPLY MAKE CUBANS MORE DESPERATE
AND MORE SUSCEPTIBLE TO CASTRO'S INFLUENCE.

THANT AND LOUTFI BOTH EXPRESSED STRONG CONVICTION THAT
ALL OFFENSIVE WEAPONS AND ALL SOVIET MILITARY WILL DEPART.
IN REPLY TO OUR INQUIRIES HE WAS UNABLE MAKE ANY SUGGESTION
IN REGARD TO VERIFICATION. HE OBVIOUSLY, HOWEVER, HAD IN
MIND AT LEAST SOME US OVERFLIGHTS SINCE HE URGED WE NOT MAKE
ANY BEFORE FRIDAY WHEN DISMANTLING WILL PRESUMABLY BE COMPLETE.

NARASIMHAN INQUIRED WHETHER IT IS STILL OUR DESIRE THAT UN
PROCEED TO ORGANIZE RED CROSS INSPECTION AND WE INFORMED HIM
THAT IT IS. HE WAS INTERESTED TO KNOW HOW THIS WOULD BE
FINANCED.

STEVENSON

HC

Note: Passed White House, 11/1/62, 1:49 a.m., RNL

Advance copy to SS, SS-O and INR (TEM)
Relayed Principle Officers Executive Committee per SS-O

CONFIDENTIAL

DOCUMENT 62: Adlai Stevenson's report on New York meeting with Anastas Mikoyan,
November 2, 1962.

PAGE 1 OF 4

=116

INCOMING TELEGRAM   *Department of State*

41

Action

SS

Info

TOP SECRET

FROM: NEW YORK

TO: Secretary of State

NO: 1604, NOVEMBER 2, 1 A.M.

PRIORITY

EYES ONLY FOR THE SECRETARY

Control: 433

Rec'd: NOVEMBER 2, 1962
1:52 A.M.

MCCLOY, STEVENSON AND AKALOVSKY MET WITH MIKOYAN, KUZNETSOV,
ZORIN, DOBRYNIN, MENSHIKOV AND ZHUKOV FROM 7 TO
11 PM THURSDAY NIGHT. MIKOYAN STARTED IN AGGRESSIVE MOOD,
INSISTING ON SUSPENDING QUARANTINE NOW, SAYING THAT WAS
U THANT'S INTENTION. WE REPEATED THAT THE AGREEMENT WAS
EMBODIED IN THE CORRESPONDENCE BETWEEN CHAIRMAN KHRUSCHEV
AND PRESIDENT KENNEDY AND LEFT NO UNCERTAINTY THAT THE HAIL
AND PASS QUARANTINE COULD NOT BE SUSPENDED UNTIL THE RED
CROSS INSPECTION WAS IN EFFECT. THIS SEEMED TO BOTHER MIKOYAN
CONSIDERABLY, BUT AFTER SOME FURTHER DISCUSSION HE DROPPED
THE MATTER. WHEN ASKED HOW FAR AWAY THE NEAREST SOVIET SHIPS
WERE, HE REPLIED FOUR OR FIVE DAYS. WE POINTED OUT THAT IN
THAT EVENT, IF RED CROSS INSPECTION WAS ESTABLISHED QUICKLY,
FEW IF ANY SOVIET SHIPS WOULD HAVE TO PASS THE PRESENT
QUARANTINE. HE SAID THANT HAD AGREED WITH HIM THAT THE US
SHOULD SUSPEND QUARANTINE DURING THE INTERVAL.

MIKOYAN THEN ASKED IF WE WERE WORKING NOW TO FORMALIZE THE
AGREEMENT BETWEEN US. WE REPLIED THERE WERE ONLY THREE QUES-
TIONS: RED CROSS INSPECTION, INSPECTION AND VERIFICATION OF
REMOVAL OF WEAPONS, AND THE GUARANTEE TO CUBA; AND SAW ONLY
ONE DIFFICULTY IN REACHING AN AGREEMENT, NAMELY CASTRO'S
REJECTION OF VERIFICATION. MIKOYAN MADE LONG SPEECH INSISTING
ON LINKING CASTRO'S FIVE POINTS WITH SOVIET-US AGREEMENT AND
CHARGED US WITH DRAWING ATTENTION TO ONLY "TEMPORARY" QUESTIONS
WHILE

Eyes only

Cat. A - Caption removed.
transferred to

Cat. B - Transferred to O. F/ORG
with additional access
controlled by S/S

Cat. C - Caption and custody
retained by S/S

Reviewed by: Elijah Kelly Jr.

Date: 2/10/92   19___

DOCUMENT 62: Adlai Stevenson's report on New York meeting with Anastas Mikoyan, November 2, 1962.

PAGE 2 OF 4

TOP SECRET

-2- 1604, NOVEMBER 2. 1 A.M., FROM NEW YORK

WHILE OVERLOOKING "CARDINAL" QUESTIONS. HE SAID WE OBVIOUSLY
DID NOT WANT TO HEAR ABOUT INTERESTS OF OTHERS AND WERE
ONLY CONCERNED WITH OUR OWN INTERESTS. HE WENT ON TO SUGGEST
CERTAIN REPORTS SHOULD BE MADE TO UNITED NATIONS AND THAT A
FORMAL DOCUMENT OR PROTOCOL SHOULD BE EXECUTED, AND THAT HE
WANTED NEGOTIATIONS TO COMMENCE FORMALLY ON BASIS OF THE LETTERS
INCLUDING CASTRO'S FIVE POINTS, BETWEEN THE US, SOVIET AND
U THANT. LATER HE ASKED IF CUBA SHOULD NOT BE INCLUDED IN
THE DISCUSSIONS, REPEATING AGAIN AND AGAIN THAT WE MUST DISCUSS
THE GUANTANAMO AND THE OTHER POINTS RELATING TO NORMALIZING
THE SITUATION IN THE CARIBBEAN WITH UN PRESENCES IN CUBA,
IN THE US AND IN OTHER PARTS OF THE AREA, TO SEE THAT AGREEMENT
ADHERED TO. CASTRO, HE SAID, WAS PRIME MINISTER OF INDEPENDENT
STATE AND WE CAN'T EVADE ASSURANCES OF NON-AGGRESSION AGAINST
CUBA, THAT WE WERE WITHDRAWING FROM OUR COMMITMENTS AND MUST
DISCUSS EVERYTHING, THAT THEY MUST KNOW THE US POSITION IN
ORDER TO TELL CASTRO.

WE REPEATED OVER AND OVER THAT WE MUST STICK TO THIS PROBLEM
AND THIS PROBLEM ONLY AND COULD CONSIDER NO OTHER QUESTIONS.
WE ADDED THAT CASTRO COULD RAISE ANY QUESTIONS HE PLEASED AND
THAT THEY WOULD BE DEALT WITH AT THE RIGHT TIME AND THAT WE
WERE CONCERNED WITH ONE QUESTION ONLY AND THAT WAS BETWEEN THE
AND SOVIET UNION. HE WENT BACK AGAIN AND AGAIN TO HIS
INSISTENCE THAT WE WERE BY-PASSING THE OTHER SIDE, INCLUDING
LIFTING THE BLOCKADE AND NORMALIZING THE SITUATION, THAT THE
WHOLE UNDERSTANDING WOULD HAVE TO BE FORMALIZED IN DOCUMENTS
REGISTERED WITH THE UNITED NATIONS AND APPROVED BY THE SECURITY
COUNCIL, AND THAT WE CAN'T DISREGARD THE DEMANDS OF CASTRO.
FOLLOWING OUR INSISTENCE THAT WE CAN NEGOTIATE ONLY ONE PROBLEM
AND THAT ANY DISCUSSION OF GUANTANAMO IN CONNECTION WITH IT WAS
OUT OF THE QUESTION, HE REMARKED THAT THE SOVIET UNION HAD
NEVER RAISED GUANTANAMO, WHICH WAS A CUBA-US PROBLEM, BUT
THAT THE US SHOULD DISCUSS THE OTHER FOUR POINTS.

WE EXPLAINED TO HIM THAT WE NEEDED NO DOCUMENTS EXCEPT THE
DECLARATIONS OF USSR, US AND SYG BEFORE SECURITY COUNCIL
AFTER TRANSACTION COMPLETED. FOR THAT PURPOSE CUBA WAS NOT
A NECESSARY PARTY, ESPECIALLY IF IT REFUSED ANY UNITED NATIONS

INSPECTION

TOP SECRET

DOCUMENT 62: Adlai Stevenson's report on New York meeting with Anastas Mikoyan, November 2, 1962.

PAGE 3 OF 4

TOP SECRET

-3-   1604, NOVEMBER 2, 1 A.M., FROM NEW YORK

INSPECTION AS KHRUSHCHEV HAD PROMISED.

WE THEN TURNED TO OTHER FORMS OF INSPECTION AND VERIFICATION, BY AIR RECON AND TABLES OF ORGANIZATION, AND SUGGESTED HE COULD ARGUE WITH CASTRO THAT A UN PRESENCE WOULD BE AN ASSURANCE TO CASTRO AGAINST INVASION IN INTERIM AS WELL AS AN ASSURANCE TO US. MIKOYAN WAS AT PAINS TO SAY THAT THIS MEETING WAS NOT A FINAL NEGOTIATION, BUT MERELY AN EXPLORATION TO SEE WHAT EVERYONE HAD IN MIND. WE SAID THAT WE FELT TIME WAS OF THE ESSENCE AND THAT WE COULD AGREE UPON MODALITIES OF THE RED CROSS INSPECTION DIRECTLY OR THROUGH OUR DEPUTIES ALMOST AT ONCE, ON BASIS OF THANT'S PROPOSALS. WE ADDED THAT WE COULD SEE NO NECESSITY FOR DOCUMENTARY AGREEMENT ON AERIAL INSPECTION, BUT WANTED ASSURANCES FROM HIM THAT OUR PLANES WOULD NOT BE FIRED ON IF THAT WAS THE ONLY FORM OF INSPECTION AND VERIFICATION AVAILABLE TO US. THEY REPLIED THEY COULD NOT GUARANTEE THAT THE GUNS WOULD NOT SHOOT, BE-CAUSE CUBA WAS AN INDEPENDENT COUNTRY OVER WHICH THEY HAD NO CONTROL, AND ADVERTED AGAIN TO FACT THAT WE SHOULD CONSIDER EVERYTHING, BUT THAT AT LEAST THIS TALK HAD SERVED TO EXPOSE OUR DIFFERENCES. (LATER IN A SUMMARY WE HAD FEELING WE WERE REALLY VERY CLOSE TOGETHER AND THAT IF MIKOYAN WOULD DROP HIS EFFORT TO LINK CASTRO'S FIVE POINTS OUR DIFFERENCES WERE FEW.)

WHEN WE TRIED TO GET DOWN TO DETAILS OF THE RED CROSS AND AERIAL INSPECTION MIKOYAN SAID HE WAS NOT SPECIALIST AND THESE -WERE DETAILS, THAT HE HAD BROUGHT A GENERAL AND COLONEL TO HELP KUZNETSOV, REPEATING AGAIN AND AGAIN THAT HE COULD GIVE US NO GUARANTEE REGARDING THE SECURITY OF OUR OVER-FLIGHTS. WE REMINDED HIM KHRUSHCHEV HAD AGREED TO UN INSPECTION AND THAT WE UNDERSTOOD HIS DIFFICULTIES IF CUBA REFUSED, IN VIEW OF ITS INDEPENDENCE, AND WERE TRYING REACH ACCOMMODATION FOR QUICK AND SATISFACTORY RESULTS. HE REVERTED AGAIN TO ARGUMENT THAT IF WE INSISTED ON UN INSPENTION IN CUBA, IT HAD A RIGHT TO INSIST ON INSPECTION OF REFUGEE CAMPS AND TRAINING ACTIVI-TIES ANYWHERE. HE WAS ASSURED THAT THERE WERE NO SUCH CAMPS ANY LONGER AND THAT US WAS NOT ENGAGED IN SUCH ACTIVITIES. LIKEWISE WE TRIED REASSURE HIM ABOUT TRAINING OF CUBAN CITIZENS IN THE ARMY AND THAT US WANTED TO REGULARIZE RELATIONS IN CARIBBEAN FOR PROTECTION OF OTHERS AS WELL AS CASTRO, BUT THAT THIS WAS A SEPARATE MATTER THAT HAD NOTHING TO DO

WITH THIS

TOP SECRET

DOCUMENT 62: Adlai Stevenson's report on New York meeting with Anastas Mikoyan, November 2, 1962.

PAGE 4 OF 4

TOP SECRET

-4- 16Ø4, NOVEMBER 2, 1 A.M., FROM NEW YORK

WITH THIS QUESTION. MIKOYAN QUICKLY ASKED IF WE WERE REFERRING
TO POSSIBLE RESTORATION ECONOMIC AND DIPLOMATIC TIES WITH CUBA,
AND WE EXPLAINED REGIONAL ARRANGEMENTS IN THIS HEMISPHERE
THROUGH OAS AND THAT SUCH MATTERS WERE NOT EXCLUDED FROM
FUTURE CONSIDERATION IF OTHER AGGRAVATIONS COULD BE RELIEVED,
BUT THAT WE MUST GET THE ONE QUESTION BEFORE US PROMPTLY
RESOLVED.

FYI. WITH REGARD TO SAM SITES, WE HAD CLEAR IMPRESSION THEY
INTENDED TO LEAVE THEM IN CUBA, AND THEY ALSO SAID THEY HAD
GIVEN THESE GUNS TO A NUMBER OF OTHER COUNTRIES, INCLUDING
INDONESIA AND UAR.

MEETING BECAME MORE CORDIAL AND FRIENDLY AS IT PROCEEDED AND
WAS EXCLUSIVELY DOMINATED BY MIKOYAN. HE SAID HE DID NOT
KNOW WHETHER HE WAS COMING BACK THROUGH NEW YORK ON WAY HOME,
BUT WE HAD IMPRESSION HE INTENDED TO.

THEIR ESTIMATE OF TIME TO COMPLETE REMOVAL WAS TEN TO FIFTEEN
DAYS, INCLUDING THE IL-28'S.

AT ONE POINT HE REPEATED KHRUSHCHEV'S STATEMENT THAT WHAT WE
CALL OFFENSIVE WEAPONS HAD BEEN GIVEN TO CUBA TO DETER US
AGGRESSION, BUT THAT IF NON-AGGRESSION WAS GUARANTEED THEY
WOULD BE WITHDRAWN AND THAT THEY WOULD SHIP NO MORE WEAPONS.

IN SUMMARIZING OUR CONCLUSIONS, WE REVIEWED THE PROCEDURE
BEFORE THE SECURITY COUNCIL AND THEY SUGGESTED WE EXCHANGE
DRAFTS OF DECLARATIONS, WHICH SEEMED TO US TO INDICATE ACCEP-
TANCE OF THIS PROCEDURE, ON THE WHOLE OUR FEELING WAS THAT
WE HAD LEFT NO DOUBT THE FIVE POINTS AND WEAPONS TRANSACTION
COULD NOT BE LINKED AND THAT HE WILL MEET CASTRO WITH A CLEAR
IMPRESSION OF OUR POSITION, AND UNDERSTAND WE WILL INSIST ON
INTERIM INSPECTION BY OUR MEANS IF AN AGREEMENT FOR UN PRESENCE
CANNOT BE REACHED. IT IS OUR INTENTION TO PROCEED AS PROMPTLY
AS POSSIBLE WITH KUZNETSOV AND HIS DEPUTY MOROZOV TO TRY
COMPLETE MODALITIES ON RED CROSS INSPECTION PENDING MIKOYAN'S
RETURN.

STEVENSON

SMD
Note: Passed Principle Officers Executive Committee 11/2/62
Advance copies to SS/O and SS/DO

TOP SECRET

DOCUMENT 63: Bromley Smith, "Summary Record of NSC Executive Committee Meeting,"
November 2, 1962.

PAGE 1 OF 4

~~TOP SECRET - SENSITIVE~~

2

Summary Record of NSC Executive Committee Meeting No. 17,
November 2, 1962, 11:00 AM

The President referred to a newspaper story by Roland Evans which
reported details of Khrushchev's private letter of October 26. The
President said the White House had already issued a denial that
the U.S. Government believed this letter was written by an agitated
or an overwrought man. He directed that all copies of the letter
be returned to the State Department. He added that apparently
a copy of the letter had gone to an allied embassy in Washington.
He reaffirmed an earlier instruction that the only sources of
information on the Cuban situation are Mr. Bundy and Mr.
Sorensen. He indicated his unhappiness with the amount of
information which had been given to the press without authorization. He directed that all aerial reconnaissance information
be kept out of the Top Secret CIA Bulletin until after he had
seen it. He would then decide what circulation within the
government was to be given the reconnaissance information.
He restated his view that we must make information available
to the press in our own way rather than have it leak out.

Director McCone then summarized the intelligence memorandum.
▓▓
▓▓▓▓▓ In conclusion, he reported on the current Soviet test
series. ▓▓▓▓▓▓▓▓▓▓▓▓▓▓▓▓▓▓▓▓▓▓▓▓▓▓ including one
yesterday of an estimated 1.2 megaton, at an altitude of fifty
nautical miles.

Under Secretary Ball reported on a dinner meeting held last
night in New York between our officials and Mikoyan, Zorin
and Kuznetsov. He said Mikoyan started with a very hard
position, but modified this somewhat later in the evening. He
repeatedly attempted to tie Castro's five points to the agreement
between President Kennedy and Khrushchev. He proposed
that there be a formal exchange of documents which would
conclude the Cuban missile negotiations. We opposed such
a proposal and suggested instead that there be a UN Security
Council meeting which would be called to hear three unilateral
declarations -- one by U Thant, another by the Soviets, and
a third by the U.S.

TOP SECRET
~~SENSITIVE~~

SANITIZED

NLK-80-29

BY ___ NAFS. DATE 10/9/84

DOCUMENT 63: Bromley Smith, "Summary Record of NSC Executive Committee Meeting," November 2, 1962.

PAGE 2 OF 4

TOP SECRET - SENSITIVE - 2 -

There was a discussion of some UN presence in the form of a peace commission. The Russians were ambiguous on the status of the SAM sites. One of the Russians said that the Cubans might agree to the dismantlement of the SAM sites in return for our promise to stop overflights. The IL-28 bomber issue was not pinned down in the conversations. The Russians said repeatedly that they could not force Castro to accept on-site inspection. There was no decision on how inspection will be carried out after the missiles have been withdrawn. Mikoyan did not ask us not to overfly, but he did admit that he could not get Castro to accept ground inspection.

Deputy Secretary Gilpatric urged that we insist upon UN inspection as promised by Khrushchev. He noted that KOMAR missiles have been given to the Cubans and recommended that we keep our quarantine until a satisfactory substitute was in place.

The President decided that in ivew of the unsatisfactory discussions with the Cubans and the Russians, he would cancel his planned press conference in order not to be obliged to reply to questions about what guarantees we have that Russian missiles had been withdrawn from Cuba. Under Secretary Ball read a six-point statement which he recommended the President issue in lieu of a press conference.

Secretary Rusk suggested that we not call attention to the IL-28 bombers at this point because we may want to retaliate against these planes if one of our reconnaissance planes is shot down.

The President directed that a statement be prepared for issuance by the White House or the State Department. It should include what the Russians have agreed to and what we have agreed to. He asked what had been discussed in New York about the quarantine and about our overflights. Deputy Secretary Gilpatric reported that UN officials have given up on a UN surveillance system because Castro won't accept it.

The President asked how we were going to check on Soviet missiles being withdrawn.

TOP SECRET-SENSITIVE

DOCUMENT 63: Bromley Smith, "Summary Record of NSC Executive Committee Meeting," November 2, 1962.

PAGE 3 OF 4

TOP SECRET - SENSITIVE - 3 -

Secretary Rusk said we could ask the ████████████ in Cuba check on Soviet equipment there, and where it was being moved to in Cuba.

The President noted that inspection of incoming material could be achieved, but we must develop some way of inspecting outgoing Soviet missiles.

The President asked that instructions to McCloy be prepared which would lay down the line he is to follow for the next three days.

Secretary McNamara recommended that we continue limited but daily overflights. He asked authorization for two flights of two planes each to cover different areas than were photographed yesterday. Targets would include Cuban ports and the IL-28 airfield. He opposed high altitude flights until we are certain that the Soviets do control the SAM sites. In answer to a question, he said we could use a drone for overflights, but the Air Force was opposed because of the possible loss and compromise of the highly classified drone.

In answer to a question, Director McCone said it was conceivable but improbable that missiles fired from SAM sites in Cuba could reach the U.S.

The President authorized the release to the press of the pictures of the missile sites taken yesterday, but not the pictures of the IL-28 bombers. He agreed that the quarantine should be continued until a satisfactory substitute was found.

Secretary McNamara reported on the current shipping situation and recommended that our ships hail all Bloc ships crossing the quarantine line but board none of them. He said Admiral Dennison had asked permission to board a Soviet ship, but had been denied this authority. The President agreed that we should not now board Bloc ships.

The President again called attention to the necessity of inspecting Soviet ships leaving Cuba with Soviet missiles as cargo. This inspection must be carried out either by the International Red Cross or by the U.S.

TOP SECRET-SENSITIVE

DOCUMENT 63· Bromley Smith, "Summary Record of NSC Executive Committee Meeting,"
November 2, 1962.

PAGE 4 OF 4

~~TOP SECRET - SENSITIVE~~ - 4 -

The President then turned to a discussion of atomic testing.
He asked that consideration be given to what we will say publicly
when our current test series ends and what we should say about
our plans for future tests. He asked whether we should announce
that we were prepared to halt tests until there was a test ban
agreement. He said he opposed any pledge to refrain from
testing for an indefinite period.

In response to the President's question, Mr. Bundy stated that
our scientists doubt that the "black box" method of detecting
nuclear tests is promising. The President asked that he be
provided an evaluation of these unmanned seismic stations as
a means of monitoring an atomic test ban.

Acting USIA Director Wilson asked the President for guidance
for USIA during the next few days. The President instructed
that USIA emphasize that Castro was obstructing peace in the
Caribbean by blocking UN inspection measures. For the time
being, USIA should not use the theme that Castro is a Soviet
stooge.

The President asked for a report on the fighting between the
Indians and the Communist Chinese, along with an estimate
of what we thought would develop in this area.

Bromley Smith

~~TOP SECRET - SENSITIVE~~

DOCUMENT 64: President Kennedy's letter to Premier Khrushchev on inspection and verification issue, November 3, 1962.

PAGE 1 OF 2

UNCLASSIFIED

~~SECRET~~

November 3, 1962

②

Dear Mr. Chairman:

I wish to thank you for your letter of October 30.
I am commenting now only on a problem raised in
your letter which relates to the Cuban affair.

With respect to the quarantine on shipments to Cuba,
I am hopeful that arrangements can be worked out
quickly by the United Nations which would permit its
removal. We were happy to agree to your suggestion
that the International Committee of the Red Cross
undertake responsibility for inspection. You are,
of course, aware that Premier Castro has announced
his opposition to measures of verification on the
territory of Cuba. If he maintains this position
this would raise very serious problems. So far as
incoming shipments are concerned, I understand
that efforts are being made to have the International
Red Cross carry out the necessary measures at sea
and I hope that these will be successful. In the
meantime, perhaps the existence of the quarantine
can be of assistance to Mr. Mikoyan in his negotiations
with Premier Castro. I should also like to point out
that in an effort to facilitate matters, I instructed our
delegation in New York to inform your representative
there, Mr. Kuznetsov, that for the next few days
any Soviet ships in the quarantine area would be
passed without inspection and only the hailing procedure which was carried out in the case of your
vessel, the Bucharest, would be applied.

~~SECRET~~

UNCLASSIFIED

IS/FPC/CDR   Date: 1/9/92

MR Cases Only:
EO Citations _____

( ) CLASSIFY as   ( ) S or ( ) C
( ) DOWNGRADE TS to ( ) S or ( ) C

DOCUMENT 64: President Kennedy's letter to Premier Khrushchev on inspection and verification issue, November 3, 1962.

PAGE 2 OF 2

~~SECRET~~   -2-

I am hopeful we can dispose of this pressing
matter quickly so that we can go on in a better
atmosphere to the broader questions.   We both
must make our best efforts to this end.

                    Sincerely,

                    /s/ JFK

His Excellency
      Nikita S. Khrushchev
            Chairman of the Council of Ministers
                  of the Union of Soviet Socialist Republics
            Moscow

~~SECRET~~

UNCLASSIFIED

DOCUMENT 65: Bromley Smith, "Summary Record of NSC Executive Committee Meeting,"
November 5, 1962.

PAGE 1 OF 2

Summary Record of NSC Executive Committee Meeting No. 20
November 5, 1962 -- 10:00 A.M

Director McCone presented the intelligence summary. He then compared
our figures on strategic missiles in Cuba with the Russian figures which
Kuznetsov gave to McCloy yesterday. Kuznetsov says the Russians sent
forty-two missiles to Cuba. We had estimated that there were forty-eight
Soviet missiles in Cuba, thirty-three of which we have actually seen.

Secretary McNamara reported on the aerial reconnaissance missions of
yesterday. Two U-2 missions aborted yesterday because of mechanical
failure. Five more U-2s are flying today.

Secretary Rusk reported on the McCloy/Kuznetsov conversation yesterday.
The Russians are prepared to give us an actual missile inventory, including
the shipping schedules, so that we can count the missiles on their way out.
Secretary Rusk said he continued to believe that we must have inspection
arrangements on the ground in Cuba. We need a UN presence in Cuba,
plus a Latin American atom-free treaty zone, if Castro will accept such.
If not, we must refuse to give a commitment not to invade and we must
continue aerial reconnaissance missions ▓▓▓▓▓▓▓▓▓▓▓▓▓▓▓▓▓▓▓▓
▓▓▓▓▓▓▓▓▓▓ We are unable to put forward an inspection plan
until we know what Mikoyan has proposed to the Cubans and what Castro
has agreed to accept.

The President recalled that Zorin wanted a protocol covering the agreement on the withdrawal of the Soviet missiles. He asked that thought be
given to how this might be done.

Secretary Rusk called attention to the difficulty of legislating on Communist
subversion in the hemisphere.

The President asked:

    1. How we would get a guarantee that no Soviet submarine base
would be built in Cuba.

    2. How to get out the IL-28 bombers.

    3. What was our position if a demand were made that UN observers
inspect refugee camps in the U.S. and in other areas where Cuban nationals
might receive military training.

DOCUMENT 65: Bromley Smith, "Summary Record of NSC Executive Committee Meeting,"
November 5, 1962.

PAGE 2 OF 2

- 2 -

    4. How the U.S. or the UN would continue reconnaissance flights.

The President's basic questions was how much should we give for a permanent UN presence in Cuba. He believed that we should keep open the question of accepting UN observers in the U.S. until we knew exactly what we would get in return.

Secretary Rusk emphasized that all arrangements arising out of the current situation must focus on Cuba. Comparable actions such as inspection in Cuba in return for the UN investiagation of complaints about the U.S. were difficult, not only for the U.S., but for other members of the OAS. As to future assurances, we want a permanent UN presence in Cuba for which we would guarantee that we would not invade. For us, the UN presence would be a guarantee against the reintroduction of strategic missiles. We should think about overflights of Cuba and the U.S. and about a UN presence in Florida as well as in Cuba.

Mr. Bundy said that the UN route to the demilitarization of Cuba would lead to a realignment of our relations with Castro.

Secretary Rusk said we must under all circumstances continue to overfly Cuba. The President asked how we could continue to overfly as long as the SAM sites were operational. Secretary Rusk replied that our overflights would continue by tacit agreement of the Cubans and the Russians.

The President asked whether a group was at work on what to tell McCloy in answer to questions raised by Kuznetsov. He believed that if Mikoyan asks Kuznetsov about our future assurances with respect to Cuba, McCloy should be in a position to respond. Secretary Rusk preferred to delay sending our final position to McCloy until after we knew what took place in Havana.

The President agreed that no release should be made to the press of pictures which reveal Soviet activity yesterday in Cuban ports. He added that we might have the International Red Cross inspect incoming ships and we would look at ships leaving Cuba. He agreed that we could delay reaching a final position on the permanent arrangements, but we should not discuss any arrangements for the time being with Mikoyan.

                                        Bromley Smith

~~SECRET~~

Dear Mr. President,

I have just received information from Mr. V. Kusnetsov, our representative at the negotiations in New York for liquidation of the tense situation around Cuba, that Mr. Stevenson handed him a list of weapons which your side calls offensive. I have studied the list and, I must confess, the approach of the American side to this matter has seriously worried me. In such a move, I will say frankly, I see a wish to complicate the situation, because it is impossible indeed to place into the category of "offensive" weapons such types of weapons which have always been reffered [sic] to as defensive weapons even by a man educated militarily—by a common soldier, not to say of an officer.

It is hard for us to understand what aim is being pursued by the introduction of that list, by setting forth such a demand—in any case it must be some other aim, but not a desire for a speediest clearing of the atmosphere. And it is being done at a moment when we have already agreed with you on the main questions and when we on our part have already fulfilled what we agreed upon—have dismantled rocket weapons, are loading them now on ships and these weapons will soon be shipped from Cuba. That is why I feel greatly concerned with the advancing of such demand by the American side, concerned with its possible consequences, if necessary reasonableness is not displayed.

The demand which has been set forth is evidently pursuing, as I have already said, some other aims and that—I would wish, Mr. President, that you understand me correctly—can lead not to the betterment of our relations but, on the contrary, to their new aggravation. We should understand the position each side is in and take it into consideration but not overburden, not complicate our relations, e specially at such an important moment when measures are being taken to eliminate the accute [sic] tension and bring these relations to a normal state.

That is why I would ask you, Mr. President, to meet our anxiety with understanding, to take measures on your side in order not to complicate the situation and to give your representatives a directive to eliminate the existing tension on the basis upon which both of us have agreed by having exchanged public messages. You spoke to the effect that missiles which you called offensive should be removed from Cuba. We agreed to that. You in your turn gave assurances that the so-called "quarantine" would be promptly removed and that no invasion of Cuba would be made, not only by the U.S. but by other countries of the Western hemisphere either.

Let us then bring the achieved understanding to a completion, so that we could consider that each side has fulfilled its pledges and the question has been settled. If, however, additional demands are made, then that means only one thing—the danger that the difficulties on the way to eliminating tension created around Cuba will not be removed. But that may raise then new consequences.

I think that you will understand me correctly. For you and I will evidently have to deal not only with the elimination of the remnants of the present tension—there lies ahead for you and me a great, serious talk on other questions. Why then start now complicating the situation by minor things. May be [sic] there exist some considerations, but they are beyond our comprehension. As for us, we view the introduction of additional demands as a wish to bring our relations back again into a heated state in which they were but several days ago.

Sincerely,

N. Khrushchev

DOCUMENT 67: President Kennedy's letter to Premier Khrushchev, November 6, 1962 (transcribed for legibility).

PAGE 1 OF 2

November 6, 1962

Dear Mr. Chairman:

I am surprised that in your letter, which I received yesterday, you suggest that in giving your representative in New York a list of the weapons we consider offensive there was any desire on our part to complicate the situation. Our intention was just the opposite: to stick to a well-known list, and not to introduce any new factors. But there is really only one major item on the list, beyond the missiles and their equipment, and that is the light bombers with their equipment. This item is indeed of great importance to us.

The solution of the Cuban affair was established by my letter to you of October twenty-seventh and your reply of October twenty-eighth. You will recall that in my letter of October twenty-seventh, I referred to "all weapons systems in Cuba capable of offensive use." You will also recall that in my broadcast address of October twenty-second, in addition to medium-range ballistic missiles, I mentioned specifically "jet bombers capable of carrying nuclear weapons," as "an explicit threat to the peace and security of all the Americas." Finally, my proclamation of October twenty-third entitled "Interdiction of the Delivery of Offensive Weapons to Cuba" specifically listed bomber aircraft. These facts were all known at the time of our exchange of letters on Cuba, and so it seems clear to me that our exchange of letters covers the IL-28s, since your undertaking was to remove the weapons we described as offensive.

Your letter says—and I agree—that we should not complicate the situation by minor things. But I assure you that this matter of IL-28s is not a minor matter for us at all. It is true, of course, that these bombers are not the most modern of weapons, but they are distinctly capable of offensive use against the United States and other Western Hemispheric countries, and I am sure your own military men would inform you that the continued existence of such bombers in Cuba would require substantial measures of military defense in response by the United States. Thus, in simple logic these are weapons capable of offensive use. But there is more in it than that, Mr. Chairman. These bombers could carry nuclear weapons for long distances, and they are clearly not needed, any more than missiles, for purely defensive purposes on the island of Cuba. Thus in the present context their continued presence would sustain the grave tension that has been created, and their removal, in my view, is necessary to a good start on ending the recent crisis.

I am not clear as to what items you object to on the list which Ambassador Stevenson handed to Mr. Kuznetsov. I can assure you I have no desire to cause you difficulties by any wide interpretation of the definitions of weapons which we consider offensive and I am instructing my representative in New York to confer promptly with Mr. Kuznetsov and to be as forthcoming as possible in order to meet any legitimate complaints you may have in order to reach a quick solution which would enable our agreement to be carried to completion. I entirely agree with your statement that we should wind up the immediate crisis promptly, and I assure you that on our side we are insisting only on what is immediately essential for progress in this matter. In order to make our position clear, I think I should go on to give you a full sense of the very strong feelings we have about this whole affair here in the United States.

These recent events have given a profound shock to relations between our two countries. It may be said, as Mr. Kuznetsov said the other day to Mr. McCloy, that the Soviet Union was under no obligation to inform us of any activities it was carrying on in a third country. I cannot accept this view; not only did this action threaten the whole safety of this hemisphere, but it was, in a broader sense, a dangerous attempt to change the world-wide *status quo*. Secret action of this kind seems to me both hazardous and unjustified. But however one may judge that argument, what actually happened in this case was not simply that the action of your side was secret. Your Government repeatedly gave us assurances of what it was *not* doing; these assurances were announced as coming from the highest levels, and they proved inaccurate.

I do not refer here only to the TASS article of September, but also to communications which were addressed to the highest levels of our Government through channels which heretofore had been used for confidential messages from the highest levels of your Government. Through these channels we were specifically informed that no missiles would be placed in Cuba which would have a range capable of reaching the United States. In reliance upon these assurances I attempted, as you know, to restrain those who were giving warnings in this country about the trend of events in Cuba. Thus undeniable photographic evidence that offensive weapons were being installed was a deep and dangerous shock, first to this Government and then to our whole people.

In the aftermath of this shock, to which we replied

DOCUMENT 67: President Kennedy's letter to Premier Khrushchev, November 6, 1962 (transcribed for legibility).

PAGE 2 OF 2

with a measured but necessary response, I believe it is vital that we should re-establish some degree of confidence in communication between the two of us. If the leaders of the two great nuclear powers cannot judge with some accuracy the intentions of each other, we shall find ourselves in a period of gravely increasing danger—not only for our two countries but for the whole world.

I therefore hope that you will promptly recognize that when we speak of the need to remove missiles and bombers, with their immediate supporting equipment, we are not trying to complicate the situation but simply stating what was clearly included in our understanding of October twenty-seventh and twenty-eighth. I shall continue to abide fully by the undertakings in my letter of October twenty-seventh, and specifically, under the conditions stated in that letter I will hold to my undertaking "to give assurances against an invasion of Cuba." This undertaking has already come under attack here and it is likely to become increasingly an object of criticism by a great many of my countrymen. And the very minimum that is necessary in regard to these assurances is, as we agreed, the verified removal of the missile and bomber systems, together with real safeguards against their reintroduction.

I should emphasize to you directly, Mr. Chairman, that in this respect there is another problem immediately ahead of us which could become very serious indeed, and that is the problem of continuing verification in Cuba . Your representatives have spoken as if this were entirely a problem for the Castro regime to settle, but the continuing verification of the absence of offensive weapons in Cuba is an essential safeguard for the United States and the other countries of this hemisphere, and is an explicit condition for the undertakings which we in our turn have agreed to. The need for this verification is, I regret to say, convincingly demonstrated by what happened in Cuba in the months of September and October.

For the present we are having to rely on our own methods of surveillance, and this surveillance will surely have to be continued unless, as we much prefer, a better and durable method can be found. We believe that it is a serious responsibility of your Government to insure that weapons which you have provided to Cuba are not employed to interfere with this surveillance which is so important to us all in obtaining reliable information on which improvements in the

situation can be based. It was of great importance, for example, for me last week to be able to announce with confidence that dismantling of missiles had begun.

Finally, I would like to say a word about longer range matters. I think we must both recognize that it will be very difficult for any of us in this hemisphere to look forward to any real improvement in our relations with Cuba if it continues to be a military outpost of the Soviet Union. We have limited our action at present to the problem of offensive weapons, but I do think it may be important for you to consider whether a real normalization of the Cuba problem can be envisaged while there remains in Cuba large numbers of Soviet military technicians, and major weapons systems and communications complexes under Soviet control, all with recurrent possibility that offensive weapons might be secretly and rapidly reintroduced. That is why I think there is much wisdom in the conclusion expressed in your letter of October 26th, that when our undertakings against invasion are effective the need for your military specialists in Cuba will disappear. That is the real path to progress in the Cuban problem. And in this connection in particular, I hope you will understand that we must attach the greatest importance to the personal assurances you have given that submarine bases will not be established in Cuba.

I believe that Cuba can never have normal relations with the other nations of this hemisphere unless it ceases to appear to be a foreign military base and adopts a peaceful course of non-interference in the affairs of its sister nations. These wider considerations may belong to a later phase of the problem, but I hope that you will give them careful thought.

In the immediate situation, however, I repeat that it is the withdrawal of the missiles and bombers, with their supporting equipment, under adequate verification, and with a proper system for continued safeguards in the future, that is essential. This is the first necessary step away from the crisis to open the door through which we can move to restore confidence and give attention to other problems which ought to be resolved in the interest of peace.

Sincerely,

His Excellency
Nikita S. Khrushchev
Chairman of the Council of Ministers
    of the Union of Soviet Socialist Republics
Moscow

~~TOP SECRET~~ - SENSITIVE

Summary Record of NSC Executive Committee Meeting No. 22,
November 7, 1962 -- 5:00 PM

Deputy Director Carter of CIA summarized the current intelligence.
Deputy Secretary Gilpatric explained our method of inspecting outgoing
missiles. We will have pictures certainly of missiles aboard six outgoing Soviet ships. About 90 percent of the missile erectors have been
moved to Cuban ports. Some Soviet troops are leaving. Photographs
will be available in Washington tomorrow.

The President asked whether we should say something tonight about the
outgoing missiles. Mr. Salinger said he thought something had to be
said. The President authorized the Defense Department to say that
ships with missiles are leaving Cuba. The President suggested that an
attempt be made to take pictures of a passenger boat returning to the
Soviet Union with Russian troops.

Secretary McNamara reported there had been no reaction to today's aerial
reconnaissance mission. The weather was bad. A request was made and
permission granted to fly five U-2 flights and twelve low-level flights, some
to photograph cave areas.

Secretary Rusk said we were heading toward a UN Security Council meeting
during which the Russians would announce that there are no Soviet missiles
in Cuba. Secretary General U Thant has put forward a suggestion that the
five Latin American Ambassadors in Havana be named as inspectors and
travel throughout Cuba. Our problem is how to manage recurrent rumors
in the U.S. and Latin America that the Russians are not moving out their
missiles but merely putting them into caves. He said we must have evidence
to reply to such allegations.

Secretary Dillon asked whether we were trying to get a bargain with the
Russians or avoid one. The President replied that we have a little time
now and we should play out our negotiations slowly. He said we wouldn't
invade with the Soviet missiles out of Cuba. We might make a formal
commitment not to invade when the Soviets comply fully by removing the
IL-28 bombers and we have assurances that there will be no reintroduction
of strategic missiles. We must continue aerial reconnaissance until a UN
substitute is in place or until we have ground inspection. He asked State
to draft a statement covering our plans for continuing inspection. He said
our posture with the Soviets should be such as to avoid the appearance of
holding back in the light of the rapid withdrawal of Soviet missiles.

DECLASSIFIED
NLK-80-29
By [signature] NARS, Date 10|9|84

~~TOP SECRET~~ - SENSITIVE

~~TOP SECRET~~ - SENSITIVE   - 2 -

Mr. Bundy said the only weapons in the proclaimed list which we must really get out are the IL-28 bombers. Secretary McNamara agreed.

The President said we must continue aerial surveillance. The Soviets say that inspection is now a Cuban problem. But we must make clear to the Russians that if they retaliate against our surveillance planes they will be held responsible. We are supporting a Latin American atom-free zone. The UN is discussing a proposal to send teams to carry out on-the-ground inspection in Cuba. If we get the IL-28 bombers out we might be prepared to lift the quarantine.

The President then asked for a memorandum spelling out what the Russians had agreed to and what we had agreed to.

Secretary Rusk said the proposal to use the Latin American Ambassadors in Havana as inspectors is a help but it is not complete. The President said these Ambassadors could look at caves and inspect possible Soviet submarine base sites. The problem is how we can hurt Castro without a quarantine which stops Soviet ships.

Secretary Rusk said we might ask the Latin American States to break relations and we might tell our allies to get their ships out of the Cuban trade.

Mr. Nitze circulated a Defense Department paper on what we would do if a reconnaissance plane were shot down. General Taylor orally stated the Chiefs' views. We must first find out whether a shoot-down is an isolated incident or whether it is the first of a series of actions undertaken with deliberate intent. We have a choice of hitting the offending source or if the shoot-down were deliberate, an air attack destroying the IL-28 bombers and the SAM sites. The President asked at what point we would give up low-level reconnaissance missions. We appeared to be running out of targets. He asked for a surveillance plan adequate to meet our interests on the assumption that the bombers remain and on the assumption that the bombers are taken out. He asked the group to meet again tomorrow to decide whether we should go to the mat on the IL-28 bombers or whether we should say the Soviets have now completed their agreement to remove the missiles and move on to other problems.

                                        Bromley Smith

                    ~~TOP SECRET - SENSITIVE~~

DOCUMENT 69: Premier Khrushchev's letter to President Kennedy, November 11, 1962 — received in Washington the following day (cover letter).

PAGE 1 OF 4

November 13, 1962

~~SECRET — EYES ONLY~~

Dear Foy:

I enclose a copy of the latest message from Khrushchev to the President, which was received on November twelfth.

This was handed to us as an oral message. Oral reply to Soviet Ambassador said if they would give the order to start removing IL-28's at once to be completed in about three weeks, we would announce removal of quarantine at once.

Sincerely yours,

Llewellyn E. Thompson

The Honorable Foy D. Kohler
American Ambassador
Moscow
RUSSIA

Enclosure

~~SECRET — EYES ONLY~~

LET:mac

IS/FPC/CDR   Date: 1/9/92

MR Cases Only:
EO Citations

( ) CLASSIFY as   ( ) S or ( ) C
( ) DOWNGRADE TS to ( ) S or ( ) C

DOCUMENT 69: Premier Khrushchev's Letter to President Kennedy, November 11, 1962
—received in Washington the following day (State Department translation).

PAGE 2 OF 4

Dear Mr. President,

I would like to express my satisfaction that the mutual obligations taken in accordance with the exchange of messages between us are being carried out by both your side and our side. One can say that certain favourable results are already seen at this time. We appreciate your understanding of the situation and your cooperation in carrying out the obligations taken by our side. We, on our part, will always honor our obligations. And I would like to inform you that our obligations with regard to dismantling and removal of both missiles and warheads have already been fulfilled.

We appreciate that we have come to an agreement with you regarding the mutually acceptable means for your side to ascertain that we really carry out our obligations. What has already been achieved in the course of negotiations between our representatives—Kuznetsov, McCloy and Stevenson—and the cooperation reached in the process of these negotiations is a good thing. The same should be said about the cooperation between captains of our ships, which were taking out missiles from Cuba, and corresponding U.S. ships. This is very good, this has created an impression that your side also wishes to cooperate in eliminating the remnants of tension which only yesterday was very dangerous for both our two peoples and for the peoples of the whole world.

Thus, if we proceed from our understanding which was expressed in your message of October 27 and in our reply of October 28, then we, the Soviet side, have carried out our obligations and thereby have created possibility for complete elimination of tension in the Caribbean. Consequently, now it is your turn, it is for your side to carry out precisely your obligations. We have in mind that apart from the long term obligations that the United States itself will not attack Cuba and will restrain other countries of the Western Hemisphere from doing that, the most important thing which is required to-day [sic] is to give moral satisfaction to world public opinion and tranquillity to peoples. And what is required from your side to that end is to lift the so-called quarantine and of course to stop violating the territorial waters and air space of Cuba. If this continues confidence in your obligations will thus be undermined which can only grieve world public and throw us back to the positions to which we must not return after the liquidation of such a dangerous situation. To say nothing of the fact that it would hamper us in the future.

At present, we must—and we are convinced in that—look forward and draw necessary conclusions from what has happened up till now and from the good which followed due to the effort of both sides. Therefore, we believe that conditions are emerging now for reaching an agreement on the prohibition of nuclear weapons, cessation of all types of nuclear weapons tests and all other questions which are ripe and require solution. You have already ended your tests and we shall probably also end our tests in November or at least before the end of this year.

Now it is also necessary to think of some real measures with regard to the question of ensuring more stable security in the world. In this connection we attach great importance to your statement that the US is ready to support idea of a non-aggression pact between NATO and the Warsaw treaty countries. but the basic question, of course, remains that of disarmament, of destroying the whole war machine of states. To give more assurance on the first stage it might be expedient to return to the proposals forwarded by us some time ago on the establishment of observation posts on mutual basis at airfields, in major sea-ports, at railway junctions, on highways. This would exclude a possibility of a surprise attack if any side does not behave honestly, if it wants to concentrate military equipment and its troops for an attack. Precisely this is pursued by the suggestion made recently by Mr. Thant.

It goes without saying that the question of a German peace treaty still remains and we can not [sic] escape from solving it. Moreover what we and you have lived through makes a speediest solution of this question still more imperative.

Now the elections in your country, Mr. President, are over. You made a statement that you were very pleased with the result of these elections. They, the elections, indeed, were in your favor. This success does not upset us either—though that is of course your internal affair. You managed to pin your political rival, Mr. Nixon, to the mat. This did not draw tears from our eyes either.

I do not name other unresolved questions, we have plenty of them, I name only the main problems, on the solution of which the destinies of the world largely depend.

Now about the matter that, as you state, worries you today about the IL-28 planes which you call an offensive weapon. We have already given you our clarification on this point and I think you can not [sic] but agree with us. However, if you do not agree—and this is your right—ask your intelligence after all and let it give you an answer based not on guesswork but on facts. If it really knows anything it must tell you the truth and namely that it is long since the IL-28's have been taken out of production and out of use in our armed forces. And if some planes still remain now—and a certain number of them have been brought by us to Cuba—that was done as a result of your action last year when you increased the budget and called up reservists. We on our part had to take measures in response at that time, having postponed taking those planes out of use as well.

Had there been no such action on your part we would not have IL-28's in existence because they would have been used for scrap. Such is this "formidable offensive" weapon. If your intelligence is objective it must give a correct appraisal of these 12-year old planes and report to you that they are incapable of offensive actions. We brought them to Cuba only because they can be used as a mobile means of coastal defense under the cover of anti-aircraft fire from their own territory. They can not however fly beyond the limits of that cover since they will be immediately destroyed either by modern anti-aircraft means or by simple conventional artillery; not to speak of interceptors before which they are entirely defenseless. But all this must be known not only to the intelligence but to all engaged in military matters.

Nevertheless we regard your concern with understanding though on our part we share the desire of the Government of Cuba to possess defensive weapons which would permit to defend the territorial integrity of its country.

Therefore if you met this with understanding and if we agreed with you on solving other questions in implementing the mutually assumed obligations then the question of IL-28 bombers would be solved without difficulties.

In what way should this cooperation, in our understanding, find its expression and what would facilitate the solution of this question?

We state to you that these bombers are piloted solely by our fliers. Consequently you should not have any fears that they can be used to do harm to the United States or other neighbouring countries in Western Hemisphere. And since you and your allies in Western Hemisphere have taken an obligation not to invade Cuba then it would seem this weapon should not pose any threat for you. Moreover we are aware of what military means are in your possession. If the enemy were threatening us with such weapon we would ignore that threat completely for it would cause us no anxiety whatsoever.

But because you express apprehension that this weapon can be some sort of a threat to the US or other countries of Western Hemisphere which do not possess adequate defensive means we state to you as a guarantee that those planes are piloted by our fliers and therefore there should be no misgivings that they could be used to the detriment of any state.

As you ascertained yourself we have removed the missiles, we also removed everything else related to missiles, all the equipment necessary for their use and recalled the personnel manning those missiles. Now that the missiles are removed the question of IL-28's is an incomprehensible argument because the weapon as I have already said is of no value as a combat weapon at present, to say nothing of the future. Let us come to an agreement on this question as well, let us do away with tension, let us fulfill the mutual pledges made in our messages. Your brother Robert Kennedy mentioned as one variant of solving the question of IL-28 aircraft that those planes should be piloted by Soviet fliers only. We agree to this. But we are also ready to go further—we will not insist on permanently keeping those planes on Cuba. We have our difficulties in

DOCUMENT 69: Premier Khrushchev's Letter to President Kennedy, November 11, 1962
—received in Washington the following day (State Department translation).

PAGE 4 OF 4

this question. Therefore we give a gentleman's word that we will remove the IL-28 planes with all the personnel and equipment related to those planes, although not now but later. We would like to do that some time later when we determine that the conditions are ripe to remove them. We will advise you of that.

I think that an agreement on such basis will enable us to complete the elimination of all the tension that existed and will create conditions for life to resume its normal course, that is the blockade would be immediately removed; the pledges of the sides would be registered in the appropriate documents in the United Nations Organization; non-invasion of Cuba and strict observance of her sovereignty guaranteed; the UN posts established in the countries of the Caribbean so that neither one nor the other side would indeed undertake any unexpected actions to the detriment of another state.

This would be the best solution which can be anticipated especially having in mind the tension that we have lived through and the abyss we came to. And I believe, Mr. President, that you yourself understand that we were very close to that abyss. But you and we soberly and wisely appraised the situation and maintained self-control. Let us now give a complete satisfaction to the public.

What happened should now prompt us to make new great efforts so that no repetition of such events should be allowed because if we succeeded in finding a way out of a dangerous situation this time, next time we might not safely untie the tightly made knot. And the knot we are now untieing [sic] has been tied rather tightly, almost to the limit.

We displayed an understanding with regard to the positions of each other and came out of a critical situation through mutual consessions [sic] to the satisfaction of all peoples of the world. Let us now give joy to all peoples of the world and show that this conflict really became a matter of yesterday, let us normalize the situation. And it would be good if on your part efforts were made to make the normalization a complete, real normalization and it is necessary to do this in the interests of all peoples and this is within our power.

Sincerely

DOCUMENT 70: President Kennedy's oral message to Premier Khrushchev, regarding the IL-28 aircraft, November 12, 1962.

PAGE 1 OF 1

<u>Unofficial translation</u>

During the second meeting with A.F.Dobrynin on the evening of November 12, R.Kennedy, under instruction from the President, formulated the US proposal in this way: "N.S.Khrushev and the President agree in principle that the IL-28 aircraft shall be withdrawn within a certain period of time. Following this agreement the US will immediately, even tomorrow, lift all quarantine, without waiting for the completion of the aircraft pullout. The US side would, of course, prefer that the agreed time period for withdrawing the IL-28 aircraft were made public. However, if the Soviet side has any objections to making it public, the President will not insist. N.S.Khrushev's word would be quite suffice. As for the period of time, it would be good if the aircraft were withdrawn within, say, 30 days". (This proposal was received in Moscow on <u>November 13</u>).

(The Department of State has been unable to locate an original version of President Kennedy's November 12, 1962 message. The above version was furnished to the Department by the Soviet Embassy in late 1991.)

DOCUMENT 71: Premier Khrushchev's Letter to President Kennedy, regarding removal of the IL-28
aircraft, November 14, 1962 (State Department translation).

PAGE 1 OF 2

I have read with great satisfaction the reply of the President of the United States and I agree with the considerations expressed by the President. It is of particular pleasure to me that we seem to have the same desire to liquidate as soon as possible the state of tension and normalize the situation so that to untie our hands for normal work and for solving those questions that are awaiting their solution. And this depends in the main on agreement between us—the two greatest powers in the world with whom special responsibility for ensuring peace lies to a greater degree than with other countries.

The question of the withdrawal of the IL-28's within mentioned 30 days does not constitute any complicated question. Yet this period will probably not be sufficient. As I already said in my oral message I can assure the President that those planes will be removed from Cuba with all the equipment and flying personnel. It can be done in 2-3 months. But for me, for our country it would be a great relief if the state of tension that evolved in the Caribbean were liquidated as soon as possible. I have in mind what I have already said, namely: to lift immediately the quarantine that is blockade; to stop the flights of the US planes over Cuba; to write down the mutual committments [sic] ensuing from the messages of the President and mine of October 27 and 28 to which end your representatives and ours have to prepare with the participation of the UN acting Secretary General U Thant an appropriate document. This is the main thing now.

You understand that when we say that it is necessary to announce now the withdrawal of the IL-28's at the time when your planes are flying over Cuba it creates for us no small difficulties. I have no doubt that you will understand—and the Cuban Government understands this—that such actions constitute violation of sovereignty of the Cuban state. Therefore it would be a reasonable step to create in this respect also conditions for the normalization of the situation and this in a great degree would make it easier to meet your wish of expediting the withdrawal of the IL-28 planes from Cuba.

If we attained all that now and if this were announced, then more favourable conditions would be created for our country to solve the question of time table for the withdrawal of IL-28 planes.

Now our main difficulties lie precisely in the fact that, as it is well known to everybody and it is being rightfully pointed out to us, we have removed from Cuba missiles and warheads, that is, we have fulfilled our committments [sic] while the US is not carrying out its committments [sic] —the quarantine continues, the US planes continue to fly over Cuba and there is no agreement that would register the pledges of the US. And all this finds ears that are listening and listening attentively. It is difficult for us to give explanations to such unjustifiable state of affairs. Therefore to carry out the final procedure after the missiles and warheads have been removed, already now the quarantine must be lifted, the flights of the American planes over Cuba must be stopped and mutual committments [sic] of the sides must be written down in an appropriate document with the participation of the UN.

It is hard to say for me what specific agreement is possible on the question of UN observation posts. But we as well as the Government of Cuba have already expressed a desire to come to terms on this question. If the question of the observation posts is of interest to the US—and I think it must be of interest—then I consider it wise to come to an agreement on this. I think that the Government of Cuba will not object to the UN posts, of course on the condition of respect for the sovereignty of Cuba, on the condition of treating her as equal which must mean that on the territory of other countries of the Caribbean and in a corresponding region of the US there will be also set up similar UN posts, that is on the condition that reciprocity will be observed in this question.

You understand, Mr. President, that no country can assume unilateral committments [sic], and it would be wise to make them mutual.

I have already said that perhaps it will be necessary for us in the negotiations on disarmament between our countries at the first stage to return to our proposals providing for the establishment of posts at airfields, in major sea-ports, at railway junctions, on highways in order to give guarantees to all the countries of the world that no country will be able to secretly concentrate troops and get prepared for an attack against or envasion [sic] of another country. It is wise, it appeals to us.

If you would give your representatives—McCloy, Stevenson and others—appropriate instructions on the question of UN posts in the Caribbean region and adjoining regions of the US—and our representatives have such instructions—and if they would come to an agreement then all this could be made public. Then there would be removed the difficulties connected with making a public announcement on the withdrawal of IL-28 planes and we would name then specific dates. These dates will be probably much closer than those which I name and maybe even closer than those which were named by you.

That is why we should make a final step in this direction. Then we would really cut the knot which was tied tightly enough and having cut it we would create normal relations between our countries to which our people aspires [sic] and which your people, we are sure of that, also wants.

I will allow myself to express some other considerations and I believe you will not take offence and will not consider that I intrude too much into the sphere of your internal affairs. Voting in the elections to the Senate, the House of Representatives and in gubernatorial elections which just took place has resulted in the defeat of your formal rival who was clearly preparing again for the next presidential elections. It is significant that as a result of the elections precisely those candidates were defeated who, if I may use such an expression, were making most frenzied bellicose speeches.

This indicates that the American people already begins [sic] to feel that if the arms race continues further, if a reasonable solution is not found and an understanding is not achieved between our countries then our peoples will feel still more strongly the threat of the dreadful catastrophe of a thermonuclear war.

Let us then not keep people of peace all over the world in suspense, let us give them joyous satisfaction. Having cut the knot in the Caribbean we would thereby immediately create better conditions and would reinforce people's hope for coping with other questions which are now awaiting their solution. Peoples expect wisdom from us, first of all from our two states. Of course our two states can not do everything, but all that depends on us in the sense of reaching an understanding will be of decisive importance. Needless to prove that other states would be also satisfied. And he who was especially displeased will have to agree after this understanding is reached that there is no other way, that the way to peace is the wisest and the only way of meeting the aspirations of all states, all peoples.

Sincerely,

November 15, 1962

⑦

I am glad to learn of your assurance of agreement that the IL-28s should be withdrawn.   All that remains is to reach understanding on the timing.

Let me review the undertakings in my letter of October twenty-seventh and your letter of October twenty-eighth.   You agreed to remove the weapons systems we described as offensive and with suitable safeguards to halt the further introduction of such weapons into Cuba.   On our side, we undertook to agree to remove the quarantine measures in effect and to give assurances against an invasion of Cuba.   There were two conditions attached to our undertaking.   The first was that the weapons systems would be removed "under appropriate United Nations observation and supervision," and, second, that there would be established "adequate arrangements through the United Nations to ensure the carrying out and continuation of these commitments."

I cannot agree with your statement that you have fulfilled your commitments and that we have not fulfilled ours.   Let us recall what, in fact, has occurred.   You have removed a certain number of missiles from Cuba -- not under United Nations supervision -- but you did cooperate in arrangements which enabled us to be reasonably sure that forty-two missiles were in fact taken out of Cuba.   There has been no United Nations verification that other missiles were not left behind and, in fact, there have been many reports of their being concealed in caves and elsewhere, and we have no way of satisfying those who are concerned about these reports.   The IL-28's are still in Cuba and are of deep concern to the people of our entire Hemisphere.   Thus, three major parts of the undertakings on your side -- the removal of the IL-28's, the arrangements for verification, and safeguards against introduction -- have not yet been carried out.

We suppose that part of the trouble here may be in Cuba.   The Secretary General of the United Nations was not allowed to make arrangements for the experts he took with him to Cuba to verify removal of the offensive weapons; the Cuban Government did not agree to international Red Cross inspection at ports; they have refused the Secretary General's suggestion that the Latin American Ambassadors in Havana undertake this verification; they have rejected a further suggestion of the Secretary General concerning the use of various non-aligned Chiefs of Mission in Havana for this purpose.   It is difficult for me to understand why the Cubans are

DOCUMENT 72: President Kennedy's letter to Premier Khrushchev, November 15, 1962.

PAGE 2 OF 4

-2-

so resistant to the series of reasonable proposals that have been made to them by U Thant unless, for reasons of their own, they are determined to see the crisis prolonged and worsened. We both have means of influencing the Cuban Government and I do not believe that we can allow that Government to frustrate the clear understandings our two governments have reached in the interests of peace.

In these circumstances we have so far been patient and careful, as we have been, indeed, at every stage. As you know from your own reports, we have always applied the quarantine with care and with regard for the position of others, and in recent days we have relied on the oral assurances of the masters of your ships and other ships. Moreover I myself held back orders for more forceful action right to the limit of possibility during the week of October 27th and 28th. But we cannot make progress from here -- or avoid a return of danger to this situation -- if your side now should fall into the mistake of claiming that it has met all its commitments, and refusing to help with the real business of carrying out our purpose of untying the Cuban knot.

What, in these circumstances, should be done? We are entitled to insist on removal of the IL-28's and on safeguards against reintroduction of offensive weapons before we lift the quarantine or give assurances of any sort. But we are interested in making rapid progress, step-by-step, and that is why we have proposed an arrangement more favorable from your standpoint: that as soon as you give the order for the removal of the IL-28's and their men and equipment, to be completed within thirty days, (and I am glad you say the length of time is not the real problem) we will announce the lifting of the quarantine. That is more than we agreed to on October twenty-seventh and twenty-eighth, but we wish to end this crisis promptly.

Beyond that, we are quite willing to instruct our negotiators in New York to work closely with yours in order to reach agreement on other matters affecting this problem. We believe, again, that these matters should follow the removal of offensive weapons systems, but just as we have been able to discuss other matters while a number of missiles were leaving, we believe the urgently needed talks can and should go forward while the bombers are leaving. We do not insist that everything wait its exact turn -- but only that the essential first steps be clearly going forward.

But what is most urgent, after we can agree that offensive weapons

-3-

are leaving, and after the quarantine is lifted, is to make some
real progress on continuing observations and verification. It will
be essential to have such arrangements -- and this again is clear
in the letters of October 27 and 28 -- before our assurances can be
more formally stated. Our undertaking on this point remains
firm and clear, and we want nothing better than to be able to give
our assurances, just as we said we would, when the necessary
conditions exist.

In the absence of any arrangements under the United Nations or
otherwise for international verification or safeguards, we have of
course been obliged to rely upon our own resources for surveillance
of the situation in Cuba, although this course is unsatisfactory.
Just today we learned of new threats by Castro against this necessary
surveillance. I should make it very clear that if there is any interference with this surveillance, we shall have to take the necessary
action in reply, and it is for just this reason that it is so urgent to
obtain better safeguards.

We note with interest that in your last message the arrangement of
observation and verification is enlarged from Cuba to include certain
other areas. This is a substantial change from the terms of our
exchange of messages, and as we see it any such wider arrangements
would necessarily require careful discussion. For example, if we
move outside Cuba to observe what is happening in other countries
which have been involved in the recent tensions, there might have
to be observation posts at the appropriate ports in the Soviet Union
from which weapons could be shipped to Cuba, as well as in appropriate
places in the United States. This is a matter which deserves close
study and it may offer a chance of real progress in the long run, but
for the immediate future it seems to us better to work within the
framework of our understanding of October 27 and 28.

We also think that the Brazilian proposal for a verified Denuclearized
Zone in Latin America could, with the cooperation of Cuba and if
acceptable to the other Latin American countries, in the long run
offer an acceptable means for a broader approach. However, the
immediate problem is, I repeat, the carrying out of our understanding
with regard to verification that offensive weapons have in fact been
removed from Cuba and the establishing of safeguards against their
reintroduction pending the coming into effect of longer-term arrangements.
Even apart from our understanding, given the history of this matter,
I am sure, Mr. Chairman, that you can understand that this is a real

-4-

necessity if we are to move to the settlement of other matters.

But the first step is to get the bombers started out, and the quarantine lifted -- for both are sources of tension. Meanwhile discussion can continue on other aspects of the problem.

DOCUMENT 73: General Maxwell Taylor, "Chairman's Talking Paper for Meeting with the President," November 16, 1962.

PAGE 1 OF 3

~~TOP SECRET~~

SANITIZED
Cuba VERSION

CHAIRMAN'S TALKING PAPER FOR MEETING WITH THE PRESIDENT

16 November 1962

1. The Chiefs appreciate the opportunity to discuss some aspects of the current negotiations bearing on the IL-28's and other matters related to Cuba. To lead-off, they would like to express their unqualified support for the insistence of our government upon the withdrawal of the IL-28's. While these aircraft are of less military significance than the IRBM's and MRBM's which have withdrawn, their continued presence in Cuba would present a long-term threat to the continental United States, would consequently require a higher level of air defense of our southeastern states and would give deep concern to many parts of Latin America. These factors added to the public statements of our Government on the need for their withdrawal convince the Joint Chiefs of Staff that the IL-28's must go.

2. The Chiefs are aware of the offer to exchange a lifting of the quarantine for Khrushchev's removal of the IL-28's and will regret the possible loss of this useful naval tool if the offer is accepted. If the Soviets decline the offer, the quarantine will provide an immediate means to apply pressure both on Khrushchev and on Castro not only to remove the IL-28's but also to obtain other ends such as the withdrawal of Soviet technicians and the acceptance of an inspection system. After appropriate warning to Khrushchev of our intentions, the Chiefs would favor a general extension of the quarantine to include a complete blockade of POL products. Concurrently, we should continue air surveillance and withhold any assurance against the invasion of Cuba. If the expanded quarantine did not succeed in obtaining the withdrawal of the IL-28's, we should be prepared to take them out by air attack.

3. Even if the IL-28's are negotiated out of Cuba, there will remain weapons systems of significant military importance; the MIG's, the SAM's, the air defense control system, and the large stocks of modern Army equipment which we have seen in our recent photography. The air defense weapons will be a constant threat to our air surveillance of Cuba while the Army weapons may be used against Guantanamo or against any invasion attempt. But more important than this equipment are the thousands of Soviet military personnel who remain in Cuba to man it. The Soviet presence in Cuba poses a particularly sensitive problem to the United States. When the extent of this presence is known and the weapons systems remaining in Soviet hands are thoroughly appreciated, it will be clear to the Western Hemisphere that it has indeed been invaded and remains invaded

E.O. 11652

JCS ltr. 2/24/75 NLK-75-98
By MFD RAPS, Date 3/12/75

~~TOP SECRET~~

Copy .... of .... Copies

Page .... of .... Pages

DOCUMENT 73: General Maxwell Taylor, "Chairman's Talking Paper for Meeting with the President," November 16, 1962.

PAGE 2 OF 3

TOP SECRET

by the Soviet Union. Under these conditions, we may anticipate a loud popular demand in the United States and in Latin America for the removal of the Soviet personnel and neutralization of their weapons. The Joint Chiefs of Staff feel that the United States should generate now all the pressure possible to get the Soviet personnel out, feeling that their eviction is far more important than that of the equipment.

4. The Chiefs are very much interested in the terms in which any assurance to Castro may eventually be couched, feeling that it would be damaging to our national interest and to the sense of security of our Latin American allies to create the impression of underwriting Castro for an indefinite period without careful qualification. If it is considered necessary to give Castro any assurance, the Chiefs feel that it should be tied to Khrushchev's proposal in his 26 October letter to withdraw Soviet forces from Cuba, and to cease giving military aid to Castro. Also the assurance should be given without affecting our commitments under the Rio Pact and should be linked to concurrent good behavior on the part of Castro and to acceptance by the Castro government of continued air surveillance.

5. The Chiefs recognize both the importance and the difficulty of obtaining an adequate verification system in Cuba. While sympathetic with their purpose, the Chiefs do not like two of the current proposals for inspection and verification.

6. In summary, the Joint Chiefs of Staff recommend at this juncture:

a. That the IL-28's be removed from Cuba, preferably by negotiation -- otherwise by blockade followed, if need be, by military action.

- 2 -

TOP SECRET

Copy .... of .... Copies

Page .... of .... Pages

DOCUMENT 73: General Maxwell Taylor, "Chairman's Talking Paper for Meeting with the President,"
November 16, 1962.

PAGE 3 OF 3

~~TOP SECRET~~

b.   That the removal of Soviet personnel from Cuba be made
an immediate objective of negotiations with the USSR.

c.   That any assurance to Castro be hedged by conditions
protecting our obligations under the Rio Pact and linking the
duration of the assurance to good behavior by Castro and the
acceptance of air surveillance.

d.

– 3 –

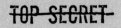 ~~TOP SECRET~~

Copy .... of .... Copies

Page .... of .... Pages

DOCUMENT 74: Roger Hilsman, State Department Bureau of Intelligence and Research memorandum, "Negotiations on Cuba: The Advantages of Stalemate," November 17, 1962.

PAGE 1 OF 5

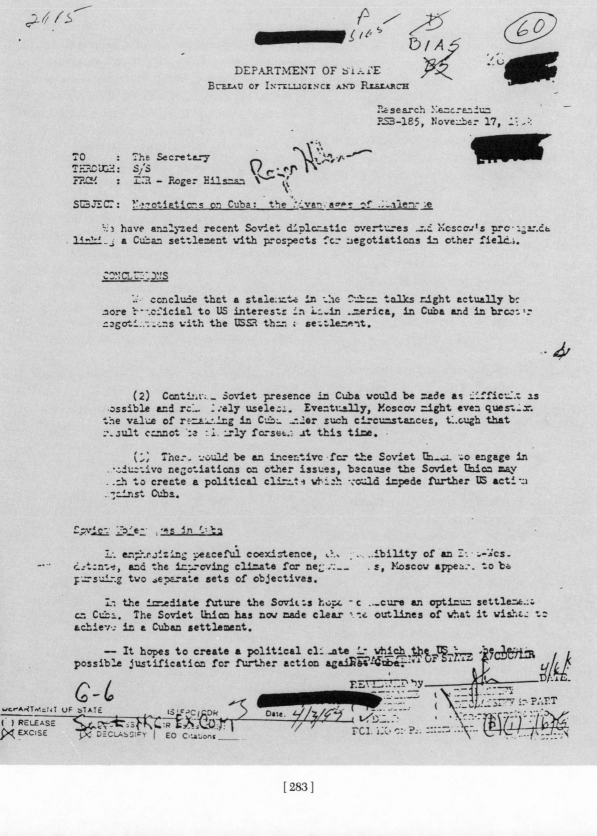

DEPARTMENT OF STATE
BUREAU OF INTELLIGENCE AND RESEARCH

Research Memorandum
RSB-185, November 17, 1962

TO   : The Secretary
THROUGH : S/S
FROM   : INR - Roger Hilsman

SUBJECT: Negotiations on Cuba: the Advantages of Stalemate

We have analyzed recent Soviet diplomatic overtures and Moscow's propaganda linking a Cuban settlement with prospects for negotiations in other fields.

CONCLUSIONS

We conclude that a stalemate in the Cuban talks might actually be more beneficial to US interests in Latin America, in Cuba and in broader negotiations with the USSR than a settlement.

(2) Continued Soviet presence in Cuba would be made as difficult as possible and relatively useless. Eventually, Moscow might even question the value of remaining in Cuba under such circumstances, though that result cannot be clearly foreseen at this time.

(3) There would be an incentive for the Soviet Union to engage in productive negotiations on other issues, because the Soviet Union may wish to create a political climate which would impede further US action against Cuba.

Soviet Objectives in Cuba

In emphasizing peaceful coexistence, the possibility of an East-West détente, and the improving climate for negotiations, Moscow appears to be pursuing two separate sets of objectives.

In the immediate future the Soviets hope to secure an optimum settlement on Cuba. The Soviet Union has now made clear the outlines of what it wishes to achieve in a Cuban settlement.

— It hopes to create a political climate in which the US has the least possible justification for further action against Cuba.

DEPARTMENT OF STATE
Bureau of Intelligence and Research

TO : The Secretary
THROUGH: S/S
FROM : INR - Roger Hilsman

SUBJECT : *Negotiations on Cuba: the Advantages of Stalemate*

We have analyzed recent Soviet diplomatic overtures and Moscow's propaganda linking a Cuban settlement with prospects for negotiations in other fields.

CONCLUSIONS

We conclude that a stalemate in the Cuban talks might actually be more beneficial to US interests in Latin America, in Cuba and in broader negotiations with the USSR than a settlement.

[5 lines excised]

(2) Continual Soviet presence in Cuba would be made as difficult as possible and relatively useless. Eventually, Moscow might even question the value of remaining in Cuba under such circumstances, though that result cannot be clearly foreseen at this time.

(3) There would be an incentive for the Soviet Union to engage in productive negotiations on other issues, because the Soviet Union may wish to create a political climate which would impede further US action against Cuba.

Soviet Objectives in Cuba
In emphasizing peaceful coexistence, the possibility of an East-West detente, and the improving climate for negotiations, Moscow appears to be pursuing two separate sets of objectives.

In the immediate future the Soviets hope to secure an optimum settlement on Cuba. The Soviet Union has now made clear the outlines of what it wishes to achieve in a Cuban settlement.

—It hopes to create a political climate in which the US has the least possible justification for further action against Cuba.

—It clearly wishes to drive the best bargain it can on US assurances to the Castro regime. And no matter how qualified the non-invasion assurance it finally obtained might be, the Soviet Union would attempt to interpret it in a fashion calculated to create a presumption that the US was acting in bad faith if any untoward events occurred in Cuba.

—It seeks to reduce to an absolute minimum, and would wish to avoid entirely if it could, any provision for on-site inspection or continuing UN presence in Cuba.

—However, Moscow is apparently willing to trade off at least some elements of its actual or potential military presence (the IL28s, for example) if it can thereby end the quarantine, minimize verification and maximize the acceptance of the Castro regime.

The Soviet Union almost certainly expects Castro to be disgruntled at the conclusion of the crisis. The Soviets probably estimate that even the most favorable terms which they can hope to obtain from the US will not leave the Cubans content, and Castro will continue to feel that he has been sold out to the Soviets. But the Soviets probably also calculate that their best chance for improving relations with Castro is to obtain a negotiated settlement with the US. If the Soviets can assure the safety of the Castro regime, they probably believe that they can in time use economic aid and political support to re-establish satisfactory rapport with the Cubans.

At the same time the Soviet Union will have succeeded in preserving a communist regime in Latin America as a foothold and as an example to other potential communist regimes. If the Soviet Union can thus assure Cuban security security [sic], it will do much to offset the damage to Soviet prestige involved in the missile withdrawal. The Soviets probably reckon that bloc critics would have less cause for thinking the USSR had been defeated if it could demonstrate that retreat was a sound tactic for preserving a communist foothold in Latin America.

Soviet Objectives in Other Negotiations

More broadly, the Soviets appear to be interested in using a Cuban settlement as a starting point from which to pursue other objectives vis-a-vis the West. These broader objectives are far less clearly visible than Soviet goals for a Cuban settlement; they may, in fact, still be under review in Moscow.

For the moment the Soviet Union has advanced only two more or less concrete negotiating proposals, on the temporary presence of Western troops in West Berlin under a UN flag and on the use of "black boxes" to monitor a test-ban. These proposals had evidently been planned for some time prior to the Cuban crisis.

Moscow's present emphasis on the possibility of negotiated settlements could be nothing more than a tactical ruse to lure the US into a more favorable Cuban settlement. At the other extreme Moscow could conceivably have radically altered its view of the world in the three weeks since it decided that it would have to withdraw its missiles from Cuba; the Soviets may have concluded that given their strategic inferiority and the grim prospect of an endless and economically debilitating arms race, the time has come for a far-reaching settlement of outstanding issues such as Berlin and a start on general disarmament.

While neither of these extreme possibilities can be entirely ruled out on the basis of the evidence presently at hand, both appear improbable. On balance, past Soviet performance and the few indications of Soviet intentions that we have, point to an effort to engage the US in negotiations on a series of topics both for the sake of the atmospheric gains to be derived from the negotiating process itself and in the hope of obtaining some agreements on acceptable terms. While Moscow appears willing to make some initial concession in order to get negotiations started, there is yet little indication of how far the Soviets may be willing to go in order to secure agreements.

Negotiated Settlement

Broadly speaking there are two principal alternatives by which the present negotiations in New York may be concluded—either a negotiated agreement or a stalemate in the talks.[1]

A negotiated settlement of the Cuban crisis would provide the Soviet Union with much or all that it could hope to achieve in Cuba under present circumstances.

Initially Castro's dissatisfaction would be maximized. He would regard any Soviet concessions in the negotiations as selling out his interests to the US.

But the Castro regime would be substantially safeguarded from invasion, and by implication, at least, from other US actions against it. Soviet presence in Cuba, as a donor of economic assistance, a sponsor of subversive activities elsewhere in the hemisphere, and probably as a military protector as well would be assured. The cause of Castro's dissatisfactions would be a single event which would tend to be obscured by sub developments, and with time Castro would have little choice but to reconcile himself to the *status quo*.

Communist China would doubtless support and encourage Castro in any charges of Soviet duplicity and disloyalty to principles of international communism. But as Castro's relations with Moscow improved, there would be less opportunity for Peiping to attempt to manipulate Soviet-Cuban differences for the purpose of attacking Soviet policies. Similarly, Peiping's ability to play up Moscow's withdrawal of its missiles as a defeat for Soviet policy would be reduced as the demonstrable fact of continued communist presence in Latin America gradually overshadowed the withdrawal itself.

Moscow would be free to use the Cuban settlement as a point or departure for other negotiations, but once they had gotten what they could in Cuba. The Soviet Union would feel little need to make concessions to the US on other issues for the sake of Cuba.

[words illeg]

The other major alternative would be to leave the Cuban crisis unresolved. Since the US is not likely to

---

1. We omit as infeasible under present circumstances a US invasion of Cuba. Obviously, in case of invasion the USSR would have to withdraw from meaningful negotiations with the US for a protracted period of time.

DOCUMENT 74: Roger Hilsman, State Department Bureau of Intelligence and Research memorandum, "Negotiations on Cuba: The Advantages of Stalemate," November 17, 1962 (transcribed for legibility).

PAGE 4 OF 5

obtain its maximum demands for on-site inspection and continuing UN presence in Cuba, it could refuse to issue a non-invasion guarantee.[1] Depending on whether or not the IL-22s were removed, the US might lift or maintain the quarantine on offensive weapons. Aerial surveillance would of course continue. The US would neither take immediate action to upset the present *status quo* to which Moscow's prestige is heavily committed, nor would it commit itself to the preservation of the Castro regime and the Soviet presence in Cuba. In effect, the present crisis with the possibility of further US action against Cuba would be perpetuated. The talks in New York would soon be obviously futile and would probably be allowed to peter out.

Effect on the Soviet Position in Cuba
There would be little immediate effect on the Soviet position in Cuba. While the Soviets would almost certainly prefer the advantages of a clear-out settlement and some form of explicit US commitment to Cuba's safety the basic Soviet interest in maintaining a presence in Cuba would not at the outset be affected. There might well be no occasion for a dramatic response on Moscow's part as the New York talks drifted into stalemate, and the US took no direct action to upset the *status quo*.

This approach would not be calculated either to force the Soviets out of Cuba or to bring down the Castro regime.

[8 lines excised]

As time went on the Soviet presence in Cuba would be made more expensive and difficult. Castro would have less immediate cause for dissatisfaction than he would under a negotiated agreement, but the sources of his discontent would remain, and over the long run Cuban-Soviet tensions would be reinforced.

Failure to obtain a guarantee of Cuba's security from the US would tend to encourage Soviet-Cuban differences over policy toward the US and the degree of Moscow's commitment to the defense of Cuba. Precisely because the future was uncertain, Cuba would seek more assurance from Moscow while the Soviets would be chary of extending commitments which they might be reluctant to fulfill.

Continuation of US surveillance, and the quarantine if maintained, would be another source of Soviet-Cuban differences. Castro would doubtless demand action which the Soviet Union was unwilling to take. The continuation of overflights and the quarantine would of course subject the US to a risk of incidents. These activities would however, provide a higher degree of assurance that Soviet offensive weapons were not reintroduced than would be afforded by any foreseeable agreement, and they could by changes in frequency, procedures etc be manipulated to stir up contention in Soviet Cuban relations.

Continued tension would tend to maximize the economic burden of Soviet aid to Cuba. Moscow would find itself in more frequent need to bribe the Cubans as disputes on other issues continued. At the same time there would be less possibility of Cuban trade with the free-world, and the burden of maintaining Cuba would fall exclusively to the bloc.

If Soviet-Cuban differences continued, Peiping would almost certainly wish to exploit them and the Cubans might seek to play off Moscow and Peiping.

At the same time the utility of Cuba to the USSR would diminish. Under the constant threat of US counteraction Moscow would have to be more circumspect about attempting to use Cuba either as a base for Soviet military forces or as a staging area for subversion in Latin America.

If the Soviets found themselves sufficiently uncomfortable in Cuba, and the utility of their remaining declined, the Soviet Union might at some future point decide that the game was no longer worth the candle, though that result cannot be assured by the simple expedient of perpetuating a chronic crisis.

Effect on US-Soviet Relations
At first glance it might seem that continued tension

---

1. The US would be spared the problems which a guarantee for Castro would create for US policy in Latin America. No matter how carefully it was worded, a guarantee for Castro would be regarded by many Latin American governments as a recognition of the legitimacy of the Castro regime and as a tacit acceptance of communism in Latin America.

over Cuba would not be conducive to negotiations on other issues. Obviously, Moscow would prefer a more secure toehold in Cuba, and the Soviet Union might at some early point wish to show its displeasure by putting off some negotiations in which it had only a limited interest in order to make a point of alleged US bad faith.

But Moscow has important interests to be served by negotiations with the West (in many instances this is true even of negotiations which the USSR does not expect will eventuate in any agreements), and the Soviets will not long allow potential diplomatic advantages to be wasted for the sake of interests which are more Castro's than the Soviet Union's. And if Moscow has in fact made a fundamental and radical reappraisal of the desirability of far-reaching settlements with the West (which we doubt), the USSR would be all the more impatient to get down to negotiations.

Whatever Moscow's aspirations for agreements with the West may be, continuation of a simmering crisis over Cuba would impel the Soviets toward creating an atmosphere of detente, and giving at least an appearance of being forthcoming in negotiations. For so long as the threat of further US moves against Cuba remains, the Soviets will have a motive for attempting to maintain a political climate in which the US might be inhibited from taking action.

DOCUMENT 75: Prime Minister Castro's Letter to U.N. Secretary General U Thant, withdrawing opposition to removal of IL-28 aircraft, November 19, 1962.

PAGE 1 OF 2

UNITED NATIONS
Press Services
Office of Public Information
United Nations, N.Y.

(For use of information media—not an official record)

Press Release SG/1379
20 November 1962

TEXT OF COMMUNICATION DATED
19 NOVEMBER 1962 FROM PRIME MINISTER
FIDEL CASTRO OF CUBA TO
ACTING SECRETARY-GENERAL U THANT

Following is the text of a communication* from Prime Minister Fidel Castro to Acting Secretary-General U Thant, as transmitted to the United Nations by the Permanent Mission of Cuba:

The Permanent Mission of Cuba to the United Nations presents its compliments to the United Nations Secretary-General and has the honour to transmit to him, upon the instructions of the Revolutionary Government of Cuba, the following message:

"U Thant,
Acting Secretary-General of the United Nations
"Your Excellency:

"The Government of the United States and the most reactionary section of the press of that country are endeavouring to create the impression that the Government of Cuba wishes to hamper and sabotage the possibilities for a peaceful solution of the present crisis.

"This attitude is based on two absolutely legitimate decisions of our people:

"The first: not to accept the unilateral inspection of our land whereby the Government of the United States wishes to decide questions which are entirely within our jurisdiction as a sovereign nations.

"The second: not to be prepared to permit invasion of our air space which are injurious to our security and offensive to our national dignity.

"The Government of Cuba has not created the

slightest obstacle to the negotiations which are taking place. This has been and it is our position. Our attitude to the threats and insults of the Government of the United States is something very different.

"The United States has now made the IL-28 medium bombers stationed on Cuban territory the crux of the problem.

"These planes are the property of the Soviet Government. They were brought to Cuba for the defence of our country when faced with aggression. Owing to their limited speed and low flight ceiling, their are antiquated equipment in relation to modern means of anti-aircraft defence.

"It is clear that the position of the Government of the United States in demanding the withdrawal of these planes merely constitutes a pretext for maintaining tension, prolonging the crisis and continuing its policy of force. Nevertheless, if the Soviet Government considers it desirable for the smooth conduct of the negotiations and the solution of the crisis to withdraw these planes, the Revolutionary Government of Cuba will not object to this decision.

"At the same time high officials of the Government of the United States have declared that military aircraft of that country will continue violating Cuban sovereignty and invading our air space.

"These illegal and aggressive acts are in flagrant contradiction with international law and the United Nations Charter.

"Cuba possesses a legitimate and indisputable right to defend its territory against such violations and it repeats the warning that to the extent of the fire power of our anti-aircraft weapons any war plane which invades Cuban air space can do so only at the risk of being destroyed.

"If during the perpetration of such arbitrary acts against our country, an incident should occur, the responsibility will fall wholly upon the Government of the United States.

"We wish to tell you once again, Mr. Secretary-General, that we are prepared sincerely to consider

---

* Unofficial translation from Spanish.

DOCUMENT 75: Prime Minister Castro's Letter to U.N. Secretary General U Thant, withdrawing opposition to removal of IL-28 aircraft, November 19, 1962.

PAGE 2 OF 2

a broad solution which will resolve the present tension once for all.

"We believe that this will be beneficial for all the peoples affected by the present situation, just as any conflict would be harmful to all. The moment has arrived when it will become clear who wants peace and who does not want peace. Cuba will never be an obstacle to a just and decent solution, acceptable to all. Cuba is simply defending its sovereignty, the right of self-determination of its people, the legal equality of all States, large or small, the right of every nation to work, to progress and to live in peace; to respect and be respected.

"If the Government of the United States, despite the sober attitude of the Soviet Union and the readiness of Cuba to promote a worthy and stable peace, insists on its acts of force against our country, no one need have any illusions about the inevitable result of this policy.

"Cuba will not give in to a policy of force. Its Revolution will remain firm, its people will resist,

cost what it may. Let our enemies not deceive themselves. With the strength born of right and patriotism we shall make the aggressors, if they attack us, pay very dearly for their crime.

"The United States is constantly threatening our country with war. It would be a war without glory and without honor, against a people who will never admit to defeat.

"May I assure you once again of my highest consideration,

> Fidel Castro Ruz
> Prime Minister of the
> Revolutionary
> Government of Cuba"

The Permanent Mission of Cuba to the United Nations takes this opportunity of repeating to the Secretary-General of the United Nations the assurance of its highest consideration.

> New York,
> 19 November 1962

DOCUMENT 76: Premier Khrushchev's Letter to President Kennedy, announcing withdrawal of the IL-28 aircraft from Cuba, November 19, 1962—received in Washington the following day (State Department translation).

PAGE 1 OF 4

I have studied attentively your considerations which were forwarded through our Ambassador in Washington in the evening of November 15. I wish first of all to express satisfaction with regard to your statement that the United States is also interested in the achievement of a rapid progress in untying the Cuban knot. This is our great desire too. It is good that you have confirmed once again that the U.S. committment [sic] to give assurance of non-invasion of Cuba, which was agreed upon in the exchange of messages on October 27 and 28 remains firm and clear. I fully share also the thought expressed by you about the necessity to act with caution, to take into consideration the position of others. Now when we speak of eliminating the remnants of the crisis this is as important as at any of its past stages.

I always believed and believe now that both of us are guided by the realization of the immense responsibility for the peaceful settlement of the crisis over Cuba being completed. The basis for such settlement already exists: the sides have achieved an agreement and have taken upon themselves certain obligations. It is precisely where we proceed from.

What have we agreed upon? In brief our agreement has come to the following.

The Soviet Union removes from Cuba rocket weapons which you called offensive and gives a possibility to ascertain this. The United States of America promptly removes the quarantine and gives assurances that there will be no invasion of Cuba, not only by the US but also by other countries of the Western Hemisphere. This is the essence of our agreement.

Later on you raised the question of removal of IL-28 planes from Cuba. I think you could not but feel the precariousness of that request. Now, of course, there may appear those who would wish to rummage in the wordings and to interpret them in different ways. But you and we do know well what kind of weapons they were that set the forest on fire, they were missiles. It was not accidental, indeed, that in our and your messages of October 27 and 28 there was not a single mention of bomber planes and specifficaly [sic] of IL-28's. At the same time those messages have direct reference to rocket weapons.

By the way, you yourself refer not to direct obligations of the sides but to the understanding implied by the American side in the expression "offensive weapons" mentioned in the messages and in this connection you recall your TV address of October 22 and you proclamation of October 23. But you will agree, Mr. President, that messages that fix the subject of agreement and unilateral statements of the US Government are two different things indeed.

I informed you that the IL-28 planes are twelve years old and by their combat characteristics they at present cannot be classified as offensive types of weapons. In spite of all this, we regarded your request with understanding. We took into consideration that you made certain statements and therefore the question of removal of IL-28 planes assumed for you as President a certain significance and probably created certain difficulties. We grant it. Since you might really have your difficulties in this question we moved in your direction having informed you of our consent to remove these planes from Cuba. What is the situation now if to summarize it in short and to speak of the main?

We have dismantled and removed from Cuba all the medium range ballistic missiles to the last with nuclear warheads for them. All the nuclear weapons have been taken away from Cuba. The Soviet personnel who were servicing the rocket installation have also been withdrawn. We have stated it to your representatives at the negotiations in New York too.

The US Government was afforded the possibility to ascertain the fact that all 42 missiles that were in Cuba have really been removed.

Moreover, we expressed our readiness to remove also the IL-28 planes from Cuba. I inform you that we intend to remove them within a month term and may be [sic] even sooner since the term for the removal of these planes is not a matter of principle for us. We are prepared to remove simultaniously [sic] with the IL-28 planes all the Soviet personnel connected with the servicing of these planes.

What can be said in connection with the committments [sic] of the American side? Proper consideration through the UN of the committment [sic] not to invade Cuba—and it is the main committment [sic] of your side—so far is being delayed. The quarantine has not been lifted as yet. Permit me to express the hope that with receipt of this communication of mine you will issue

DOCUMENT 76: Premier Khrushchev's Letter to President Kennedy, announcing withdrawal of the IL-28 aircraft from Cuba, November 19, 1962—received in Washington the following day (State Department translation).

PAGE 2 OF 4

instructions to the effect that the quarantine be lifted immediately with the withdrawal of your naval and other military units from the Caribbean area.

Furthermore, your planes still continue to fly over the Cuban territory. It does not normalize the situation but aggravates it. And all this is taking place at the time when we have removed the missiles from Cuba, have given you the possibility to ascertain it through appropriate observation and when we declare our intention to remove the IL-28 planes from Cuba.

I will not conceal that lately I have to hear more and more often that we are too trustful with regard to the statements of the US readiness to carry out its part of the agreement on Cuba and that the American side will under various pretexts evade the fulfilment [sic] of the obligations which it assumed. Ido [sic] not want to believe this and I proceed from something different: the President has given his word and he will keep it as well as we keep our word. But in such an acute and delicate question which we face there cannot but exist the limits beyond which the trust begins losing its value if it is not being strengthened with practical steps towards each other. All this should be mutually taken into consideration to sooner crown with success our efforts in settling the conflict.

I understand, of course, that some time is needed to formalize through the U.N. the agreement on the settlement of the conflict in the Caribbean area,including [sic] committments [sic] of non-invasion of Cuba. But this time should be measured by days, not by weeks and, of course, not by months.

Of all the committments [sic] based on the agreement achieved between us in the course of the exchange of messages you declare of your readiness to remove the quarantine immediately as soon as we agree on the term for the removal of IL-28's, without waiting for their removal.

Moving in your direction and taking the decision on the removal of IL-28 planes from Cuba we presume that we have grounds to count on similar understanding on your part also in the questions of the flights of American planes over Cuba and in promptest formalizing through the U.N. of the U.S. committments [sic].

As for the discontinuance of flights of American planes over Cuba you yourself can see better how this should be done. In my opinion, actual discontinuance of such flights over Cuba would already be a major step forward and would bring about a great easing in the situation, the more so that our missiles have been removed and your side has ascertained this.

They say that so far as it is a matter of formalizing the committments [sic] through the U.N. it is difficult for the American side to accept the form of a protocol we are suggesting in which the committments [sic] of the sides are to be fixed. We do no[t] attach decisive significance to a form. Other forms are not excluded either. For instance, a declaration (or declarations) which would be confirmed by the U.N. It is the contents [sic] of the document which is important and also that the committments [sic] of the sides be formalized through the U.N. without delay.

I heard that Americans have a rule: in any business each side should approach with the same standard the fulfilment [sic] of both its own obligations and the obligations of its counterpart and not use "double standard" —one for itself and another for the others. This is a good rule and if it is observed this promises a prompt settlement of the Cuban conflict. Let us follow this good American rule.

Now about the conditions which you set forth with regard to carrying out the verification and measures of further observation.

Yes, we really agreed to the effect that U.N. representatives could ascertain the removal from Cuba of rocket weapons which you called offensive. But we stipulated however that this question can be solved only with the consent of the Government of Cuba. We could not take an obligation for the Government of Cuba and your reference, Mr. President, that we allegedly took such an obligation, of course, does not reflect the real situation. I believe that you see for yourself the weakness of such a reference.

But what is the main thing in connection with the question of verification with regard to the missiles removed by us that is evaded in your communication? The main thing is that under agreement with you we gave you the possibility to carry out verification of the removal of our rockets in the open sea. We did that and that was an act of

DOCUMENT 76: Premier Khrushchev's Letter to President Kennedy, announcing withdrawal of the IL-28 aircraft from Cuba, November 19, 1962—received in Washington the following day (State Department translation).

PAGE 3 OF 4

goodwill on our part. You will agree that we took this step in the circumstances when no promise had been made by us with regard to this matter in our messages. We did something more in comparison with what had been said by us in the message with regard to verification.

It is clear that the said verification of the removal of the missiles conducted in accordance with the arrangement between us substitutes [sic] the verification of which you spoke in your message and I would say, in a more effective form at that because the American side was observing the missiles we were shipping out, so to say, at the final stage of their removal. While even verification of the dismantling would mean observing only the first stage of their removal from Cuba.

As a result the American side, as it itself so declared, had every opportunity to count the missiles put on our ships, to photograph them and to ascertain their removal.

Thus a way out was found and not a bad one, and the question of the verification must, of course, belong to the past. Now no one can doubt that we have carried out our committment [sic] with regard to the dismantling and shipping of the missiles from Cuba which were a subject in our correspondence. The fact of the removal of those missiles has been officially confirmed also by the U.S. Department of Defense.

As for the rumours [sic] alleging that the missiles may have been left in Cuba somewhere in the caves, one can say that we do not live in the cave-man age to attach great significance to the rumours [sic] of this sort. If someone is spreading rumours of this kind he is doing that deliberately [sic] to create difficulties in the negotiations.

As far as the question of the American side ascertaining our removing the IL-28 planes from Cuba is concerned, we do not see any problem here. In this respect you and we have the paved way and let us take that way. We have no objections against applying also to this case the procedure agreed upon between us for observation of the removal of the missiles though, speaking frankly, one could do without it. But if you want your naval vessels and helicopters to spend several hundred tons of fuel sailing and somersaulting around our ships carrying the IL-28 planes, let us then consider that such

possibility exists.

I will tell you frankly that it was part of our plans, and we believe that we will do it at a proper time, to ship out of Cuba those groups of our military personnel which although were not directly involved in servicing the rocket weapons now removed, still had something to do with guarding those installations. We will do this upon the arrival of our ships. But I must say that the strength of those groups in Cuba is not significant.

You raise the question as to what to do next, how to ensure that those types of weapons on the removal of which we have agreed are not brought back to Cuba. I believe that with respect to non-introduction of such weapons in the future you and I do not have any differences. We are prepared to give firm assurance with regard to this matter.

However, you speak not only about this. You now want some permanent supervision to be established, in Cuba or over Cuba. But where was it taken from that we gave our consent to permanent supervision? The question has never been put that way in the exchange of messages. And generally, how can one take as a normal thing an establishment, and without any reciprocity at that, of some permanent supervision over a sovereign state?

If we are to show serious concern that no unexpected steps are taken on either side to the detriment of each other, then as I already said, the proposal of the U.N. Acting Secretary General U Thant on the so-called "presence of the U.N.," i.e. on establishing U.N. posts in the countries of the Caribbean area would meet this task. This proposal of U Thant was also supported as is known by the Government of the Republic of Cuba. We believe it to be a reasonable basis on which it is possible to come to an agreement. And it would be good if that idea was accepted by you and put into life.

To tell the truth, I am somewhat surprised that in connection with the idea of "presence of the U.N." in the Caribbean area you are talking for some reason about setting up observation posts at the ports in the Soviet Union. May be [sic] you have in mind the proposals which we submitted during the negotiations on the problem of disarmament and on the problem of prevention of surprise attack in 1955 and 1958. But those proposals had nothing to do and cannot have anything to do with the question of

DOCUMENT 76: Premier Khrushchev's Letter to President Kennedy, announcing withdrawal
of the IL-28 aircraft from Cuba, November 19, 1962—received in Washington the following day
(State Department translation).   PAGE 4 OF 4

Cuba since that question simply did not exist at that time. Incidentally, I have already told you that in our opinion it would be useful to get back to considering the proposals to set up on a mutual basis the observation posts at airfields, major sea-ports, railway junctions and auto routes. We have given our representatives at the negotiation on disarmament in Geneva the necessary instructions. I repeat—we would like to come to an agreement on this question and if you give such instructions to your representatives at the negotiations on disarmament we will only greet that.

Such is our viewpoint on the three questions raised by you: on the removal of the IL-28 planes, on organizing the verification and on non-introduction to Cuba of such weapons which in accordance with the agreement are removed from Cuba.

How should we deal with the matter now so that we and you could soon bring joy to humanity with the news that the crisis over Cuba is completely liquidated?

The Government of the USA in view of the agreement reached on the IL-28 planes should immediately remove the quarantine which corresponds to your own statement as well.

It is necessary to stick to generally recognized international norms and rules fixed in the UN Charter—not to violate the territorial waters and air space of sovereign states and stop the flights of American aircraft over Cuba. I will tell you frankly, Mr. President, that I met with some relief the report that during the last one-two days the flights of American planes over Cuba did not take place. It is good if it promises maintaining of such wise decision in the future as well.

Let both of us agree, Mr. President, also that our representatives in New York be given at once the instructions to immediately proceed with working out an agreed document (or documents) that would formalize through the UN the committments [sic] of the sides.

As we see the matter this will require only a few days if, of course, all the sides want to have speediest liquidation of the aftermath of a tense and dangerous situation evolved in the Caribbean area, the situation that really brought humanity to the brink of thermonuclear war.

One more point. I have read V. Kuznetsov's report on his talk with A. Stevenson from which I learned that the American side is going to give us a draft of its document stating the US commitments [sic] of non-invasion of Cuba. Our draft of the document on settling the conflict has been already forwarded to your representatives. Naturally, we will study your document with utmost attention. Let us hope that as a result of the negotiations we will manage to formalize the achieved agreement so that it satisfy all the sides.

Your brother Robert Kenendy through our Ambassador Dobrynin in Washington and Mr. McCloy through our representatives in New York expressed a desire to get promptly our answer to the considerations expressed by you on the question of the removal of IL-28 planes from Cuba. Well, I think, this answer of mine gives you not a bad material for your statement at your press-conference. However, I hope, Mr. President, that your statement will not be one-sided but will respond to mutual understanding of the situation with regard to immediate steps to remove the quarantine and to discontinue the flights of American planes over Cuba as well as with regard to the immediate formalizing through the UN of the committments [sic] of the sides on the final liquidation of the crisis evolved in the Caribbean area.

In conclusion I wish to stress that much time has already passed since an agreement was reached between us and it is not in the interests of our countries, not in the interests of peace to delay the fulfillment of the agreement that has been reached and the final settlement of the Cuban crisis. Such is our conviction.

DOCUMENT 77: McGeorge Bundy, "Summary Record of NSC Executive Committee Meeting, November 20, 1962.

PAGE 1 OF 2

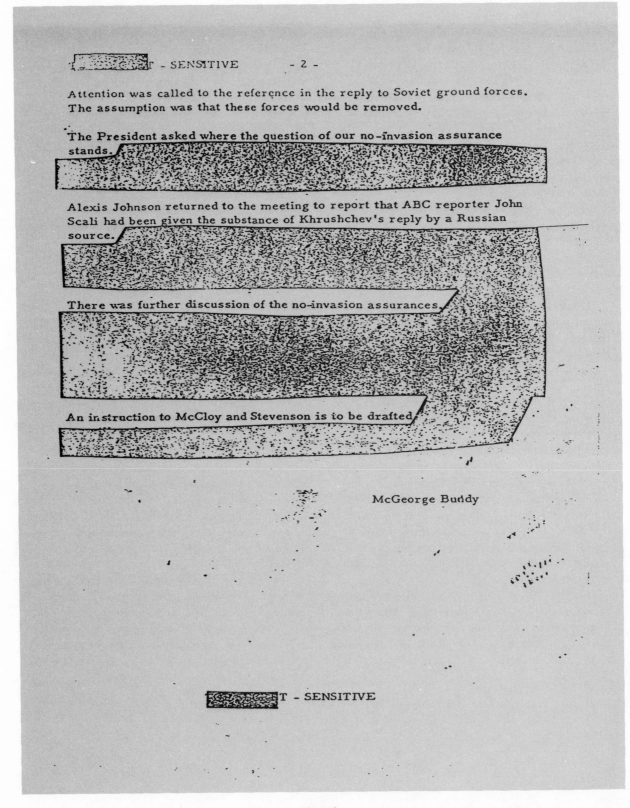

T - SENSITIVE   - 2 -

Attention was called to the reference in the reply to Soviet ground forces. The assumption was that these forces would be removed.

The President asked where the question of our no-invasion assurance stands.

Alexis Johnson returned to the meeting to report that ABC reporter John Scali had been given the substance of Khrushchev's reply by a Russian source.

There was further discussion of the no-invasion assurances.

An instruction to McCloy and Stevenson is to be drafted.

McGeorge Bundy

T - SENSITIVE

DOCUMENT 77: McGeorge Bundy, "Summary Record of NSC Executive Committee Meeting, November 20, 1962.

PAGE 2 OF 2

████ET - SENSITIVE

Summary Record of NSC Executive Committee Meeting No. 28
November 20, 1962 -- 3:30 PM

Khrushchev's reply was read to the group, the President not having yet arrived.

A statement to be made by the President at his 6:00 PM press conference was discussed and approved. The following decisions were reached:

    a. The quarantine is to be lifted immediately and a proclamation revoking it is to be prepared.

    b. U.S. naval forces in the Caribbean will remain there for the time being and carry out normal exercises. Ships in the area will not be removed because it is normal for some to be always on station in the Caribbean. Latin American ships which are in the quarantine force will be asked to stay and participate in exercises.

    c. Secretary McNamara recommended, and the President agreed, that there would be no low-level reconnaissance missions flown tomorrow.

    d. High-level flights averaging not more than one a day will continue intermittently because of the importance of knowing that the IL-28 bombers are actually being removed.

Two other actions are to be taken without public notice:

    a. The SAC air alert will be terminated and all other military forces will be put on a reduced alert basis.

    b. TAC planes concentrated along the coast will be deployed inland.

Secretary McNamara recommended that within forty-eight hours we announce that the air reserves called up for the Cuban crisis would be released before Christmas.

The OAS Organ of Consultation meeting will be called off. The State Department will call in the Latin American Ambassadors before the President's press conference to brief them on the Russian reply.

████ET - SENSITIVE

SANITIZED

DOCUMENT 78: President Kennedy's letter to Premier Khrushchev, acknowledging an end to the crisis, November 21, 1962.

PAGE 1 OF 1

November 21, 1962

MESSAGE FOR CHAIRMAN KHRUSHCHEV

Dear Mr. Chairman:

I have been glad to get your letter of November 20, which arrived in good time yesterday. As you will have seen, I was able to announce the lifting of our quarantine promptly at my press conference, on the basis of your welcome assurance that the IL-28 bombers will be removed within a month.

I am now instructing our negotiators in New York to move ahead promptly with proposals for a solution of the remaining elements in the Cuban problem. I do not wish to confuse the discussion by trying to state our present position in detail in this message, but I do want you to know that I continue to believe that it is important to settle this matter promptly and on reasonable terms, so that we may move on to other issues. I regret that you have been unable to persuade Mr. Castro to accept a suitable form of inspection or verification in Cuba, and that in consequence we must continue to rely upon our own means of information. But, as I said yesterday, there need be no fear of any invasion of Cuba while matters take their present favorable course.

January 7, 1963.

His Excellency U Thant,
    Secretary General,
        United Nations, New York.

Dear Mr. Secretary General:

On behalf of the Governments of the United States of America and the Soviet Union we desire to express to you our appreciation for your efforts in assisting our Governments to avert the serious threat to the peace which recently arose in the Caribbean area.

While it has not been possible for our Governments to resolve all the problems that have arisen in connection with this affair, they believe that, in view of the degree of understanding reached between them on the settlement of the crisis and the extent of progress in the implementation of this understanding, it is not necessary for this item to occupy further the attention of the Security Council at this time.

The Governments of the United States of America and of the Soviet Union express the hope that the actions taken to avert the threat of war in connection with this crisis will lead toward the adjustment of other differences between them and the general easing of tensions that could cause a further threat of war.

Sincerely yours,

ADLAI E. STEVENSON
Permanent Representative
  of the United States to
  the United Nations

V. KUZNETSOV
First Deputy Minister
  of Foreign Affairs
  of the U.S.S.R.

PART IV

THE CUBAN MISSILE CRISIS:
POSTMORTEMS

Even before the Cuban missile crisis actually ended, U.S. national security agencies began to assess the lessons of the conflict and its implications for the future. The various military and civilian bureaucracies produced numerous after-action reports, chronologies, retrospectives, policy studies, and even a two-hundred-page narrative meant to serve as the official internal history of the crisis.[1] These postmortems did not address the profound issues raised by the world's brush with nuclear holocaust; they were, for the most part, pragmatic evaluations of the political and military impact of the crisis on the United States' ability to project its power throughout the world.

One of the earliest assessments, "Significance of the Soviet Backdown for Future U.S. policy," written by State Department analyst Raymond Garthoff on October 29, 1962, concluded that the United States would "emerge from this confrontation with increased prestige world-wide," bolstering the confidence of European allies and enhancing Washington's ability to assert its interests in other international arenas of conflict—such as Berlin. The Soviet Union, in contrast, emerged from the crisis with its intentions "unmasked" and its "inability to force its will clearly demonstrated." Over the long term, Garthoff suggested, the political result of the crisis might be a Soviet responsiveness to "finding peaceful solutions" to a range of international problems. Militarily, though, these dangerous events might "set in motion a redou-

bled Soviet effort to close the gap...of a secure second strike capability" (Document 80).

Garthoff was prescient on both counts. Diplomatically, U.S.-Soviet relations gradually warmed in the period following the crisis. Several bilateral agreements were struck, including a "hot-line" agreement—modernizing the grossly inadequate communications systems between the Kremlin and the White House, which had plagued Kennedy and Khrushchev during the conflict—and a limited test-ban treaty. More significant, tensions over Berlin eased as the United States and the Soviet Union worked toward a peaceful accommodation on one of the key disputed regions of the Cold War.

Militarily, the constraints imposed during the crisis by Moscow's significant strategic inferiority clearly galled Soviet leaders into making a massive investment toward a credible nuclear capability. "We will honor this agreement. But I want to tell you something," Soviet Deputy Foreign Minister Vasily Kuznetzov warned U.S. negotiator John McCloy in December 1962. "The Soviet Union is not going to find itself in a position like this ever again."[2] As the missile crisis came to an end, the costly and dangerous nuclear arms race between the superpowers dramatically accelerated.

For the Pentagon's Office of International Security Affairs (ISA), the key lessons of the missile crisis addressed the "integrated use of national power" and better preparedness for future conflict. The drafters of "Some Lessons From Cuba" began with certain assumptions that have since been challenged by historical scholarship; for example, that the Cuba case was what Walt Rostow called a "controlled conflict." This case was unique because "the problem of controlling the development of events…was in some respects simpler here than can be expected as a rule," stated the paper—a flawed characterization given what is now known about the misjudgments, miscommunications, misinterpreted signals, and inadvertent military and covert operations that plagued the crisis. The ISA's analysis was also based on the premise that Soviet motives in putting missiles in Cuba were, first among others, "to display to the world, and especially to our allies, that the U.S. is too indecisive or too terrified of war to respond effectively to major Soviet provocation." The crucial lesson, therefore, was that U.S. decisiveness to respond with "serious military action"—to destroy the missiles and/or invade Cuba—was responsible for the successful outcome of the crisis. Conclusion: "The Soviets saw they were going to face conflict in Cuba and lose," therefore they withdrew (Document 81).

ISA analysts minimized the threat of nuclear conflagration. To be sure, the United States had demonstrated its willingness "to take risks of nuclear consequences." But the possibility of nuclear war drew greater attention "than was warranted by its likelihood." "Our public statements exaggerated the risks of nuclear war," according to the postmortem. "Our public stance should have de-emphasized the nuclear risks to the extent possible (even if we weren't entirely sure)."

Soviet officials viewed the crisis considerably differently than did their U.S. counterparts. Substantive internal government documentation of the "Caribbean crisis" has yet to be released, but a lengthy private letter from Khrushchev to Castro, dated January 22, 1963, and released during the Havana conference in January 1992, captures the thinking of the Soviet leader at the time.

In his letter, Khrushchev sought to repair the "mark…in the relations between our states" left by the outcome of the crisis. The Soviets believed, as did the Cubans, that the United States was preparing for an invasion. The purpose of placing the missiles in Cuba, he affirmed, was to "place the imperialists of the United States in the dilemma of having to renounce the invasion or unleash thermonuclear war," and to defend Cuba "on behalf of the common Marxist-Leninist cause" (Document 82).

The threat of nuclear war, Khrushchev claimed in trying to put the best face on Kennedy's noninvasion pledge, had forced the United States to "retreat [and] renounce the invasion." But, the "correlation of forces" in the Caribbean was such that it made no sense for the Soviets or Cubans to go to war with the United States if it could be avoided. A victory for global socialism, he predicted, would come not through unleashing a thermonuclear war, but "in winning the contest of peaceful competition" between capitalism and communism.

From the Cuban perspective, the outcome of the *"crisis de Octubre"* was the worst of both worlds: a victory for the enemy and a betrayal by an ally. Instead of relief that a nuclear confrontation over Cuba had been avoided, Fidel Castro reminisced to conferees in Havana that when news of the withdrawal arrived "it provoked a great indignation because we realized that we had become some type of game token.…[A] series of steps had been taken without including us…We had to endure the humiliation." Castro's indignation at being a bargaining chip would no doubt have been even greater had he known that Khrushchev had used the Cuban missiles to extract U.S. concessions on the Jupiters—something Castro did not learn until his visit to Moscow in April 1963.

Cuban government documentation on the crisis remains unpublished, but the lengthy statements made by Fidel Castro at the January 1992 conference, and translated by the CIA's Foreign Broadcast Information Service, constitute a veritable oral history from the sole surviving leader from the October 1962 crisis

(Document 83). In the end, Castro declined to draw his own conclusions: "There is a lot of material to study, to mull over, many things to reflect on....As a Soviet man once said, never has a problem been so seriously discussed as this one has, from which important lessons can be derived."

Yet none of the contemporary evaluations of the crisis, whether U.S., Soviet, or Cuban, attempted to address the ultimate lessons of the events of 1962. Those lessons center on the morality of nuclear weapons as a military or political tool. As Theodore Sorensen notes, Robert Kennedy was keenly aware of this issue and, in his unfinished memoir had intended to explore this "basic ethical question: What, if any, circumstances or justification gives this government or any government the moral right to bring its people and possibly all peoples under the shadow of nuclear destruction?"[3] Thirty years after the missile crisis, that question remains.

NOTES

1. This report was declassified in 1985. See Franklin Sieverts, "The Cuba Crisis, 1962" August 22, 1963, in the National Security Archive, *The Cuban Missile Crisis, 1962: The Making of U.S. Policy*.

2. Kuznetsov is quoted in Kai Bird, *The Chairman: John J. McCloy and the Making of the American Establishment* (New York: Simon and Schuster, 1992), p. 539

3. Robert F. Kennedy, *Thirteen Days: A Memoir of the Cuban Missile Crisis* (New York: W. W. Norton, 1969), p. 128.

~~SE CRET~~ ✓ October 29, 1962

McGB:

　　Attached by Ray Garthoff is the best quick assessment of Soviet backdown of those I've seen.

　　I'd underline his conclusion that we should take the initiative now to offer negotiations on other main East-West issues. Above all, we may have a first class chance of getting some kind of a viable standstill arrangement on Berlin.

　　Now would be the time to beat up Adenauer (here Monday) and offer the Soviets a deal. If they don't take it, we're no worse off (and look good for having made the effort). If they do take it, so much the better.

RWK

Attach. Garthoff paper
dtd 10/29/62, subj. Sig of
Soviet Backdown for Future
US Policy

DECLASSIFIED
E. O. 12356, Sec. 3.3
US ARCHIVIST (NLK-83-32)
FWH, MARS. Date 5/16/83　　~~SECRET~~

DOCUMENT 80: Raymond Garthoff, "Significance of the Soviet Backdown for Future U.S. Policy"
(with cover page from Robert W. Komer), October 29, 1962.

PAGE 2 OF 4

DEPARTMENT OF STATE

DEPUTY UNDERSECRETARY

G/PM

SECRET

October 29, 1962

MEMORANDUM

SUBJECT: Significance of the Soviet Backdown
for Future US Policy

1. Short-Run Effects

Political - The short-run effects should be very
favorable to the US. Unquestionably the US will emerge from this
confrontation with increased prestige world-wide. The Soviet action
should demonstrate once again the offensive nature of Soviet motivations more clearly than anything we could say. It should also demonstrate that the Soviets are not prepared to risk a decisive military
showdown with the US over issues involving the extension of Soviet
power. (We should be clear however that this is not to be confused
with Soviet lack of willingness to "go to the mat" over an interest
vital to Soviet security.) More specifically, short-run political
effects should include the following:

a. Soviet ability to penetrate Latin America should
suffer a reversal, though a base for future penetration may remain
in Cuba for some time. Soviet intentions have been unmasked, and
Soviet inability to force its will clearly demonstrated. Our
problems in assisting Latin America to achieve a higher state of
political and economic development will still require all of our
best efforts. However, our efforts should be focused on the fundamental nature of the problem, and it is important that we continue to
pursue our Latin American country internal programs, along with our
broader development programs.

b. NATO should be strengthened. The firmness of the
US stand, and perhaps even more importantly the categorical refusal
to barter NATO assets for immediate US security interests, should
provide assurance of US commitment to the Alliance.

c. Our position on Berlin should be greatly strengthened.
Our resolute willingness to act in Cuba should result in a complete re-
assessment by the Soviets as to how far they can safely push US will
in general, including Berlin. Similarly it should provide our Allies
with fortitude for meeting Soviet threats.

DOCUMENT 80: Raymond Garthoff, "Significance of the Soviet Backdown for Future U.S. Policy" (with cover page from Robert W. Komer), October 29, 1962.

PAGE 3 OF 4

SECRET

-2-

d. The effect upon the neutrals is more difficult to estimate, but in general is favorable. It must raise in the minds of many of the neutrals who may have a pro-Communist leaning a question as to how far they may safely "get in bed" with the Soviets and still protect their own national interests.

e. While there is probably very little immediate effect on Soviet Satellite relations, it cannot help but plant the seed of doubt as to Soviet omnipotence. This could have important implications for the future.

f. The effect on the USSR can be beneficial, but this will depend on how we further use our present strong position. It is conceivable that within the Soviet leadership the events of the past several days may be considered so serious a setback that changes may occur in the current Soviet leadership.

Military - The military benefits secured as a result of the Soviet backdown are similarly immense. Agreement not to proceed with additional missiles, and to dismantle existing missiles and launch facilities, cancels out the temporary increase in capability vis-a-vis the continued United States, which the Soviets achieved in their short-lived attempt to offset the current US nuclear strategic advantage.

2. Long-Run Effects

Political - An analysis of long-run effects is of course more uncertain. Unquestionably the Soviet defeat will have its impact on Soviet thinking and policymaking. Over the long run, one effect may be to make the Soviets far more responsive to our efforts at finding peaceful solutions to the whole range of world problems. However, and this is an important qualification, this effect is certain to take a considerable period of time. We should not delude ourselves into believing that great and rapid changes will result in Soviet policy. People and governments simply do not and cannot change that quickly, even assuming the stimulus for doing so. Thus while it is useful to explore all avenues of solutions to world problems, such as disarmament, we must not expect quick or easy solutions. We would expect that the US will meet with the usual Soviet criticism, resistance, and negotiatory pressure. In short, we must not slip into euphoria over the successful course of events, assuming it continues to develop favorably.

SECRET

[305]

DOCUMENT 80: Raymond Garthoff, "Significance of the Soviet Backdown for Future U.S. Policy" (with cover page from Robert W. Komer), October 29, 1962.

PAGE 4 OF 4

SECRET

-3-

<u>Military</u> - Viewed in its long-run perspective, the Soviet backdown does not affect the Soviet military position in any important essential other than, of course, the important removal of the missiles from Cuba and awarness in Moscow of US refusal to permit <u>any</u> such venture. It is possible that the effect of these events might be to set in motion a redoubled Soviet effort to close the gap to development by the Soviets of a secure second strike capability.

3. <u>General Conclusion</u>

Our over-all preliminary conclusion may be summarized as follows:

a. We have in the recent situation gained broad political and military assets, on which we should attempt to capitalize. We have probably gained important, but less definitive, long-range benefits.

b. In these circumstances, it is vitally important that the US take the initiative in offering to negotiate on major issues between East and West. Without being bellicose on the basis of our new-found strength, nor on the other hand making concessions which would adversely affect our position of strength, we should press for fair but safeguarded solutions to outstanding problems.

If we have learned anything from this experience, it is that weakness, even only apparent weakness, invites Soviet transgression. At the same time, firmness in the last analysis will force the Soviets to back away from rash initiatives. We cannot now, nor can we in the future, accept Soviet protestations of "peaceful" coexistence at face value. The words may sound the same, but the meaning is different. Their willingness to cooperate in common endeavors can only be judged by performance. The difficult task for US policy in the future is to strike the correct fine balance between seeking cooperation from a forthcoming posture, while retaining the necessary strength and skepticism to insure ourselves and our friends against future duplicity.

— Garthoff

SECRET

~~UNCLASSIFIED~~ 1-0648

DEPARTMENT OF STATE
Counselor and Chairman
Policy Planning Council
Washington

~~SECRET~~

November 15, 1962

TO: U - Mr. George Ball

THROUGH: S/S

FROM: S/P - W. W. Rostow

SUBJECT: Some Lessons From Cuba.

As background to your talks in Europe, I believe
you will wish to read carefully this preliminary paper
on some lessons from the Cuba crisis. I would warn
you, however, against paragraph 22 which I believe to
be incorrect and the product of nineteenth century
international law thinking.

It is envisaged that we may develop a version of
this paper for later presentation to the Quadripartite
Group here and possibly to some group on the occasion
of the December NATO meeting. Nevertheless, it may
serve you well ad interim.

PORTIONS
DECLASSIFIED BY: DOS + OASD(IA)
ON: 31 OCT 89

STATE DOC 834   OASD(PA) OFOISR
                 88 FOI 1267
                 88 FS 171
~~SECRET~~   DOC # 6 (R)

[307]

F78C011-0649

ISA DRAFT

November 14, 1962

SOME LESSONS FROM CUBA

In drawing lessons from the Cuban experience one should generalize with caution. The Cuban case, like all cases, was unique. Developments were influenced by a number of peculiarities not apt to reappear in the next crisis. Thus, the problem of controlling the development of events, for example, was in some respects simpler here than can be expected as a rule. A lot of operational information was quickly at hand to us but not to the Soviets, the focal military actions had few effects outside the immediate area which was dominated by U. S. power, and escalation barely got started. Each feature aided control.

Two limits of the observations to follow deserve notice. First, they cover only a portion of the lessons learned, being concerned mostly with political-military aspects at the national level. Lessons of importance for policy makers and bearing on the integrated use of national power are sought here. Many other lessons of a different sort no doubt are there to be learned. Second, the data on which the material below is based have some gaps. Some of the more closely held material may bear other lessons or have impact on these.

1. Soviet Objectives

It seems likely that the Soviet decision makers agreed on putting missile and bomber bases in Cuba without agreeing completely on the objectives for doing so. The list below includes some plausible, consistent, objectives:

a. To display to the world, and especially to our allies, that the US is too indecisive or too terrified of war to respond effectively to major Soviet provocation, even when possessing great local superiority backed by nuclear superiority. US acceptance of Soviet action in Cuba would then set the stage for action on Berlin and would weaken US alliances.

b. To step up suddenly the Soviet ability in a first strike to deliver nuclear weapons against our nuclear strike forces, especially our command and control systems.

c. To contrast an expanding USSR with a receding US:

(1) by breaking through the ring of US bases around the USSR.

(2) by suddenly creating a base posture more nearly symmetric to that of the US.

Downgraded at 12 yr. intervals.
Not automatically declassified.
DOD DIR. 5200.10   SECRET

~~SECRET~~   F78C011-0650

(3) and by seeming to make up deficiencies in intercontinental nuclear capability.

d. In the course of making a forward step toward Berlin to
discover empirically in a less explosive arena the US determination to
fight.

e. To deter a US invasion of Cuba--or, at least, to use this
argument with Castro.

f. As a fall back position, in the face of a strong US reaction,
to enter into a negotiation on Soviet bases in Cuba vs. US bases abroad.

Finally, it seems unlikely that the Soviets would have undertaken
this Cuban excursion without thinking there was enough of a chance of
only a feeble US reaction. Something for us to reflect on is what in our
behavior over the past year led them to think they could get away with
it or would not be badly hurt by trying.

2. Renewed Credibility of Soviet Expansionism

In the last few years, the West has tended to fear Soviet expansion
less and less. In Cuba, the Soviets made their first long distance leap
into "third areas," first politically, then in concrete military power.
Moreover, this deployment threatened the main nuclear force of NATO. Now
not only their Premier travels across oceans but also their missiles.
They deployed forces to threaten the Atlantic deterrent, a major military
move to signal a dramatic shift in the "relationship of forces" on a
world scale. No longer are the Soviets confining their expansionist
activities to political, economic, and military efforts against only the
underdeveloped regions. It should now be clearer to our European Allies
that the Russians were willing to make a major move with significant
military implications against the West.

3. US Nuclear Threshold

The US did not launch nuclear weapons, nor come close to doing so.
It did apply limited, non-shooting force, and it was actively preparing
to launch non-nuclear combat operations. It was of course prepared to
face such risks of escalation by the Soviet Union as these actions might bring.
The Soviets, our Allies, other nations, and we ourselves have seen that nuclear
retaliation by the US requires more serious provocation that the sudden appearance of a nuclear base 90 miles from our shores.

4. How Far the Nuclear Writ Runs

Our nuclear strength was a continuous restraint on the Russians against
a nuclear attack or, perhaps, a markedly broadened non-nuclear operation.
However, over-all, and especially local, US nuclear superiority did not
deter the Soviets from military and nuclear intrusion into Cuba.

2

~~SECRET~~

~~SECRET~~   F780011-0651

5. How Far the Non-nuclear Writ Runs

Nor were the Soviets put off by the immense US superiority in non-nuclear strength usable locally. At the outset, the Soviets clearly lacked conviction that the US was determined to use force on this issue. Once we decided to use force, however, we faced the Soviets with an impossible military problem locally. Moreover, they could not be certain how far a local conflict would escalate, and they know it to be generally true that any direct US-USSR conflict would be carried out against the background of a possible nuclear war. Demonstrated US willingness to begin non-nuclear combat action against a nuclear-armed opponent surely made evident to the Soviets that the US was willing to take risks of nuclear consequences.

6. Soviet Advance and Withdrawal

The Soviets undertook a limited-objective, limited-means operation. By deploying nuclear strike forces, they used bold means to widen the struggle with the US, but they took care not to let widespread shooting start (they did shoot down a U-2). In making the confrontation military and injecting the nuclear element, they evidently did not credit an immediate US nuclear reply. When opposed with the certainty that we would use non-nuclear force they backed off, probably because (a) in non-nuclear combat in the area of Cuba, defeat was certain; (b) there was a high risk of escalation into nuclear war if conflict were extended to areas where the local balance of forces was favorable to them.

It is possible that some Soviet actions were responses to signals that we did not intend to send. One example might be the straying of the U-2 over Russia, and another the apparent interpretation by a Soviet ship captain of night photography with a flash cartridge as an attack on him. On the other hand, one signal that was intended to be heard loud and clear was sent by the President on September 4th and repeated on September 13th: the warning that we wouldn't tolerate bombardment vehicles in Cuba. This signal was met initially by an elaborate attempt at deception probably accompanied by a belief that faced with a _fait accompli_ we would back down.

On withdrawal, the timing of their decision gives us probably our best clue. It did not come on the heels of the President's speech, with its mention of "full retaliatory response upon the Soviet Union," and the immediate SAC alert which followed. It came instead when non-shooting coercion had already been applied, and when it must have seemed unmistakable that the US was on the point of using shooting force to enforce the quarantine and probably either to destroy Soviet systems in Cuba or to invade the island. It is probable that the most impressive thing was confirmation through their intelligence channels that we had taken all the measures consistent with serious military action.

The Soviets saw they were going to face conflict in Cuba and lose.

3

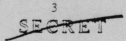

F78GG11-0G52

7. Our Views of Soviet Advance and Retreat

The crisis highlighted some contrasting American views of likely Russian calculations. On one view of the Kremlin, when the Russians advance and then withdraw, one faction in the Kremlin pressed the advance and another led the retreat. An alternative interpretation regards decisions on advance, and retreat in the event the advance is unsuccessful, as mutually consistent policy. There is undoubtedly disagreement in the Kremlin, but it is not necessary to assume that Khrushchev is in either an "advance" faction or a "retreat" faction.

Divergent views on how the Soviets calculate in withdrawal, particularly, led to contrasting US policy recommendations as to concession, standstill, or pursuit of the Russians in retreat.

According to the first view of the Kremlin in retreat, as the magnitude of the withdrawal increases, so does the psychological cost of the act--until the readiness to retreat gives out. Hence we must be careful not to ask for too much, or we must soften deprivations with indulgences (for example, the "pledge" not to invade, commendations of the other side, Lippmann's proposal to trade Turkish bases) if we want to have the opponent retreat at all.

In the other conception Soviet leaders view it as impermissible to concede an iota more than the situation "forces" them to do, it is also obligatory to engage in whatever degree of withdrawal is required to prevent even worse damage or annihilation. The graver the penalty we impose on them for not withdrawing, and the more certain we make it appear the penalty will actually be applied, the more probable becomes their compliance and in fact the easier we make it for them to withdraw.

Clearly, a wide variance in policy recommendations resulted.

8. Nuclear Risks

While Khrushchev could know that he was not going to use nuclear weapons and that he would lose in Cuba, the US Government was obliged to take into account other possible outcomes. The possibility of nuclear war drew therefore a share of attention proportionate perhaps to its gravity but greater than was warranted by its likelihood, given the assumption that Soviet policy conforms to Soviet interests and known strategy. Concern with remote nuclear possibilities not only prompted consideration of some highly improvident courses of action but also counseled hesitation on pursuing our interest on immediate inspection and on withdrawal of IL-28's.

Certainly our public statements exaggerated the risks of nuclear war. We could get our way without initiating the use of nuclear weapons. This burden was entirely on Khruschev. And for him such a

4

DOCUMENT 81: Defense Department review, "Some Lessons From Cuba," November 15, 1962.

PAGE 6 OF 12

SECRET   F780011-0653

decision would be suicidal. Our public stance should have de-emphasized
the nuclear risks to the extent possible (even if we weren't entirely sure).

9.

10. The Role of Intelligence

We had timely, reliable intelligence data, and it helped immensely.
Soviet performance was probably hampered by a paucity and slowness of

5

SECRET

intelligence. And thanks to our continuing prior surveillance, we had
a solid factual basis for evaluating new material. Both in laying the
intelligence base and in getting the new facts swiftly, air reconnaissance
was a priceless asset. US conduct of future crises elsewhere would be
substantially helped if a similarly solid base of intelligence data
were created before that geographical area attracted intense interest.

11. Reconnaissance and Stability

In the last few years, it has been common for peacetime surveillance
to be called provocative. The Cuban experience has abruptly changed
the world's image of outside surveillance. Reconnaissance and inspection
are widely viewed today as major tools toward preventing violence. Our
reconnaissance aided control and stability. For a time the US should be
able to conduct, and urge others to conduct, fuller reconnaissance of
more areas. Aerial reconnaissance of China, for example, is less likely
to meet with widespread opposition if the matter were to become public;
the common good could be more plausibly argued than before Cuba.

12. Control

Control over the Cuban operation was affected by many unique
features. Developing swiftly, and initially in deep secrecy, with US
forces vastly overmatching those of the Soviet, the Cuban problem
permitted continuous, intense, central control. Before military moves
had much more than begun, Washington and Moscow were exchanging notes.
The military actions provided time for communications, had delimited
scope and well-defined terminal points, and the method of exchanging
notes provided time for thought and evaluation. (This suggests that the
purple telephone, between President and Premier, might not be an unmixed
blessing.) All this made the control problem simpler, as did the exceptionally good intelligence and operational information available. But it
still was not easy, even with centralized control, for decisions to be
made and translated into action at the pace required to keep the US in
control of the situation.

In most military operations of a large scale, it will ordinarily be
necessary and more efficient to decentralize control over execution to
a greater extent than in Cuba. Especially will this be true where overseas
operations are involved. But the Cuban operation points up some difficulties that delegation would bring. Even where the interconnection of political
and military aspects is thoroughly appreciated, not all significant political
and military information can be quickly accessible in the field. Even where
workable packages of delegated control have been arranged, accidental or unfore-
seeable events may interrupt the process. It is often useful to design

6

DOCUMENT 81: Defense Department review, "Some Lessons From Cuba," November 15, 1962.

PAGE 8 OF 12

F780011-0655

operations so that control can be transferred, new instructions issued, and communications with opponents occur. In all such operations there is the problem of clarity about what matters will be dealt with at what levels. Cuba shows how helpful it would be to have in advance a common understanding on whether, for example, the executive agent concept will be used for command of military forces, and, if so, what matters will be decided above, at, and below the executive agent. Delegation is also less easy to manage where Allies are intimately involved, and especially their military forces. The desirability of Allied agreement that the US President must in serious crises act as Commander-in-Chief for the Alliance as a whole has become still more evident.

13. Allied Reactions

The NATO Allies were remarkably willing for the US to manage the Cuban operations, with fewer complaints about our putting them into jeopardy than seemed likely before the event. This was true despite rather than because of our consultation which was little and late. The relatively favorable NATO reactions stemmed mostly from the attitude that this was an American show, despite the fact that their interests were very much at stake and that they might have become directly involved at any time. Fortunately, the US had become, through continuing contacts and discussions in NATO, reasonably well equipped to judge the acceptability to its Allies of various courses of action. This was essential, for we needed one, and only one, hand on the valve to apply increasing pressures with the least risk of unwanted escalation.

The Latin American attitude was determined by shock at the Soviet move, fear of what might follow, the deflation of Castro's pretensions, and respect for the vigorous action by the US. This attitude is unlikely to persist in full strength, but perhaps it will last long enough to help bring about change in Cuba. Moreover, there is no reason to believe that a high degree of unity cannot be generated in similar situations in the future.

14. Politico-Military Inseparability

The military and the political aspects of every action of both sides were closely interwoven: at the outset, our assessment of Soviet objectives, our reconnaissance activities, expected Soviet reactions, and timing of our moves. As the political situation developed through OAS action, initial UN discussions, and first Soviet reactions, it was considered politically desirable to make detailed changes in such military matters as rules of engagement, instructions for conduct of the search, and even the selection of which approaching vessels to handle first. The

7

SECRET

S̶E̶C̶R̶E̶T̶   F780011-0656

planning of possible strikes or assaults was subject to many specific
political restrictions, owing to expected effects on the Cuban people,
the Castro government, the OAS, NATO governments and populations, and
US public opinion.

Thus, at no stage in the operation as executed or foreseen did the
problem ever seem wholly political or wholly military. Advisors and
decision-makers at the seat of government, whether diplomats, military
men, or political officials, at every stage found it essential to take
into account factors which might ordinarily seem beyond their individual
spheres of cognizance. It was not possible to predict at what point
a political detail would require change in minor military details normally
left to be decided in the field; similarly, military detail at unexpected
times necessarily altered political decisions and actions, large and
small. In the basic policy decisions at high levels, there was complete
interdependence of military and political factors. The selection of the
objective was a combined problem. Only out of the interplay of military
capabilities and limitations with the political elements of the setting
could courses of action be set up and choices made.

15. Alliance Indivisibility

The defense of the Alliance is not geographically divisible.
Although the Caribbean is outside the NATO area, Soviet action there
affected the US not only as homeland but also as Alliance arsenal. The
US was acutely aware that Alliance nuclear strength was threatened and
that Berlin repercussions might follow US actions over Cuba. The Soviet
attempt to connect their bases in Cuba with NATO bases in Turkey underlined the fact of indivisibility.

16. Inspection and the United Nations

The crisis has prompted the spontaneous emergence of ad hoc arms
control proposals from many sources. Both internal and external pressures
have developed for their hasty implementation unsupported by prior
analysis and planning. These pressures contrast strikingly with the
lack of preparations for rapidly implementing even temporary inspection
arrangements with competent neutral observers and adequate modern equipment. One of the lessons of the crisis is that many proposals for
international inspection considered abstractly are, in the event,
woefully inadequate to meet our needs for information in a crisis. Once
again the United Nations has been proved not a reliable or quickly
responsive device to verify Soviet performance of an agreement. Even
when we push an exceptionally strong case with insistent force, the
results are inadequate. The neutral powers are eager to avoid enmity

8

S̶E̶C̶R̶E̶T̶

~~S E C R E T~~   F78OO11-0657

and damaging responses from great powers. The UN Secretariat is not in
a position to act against member nations without their consent and in any
case lacks the technical capacity to inspect. Perhaps the latter defect
can be corrected.

17. Secrecy in Planning

It has been shown possible to conduct over a period of at least a
week an intensive analytic and planning activity at a high level without
having its nature revealed in the press. Furthermore, judging from the
apparent confusion produced in Moscow by the President's speech of 22 October, it would appear that Soviet intelligence was surprised. In the
climactic stages of the planning, many people and many widely separated
locations were involved, yet security still remained very tight. The
effect of this was to deny to the Soviets much opportunity for political
pre-emption, by announcing commitments or conditions prior to the
President's speech. Such actions by the Soviets, putting us in the
position of reacting rather than initiating, could have restricted US
freedom of action and substantially changed the effect produced on
Allied governments and public opinion. Several conditions offered
unique opportunity for avoiding press attention over the first five
or six days. That the problem itself was unknown to the public was
foremost. The special system for handling key intelligence information
helped greatly. Perhaps third was the fact that the problem quickly
became an operational one involving the risk of American casualties;
people were therefore much more conscious of security than normally.
It would be imprudent to conclude from the Cuban experience, fortified
as our security was by luck, that this degree of secrecy is routinely
attainable. It should be noted that security deteriorated rapidly
when the problem passed into the stages of finally closing the deal;
here the press was less restrained.

However, secrecy was achieved at a cost in effectiveness. Severe
restrictions were applied to the dissemination and availability of
sensitive information. The result was some reduction in coordination,
in governmental capacity for analysis of events and trends, and in the
possibilities of intelligent initiatives.

18. The Importance of Communications and Information

It is important that information of importance to national decisions
move with great speed to the locations where these decisions are made.
Part of the problem is mechanical. Effective execution of much political
planning on Cuba was hampered by imperfections in the communications
system. Major improvements in communication, especially for the State
Department, are clearly called for. But there is also need for discrim-
ination. Sending too much information to the top slows not speeds the

9

~~S E C R E T~~

S̶E̶C̶R̶E̶T̶   F780611-0658

process. And operating levels need to know what policy levels are concerned about. This need conflicts with the need for secrecy.

While it is not a cardinal necessity that all advisors whom the President consults have the same information, it is highly undesirable that their advice diverge merely because some lack certain key facts. Whether this actually ever occurred in the Cuban operation is not so significant as the fact that it was certainly possible. The handling of factual data in Washington is susceptible of much improvement, particularly at the boundary where diplomatic and military data intersect. Improvements here could prevent future troubles, possibly serious ones.

19. Prior Analysis of Contingencies

Each of the high-level decisions during the Cuban operation involved a choice among alternatives, but more searching contingency planning beforehand would have permitted more informed, thorough comparison. Actions to cause removal of offensive weapons from Cuba have effects upon the tenure of Castro, the orientation of the Cuban people, and the general question of how far we can go toward aiding resistance in Communist satellites, for example, as well as upon more direct and crucial issues of US-Soviet power confrontation. These and other relationships were noted during the recent decision-making processes, but in the heat of immediate problems they were often treated anxiously not analytically, without benefit of as balanced and searching an examination as prior planning would permit.

20. Overseas Bases

Judging by the repercussions in the Communist world, the Soviet setback in Cuba was more than a local one. And not because of the importance of the base in Cuba. Retreat in Cuba suggests retreat closer to home. The lesson for us should be clear. No matter how valueless an overseas base, the time to give it up is before or well after a crisis-- not during it--if we want to have allies believing that association with us is to their interest. With few exceptions, however, ridding ourselves of bases should not be a consuming concern; as we increase the emphasis on non-nuclear forces to meet the more likely contingencies abroad, overseas bases will become more, not less, important.

21. Power at Sea

The ease with which the US was able to apply its will on the high seas, little hampered by prospects of local enemy action, shows vividly how immense is our superiority at sea. While this is especially so in

10

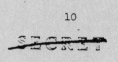

S̶E̶C̶R̶E̶T̶

DOCUMENT 81: Defense Department review, "Some Lessons From Cuba," November 15, 1962.

PAGE 12 OF 12

SECRET   F780011-0659

the Caribbean where our naval power is supplemented by shore-based air power, everywhere, except in waters subject to Soviet-based air control, our naval superiority is very pronounced indeed. Cuba in particular is a hostage to the US Navy. US manipulation of a few among the great many available non-nuclear naval moves, in concert with a carefully managed program of political moves, forced the Soviets into a reactive position. Our power at sea, visibly capable of destroying enemy sea forces but used instead to apply political-military pressures, permitted us to retain the initiative and to succeed.

22. The Moral Element

The US broke the strict bounds of legality in invoking the quarantine, but the nation recognized quickly that its government was acting with great restraint to defend an important national interest. This increased the strength of public support. More importantly, the action is not likely to leave bad after-effects when there is time for reflection and discussion about its morality. A similar recognition abroad similarly expanded the base of the whole-hearted support which Allied governments gave.

11

SECRET

DOCUMENT 82: Premier Khrushchev's letter to Prime Minister Castro, reviewing the crisis, January 31, 1963.

PAGE 1 OF 11

[Nikita Khrushchev to Fidel Castro, 31 January 1963]

Dear comrade Fidel Castro:

For some time I have been considering the idea of writing you this letter. Now, on my way to Moscow from Berlin, where I attended the Congress of Socialist Unity Party of Germany, I write to you. Our train is crossing the fields and forests of Soviet Byelorussia and it occurs to me how wonderful it would be if you could see, on a sunny day like this, the ground covered with snow and the forests silvery with frost.

Perhaps you, a southern man, have seen this only in paintings. It must surely be fairly difficult for you to imagine the ground carpeted with snow and the forests covered with white frost. It would be good if you could visit our country each season of the year; every one of them, spring, summer, fall, and winter, has its delights.

Cuba is a country of eternal summer. I remember that during our talk in New York, we reacted differently to the weather of that city: I was choking with heat, but you told me you felt chilly.

Nevertheless, all these thoughts about nature should not carry us away from the principal theme of this letter. The most important is the strong desire my comrades and I feel to see you and to talk, to talk with our hearts open. We have much to talk about. We hope that this meeting, this conversation, will not be delayed for long. We would like the meeting to take place as soon as possible.

Why? Well, because we have lived through a very important stage, one that represents a landmark in the historical development of Cuba, the Soviet Union, and the other socialist countries. For the first time since the end of the Second World War we have been close, very close, to war. Cuba has found itself at the center of the acute crisis in the Caribbean.

We understand that the extreme gravity of the crisis has now passed, but the danger of a confrontation has not yet ended. You understand this very well, and we fully share your worry and view the situation as you do.

But, what is most important today? Why do we need to meet and talk frankly?

The gravity of the crisis created by North American imperialism in the Caribbean has ended. But it seems to me that this crisis has left a mark, although barely visible, in the relations between our states—Cuba and the Soviet Union— and in our own personal relationship. Speaking frankly, these relations are not what they were before the crisis. I will not conceal the fact that this troubles and worries us. And it seems to me that the development of our relations will depend, in large part, on our meeting. At present, a mode of communication such as correspondence is insufficient. Nothing can substitute for a personal conversation. It is precisely through such a talk that we can overcome more easily and quickly any misunderstanding of each other's positions and reach an understanding.

It is for this reason that people, while also using various means of communicating and exchanging views, also try to meet personally, have personal contacts, personal conversations. You already know that our enemies meet fairly often, even more often than we do.

We should meet. During the Caribbean crisis, our viewpoints did not always coincide, we did not see the different stages of the crisis in the same way; it was clear that we viewed the ways to solve it differently. After our known statement, you even said publicly that during the development of the crisis there had emerged certain differences between the Soviet government and the Cuban government. You can understand that for us this was no cause for joy. Now the tensions have diminished; and now that we have entered into a new phase in the relations between Cuba and the Soviet Union,

DOCUMENT 82: Premier Khrushchev's letter to Prime Minister Castro, reviewing the crisis, January 31, 1963.

PAGE 2 OF 11

on one hand, and [between the Soviet Union and] the United States of North America, on the other, there are still gaps, which are difficult to assess, in our relations with Cuba.

That is why we want to meet—to even out, to close the gaps in our relations, whatever their extent; even if they are only small, we would try to smooth them out. In the relations between two socialist states there must be no rough edges; our relations must be truly fraternal.

Now that some time separates us from the acute stages of the crisis and we can proceed with a calm analysis of all its aspects, I shall permit myself, dear friend, to recall some events and examine the events that took place.

I would like to state frankly, so there is no doubt in your mind, why it is that we proposed to deploy our ballistic missiles in Cuba. I want to tell you this because even the representatives of certain socialist states are thinking in a rather curious way, distorting not only our initial steps but also those we took later, and obscuring their positions with vigorous revolutionary phrases regarding persistance in the face of common class enemies, and other Marxist slogans. Why then do they take the liberty to judge the steps of other governments when, as you know perfectly well, they didn't actually do anything to help Cuba when it faced mortal danger?

You may have observed that certain people and groups, and even the leaders of certain socialist countries, who limited themselves to observing the crisis, started to get agitated and to pontificate on to the ways in which one should have acted during the crisis, criticizing those who carried the burden of the struggle. They say that we should have proceeded in this or that way, taken such-and-such a step, although they themslves took no steps and held themselves at the sidelines of the real struggle. We may rightly ask these critics why they, at the height of the crisis, did not take any step—verbal or material—that would have demonstrated their

willingness to aid Cuba, to march with her if war broke out.

In those days, those critics gave no proof of any such willingness and limited themselves to cursing capitalism and imperialism. Were we to compete with them in this practice, we would win the contest easily: it is well known that the Russian language has an enormous number of insults.

In the first days of the revolution, we hurled prodigious vituperations against imperialism; but then we were the only socialist country; and our economic and military strength was weak. Today things are different: the Soviet Union is no longer the only socialist state, and there is a powerful socialist world system, the community of socialist states. This is why the Republic of Cuba is not alone. When it put itself under the banner of Marxism-Leninism, Cuba joined the community of socialist countries. We applauded it and we continue to do so—and not only with words.

Our country, which fought difficult battles to save the achievements of the October Revolution, repelled the intervention by fourteen states, and played a decisive role in the defeat of the Hitlerian war machine; our country, which went unrecognized by the United States for seventeen years and which other countries also did not recognize for a long time, has a very clear idea of the difficulties that confront the Cuban people, their leader, and his comrades in their efforts to defend the Cuban Revolution, to safeguard the right of the Cuban people to decide its own destiny when it has next to it a neighbor as strong, aggressive, and implacable as North American imperialism.

We were the first to know of the infinite vileness of the methods and ways of fighting of the enemy. When Churchill, who headed the crusade to strangle the October Revolution, was unable, with all his allies, to bring the Soviet nation to its knees through intervention, they turned to economic blockade. They were sure that we would lack the

DOCUMENT 82: Premier Khrushchev's letter to Prime Minister Castro, reviewing the crisis, January 31, 1963.

PAGE 3 OF 11

means, the strength, and the cadres needed to rebuild our shattered economy. They believed that Soviet Russia would disintegrate by itself, that hunger would smother it, that typhus would kill it, and that the experiment of building socialism would collapse.

But what happened? Under the leadership of the Bolshevik party, headed by the great Lenin, the peoples of the Soviet Union demonstrated their organizational and combative spirit, they defeated the White Guards, they expelled the interventionists from the country, and they overcame all of their economic difficulties. The socialist way was so effective, so productive, that we made the backward Russia of the Tsars—a country that could not even dream of competing with the most advanced capitalist countries of Western Europe—into a country that in terms of its overall industrial production is second in the world, and one in which the development of science and technology cedes nothing to the most advanced capitalist country, the United States of North America, if it does not surpass it. If we take as our yardstick the conquest of the cosmos, it is known that the North Americans have been unable to catch up with us in terms of the throw weight of the rockets and in terms of flights by cosmonauts around the earth.

Guided by the doctrine of Marxism-Leninism, communists have demonstrated their capacity to create material value on a new, socialist, base, as well as their capacity to develop culture, to elevate science to a level that is now the summit for all the states in the world. It is not by chance that after we launched our ships into space, the United States sent a delegation to our country to study our public education system, our preparation of engineers and of scientific personnel. That delegation developed a very high appreciation of our education system. In the Soviet Union we graduate three times as many engineers as did the United States, which is evidence of the intellectual development of society and of the way in which the peoples' knowledge has been extended. And the greater our knowledge, the earlier we will assure the final victory.

When the Cuban Revolution took place, its enemies were seized with panic. They saw that a socialist Cuba could be guiding star, a magnet for all Latin American countries, for all peoples fighting for their independence and liberty. The peoples that have merely achieved their political liberation from the colonial yoke, but who have not yet managed to become the true proprietors of their countries, see in Cuba a model for the solution of their social problems.

This is why we are firmly convinced that the United States of North America will never resign itself to the existence of a socialist Cuba. We knew that they would do all they could to eliminate socialist Cuba and to maintain the capitalist system in all the countries of the western hemisphere. Precisely with this end in mind they went to the archives, and dusted off the Monroe Doctrine, which they had practically renounced.

You know as well as I do that the Monroe Doctrine proclaims that America should not involve itself in Europe and Asia and that Europe and Asia should not involve itself in the affairs of the western hemisphere. Today, the United States has reserved itself the "right" to involve itself in the affairs of Europe, Asia, and the other continents, forming military alliances of imperialist countries to carry out a third world war. Nevertheless, it would hold the part of the Monroe Doctrine referring to the western hemisphere to remain in effect so as to suffocate liberating revolutions, to erect a barrier against socilism.

The leadership of the Soviet state—the presidium of the central committee and the government—often changed its views in looking for the most effective way to help Cuba. When the Yankees announced the economic blockade against Cuba, when they left it without fuel, without other

[321]

DOCUMENT 82: Premier Khrushchev's letter to Prime Minister Castro, reviewing the crisis, January 31, 1963.

PAGE 4 OF 11

materials and essential products, when the republic felt an acute need for prepared cadres and was running into enormous difficulties, we gave you, without hesitation, a fraternal helping hand to aid you in all areas.

The truth is that people who have lost their communist consciousness now accuse the Soviet Union of giving aid with mercantile goals in mind. But such accusations are motivated by ill will; the accusers have lost their common sense, the capacity to consider the question in a sensible way. We can take any dispute about this and present real facts that prove just how unfounded that accusation is.

I don't think that there is any proof lacking that, in aiding Cuba, we are not pursuing any self-serving ends. Only a madman would think that we are getting rich or profiting from it. In giving Cuba great material aid, we do it consciously because we are communists. We ourselves have suffered immense difficulties in our struggle for socialism, and we know from experience that it is not easy to create a new society. We have given aid to Cuba, and we will continue to give it. We are looking forward.

With the failure of its plans to strangle Cuba through the economic blockade and through the breaking of diplomatic relations, North American imperialism started to prepare armed invasion and, in 1961, unleashed its mercenaries against Cuba.

But North American imperialism underestimated the cohesion, the will to triumph, and the degree of organization of the Cuban people, its faithfulness to the ideas of liberty and independence, it trust in its leaders, its trust in you, dear Fidel. You defeated the enemy. All of us, all socialist countries, and all progressive men are proud of your glorious victory.

It was clear to us that the North Americans, having been defeated once, would not resign themselves to it, that they would change tactics and more or less *repeat* the invasion. However, it would be a much better prepared invasion, hence much more dangerous, since they would take into account

the lessons from the first defeat. The North Americans themselves even spoke openly of this. For example, in their conversations with our representatives, they would frequently recall the events of 1956 in Hungary. They took them as an example of energetic measures, trying to find in them some justification for their measures against the Cuban Revolution. You, they told us, proceeded in this way in your own self-interest, because Hungary is close to your borders; but we also have the right to undertake such energetic measures against Cuba, which is close to our country. Naturally, our representatives emphatically rejected such "foundations" for a new invasion against Cuba.

Our party and our government saw that they were moving, in effect toward an invasion. And you, Cuban comrades, as was shown in you statements, understood and felt the real danger of such an act of aggression, and you, exhorted the people to defend the revolutionary conquests.

We considered, and we still consider, that your slogan of *"Patria o Muerte"* [Fatherland or Death] was completely just, revolutionary. But, at the same time, we understood that it was impossible to restrain imperialism with only a heroic readiness to resist unto death. It was clear that the imperialists wanted to prepare the Cuban people for death, not for victory. And the imperialists of the United States disposed themselves of great forces to move on little Cuba, and Cuba naturally cannot confront such a war machine for long.

How could one help Cuba in this situation?

Some chose the path of revolutionary slogans. In the days of the crisis, they expressed their support for the Declaration of 1957 and the Declaration of 1958 of the eighty-one parties but, in fact, they did not lend any effective support, aside from protests and solidarity demonstrations with Cuba. These men, naturally, pronounced not a few just words on the heroism of the Cuban people, of its maximum leader, of his comrades in arms, of their intrepidness

DOCUMENT 82: Premier Khrushchev's letter to Prime Minister Castro, reviewing the crisis, January 31, 1963.

PAGE 5 OF 11

and readiness to die but not to surrender to the enemy. Yet, could aggression be contained by giving Cuba only that kind of help and insulting imperialism? You know very well that to proceed like that is not to take the primary, decisive measures.

We took another path. We decided to go to face the danger, to take measures that would place the imperialists of the United States in the dilemma of having to renounce to the invasion of Cuba or to unleash thermonuclear war. To defend Cuba we proposed the installation of the missiles. If North American imperialism had unleashed the invasion, no protest of ours, no three-shift, three-week or even three-month demonstration would have stopped them. Only one thing could restrain them: the fear, the knowledge that if they began the invasion, the missiles would carry out their mission and the cities of North America would be left in ruins. We understood that placing such a weapon in Cuba was the most efficient way of defending it during that time.

We considered that Cuba needed the means that would make the United States renounce any armed invasion of the island.

We examined this question several times and we decided to propose the installation of the weapons, you know, serviced by our personnel. We started with the premise that the missiles would be in the hands of Soviet military units. We also want to stick to that system in the future. The aim was for our enemies to hold themselves to the same position, if only for a certain amount of time. It is clear that in the end, West Germany will also, probably, have such a weapon, but we are interested in pushing this into the future.

When this question was decided, we took into account that the imperialists could take advantage of such a step, to use it as a pretext to turn up the heat, to put the world on the brink of war, or even unleash war. And we took decisive steps on behalf of the defense of Cuba, on behalf of the whole socialist camp and of the proletarian solidarity of Marxist-Leninist parties. What could be more perfect, from the point of view of fulfilling proletarian internationalist duties, than the actions undertaken by our country on behalf of another socialist country, on behalf of the common Marxist-Leninist cause? We understood that our country could see itself dragged into a war in the Caribbean, which would have given the conflict a global character. I'm not just speaking of the fact that our men, who, with your agreement, arrived on the island in the thousands along with the new types of weapon, that they would have shared the fate of the fighters in Cuba. That is clear to all. And we sent them with a clear notion of our internationalist duty.

These are not resolutions, they are not insults against imperialism, with which one cannot weaken it. As a Byelorussian proverb says: You can insult the master, but with that he only gets fatter. And so it is effect. You can insult imperialism as much as you like, but that won't make it wither, it won't make it weaker, nor will it diminish its insolence. Imperialism takes into account only real forces. It does not recognize anything else. That is why one can call it a paper tiger, dung, whatever you like; but if you do not let imperialism know that behind those words expressing our indignation there is a force, they will not be stopped by them nor will their insolence and aggressiveness be diminished.

We consider as a real force, in the first place, the economy, when the people are united around their leaders. Only with a firm economic base can you create the necessary weaponry.

We, the socialist countries, appreciate more than anything else the goodness of peace and dedicate all our forces to promote it. But we must never forget the existence of the imperialist camp and its aspirations to strangle the socialist countries. That is why we must observe the proper proportion of expenses, diversify the economy, which is also the

DOCUMENT 82: Premier Khrushchev's letter to Prime Minister Castro, reviewing the crisis, January 31, 1963.

PAGE 6 OF 11

fundamental base of military might; but we must do so without skimping on resources to create the most modern armed forces and the most modern equipment, which must be at a necessary level, even more, superior to our enemy's.

Without this, we cannot guarantee peaceful coexistence; without basing oneself on such real premises, it is impossible to safeguard peace worldwide.

Because of this, those who say that we are begging for peace are consciously distorting our position, or they simply do not understand what they're saying. As is said, only God knows what moves them: ill-will or incomprehension.

Some are now daring to slander us, claiming that in resolving the conflict in the Caribbean we guided ourselves exclusively by our own self-serving interests. That is the greatest offense against the Soviet people! We sent Soviet citizens to Cuba knowing that an attack could be unleashed against it. Had there been such an attack our men would have fought to the end along with the Cuban brothers, and if it had been necessary, would have burned in the fires of war.

Those who make such statements can only be men who, while calling themselves Marxist-Leninist, do not truly value that title. It is obvious, that while pursuing their own egotistical and adventurist ends, they dare to slander the Soviet Union—the first country to revolt, to build socialism, and to set an unyielding example in the face of the enemy in the fight against its own bourgeoisie and landowners, and a country that now gives the same unyielding example in the fight against imperialism. Doubtlessly, you know that the Soviet Union has extended, and extends, immense aid, even in weaponry, to peoples fighting for their liberation from imperialism.

Honest men cannot hear, without indignation, such slanderous statements about the Soviet Union. Such men are gladdened and proud of our successes, of our Leninist internationalist policy.

As you can see, dear comrade Fidel, I have gotten carried away and am now writing you a very long letter. You will understand, I hope, that I feel the need to do so. As we say among ourselves, among us Russians, one feels the desire to let off steam when talking to a comrade, to a friend, to a brother. Although we are carrying out this conversation at a distance, I'd like this letter to express my feelings. I hope that when you come to our country—and if you want to bring your comrades with you we would be happy—we will have more than one fraternal conversation.

I will not hide from you, it would be senseless to do so, that any imprudent step or even any roughness in our relations could today generate several problems. One ill-advised step or one wrong sentence could make us, and you, think. It is possible that under normal conditions, no one would attach any importance to this; but under the conditions that have now been created, I would say that serenity and self-control are necessary. You will understand, as is natural, that we, like you, have reason to be in a good mood. With you, we have stopped an aggressor poised to invade Cuba and, despite the mobilization it carried out, its concentration of immense forces, it did not dare to attack the isle of freedom. We cannot underestimate the aggressive imperialist forces that were ready to attack your republic. Those forces were superior to Cuba's, including our troops on your territory, who, comrade Fidel, would have fought shoulder-to-shoulder with your heroes and, had it been necessary, would have died with them for the cause of the revolution.

When Marshal Malinovsky was asked what Cuba could do to respond to an attack from the United States, he answered frankly, although it was very difficult for him to give this answer: "If we speak of the correlation of forces existing in the Caribbean, and we know what Cuba has at its disposal and we

DOCUMENT 82: Premier Khrushchev's letter to Prime Minister Castro, reviewing the crisis, January 31, 1963.

PAGE 7 OF 11

know our capacities there—he said—we could say that, with such a correlation of forces, it is impossible, unfortunately, to hold. And if hostilities start, it is very unlikely that Cuba will be able to resist for long because the forces are so unequal."

It may be that you do not agree with us. We too would have wished that the situation had been different. But, dear friend Fidel, you are a military man, I also spent almost the entire Second World War at the front and took part in the civil war: there is a real correlation of forces and it is impossible to escape it. When Hitler attacked our country, we retreated for a long time, we lost one city after another and left behind millions of exhausted beings under the enemy yoke. It was very bitter for us, but in that first period maledictions did not help us, neither did appeals, nor tears nor ire. Only when we became stronger militarily did we start to defeat the fascists. Twenty million dead: this was the offering of the Soviet people on the alter of victory. In other words, since we knew the correlation of forces that prevailed in the Caribbean, we thought that Marshal Malinovsky had calmly evaluated the existing situation.

But, why did the enemy—the North American aggressor—retreat, renounce the invasion? It is clear that they were not stopped just by the forces of Cuba, including the forty-two medium-range missiles we installed there. The principal thing that stopped North American imperialism was the powerful forces of the Soviet Union; they were deterred by the fact that an attack against Cuba would have meant a world war in which many countries would have been blown up. The United States of North America would have also suffered terrible damages.

As you will understand, we do not want to minimize in the slightest the important role played by the firm decision and willingness of the Cuban people to defend the conquests of the revolution.

This is what stopped the enemy—not the curses and insults against imperialism, not the resolutions, although we considered the unmasking and insulting of imperialism to be useful and necessary in the struggle against the enemy. But one cannot think it possible to achieve victory over any enemy with mere insults, and even with heroism. Communists esteem qualities as important to revolutionaries as will and heroism; but if they are not supported with effective forces, these qualities are not as feared by the imperialist camp. I stress once again that the enemy can only be deterred by effective forces—he's deterred by the fear of losing the war. Even if he is confident of winning, he also has other calculations: he takes into account the colossal losses and understands that such losses, under actual conditions, would reduce his victory to nothing, and that his territories would be left a field strewn with corpses, and contaminated by radioactivity.

It's said that we cannot believe the enemy. We have always held, do hold, and always will hold this position.

It is clear to any Marxist-Leninist that North American imperialism will not renounce its plans to end the socialist regime in Cuba, to abolish the revolutionary order in your country, and to restore capitalism and reaction there. While there are two systems—the socialist one, which is edifying life on the basis of Marxist-Leninist doctrine, and the capitalist one—those systems will be antagonistic, and the struggle between them will not cease; it will not cease until one of the two achieves total victory.

We Marxist-Leninists are profoundly convinced of our victory. Not only do we hold that conviction, but the steps toward the final triumph in the building of communism are firmly calculated, in accordance to the Program of the CPSU [Communist Party of the Soviet Union]. That period has been set at twenty years for the Soviet Union. It is true that it will still not be total communism, but the material and technological basis for communism will by then

DOCUMENT 82: Premier Khrushchev's letter to Prime Minister Castro, reviewing the crisis, January 31, 1963.

PAGE 8 OF 11

have been created. The other socialist countries will also advance during that time with the Soviet Union, increasing their economic might. Nor should we weaken; rather, we should strengthen our military might. Speaking frankly, at this time, there are few hopes of reaching a disarmament agreement.

This last observation does not mean, however, that we should renounce our efforts in the struggle for peace, or replace our slogan in the struggle for disarmament with one for the struggle for rearmament. With such an aim we would neither attract the masses nor be an attractive force for workers and for all friends of peace. If we put at the forefront not the struggle for disarmament but the struggle for the unleashing of war and for the destruction of capitalism through war, instead of through peaceful competition, we would practically be exhorting people to die. People go to their deaths when there is no other way out. Just that—when there is no other way out.

But we do have a way out! We our sure that we are right—and not only of our reason, but also of the possibilities for victory. These possibilities we have proven with the socialist construction in practice, with the very fact of our existence. Forty years ago, the Soviet Union ranked among the lowest of the European countries in terms of economic development; today we hold second place in the world, and by 1970, by what we see, we will be in first. We have also succeeded in making the words "peace" and "socialism" inseparable in the minds of all the peoples in the world.

Does that not encourage us? Should this incite us into adventure, into unleashing a thermonuclear world war? Why should we follow the principle of all or nothing? One acts in this way only when there is not way out. Desperation and pessimism are for imperialist circles. They are the ones who, having lost faith in winning the contest of peaceful competition, can take risks and unleash war; such aggressive forces exist.

But we do not need a world war to achieve the victory of the communist cause. We communists have better prospects; we hold firm convictions, and this certainty is based not in words, but in real facts.

In conditions of peace, socialism deploys to the fullest its forces and demonstrates its advantages in all fields, even in fields as decisive as the powerful growth of the economy, worker productivity, and the material and cultural level of the masses.

On the other hand, peaceful coexistence does not free capitalism from its insoluble contradictions—it contributes to sharpening the workers' class struggle, of the workers against the exploiters, and contributes to the rise of the national liberation movement.

You may have noticed that the strongest labor conflicts and the national liberation struggles of greatest scope have taken place over the past ten or fifteen years, that is to say, during the period of peaceful coexistence. Under the conditions of peaceful coexistence of nations with different social regimes, democratic revolutions, national liberation revolutions, and socialist revolutions, are not only possible but certain, including, of course, the revolutions in Latin America, which Cuba precipitated. That is why we make all efforts to avoid the eruption of a thermonuclear world war. We are not interested in unleashing a war.

But we are ready to carry out a counterstrike. If imperialism tries to liquidate us with war, we can liquidate the imperialist forces and, in this way, end imperialism forever. It will be, as is written in the documents of our Party, in the Communist party program, and in the declaration of fraternal communist parties, the last war ever unleashed by imperialism.

I have already told you, comrade Fidel, that there now exists, in our relations with you, a certain amount of resentment, and that this harms the cause, and naturally, harms Cuba and harms us. Allow me to tell you without beating around the

DOCUMENT 82: Premier Khrushchev's letter to Prime Minister Castro, reviewing the crisis, January 31, 1963.

PAGE 9 OF 11

bush: this harms our party and our country, but these difficulties cannot benefit you either, because we can imagine how many different matters and preoccupations confront you regarding the development of the country's economy and many other matters.

All of this I say from the heart. This is why we would very much like you to come to our country. We have been inviting you to come for some time, but in the recent past events have taken such a course that we ourselves advised you to delay your visit somewhat. Then we worried greatly that North American imperialism could profit from your absence and invade Cuba.

Now we believe—and we are sure of this— that the enemy will not try to take advantage of your absence from the country and your visit to Moscow to attack Cuba. There are, in spite of everything, commitments that the United States of North America has undertaken through the statement of their president. Obviously, one cannot trust them and take it as an absolute guarantee, but neither is it reasonable to ignore them totally. This declaration of the president of the United States is now kind of international document, registered at the United Nations. The crisis in the area of the Caribbean Sea and the desire of North American imperialism to deploy armed forces in Cuba have become a world crisis. Now you relations with the United States of North America are not simply relations between only two countries, between Cuba and the United States; no, this matter is a global question now. However brazen, the aggressor will be forced to take this into account in some way.

Naturally, imperialism can change its tactics in its struggle to obtain its objectives. It will not renounce the objective it has set itself—fighting against socialism—and this should not surprise us, because we too speak openly of the global victory of socialism. We speak of peaceful coexistence and of the inevitable triumph of communism all over the globe. And we say at the same time, "Long live peaceful coexistence!" and "Long live communism!"

We want to reach this great objective in the conditions of peaceful competition. In the atmosphere of peaceful coexistence we are demonstrating the superiority of socialism compared to capitalism and, in this way, we attract more and more the peoples of the capitalist countries to the struggle within each country against the domination of capital—for its defeat, for the establishment of the dictatorship of the proletariat, and for the victory of peace, democracy, and socialism.

As has already been said, peaceful coexistence contributes to the development of the class struggle of the peoples of Latin America, Africa, and Asia, which also changes to a great degree the correlation of forces at the global level in favor of socialism. We have helped, and will help with all means, the peoples in their just struggle against imperialism.

Not long ago, Kennedy assembled all the counterrevolutionary crowd that you expelled from Cuba, along with other scum, and perorated before them, promising the participants of the invasion to return to Havana the banner they had given him, when another government is in power there. That does not discourage us in the least. You will surely recall that when I was in the United States I told them without evasion that capitalism would be buried. But I said that the gravedigger would be the North American working class. This class will bury North American imperialism on its own.

The Soviet Union does not exclude the possibility of furious action by North American imperialism. It would be stupid not to see the danger. But today, after the acute crisis in the area of the Caribbean Sea, there are reasons to believe that you have won a truce and that you will take advantage of it for peaceful construction. One must use this truce, above all, to expand the economy and agricultural production: this will allow you to improve the

DOCUMENT 82: Premier Khrushchev's letter to Prime Minister Castro, reviewing the crisis, January 31, 1963.

PAGE 10 OF 11

people's living standards. It is precisely this revolutionary example of Cuba's that the North American monopolists and imperialists most fear. That is why they want to strangle Cuba.

From this, it seems to us, important tasks can be derived today for the Republic of Cuba. One must concentrate efforts in the development of the economy and culture, in increasing the living standards of the masses. And we, comrade Fidel, are ready to cooperate with you. The Soviet Union is doing, and will do, everything possible to develop this cooperation. This cooperation requires us to give aid to your Republic. In making its contribution to strengthening the economy of the Republic of Cuba and its might, the Soviet Union is in no way guided by any self-interested calculations. When we help to strengthen the economy and defense of Cuba, we consider it to be a contribution to the common cause of developing and strengthening revolutionary forces, of strengthening the unity of socialist countries. With joint efforts we open in the new continent the road to a new world, the world of socialism.

Revolutionary Cuba is a brilliant star in the western hemisphere. The more developed its economy and culture, and the higher the material well-being of the Cuban, people the brighter the light of the beacon that attracts the working class, the peasants, and the working intellectuals of Latin American, African, and Asians countries; they are encouraged by the struggle for liberty and for a better life.

These are, comrade Fidel, my sincere judgments.

Now I would like to tell you, comrade Fidel, what the best time, in our opinion, would be for you to come to the Soviet Union. From our point of view, the season of the year is of no great importance. But taking into account the tropical climate of Cuba, and remembering that you felt physically cold in New York, we must also take into account our Russian winter. In what concerns political warmth, our

country cannot be compared to any continent, the geographical position of our country notwithstanding: the burning feelings of friendship between us also create tropical conditions in any season for the visitors from brother countries. But for the time being the most important thing is to free you from the physical sensation of coldness. Because of this it might be most convenient for you to come to our country at the beginning of spring, so that you could take part in the May Day festivities.

At another time you wanted to come to the Soviet Union precisely for the First of May, to watch our demonstration and parade. Because of this it would be good if you could come before the First of May so that you could get to know our cities, what we are building, our people. I would gladly travel with you through the country, and accompany you in your travels to certain cities. We could talk during those trips and then we could celebrate the First of May in Moscow, where you could see the parade and the demonstration.

Before the First of May we could go hunting. The hunt of animals with valuable furs will end soon in our country, in January, but in the spring we also have many kinds of good game. For nature lovers, the hunt does not depend so much on the number of animals bagged, but rather on the poetry of the landscape. This would be very good for resting. We also can go fishing. They have told me that on your leisure time, though it is infrequent, you are a fan not only of hunting but also of fishing. We can guarantee one or the other.

In a word, you choose the time that is most convenient for you. May Day with your participation would be an even more joyous holiday for Muscovites and for all the peoples of the Soviet Union. The popularity of your revolution, and your own personal popularity as leader of the Cuban Revolution, is very high among our peoples. The Soviets value you greatly and admire your revolutionary audacity. The Cuban Revolution has

DOCUMENT 82: Premier Khrushchev's letter to Prime Minister Castro, reviewing the crisis, January 31, 1963.

PAGE 11 OF 11

conquered the hearts of our people. You will feel this heat when you come to our country and meet with the people in any place: in the city, in the factory, the Kolkhoz and Sovkhoz, in every place you go.

I will not hide from you, comrade Fidel, that I myself had great desires to make a trip to Cuba. Before the crisis my comrades and myself had already decided to go to Cuba in January to talk to you, to travel and see the your land, to talk with the Cuban brothers, and mainly to share with you the experience of presumptuous, if I say that after the victory of the revolution we have lived forty-five years and have accumulated a certain amount of experience. You cannot be in full agreement with that experience; we ourselves would not repeat everything if we had to start over. But the value of experience resides not only in what is useful, but also in not repeating what was mistaken, and at times, harmful.

Now, having overcome the crisis, successfully overall, through joint efforts we have prevented the North American invasion, we have preserved revolutionary Cuba without losses and pushed away the eruption of a world war; the situation has improved measurably. By overcoming the crisis we have gained time. Perhaps for one or two years, and we think that even for five or six, the situation will be more favorable for Cuba than before the crisis. And gaining time is a very important factor because the correlation of forces is everyday more favorable to socialism, which is immensely important for the development of the Cuban revolution.

I thought that after ending this tension I could go see you in Cuba. But circumstances are such that, as far as I can see, I should not go. We have reached that conclusion because it could be falsely interpreted in your country and in other countries. Many will ask: Why is Khrushchev going to Cuba if comrade Mikoyan has just been there? Mikoyan's visit was interpreted in a twisted way in some countries, even in some socialist countries. And if, after this, Khrushchev shows up over there, they will say that obviously the relations between the Soviet Union and Cuba have become such that Khrushchev's visit was necessary.

Now, I reaffirm my great wishes to go to your country if you invite me. I'm sure that such a trip would be advantageous. but we will talk about that when you come to the Soviet Union, and together we can select the time or my visit to Cuba.

Currently, we are occupied with our internal matters. The Central Committee of the CPSU has just begun a great reform of the organic structure of our Party and is improving the leadership of the national economy. More specifically, we are devoting the Party's and peoples' efforts to the development of the economy, the growth of agriculture, industry, construction, science, and technology. Naturally, there is enough to do here, we cannot complain of not having enough work. When you come to Moscow we will talk frankly about all matter of interest.

Please accept, comrade Fidel, a cordial communist greeting on behalf of my comrades and myself.

January 31, 1963   N. Khrushchev

FBIS-LAT-92-043-S
4 March 1992

CARIBBEAN   11

Castro Addresses Conference

*CM0304154092 Havana Cubavision Television
in Spanish at 2233 GMT 28 Feb 92*

[Fourth of four parts of the special program: "Reflections on a Crisis," a tripartite conference on the Cuban Missile Crisis held in Havana from 9 to 12 January—recorded]

[Text] Well, another surprise. I thought that this morning we were going to discuss a point brought up by the American delegation, and that my speech might be in the afternoon. I think I can make an effort, in any case. If this is what you prefer, in that case, I will speak. Maybe I will need a little help, some paper.

Check and see if the five points are anywhere around there. [speaking to unidentified aide]

I think I have the essential ideas to speak right now. If I do not speak long, do not think that it is because I do not want to provide information, but really because I do not want to make a traditional two-and-a-half, or three-hour speech. I want to summarize ideas as much as possible. I want to concentrate on those things that I believe are essential. I must keep in mind everything that has been discussed in the two previous days. I do not want to repeat any of those issues.

I believe that many things have been clarified here. I believe that the meeting has been truly fruitful, at least for me, since I did not have an opportunity to participate in the previous meetings. I do not know everything that has been discussed. I only know it in very general terms. That is why I think that I should limit myself to those things that, by their character, have not been discussed in other meetings.

I should begin by saying that in analyzing a period such as this one, it is necessary to analyze or report the involvement in it of different personalities. Two of them were very important personalities of our time. They were Khrushchev and Kennedy. They were two people for whom I have great respect. I respect Khrushchev for his demonstrations of friendship toward Cuba in extremely difficult times. I always thought that he was pleasant. I had the opportunity to get to know him personally. I remember at the United Nations when, as a result of a meeting of heads of state at the United Nations, Khrushchev came to visit me at the Teresa Hotel, where I was practically in confinement in those days because of the atmosphere of intense hostility that I found there, and because I had been virtually thrown out of my other hotel. I had two alternatives, to either set up a tent in the UN front yard or to go to the Teresa Hotel. I was warmly welcomed at the Teresa Hotel. I was visited there by many heads of states, among them Khrushchev, which was a great honor.

Khrushchev was extraordinarily good to us. Always, when we requested something from him, he made every possible effort at his disposal to approve our requests. He

DOCUMENT 83: Foreign Broadcast Information Service, transcript of Fidel Castro's remarks at the Havana conference on the Cuban missile crisis, January 11, 1992.

PAGE 2 OF 16

gave me the impression of being basically a peasant; that was the impression he gave. A clever peasant, and not only a clever peasant, he was an intelligent, very intelligent man. He was a daring and courageous man. Those were the personal impressions I got from him.

I also have an opinion of the personal qualities of Kennedy, apart from the conflicts that emerged between his administration and ours. He was a talented man and also courageous. A man with the ability to lead his country. He made mistakes but also did things right. He was the central character in charge of directing the United States during the October Crisis. He had new ideas—some of them were brilliant, or very intelligent—such as the idea of the Alliance for Progress.

It is my opinion that with the authority he attained precisely after the October Crisis—which was when he consolidated his leadership in the United States—he could have been one of the presidents, or maybe the president, in the best position to rectify certain aspects of the U.S. policy toward Cuba. I had proof of this precisely on the day of his death. I was talking that morning with a French reporter, Jean Daniel, who had interviewed him at length and whom he asked to come to Cuba to talk with me. He conveyed a message to me and, as we were talking, the news of the attack in Dallas was heard on the radio. You can see how many coincidences have occured in all of this. From what that reporter told me, I could see a man who was pondering the possibility of holding talks, finding some solutions to the problems with Cuba, since he began by saying, actually talking or asking, he conveyed to me to what degree we had been in danger of a nuclear war.

Was I aware of this? He truly wanted, regarding all these issues, an exchange of opinions that really became unnecessary. We were in the middle of our conversation when the news of his death arrived. I think Kennedy was a capable man because of his authority, because of his ability to correct certain aspects of U.S. policy toward Cuba. I have explained this, and I say it with lots of sincerity, to justify why I feel real respect and admiration for these historic figures, and because I do not have the least intention of saying things to hurt anyone, or to defame anyone's memory.

In relation to the most immediate antecedents of the problem that would emerge afterwards, we have the issue of the Bay of Pigs. However, I do not blame Kennedy for the Bay of Pigs. Kennedy received a legacy from the previous administration. Decisions had already been made; everything was already prepared. Kennedy was still new in office; he had just been sworn in. He knew that it was a very serious problem; he had made certain pledges regarding Cuba in some speeches during the electoral campaign.

The impression I have is that he did not like that operation. It is true that he had constitutional authority to have stopped it, but constitutional authority alone is not enough. Sometimes you need moral authority and a considerable amount of political authority to solve certain problems, which U.S. administrations usually do not have during the first few weeks of government, and sometimes do not have even during the entire first presidential term. You are aware that many times it is said that a president cannot solve this or that problem in his first term because the next elections are still pending, but that he could solve it during a second term. Therefore, I do not blame him for the Bay of Pigs invasion.

Somehow, we have to acknowledge that he remained very composed regarding these events. As has been stated here, the whole thing became a disaster, a political disaster that, because of its scope, cannot be compared to a military disaster, with other military disasters. From the military point of view, and the scale of the battles, it also became a disaster. It was a difficult trial for Kennedy, and I would say that he showed courage at the time. I have not forgetten what he said when he assumed total responsibility for it: Victory has many fathers, but defeat is an orphan.

He could have made the decision to order U.S. troops and squadrons to participate. The Bay of Pigs' battles were held within view of the U.S. aircraft carriers and warships that were three miles from our coasts. I saw this personally when we entered Giron as it was getting dark that 19 April 1961. The squadron was out there with all its lights off, in full combat gear. They witnessed everything and were ready to enter into action. The invasion plans even presupposed the intervention of military forces later on. The goal was to establish a government, recognize it, and support it with troops. In other words, the invasion plans included the premise of using military force against our country, the intervention and invasion of our country because, naturally, those troops that disembarked, and those forces did not have the support of our people and could not do anything but maybe sustain their hold on a piece of territory and create in Cuba something like Taiwan or the like, nothing else. But we know that the plan presupposed a recognition after the recognition. The intervention always occurred within this framework.

In other words, if Kennedy had not been a composed and courageous man at the time, if he had not realized how mistaken the plan was from every point of view, military and political.[sentence as heard] Kennedy, undoubtedly, was very concerned with Latin American public opinion. He did not want to begin his administration with an event of that nature and decided not to give the order for U.S. forces to intervene.

That would have been a very bloody war, and I do not know if the number of Cuban casualties would have been as high, maybe, as if an intervention had occurred during the months of the 1962 October Crisis. There are no doubts that that war would have had a different character and unpredictable consequences. Despite that, casualty estimates were prepared. At the time, April 1961, we had hundred of thousands of armed men and women in our country. Weapons were distributed

DOCUMENT 83: Foreign Broadcast Information Service, transcript of Fidel Castro's remarks at the Havana conference on the Cuban missile crisis, January 11, 1992.

PAGE 3 OF 16

FBIS-LAT-92-043-S
4 March 1992

CARIBBEAN   13

throughout the country, in the mountains, the plains, in the cities, everywhere. An enormous resistance would have been put up by the people, who were armed and had just come out of a war. All the guerrilla traditions were still fresh.

Our people would have had to fight a well-equipped army that numbered up to 80,000 men-in-arms, yet by the end of the war we barely had 3,000 battle weapons. At that time, we could estimate that we had approximately 300,000 men and women armed or capable of taking up arms, or in different ways organized and prepared. We also already had some infantry cannons, some tanks, on which the soldiers received quick, accelerated training. I would ask the first advisers—at that time we already had some specialists teaching us how to use the weapons, advisers from Czechoslovakia and the USSR; there was a large number of cannons and anti-aircraft artillery guns—and we asked them if they could train all the necessary personnel. The training program would have taken years, yet we did it in weeks, because what our comrades would learn in the morning, they would go and teach in the evening in the other camps that we organized. There was a great exhilaration among the people. Maybe, we might still be fighting if there had been an intervention in 1961.

This may have meant a cost of hundreds of thousands of lives for our country. A prolonged struggle would have also resulted in considerable losses for the invaders of our territory. This is why I said that, on the contrary, we should credit Kennedy with the common sense and wisdom to have not ordered the intervention of the U.S. troops at the time. I know of presidents who would not even think for three minutes about ordering the intervention of U.S. troops. I tell you this so you can understand the reason for our opinion of the conduct of President Kennedy at the time. In Giron, we find the antecedents of the October Crisis because there is no doubt that, for Kennedy, it meant a severe political blow. He was embittered by this event. He was very upset. And afterwards, the issue of Cuba had a special meaning for him. This was reflected in the relations between the two countries.

I am not going to talk about the clandestine operations, acts of sabotage, that were continuous during that period. I am not going to make reference to the problems related to assassination plots. Unfortunately, all these things happened in one way or another during that period, but are not the subject of our analysis. But Kennedy was left very bitter about Cuba, determined to end in one way or another the revolutionary process in Cuba. He also used political instruments and strategies. I cite, as I used to, the example of the Alliance for Progress designed to change objective conditions, because he knew that the objective conditions in Latin American were, as they still are nowadays, favorable for social explosions. He wanted to deal with it from that angle.

We should remember that the Bay of Pigs crisis was followed by a meeting between Kennedy and Khrushchev. According to the news we received, Khrushchev heard with concern the Kennedy statements regarding Cuba. We still need to find out, through some of the figures that were there, if that was when Hungary was discussed, because Kennedy made reference to Hungary—that they had solved the problem in Hungary and that the U.S. still had not been able to solve the problem of Cuba. I do not have the menas to clarify this now, if this was mentioned in the Vienna talks. Darusenkov thinks that yes, it was in Vienna. There was also a later version saying that in a conversation of Khrushchev's son-in-law, whom I believe was the director of PRAVDA, (Aksuvey), forgive me if I do not pronounce the last name correctly; director of IZVESTIYA, right? He was traveling and made some remarks in the United States. I have heard comrades talk about the conversation between (Aksuvey) and Kennedy, and the subject of Hungary was mentioned—the same problem they did not know how to solve—and they took it as a warning, as a firm statement that they were planing to solve by one means or another the problem of Cuba. I remember that (Aksuvey) visited us, I do not remember the exact date either, if it was after the Washington trip. Maybe Oleg [Darusenkov] remembers this. But we have to clarify in which of the two conversations, or if on both occasions, the issue of Hungary was mentioned.

I do know, and I am aware of the great concern that Khrushchev felt after those conversations. It was a frequent subject, long before any idea about installing missiles existed. Of course, we were asking for more weapons. We were willing to defend ourselves. We asked for more weapon supplies. We signed certain accords on weapon supplies for our Armed Forces. That was the situation up to May 1962. Here we have already talked about some of the antecedents.

Aleksandr, for many years an ambassador in our country, and ambassador during the crisis, has talked about this, and other members of the Soviet delegation have provided details here of the conversations that took place regarding the missiles when we did not have any news about it.

We received news of an upcoming visit by (Rachido), who was the leader of the party in Uzbekistan, and who had already visited us and spent several months in Cuba providing cooperation in matters of agriculture, irrigation, etc. He was bringing along a marshal, Belyusofov or Belysofov, [corrected by unidentified speakers] Bydiusuv. I am appalling in English, but I think that in terms of pronunciation I am even worse in Russian. Bydiusov. His war name was Petrov? Well, Petrov Bydiusov—undoubtedly a very smart and energetic man—I believe that he later died in an airplane crash in Yugoslavia. He accompanied (Rachido), but he was the one basically entrusted with the issue of the missiles. Naturally he did not begin talking about missiles right at the beginning. We met with him right away. He did not begin by talking about missiles. He began by talking

DOCUMENT 83: Foreign Broadcast Information Service, transcript of Fidel Castro's remarks at the Havana conference on the Cuban missile crisis, January 11, 1992.

PAGE 4 OF 16

about the international situation, the situation of Cuba, the risks facing Cuba, and at one point he asked me what would be required to prevent a U.S. invasion. That was the question he asked me. I immediately answered him. I told him: Well, if the United States knows what an invasion of Cuba would mean with the Soviet Union, that would be, in my opinion, the best way to prevent an invasion of Cuba. That was my answer.

To corroborate this with documentation, you can, if you want, see the version that I wrote six years later and what I said in a report to the Central Committee in 1968. A Soviet military delegation came to visit around that time, headed by a marshal. He asked us how we believed the problem of an invasion could best be prevented. We told him that by adopting measures that unquestionably expressed to imperialism—forgive me for using that word, but that is how it was said, literally [muffled laughter]—that any aggression against Cuba would mean not only war with Cuba. Since the man already had his ideas ready, he said: But, specifically how? We have to perform concrete acts to indicate this.

He already had the mission to propose the installation of strategic missiles, and perhaps he was even afraid that we might refuse. We might have said: Well, the missiles here could mean, or could be used as a reason for criticism and campaigns against Cuba and the revolution in the rest of Latin America. But we did not have any doubts. First of all, when the issue of the missiles was first brought up, we thought that it was something beneficial to the consolidation of the defensive power of the entire socialist bloc, that it would contribute to this. We did not want to concentrate on our problems. Subsequently, it represented our defense. Subsequently. But really, the comrades who participated were the comrades of the directorate, who met to analyze this problem and make a decision. And how was it presented: That in our opinion it would strengthen the socialist bloc, the socialist bloc.

If we held the belief that the socialist bloc should be willing to go to war for the sake of any other socialist country, we did not have any right to consider something that could represent a danger to us. The questions of propaganda stayed within us, but we also saw the real danger of any crisis that could emerge, but without any hesitation, and honestly, thinking in a truly internationalist manner. All the comrades decided to give an immediate response. Keeping in mind the affirmative answer—with an enormous trust in a country that we believed was experienced in many things, even in war, and in international affairs—we told, we stated to them the usefulness of signing a military accord. Then, they sent an accord bill. I already talked about that.

Here I have what I said, textually, in a private conversation in 1968, regarding the antecedents of the October Crisis. In all truth and summarizing, we, from the beginning, saw it as a strategic operation. I am going to tell the truth about how we thought. We did not like the missiles. If it was a matter of our defense alone, we would not have accepted the missiles here. But do not think

that it was because of the dangers that could come from having the missiles here, but rather because of the way in which this could damage the image of the revolution. We were very committed to the image of the revolution in the rest of Latin America.

The fact that the presence of the missiles would turn us into a Soviet military base would have a high political cost for our country's image, which we valued so highly. So if it had been for our defense—and I say this here with all honesty, Aleksandr knows this—we would not have accepted the missiles. But we really saw in the issue of the missile installation something that would strengthen the socialist bloc, something that would help in some way to improve the so-called correlation of forces. That was how we perceived it immediately, immediately, instantaneously.

We did not argue about this. It would not have made sense, because if we had argued about what they were for, in fact, the conclusion we would draw would be that they should not be brought. In fact, we would have refused to accept the missiles because, of course, their presence was not presented in those terms. That was what we perceived immediately. Then we asked a few questions about what kind of missiles and how many. We did not have any practical knowledge about these things, and we were informed that they would deploy 42 missiles. From what has been shown here, it seems there were 36 operational missiles and six for testing. But they told us there would be 42 missiles. We asked for time because we had to meet with the leadership and to inform them about all this before coming to a decision, but we said we would do this quickly.

In fact, when this meeting was over, we organized a meeting of the leadership, and we analyzed the matter in the terms that I have explained. We said that the presence of the missiles had this and that significance. We also were not unaware—and for me it was obvious—that the presence of the missiles was going to give rise to great political tension. That was obvious. But we saw this matter from the angle of our moral, political, and internationalist duties. That was how we understood it.

There was talk about the missiles in a different sense. After the Bay of Pigs invasion, there had been talk about missiles. You would have to review all of Nikita's statements. He insinuated more than once that an invasion of Cuba could be responded to with the use of missiles. He insinuated this more than once, publicly, to such an extent that everyone here was talking about the Soviet missiles before the crisis, after the Bay of Pigs, as if they were their property. Many comrades talked about the missiles in their speeches. However, I refrained from saying a single word about missiles, because it did not seem right to me that our people, our populace, should place their hopes for defense in support from abroad. Our populace should be totally prepared—as it is today, and today more than ever—to develop their confidence in themselves and their ability to struggle and resist without any foreign support.

DOCUMENT 83: Foreign Broadcast Information Service, transcript of Fidel Castro's remarks at the Havana conference on the Cuban missile crisis, January 11, 1992.

PAGE 5 OF 16

FBIS-LAT-92-043-S
4 March 1992   CARIBBEAN   15

That is why I did not talk about the Soviet missiles as a possible aid in any of my speeches, and there are quite a few in that period. Nikita encouraged this matter a lot with his public statements. As was also acknowledged here yesterday, even in the United States, even Kennedy said in his campaign that he thought that there was an imbalance in strategic missiles. Throughout the world, people thought there was an imbalance in strategic missiles. It was known that the Americans had a very powerful air force, but that the Soviet Union had made great progress in the area of rocketry.

During those days, there were spectacular technical achievements like the space flights. The first space flight was made by a Soviet pilot, in a space capsule. All of that had an enormous effect on world opinion, and from what I can see, it also had an enormous effect in the United States. It is not at all strange that we would have more or less similar ideas about the combat capacity of each of the great powers in this area of nuclear missiles.

But everyone thought this, and assuming that the USSR had many more missiles than they had, we perceived that the presence of these missiles here in Cuba meant a modification...[changes thought] not a change; we cannot talk about a change in the correlation of forces, but it was a considerable improvement in the correlation of forces in favor of the socialist countries that we saw as our allies, friends, and brothers—sharing a common ideology.

Of course, we never saw the missiles as something that could one day be used against the United States, in an attack against the United States, an unjustified attack or a first strike. I remember that Nikita was always repeating: that they would never make a first strike, a nuclear strike. This issue was an obsession of his. He was constantly talking about peace. He was constantly talking about negotiations with the United States, of ending the Cold War, the arms race, etc.

So to judge the mood of that time, one should understand what was thought about this and about the strength of each of the great powers. But we saw that this improved the situation of the socialist bloc, and we really saw the issue of Cuba's defense as a secondary matter, for the reasons I have explained. So that was how we saw it, and we have continued to have this perception throughout all these years. That is why I read this speech 24 years ago. If one sees that the correlation ....[rephrases] Knowing what one knows now, one can see the practical military importance these rockets had, because they really turned medium-range missiles into strategic missiles.

When we returned to the meeting with the marshall and (Rachidov), we gave them our answer. It was in these words.... [changes thought] Unfortunately, this was not recorded. It should have been recorded, but recordings were very underdeveloped at that time. Those little recorders that many people have now that they can put in their pocket did not exist. Today everything is recorded. So this meeting is being recorded, and whenever we have visits by heads of state. We asked Gorbachev the last visit we had from him, and we agreed that everything we talked about should be recorded. We ask permission of the person with whom we are talking, as a rule, right? Of course, there are those who are more in the habit of recording and those who are less in the habit. But our meetings are being recorded, and you already....[changes thought] The meetings with U Thant were recorded, by mutual agreement and all that. If one thinks about history, one sees how many details and things could have been recorded and kept.

But we answered them with these words: that if it was to strengthen the socialist bloc, yes, if it was to strengthen the socialist bloc, and also—and I put this in second place—if it would contribute to Cuba's defense, we were willing to receive all the missiles that might be needed. To be more faithful, we said that we were willing to receive up to 1,000 missiles, if they wanted to send them. Those were our words, verbatim. I used the words: 1,000. I said: This is our resolution. It has been made. [words indistinct], as they say a Roman general said in ancient times—I think it was Julius Caesar. If the decision has already been made, it has already been made. But it was made in that spirit and with that intention. This may also explain why we felt so indignant about the later development of events, about what happened. Because we practically took an attitude of rebellion and intransigence about the crisis.

Then there was the whole process that has been talked about that has been so clearly explained by the Soviet military officer—how they organized it. In a few months, they began a great movement of weapons and troops. From a logistics point of view, it was a perfect operation. We can see this, not only from theoretical considerations, but because we have also found ourselves forced to send troops abroad, as we did in Angola, for example.

I remember the first time we sent 36,000 men in a few weeks with a large part of their weaponry. But I also remember what we did after Cuito Cuanavale, when we increased our forces to 53,000 men. We have some experience in transporting troops in our ships. There was not a single Soviet ship in this operation. We transported our troops and weapons. We were all alone in Cuito Cuanavale. That was also true of the operation in Angola in 1975. That was a decision of ours. The only thing that came from the Soviet Union was worries. They conveyed them to us in 1975, but it was an absolutely free and sovereign decision by our country.

A crisis situation arose in Cuito Cuanavale that forced us to send large numbers of troops, and we did so with decisiveness, because one must do things decisively. Otherwise, one will be defeated. If 20,000 are needed and you send 10,000, the most likely thing is that you will be defeated. We were facing the South Africans. They are very powerful. They manufacture weapons. They have good training, good equipment, and very good aircraft. We prepared for battle with the South

DOCUMENT 83: Foreign Broadcast Information Service, transcript of Fidel Castro's remarks at the Havana conference on the Cuban missile crisis, January 11, 1992.

PAGE 6 OF 16

Africans. To give you an idea, when our troops advanced, they had 1,000 antiaircraft weapons, so that they could have superiority in antiaircraft weapons. So we also have some experience in troop movements, and we know what it means to carry out an operation. Of course, there were no missiles in this case, but we did have to send all kinds of heavy weapons. This operation with the missiles was carried out very efficiently by the Soviet Armed Forces and in a very short time. They fulfilled completely the mission that had been assigned to them.

Well, the motivations still need to be clarified. Here opinions have been given on this point by almost all the Soviets. They really have summarized what was talked about in the Soviet Union, and what was said in the Soviet Union, and the reasoning Nikita always used. I have already said that Nikita was very shrewd about how he presented the problem to the other CPSU leaders, and how he really thought, or if there was another CPSU leader who knew Nikita's most personal intentions. In the light of the facts we know today about the true correlation of forces, we can clearly see that it was a necessity. I am not criticizing Khrushchev. Really, I am not criticizing him for the fact that he wanted to improve the correlation of forces. It seems absolutely legitimate to me, absolutely legal—if we are going to talk in terms of international law—absolutely moral, to want to improve the correlation of forces between the socialist bloc and the United States.

If what they really had was 50 or 60 missiles, there is no doubt that the presence of those 42 missiles significantly improved the situation. It almost doubled the effective assets. We have not talked about the submarines here. You probably also know how many missiles the Soviets had on the submarines and their ability to move with their submarines and also carry out strikes, because I know they had submarines with nuclear missiles. This information has not come out here, how many they had at that time. But there is no doubt that the missiles on land were doubled.

If we had known that the correlation of forces, which we did not know—I repeat—perhaps we would have suggested ....[rephrases] If they had talked to us in those terms, of improving the correlation of forces, perhaps we would have advised prudence. Because I think, of course, that if you have 50 missiles, you have to be more prudent than if you have 300. That is clear. If we had had that information, and if they had talked to us in strategic terms, we would surely have advised prudence because I say, and I repeat, that we were not concerned about defending the country. If that were not true, what kind of situation would we be in today? We do not receive missiles or anything, and here you can see that we are all unworried. The United States is much more powerful. I do not know what kinds of conventional weapons and smart weapons and all those things that it has, and you can see that we are calm here. We have confidence in ourselves. We have confidence in our ability to fight, and we are proud of this confidence and ability to fight.

I say that it is a mystery. We do not know Nikita's most personal thoughts. But that was how we understood it, and how the other members of the Soviet leadership understood it. As I have said, he was very shrewd. He could present something in one set of terms and think in another set. But I could not find any other explanation and, even today, I cannot find any other explanation. Of course, it is true that Nikita loved Cuba and admired Cuba a lot. He felt special affection for Cuba. We would say that he was fond of Cuba, in his feelings, his emotions, and all. Because Nikita was also a man of political thinking. He had a political theory and doctrine, and he was consistent with that doctrine. He thought in those terms, between capitalism and socialism. He had very solid convictions. He even thought, in my opinion erroneously, that one day socialism would surpass capitalism by peaceful means.

I say that this is a possibly mistaken concept, because I do not think that the aim of a socialist society should be consumption. I do not think Third World countries need to imitate capitalism in consumption. I always wonder what would happen in the world if every Chinese family had a car, and every Indian family also had a car, and every family in Bangladesh, Pakistan, and all those other places had a car. If they reached such a level of development, how much longer would the oil and fuel last? How much longer would the atmosphere tolerate this poisoning and all these phenomena we know about?

That is why I say that there is a mistake in this concept of socialism. Socialism should solve people's basic problems—education, health, culture, housing, food—all the essential material needs, and not be the idea that everyone should have a car or consumer objects. They should have what they can have, what the environment can tolerate. We have a different concept of socialism, but he was a man of profound political convictions. I do not think that Nikita wanted war. The farthest thing from his mind was war, especially nuclear war. He was very aware of what a nuclear war would mean for the Soviet Union. He did have an obsession about reaching some kind of parity.

I think that the words, the reasoning yesterday by Mr. McNamara was excellent when he said that parity existed at all times after the first moment when there was the capacity to make a response that would cause terrible damage. But even if all the nuclear weapons were launched against one country, the world would be annihilated just the same. Because the contamination this would cause—and the problems of all kinds that this would cause—would be such that, even if only 10,000 of the 50,000 warheads are used and are used in only one place, the world will be finished. This reasoning about when parity really exists seems wise to me, because parity exists as soon as there is the capacity to respond by doing enough damage so that it would be unacceptable to someone who is thinking about launching a nuclear attack.

DOCUMENT 83: Foreign Broadcast Information Service, transcript of Fidel Castro's remarks at the Havana conference on the Cuban missile crisis, January 11, 1992.

PAGE 7 OF 16

FBIS-LAT-92-043-S
4 March 1992

CARIBBEAN

17

I tried to find out how this was discussed in the leadership of the CPSU and the Soviet Government when I traveled to the USSR in 1963. But, in fact, I was unable to clarify this. I asked a lot of questions of as many Politburo members as I met with: Kosygin, Gromyko—I do not remember if Gromyko was a Politburo member. I asked all of them one by one: Tell me, how was that decision made? What were the arguments that were used? I really was not able to get a single word out of them. They often did not answer my questions. Of course, you cannot be impertinent and say: Listen, answer me! For all my questions, I was not able to get a clear answer about the possibility that the strategic argument had been used among the Soviet leadership. That was our perception and our conception of the problem. I should say this, really.

The agreements were put into effect immediately. After the verbal agreement, it was necessary to formalize it, but it was already in effect. That was how a draft was drawn up in the USSR; Aleksandr has spoken about this. This draft was sent to Cuba. Politically, the draft was erratic, in the sense that there was no clear foundation established about the matter. It did not talk about strategic weapons, of course. I modified it, using some of points. I took some away, some of the considerations, and I established the political foundation for the agreement, which in my opinion was unobjectionable. The articles of the agreement were not mentioned. It said: The Soviet Union will send to the Republic of Cuba armed forces to reinforce its defenses in the face of a danger of foreign aggression, and thus contribute to maintaining world peace. The type of Soviet troops, and the areas where they will be stationed on the territory of the Republic of Cuba, will be set by the representatives named in accordance with Article 11 of this agreement.

Article 11 talks about the representatives. There is no mention of the kind of strategic weapons, and this agreement could have been mentioned... [pauses] could have been published, and no one could have challenged the legality and morality of this agreement. Of course, it was not essential to bring the missiles here to defend Cuba. That argument was not included, because we could have made a military pact with the USSR saying that an attack on Cuba would be equivalent to an attack on the USSR. The United States has a lot of these pacts throughout the world, and they are respected, because the word of nations is respected and because the risks involved in violating the treaties or disregarding the treaties are taken into consideration.

That is why I say that you should know this. The USSR could have declared that an attack on Cuba would be equivalent to an attack on the USSR. We could have had a military agreement. We could have been able to achieve the aim of the defense of Cuba without the presence of the missiles. I am absolutely convinced of this. This is one of the things that reaffirms the conviction we had at that time and that we have kept until now, even though there is not a single bit of proof that a different argument was used. That is why the comrades

in the Soviet delegation—I can no longer say Soviet, from the CIS—but I mean those who participated in the delegation from the armed forces and the country that participated in this crisis, have spoken, in my opinion, with absolute honesty about the reasoning and concepts that prevailed there in the Soviet Union.

All this brought, or gave rise to, a great effort in the period when the missiles were installed, because there were people living in the places that had been chosen. There were farmers, buildings, and things. We had to clean them out, rid the places of obstacles. We appointed a comrade, a party and government official, to attend exclusively to everything connected with the negotiations to free the land to install the missiles, and it was quite a bit of land. I do not have the figures fresh in my mind, but hundreds of families had to move. We had to arrange this with them, find land for them, give them benefits. All of this was negotiated, and all as much in secret as possible, without being able to explain what it was for.

[Text] There were all kinds of leaks. Well, we had to adopt a measure. All those who knew something knew that they had the duty to consider themselves quarantined. So sometimes, groups of officials came and said: Listen, I have found something out. I have come to stay here now. Because in such-and-such a place, and while talking with someone, a Soviet official often...[changes thought] because you can imagine, there were a lot of troops, 42,000 men, and they establish relations, and some talk to some people, others talk to other people, or another person sees something. So we adopted the method that is used in cases of serious epidemics, which is to quarantine the infected people. Everyone who knew something was infected and was quarantined.

Of course, there were large troop movements, and there began to be talk relatively early that there might be offensive weapons, other sorts of weapons or missiles. In addition, when the missiles began to arrive, those devices are so large....[pauses] I think the current ones must be more modern and smaller. Maybe they can be carried in a suitcase. I do not know what the technology is like; other people know more than we do about this problem. However, those were such enormous devices, approximately 25 meters long, no one knows for sure, that it could occupy an entire block. When such big devices were unloaded, no matter how hard one tried to hide and move through in the streets, everyone knew about it.

That was the best kept secret in history, I would say, because several million Cubans knew it. It was something that really could not be hidden. I imagine that the Central Intelligence Agency must have received letters, because there were spontaneous informers here. They were people who were not with the revolution, and they sympathized with the United States, or they were against the revolution. There were these spontaneous informers. But no one knew anything for sure. No one had any proof.

DOCUMENT 83: Foreign Broadcast Information Service, transcript of Fidel Castro's remarks at the Havana conference on the Cuban missile crisis, January 11, 1992.

PAGE 8 OF 16

18   CARIBBEAN

FBIS-LAT-92-043-S
4 March 1992

I: was a truly intense process, truly intense work. We had to see to an infinite number of details and solve an infinite number of issues to keep it a secret. All this did not happen....[rephrases] Other things happened that have already been mentioned here. I am not going to repeat them. Raul's trip to Moscow, the trip of Che [Guevara] and (?Aragoni) to the Soviet Union when he delivered the final draft that was accepted. Our draft was accepted, just as it was, without adding or deleting one comma. I have already talked about this. We should remember that a tremendous atmosphere was being created, which seemed negative to us. Therefore, we thought that we should come out with the law on our side, and simply publish this military agreement. The secrecy put us at a disadvantage. It put us at a political and practical disadvantage. It did both things.

But we should distinguish between secrecy—many military operations have to be done in secret, the operation itself, not the basis for an operation—and the information that was given about it. I think this is an important point. There was a big mistake made here, a really big mistake. Not only the mistake about the secrecy, which is one thing that harmed us, but also the information that was given to Kennedy, going along with the game about the category of the weapons, whether they were offensive or defensive.

If you want to verify this, you will see that in none of the Cuban statements—and there were several—did we ever go along with the game relating to the category of the weapons. We refused to go along with that game and, in public statements the government made and in the statements at the United Nations, we always said that Cuba considered that it had a sovereign right to have whatever kind of weapons it thought appropriate, and no one had any right to establish what kind of weapons our country could or could not have. We never went along with denying the strategic nature of the weapons. We never did. We did not agree to that game. We did not agree with that approach. Therefore, we never denied or confirmed the nature of the weapons; rather, we reaffirmed our right to have whatever type of weapons we thought appropriate for our defense.

In contrast, to tell the truth, Khrushchev went along with the game of categorizing the weapons. He turned it into something intentional. Since he did not have any intention of using the weapons in an offensive operation, he believed that it was the intention that defined the nature of the weapons. But it was very clear that Kennedy did not understand it that way. Kennedy did not understand the issue of intentions but rather the issue of type of weapons, whether they were strategic weapons or not. That was the issue. It can be seen very clearly that Kennedy was convinced that strategic weapons were not going to be brought to Cuba.

Because of this, I would say that there was something more than shrewdness here. Deception was involved here. I think the two things—the secrecy about the military agreement and the deception—were two facts, two facts that did harm. Because I think a different approach should have been adopted, and not the approach of deceit. It did us a lot of harm because, in the first place, Kennedy had a lot at stake. He had already suffered the setback of the Bay of Pigs. He was entering his second year. There were elections. Khrushchev did not want to affect those elections. That is very clear. Perhaps this was one of the factors he used in deciding not to publish the agreement. It is possible that he was counting on not doing anything that would hurt (?Kennedy) in the elections, but he did the worst thing. It was not anticipated that what was happening could become known.

So, in my opinion, Kennedy trusted in what he was told. This is seen in all his public statements. It was like a relief to him to think: Well, they are filling that country with tanks or cannons or who knows what, but there are no strategic weapons there. He thought according to a rationale; he made calculations according to a rationale. This naturally gave him, not legal force, but it gave him the opportunity to present himself to world public opinion as one who had been deceived, saying: They have told me this, they have told me that, they have repeated this to me many times.

So in the eyes of world public opinion, Kennedy gained moral force, not legal force. But he said: They assured me of this, but it has turned out otherwise. He was put in a difficult personal situation—which was something Khrushchev would not have wanted but that, in fact, occurred. He presented himself as one who had been deceived, who had been assured of this, that, or the other, while the truth was something else. That was one of the advantages he was given, not by the secrecy itself but by the secrecy plus the deception.

What other advantage did it give him? That when the missile sites were finally discovered on 14 October, the United States had an enormous advantage because they held the secret in their hands. They could take the initiative. The initiative in the military realm was put into the hands of the United States because they knew what was happening and could afford to choose one option or another, a political option, a quarantine, or a surprise air attack on those installations.

I think that was a very dangerous moment, from the military point of view—even if it was illegal, arbitrary, and unjust, or even immoral from any point of view because you have to comply with international laws. You do not have the right to attack any country or invade any country. But, well, he had the choice in his hands. There could have been a surprise strike when no one was expecting it. Of course, the Soviet military officer explained something here that is extremely important. The nuclear warheads were not in the same place. They were a considerable distance away—which was the right thing, the elementary thing; just as I had told the Soviet officer not to put all the missiles in the same place—that

DOCUMENT 83: Foreign Broadcast Information Service, transcript of Fidel Castro's remarks at the Havana conference on the Cuban missile crisis, January 11, 1992.

PAGE 9 OF 16

was on 26 October, already in the middle of the crisis—so that they would not all be destroyed and some capability could be kept.

It is unquestionable that the Soviet military took these elementary measures, but I fear that a large part, or almost all, of the surface-to-air missile units and all the installations that were in view could have been destroyed in a totally surprise attack. Because those antiaircraft missiles really fired above 1,000 meters. They did not have defenses. The defenses of those installations were strengthened against the low-altitude overflights when we mobilized all our batteries and devoted them to defending those installations. These were conventional batteries. But at that time, they were very vulnerable. Of course, things changed later. The situation improved. But the United States had eight days—or from 16 October when it was reported to them, six days—to act before making this information public. I think this was an extremely dangerous time, not only from the political point of view but also militarily, the way the issue was handled in these two respects. In my opinion, these were negative respects, but that was how it was handled.

I have already explained the position we took. We had our views. We do not know about the others. The crisis broke out on 22 October, but in the morning we issued a combat alert to all forces when we saw the movement and the meeting, all the information that reached us publicly. We also realized that it was about the missiles. We did not lose a single minute, and we issued a maximum combat alert to all our forces that same day before Kennedy spoke. We had already mobilized the forces, our forces. We also warned the Soviets about the situation.

Essentially, the crisis erupted on the night of 22 October, and defense preparations occupied almost all of our time after that. We dedicated ourselves to feverishly working day and night on things that I have already talked about: the mobilization of our forces, the protection of the missile bases, and also the medium range surface-to-air missiles. We assigned to all the Soviet facilities practically all of our anti-aircraft batteries. We thought that it was the most important thing to defend from the beginning of the crisis.

What was Khrushchev's mood once the crisis was declared? What mood was he in? He was in a very combative, very determined mood. Therefore, he sent a letter on 23 October. I am declassifying this also. Does this business of declassifying have anything to do with the theory of class struggles or what? [laughter]

Khrushchev said: [Begins quoting letter] Dear Comrade Castro, the Soviet Government has just received from U.S. President Kennedy, the following document, of which we attach a copy. We consider this declaration of the U.S. Government and Kennedy's speech on 22 October—Oh, alright. They are telling me to go slowly. Thanks—The Soviet Government has just received from U.S. President Kennedy the following document, a copy

of which we have attached. We consider this declaration by the U.S. Government and Kennedy's speech on 22 October as an inconceivable interference in the internal affairs of the Republic of Cuba, and a violation of the norms of international law, and of the basic rules that govern relations between states, and as a blatant act of provocation against the Soviet Union.

The Republic of Cuba has the total right, as any other sovereign state, to defend itself and to choose allies as it wishes. We reject the blatant demands of the U.S. Government for control over the shipment of weapons to Cuba and their aspiration to determine what type of weapons the Republic of Cuba can possess. The U.S. Government knows quite well that no sovereign state will permit another state to meddle in its relations with other states, nor will it render an account of pending measures until its national defense reaches a point of strength.... [corrects himself] toward the strengthening of its national defense. In response to Kennedy's speech, the Soviet Government states its most emphatic protest against the piracy [piratescas] actions of the U.S. Government and depicts these actions as treacherous and aggressive—See, this is all in one paragraph—piracy, treacherous, and aggressive actions in regards to sovereign states, and declares its decision to actively fight against such actions.

We have given instructions to our UN Security Council representative to urgently present to the Council the issue of the violation by the United States of the norms of international law and the UN Charter and to state an emphatic protest against the aggressive and treacherous actions of U.S. imperialism. As a result of the situation created, we have instructed the Soviet military representatives in Cuba on the need to adopt corresponding measures and to be completely ready, ready for combat.

We are sure that the actions undertaken by the American imperialists with the intention of taking away the legitimate right of the Republic of Cuba to strengthen its defensive power and the defense of its territory, will provoke the irate protest of all peace-loving countries.—The truth is that there were really no big protests because politically adverse conditions had arisen due to the procedures used. All of this is in parenthesis. This is what I am saying.—Will provoke the irate protest of all peace-loving countries and will move into action the widest masses in defense of the just cause of revolutionary Cuba. [ends quoting letter]

This could have been accomplished, in part, if we had done things openly. All of this is true because we were within our most absolute right to do so. And if we had the right, how were we going to act in a way that made it seem that we did not have this right, that made it seem that we were doing something wrong. I am analyzing this in terms of ethics, politics, legality—not in terms of force, correlations of force, or in military terms.

[Continues quoting letter] We send to you, Comrade Castro, and to all your comrades in arms, our warmest

DOCUMENT 83: Foreign Broadcast Information Service, transcript of Fidel Castro's remarks at the Havana conference on the Cuban missile crisis, January 11, 1992.

PAGE 10 OF 16

greetings and express our firm believe that the aggressive plans of the U.S. imperialists will be thwarted. [ends quoting letter]

The other thing is the declaration. This is the letter that we received on the 23d, and nothing else.

It contained a clear and firm commitment to fight against the piracy, treacherous, and aggressive actions [words indistinct]. What was ahead was combat. I could not imagine any withdrawal. To tell the truth, the idea of a withdrawal never crossed our minds. We did not think it was possible. And Khrushchev, who is the one who knew how many missiles and nuclear weapons he had available and all those things, sent us this letter on the 23d. We, of course, told ourselves: The issue is clear, things are clear, and we went ahead with our preparations. Then, the time came when I wrote the letter, when we had already taken all the humanly possible measures. I met with the Soviet military command, as I have explained before. It reported that everything was ready, all the weapons that were mentioned here, that the Soviet officer explained here, and with lots of willingness.

A truly strange phenomenon occurred among the Soviet troops in a situation such as that one, in which the people were in extreme danger and at the same time remained totally calm. The Soviet and Cuban troops remained totally calm among the Cuban people. if you conducted a poll of the Cuban people and asked: Should we return the missiles? Ninety percent would have answered no. Our people maintained a calm and intransigent position regarding this issue. That same day, the 26th, we notified the Soviet officers that low-altitude overflights were unacceptable, as I mentioned before and, therefore, our batteries were going to open fire, and we wanted them to be informed.

According to the accord, there were two armies and two commands, we commanded our forces and our country. We said, well, we cannot continue to tolerate this. This is extremely dangerous. I already mentioned this. I should not repeat it. Essentially, on the morning of the 27th, when the U.S. aircraft arrived—this was an daily occurrence early in the morning—they faced the fire from our antiaircraft batteries. The Soviet antiaircraft missile unit shot down the aircraft in the eastern part of the country; naturally, it was a moment of great tension. But in reality, it was clear, that when we were meeting, or even before we met, on the 26th, when we met with the Soviet officers and were sending a message to Khrushchev, he had already sent a message to Kennedy. You are well aware of all of this. His message proposed the basis for a solution—which was the withdrawal of the missiles in return for guaranties toward Cuba, of not attacking Cuba. Later, the next day, he sent another message and from what I am told, the message on that second day added to the issue of the guaranty for Cuba the issue of missiles in Turkey.

Of course, when this news arrived, the news arrived here on the 28th, it provoked a great indignation because we realized that we had become some type of game token. We not only saw a unilateral decision; a series of steps had been taken without including us. They could have told us; there was the message on the 26th and on the 27th. There had been time, but we heard on the radio on the 28th that an agreement had taken place. We had to endure the humiliation. I understood the Soviet officer when he said that it was the most painful decision that he had to obey in his life, the issue of the inspection of the ships.

We found out about the agreement on the 28th. I believe that there was a message on the way, informing us after the fact. It arrived one or two hours later through the embassy. The reaction of all the people, of all the people, all the cadres, of all the comrades was of profound indignation, it was not a feeling of relief. Then, the political decision that we immediately took was to issue the five-point demands on that same day, the 28th.

Do we have it around here? Check and see where our five-points are. [speaking to unidentified aide]

There were five points, very simple and easy to remember.

1. The end of the economic blockade and of all the economic and trade pressure measures that the United States implemented throughout the world against our country;

2. The end of all subversive actions, shipment and infiltration of weapons and explosives by air or sea, organization of mercenary invasions, infiltration of spies and saboteurs, actions that are carried out from U.S. territory and certain accomplice countries;

3. The end to all pirate attacks conducted from existing bases in the United States and in Puerto Rico:

4. The end of all violations of our airspace and waters by U.S. aircraft and warships;

5. The withdrawal from the Guantanamo Naval Base and the return of the territory occupied by the United States.

These were the five points that we issued on the 28th as our demands.

We would not have opposed a solution. If there was a real danger of war, if we would have known that Nikita was willing to withdraw the missiles and find a solution on that basis, and on a truly honorable basis, we would not have refused. Logically, there was no purpose in insisting on a situation or a solution, but it had to be an acceptable and honorable solution.

The simple solution to withdraw the missiles because the United States had given its word that it would not attack Cuba is incongruent with all the steps taken and it was incongruent with the existence of a situation in our

DOCUMENT 83: Foreign Broadcast Information Service, transcript of Fidel Castro's remarks at the Havana conference on the Cuban missile crisis, January 11, 1992.

PAGE 11 OF 16

FBIS-LAT-92-043-S
4 March 1992

CARIBBEAN   21

country that had to be overcome. It would have been enough if Nikita had said: Would you agree to the withdrawal of the missiles if satisfactory guaranties are given to Cuba? Cuba was not a stumbling block to that solution. Cuba would have helped but would have said the minimum guarantees we want are these. Not a guarantee that they would not invade us, I believe that the whole world, anyhow, would have seen with relief the beginning of the solution of the crisis because the consent by Nikita to withdraw the missiles would already have produced relief.

The people would have thought that it was reasonable to find an agreement on a basis related to Cuba, because if Cuba was the motive for the missiles, Cuba should have been kept in mind instead of the missiles in Turkey. But it is evident that the missiles in Turkey were present in Nikita's mind, because he said that he was in the Baltic Sea, near Turkey, and thought about those missiles or so the story goes. The Black Sea? [corrected by unidentified aide] And thought about the missiles in Turkey and all that. And in the end, he ends up also thinking about the missiles in Turkey for whatever reasons, because someone might have suggested that they could be included. But from the political and international point of view, for the honest people, the peace-loving people, those people in the world that sympathized with Cuba, or with independence, or whatever, it made no sense to propose an exchange of missiles in Cuba with missiles in Turkey. If the reason was the defense of Cuba, what did Turkey have to do with the defense of Cuba? Absolutely nothing.

The demands that Cuba made were completely reasonable, a good negotiation point could have been found, and the missiles could have been withdrawn, if that was the condition required to preserve the peace because peace was really threatened. I believe that the procedures used promoted those actions that endangered peace. I already explained them. We were already at that point on the 28th, when another solution was not possible anymore. A commitment had been made, Cuba had been ignored, Turkey had been mentioned; then we issued our five points.

We have already talked about the trip by U Thant. The Soviet Government asked us to please hold our fire, to not shoot anymore. We agreed, right, but as long as the negotiations last, only as long as the negotiations; only as long as the negotiations [repeats] are taking place will we maintain that cease-fire order, the order to not fire against the low-altitude overflights. Because immediately afterwards, on the 27th, the aircraft stopped flying. After our batteries on the 27th.... [changes thought] There were no more sorties that afternoon, there were no more overflights. There were none on the 28th. But later, after the batteries went silent, they began to conduct overflights again while the negotiations were taking place, and it was very humiliating. Given the frame of mind of our people, to watch those aircraft flying at 100 meters was extremely irritating and demoralizing even for the artillery soldiers and everyone else. You have to

really understand the Cuban personality to comprehend the harmful effect to our morale of events of this nature.

Then U Thant came to visit. I fully explained to him our position, even the five points, and especially our categorical opposition to the inspections. I told him that we did not accept—because the USSR is a sovereign country and so were we—and that no one could authorize an inspection of our territory if we did not authorize it. And we told him, there is not going to be any inspection. That was one of our reactions because we were in disagreement with the manner in which... [changes thought] with the outcome of the crisis. When U Thant came, I explained to him all our positions.

He definitely did not go beyond three proposals. He proposed that we accept a group of UN representatives and all that, a UN reconnaissance plane crewed by people acceptable to the Cuban, Russian, and American Governments. We really were not in the mood for overflights in those days.

[Begins quoting U Thant message] So, the United States has told me that if this system is put into practice, I will make a public statement, in the Security Council if necessary, because they will not continue to have aggressive intentions against the Cuban Government, and they will guarantee the integrity of the nation's territory, etc. [ends quoting]

Where is my response? I told him, precisely: We do not understand why this is being asked of us, because we have not violated anyone's rights. We have not carried out any attack on anyone at all. All our actions have been based on international law. We have been the victims of an embargo, in the first place, which is an illegal act; and in the second place, of an attempt to determine from another country what we have the right to do or not do within our borders. Cuba is a sovereign state.—I am reading the essential things—The United States has been repeatedly violating our airspace without any right. We can accept anything that complies with the law and that does not involve a reduction in our status as a sovereign state. I understand that this business about the inspections is one more attempt to humiliate our country. Therefore, we do not accept it. This demand for inspections is to validate their attempt to violate our right to act within our borders with complete freedom, to decide what we can and cannot do within our borders.

The threat of launching a direct armed attack is absurd. If Cuba were to strengthen itself militarily to a degree that the United States takes on itself to determine. [sentence as heard] We do not have the least intention of accounting to or consulting the U.S. Senate or House about the weapons we think it appropriate to acquire or the measures to be taken to fully defend our country. We have not yielded, nor do we intend to yield any sovereign prerogative to the U.S. Congress. We can negotiate with all sincerity and honor. It would not be honorat : if we accepted negotiating about a sovereign right of our country.

DOCUMENT 83: Foreign Broadcast Information Service, transcript of Fidel Castro's remarks at the Havana conference on the Cuban missile crisis, January 11, 1992.

PAGE 12 OF 16

Then U Thant explained. He said: All actions by the United Nations on Cuban territory can only be undertaken with the consent of the Cuban Government and people. Here, in essence, are some other ideas U Thant presented. They are very interesting. He said: My colleagues and I [words indistinct] what I have said.

[Quoting from own letter] In the first place, our government does not have the least doubt of the great intention, disinterest, and honesty with which the current UN Secretary General is working. We do not have any doubts about your intentions, good faith, and extraordinary interest in finding a solution to this problem. I understand the interest all of us should have in peace, but the road to peace is not the road of sacrificing the rights of peoples, violating the rights of peoples, because that precisely the road that leads to war. The road to peace is the road of guaranteeing the rights of peoples and the willingness of peoples to resist when defending those rights.

Here I said: The road to the last world war was the road set by the annexation of Austria, the dividing up of Czechoslovakia, acts of German imperialism that were tolerated and that led to that war. That is why it is difficult to understand how one can talk about an immediate solution without reference to future solutions, when what is of greatest interest is not paying any price for peace now, but rather, guaranteeing peace in a definitive way.

I said: Cuba is not Austria nor southeastern Czechoslovakia—it is southwestern, right? I said southeastern, that appears here—Cuba is not Austria nor southeastern Czechoslovakia nor the Congo. We have the very firm determination to defend our rights through any difficulties and any dangers.

I hope [name indistinct] has not underlined anything more here, because otherwise this will drag on too long. Here I said: The Soviet Government's decision to withdraw the strategic weapons they brought to defend Cuba should have been enough for them. The Cuban Government has not impeded the withdrawal of those weapons. If, in addition to that, the United States wants to humiliate our country, they will not succeed. We have not hesitated a single minute in our determination to defend our rights.

I added: We also oppose the inspections at our ports. I ask if the Soviet Union has authorized inspections of its ships at sea, why would it then be necessary to inspect them again in Cuban ports? Regarding this, I want to say, in the first place, that the United States has no right to invade Cuba, and one cannot negotiate based on a promise not to commit a crime, based on the simple promise not to commit a crime—I repeat—and that given the threat of this danger, we trust more in our determination to defend ourselves than in the U.S. Government's words.

I said: Why not value equally the public pledge made to the United Nations by the Soviet Union to withdraw the strategic weapons it had sent to defend the Republic of Cuba? Those are, in essence, the ideas I presented.

Now, U Thant said some interesting things. U Thant said: My colleagues and I—I am also reading the essential parts—think that the blockade was illegal, that no state can permit a blockade that is not only military, or even an economic one. [sentence as heard] This is using the imposition of a great power's force against a small country. I also told him that the air reconnaissance that was being done over Cuba was illegal and inadmissible. These three things—economic embargo, military blockade, and air reconnaissance—are illegal.

Here he said: The Pentagon, the Central Intelligence Agency ....[rephrases] There are three forces in the United States: the Pentagon, the CIA, and the State Department. This will not please the man who looks like Hemingway much. [referring to Ray Cline] U Thant said: In my opinion, the Pentagon and the CIA have more power than the State Department. Ah, this will not please [Edwin] Martin much. [laughter] If the CIA and the Pentagon continue to have that power, I see the future of the world very black. That is what U Thant said. Well, I hope they do not have any monument to U Thant there in the United States. Now they will take it away [chuckles] with a crane. [laughter]

[Continues quoting U Thant] I said to the United States that if they do anything drastic, I would not only report them to the Security Council but would accuse the United States in the Security Council. Even though the United States has the vote and the veto, there can still be a moral sanction. I also told them I would resign my post, because if the United Nations cannot stop a great power in an attack against a small country, I do not want to be the secretary general. I warned them that they should not make any attack on Cuba, because that would be the end of the United Nations. My aim is to achieve peace and ensure the continuation of the United Nations.

He said: I am thinking about the first proposal by Khrushchev about the dismantling and inspection accepted by the Soviet Union. Since Your Excellency considers that the Soviet Union was referring to having the inspections performed outside Cuba, I believe this might create some division or misunderstanding between the Soviet Union and Cuba. That is what he said. There are other things of interest in my opinion but in essence, that is what U Thant said. That was on 31 October, that meeting, on 30 and 31 October.

Then Mikoyan visited two or three days after U Thant. Do you remember, Aleksandr? [Alekseyev answers: "4 November; he arrived in Cuba on 2 November, and the first meeting was on 4 November."] He arrived in Cuba on 2 November. The lengthy negotiations or talks with Mikoyan began, based on the positions taken by the Soviet Union and the positions we had taken. Those negotiations were very difficult, because first we talked about the missiles. Then we talked about the IL-28's.

DOCUMENT 83: Foreign Broadcast Information Service, transcript of Fidel Castro's remarks at the Havana conference on the Cuban missile crisis, January 11, 1992.

PAGE 13 OF 16

Then we talked about other things. It seemed interminable. I have already talked about this here. I should not repeat it.

A really unpleasant incident happened when the talks with Mikoyan started. The news came from the USSR that his wife had died. They gave him the choice of returning to the USSR, and he really made a very generous gesture. He decided, well.... [rephrases] He received the news. Of course, it had a great impact on him. They had been very close, married for a long time. Mikoyan cried, but he decided to stay in the country and continue the talks instead of returning to the USSR. It was also very hard for us to receive that news, at a time when we were beginning talks that were not easy at all.

He stayed about three weeks, and we discussed this. As you have seen and heard in recent days—at least many of us have, some of you surely knew it before—the letters have been published. [speaking to unidentified aide] See if you can help me find the letters. I had them right here. Here they are. Here are the letters in translation. On the first day, I was able to reach my goal of reading 85 pages of them, early in the morning. That is why I was a little sleepy here in the meeting yesterday. These letters were really very interesting. Here you can see when the problem of the IL-28's came up, the discussions.

With the same honesty I have spoken with up to now I should say that I see a difference here between Kennedy's and Khrushchev's conduct, in this correspondence. It must be said that Khrushchev conducted himself very well, with great dignity. You can see that he is anxious to solve not only these problems but also many others. I see here a noble, thoughtful, capable, intelligent Khrushchev, who uses profound arguments, not just with respect to the crisis, but also with respect to world peace.

In contrast, we can see a harsh Kennedy. The same nobility is not reflected in these letters in Kennedy's case. You can see that he squeezes Khrushchev, squeezes him more and more, and the further away the missiles were, the more he squeezed him. That is what I see in these letters. It is not the same thing to discuss when the missiles were here as when they have been taken out. So Kennedy's language became harsher as the ships left for the Soviet Union with the missiles. He presented new demands and talked about verification. He talked about continued guarantees. He insisted on this. You can see that he was reluctant to formalize the pledges he had made to Khrushchev. He used very subtle words. He said one thing in one place, and then tried to soften it with other words elsewhere. You can see Khrushchev struggling so that the pledges Kennedy had been made would be fulfilled and formalized.

It is unquestionable that Khrushchev's position was much weaker at that stage, from an objective point of view, especially after 20 November, when the missiles

had been withdrawn. Naturally, we did not know anything about this exchange. We did not have any information about this. But we still had a problem. The days went by, and the planes continued their overflights. That was intolerable. We finally informed Mikoyan that we had no alternative but to fire at the planes flying at low altitudes. We issued the appropriate instructions about this matter.

I knew that there would be a U.S. counterattack. Since I was responsible for that order, I went to one of our air bases and spent the morning there. That was the next day; I do not know if it was on 16 November. I believed it was a moral duty if there was a reprisal against that base.... [rephrases] The planes passed over that base at 1000, and I considered that I had a moral duty, not to commit suicide there, but to be with the troops that were going to fire. I went to one place, but many places were going to fire.

We had warned Mikoyan about 24 hours before—24 or 48 hours before—so that he could inform the Soviets. We were waiting for the planes at that antiaircraft battery that morning, and fortunately the planes did not come. That was the best thing that could have happened, right? For the planes not to fly, because they would have been shot down. Because there were so many batteries there that it would have been impossible not to hit the planes. Even though our gunners were not very expert, the planes had been flying very low and relatively slowly, at the minimum possible speed and at about 100 meters altitude. They would come by like that. But they did not come.

I know that in one of the letters—the one on 15 November—Kennedy told Khrushchev that.... [changes thought] because he mentions me every once in a while, always trying to cause some friction between the Soviets and us, or make the Soviets punish us in some way. He would say that Castro was the bad guy, and wanted war or who knows what. He said that he had received news that we were going to fire against the low-altitude overflights. It is possible.... [rephrases] I imagine that Mikoyan in some way communicated to someone, through some channel, that we had decided to fire. It seemed stupid to me that the United States would continue with those flights because Kennedy really was so pleased with the results he had obtained that he had no reason to complicate that whole situation by doing something that made no sense at that time, except to humiliate us.

There were people among the antiaircraft troops who made cartoons, drawing spiderwebs and things. The Cubans who were at the antiaircraft batteries had a sense of humor. [unidentified aide hands letter to Castro] Yes? To U Thant? Where? What day was this? On 15 November, a letter from the prime minister [Castro] to Acting UN Secretary General Mr. U Thant says that we will not tolerate further low-altitude overflights over Cuba, since these serve U.S. military plans against the revolution and demoralize our national defense. We

DOCUMENT 83: Foreign Broadcast Information Service, transcript of Fidel Castro's remarks at the Havana conference on the Cuban missile crisis, January 11, 1992.

PAGE 14 OF 16

assert that groups of sabotage and subversion have been introduced into Cuba, which proves the military usefulness of the overflights for the United States.

Yes, we also informed U Thant about this on 15 November. So, fortunately, I think the attitude adopted by the administration was reasonable, not to cause a conflict. They understood that it was unnecessary and senseless, and that our reaction was natural. This might have interrupted the withdrawal of the missiles or something, and made the situation more complicated. So they did not send the flights. They did not authorize the low-altitude overflights any more.

Then they approached the coasts, and there were some enormous exchanges of fire because some came close to the coasts, and all the batteries fired at them when they got near. But, in general, the low-altitude overflights ended by mid-November, and the U-2 remained. People could not see the U-2. We were not in agreement with the U-2 overflights, but we could do nothing about them. It was a long process. Then, they finally turned over to us those antiaircraft batteries when our personnel had learned how to use them. We had to take a lot of boys out of the universities, or recent graduates, to learn to handle all those missiles, which were for targets higher than 1,000 meters. But when the Soviets turned them over to us, they did it on the condition that we not fire at the U-2. We found ourselves in the dilemma of either going without antiaircraft batteries or pledging not to fire at the U-2. We had to promise not to. It was quite a while later when they turned those surface-to-air missiles over to us.

That is the only thing I can say, basically, concerning Cuba in those days. These letters refer to it. Towards the end of the year, things were a little better. In December, things got better. Now, were these the only letters? No, I had three more pieces of paper. That one was on the IL-28's, but we have already talked about that. I think these letters are really very revealing. At that moment.... [rephrases] The circumstances had changed. Khrushchev was one man before the crisis, and a different one afterwards. Kennedy was one man before the crisis, and a different one afterwards. Kennedy behaved with great nobility and elegance and believed what they told him, and Khrushchev fed the deception, the theory that there were no offensive weapons. He went along with that game. Afterwards, in the other stage, we can see a very noble, frank, sincere Khrushchev and a harsher Kennedy who, in short, squeezes him—to use an elegant word.

But the effort Khrushchev made was admirable. He behaved with great elegance. He did not make concessions concerning Cuba, in the face of all the.... [changes thought] Except that at one time he said that it was a question of the Spanish character, but he did not say it in pejorative terms, according to what I have read there. On the other hand, he makes a rather rude reference to Eisenhower. That is the only little part of the letter that I do not like. It is not that I am an Eisenhower sympathizer—not at all. We are very far apart ideologically.

But the way he said it, the phrase he used—about an old man who has one foot in the grave should not interfere with our plans—was not very elegant. It was not an elegant way of saying it. Then Kennedy, of course, defends Eisenhower, saying that the two problems have nothing to do with each other.

But I think public knowledge has been enriched with this. Now we have to ask the State Department to continue declassifying things, more letters. Because the one from 1963 is still missing. It may contain interesting things, from what I remember. Let me find the letter. Now, three more months had gone by, and on 31 January—almost four months later, right? November, December, January: three months and a bit—on 31 January 1963, Khrushchev wrote me a lengthy letter, really a wonderful letter. It is 31 pages long. I am not going to read it, of course, but it can be handed out to anyone because it is a beautiful, elegant, friendly, very friendly letter. Some of its paragraphs are almost poetic. It invites me to visit the Soviet Union. He was travelling from Berlin to Moscow by train, where a conference was taking place.

You can see in his letter.... [changes thought] It was written by him, because he was a man who knew how to express himself very well, write very well, and he wrote a persuasive letter. Tempers had been cooling down by then; they had been quite hot. I accepted the trip. You know, I got there by a miracle, because I had to fly in a TU-114 plane. It was a 16-hour flight. I think that is a kind of bombardment in a plane like that. [Words indistinct] I arrived in Murmansk on a direct flight from Havana in 16 hours. That plane had four propellers, and it shook and vibrated, and we had to land blind. It was lucky that Khrushchev, who was very concerned about details, had sent the best pilot in the Soviet Union because he was the only man who would have been able to land in the middle of the mountains in Murmansk with such a fog that you could not see for five meters. On the third try, we finally landed. Mikoyan was waiting for me there in Murmansk with a delegation. I spoke by telephone with Khrushchev for a short time.

That was the first time I visited the Soviet Union. I can say that my part in all this could have ended that day we landed in Murmansk. [chuckles] I said: If this crashes, we will never even know why. I was sitting with the pilots watching the operation. Suddenly I said: I will get out of here. I do not want it to happen that instead of helping, I make things more complicated. I stayed sitting down until that monster landed. It was an enormous plane.

This is how I first visited the USSR.

There is an excellent letter. This is why I said that I know Khrushchev well. It contained outstanding feelings. It was friendly; he was concerned for Cuba. I appreciated this letter very much. Then the invitation to visit the USSR was made. In the USSR, we talked about this, as I have already told you. I had my theory on what the goal was. I was trying to find out what had been discussed, yet

DOCUMENT 83: Foreign Broadcast Information Service, transcript of Fidel Castro's remarks at the Havana conference on the Cuban missile crisis, January 11, 1992.

PAGE 15 OF 16

FBIS-LAT-92-043-S
4 March 1992

CARIBBEAN

25

not once he did talk about the terms, he and all the others, as a rule. I was not able to clarify the issue. But for hours he read many messages to me, messages from President Kennedy, messages sometimes delivered through Robert Kennedy, and other times through Thompson, that is the name I remember. There was a translator, and Khrushchev read and read the letters sent back and forth.

I have read this with great interest to find out if any of the issues touched in the messages were from that trimester, but they were not, they belong to a later period. They probably belong to the first trimester of 1963: January, February, March, and April, the first quarter of the year, because I arrived in the Soviet Union toward the end of April.

Khrushchev was sitting with me in (Savidova), a remote hunting reserve. He liked hunting very much. He tried to do so whenever he had a chance, he did not have much time available, he was a hard worker. We sat in the patio. It was already spring. It was almost spring, and you can be outside with a coat on in spring in the Soviet Union. He kept reading the letters. The messages continued on and on, discussing the security of Cuba.

There was a moment when Khrushchev..... [changes thought] There were two moments of interest to me. There was a moment when Khrushchev was reading and the other man was translating, when there was a phrase in which they said: Something is going to happen, in reference to Cuba. Then when Khrushchev later read his reply, it said—I have not forgotten the phrase, even though it was not recorded—that something is going to happen, something unbelievable. That was the word used by Khrushchev in his reply. Therefore, it seems that, at a certain point, the mood was getting heated again when they told him—regarding Cuba—that something was going to happen, and he says that something is going to happen but it will be something unbelievable. As if to say that there would be a war if it is not fulfilled. [sentence as heard]

You have seen from his letters that he writes with dignity, with elegance but with dignity. I have not forgotten that phrase. Khrushchev kept on reading and reading. There was a moment when I believe that he said something that he did not want me to hear. Anyone can make a mistake, even me, while reading letters. But here no one had highlighted for him the essential ideas, and there was a moment when he read a message from the other side: We have fulfilled all our pledges—take notice of these words—and have withdrawn or are withdrawing, or are going to withdraw the missiles from Turkey and Italy. I remember it well, that he not only said Turkey but also said Italy. I always kept that in my mind. Once I asked the Soviets if in the documents or the papers there was finally something to this effect. I sent a query to Gromyko, since there was a new campaign in the United States because we were going to receive some MiG-23 or some other planes of that kind. They were

always examining to see if 1962 accords were being violated. I was told that the issue of Turkey appeared, but not Italy.

But in that message that Nikita was reading and that the translator was translating it said: We have withdrawn, are withdrawing, are going to withdraw. This refers to the withdrawal of the missiles from Turkey and Italy. I told myself, well, this has not been discussed publicly. This must have been some kind of gift or concession made—maybe in this case by Kennedy—to help Khrushchev. There had been times when Khrushchev had wanted to help Kennedy, but other times he had wanted to hurt him—or did not want to but did anyway—and other times it was Kennedy who had wanted to hurt Khrushchev.

I only know and remember that phrase. When I heard that phrase, it was the last thing that Nikita wanted me to hear, since he knew my way of thinking, and that we were completely against being used as an exchange token. This was contradictory to the theory that the missiles were sent for the defense of Cuba. Withdrawing missiles from Turkey had nothing to do with the defense of Cuba. That is quite clear, it is a matter of simple logic. Cuba was defended by saying: Please, remove the naval base; please, stop the economic blockade and the pirate attacks. Withdrawing missiles from Turkey was in total contradiction to the theory that the essential goal had been the defense of Cuba.

When this was read, I looked at him and said: Nikita, would you please read that part again about the missiles in Turkey and Italy? He laughed that mischievous laugh of his. He laughed, but that was it. I was sure that they were not going to repeat it again because it was like that old phrase about bringing up the issue of the noose in the home of the man who was hung.

There were two points, and this is why I am going to leave it to the researchers to investigate this. We will await with interest the day when this is declassified, now that everything is being declassified, or as it also is called, the deideologizing [chuckles] of international relations. It is better if all these documents come to light once and for all.

Of course, this situation in 1962, despite efforts by both parts, and we also tried to completely overcome the incident, tried to save the relations with the Soviet Union, tried to stop it from getting any more embittered. Yet the 1962 incidents affected for many years the relations between the Soviet Union and Cuba. We are putting all these documents at the disposal of historians and, if you think so, we can make photocopies.

No, this document also. [speaking to unidentified aide]

I believe that the text of this accord has never been made public. I do not know if it is of any interest to historians. We can have it typed or make photocopies. What was that? Not typed, photocopies? We will make copies for the historians. This is now declassified.

DOCUMENT 83: Foreign Broadcast Information Service, transcript of Fidel Castro's remarks at the Havana conference on the Cuban missile crisis, January 11, 1992.

PAGE 16 OF 16

You are in charge of providing this. [speaking to unidentified aide]

This letter also, the one sent on the 23d; someone might be interested in it.

Yes. [speaking to unidentified aide]

I do not remember anything else that, in my opinion, might be of concrete and specific interest in relation to the studies that you are conducting. If any more papers or anything else of interest surfaces, we can give them to you. We do not have anything to hide with respect to this whole problem of the October Crisis, and if it can be of use or contribute to clarifying the facts and to drawing the pertinent conclusions. I am not going to draw conclusions here about all this. There is a lot of material to study, to mull over, many things to reflect on, thanks in part to the constructive efforts made by bringing this to light. As a Soviet man once said, never has a problem been so seriously discussed as this one has, from which important lessons can be derived. Thank you very much. [applause]

THE CUBAN MISSILE CRISIS

A CHRONOLOGY OF EVENTS

SOURCE NOTES

This chronology describes key events relating to the Cuban missile crisis. It begins in 1959 and describes the evolution of relations between the United States, the Soviet Union, and Cuba in the period before the missile crisis, focusing particularly on the Soviet military buildup in Cuba during 1962. The chronology also provides a day-by-day (in some cases, hour-by-hour) account of the October missile crisis and the continuing crisis over Soviet IL-28 bombers in Cuba, which extended well into November 1962. Additional entries in the chronology trace the aftermath of the missile crisis with regard to U.S.-Cuban relations.

All times cited in the chronology are Eastern Daylight Time, unless otherwise noted. Square brackets in quoted text indicate either editorial clarifications or sections excised by government declassification reviewers.

Each entry is followed by a citation for its sources. Documents that are included in this reader are cited by number. Documents that appear in the National Security Archive's microfiche collection, The Cuban Missile Crisis, 1962: The Making of U.S. Policy, are cited by document title and date. Books and periodicals are cited in an abbreviated form, often with references to specific sections or pages. A few unpublished sources and documents that do not appear in the document collection are also cited in this manner. For a listing of the abbreviated titles used in this chronology, see the "Abbreviations" section on pages 399–400.

January 1, 1959: Fidel Castro assumes power in Cuba, the culmination of the six-year revolution that toppled the government of General Fulgencio Batista.

October 28, 1959: Turkey and the United States sign an agreement for the deployment of fifteen nuclear-tipped Jupiter missiles in Turkey. June 1, 1961, is tentatively set as a target installation date for the first launch site. (*Jupiters in Italy and Turkey*, 10/22/62)

February 4–13, 1960: Soviet First Deputy Prime Minister Anastas Mikoyan visits Cuba and attends the opening of a Soviet trade exhibit in Havana. During his trip, Mikoyan negotiates economic and trade agreements that help Fidel Castro wean Cuba away from economic dependence on the United States. (*The Military Buildup in Cuba*, 7/11/61)

May 7, 1960: The Soviet Union and Cuba establish diplomatic relations. (Halperin, p. 77)

July 8, 1960: The United States suspends the Cuban sugar quota, effectively cutting off 80 percent of Cuban exports to the United States. The following day, the Soviet Union agrees to buy sugar previously destined for the U.S. market. On October 6, citing the suspension of the sugar quota, Cuba nationalizes approximately one billion dollars in U.S. private investments on the island. (*NYT*, 8/7/60; Brenner, p. 528)

August 16, 1960: The first assassination plot by the United States against Fidel Castro is initiated when a CIA official is given a box of Castro's favorite cigars and told to poison them. It is unknown whether any attempt was later made to pass the cigars on to Castro. The plan becomes one of at least eight assassination plots against the Cuban leader devised by the U.S. government between 1960 and 1965, according to a 1975 Senate investigation. (*Alleged Assassination Plots Involving Foreign Leaders*, 11/20/75, p. 73)

August 28, 1960: The United States imposes an embargo on trade with Cuba. (Brenner, p. 528)

September 1960: The first large Soviet Bloc arms shipment arrives in Cuba. Soon afterward, Czech and Soviet technicians are reportedly assisting the Cuban military in assembling equipment and installing weapons such as antiaircraft batteries. Soviet Bloc personnel also begin to be employed as military instructors, advisers, and technicians. (*The Military Buildup in Cuba*, 7/11/61)

December 19, 1960: Cuba and the Soviet Union issue a joint communiqué in which Cuba openly aligns itself with the domestic and foreign policies of the Soviet Union and indicates its solidarity with the Sino-Soviet Bloc. (*NYT*, 12/20/60)

January 2, 1961: Soviet Premier Nikita Khrushchev tells a gathering at the Cuban embassy in Moscow: "Alarming news is coming from Cuba at present, news that the most aggressive American monopolists are preparing a direct attack on Cuba. What is more, they are trying to present the case as though rocket bases of the Soviet Union are being set up or are already established in Cuba. It is well known that this is a foul slander. There is no Soviet military base in Cuba." (Abel, p. 15)
January 3, 1961: The United States and Cuba sever diplomatic and consular relations. The United States turns over the handling of its affairs to the Swiss embassy, and the Cuban government refers its affairs to the embassy of Czechoslovakia. (*NYT*, 1/4/61)

January 20, 1961: John F. Kennedy is inaugurated as the thirty-fifth president of the United States.

April 12, 1961: On the eve of the invasion of Cuba at the Bay of Pigs, President Kennedy decides that U.S. armed forces will not take part in the operation. Any conflict that takes place, Kennedy tells his aides in private, will be "between the Cubans themselves." (Sorensen, p. 298)

April 14, 1961: Early in the morning, a group of B-26 bombers piloted by Cuban exiles attack air bases in Cuba. The raid, coordinated by the CIA, is designed to destroy as much of Castro's air power as possible before the scheduled landing of a force of U.S.-trained Cuban exiles. However, to keep the U.S. connection from becoming public, an additional set of airstrikes on Cuban airfields is canceled. (Sorensen, pp. 300-302)

April 17–18, 1961: With U.S. direction, training, and support, a group of about fourteen hundred Cuban émigrés attempt an invasion of Cuba at the Bay of Pigs. Cuban government aircraft that survived the earlier airstrikes are able to pin the invasion force on the beachhead, and without additional supplies of ammunition, the invaders are quickly crushed by Cuban ground forces. Of the anti-Castro émigrés, 114 are killed and 1,189 are captured. In response to the invasion, Fidel Castro orders the arrest of some two hundred thousand suspected dissidents to prevent internal uprisings. (Wyden, p. 303)

April 19, 1961: In a memo for the president, Attorney General Robert Kennedy warns, "if we don't want Russia to set up missile bases in Cuba, we had better decide now what we are willing to do to stop it." Robert Kennedy identifies three possible courses of action: (1) sending American troops into Cuba, a proposal "you [President Kennedy] have rejected...for good and sufficient reasons (although this might have to be reconsidered)"; (2) placing a strict blockade around Cuba; or (3) calling on the Organization of American States (OAS) to prohibit the shipment to Cuba of arms from any outside source. He concludes that "something forceful and determined must be done....The time has come for a showdown for in a year or two years the situation will be vastly worse." (Schlesinger, p. 471)

April 19, 1961: In continuing correspondence with President Kennedy after the Bay of Pigs invasion, Premier Khrushchev assures Kennedy that the Soviet Union "does not seek any advantages or privileges in Cuba. We do not have any bases in Cuba, and we do not intend to establish any." Khrushchev, however, also warns against arming Cuban émigrés for future attacks on Cuba. Such a policy of "unreasonable actions," he writes, "is a slippery and dangerous road which can lead the world to a new global war." (*Soviet Public Statements with Respect to Cuban Security,* 9/10/62)

April 27–28, 1961: While at a Central Treaty Organization (CENTO) meeting in Ankara, Turkey, Secretary of State Dean Rusk privately raises the possibility of withdrawing the U.S. Jupiter missiles from Turkey with Turkish Foreign Minister Salim Sarper. Sarper objects to Rusk's suggestion, pointing out that the Turkish Parliament has just approved appropriations for the missiles and that it would be embarrassing for the Turkish government to inform Parliament that the Jupiters now are to be withdrawn. Upon returning to Washington, D.C., Rusk briefs President Kennedy on his discussion with Sarper, and Kennedy accepts the idea of some delay in removing the Jupiters. (*Recollection by Dean Rusk of Negotiating Channel through Andrew Cordier and Details of Negotiations To Remove Jupiters Prior to Crisis,* 2/25/87)

June 3–4, 1961: President Kennedy meets with Premier Khrushchev in Vienna. On the second day of the summit, Khrushchev delivers an ultimatum on the status of Berlin, a continuing source of tension between the two superpowers. Khrushchev threatens to "normalize" the situation in Berlin (and consequently cut Allied access to West Berlin) if the city's status is not resolved within six months. Kennedy tells reporters after the meeting that Khrushchev's demands had made the prospects for war "very real." (Sorensen, p. 549)

June 13, 1961: General Maxwell Taylor submits a report on U.S. limited war programs that President Kennedy had ordered following the Bay of Pigs invasion. Concluding that there is "no long term living with Castro as a neighbor" and that Cuban subversion "constitutes a real menace" to Latin American nations, Taylor calls for the creation of a new program of action against Cuba, possibly employing the full range of political, military, economic, and psychological tactics. (*The Taylor Report on Limited War Programs,* 6/13/61)

August 12–13, 1961: Soviet forces aid the East Germans in erecting the Berlin Wall. U.S.-Soviet tensions over the Berlin situation flare up throughout this period, culminating in a sixteen-hour confrontation between U.S. and Soviet tanks at the Berlin border on October 27–28. However, the construction of the Berlin Wall staunches the destabilizing flow of East Germans to the West, and Nikita Khrushchev allows his "deadlines" on resolving the Berlin question to pass without further incident. (Betts, pp. 255–57)

September 21, 1961: An interagency report on Soviet nuclear capabilities, National Intelligence Estimate (NIE) 11-8/1-61, is disseminated within the government. The NIE and later intelligence reports show for the first time that the Soviet ICBM program is far behind previous U.S. estimates. Only some ten to twenty-five Soviet ICBMs on launchers are believed to exist, with no major increase in Soviet ICBM strength expected in the near future. (*But Where Did the Missile Gap Go?,* 5/31/63, p. 15)

October 21, 1961: In a major speech cleared by Rusk, Bundy, and President Kennedy, Deputy Secretary of Defense Roswell Gilpatric publicly deflates the "missile gap" hypothesis—the theory that the United States is dangerously behind the Soviet Union in its nuclear capabilities. Gilpatric tells his audience in Hot Springs, Virginia, that the United States actually possessed a substantially larger nuclear arsenal than the Soviet Union. (*Address by Roswell Gilpatric, Deputy Secretary of Defense before the Business Council at the Homestead, Hot Springs, Virginia,* 10/21/61; Hilsman, p. 163)

November 30, 1961: President Kennedy authorizes a major new covert action program aimed at overthrowing the Cuban government. The new program, code-named OPERATION MONGOOSE, will be directed by counterinsurgency specialist Edward G. Lansdale under the guidance of Attorney General Robert Kennedy. A high-level interagency group, the Special Group Augmented (SGA), is created with the sole purpose of overseeing Mongoose. (*The Cuba Project*, 3/2/62; *Alleged Assassination Plots Involving Foreign Leaders*, 11/20/75, pp. 139, 144)

Late 1961 or early 1962: William K. Harvey is put in charge of Task Force W, the CIA unit for OPERATION MONGOOSE. Task Force W operates under guidance from the SGA and subsequently will involve approximately four hundred Americans at CIA headquarters and its Miami station, in addition to about two thousand Cubans, a private navy of speedboats, and an annual budget of some $50 million. Task Force W carries out a wide range of activities, mostly against Cuban ships and aircraft outside Cuba (and non-Cuban ships engaged in Cuban trade), such as contaminating shipments of sugar from Cuba and tampering with industrial products imported into the country. (*Alleged Assassination Plots Involving Foreign Leaders*, 11/20/75, p. 140; Branch)

January 1, 1962: The New Year's Day parade in Cuba provides U.S. intelligence sources with the first reliable intelligence on the extent of Soviet Bloc arms deliveries to Cuba. Aircraft in the possession of the Cuban Revolutionary Air Force are estimated to include around sixty Soviet-built jet fighters, primarily MiG-15 and MiG-17 aircraft with a limited number of somewhat more advanced MiG-19 planes. Small numbers of helicopters and light transport aircraft are also believed to have been provided to Cuba. (*CINCLANT Historical Account of Cuban Crisis*, 4/29/63, pp. 6–8)

January 18, 1962: Edward Lansdale outlines "The Cuba Project," a program under OPERATION MONGOOSE aimed at the overthrow of the Castro government. Thirty-two planning tasks, ranging from sabotage actions to intelligence activities, are assigned to the agencies involved in Mongoose. The program is designed to develop a "strongly motivated political action movement" within Cuba capable of generating a revolt eventually leading to the downfall of the Castro government. Lansdale envisioned that the United States would provide overt support in the final stages of an uprising, including, if necessary, using military force. (*The Cuba Project*, 1/18/62; *Alleged Assassination Plots Involving Foreign Leaders*, 11/20/75, p. 142)

January 19, 1962: A meeting of the SGA is held in Robert Kennedy's office. Notes taken by CIA representative George McManus contain the following passages: "Conclusion Overthrow of Castro is Possible...a solution to the Cuban problem today carried top priority in U.S. Gov[ernment]. No time, money, effort—or manpower is to be spared. Yesterday...the president indicated to [Robert Kennedy] that the final chapter had not been written—it's got to be done and will be done." McManus attributes the phrase "top priority in the U.S. government—no time, money...to be spared" to Attorney General Kennedy. (*Alleged Assassination Plots Involving Foreign Leaders*, 11/20/75, p. 141)

January 22–30, 1962: A conference of the OAS is held in Punta del Este, Uruguay. At the close of the conference on October 30, the foreign ministers from the twenty-one American republics vote to exclude Cuba "from participation in the inter-American system." The measure is approved fourteen-to-one, with six abstentions. Another resolution is also adopted prohibiting OAS members from selling arms to Cuba and setting measures for collective defense against Cuban activities in the hemisphere. (*U.S. Policy toward Cuba and Related Events 1 November 1961 – 15 March 1963*, 3/16/63, pp. 9–10; Sorensen, p. 669–70)

February 1962: The Joint Chiefs of Staff (JCS) establishes a "first priority basis" for the completion of all contingency plans for military action against Cuba. (*USCONARC Participation in the Cuban Crisis*, 10/63, p. 17)

February 20, 1962: Edward Lansdale presents a six-phase schedule for OPERATION MONGOOSE designed to culminate in October 1962 with an "open revolt and overthrow of the Communist regime." The basic plan includes political, psychological, military, sabotage, and intelligence operations as well as proposed "attacks on the cadre of the regime, including key leaders." Lansdale notes that a "vital decision" has not yet been made regarding possible U.S. military actions in support of plans to overthrow Fidel Castro. (*Alleged Assassination Plots Involving Foreign Leaders*, 11/20/75, pp. 143–44)

February 26, 1962: At a meeting of the SGA, the scale of Lansdale's "Cuba Project" is sharply reduced, and Lansdale is directed to develop a detailed plan for an intelligence-gathering program only. On March 1, the SGA confirms that the immediate objective of the program would be intelligence collection and that all other actions would be inconspicuous and consistent with the U.S. overt policy of isolating Castro and neutralizing Cuban influence in the hemisphere. (*Document 6, Guidelines for Operation Mongoose,* 3/14/62; *Alleged Assassination Plots Involving Foreign Leaders*, 11/20/75, p. 145)

March 14, 1962: Guidelines for OPERATION MONGOOSE are approved by the SGA. Drafted by Maxwell Taylor, they note that the United States would attempt to "make maximum use of indigenous resources" in trying to overthrow Fidel Castro but recognize that "final success will require decisive U.S. military intervention." Indigenous resources would act to "prepare and justify this intervention, and thereafter to facilitate and support it." Kennedy is briefed on the guidelines on March 16. (*Document 6, Guidelines for Operation Mongoose*, 3/14/62; *Alleged Assassination Plots Involving Foreign Leaders*, 11/20/75, pp. 145–47, 159)

April 1962: U.S. Jupiter missiles in Turkey become operational. All positions are reported "ready and manned" by U.S. personnel. (*History of the Jupiter Missile System*, 7/27/62)

Late April 1962: While vacationing in the Crimea, across the Black sea from Turkey, Khrushchev reflects on the Turkish missiles and reportedly conceives the idea of deploying similar weapons in Cuba. Soviet sources have identified three reasons that might have led Khrushchev to pursue the idea seriously. The deployment of missiles in Cuba would: (1) perhaps most important, increase Soviet nuclear striking power, which lagged far behind that of the United States; (2) deter the United States from invading Cuba; and (3) psychologically end the double standard by which the United States stationed missiles on the Soviet perimeter but denied the Soviets a reciprocal right.

Upon returning to Moscow, Khrushchev discusses the idea with First Deputy Prime Minister Anastas Mikoyan. Although Mikoyan is opposed, Khrushchev asks a group of his closest advisers, including Frol Kozlov, Commander of the Strategic Rocket Forces (SRF) Sergei Biryuzov, Foreign Minister Andrei Gromyko, and Marshal Malinovsky to evaluate the idea. The group proposes that a mission be sent to Cuba to see if Fidel Castro would agree to the proposed deployment and to determine whether the deployment could be undertaken without being detected by the United States. (Garthoff 1, p. 13)

May 1962: Deliberations regarding the possible installation of missiles in Cuba continue in Moscow. In early May, Khrushchev informs the newly designated ambassador to Cuba, Aleksandr Alekseyev, of the plan. Although Alekseyev expresses concern over the idea (as did Gromyko and Mikoyan at different times), it is decided that Alekseyev and Marshal Biryuzov should secretly travel to Cuba to explore the question with Castro. (See May 30, 1962, entry.)

Following further discussions in May and June, Khrushchev authorizes Soviet military officials to decide independently on the exact composition of nuclear forces to be deployed in Cuba. The military proposes a force of twenty-four medium-range ballistic missile (MRBM) launchers and sixteen intermediate-range (IRBM) launchers; each of the launchers would be equipped with two missiles (one serving as a spare) and a nuclear warhead. Soviet officials also decide that a large contingent of Soviet combat forces should be sent to Cuba. The proposed Soviet contingent includes four elite combat regiments, twenty-four advanced SA-2 surface-to-air missile (SAM) batteries, forty-two MiG-21 interceptors, forty-two IL-28 bombers, twelve Komar-class missile boats, and coastal defense cruise missiles. (Garthoff 1, pp. 12–18)

May 8, 1962: A multiservice military exercise designed to test contingency planning for Cuba begins. The operation, codenamed Whip Lash, concludes on May 18. Another U.S. military exercise in the Caribbean known as Jupiter Springs is planned for sometime in the spring or summer. Soviet and Cuban sources have suggested that the series of U.S. military exercises conducted in the region throughout the year are perceived as additional evidence of U.S. intentions to invade Cuba. (*operation mongoose, 4–10 May*, 5/10/62; Garthoff 1, p. 31)

May 29, 1962: Sharif Rashidov, an alternate member of the Soviet Presidium, arrives in Cuba with a delegation, ostensibly on a ten-day mission to study irrigation problems. The presence of the ambassador-designate in Cuba, Aleksandr Alekseyev, Marshal Biryuzov, and two or three military experts is not known to the United States. Shortly before the departure of the delegation, Premier Khrushchev informs all Presidium members that the Soviet Union plans to deploy nuclear missiles in Cuba and that Biryuzov and Alekseyev will broach the idea with the Cuban government.

On the evening of its arrival, the Soviet delegation meets with Fidel Castro and his brother Raúl, the Cuban minister of defense. Expressing their concern over the possibility of a new U.S. invasion of Cuba, the Soviet officials state that the Soviet Union is prepared to assist Cuba in fortifying its defenses, even to the extent of deploying nuclear missiles on Cuban soil. Castro responds by calling the idea "interesting," but tells the group that he will need to consult with his colleagues before providing a final answer. (Alekseyev, pp. 7–8)

May 30, 1962: After conferring with Raúl Castro, Che Guevara, Osvaldo Dorticos and Blas Roca, Fidel Cas-

tro informs the visiting Soviet officials that Cuba will accept the deployment of nuclear weapons. Since the crisis, Castro and other Cuban sources have suggested that this decision was made not only because the missiles would serve to deter a U.S. invasion but also because the Cuban government wished to shift the "correlation of forces" in favor of socialism. In addition, Havana felt indebted to the Soviet Union for its support of the Cuban revolution.

July 2, 1962: Raúl Castro and a high-level Cuban military delegation arrive in Moscow, where they are met at the airport by Marshal Rodion Malinovsky and Anastas Mikoyan. Nikita Khrushchev subsequently meets with Raúl Castro on July 3 and 8. During these discussions, detailed arrangements are made for the missile deployment. According to the formal agreement, which is renewable every five years, the missiles and their servicing will be completely under the jurisdiction of the Soviet military command. Raúl Castro spends a total of two weeks consulting with Soviet officials before returning to Cuba on July 17. (Alekseyev, p. 9; Medvedev, p. 184; Garthoff 2, p. 67)

July 15, 1962: Around this time, Soviet cargo ships begin moving out of the Black Sea for Cuba with false declarations of their destinations and reporting tonnages well below their capacities. Aerial reconnaissance of the ships in the following months showing them "riding high in the water" would confirm that the vessels carried unusually light cargo, typically a sign that military equipment is being transported. (*The Soviet Bloc Armed Forces and the Cuban Crisis: A Chronology July–November 1962*, 6/18/63, p. 1)

July 17, 1962: Raúl Castro leaves Moscow after two weeks of secret talks with Nikita Khrushchev and other high-ranking Soviet officials on the scheduled deployment of Soviet nuclear missiles in Cuba. (See entry for July 2, 1962, above.) Although aware of the military makeup of the Cuban delegation, the fact that no public communiqué is issued after the visit leads the U.S. intelligence community at first to believe that the mission had failed. Upon his return to Cuba, Raúl Castro tells a gathering that neither internal uprisings nor exile landings are a threat, only a U.S. invasion, which, he said, "we can now repel." (*Forwarding of and Comments on CIA Memo on Soviet Aid to Cuba*, 8/22/62; Allison, p. 48; Garthoff 2, p. 67)

July 25, 1962: Edward Lansdale provides the SGA an assessment of Phase One of OPERATION MONGOOSE. Some successes are reported, such as the infiltration of eleven CIA guerrilla teams into Cuba, including one team in Pinar del Río Province that has grown to as many as 250 men. Nonetheless, Lansdale warns that "time is running out for the U.S. to make a free choice on Cuba." (Document 7, Brig. Gen. Edward Lansdale, *Review of operation mongoose*, 7/25/62)

July 26, 1962: On the ninth anniversary of the 26th of July Movement, Fidel Castro states that "mercenaries" no longer pose a threat to Cuba: President Kennedy had already "made up his mind" to invade Cuba, he asserts, but Cuba has acquired new arms to beat back such a direct attack. (Draper, p. 39; CR, 1/30/63)

August 1962: U.S. intelligence receive several reports of Soviet missiles in Cuba during the month, all of which are either linked to SAM or cruise missiles or shown to be incorrect. After late August, numbers of such reports increase, as do reported sightings of MiG-21s and IL-28s. (*The Cuban Crisis, 1962, ca. 8/22/63*, pp. 10–11)

August 10, 1962: After examining CIA reports on the movement of cargo ships from the Black and Baltic seas to Cuba, CIA Director John McCone dictates a memorandum for the president expressing the belief that Soviet MRBMs are destined for Cuba. McCone's memorandum is sent over the objections of subordinates concerned that McCone has no hard evidence to back up his suspicions. (*Chronology of John McCone's Suspicions on the Military Build-up in Cuba Prior to Kennedy's October 22 Speech*, 11/30/62; *Recollection of Intelligence Prior to the Discovery of Soviet Missiles and of Penkovsky Affair*, n.d.)

August 13, 1962: Aleksandr Alekseyev arrives in Havana to take up his post as the Soviet ambassador to Cuba. Alekseyev delivers to Fidel Castro the text of the agreement governing the missile deployment that Raúl Castro had worked out during his June visit to Moscow. Castro makes a few corrections in the text and gives it to Che Guevara to take to Moscow in late August. The text calls for "taking measures to assure the mutual defense in the face of possible aggression against the Republic of Cuba" (see August 27, entry). (*The Soviet Bloc Armed Forces and the Cuban Crisis: A Chronology July–November 1962*, 6/18/63, p. 6; Alekseyev, p. 10; *Draft Agreement between the Government of the Republic of Cuba and the Government of the Union of Soviet Socialist Republics on military cooperation for the defense of the national territory of Cuba in the event of aggression*)

August 17, 1962: On the basis of additional information, CIA Director John McCone states at a high-level meeting that circumstantial evidence suggests that the Soviet Union is constructing offensive missile installations in Cuba. Dean Rusk and Secretary of Defense Robert McNamara disagree with McCone, arguing that the buildup is purely defensive. (*Chronology of John McCone's Suspicions on the Military Build-up in Cuba Prior to Kennedy's October 22 Speech*, 11/30/62)

August 20, 1962: Maxwell Taylor, the chairman of the SGA, informs President Kennedy in a memo that the SGA sees no likelihood that the Castro government can be overthrown without direct U.S. military intervention. Taylor reports that the SGA recommends a more aggressive OPERATION MONGOOSE program. Kennedy authorizes the development of aggressive plans aimed at ousting Castro, but specifies that no overt U.S. military involvement should be made part of those plans (see entry for August 23, 1962, below). (*Alleged Assassination Plots Involving Foreign Leaders*, 11/20/75, p. 147)

August 23, 1962: President Kennedy calls a meeting of the National Security Council (NSC) to air John McCone's concerns that Soviet missiles were in the process of being introduced into Cuba. Although Dean Rusk and Robert McNamara argue against Mc-

Cone's interpretation of the military buildup in Cuba, Kennedy concludes the meeting by saying that a contingency plan to deal with a situation in which Soviet nuclear missiles are deployed in Cuba should be drawn up.

Kennedy's instructions are formalized in National Security Action Memorandum (NSAM) 181, issued that same day. Kennedy directs that several additional actions and studies to be undertaken "in light of the evidence of new bloc activity in Cuba." Papers are to consider the pros and cons of a statement warning against the deployment of any nuclear weapons in Cuba; the psychological, political, and military effect of such a deployment; and the military options that might be exercised by the United States to eliminate such a threat. In addition, Kennedy requests that the Defense Department investigate what actions could be taken to remove U.S. Jupiter nuclear missiles from Turkey. With regard to Mongoose, Kennedy orders that "Plan B Plus," a program aimed at overthrowing Castro without overtly employing the U.S. military, be developed "with all possible speed." (*Document 12, National Security Action Memorandum 181, on Actions and Studies in Response to New Soviet Bloc Activity in Cuba*, 8/23/62; *Recollection of Intelligence Prior to the Discovery of Soviet Missiles and of Penkovsky Affair*, n.d.; *Chronology of John McCone's Suspicions on the Military Build-up in Cuba Prior to Kennedy's October 22 Speech*, 11/30/62)

August 26, 1962: Che Guevara, Cuba's Minister of Industries, and Emilio Aragonés Navarro, a close associate of Fidel Castro, arrive in the Soviet Union. On August 30, Guevara and Aragonés meet with Nikita Khrushchev at his dacha in the Crimea, where Guevara delivers Castro's amendments to the Soviet-Cuban agreement governing the deployment of missiles in Cuba. Although Guevara urges Khrushchev to announce the missile deployment publicly, the Soviet premier declines to do so. The agreement is never signed by Khrushchev, possibly to preclude the Cuban government from leaking it. Following additional talks in Prague, Guevara and Aragonés return to Cuba on September 6. (*Evidence of Soviet Military Commitment To Defend Cuba*, 10/19/62; *Visit to the Soviet Union by Che Guevara and Emilio Aragonés*, 8/31/62; Alekseyev, pp. 9–10; Garthoff 1, p. 25)

August 29, 1962: A high-altitude U-2 surveillance flight provides conclusive evidence of the existence of SA-2 SAM missile sites at eight different locations in Cuba. Additional reconnaissance shortly thereafter also positively identifies coastal defense cruise missile installations for the first time. However, U-2 photography of the area around San Cristóbal, Cuba, where the first nuclear missile sites are later detected, reveals no evidence of construction at this time. (*CINCLANT Historical Account of Cuban Crisis*, 4/29/63, pp. 7–8; *Interim Report by the Preparedness Investigating Subcommittee on the Cuban Military Buildup*, 5/9/63, p. 6; *The Soviet Bloc Armed Forces and the Cuban Crisis: A Chronology July–November 1962*, 6/18/63, p. 7)

August 29, 1962: At a news conference, President Kennedy tells reporters: "I'm not for invading Cuba at this time…an action like that…could lead to very serious consequences for many people." Kennedy repeats that he has seen no evidence that Soviet troops were stationed in Cuba and stated that there was "no information as yet" regarding the possible presence of air defense missiles in Cuba. (*President's News Conference of August 29, 1962*, 8/29/62)

August 31, 1962: President Kennedy is informed that the August 29 U-2 mission has confirmed the presence of SAM batteries in Cuba. (Sorensen, p. 670)

August 31, 1962: Senator Kenneth Keating tells the U.S. Senate that there is evidence of Soviet "rocket installations in Cuba." Keating urges President Kennedy to take action and proposes that the OAS send an investigative team to Cuba. Although Keating's sources of information remain unclear, it appears that he simply made firm declarations based on rumors and reports that U.S. intelligence officials consider too "soft" to be definitive. (*Soviet Activities in Cuba*, 8/31/62; Paterson 1, p. 98)

First week of September 1962: Soviet troops belonging to four elite armored brigades are believed to have begun arriving in Cuba at this time. Troops belonging to the combat groups continue to embark through the second week of October. However, U.S. intelligence does not recognize the existence of the organized combat units until the middle of the missile crisis, on October 25 (see entry for that date). (*The Soviet Bloc Armed Forces and the Cuban Crisis: A Chronology July–November 1962,* 6/18/63, p. 13)

September 3, 1962: At President Kennedy's request, senior State Department official Walt Rostow submits his assessment of the Soviet military buildup. According to Rostow, while the SAMs do not pose a threat to U.S national security, a "line should be drawn at the installation in Cuba or in Cuban waters of nuclear weapons or delivery vehicles...." Rostow recommends that current OPERATION MONGOOSE activities be intensified but also suggests studying the possibility of having independent anti-Castro groups oust Castro with minimal U.S. assistance. (Document 14, *W. W. Rostow's Memorandum to the President, Assessing Soviet Military Aid to Cuba,* 9/3/62)

September 4, 1962: Following a discussion between President Kennedy, Dean Rusk, and Robert McNamara, during which they review evidence that SAM sites and possibly a submarine base are under construction in Cuba, Attorney General Robert Kennedy meets with Soviet Ambassador Anatoly Dobrynin. Dobrynin tells the attorney general that he has been instructed by Premier Khrushchev to assure President Kennedy that there would be no surface-to-surface missiles or offensive weapons placed in Cuba. After his meeting with Dobrynin, Robert Kennedy relates the conversation to the president and suggests issuing a statement making it clear that the United States will not tolerate the introduction of offensive weapons into Cuba. (Kennedy, pp. 24–26)

September 4, 1962: President Kennedy releases a statement revealing that SAMs and substantially more military personnel than previously estimated have been detected in Cuba. Kennedy also declares:

"There is no evidence of any organized combat force in Cuba from any Soviet Bloc country; of military bases provided to Russia; of a violation of the 1934 treaty relating to Guantánamo; of the presence of offensive ground-to-ground missiles; or of other significant offensive capability....Were it otherwise the gravest issues would arise." (*President Kennedy's Statement on Soviet Military Shipments to Cuba,* 9/4/62)

September 7, 1962: Soviet Ambassador Dobrynin assures U.S. Ambassador to the United Nations Adlai Stevenson that "only defensive weapons are being supplied" to Cuba. (The Soviet Bloc Armed Forces and the Cuban Crisis: A Chronology July–November 1962, 6/18/63, p. 13)

September 7, 1962: The U.S. Tactical Air Command (TAC) establishes a working group to begin developing plans for a coordinated air attack against Cuba to be launched well before an airborne assault and amphibious landing. Joint Chiefs of Staff (JCS) military planners have, until then, made no provision for such an operation. (*The Air Force Response to the Cuban Crisis 14 October–November 1962,* 1/63)

September 11, 1962: TASS releases an authorized Soviet government statement condemning U.S. overseas bases and denying any intention of introducing offensive weapons into Cuba. The statement declares: "The arms and military equipment sent to Cuba are intended solely for defensive purposes.... [T]here is no need for the Soviet Union to set up in any other country—Cuba for instance—the weapons it has for repelling aggression, for a retaliatory blow." (*Soviet Statement on U.S. Provocations,* 9/11/62)

September 13, 1962: President Kennedy, speaking at a news conference, states that Fidel Castro, "in a frantic effort to bolster his regime," is attempting to "arouse the Cuban people by charges of an imminent American invasion." The president reiterates that new movements of Soviet technical and military personnel to Cuba do not constitute a serious threat and that "unilateral military intervention on the part of the

United States cannot currently be either required or justified." Nevertheless, he again warns that if Cuba "should ever attempt to export its aggressive purposes by force...or become an offensive military base of significant capacity for the Soviet Union, then this country will do whatever must be done to protect its own security and that of its allies." (*The President's News Conference of September 13, 1962, 9/13/62*)

September 15, 1962: The *Poltava*, a Soviet large-hatch cargo ship, docks at the port of Mariel, Cuba, apparently carrying the first MRBMs to be deployed. U.S. intelligence sources report what appears to be unloading of MRBMs at that port September 15–17 and the movement of a convoy of at least eight MRBMs to San Cristóbal, where the first missile site is constructed. (*The Soviet Bloc Armed Forces and the Cuban Crisis: A Chronology July–November 1962*, 6/18/63, p. 15; Allyn, p. 152)

September 19, 1962: The United States Intelligence Board (USIB) approves a report on the Soviet arms buildup in Cuba. Its assessment, Special National Intelligence Estimate (SNIE) 85-3-62, states that some intelligence indicates the ongoing deployment of nuclear missiles to Cuba. In particular, the report notes: (1) two large-hatch Soviet lumber ships, the *Omsk* and the *Poltava*, had been sighted "riding high in the water," suggesting that they carried military cargo; (2) intelligence accounts of sightings of missiles and a report that Fidel Castro's private pilot, after a night of drinking in Havana, had boasted, "We will fight to the death and perhaps we can win because we have everything, including atomic weapons"; and (3) evidence of the ongoing construction of elaborate SA-2 air defense systems.

The report asserts that the Soviet Union "could derive considerable military advantage from the establishment of Soviet medium and intermediate range ballistic missiles in Cuba...." However, it concludes that "the establishment on Cuban soil of Soviet nuclear striking forces which could be used against the U.S. would be incompatible with Soviet policy as we presently estimate it...[and the Soviets] would almost certainly estimate that this could not be done without

provoking a dangerous U.S. reaction." (Document 13, *CIA National Intelligence Estimate, The Military Buildup in Cuba*, 9/19/62)

September 20, 1962: A Senate resolution on Cuba sanctioning the use of force, if necessary, to curb Cuban aggression and subversion in the western hemisphere, passes the Senate by a vote of eighty-six to one. The resolution states that the United States is determined "to prevent the creation or use of an externally supported offensive military capability endangering the security of the U.S." and to "support the aspirations of the Cuban people for a return to self-determination."

In the House of Representatives, a foreign aid appropriations bill is approved with three amendments designed to cut off aid to any country permitting the use of its merchant ships to transport arms or goods of any kind to Cuba. (*Joint [Congressional] Resolution Expressing the Determination of the United States with respect to the Situation in Cuba*, 10/3/62; *CR*, 1/31/63)

September 21, 1962: In a speech to the U.N. General Assembly, Soviet Foreign Minister Andrei Gromyko charges the United States with whipping up "war hysteria" and threatening to invade Cuba. Gromyko states that "any sober-minded man knows that Cuba is not...building up her forces to such a degree that she can pose a threat to the United States or...to any state of the Western Hemisphere." Gromyko further warns that any U.S. attack on Cuba or on Cuba-bound shipping would mean war. (*Statement by Andrei Gromyko before the U.N. General Assembly Including Comments on U.S. Policy toward Cuba*, 9/21/62)

September 27, 1962: The plan for a coordinated tactical air attack on Cuba in advance of an airborne assault and amphibious landing is presented to Curtis LeMay, the Air Force chief of staff. The concept is approved and October 20, is set as the date when all preparations needed to implement such an attack should be completed. (*The Air Force Response to the Cuban Crisis 14 October–24 November 1962*, 1/63, Tab B-2)

September 28, 1962: Navy air reconnaissance aircraft observing Cuba-bound ships photograph ten large shipping crates on the decks of the Soviet vessel *Kasimov.* After studying the size and configuration of the crates, photoanalysts determine that the containers hold Soviet IL-28 light bomber aircraft. The IL-28s are over twelve years old and have been removed almost entirely from the Soviet Air Force in 1960. Although technically capable of carrying nuclear payloads, the aircraft have never been given a nuclear delivery role. (*The Soviet Bloc Armed Forces and the Cuban Crisis: A Chronology July–November 1962,* 6/18/63, p. 16; *Interim Report by the Preparedness Investigating Subcommittee on the Cuban Military Buildup,* 5/9/63, p. 7; *Department of Defense Press Conference of Robert McNamara,* 2/28/63, p. N-1; Garthoff 1, p. 104)

October 1, 1962: Secretary McNamara meets with the JCS for a briefing on the latest intelligence on Cuba and to discuss intensified Cuban contingency planning. Defense Intelligence Agency analysts inform the group that some intelligence points to the possibility that MRBMs have been positioned in Pinar del Río Province. After the meeting, Admiral Robert Dennison, commander-in-chief of the U.S. Atlantic Command (CINCLANT), is directed by McNamara "to be prepared to institute a blockade against Cuba." The commanders-in-chief of the U.S. Navy and the U.S. Air Force under the Atlantic Command are also directed to preposition military equipment and weapons needed to execute the airstrike plan. (*US-CONARC Participation in the Cuban Crisis,* 10/63, p. 8; *CINCLANT Historical Account of Cuban Crisis,* 4/29/63, p. 39; *Department of Defense Operations during the Cuban Missile Crisis,* 2/12/63, p. 2)

October 2, 1962: As a result of his meeting with the JCS the previous day, Robert McNamara sends a memo to the JCS outlining six circumstances in which military action against Cuba may be necessary:

a. Soviet action against Western rights in Berlin....
b. Evidence that the Castro regime has permit-

ted the positioning of bloc offensive weapons on Cuban soil or in Cuban harbors.
c. An attack against the Guantánamo Naval Base or against U.S. planes or vessels outside Cuban territorial air space or waters.
d. A substantial popular uprising in Cuba, the leaders of which request assistance....
e. Cuban armed assistance to subversion in other parts of the Western Hemisphere.
f. A decision by the President that the affairs in Cuba have reached a point inconsistent with continuing U.S. national security.

McNamara asks that future military planning cover a variety of these contingencies, and place particular emphasis on plans that would assure that Fidel Castro is removed from power. (*CINCLANT Historical Account of Cuban Crisis,* 4/29/63, pp. 41–42; Johns, pp. 81–82)

October 4, 1962: The SGA meets to discuss the progress of OPERATION MONGOOSE. According to minutes of the meeting, Robert Kennedy states that the president was "concerned about progress on the MONGOOSE program" and believed that "more priority should be given to trying to mount sabotage operations." The attorney general also expresses the president's "concern over [the] developing situation," and urges that "massive activity" be undertaken within the MONGOOSE framework. The group agrees that plans for the mining of Cuban harbors and for capturing Cuban forces for interrogation should be considered. (*Memorandum of Mongoose Meeting Held on Thursday, October 4, 1962,* 10/4/62; *Alleged Assassination Plots Involving Foreign Leaders,* 11/20/75, p. 147)

October 6, 1962: CINCLANT directs increased readiness to execute an invasion of Cuba. On October 1, CINCLANT orders military units to increase their readiness posture to execute Oplan 312, the airstrike on Cuba. With the new orders, the prepositioning of troops, aircraft, ships, and other equipment and supplies are directed to increase readiness to follow an airstrike with a full invasion of the island using one of two U.S. invasion plans known as Oplan 314 and

Oplan 316. (*CINCLANT Historical Account of Cuban Crisis*, 4/29/63, p. 40)

October 8, 1962: Cuban President Dorticós, addressing the U.N. General Assembly, calls upon the United Nations to condemn the U.S. trade embargo against Cuba. Near the end of his address, Dorticós declares: "If...we are attacked, we will defend ourselves. I repeat, we have sufficient means with which to defend ourselves; we have indeed our inevitable weapons, the weapons which we would have preferred not to acquire and which we do not wish to employ." The speech is interrupted four times by anti-Castro demonstrators. (*Address by H.E. Dr. Osvaldo Dorticós, President of the Republic of Cuba*, 10/8/62; Szulc, p. 646)

October 13, 1962: State Department Ambassador-at-Large Chester Bowles has a long conversation with Soviet Ambassador Dobrynin. Bowles, after having been briefed by Thomas Hughes of the State Department Bureau of Intelligence and Research, tells Dobrynin that the United States "had some evidence" indicating that Soviet nuclear missiles were in Cuba. Dobrynin, who had not been told of the missile deployment by the Kremlin, repeatedly denies that the Soviet Union harbored any intention of placing such weapons in Cuba. (*Ambassador Bowles Visit to Nkrumah*, 11/2/62; *Oral History Interview with Chester Bowles by Robert Brooks*, 2/2/65; Hilsman 1, p. 166)

October 14, 1962—early morning: A U-2 aircraft flies over western Cuba from south to north. The reconnaissance mission, piloted by Major Richard Heyser, is the first Strategic Air Command (SAC) mission after authority for the flights is transferred from the CIA to the air force. The photographs obtained by the mission provide the first hard evidence of MRBM sites in Cuba. (Bundy, p. 301)

October 15, 1962—morning: Quick readout teams at the National Photographic Interpretation Center (NPIC) in Washington analyze photos taken by Richard Heyser's U-2 mission. Late in the afternoon,

one of the teams finds pictures showing the main components of a Soviet MRBM in a field at San Cristóbal. Analysis of reconnaissance photos during the day also identifies all but one of the remaining twenty-four SAM sites in Cuba. Other photographs of San Julián airfield show that IL-28 light bombers are being uncrated. (*The Soviet Bloc Armed Forces and the Cuban Crisis: A Chronology July–November 1962*, 6/18/63, p. 40; Cline, p. 89; Prados, p. 110)

October 15, 1962—late afternoon: A senior officer at NPIC phones CIA Deputy Director of Intelligence Ray Cline to inform him of the discovery. The officials at NPIC have tried to contact CIA Director McCone but are unable to reach him en route to Los Angeles. Cline requests that NPIC completely recheck the photographs and consult with missile experts outside of the agency. Cline asks that he be called again between 8:00 and 10:00 P.M. to be informed of the results of these additional analyses. (Cline, p. 89)

October 15, 1962—evening: Key Kennedy administration officials are tracked down in Washington and briefed about the discovery of the missiles. National Security Advisor McGeorge Bundy, who is given the news by Ray Cline, decides to wait until morning to alert President Kennedy. Bundy later states that he chose to wait because it was not possible to prepare a presentation information until morning and because he feared that a hastily summoned meeting at night would jeopardize secrecy. (*Explanation of Why McGeorge Bundy Did Not Inform President Kennedy of the Missiles in Cuba until the Morning of October 16*, 3/4/63; Cline, pp. 90–91)

October 15, 1962: The SGA orders the acceleration of covert activities against Cuba. In particular, the group agrees that "considerably more sabotage should be undertaken" and that "all efforts should be made to develop new and imaginative approaches with the possibility of getting rid of the Castro regime." (*Alleged Assassination Plots Involving Foreign Leaders*, 11/20/75, p. 147)

A major U.S. military exercise named PHIBRIGLEX-62 is scheduled to begin. The two-week long maneuver was to have employed twenty thousand Navy personnel and four thousand Marines in an amphibious assault on Puerto Rico's Vieques Island and the overthrow of its imaginary tyrant, "Ortsac"—"Castro" spelled backwards. However, because of the impending crisis, Phibriglex-62 is used primarily as cover for troop and equipment deployments aimed at increasing military readiness for a strike on Cuba. (*CINCLANT Historical Account of Cuban Crisis*, 4/29/63, p. 2; *The Cuban Crisis, 1962*, ca. 8/22/63, pp. 72–73; Allison, p. 47)

October 16, 1962—8:45 A.M.: McGeorge Bundy informs President Kennedy that "hard photographic evidence" has been obtained showing Soviet MRBMs in Cuba. Kennedy immediately calls an 11:45 A.M. meeting and dictates the names of the fourteen or so advisers he wants present. This is the group that becomes known as the "ExComm"—the Executive Committee of the National Security Council. Later that morning, President Kennedy briefs his brother Robert, who expresses surprise at the news. Kennedy also telephones John McCloy, a Republican lawyer who acted as a private adviser to the president. McCloy recommends that the president take forceful action to remove the missiles, even if that involves an airstrike and an invasion. (Abel, pp. 44–45; Issacson, p. 620)

October 16, 1962—11:15 A.M.: President Kennedy confers for half an hour with Charles Bohlen, the former U.S. ambassador to the Soviet Union who has just been appointed ambassador to France. Bohlen later recalls that at this early stage in the crisis, "there seemed to be no doubt in [Kennedy's] mind, and certainly none in mine, that the United States would have to get these bases eliminated…the only question was how it was to be done." Bohlen participates in the first ExComm meeting later that morning but leaves for France on the following day. (*The President's Appointment Book*, ca. 11/22/62; *Interview with Charles E. Bohlen by Arthur Schlesinger: Excerpts on the Cuban Crisis*, 5/21/64)

October 16, 1962—11:50 A.M.: The first meeting of the ExComm convenes. Photographic evidence is presented to the group, including pictures of missile sites under construction with canvas-covered missile trailers. The missiles are initially identified by photoanalysts as nuclear-tipped SS-3s by their length; by evening, the MRBMs are correctly identified as longer range SS-4 missiles. No nuclear warheads are reported seen in the area. CIA photoanalyst Sidney Graybeal informs the group that "we do not believe [the missiles] are ready to fire." The first part of the noon meeting covers questions regarding the validity and certainty of the evidence, Soviet military capabilities in Cuba and what additional U.S. surveillance might be required. Further U-2 flights are ordered, and six U-2 reconnaissance missions are flown during the day. In the freewheeling discussion, participants cover a number of different options for dealing with the Cuban situation. The principle options discussed are: (1) a single, surgical airstrike on the missile bases; (2) an attack on various Cuban facilities; (3) a comprehensive series of attacks and invasion; or (4) a blockade of Cuba. Preliminary discussions lean toward taking some form of military action. As discussions continue on proposals to destroy the missiles by airstrike, Robert Kennedy passes a note to the president: "I now know how Tojo felt when he was planning Pearl Harbor." (*Transcript of October 27 Cuban Missile Crisis ExComm Meetings*, 10/27/62; Kennedy, pp. 30–31)

October 16, 1962—afternoon: McNamara, Deputy Secretary of Defense Roswell Gilpatric, and the JCS hold a luncheon meeting to begin preparing the military for any actions that might be ordered. At the State Department, additional discussions continue with Dean Rusk, Under Secretary of State George Ball, Adlai Stevenson, Assistant Secretary of State for Inter-American Affairs Edwin Martin, Deputy Under Secretary of State U. Alexis Johnson, and State Department Soviet specialist Llewellyn Thompson. (*Chronology of the Cuban Crisis October 15–28, 1962*, 11/2/62, p. 1; Taylor, p. 269)

The USIB meets to examine U-2 photographs and to coordinate intelligence on the crisis. During the meeting, the USIB directs the Guided Missile and Astronautics Intelligence Committee (GMAIC) to prepare an immediate evaluation of the Soviet missile sites. The GMAIC concludes that the missiles are clearly under Soviet control and that there is no evidence that nuclear warheads are present in Cuba. It also concludes that the missile installations thus far identified do not appear to be operational. (*The Cuban Crisis, 1962*, ca. 8/22/63, p. 36)

The SGA convenes in the White House prior to the second ExComm meeting. According to Richard Helms's notes, Robert Kennedy expresses President Kennedy's "general dissatisfaction" with progress under the MONGOOSE program. The SGA discusses but rejects several alternatives for eliminating the newly discovered Soviet missile sites in Cuba, including a proposal to have Cuban émigrés bomb the missile sites. (*Alleged Assassination Plots Involving Foreign Leaders*, 11/20/75, p. 146; Hurwitch, p. 33)

October 16, 1962—6:30 P.M.: At the second ExComm meeting, Marshall Carter states that the missiles could be "fully operational within two weeks," although a single missile might achieve operational capability "much sooner." After the intelligence report is presented, Robert McNamara outlines three broad options for action. The first is "political," involving communications with Fidel Castro and Premier Khrushchev; the second is "part political, part military," involving a blockade of weapons and open surveillance; the third is "military" involving an attack on Cuba and the missile sites. The ExComm members debate, but do not resolve, which option should be used. (Document 16, *Transcript of the Second Executive Committee Meeting*, 10/16/62)

October 16, 1962: Premier Khrushchev receives U.S. Ambassador to the Soviet Union Foy Kohler for a three-hour conversation on a variety of subjects. Khrushchev reassures Kohler that the Cuban fishing port that the Soviet Union has recently agreed to help build will remain entirely nonmilitary. Khrushchev adds that the Cuban government has announced the agreement without consulting Soviet officials, and that when he learned of the leak, he "cursed them and said they should have waited until after the U.S. elec-

tions." Once again, Khrushchev insists that all Soviet activity in Cuba was defensive and sharply criticizes U.S. bases in Turkey and Italy. (*Report on Khrushchev-Kohler Meeting, October 16 (Part IV: Discussion of U-2, Cuban Fishing Port, Nuclear Test Ban and U.S. Elections) In Two Sections*, 10/16/62; Sorensen, p. 691; Hilsman 1, p. 166)

October 17, 1962—morning: Adlai Stevenson writes to President Kennedy that world opinion would equate the U.S. missiles stationed in Turkey with Soviet bases in Cuba. Warning that U.S. officials could not "negotiate with a gun at our head," he states, "I feel you should have made it clear that the existence of nuclear missile bases anywhere is negotiable before we start anything." Stevenson suggests that personal emissaries should be sent to both Fidel Castro and Premier Khrushchev to discuss the situation. (*Document 19, U.N. Ambassador Adlai Stevenson's Opinions Against an Airstrike on Cuba*, 10/17/62)

October 17, 1962—morning: Further debate on the Cuban situation takes place at the State Department. Dean Acheson and John McCone attend discussions for the first time, though President Kennedy and Vice President Johnson are absent. By this time, Robert McNamara has become the strongest proponent of the blockade option. McNamara reports that a "surgical" airstrike option is militarily impractical in the view of the JCS and that any military action would have to include attacks on all military installations in Cuba, eventually leading to an invasion. McNamara urges seeking alternative means of removing the missiles from Cuba before embarking on such a drastic course of action. However, critics of the blockade, led primarily by Dean Acheson, argue that a blockade would have no effect on the missiles already in Cuba. Airstrike proponents also express concern that a U.S. blockade would shift the confrontation from Cuba to the Soviet Union and that Soviet counteractions, including a Berlin blockade, might result. (*Chronology of the Cuban Crisis October 15–28, 1962*, 11/2/62, p. 2; Kennedy, pp. 34–35)

October 17, 1962: Around this time, Georgi Bolshakov, a Soviet embassy official who served as an authoritative back channel for communications between Soviet and U.S. leaders, relays a message from Premier Khrushchev to Attorney General Robert Kennedy that the arms being sent to Cuba are intended only for defensive purposes. Bolshakov had not been told by Khrushchev that the Soviet Union is actually in the process of installing MRBMs and IRBMs in Cuba. By the time Bolshakov's message reaches President Kennedy, he has been fully briefed on the Soviet missile deployment. (Hilsman, p. 166; Kennedy, p. 27; Schlesinger, pp. 499–502)

An SS-5 IRBM site, the first of three to be identified, is detected in Cuba. The SS-5s have ranges of up to 2,200 nautical miles, more than twice the range of the SS-4 MRBMs. The GMAIC estimates that the IRBM sites would not become operational before December but that sixteen and possibly as many as thirty-two MRBMs would be operational in about a week. No SS-5 missiles actually reach Cuba at any time, although this is not completely confirmed by U.S. officials during the crisis. (*The Cuban Crisis, 1962*, ca. 8/22/63, p. 36; *Department of Defense Press Conference of Robert McNamara*, 2/28/63, p. F-2; Garthoff 1, p. 209)

October 18, 1962—11:00 A.M.: The ExComm convenes for further discussions. The JCS, attending part of the meeting, recommends that President Kennedy order an airstrike on the missiles and other key Cuban military installations. However, Robert Kennedy responds by asking whether a surprise air attack would be a morally acceptable course of action. According to Robert Kennedy, the ExComm spent "more time [deliberating] on this moral question during the first five days than on any other single matter." (Kennedy, pp. 38–39; Taylor, p. 269)

October 18, 1962—2:30 P.M.: More discussions take place in Dean Rusk's conference room at the State Department. President Kennedy, who does not attend the talks, confers privately with Dean Rusk and Robert McNamara at 3:30 P.M. During the day, Kennedy also meets privately with Dean Acheson for

over an hour. When the president raises his brother's concern over the morality of a "Pearl Harbor in reverse," Acheson reportedly tells Kennedy that he was being "silly" and that it was "unworthy of [him] to talk that way." Acheson again voices his opinion that the surgical airstrike is the best U.S. option. Acheson, however, is in the minority in dismissing the Pearl Harbor analogy. Although Paul Nitze also recalls thinking that the analogy was "nonsense," others like George Ball find it persuasive. In some cases, as with Secretary of the Treasury Douglas Dillon, the moral argument becomes the deciding factor behind their support for the blockade. (Blight, pp., 142, 152; Schlesinger, p. 508; Issacson, p. 622)

October 18, 1962—5:00 P.M.: Andrei Gromyko and President Kennedy meet at the White House. Gromyko states that Premier Khrushchev plans to visit the United Nations following the U.S. elections in November and that he believes a meeting with Kennedy at that time would be useful. After Kennedy agrees to meet the Soviet Premier, Gromyko turns the discussion to Cuba, charging that the United States is "pestering" a small country. According to the minutes of the meeting, "Gromyko stated that he was instructed to make it clear...that [Soviet military] assistance, [was] pursued solely for the purpose of contributing to the defense capabilities of Cuba....If it were otherwise, the Soviet Government would never had become involved in rendering such assistance." Kennedy has decided not to discuss U.S. awareness of the missiles with Gromyko. So, without taking exception to Gromyko's claim, Kennedy responds by reading a portion of his September 4 statement warning against the deployment of offensive weapons in Cuba. After a discussion of other issues, the meeting ends at 7:08 P.M. Following the talk with Gromyko, Kennedy directs Llewellyn Thompson to inform Ambassador Dobrynin that a summit would not in fact be appropriate at that time. Kennedy then meets with Robert Lovett, a former government official brought in to give advice in the crisis. Lovett warns that an airstrike would appear to be an excessive first step. He argues that a blockade is a better alternative, although he expresses a preference for blocking the movement of all materials into Cuba except for food and medicine, rather than limiting the quarantine to offensive weapons. (*The Cuban Crisis, 1962*, ca. 8/22/63, pp. 56-58; *Memoranda of Conversations on Kennedy-Gromyko Meeting [in Four Parts]*, 10/18/62; Bundy, p. 399; Garthoff 1, p. 48)

October 18, 1962—9:00 P.M.: Meeting at the White House, the ExComm presents its recommendations to President Kennedy. By this time, most members of the committee support the blockade option. As the meeting progresses however, individual opinions begin to shift and the consensus behind the blockade breaks down. Kennedy directs the group to continue its deliberations. (Kennedy, pp. 43-44)

October 18, 1962—evening: Robert Kennedy phones his deputy, Nicholas deB. Katzenbach, to request the preparation of a brief establishing the legal basis for a blockade of Cuba. The legality of a blockade is also examined independently at the State Department by Leonard C. Meeker, the deputy legal adviser. (*NYT*, 11/3/62)

October 18, 1962: The first of a series of daily "Joint Evaluation" intelligence reports is disseminated. The evaluation, the product of collaboration between the Joint Atomic Energy Intelligence Committee (JAEIC) and the Guided Missile and Astronautics Intelligence Committee (GMAIC), states that the MRBMs in Cuba could probably be launched within eighteen hours. (*The Cuban Crisis, 1962*, ca. 8/22/63, pp. 45–46, 53)

October 19, 1962—11:00 A.M.: At the State Department, Nicholas Katzenbach and Leonard Meeker provide the ExComm with their legal opinions regarding a blockade of Cuba. As the meeting progresses, it becomes apparent that sharp disagreements about how the United States should proceed still exist. In order to provide clear options to President Kennedy, the ExComm decides that independent working groups should be established. Separate groups are to develop the blockade and airstrike options, drafting speeches for each plan and outlining

possible contingencies. (*The Cuban Crisis, 1962*, ca. 8/22/63, p. 63; Document 21, *Minutes of October 19, 1962, 11:00 A.M. ExComm Meeting*, 10/19/62; Schlesinger, p. 515)

October 19, 1962—early afternoon: Discussions continue in the ExComm. The papers developed by the separate working groups are exchanged and critiqued. In the course of this process, airstrike proponents begin to shift their support to the blockade option. The airstrike speech is abandoned, and Theodore Sorensen agrees to try to put together a speech for President Kennedy on the blockade. Sorensen completes the speech at 3:00 A.M. the following day. (*Chronology of the Cuban Crisis October 15–28, 1962*, 11/2/62, p. 3; Kennedy, pp. 45–47; Sorensen, pp. 692–93)

October 19, 1962—8:40 P.M.: U. Alexis Johnson and Paul Nitze meet to develop a specific timetable for carrying out all of the diplomatic and military actions required by the airstrike or the blockade plan. The schedule includes raising military alert levels, reinforcing Guantánamo naval base and briefing NATO allies. All timing revolves around the "P Hour"—the time when President Kennedy would address the nation to inform Americans of the crisis. (*Quarantine*, 10/20/62; Blight, p. 145; Johnson, pp. 383–86)

October 19, 1962—evening: Responding to questions about an article by Paul Scott and Robert Allen dealing with Soviet missiles in Cuba, a Defense Department spokesperson replies that the Pentagon has no information indicating that there are missiles in Cuba. Reports that emergency military measures are being implemented are also denied. (*Chronology of the Cuban Crisis October 15–28, 1962*, 11/2/62, p. 4; *The Cuban Crisis, 1962*, ca. 8/22/63, p. 71a)

October 19, 1962: SNIE 11-18-62, entitled "Soviet Reactions to Certain U.S. Courses of Action on Cuba," reports that a direct approach to Premier Khrushchev or Fidel Castro is unlikely to halt the ongoing deployment of missiles to Cuba. On the other hand, a total blockade of Cuba, the SNIE projects, would "almost certainly" lead to "strong direct pressures" elsewhere by the Soviet government. Any form of direct military action against Cuba would result in an even greater chance of Soviet military retaliation. In such a situation, the report notes, there exists "the possibility that the Soviets, under great pressure to respond, would again miscalculate and respond in a way which, through a series of actions and reactions, could escalate to general war...." The SNIE is read by President Kennedy and most of the main policy planners the following day. SNIE 11-19-62, produced on October 20, draws similar conclusions. (*Soviet Reactions to Certain U.S. Courses of Action on Cuba*, 10/19/62; Document 24, *CIA SNIE, Major Consequences of Certain US Courses of Action on Cuba*, 10/20/62; *The Cuban Crisis, 1962*, ca. 8/22/63, p. 68)

October 20, 1962—9:00 A.M.: ExComm meetings continue at the State Department. Final planning for the implementation of a naval blockade is completed, and Theodore Sorensen's draft speech for President Kennedy is amended and approved. As McNamara leaves the conference room, he reportedly phones the Pentagon and orders four tactical squadrons to be readied for a possible airstrike on Cuba. McNamara explains to an official who overhears the conversation, "If the president doesn't accept our recommendation, there won't be time to do it later." (*Chronology of the Cuban Crisis October 15-28, 1962*, 11/2/62, p. 4; *The Cuban Crisis, 1962*, ca. 8/22/63 p. 71b; Abel, p. 93)

October 20, 1962—2:30 P.M.: President Kennedy meets with the full group of planning principals. He notes that the airstrike plan as presented is not a "surgical" strike but a massive military commitment that could involve heavy casualties on all sides. As if to underscore the scale of the proposed U.S. military attack on Cuba, one member of the JCS reportedly suggests the use of nuclear weapons, saying that the Soviet Union would use its nuclear weapons in an attack. President Kennedy directs that attention be focused on implementing the blockade option, calling it the only course of action compatible with American principles. The scenario for the full quarantine operation, covering diplomatic initiatives, public statements,

and military actions, is reviewed and approved. Kennedy's address to the nation is set for October 22, at 7:00 P.M.

Adlai Stevenson, who has flown in from New York, enters the discussion late. He proposes that the quarantine be accompanied by a U.S. proposal for a settlement involving the withdrawal of U.S. missiles from Turkey and the evacuation of Guantánamo. The proposal is promptly attacked by several of the participants who believe it concedes too much. President Kennedy is among those critical of Stevenson's proposal. According to minutes of the meeting, Kennedy "agreed that at an appropriate time we would have to acknowledge that we were willing to take strategic missiles out of Turkey and Italy if this issue was raised by the Russians.... But he was firm in saying we should only make such a proposal in the future." After the meeting adjourns at 5:10 P.M., President Kennedy tells Theodore Sorensen that he is canceling the remainder of his midterm election campaign trip. Kennedy instructs Sorensen to redraft the quarantine speech, although he notes that he would not make a final decision on whether to opt for the quarantine or an airstrike until he has consulted one last time with air force officials the next morning. (*The Cuban Crisis, 1962*, ca. 8/22/63, pp. 74–77; Schlesinger, p. 515; Kennedy, p. 48; Sorensen, pp. 1–3)

October 20, 1962—late night: James Reston, Washington Bureau Chief for the *New York Times*, phones George Ball and McGeorge Bundy to ask why there is such a flurry of activity in Washington. Reston is given a partial briefing on the Cuban situation but is requested to hold the story in the interests of national security. (*The Cuban Crisis, 1962*, ca. 8/22/63, p. 83a)

October 20, 1962: The intelligence community prepares another SNIE reviewing the possible consequences of certain courses of action that the United States could follow with regard to Cuba. The study, numbered SNIE 11-19-62, describes the status of armaments deployed in Cuba. It is estimated that sixteen launchers for SS-4 MRBMs are operational and that these operational missiles could be fired within eight hours of a decision to launch. The inventory of other major Soviet weapons identified in Cuba by the SNIE includes: (a) twenty-two IL-28 jet light bombers; (b) thirty-nine MiG-21 jet fighters; (c) sixty-two less advanced jet fighters; (d) twenty-four 24 SA-2 missile sites; (e) three cruise missile sites for coastal defense; and (f) twelve Komar-class cruise missile patrol boats. (Document 24, *CIA SNIE, Consequences of Certain U.S. Courses of Action on Cuba*, 10/20/62)

A nuclear warhead storage bunker is identified at one of the Cuban MRBM sites for the first time. U.S. intelligence proves unable to establish definitively whether warheads are actually in Cuba at any time, however, and the ExComm believes it prudent simply to assume that they are. Soviet sources have recently suggested that twenty of a planned deployment of forty nuclear warheads reached the islands but that none of the warheads were ever actually "mated" to the missiles. (*Chronology of JCS Decisions Concerning the Cuban Crisis*, 12/21/62; Garthoff 1, pp. 37–42)

October 21, 1962—10:00 A.M.: President Kennedy meets with secretaries Rusk and McNamara. After a brief discussion, Kennedy gives final approval to the quarantine plan. Around this time, White House Press Secretary Pierre Salinger is informed of the crisis for the first time by McGeorge Bundy. (*The Cuban Crisis, 1962*, ca. 8/22/63, pp. 78–79a)

October 21, 1962—11:30 A.M.: At a meeting in the Oval Office, the commander of the Tactical Air Command (TAC), General Walter C. Sweeney, meets with President Kennedy and other top officials to discuss the air attack concept. Sweeney tells the group that to eliminate the missiles in Cuba, TAC believes that additional strikes are required on, at a minimum, Soviet SAM sites and MiG airfields, and that altogether several hundred bombing sorties would be required. After carrying out all these strikes, Sweeney states, he can only guarantee that 90 percent of the Soviet missiles would be destroyed. Although Kennedy has apparently finalized plans for the quarantine before Sweeney's briefing, he nonetheless directs that the military be prepared to carry out an airstrike anytime after the morning of October 22. (Document 25, *Robert McNamara, Notes on Military Briefing for President Kennedy*, 10/21/62)

October 21, 1962—2:30 P.M.: The president convenes a formal meeting of the National Security Council. Admiral George Anderson briefs the gathering on the quarantine plans and procedures that he has drawn up earlier in the day. Anderson explains that each ship approaching the quarantine line will be signaled to stop for boarding and inspection. If the ship does not respond, a shot will be fired across the bow. If there is still no response, a shot will be fired into the rudder to cripple the vessel. President Kennedy expresses concern that such an action might unintentionally destroy the boat, but Anderson reassures the president that it is possible to cripple a ship without sinking it. Kennedy concludes the meeting by observing that the United States might be subjected to threats in the following days but that "the biggest danger lay in taking no action."

Midway through the ExComm session, Kennedy and Robert Lovett leave the room briefly to hold a private conversation. Kennedy asks Lovett if he thinks that Adlai Stevenson is capable of handling negotiations at the United Nations. Lovett replies that he does not think Stevenson is right for the job and recommends that Stevenson be assisted by John McCloy. Kennedy agrees, and Lovett arranges to have McCloy flown from Germany to the United States. (*The Cuban Crisis, 1962*, ca. 8/22/63, p. 81; *Department of Defense Operations during the Cuban Missile Crisis*, 2/12/63, p. 2; Issacson, p. 627; Sagan, p. 112)

October 21, 1962: Despite White House precautions, several newspapers have by this time pieced together most of the details of the crisis. Pierre Salinger notifies President Kennedy in four separate calls during the day that security is crumbling. To keep the story from breaking, Kennedy phones Max Frankel at the *New York Times* and Philip Graham at the *Washington Post* and asks Robert McNamara to call John Hay Whitney, the publisher of the *New York Herald Tribune*. All three agree to hold their stories. (*The Cuban Crisis, 1962*, ca. 8/22/63, pp. 83a–b; Abel, p. 102; Detzer, p. 169)

October 22, 1962—10:55 A.M.: The State Department transmits a special "go" message to most U.S. diplomatic posts abroad instructing envoys to brief foreign heads of government or foreign ministers about the Cuban missile crisis. (*Instructions to Brief Foreign Minister and Chief of State on the Situation in Cuba upon Receipt of the "Go" Signal*, 10/21/62)

October 22, 1962—11:00 A.M.: Dean Acheson briefs Charles de Gaulle and delivers President Kennedy's letter on the Cuban situation. Acheson is not able to provide de Gaulle with a copy of Kennedy's speech because only part of the text has arrived. After Acheson concludes his summary of the contents of the letter, de Gaulle declares, "it is exactly what I would have done....You may tell your President that France will support him." At about the same time, U.S. Ambassador to Great Britain David Bruce briefs Prime Minister Harold Macmillan and Lord Home, the British foreign minister. Bruce also fails to receive a complete copy of Kennedy's speech and briefs MacMillan without it. MacMillan's initial reaction upon seeing the photos of the missiles sites reportedly is to remark: "Now the Americans will realize what we here in England have lived through for the past many years." He hastens to assure Bruce that he will assist and support the United States in any way possible. (*Briefing of Charles de Gaulle by Dean Acheson*, 10/23/62; Abel, p. 112; *Briefing of British Prime Minister Harold MacMillan on the Cuban Situation*, 10/22/62; Cooper)

The ExComm meets with President Kennedy for a brief discussion. The president directs that personal messages be sent to commanders of Jupiters missiles in Italy and Turkey instructing them to destroy or render inoperable the Jupiters if any attempt is made to fire them without Kennedy's authorization. During the meeting, State Department Legal Advisor Abram Chayes successfully suggests changing the legal justification for the blockade presented in Kennedy's speech. Instead of basing the action on the U.N. charter, which assures a country's inherent right of self-defense in case of armed attack, Chayes suggests citing the right of the OAS to take collective measures to protect hemispheric security. In addition, Kennedy accepts Leonard Meeker's suggestion that the limited nature of the "blockade" be stressed by calling it a "quarantine." (*The Cuban Crisis, 1962*, ca. 8/22/63, p. 89; *Chronology of JCS Decisions Concerning the Cuban Crisis*, 12/21/62; Abel, p. 115)

October 22, 1962—12:00 noon: SAC initiates a massive alert of its B-52 nuclear bomber force, guaranteeing that one-eighth of the force is airborne at any given time. B-52 flights begin around the clock, with a new bomber taking off each time another bomber lands. The alert is directed to take place quietly and gradually and to be in full effect by October 23. SAC also begins dispersing 183 B-47 nuclear bombers to thirty-three civilian and military airfields. The Air Defense Command (ADC) also disperses 161 aircraft to sixteen bases in nine hours. For the first time in ADC history, all aircraft are armed with nuclear weapons. (*Chronology of JCS Decisions Concerning the Cuban Crisis*, 12/21/62)

October 22, 1962—2:14 P.M.: The JCS notify the State Department that U.S. military forces worldwide would go to DEFCON 3—an increased alert posture—effective at 7:00 P.M. They also state that Supreme Allied Commander, Europe (SACEUR) Lauris Norstad has been ordered to try to persuade NATO forces to assume a comparable alert posture but that he is authorized to "exercise his discretion in complying with this directive." During the day, Norstad confers with Harold MacMillan, who strongly argues against "mobilizing" European forces. Aware that an alert might weaken European support for the United States—and having received a personal message from President Kennedy stressing the need to keep the alliance together—Norstad decides not to put European forces on higher alert status. (Document 29, *Cable from Joint Chiefs of Staff Announcing DEFCON 3 Military Alert*, 10/22/62; *Text of Message to Lauris Norstad on the Impact of the Cuban Crisis on NATO*, 10/22/62; MacMillan, p. 190)

October 22, 1962—3:00 P.M.: The president reviews the crisis in a formal meeting of the National Security Council. During the meeting, attended by representatives from the Office of Emergency Planning for the first time, Kennedy formally establishes the ExComm. (*National Security Action Memorandum 196: Establishment of an Executive Committee of the National Security Council*, 10/22/62; NYT, 11/1/62)

October 22, 1962—5:00 P.M.: Seventeen congressional leaders from both parties assemble at the White House for a briefing by President Kennedy, Secretary of State Rusk and an intelligence officer. Most express support for Kennedy's blockade plan. Others, however, led by Senators Richard B. Russell and J. William Fulbright, argue that the quarantine will not compel the Soviet Union to remove the missiles from Cuba and that an airstrike or invasion should be employed instead. (*The Cuban Crisis, 1962,* ca. 8/22/63, p. 98; Kennedy, p. 55)

October 22, 1962—6:00 P.M.: Secretary of State Rusk meets with Anatoly Dobrynin. Calling the Soviet missile deployment "a gross error," Rusk hands the Soviet ambassador an advance copy of President Kennedy's speech. Rusk later recalls that Dobrynin, who had never been told by Soviet leaders of the Cuban missile deployment, aged "ten years right in front of my eyes." (*Brief Summary of Dean Rusk-Anatoly Dobrynin Meeting on October 22 Prior to President Kennedy's Speech on the Cuban Crisis,* 10/22/62; *Interview with Sergo Mikoyan on Soviet Views on the Missile Crisis,* 10/13/87; Kennedy, p. 52)

U.S. Ambassador to the Soviet Union Foy Kohler calls the Kremlin to deliver a letter from President Kennedy and the text of the speech. "I must tell you that the United States is determined that this threat to the security of this hemisphere be removed," read the president's letter. (Document 27, *President Kennedy's Letter to Premier Khrushchev,* 10/22/62; *The Cuban Crisis, 1962,* ca. 8/22/63, p. 107)

October 22, 1962—6:26 P.M.: The State Department receives a letter addressed to President Kennedy from British Prime Minister Macmillan. MacMillan warns that Premier Khrushchev, in reaction to the blockade,

> may try to escort his ships into the Caribbean and force you to attack them. This "fire-first" dilemma has always worried us and we have always hoped to impale the Russians on this horn. We must be ready for retaliatory action against Berlin [as well as for] pressure on the weaker parts of the Free World defense system.

President Kennedy phones MacMillan late that evening. During the crisis, the two leaders remain in close contact, speaking with each other over the telephone as often as three times a day. (*The Cuban Crisis, 1962,* ca. 8/22/63, pp. 106–107; MacMillan, p. 94)

October 22, 1962—7:00 P.M.: President Kennedy addresses the nation in a televised seventeen-minute speech. Announcing that "unmistakable evidence" has established the presence of Soviet MRBM and IRBM sites and nuclear capable bombers in Cuba, he states that as one of his "initial steps," a "strict quarantine on all offensive military equipment" is being put into effect. Kennedy further warns the Soviet government that the United States will "regard any nuclear missile launched from Cuba against any nation in the Western Hemisphere as an attack by the Soviet Union on the United States, requiring a full retaliatory response against the Soviet Union." According to dissident Soviet historian Roy Medvedev, Khrushchev responds to the speech by "issuing orders to the captains of Soviet ships…approaching the blockade zone to ignore it and to hold course for the Cuban ports." Khrushchev's order was reportedly reversed at the prompting of Anastas Mikoyan as the Soviet ships approached the quarantine line on the morning of October 24. (Document 28, *Text of President Kennedy's Radio/TV Address to the Nation, October 22, 1962,* 10/22/62; Blight, p. 306)

U.S. military forces worldwide, with the exception of the United States Air Forces in Europe (USAFE), are placed on DEFCON 3. ICBM missile crews are alerted and Polaris nuclear submarines in port are dispatched to preassigned stations at sea. During the president's speech, twenty-two interceptor aircraft go airborne in the event the Cuban government reacted militarily. (*Department of Defense Operations during the Cuban Missile Crisis,* 2/12/63, p. 11; *The Air Force Response to the Cuban Crisis 14 October–24 November 1962,* 1/9/63, pp. 6–7; *The Soviet Bloc Armed Forces and the Cuban Crisis: A Chronology July–November 1962,* 6/18/63, p. 108)

October 22, 1962—7:30 P.M.: Assistant Secretary of State Edwin Martin conducts a further closed-door briefing for Latin American ambassadors at the State Department. At around 8:00 P.M., Secretary Rusk speaks to a meeting of all other ambassadors in Washington. Rusk reportedly tells the group, "I would not be candid and I would not be fair with you if I did not say that we are in as grave a crisis as mankind has been in." (*The Cuban Crisis, 1962*, ca. 8/22/63, pp. 108–109; Abel, p. 125)

October 22, 1962: The first U.S. Jupiter missile site is formally turned over to the Turkish Air Force for maintenance and operation. Although the move is publicized in Turkey and probably detected by Moscow, U.S. decision-makers apparently are not aware of the action. (*Historical Highlights: United States Air Force in Europe 1945–1979*, 11/28/80, p. 61; Garthoff 1, p. 60)

Soviet Colonel Oleg Penkovsky is arrested in the Soviet Union. From April 1961 to the end of August 1962, Penkovsky has been a spy for British and U.S. intelligence services, providing them with material on Soviet military capabilities, including important technical information on Soviet MRBM and ICBM programs. Penkovsky had been given a few telephonic coded signals for use in emergency situations, including one to be used if he is about to be arrested and one to be used in case of imminent war. When he learns he was about to be arrested, Penkovsky apparently chose to use the signal for an imminent Soviet attack. Western intelligence analysts decide, however, not to credit Penkovsky's final signal, and the ExComm is not informed of Penkovsky's arrest or its circumstances. (Garthoff 1, pp. 63–65; Penkovsky, pp. 4–5)

October 23, 1962—8:00 A.M.: TASS begins transmitting a Soviet government statement. At the same time, U.S. Ambassador Foy Kohler is called to the Soviet Foreign Office and given a copy of the statement with a letter from Chairman Khrushchev to President Kennedy. Khrushchev writes:

I must say frankly that the measures indicated in your statement constitute a serious threat to peace and to the security of nations....We reaffirm that the armaments which are in Cuba, re-

gardless of the classification to which they may belong, are intended solely for defensive purposes in order to secure [the] Republic of Cuba against the attack of an aggressor.

I hope that the United States Government will display wisdom and renounce the actions pursued by you, which may lead to catastrophic consequences for world peace.

In his transmittal of the letter, Kohler notes that both the statement and the letter "avoid specific threats and are relatively restrained in tone." (Document 30, *Premier Khrushchev's Message to President Kennedy, October 23, 1962*, 10/23/62)

October 23, 1962—10:00 A.M.: At a meeting of the ExComm, President Kennedy approves plans for signing an official quarantine proclamation. In anticipation of a possible reaction to the blockade from the Soviet government, Kennedy directs John McCone to prepare an analysis of the effects of a comparable blockade on Berlin. The ExComm then examines the question of how the United States will respond if a U-2 aircraft is shot down. If such an event occurs and "evidence of hostile Cuban action" has been established, the ExComm decides that the SAM site responsible for the downing will be attacked and destroyed. Continued harassment of U-2 flights, it is agreed, would probably result in attacks on all SAM sites in Cuba. Following the ExComm meeting, President Kennedy establishes three subcommittees: another on crisis communications, one on advance planning, and the third on Berlin contingencies. (Document 31, McGeorge Bundy, *Executive Committee Minutes, October 23, 1962, 10:00 A.M.*, 10/23/62; *The Cuban Crisis, 1962*, ca. 8/22/63, p. 124; *Notes from 10:00 A.M. ExComm Meeting*, 10/23/62)

October 23, 1962—4:00 P.M.: At a special meeting of the U.N. Security Council, Adlai Stevenson issues a sharply worded statement in which he characterizes Cuba as "an accomplice in the communist enterprise of world domination." Cuban representative Mario García Incháustegui responds by denouncing the quarantine as an "act of war," and Soviet representative Valerian Zorin calls U.S. charges of missiles in Cuba "completely false." Zorin submits a draft resolution demanding an end to U.S. naval activity near Cuba and calling for negotiations to end the crisis. (*The Cuban Crisis, 1962*, ca. 8/22/63, pp. 115–22)

October 23, 1962—5:40 P.M.: Fidel Castro announces a combat alarm, placing the Cuban armed forces on their highest alert. Cuban armed forces subsequently reach a size of 270,000 men, following a massive mobilization effort. (*Statement by Castro Rejecting the Possibility of Inspection and Noting That Cuba Has Taken Measures To Repel a United States Attack*, 10/23/62; Garthoff 1, p. 66)

October 23, 1962—6:00 P.M.: The ExComm holds a brief meeting prior to the president's signing of the quarantine proclamation. The group makes slight revisions to the proclamation and approves a new message to Premier Khrushchev. ExComm members are informed that an "extraordinary number" of coded messages have been sent to Soviet ships on their way to Cuba, although the contents of these messages are not known. In addition, John McCone states that Soviet submarines have unexpectedly been found moving into the Caribbean. According to Robert Kennedy, the president ordered the navy to give "the highest priority to tracking the submarines and to put into effect the greatest possible safety measures to protect our own aircraft carriers and other vessels." (Document 32, *McGeorge Bundy, Executive Committee Record of Action, October 23, 1962, 6:00 P.M.*, 10/23/62; Kennedy, pp. 61–62)

October 23, 1962—6:51 P.M.: A new message from President Kennedy is transmitted to Premier Khrushchev via the U.S. embassy in Moscow. Kennedy, stressing that it is important that both sides "show prudence and do nothing to allow events to make the situation more difficult to control than it already is," asks the Soviet Premier to direct Soviet ships to observe the quarantine zone. (Document 33, *President Kennedy's Letter to Premier Krushchev*, 10/23/62)

October 23, 1962—7:06 P.M.: In a ceremony at the White House, the president signs Proclamation 3504, formally establishing the quarantine. CINCLANT is directed to enforce the blockade beginning at 10:00 the following morning. (*The Cuban Crisis, 1962*, ca. 8/22/63, p. 130)

October 23, 1962—8:35 P.M.: Fidel Castro tells the Cuban public in a ninety-minute television speech that Cuba will never disarm while the United States persists in its policy of aggression and hostility. Castro denies the presence of offensive missiles on Cuban soil but declares: "We will acquire the arms we feel like acquiring and we don't have to give an account to the imperialists." Castro also categorically refuses to allow inspection of Cuban territory, warning that potential inspectors "must come in battle array." (*Statement by Castro Rejecting the Possibility of Inspection and Noting That Cuba Has Taken Measures To Repel a United States Attack*, 10/23/62; OR 10/31/62)

October 23, 1962—evening: At a Soviet embassy reception in Washington, D.C., Lieutenant General Vladimir A. Dubovik appears to suggest that the captains of the Soviet ships heading for Cuba are under orders to defy the blockade. Ambassador Dobrynin, arriving late at the reception, declines to refute Dobovik's comments, saying, "he is a military man, I am not. He is the one who knows what the Navy is going to do, not I." U.S. intelligence also notes a statement by the president of TASS during the day warning that U.S. ships would be sunk if any Soviet ships are attacked. (*The Soviet Bloc Armed Forces and the Cuban Crisis: A Chronology July–November 1962*, 6/18/63, p. 50; Abel, p. 134)

At a debriefing for State Department officials, Edwin Martin emphasizes to U. Alexis Johnson the importance of preventing exile groups from creating an incident in Cuba during the crisis. Martin suggests that Johnson raise the issue of halting covert activities with CIA Director of Plans Richard Helms as well as with the ExComm. The issue of ending OPERATION MONGOOSE activities and checking the action of independent Cuban émigré groups does not, however, appear to have been seriously discussed in the Ex-

Comm. MONGOOSE activities are not in fact shut down until October 30, too late to prevent a sabotage mission against Cuba from being carried out by CIA agents on November 8 (see entries for those dates). (*U. Alexis Johnson's Agenda for the Morning ExComm Meeting*, 10/24/62)

October 23, 1962—9:30 P.M.: Robert Kennedy, at the suggestion of the president, meets with Anatoly Dobrynin in the latter's office at the Soviet embassy. According to his memorandum on the meeting, the attorney general calls the Soviet missile deployment "hypocritical, misleading, and false." Dobrynin tells Kennedy that, as far as he knows, there are still no missiles in Cuba, and said that he is not aware of any change in instructions to captains of Soviet ships steaming toward Cuba. (Kennedy, pp. 65–66; Schlesinger, p. 514)

October 23, 1962—10:15 P.M.: Robert Kennedy relates his conversation with Dobrynin to President Kennedy and British Ambassador David Ormsby-Gore, who is meeting with the president. Robert Kennedy recalled that his brother first talked about the possibility of arranging an immediate summit with Premier Khrushchev, but then dismissed the idea as useless until Khrushchev "first accepted…U.S. determination in this matter." Ambassador Ormsby-Gore then reportedly expressed concern that the naval quarantine line reportedly has been set at eight hundred miles from Cuba. Ormsby-Gore recommends drawing the interception line closer to the island in order to give the Soviet government more time to analyze their position. President Kennedy agrees and calls Secretary of Defense McNamara to shorten the line to five hundred miles. It is unclear whether the eight-hundred-mile line is ever actually planned; diaries from the quarantine commander, Admiral Alfred Ward, show that he considered even a five-hundred-nautical mile line "excessive." (*Personal History or Diary of Vice Admiral Alfred G. Ward, U.S. Navy, While Serving As Commander Second Fleet*, ca. 11/28/62; Kennedy, pp. 66–67)

October 23, 1962: Low-level reconnaissance flights over Cuba begin for the first time, supplementing high-altitude U-2 photoreconnaissance. Navy and air force F-8U and RF-101 aircraft fly some 158 low-level missions between October 23 and November 15. The Soviet Union responds to the low-altitude flights by employing camouflage where possible. (*Department of Defense Press Conference of Robert McNamara*, 2/28/63, p. H-1; *Interim Report by the Preparedness Investigating Subcommittee on the Cuban Military Buildup*, 5/9/63)

Moscow places the armed forces of Warsaw Pact countries on alert. The Soviet government also defers the scheduled release of troops in the Strategic Rocket Forces, air defense units, and the submarine fleet, and it announces that "the battle readiness and vigilance of all troops" has been raised. (*The Soviet Bloc Armed Forces and the Cuban Crisis: A Chronology July–November 1962*, 6/18/63, p. 52)

Gallup poll survey taken on October 23 shows that 84 percent of the U.S. public who know about the Cuban situation favor the blockade while only 4 percent oppose the action. At the same time, roughly one out of every five Americans believe the quarantine will lead to World War III. (Detzer, p. 192)

October 24, 1962—6:00 A.M.: A CIA report based on information as of 6:00 A.M. states that communist reaction to the U.S. quarantine against Cuba has "not gone beyond the highly critical but noncommittal statement" issued by the Soviet government on October 23. Official world reaction is reported to be generally favorable, particularly in Latin America. Surveillance of Cuba indicates continued rapid progress in completion of IRBM and MRBM missile sites. No new offensive missile sites have been discovered, but nuclear storage buildings are being assembled with great speed. (*The Crisis USSR/Cuba: Information as of 0600*, 10/25/62)

October 24, 1962—early morning: Soviet ships en route to Cuba capable of carrying military cargoes appear to have slowed down, altered, or reversed their courses. Sixteen of the nineteen Soviet ships en route to Cuba at the time the naval quarantine is announced, including five large-hatch vessels, reverse course and are returning to the Soviet Union. Only the tanker *Bucharest* continues toward the quarantine line. (*Department of Defense Press Conference of Robert McNamara*, 2/28/63, p. K-1; *Department of Defense Operations during the Cuban Missile Crisis*, 2/12/63, p. 4)

October 24, 1962—morning: William Knox, a U.S. businessman, has a 3 1/4–hour interview with Premier Khrushchev at Khrushchev's request. Khrushchev states that it is now too late for the United States to take over Cuba, and that he will eventually give orders to sink a U.S. vessel enforcing the blockade if Soviet ships are stopped. (*The Soviet Bloc Armed Forces and the Cuban Crisis: A Chronology July–November 1962*, 6/18/63; *Khrushchev's Conversation with Mr. W. E. Knox, President Westinghouse Electric International, Moscow, October 24*, 10/26/62)

October 24, 1962—9:35 A.M.: President Kennedy has a brief conversation with his brother, Robert, during which the president reportedly expresses deep concern that Soviet ships appear ready to challenge the quarantine:

> "It looks really mean, doesn't it? But then, really there was no other choice. If they get this mean in our part of the world, what will they do next?" "I just don't think there was any choice," [Robert Kennedy] said, "and not only that, if you hadn't acted, you would have been impeached." The President thought for a moment and said, "That's what I think—I would have been impeached." (Kennedy, p. 67)

October 24, 1962—10:00 A.M.: The U.S. naval quarantine of Cuba officially goes into effect. (*Interdiction of the Delivery of Offensive Weapons to Cuba*, 10/23/62)

October 24, 1962—10:00 A.M.: The ExComm meets to consider the situation in Cuba. According to Robert Kennedy's memoirs on the crisis, the meeting "seemed the most trying, the most difficult, and the most filled with tension." Robert McNamara tells the group that Soviet ships approaching the quarantine line show no indications of stopping and that two Soviet ships, the *Gagarin* and the *Komiles*, are within a few miles of the line. Naval intelligence then reports that a Soviet submarine has moved into position between the two ships. McNamara states that the aircraft carrier USS *Essex* has been directed to make the first interception, and that antisubmarine tactics, including the use of small explosives, has been ordered to prevent the Soviet submarine from interfering with the blockade.

According to Robert Kennedy, the president asks, "Isn't there some way we can avoid our first exchange with a Russian submarine—almost anything but that?" McNamara replies, "No, there's too much danger to our ships…. Our commanders have been instructed to avoid hostilities if at all possible, but this is what we must be prepared for, and this is what we must expect." At 10:25 A.M., a new intelligence message arrives and John McCone announces: "We have a preliminary report which seems to indicate that some of the Russian ships have stopped dead in the water." Dean Rusk leans over to McGeorge Bundy and says, "We're eyeball to eyeball and I think the other fellow just blinked." President Kennedy directs that no ship be intercepted for at least another hour while clarifying information is sought. (Document 36, *McGeorge Bundy, Executive Committee Record of Action*, 10/25/62; Kennedy, pp. 67-72; Schlesinger, p. 514; Abel, p. 143)

October 24, 1962—11:24 A.M.: A cable drafted by George Ball is transmitted to U.S. Ambassador to Turkey Raymond Hare and U.S. Ambassador to NATO Thomas Finletter, notifying them that the United States is considering a Turkey-for-Cuba missile trade. The cable states that while the comparison of missiles in Turkey with those in Cuba was "refutable," it is nonetheless possible that a negotiated solution to the crisis might "involve dismantling and removal" of the Jupiters. Each diplomat is requested to assess the political consequences of the removal of the Jupiters in a variety of different circumstances. Finletter presents his recommendations on October 25 (see entry for October 25, 1962—6:41

P.M.); Hare responds on October 26 (see entry for October 26, 1962—1:18 P.M.). (*Possible Soviet Reaction to Cuban Quarantine and Request for Assessments on the Possible Dismantling of Jupiter Missiles*, 10/24/62)

October 24, 1962—2:00 P.M.: In his first communication with President Kennedy and Premier Khrushchev during the crisis, U.N. Acting Secretary General U Thant sends identical private appeals to the two leaders, urging that their government "refrain from any action which may aggravate the situation and bring with it the risk of war." U Thant's plea, made at the request of more than forty nonaligned states, calls for the voluntary suspension of arms shipments to Cuba together with the voluntary suspension of the naval quarantine for between two and three weeks. (*U Thant's October 24 Letter to Kennedy Calling for a Temporary Suspension of the Quarantine and of Arms Shipments to Cuba*, 10/24/62)

October 24, 1962—5:15 P.M.: A Defense Department spokesperson announces publicly that some of the Soviet Bloc vessels proceeding toward Cuba appear to have altered their course. (Abel, p. 153)

October 24, 1962—evening: TASS releases an exchange of telegrams between British philosopher and passivist Bertrand Russell and Nikita Khrushchev. In his first public statement since the onset of the crisis, Khrushchev warns in his telegram that if the United States carries out its program of "pirate action," the Soviet Union will have no alternative but to "make use of the means of defense against the aggressor." Khrushchev also proposes a summit meeting with Kennedy to discuss how to end the conflict and "remove the threat of the unleashing of a thermonuclear war." (*Text of Khrushchev's October 24 Message to Bertrand Russell*, 10/24/62; *The Cuban Crisis, 1962*, ca. 8/22/63, p. 139)

October 24, 1962—9:24 P.M.: The State Department receives a letter for President Kennedy from Premier Khrushchev. At 10:52 P.M., the message is read to Kennedy. Khrushchev writes, "if you coolly weigh the situation which has developed, not giving way to pas-

sions, you will understand that the Soviet Union cannot fail to reject the arbitrary demands of the United States." Khrushchev warns that the Soviet Union views the blockade as "an act of aggression" and that, as a consequence, he will not instruct Soviet ships bound for Cuba to observe the quarantine. (Document 34, *Premier Krushchev's Letter to President Kennedy*, 10/24/62; *The Cuban Crisis, 1962*, ca. 8/22/63, p. 139)

October 24, 1962: At the direction of the Joint Chiefs of Staff, SAC increases its alert posture to DEFCON 2 for the first time in history. Thomas Powers, the commander-in-chief of SAC, believed, as he later wrote, that while discreet preparations had been appropriate before, it was now "important for [the Soviets] to know of SAC's readiness." Consequently, Powers decides on his own authority to transmit uncoded messages to SAC commanders noting that SAC plans are well prepared and that the alert process was going smoothly. (*The Air Force Response to the Cuban Crisis 14 October–24 November 1962*, ca. 1/63, pp. 7–8, Tab A2–A3; Garthoff 1, p. 62; Sagan, p. 108)

At the request of President Kennedy, the Defense Department drafts two separate plans to increase civil defense preparations during a possible military engagement with Cuba. The first outlines civil defense measures which could be taken in the vicinity of targets close to Cuba under attack with conventional weapons, while the second suggests measures which could be taken in response to possible nuclear attack within MRBM range.

October 25, 1962—1:45 A.M.: A message from President Kennedy for Premier Khrushchev is transmitted to the U.S. embassy in Moscow. Acknowledging Khrushchev's letter of October 24, Kennedy writes, "I regret very much that you still do not appear to understand what it is that has moved us in this matter...." Kennedy notes that he had received "solemn assurances" that no missiles bases would be established in Cuba. When these assurances proved false, the deployment of missiles in Cuba "required the responses I have announced....I hope that your government will take the necessary action to permit a restoration of the earlier situation." (Document 39, *President Kennedy's Letter to Premier Khrushchev*, 10/25/62)

October 25, 1962—7:15 A.M.: The aircraft carrier USS *Essex* and the destroyer USS *Gearing* hail and attempt to intercept the Soviet tanker *Bucharest*. Since there is no reason to suspect the ship carries contraband, the *Bucharest* is allowed to continue its voyage to Cuba. (*Department of Defense Operations during the Cuban Missile Crisis*, 2/12/63, p. 4)

October 25, 1962—morning: A syndicated column by the influential journalist Walter Lippman proposes a "face-saving" agreement whereby the United States would agree to remove Jupiters from Turkey in return for a Soviet withdrawal of missiles from Cuba. Many in the United States and the Soviet Union mistakenly interpret the proposal as a trial balloon floated by the Kennedy administration. (*Newspaper Column by Walter Lippman Suggesting That Both United States Bases in Turkey and Soviet Bases in Cuba Could Be Dismantled*, 10/25/62)

October 25, 1962—10:00 A.M.: During the morning ExComm meeting, President Kennedy authorizes the development of a program to drop propaganda leaflets over Cuba. Although leaflets are produced and approved by the ExComm, the program, later christened "Bugle Call," is never actually carried out. (*The Cuban Crisis, 1962*, ca. 8/22/63, pp. 149–50)

October 25, 1962—2:19 P.M.: In his reply to U.N. Secretary General U Thant's letter of October 23, President Kennedy avoids responding directly to U Thant's proposal that Soviet arms shipments to Cuba and the U.S. quarantine be suspended for several weeks. Concerned that acceptance of the proposal would allow Soviet military personnel to continue work on the missiles already in Cuba, Kennedy writes only that he appreciated the "spirit" of U Thant's message, adding that Adlai Stevenson is prepared to begin preliminary negotiations regarding the crisis. Also, during the day, Premier Khrushchev writes to U Thant to say that he welcomes and agrees with his proposal. Khrushchev notes that, like U Thant, he considered the Cuban crisis "highly dangerous and requiring…immediate interference by the United Nations." (*Letter from Khrushchev to U Thant Accepting U Thant's October 24 Proposal to Temporarily Suspend the Quarantine and Further Arms Shipments to Cuba*, 10/25/62; *Message from President Kennedy to U Thant Stating That United States Ships Will Avoid Confronting Soviet Vessels If the Quarantine Zone Is Respected*, 10/25/62)

October 25, 1962—2:26 P.M.: At the prompting of the United States, U Thant sends a second message to Premier Khrushchev and President Kennedy asking them to avoid direct confrontations between Soviet and U.S. ships while the quarantine remains in effect. U Thant asks that Soviet ships keep out of the quarantine zone for a limited time and that the United States instruct its vessels "to do everything possible to avoid a direct confrontation with Soviet ships in the next few days." (*Letter from U Thant to Khrushchev Requesting That Soviet Ships Avoid Challenging the United States Quarantine*, 10/25/62; Ball, p. 302)

October 25, 1962—5:00 P.M.: Dean Rusk reports on the political situation during an ExComm meeting. At the close of the meeting, CIA Director McCone indicates that some of the missiles deployed in Cuba are now operational. (Document 38, *McGeorge Bundy, Executive Committee Meeting Record of Action, October 25, 1962, 5:00 P.M.*, 10/25/62; *Nuclear-Free or Missile-Free Zones*, 10/26/62)

October 25, 1962—5:43 P.M.: The commander of U.S. quarantine forces, Admiral Alfred Ward, orders the USS *Kennedy* to proceed toward a Lebanese freighter, the *Marucla*. During the day, the freighter has been selected by President Kennedy as the first ship to be boarded by quarantine forces. The USS Kennedy informs the *Marucla* that night by radio that the ship will be boarded the following morning. (Kennedy, p. 82; Detzer, p. 230)

October 25, 1962—6:41 P.M.: The State Department receives a cable from U.S. Ambassador to NATO Thomas Finletter relaying Ankara's position on the possible withdrawal of Jupiter missiles from Turkey. Finletter reports that the Turkish representative to NATO has made it clear that his government sets "great store" by the Jupiters, and that Turkey regards the missiles "as a symbol of the alliance's determination to use atomic weapons" against either a Soviet conventional or nuclear attack on Turkey. Finletter states his belief that any arrangement that fails to substitute some other form of nuclear capability in Turkey would be rejected by the Turkish government. He adds, "in my opinion we must be most careful in working out any horse trade of this type to be sure it does not set pattern for handling future Russian incursions in other parts of the world (perhaps in other Western Hemisphere countries)." (*Turkish Position with regard to Trading Jupiters for Soviet Missiles in Cuba*, 10/25/62)

October 25, 1962: President Kennedy issues National Security Action Memorandum 199 authorizing the loading of multistage nuclear weapons on aircraft under the command of the Supreme Allied Commander, Europe (SACEUR). (*The Air Force Response to the Cuban Crisis 14 October–24 November 1962*, ca. 1/63, p. 27; *Chronology of JCS Decisions Concerning the Cuban Crisis*, 12/21/62)

October 25, 1962: A CIA sabotage team, dispatched to Cuba to destroy facilities at the Matahambre copper mine in Cuba (see entry for October 15, 1962), is prevented from executing the sabotage attack by Cuban authorities. (Garthoff 1, p. 78)

October 26, 1962—6:00 A.M.: The CIA memorandum reporting information as of 6:00 A.M. notes that construction of IRBM and MRBM bases in Cuba is proceeding without interruption. (*The Crisis USSR/Cuba: Information as of 0600*, 10/26/62)

October 26, 1962—10:00 A.M.: President Kennedy tells the ExComm that he believes the quarantine by itself will not cause the Soviet government to remove the missiles from Cuba, and that only an invasion or a trade of some sort will succeed. After discussing the airstrike option again at some length, Kennedy agrees

to apply further pressure by increasing the frequency of low-level flights over Cuba from twice per day to once every two hours. The ExComm also decides not to undertake any emergency civil defense programs at this time, although preliminary measures have been initiated. (Document 42, Bromley Smith, *Summary Record of NSC Executive Committee Meeting, October 26, 1962, 10:00 A.M.*, 10/26/62; *The Cuban Crisis, 1962*, ca. 8/22/63, pp. 165–66; Kennedy, p. 83)

October 26, 1962—morning: President Kennedy orders the State Department to proceed with preparations for a crash program aimed at establishing a civil government in Cuba after an invasion and occupation of the country. During the meeting, Robert McNamara reports to the president that the military believes that heavy casualties should be expected in an invasion; several days later, CINCLANT estimates that up to 18,484 U.S. casualties might occur during the first ten days of fighting. (*CINCLANT Historical Account of Cuban Crisis*, 4/29/63, p. 56; Kennedy, p. 85)

October 26, 1962—1:00 P.M.: John Scali, State Department correspondent for ABC News, lunches with Aleksandr Fomin at the Occidental Restaurant in Washington at Fomin's urgent request. The two have met together on several previous occasions. Fomin, officially the Soviet embassy public affairs counselor, is known to be the KGB's Washington station chief. Noting that "war seems about to break out," he asks Scali to contact his "high-level friends" in the State Department to ascertain whether the United States would be interested in a possible solution to the crisis. According to Scali's notes, Fomin's proposal runs along the following lines: "[Soviet] bases would be dismantled under [U]nited [N]ations supervision and [C]astro would pledge not to accept offensive weapons of any kind, ever, in return for [a U.S.] pledge not to invade Cuba." Following the lunch, Scali goes directly to the State Department to report on the meeting to Roger Hilsman. (Document 43, *John Scali's Notes of First Meeting with Soviet Embassy Counselor Alexandr Fomin*, 10/26/62)

October 26, 1962—1:18 P.M.: The State Department receives a cable from U.S. Ambassador to Turkey Raymond Hare warning that Turkish officials will "deeply resent" any Turkey-for-Cuba missile trade. Hare expresses his opinion that the most satisfactory resolution to the crisis would avoid the Jupiter issue altogether, but he suggests that if the missiles have to be removed it should be done gradually. Hare also acknowledges that an alternative solution could be the "dismantling of Jupiters...on [a] strictly secret basis with Soviets." (*Assessment of Consequences for the NATO Alliance If the Jupiters Are Traded for the Cuban Missiles—In Three Sections*, 10/26/62)

October 26, 1962—2:00 P.M.: U.S. Ambassador to Brazil A. Lincoln Gordon is requested to ask the Brazilian government to have the Brazilian ambassador in Havana, Luis Batian Pinto, meet privately with Fidel Castro to relay a message from the U.S. government. The message that Pinto is to give to Castro includes reassurances that the United States is unlikely to invade Cuba if the missiles are removed. (*Instructions to Secure Assistance of Brazil in Approaching Castro*, 10/26/62)

October 26, 1962—6:00 P.M.: The State Department begins receiving a message from the U.S. embassy in Moscow containing a new, private letter from Premier Khrushchev. The message arrives in four sections, with the final portion arriving at 9:00 P.M., some twelve hours after the text has been delivered to the U.S. embassy. The letter, almost certainly composed by Khrushchev himself, is, in Robert Kennedy's words, "very long and emotional." But it contains a proposal for a settlement: "I propose: we, for our part, will declare that our ships bound for Cuba are not carrying any armaments. You will declare that the United States will not invade Cuba with its troops and will not support any other forces which might intend to invade Cuba. Then the necessity of the presence of our military specialists in Cuba will disappear." (Document 44, *Premier Khrushchev's Letter to President Kennedy, Offering a Settlement to the Crisis*, 10/26/62; Kennedy, p. 86)

October 26, 1962—6:45 P.M.: John Scali tells Dean Rusk and Roger Hilsman of Aleksandr Fomin's proposal (see entry for October 26, 1962—1:00 P.M.). U.S. officials assume that Fomin's message has been initiated by the Kremlin and interpret Khrushchev's newly arrived letter in light of Fomin's offer that the Soviet Union remove its missiles under U.N. inspection in return for a U.S. noninvasion pledge. Recent information from Soviet sources suggests that, contrary to U.S. assumptions at the time, Fomin's proposal was not in fact authorized by Moscow. (Hilsman, p. 218; Garthoff 2, p. 73)

October 26, 1962—7:35 P.M.: Meeting again with Aleksandr Fomin, John Scali recites a message given to him by Dean Rusk. Scali states, "I have reason to believe that the [U.S. government] sees real possibilities and supposes that the representatives of the two governments in New York could work this matter out with U Thant and with each other. My impression is, however, that time is very urgent." Fomin assures Scali that his remarks would be communicated immediately to the "highest Soviet sources." (*Report on Meeting between John Scali and Aleksandr Fomin on October 26, 1962, 7:35 P.M.*, 10/26/62; "John Scali, ABC News," 8/13/64)

October 26, 1962—10:00 P.M.: The ExComm reconvenes in an extraordinary session to consider Premier Khrushchev's letter. Further textual analysis of the letter is ordered, and two Soviet specialists, Helmut Sonnenfeldt and Joseph Neubert, are directed to analyze the letter alongside the proposal from Aleksandr Fomin. (Abel, p. 184)

October 26, 1962—night: Unknown to any of the ExComm members, Robert Kennedy and Anatoly Dobrynin meet at the Soviet embassy, one of a series of secret meetings the two held during the crisis. (Dobrynin has since disclosed that when he defended the Soviet missile deployment by noting that the United States had stationed Jupiter missiles to Turkey, Robert Kennedy offered to introduce the Turkish missiles into a potential settlement.) The attorney general reportedly leaves the room to phone the president.

When he returns, he tells Dobrynin, "the president said that we are ready to consider the question of Turkey, to examine favorably the question of Turkey." Dobrynin reports the conversation to the Kremlin. (Allyn, p. 158)

Around this time, according to Nikita Khrushchev, "we received information from our Cuban comrades and from other sources which directly stated that this attack [on Cuba] would be carried out within the next two or three days." Khrushchev's statement may refer to a cable from Fidel Castro that was transmitted on the evening of October 26. Fearing that a U.S. invasion is imminent, Castro reportedly composes the message—dictating in Spanish to Soviet Ambassador Alekseyev, who translates the letter into Russian—while spending the night in a bomb shelter in the Soviet embassy in Havana. Khrushchev apparently understood the cable both as a warning of an impending invasion and as an attempt to get Khrushchev to launch the missiles in Cuba against the United States. According to an unpublished portion of Khrushchev's memoirs, Khrushchev recalls Castro warning that "an American invasion would take place within a few hours. Therefore, he was proposing to preempt the invasion and inflict a nuclear strike on the U.S." At the Havana Conference in January 1992, Castro states that his letter was mistranslated; that he was suggesting that if Cuba was invaded, the Soviet Union would need to defend itself from attack by using nuclear weapons. (Document 45, *Prime Minister Fidel Castro's Letter to Premier Krushchev*, 10/26/62; *The Soviet Bloc Armed Forces and the Cuban Crisis: A Chronology July–November 1962*, 6/18/63; Allyn, p. 167)

October 26, 1962: Fidel Castro orders Cuban antiaircraft forces to open fire on all U.S. aircraft flying over the island. According to one source, Castro's order reportedly replaces his standing orders to fire only on groups of two or more low-altitude airplanes. When Soviet Ambassador to Cuba Alekseyev asks Castro to recind his order, he apparently is rebuffed. (*Interview with Sergo Mikoyan on Soviet Views on the Missile Crisis*, 10/13/87; Szulc, p. 647; Allyn, p. 161)

As a result of the increased frequency of low-level reconnaissance missions, additional military targets in Cuba are identified. Military planners consequently revise air attack targeting and plans. The airstrike plan now includes three massive strikes per day until Cuban air capability is destroyed. Some 1,190 bombing sorties are planned for the first day of operations. (*The Air Force Response to the Cuban Crisis 14 October–24 November 1962*, ca. 1/63, p. 9)

October 27, 1962—6:00 A.M.: The CIA intelligence memorandum containing information compiled as of 6:00 A.M. reports that three of the four MRBM sites at San Cristóbal and the two sites at Sagua la Grande appear to be fully operational. The mobilization of Cuban military forces is reported to be continuing at a high rate, but the CIA advises that Cuban forces remain under orders not to engage in hostilities unless attacked. (Document 47, *CIA Daily Report, The Crisis USSR/Cuba: Information as of 0600 27 October 1962*, 10/27/62)

October 27, 1962—9:00 A.M.: Radio Moscow begins broadcasting a message from Premier Khrushchev. In contrast to the private message of the day before, the new message calls for the dismantling of U.S. missile bases in Turkey in return for the removal of the Soviet missiles in Cuba. While the broadcast is underway, the original copy of Khrushchev's last letter to President Kennedy is delivered to the U.S. embassy in Moscow. (*Report That Khrushchev's October 27 Letter to President Kennedy Was Delivered to Embassy at 5:00 P.M. Moscow Time*, 10/27/62)

October 27, 1962—10:00 A.M.: The ExComm meets in the Situation Room at the White House. After the usual intelligence briefing by John McCone, the minutes of the meeting record that

> McNamara reported on the positions of Soviet Bloc ships moving toward Cuba.... He recommended that we be prepared to board the *Grozny*, which is now out about six-hundred miles.... Under Secretary Ball pointed out that the Soviets did not know the extent of our quarantine zone. The President agreed that we should ask U Thant to tell the Russians in New

York where we are drawing the quarantine line. The Russians would then be in a position to decide whether to turn back their tanker or allow her to enter the quarantine zone sometime later today.

During the meeting, Premier Khrushchev's second message begins to be received. The full text of Khrushchev's formal letter came across a Foreign Broadcast Information Service ticker in the White House at 11:03 A.M. The message states in part:

> You are disturbed over Cuba. You say that this disturbs you because it is ninety miles by sea from the coast of the United States of America. But…you have placed destructive missile weapons, which you call offensive, in Turkey, literally next to us…. I therefore make this proposal: We are willing to remove from Cuba the means which you regard as offensive…. Your representatives will make a declaration to the effect that the United States…will remove its analogous means from Turkey…. And after that, persons entrusted by the United Nations Security Council could inspect on the spot the fulfillment of the pledges made….

The new letter sets the stage for a protracted ExComm discussion, which continues throughout the day, about how to respond, with the president stating that to go to war with the Soviet Union instead of accepting a trade would be "an insupportable position." (Document 48, *Premier Khrushchev's Communiqué to President Kennedy, Calling for a Trade of Cuban Missiles for Turkish Missiles*, 10/27/62; Document 49, *Transcript of Executive Committee Meetings* [edited], 10/27/62; *NSC Executive Committee Record of Action, October 27, 1962, 10:00 A.M.*)

October 27, 1962—Around 10:15 to 11:00 A.M.: A U-2 from a SAC base in Alaska strays into Soviet airspace over the Chukotski Peninsula on what was reported to be a "routine air sampling mission." The U-2 pilot apparently enters Soviet airspace as a result of a navigational error. The pilot radios for assistance and a U.S. F-102 fighter aircraft in Alaska scrambles and heads toward the Bering Sea. At the same time, Soviet MiGs take off from a base near Wrangel Island to intercept

the U-2, which eventually manages to fly out of Soviet territory with no shots being fired. Alaskan Air Command records suggest that the U.S. fighter planes are armed with nuclear air-to-air missiles.

According to one account, when Secretary of Defense McNamara hears that a U-2 was in Soviet airspace, "he turned absolutely white, and yelled hysterically, 'This means war with the Soviet Union.'" President Kennedy's laconic reaction upon hearing of the incident is simply to laugh and remark that "there is always some [son of a bitch] who doesn't get the word." (*War Room Journal*, 10/27/62; *Chronology of the Cuban Crisis October 15–28, 1962*, 11/2/62, p. 14; *Interview of David A. Burchinal*, 4/11/75, pp. 114–15; Hilsman 1, p. 221; Sagan, pp. 117–18; *Air Defense Operations*, ca. 12/62)

October 27, 1962—Around 12:00 noon: A U-2 reconnaissance plane is shot down over Cuba and its pilot, Major Rudolf Anderson, killed. Anderson had flown one of the first U-2 missions responsible for detecting the Soviet missiles. The ExComm, when informed of the downing, assumes that the attack had been ordered by the Kremlin and speculates that the move is designed to escalate the crisis. In fact, as Soviet and Cuban officials have only recently revealed, the attack is the result of a decision made by local Soviet commanders. Although a Soviet major general, Igor I. Statsenko, claims responsibility for the decision in 1987, other Soviet sources have suggested that Lt. Gen. Stepan N. Grechko and Gen. Leonid S. Garbuz are the two officers in Cuba who authorized the firing of the SAM. After the incident, Marshal Malinovsky mildly reprimands the officers and orders that no other U-2s be attacked. (*Chronology of the Cuban Crisis October 15–28, 1962*, 11/2/62, p. 14; *The Crisis USSR/Cuba: Information as of 0600 28 October 1962*, 10/28/62; Garthoff 1, p. 82–85; Allyn, pp. 160–62)

October 27, 1962—2:30 P.M.: Several ExComm members assemble in George Ball's conference room to consider possible options in light of the deteriorating crisis situation. (*The Cuban Crisis, 1962*, ca. 8/22/63, pp. 185–86)

October 27, 1962:—3:41 P.M.: F8U-1P low-level reconnaissance planes take off for afternoon missions over Cuba. Two of the six planes are forced to abort their mission due to mechanical problems. As the remaining planes fly over San Cristóbal and Sagua la Grande, Cuban troops open fire with antiaircraft guns and small arms. One of the U.S. aircraft is hit by a 37mm antiaircraft shell but manages to return to its base. (*Transcript of October 27 Cuban Missile Crisis ExComm Meetings*, 10/27/62, p. 18; U.S. Plane Cuba, 10/27/62)

October 27, 1962—4:00 P.M.: The ExComm is called back to the White House. President Kennedy orders the immediate dispatch of a message to U Thant asking urgently whether he would ascertain if the Soviet government is willing to stop work on the bases while negotiations continue to find a solution to the crisis. In the middle of the meeting, Maxwell Taylor brings in a late report confirming that the missing U-2 had been shot down over Cuba, probably by a SAM site. President Kennedy, however, decides not to retaliate but agrees that if any more surveillance planes are fired on over Cuba, the SAM sites would be attacked. Kennedy's order to call off the planned reprisal is reportedly received with disbelief in the Pentagon.

Most of the long meeting, however, centers on formulating a response to Nikita Khrushchev's most recent proposal. President Kennedy, in deliberations throughout the day, continually favors trading away the missiles in Turkey for those in Cuba as Khrushchev has offered—possibly because he secretly has hinted to the Soviet government through Robert Kennedy and Anatoly Dobrynin on October 26 that the United States would agree to such a deal. However, most of the group argues that an open trade could fragment the NATO alliance. Alternative courses of action are suggested: McNamara argues that the Jupiters in Turkey should be removed, but only as a prelude to an invasion of Cuba; Maxwell Taylor forwards the JCS recommendation simply to initiate the airstrike and invasion plans; and the State Department drafts a letter flatly rejecting the Soviet proposal.

As the meeting progresses, the idea of ignoring Khrushchev's new proposal and responding only to the October 26 letter (which did not mention the Jupiters) gradually begins to emerge. President Kennedy, initially hesitant to accept the idea because he does not believe Khrushchev would accept such a deal, finally agrees when Soviet specialist Llewellyn Thompson argues that Khrushchev might. Theodore Sorensen and Robert Kennedy leave the meeting to compose the proposed response. After forty-five minutes, they return to present the draft. The president refines the letter, has it typed, and signs it. The letter is sent that evening (see entry for October 27, 1962—8:05 P.M.).

After the ExComm meeting breaks up, a smaller group composed of President Kennedy, McNamara, Robert Kennedy, Bundy, Rusk, Llewellyn Thompson, and Theodore Sorensen meet in the Oval Office. The group agrees that the second letter to Khrushchev should be reinforced with an oral message passed through Ambassador Dobrynin. They further agree that Dobrynin should be informed that if the Soviet missiles are not withdrawn, there will be military action against Cuba. If they are removed, however, the United States will be willing to give a noninvasion pledge. Dean Rusk suggests one further component to the message: an assurance that, while there can be no public or explicit deal over the Turkish missiles, the Jupiters will in fact be removed once the Cuban crisis is resolved. The proposal quickly gains the approval of the group and the president. Concern is so acute that the assurance not be leaked to the public or to NATO that not even other ExComm members are told of the additional assurances regarding the Jupiters. (Document 49, *Transcript of the Executive Committee Meetings* [edited], 10/27/62, pp. 25–26, 39; Bundy, p. 431; Kennedy, pp. 98, 101–102; Allison, p. 225; Bundy, p. 432; *Recollection by Dean Rusk of Negotiating Channel through Andrew Cordier and Details of Negotiations To Remove Jupiters Prior to the Crisis*, 2/25/87; Bundy, p. 433)

October 27, 1962—4:15 P.M.: At Dean Rusk's request, ABC News correspondent John Scali and Soviet embassy official Fomin meet once again. When Scali asks Fomin why the October 26 proposal has been scrapped and the Jupiters introduced into the deal,

Fomin explains that the change is a result of "poor communications." He states that Premier Khrushchev's new message had been drafted before his report on the favorable U.S. reaction to the October 26 proposal had arrived. Furious at Fomin's response, Scali shouts that Fomin's explanation is not credible and that he thought it is simply a "stinking double cross." An invasion of Cuba, Scali warns, is now "only a matter of hours away." Fomin says that he and Ambassador Dobrynin are expecting a reply from Khrushchev at any moment and urges Scali to report to U.S. officials that there is no treachery. Scali replies that he does not think anyone will believe Fomin's assurances but that he will convey the message in any case. The two part ways, and Scali immediately types out a memo on the meeting which is sent to the ExComm. (*"John Scali, ABC News,"* 8/13/64; Hilsman, p. 222; Bundy, p. 439)

October 27, 1962—7:45 P.M.: Dobrynin and Robert Kennedy meet at the Justice Department. In his memoirs on the crisis, the latter recalls telling Dobrynin:

> [W]e had to have a commitment by tomorrow that [the missile] bases would be removed. I was not giving them an ultimatum but a statement of fact. He should understand that if they did not remove those bases, we would remove them....
>
> He asked me what offer the United States was making, and I told him of the letter that President Kennedy had just transmitted to Khrushchev. He raised the question of our removing the missiles from Turkey. I said that there could be no quid pro quo or any arrangement made under this kind of threat or pressure, and that in the last analysis that was a decision that would have to be made by NATO. However, I said, President Kennedy had been anxious to remove those missiles from Turkey and Italy for a long period of time. He had ordered their removal some time ago, and it was our judgment that, within a short time after this crisis was over, those missiles would be gone.... Time was running out. We had only a few more hours—we needed an answer immediately from the Soviet Union. I said we must have it the next day.

Anatoly Dobrynin has recently contradicted Robert Kennedy's account of the meeting in several ways. According to Dobrynin, Kennedy did not in fact threaten military action against the missiles sites if the Soviet government did not remove the missiles. Second, Kennedy reportedly did not say that the Jupiters had been ordered removed earlier; instead, he suggested that an explicit deal on the Turkish missiles could be struck.

After the meeting with Dobrynin, the attorney general returns to the White House. At President Kennedy's direction, McNamara instructs Secretary of the Air Force Eugene Zuckert to order to active duty twenty-four Air Force Reserve units totaling 14,200 personnel. Robert Kennedy later recalls the mood at the White House: "We had not abandoned hope, but what hope there was now rested with Khrushchev's revising his course within the next few hours. It was a hope, not an expectation. The expectation was a military confrontation by Tuesday [October 29] and possibly tomorrow...." (Allyn, p. 164; Kennedy, pp. 108–109; *Department of Defense Operations during the Cuban Missile Crisis*, 2/12/63, p. 19; Kennedy, p. 109)

October 27, 1962—8:05 P.M.: President Kennedy's letter to Premier Khrushchev drafted earlier in the day is transmitted to Moscow. The final text reads in part:

> As I read your letter, the key elements of your proposals—which seem generally acceptable as I understand them—are as follows: 1) You would agree to remove these weapon systems from Cuba under appropriate United Nations observation and supervision; and undertake, with suitable safe-guards, to halt the further introduction of such weapon systems into Cuba. 2) We, on our part, would agree—upon the establishment of adequate arrangements through the United Nations, to ensure the carrying out and continuation of these commitments (a) to remove promptly the quarantine measures now in effect and (b) to give assurances against the invasion of Cuba.

The letter is also released directly to the press to avoid

any communications delays. (*Document 51, President Kennedy's Letter to Premier Krushchev, Responding to Proposal to End the Crisis*, 10/27/62; Salinger, p. 272)

October 27, 1962—8:50 P.M.: In response to U Thant's request that Cuba stop work on the missile sites while negotiations continue, Fidel Castro indicates in a letter to the U.N. acting secretary general that he would order work to cease, provided the United States lifted the blockade. Castro also extends an invitation to U Thant to visit Cuba. U Thant accepts the invitation on October 28 and travels to Havana on October 30. (*Transmittal of Message from Fidel Castro Welcoming U Thant's Visit and Responding to U Thant's Request to Suspend Missile Base Construction*, 10/27/62)

October 27, 1962—9:00 P.M.: U Thant informs Adlai Stevenson that Soviet representative Zorin has refused to accept information about the exact location of the quarantine interception area that the United States passed on earlier in the day. (*Chronology of the Cuban Crisis October 15–28, 1962*, 11/2/62, p. 15)

October 27, 1962—9:00 P.M.: The ExComm again reviews various options for the following day, including ordering an airstrike on the missile sites in Cuba and extending the blockade to include petroleum, oil, and lubricants (POL). As the meeting comes to a close, Robert McNamara turns to Robert Kennedy. The United States had better be "damned sure," McNamara states, that we "have two things ready, a government for Cuba, because we're going to need one…and secondly, plans for how to respond to the Soviet Union in Europe, because sure as hell they're going to do something there." (*Document 49, Transcript of October 27, 1962 Executive Committee Meetings* [edited], 10/27/62, p. 82; *The Cuban Crisis, 1962*, ca. 8/22/63, pp. 189–90; *Possible Role of a Progressive Economic Blockade against Cuba*, 10/25/62)

October 27, 1962—evening: Unknown to other members of the ExComm, President Kennedy and Dean Rusk prepare a contingency plan to facilitate a public Turkey-for-Cuba missile trade. At Kennedy's instruction, Rusk phones Andrew Cordier, a former U.N. undersecretary, and dictates a statement that Cordier is to give to U Thant upon further instructions from Washington. The statement is a proposal to be made by U Thant calling for the removal of both the Jupiters in Turkey and the Soviet missiles in Cuba. During the day, Kennedy also asks Roswell Gilpatric to draw up a scenario for the early removal of the missiles from Turkey. (*Recollection by Dean Rusk of Negotiating Channel through Andrew Cordier and Details of Negotiations To Remove Jupiters Prior to the Crisis*, 2/25/87; Schlesinger, p. 520)

October 27, 1962—night: Fidel Castro meets with Soviet Ambassador Alekseyev for lengthy discussions in the Soviet embassy in Havana. Castro, Alekseyev later reports, had been briefed by him on each of the messages sent back and forth between Moscow and Washington during the crisis. Alekseyev recalls that despite Castro's "characteristic restraint, he [Castro] also evaluated the situation as highly alarming." (Alekseyev, p. 16)

October 28, 1962—12:12 A.M.: Instructions are sent to Ambassador Finletter to review the deepening crisis with the NATO allies. The cable notifies Finletter that "the situation as we see it is increasingly serious and time is growing shorter…. [T]he United States may find it necessary within a very short time in its interest and that of its fellow nations in the Western Hemisphere to take whatever military action may be necessary." (*Instructions for Briefing to NATO on Possible U.S. Action against Missile Sites and on Soviet Jupiter Trade Proposal*, 10/28/62)

October 28, 1962—6:00 A.M.: The CIA's daily update as of 6:00 A.M. reports that Soviet technicians have succeeded in making fully operational all twenty-four MRBM sites in Cuba. Construction of one nuclear bunker reportedly has been completed but none are believed to be in operation. (*The Crisis USSR/Cuba: Information as of 0600 28 October 1962*, 10/28/62)

October 28, 1962—9:00 A.M.: A new message from Nikita Khrushchev, which effectively terminates the missile crisis, is broadcast on Radio Moscow.

Khrushchev declares: "the Soviet government, in addition to previously issued instructions on the cessation of further work at the building sites for the weapons, has issued a new order on the dismantling of the weapons which you describe as 'offensive,' and their crating and return to the Soviet Union." Upon receiving Khrushchev's message, President Kennedy issues a statement calling the decision "an important and constructive contribution to peace." In a separate letter to Khrushchev, written almost immediately after the broadcast, Kennedy states, "I consider my letter to you of October twenty-seventh and your reply of today as firm undertakings on the part of both our governments which should be promptly carried out."

Although there is a sense of relief and exultation among most of the ExComm members after word of Khrushchev's decision is received, several members of the JCS are less enthusiastic. Admiral George Anderson reportedly complains, "we have been had," while General Curtis LeMay suggests that the United States "go in and make a strike on Monday anyway." In the afternoon, the Joint Chiefs instruct military commanders not to relax their alert procedures, warning that the Soviet Union's offer to dismantle the missile sites could be an "insincere proposal meant to gain time."

In Havana, Fidel Castro, who was not consulted or informed of the decision beforehand, reportedly goes into a rage upon hearing of the Soviet move, cursing Khrushchev as "son of a bitch, bastard, asshole." A few days later, Castro will publicly state in a speech at the University of Havana that Khrushchev lacked *"cojones"* (balls). After meeting with high military leaders during the morning, Castro apparently goes to San Antonio Air Force Base himself in order to shoot down a U.S. low-altitude aircraft. However, U.S. planes do not pass over the base. (Document 53, *President Kennedy's Letter to Premier Krushchev, Confirming Terms To Settle the Missile Crisis*, 10/28/62; *Statement by President Kennedy Welcoming Khrushchev's Decision to Withdraw Soviet Missiles from Cuba—Includes Text as Carried by UPI*, 10/28/62; *Summary of Items of Significant Interest Period 280701–290700 October 1962*, 10/29/62; Schlesinger, p. 524; *RN* 10/28/62; Bourne, p. 239; Szulc, pp. 649–50)

October 28, 1962—11:00 A.M.: Robert Kennedy meets

with Anatoly Dobrynin at the Soviet ambassador's request. Dobrynin notes that Premier Khrushchev has agreed to withdraw the missiles, and he tells Kennedy that the Soviet leader wants to send his best wishes to him and the president. (Kennedy, p. 110)

The ExComm meets. By this time, the full text of Premier Khrushchev's message announcing the decision to dismantle the missiles in Cuba is available. Secretary of Defense McNamara reports that the Soviet ship *Grozny* is standing still and that no other Soviet Bloc ships will be entering the quarantine zone during the day. President Kennedy directs that no air reconnaissance missions be flown during the day, and that no action be taken against any Soviet Bloc ships with regard to the unresolved question of the IL-28 bombers in Cuba. Kennedy agrees that the United States should consider the IL-28s "offensive weapons" and press for their removal, but he also suggests that the United States should not "get hung up" on this issue. (Document 59, *Summary Record of NSC Executive Committee Meeting*, 10/28/62; *Statement of Soviet Government of October 23, 1962 on Cuba*, 10/23/62)

October 28, 1962—around noon: Fidel Castro declares that the U.S. assurance of nonaggression against Cuba is unsatisfactory unless it includes additional measures. He outlines several specific demands, later to be known as his "five points." They include an end to the economic blockade against Cuba; an end to all subversive activities carried out from the United States against Cuba; a halt to all attacks on Cuba carried out from the U.S. military bases on the island of Puerto Rico; the cessation of aerial and naval reconnaissance flights in Cuban airspace and waters; and the return of Guantánamo naval base to Cuba. (Document 56, *Prime Minister Castro's "Five Points" Letter to U.N. Secretary General U Thant*, 10/28/62)

October 28, 1962—1:00 P.M.–3:00 P.M.: According to information given to U Thant by a Soviet commander several days afterward, instructions to dismantle the missiles in Cuba are received by the Soviet military in Cuba between 1:00 and 3:00 P.M. Actual dismantling of the sites reportedly begins at 5:00 P.M. (Document

61, *State Department Cable on UN Secretary General U Thant's Meetings with Castro,* 11/1/62)

October 28, 1962—1:04 P.M.: At a background press briefing, Dean Rusk cautions against any gloating at the Soviet decision, explaining that "if there is a debate, a rivalry, a contest going on in the Kremlin over how to play this situation, we don't want…to strengthen the hands of those in Moscow who wanted to play this another way." Rusk also asserts, in a reference to inspection issues and the IL-28s still in Cuba, "it is not yet the time to say this is over." (*Transcript of Background Press and Radio News Briefing, Sunday, October 28, 1962,* 10/28/62)

October 28, 1962—4:07 P.M.: The JCS asks CINCLANT to reevaluate Oplan 316, the invasion plan of Cuba, and determine what modifications should be made to the plan in light of the most recent intelligence estimates on military equipment in Cuba. CINCLANT is specifically directed to consider whether tactical nuclear weapons, both air and ground, should be included in the arsenal of U.S. forces invading Cuba. (*Summary of Items of Significant Interest Period 280701–290700 October 1962,* 10/29/62)

October 28, 1962—evening: John Scali meets with Soviet embassy official Fomin for the fourth time during the crisis. Fomin tells Scali, "I am under instructions to thank you. The information you provided Chairman Khrushchev was most helpful to him in making up his mind quickly." Fomin then adds, "And that includes your explosion of Saturday"—indicating that U.S. anger, as conveyed by Scali, toward the broadening of Soviet demands had reinforced Khrushchev's decision to accept the U.S. proposal for ending the crisis. (*"John Scali, ABC News,"* 8/13/64)

The Soviet embassy in Havana receives a lengthy telegram from the Kremlin explaining the decision to withdraw the missiles. Any other move, the message argues, would have meant "global conflagration and consequently the destruction of the Cuban revolution." The cable also stresses that "the Soviet government under no circumstances would refuse to fulfill its international duty to defend Cuba." Soviet Ambassador Alekseyev passes on the telegram to Cuban

President Dorticós, who is reportedly somewhat reassured by it. (Alekseyev, p. 17)

October 29, 1962—morning: Soviet First Deputy Premier Vasily V. Kuznetsov meets with U Thant. Kuznetsov, sent by Premier Khrushchev to New York to work out the details of a settlement to the crisis, tells U Thant that the Soviet missiles are in the process of being dismantled and shipped out of Cuba. Kuznetsov proposes that when the dismantling is completed, the Soviet Union report to the Security Council, which would then authorize a U.N. team to visit Cuba for "on-site" verification. (*The Soviet Bloc Armed Forces and the Cuban Crisis: A Chronology July–November 1962,* 6/18/63, p. 78)

As a result of an order from Robert McNamara to begin the process of removing Jupiter missiles from Turkey, an interdepartmental task force convenes under Defense Department General Counsel John McNaughton. McNaughton reportedly opens the meeting by declaring, "those missiles are going to be out of there by April 1 if we have to shoot them out." (*A Transcript of a Discussion about the Cuban Missile Crisis, 1983;* Chayes, p. 98)

October 29, 1962—10:00 A.M.: At the morning ExComm meeting, President Kennedy orders that U.S. Navy ships maintain their quarantine stations. Low-level reconnaissance flights are directed to resume, but no U-2 missions are authorized. (*NSC Executive Committee Record of Action, October 29, 1962, 6:30 P.M., Meeting No. 12,* 10/29/62)

October 29, 1962—3:30 P.M.: U Thant briefs Adlai Stevenson, John McCloy, and Charles Yost on his meeting with Vasily Kuznetsov earlier in the day. U Thant tries to convince the Americans that the quarantine should now be suspended, but McCloy and Stevenson disagree, linking the end of the quarantine to the actual removal of offensive weapons from Cuba. They do agree, however, that the quarantine could be suspended for the duration of U Thant's visit to Cuba, scheduled to begin on October 30. (*Summary of Meeting between U.S. Negotiators and U Thant on U Thant's Meeting with Kuznetsov,* 10/29/62)

October 29, 1962—10:48 P.M.: CINCLANT informs the JCS that, in view of reports that Cuban forces have nuclear-capable FROG short-range missiles, he intends to modify invasion plans so that U.S. air and ground forces engaged in operations against Cuba would also be armed with tactical nuclear weapons. CINCLANT assures the JCS that the nuclear weapons would be employed only if Cuban or Soviet forces initiated the use of nuclear weapons. The JCS agrees to allow U.S. invasion forces to be armed with nuclear-capable weapons but specifies that the actual nuclear warheads should not be introduced into Cuba without further JCS authorization. (*Summary of Items of Significant Interest Period 300701–310700 October 1962,* 10/31/62; *CINCLANT Historical Account of Cuban Crisis,* 4/29/63, p. 95; *The Air Force Response to the Cuban Crisis 14 October–24 November 1962,* ca. 1/63, p. 11; *Secretary of Defense's Report for the Congress,* 12/29/62)

October 29, 1962: The Soviet Union attempts to hammer out a formal agreement with the United States on the settlement of the missile crisis. Anatoly Dobrynin brings Robert Kennedy an unsigned letter from Premier Khrushchev explicitly spelling out the terms of the arrangement, including Robert Kennedy's pledge that the Jupiter IRBMs will be removed from Turkey. The attorney general makes no immediate response but takes the letter with him to consider the proposal. When he meets Dobrynin the following day, Kennedy rejects the idea of a written agreement involving the Jupiter missiles. (Schlesinger, pp. 522–23)

Following the ExComm's discussion of the IL-28 question on October 28, State Department analyst Raymond Garthoff recommends in a memo that "in addition to the MRBMs and IRBMs, the IL-28s should definitely be included in the items the United States wanted withdrawn from Cuba." Garthoff writes, however, that the United States can not "reasonably insist" on the withdrawal of MiG aircraft, SAMs, or nonmissile ground force weapons. Nikita Khrushchev has inadvertently opened the door to U.S. demands that additional weapon systems be removed by telling Kennedy in his October 28 letter that he would remove "those weapons you describe as

offensive." Although the crisis has centered around the deployment of Soviet missiles, the United States uses several arguments to support its contention that the bombers are also "offensive." U.S. negotiators note that the quarantine proclamation explicitly included bomber aircraft, and they point to President Kennedy's letter of October 22, which objected to the "long-range missile bases" as well as "other offensive systems in Cuba." (Document 60, *State Department Memorandum Defining Weapons That Must Be Removed from Cuba,* 10/29/62)

October 30, 1962—3:00 P.M.: Shortly after his arrival in Havana, U Thant and his aides meet with Fidel Castro, Cuban President Osvaldo Dorticós and Foreign Minister Raúl Roa. U Thant presents several verification proposals to ensure that the dismantling of the missiles is proceeding, including on-site inspection by a U.N. team, aerial inspection by U.N. reconnaissance planes, or verification by the International Committee of the Red Cross (ICRC). Castro rejects each of these proposals, saying they are "intended to humiliate the Cuban State." (*Summary of U Thant's Meeting with President Dorticos, Premier Castro and Foreign Minister Roa in Havana, October 30, 1962,* 10/30/62)

October 30, 1962: Premier Khrushchev sends President Kennedy a sixteen-page message covering the missile crisis, the naval quarantine, a nuclear test-ban treaty, and the Berlin question. The Kremlin leader requests that the United States lift the quarantine immediately, as well as the economic blockade of Cuba. He also suggests that the United States withdraw from its base in Guantánamo, Cuba. On the issue of a test-ban treaty, Khrushchev proclaims, "we now have conditions ripe for finalizing the agreement on signing a treaty on cessation of tests of thermonuclear weapons." Khrushchev also attempts to garner an agreement on Berlin that would exclude German Chancellor Konrad Adenauer, because "the next crisis...can be caused by the German question." (*Premier Khrushchev's Letter to President Kennedy,* 10/30/62)

Robert Kennedy calls Ambassador Dobrynin back to his office to discuss the letter Dobrynin had given him the day before spelling out the terms of the U.S.-Soviet agreement resolving the Cuban missile crisis. Notes he prepared for the meeting reflect his position:

Read letter—Studied it over night. No quid pro quo as I told you. The letter makes it appear that there was. You asked me about missile bases in Turkey. I told you we would be out of them—four to five months. That still holds…You have my word on this & that is sufficient. Take back your letter—Reconsider it & if you feel it is necessary to write letters then we will also write one which you cannot enjoy. Also if you should publish any document indicating a deal then it is off & also if done afterward will further affect the relationship.

Dobrynin acquiesces to Kennedy's demand and withdraws the letter. (Schlesinger, p. 523)

In Moscow, Soviet Foreign Minister Andrei Gromyko informs Foy Kohler that the Soviet Union wishes to reach an agreement as quickly as possible on the basis of the Kennedy-Khrushchev exchange of letters. Gromyko also suggests that some type of formal agreement should "codify" obligations on both sides. (*Meeting between Andrei Gromyko and Ambassador Foy Kohler, 4:00 P.M., October 30, 1962, 10/30/62*)

All operations by Task Force W, the CIA's action arm for OPERATION MONGOOSE activities, are called to an immediate halt. However, during the crisis, Director of Task Force W William Harvey ordered teams of covert agents into Cuba on his own authority to support any conventional U.S. military operation that might occur. At the end of October, a new mission is about to be dispatched. One of the operatives, concerned about a covert operation so soon after a settlement to the missile crisis has been reached, sends a message to Attorney General Robert Kennedy to verify that the mission is in order. Kennedy, angered to learn that CIA missions are continuing, chastises Harvey and asks CIA Director McCone to terminate the operations. Edward Lansdale is subsequently sent to Miami to oversee the end of MONGOOSE. However, three of ten scheduled six-man sabotage teams have already been dispatched to Cuba. On November 8, one of the teams carries out its assigned sabotage mis-

sion. (*Alleged Assassination Plots Involving Foreign Leaders*, 11/20/75, pp. 147–48)

October 31, 1962—10:00 A.M.: The ExComm reviews the lack of progress in the talks between U Thant and Fidel Castro. President Kennedy directs reconnaissance missions to resume the next day unless significant progress is made in the discussions. (*NSC Executive Committee Record of Action, October 31, 1962, 10:00 A.M., Meeting No. 14, 10/31/62*)

U Thant meets with Fidel Castro, Dorticós, and Roa for the second time during his stay in Cuba. Castro agrees to send the body of Rudolf Anderson, the pilot of the downed U-2, back to the United States. Castro claims that Anderson's plane "was brought down by Cuban anti-aircraft guns, manned only by Cubans, inside Cuban territory." Complaining about continued U.S. aerial reconnaissance, he warns that "the Cuban people can no longer tolerate such daily provocations," and that Cuba will "destroy any plane any time which intruded into Cuban airspace." U Thant is unable to obtain Castro's approval for any form of inspection of the Soviet missile withdrawal. (*Summary of U Thant's Meeting with President Dorticos, Premier Castro and Foreign Minister Roa of Cuba, 10:00 A.M., October 31, 1962, 10/31/62*)

October 31, 1962—6:00 P.M.: After hearing an update on U Thant's mission to Cuba, President Kennedy orders the resumption of low-level reconnaissance and quarantine operations but continues the suspension of U-2 flights (*NSC Executive Committee Record of Action, October 31, 1962, 6:00 P.M., Meeting No. 15, 10/31/62*)

November 1, 1962—1:00 A.M.: Adlai Stevenson reports to Washington that he has received preliminary reports from U Thant and Indar Jit Rikhye on their visit to Cuba. The U.N. officials report that relations between Cuba and the Soviet Union are, in Rikhye's words, "unbelievably bad." Rikhye states that although they have not had "definitive" discussions about the IL-28 bombers, "the Russians repeated… that they were determined to take out all equipment which the president has regarded as offensive and this would include the IL-28's...." (Document 61, *State Department Cable on Secretary General U Thant's Meetings with Castro*, 11/1/62; *Report by Rikhye on Impressions from United Nations Visit to Cuba*, 11/1/62)

November 1, 1962—10:00 A.M.: President Kennedy authorizes continued low-level reconnaissance flights over IL-28 airfields and missile bases but decides that no immediate retaliatory measures will be carried out if any U.S. aircraft are shot down. (*NSC Executive Committee Record of Action, November 1, 1962, 10:00 A.M., Meeting No. 16*, 11/1/62)

November 1, 1962—2:59 P.M.: Instructions approved by President Kennedy are issued to U.S. negotiators in New York for use in upcoming meetings with Soviet First Deputy Premier Anastas Mikoyan. Kennedy directs U.S. negotiators to stress the importance of obtaining verification, which he describes as "essential" in "view of the history of the affair." With regard to the Soviet bombers stationed in Cuba, the negotiators are told to try to "elicit a clear confirmation that the IL-28's are included [in the Kennedy-Khrushchev understanding] and are being dismantled for removal from Cuba." (*Points President Kennedy Wishes Made in Conversation with Anastas Mikoyan and Vasily Kuznetsov*, 11/1/62)

November 1, 1962—7:30 P.M.: Anastas Mikoyan meets with John McCloy and Adlai Stevenson shortly after arriving in New York. Stevenson has been instructed to provide Mikoyan with a list of weapons that the United States considers "offensive" and expects the Soviet government to withdraw. However, engrossed in discussions dealing with many matters, Stevenson and McCloy apparently forget to give the list to Mikoyan. The U.S. negotiators remedy this oversight the next day by sending Mikoyan a letter with the list attached (see entry for November 2, 1962—morning). (*Meeting between Adlai Stevenson, John McCloy and U Thant on Inspection Issues*, 11/2/62; Garthoff 3, pp. 432–33)

November 1, 1962—8:30 P.M.: Fidel Castro reports on his meetings with U Thant in a speech carried by Cuban radio and television. Castro also discusses the differences that had arisen between the Soviet Union and Cuba over the resolution of the missile crisis. Adopting a conciliatory tone, he states, "we have confidence in the leadership of the Soviet Union...more than ever, we should remember the generosity and friendship that the Soviets have shown us." Castro and Soviet Ambassador to Cuba Alekseyev meet during the day for the first time since October 27. (*Transcript of Interview with Castro on his Meeting with U Thant—in Spanish*, 11/1/62; Alekseyev, p. 19)

November 1, 1962: Photoreconnaissance shows that all MRBM sites in Cuba have been bulldozed and that the missiles and associated launch equipment have been removed. Construction at the IRBM sites appears to have stopped, and the installations are partially dismantled. U.S. intelligence further reports that work is continuing on IL-28s at San Julián airfield but that it is unclear whether the bombers are being assembled or dismantled. (*The Soviet Bloc Armed Forces and the Cuban Crisis: A Chronology July–November 1962*, 6/18/63, p. 86)

November 2, 1962—10:00 A.M.: At a meeting of the ExComm, Kennedy confirms that the United States will press for the removal of the IL-28 bombers currently stationed in Cuba. In other matters, Kennedy states that the quarantine must continue to be maintained but only by hailing all vessels entering the quarantine zone. He reconfirms orders to U.S. Navy vessels not to board Soviet Bloc ships. (Document 63, *Summary Record of NSC Executive Committee, November 2, 1962, 10:00 A.M., Meeting No. 17*, 11/2/62)

November 2, 1962—morning: In a letter to Anastas Mikoyan, Adlai Stevenson lists those items the United States considers to be "offensive weapons," adding, "we trust that the weapons you plan to remove include all those on this list." The complete list includes:

1) surface-to-surface missiles including those designed for use at sea and including propellants and chemical compounds capable of being used

to power missiles;

   2) bomber aircraft;

   3) bombs, air-to-surface rockets, and guided missiles;

   4) warheads for any of the above weapons;

   5) mechanical or electronic equipment to support or operate the above items such as communications, supply and missile launching equipment, including Komar-class motor torpedo boats. (*List of Weapons Deemed Offensive by the United States in Accordance with the Exchange of Letters between President Kennedy and Chairman Khrushchev, 11/2/62*)

November 2, 1962—5:30 P.M.: In a brief televised address, President Kennedy informs the nation that the U.S. government has concluded "on the basis of yesterday's aerial photographs...that the Soviet missile bases in Cuba are being dismantled, their missiles and related equipment are being crated, and the fixed installations at these sites are being destroyed." (*Statement of the President, November 2, 1962, the White House,* 11/2/62)

November 2, 1962: Anastas Mikoyan arrives in Havana and immediately announces his support of Fidel Castro's "five points." Castro, still angry with the Soviet decision to remove the missiles, reportedly does not want to meet Mikoyan but is persuaded to do so by Ambassador Alekseyev. Castro's anger and concern revolve around not only the lack of consultation before the Soviet decision to remove the missiles but a belief that the United States will invade Cuba despite pledges to the contrary resulting from the Kennedy-Khrushchev agreement. Because of his distrust of any agreement, Castro agrees to the missile withdrawal only after receiving assurances from the Soviet government, including a pledge to maintain one Soviet combat brigade on the island. (Blight, pp. 267–68; Khrushchev 1, p. 500)

November 3, 1962—9:00 A.M.: Anastas Mikoyan holds his first formal meeting with Fidel Castro at Castro's apartment in Havana. Castro meets alone with Mikoyan, Ambassador Alekseyev, and a Soviet interpreter. However, the talks are immediately interrupted by the news that Mikoyan's wife in the Soviet Union has died unexpectedly. Mikoyan later decides to have his son Sergo, who was accompanying him, return to Moscow while he remains in Cuba. (Alekseyev, p. 23)

November 3, 1962—4:30 P.M.: The nineteenth meeting of the ExComm focuses on inspection questions and the issue of the IL-28 bombers. Adlai Stevenson, who attends the meeting with John McCloy and Charles Yost, brings the group up to date on the slow-moving talks in New York. President Kennedy states his belief that the United States should announce that it considers the IL-28s to be offensive weapons to be withdrawn from Cuba, but he agrees that the public announcement of this position should be delayed until the next day. (*Summary Record of NSC Executive Committee Meeting No. 19, November 3, 1962, 4:30 P.M.,* 11/3/62)

November 3, 1962—8:44 p.m: President Kennedy issues additional directions to "all concerned with the present negotiations in Cuba." The formal instructions state: "We have good evidence that the Russians are dismantling the missile bases.... [But] the assembly of IL-28's continues. There is some evidence of an intent to establish a submarine-tending facility. The future of the SAM sites is unclear. We have no satisfactory assurances on verification...." Kennedy concludes, "in blunt summary, we want no offensive weapons and no Soviet military base in Cuba, and that is how we understand the agreements of October 27 and 28." (*Instructions from the President to All Concerned with Present Negotiations in Cuba,* 11/3/62; *Summary Record of NSC Executive Committee Meeting No. 19, November 3, 1962, 4:30 P.M.,* 11/3/62)

November 3, 1962: President Kennedy replies to Premier Khrushchev's letter of October 30 addressing the issue of inspection and verification before the naval quarantine can be lifted. Kennedy cites "very serious problems" if Fidel Castro cannot be convinced to allow on-site verification, and he suggests that sustaining quarantine "can be of assistance to Mr. Mikoyan in his negotiations with Premier Castro." (*Kennedy-Khrushchev Messages Exchanged on the Cuban Crisis*, 11/3/62)

November 4, 1962: John McCloy lunches with Soviet negotiators at his Stamford, Connecticut, home. Vasily Kuznetsov says all missile sites constructed by the Soviet Union were dismantled as of November 2. Kuznetsov proposes that the United States conduct at-sea inspections: the Soviet Union would give the United States a schedule for the removal of the missiles and allow the United States to bring ships alongside Soviet vessels to examine the cargo on deck. In return, the Soviet government wants the quarantine lifted and a formal protocol of U.S. guarantees, including a pledge that the United States will not invade Cuba or induce other Latin American countries to attempt an invasion. Kuznetsov also seeks a guarantee that no subversive activity will be undertaken against Fidel Castro and suggests U.N. observation in the United States as well as in Cuba. (*The Soviet Bloc Armed Forces and the Cuban Crisis: A Chronology July–November 1962*, 6/18/63, p. 89)

November 5, 1962—3:15 P.M.: President Kennedy dispatches a brief memo to Robert McNamara warning that "the Russians may try again. This time they may prepare themselves for action on the sea in the Cuban area. Does Admiral Anderson think they could build up a secret naval base which will put them on a near parity with us if we should once again blockade?" Admiral Anderson later advises McNamara that the Soviet Union could base naval forces in Cuba in several ways, but he believes that U.S. intelligence would detect all but the most "austere" buildup. Anderson repeats his earlier recommendation that submarines operating out of, or supported from, Cuban bases should be declared offensive weapons and placed on the list of prohibited materials. (*Concern over the Possible Establishment of a Soviet Submarine Base in Cuba*, 11/5/62; Johns, p. 259)

November 5, 1962: In a three-page letter to President Kennedy, Premier Khrushchev writes that he is "seriously worried" about the way in which the United States has defined "offensive weapons" that the Soviet Union is to remove from Cuba, that is, as including the IL-28s and Komar-class missile boats. Khrushchev asks Kennedy to withdraw his "additional demands," saying that the Soviet Union views them as "a wish to bring our relations back again into a heated state in which they were but several days ago." (Document 66, *Premier Khrushchev's Letter to President Kennedy, Regarding U.S. List of Offensive Weapons in Cuba*, 11/5/62)

Soviet ships begin to return the first MRBMs and associated launch equipment to the Soviet Union. The process of removing the equipment is completed on November 9. (*Department of Defense Press Conference of Robert McNamara*, 2/28/63, p. M-1)

President Kennedy hands Secretary of Defense McNamara a short memorandum expressing his concern that U.S. plans for an invasion of Cuba seem "thin." Warning that using too few troops could result in the United States becoming "bogged down," Kennedy recommends calling up three Army Reserve divisions and, if necessary, building additional divisions. As a result of the memo, McNamara tells military planners later that day that additional Army divisions might be needed for a successful invasion. The JCS meet on November 7 with CINCLANT to rectify the problem. (*U.S. Army in the Cuban Crisis*, 1/1/63)

Robert Kennedy continues to exert pressure on the IL-28 question in a meeting with Anatoly Dobrynin, telling the Soviet ambassador that "it was very clear that the...IL-28's had to go." Further pressure to remove the bombers is brought to bear by U Thant, who, at the request of the United States, raises the issue with Vasily Kuznetsov. Kuznetsov replies that the bomber question is "a new issue" and not "covered" in the Kennedy-Khrushchev understanding. (*Meeting with Soviet Representatives on On-Site and ICRC Inspection*, 11/5/62; Garthoff 1, p. 110)

An aerial encounter between a U.S. reconnaissance aircraft and Cuban-based MiG fighters occurs. Although no shots are known to have been fired, U.S. policymakers express concern that the incident suggests that more attempts to intercept reconnaissance aircraft would be made in the future. Robert McNamara, with the concurrence of the JCS, proposes that the public not be informed of the incident, but that a diplomatic protest be made to the Soviet Union. Both high- and low-altitude reconnaissance flights continue as scheduled the following day. (*Chronology of JCS Decisions Concerning the Cuban Crisis*, 12/21/62, p. 70; *Highlights of World Activities and Situations*, 11/5/62)

November 6, 1962: President Kennedy sends another letter to Premier Khrushchev regarding the U.S. definition of "offensive weapons." In it he responds to Khrushchev's accusation that the United States is trying to complicate the Cuban situation. The IL-28s are not "minor things" for the United States, Kennedy writes, asserting that the weapons are definitely capable of carrying out "offensive" missions. The president raises the issue of the four reinforced Soviet troop regiments in Cuba for the first time. He also expresses concern over possible Soviet submarine facilities, telling Khrushchev that he attaches "the greatest importance to the personal assurances you have given that submarine bases will not be established in Cuba." (*President Kennedy's Letter to Khrushchev Stressing the Importance of Removing the IL-28s and Obtaining Verification*, 11/6/62)

November 7, 1962—4:02 P.M.: A cable from U.S. Ambassador to Moscow Foy Kohler reports, "there seems to me no doubt that events of [the] past ten days have really shaken [the] Soviet leadership." One Soviet military official, Kohler recounts, "told my wife he was now willing to believe in God." Kohler reports seeing no evidence of any split within the ruling elite at a Kremlin reception held during the evening, and he states that Premier Khrushchev has privately discouraged an immediate summit with President Kennedy, saying that the two sides should not "rush" into such a meeting. (*Some Footnotes to Kremlin Reception*, 11/7/62)

November 7, 1962—5:00 P.M.: After being informed that the Soviet missiles withdrawal was continuing, President Kennedy tells the ExComm that the United States "wouldn't invade with the Soviet missiles out of Cuba." Kennedy suggests that a formal noninvasion

commitment might be issued once the Soviet Union remove the IL-28 bombers and the U.S. receives "assurances that there will be no reintroduction of strategic missiles." Apparently, some uncertainty still exists on how to handle the IL-28s, for Kennedy requests that the ExComm reconvene the next day to "decide whether we should go to the mat on the IL-28 bombers or whether we should say that the Soviets have now completed their agreement to remove the missiles and move on to other problems." (Document 65, *Summary Record of NSC Executive Committee Meeting, November 5, 1962,* 11/5/62; *Washington Embassy Reports Re Events in Cuba,* ca. 11/5/62)

November 7, 1962—9:32 P.M.: In a cable to Adlai Stevenson, Secretary of State Rusk advises, "our primary purpose is to get the MRBMs and IL-28 bombers out [of Cuba], and we would go far in reducing our list of offensive weapons in order to achieve this purpose." The United States eventually drops its demands for the removal of Komar-class missile boats in order to focus on the IL-28 bombers. (*Instructions for Negotiations Using a Minimum List of Offensive Weapons,* 11/7/62)

November 8, 1962—4:30 P.M.: The ExComm discusses the ways in which the United States can pressure Cuba into removing the IL-28 bombers. According to minutes of the meeting, President Kennedy "was inclined not to reimpose the quarantine, but he did favor pressure on our allies to keep their ships out of Cuba." Various other ideas are offered, including tightening the quarantine, initiating new covert action against Castro, and launching air attacks on the IL-28 aircraft. (*Summary Record of NSC Executive Committee Meeting No. 23, November 8, 1962, 4:30 P.M.,* 11/8/62; *Notes on 4:30 P.M. ExComm Meeting,* 11/8/62)

November 8, 1962: A six-man CIA sabotage team dispatched as part of Task Force W blows up a Cuban industrial facility (see entry for October 30, 1962). The incident is never raised in U.S.-Soviet talks and remains unknown to most if not all members of the ExComm. (Garthoff 1, p. 122)

The Defense Department announces that "all known" MRBM and IRBM Soviet bases in Cuba have been dismantled, and that a "substantial" number of missiles have been loaded aboard Soviet ships or are being moved to port areas. (*Defense Department Statement on Evidence That All MRBM and IRBM Bases Have Been Dismantled*, 11/8/62)

U Thant offers a new on-site inspection proposal in which five ambassadors to Cuba from Asian, African, European, and Latin American countries would verify the withdrawal of the missiles. Cuba rejects this proposal, as it does all other unilateral inspection formulas, on November 11. (*Discussion of Draft Letter from U Thant to Castro on Verification by Latin American Ambassadors*, 11/9/62; *U Thant's Proposal for On-Site Verification by a Group of Ambassadors in Havana—Includes Revised Copy*, 11/8/62)

November 9, 1962: The last of the ships removing Soviet MRBM missiles from Cuba leave the island. Six vessels, the *Bratsk, Dvinogorsk, I. Polzunov, Labinsk, M. Anosov,*and *Volgoles*, have left Mariel since November 5, and two ships, the *F. Kurchatov* and the *L. Komsomol* depart from Casilda during this period. During the day, five of the ships are inspected at sea, with the Soviet ships pulling canvas covers off the missile transporters to allow U.S. ships to observe and photograph their contents. Assistant Secretary of Defense Arthur Sylvester later tells reporters that the "responsible people of this government are satisfied" that the ships are in fact carrying missiles. (*Department of Defense Press Conference of Robert McNamara*, 2/28/63, p. M-1; *The Missiles Leave Cuba*, ca. 12/62; *NYT*, 11/10/62)

November 12, 1962—11:00 A.M.: Adlai Stevenson reports to the ExComm that negotiations in New York on the IL-28 issue are deadlocked. At President Kennedy's prompting, the group discusses various ways in which the United States might strike a deal with the Soviet Union over the bomber issue. The possibility of offering further noninvasion assurances, ending the quarantine, and lifting on-site inspection demands are raised as possible inducements, but the meeting ends without a firm decision on how to pro-

ceed in the negotiations. President Kennedy decides not to lower SAC alert levels at the time, with Robert McNamara noting that such a decision could send the wrong "signals" to the Soviet Union. (*Summary Record of NSC Executive Committee Meeting No. 24, November 12, 1962, 11:00 A.M.*, 11/12/62)

November 12, 1962: Premier Khrushchev sends President Kennedy a message confirming the removal of the missiles. The letter adopts a friendly tone, commenting on the outcome of the November 6, 1962 elections in the United States: "You managed to pin your political rival, Mr. Nixon, to the mat," the letter comments on the fact that Nixon lost his bid to become governor of California. "This did not draw tears from our eyes either." (Document 69, *Premier Khrushchev's Letter to President Kennedy*, 11/12/62)

November 12, 1962—night: President Kennedy instructs his brother Robert to inform Soviet Ambassador Dobrynin that Khrushchev's "word" on the IL-28s will "suffice" and the U.S. will not insist on an immediate withdrawal of the bomber planes. Robert Kennedy tells the Soviet Ambassador that the U.S would hope the planes are removed "within, say, 30 days." (Document 70, *President Kennedy's Oral Message to Premier Khrushchev, On the Subject of the IL-28 Aircraft*, 11/12/62)

November 13, 1962—morning: ExComm members continue to discuss the IL-28 issue. The group's recommendations, incorporated into a paper by U. Alexis Johnson, include a proposed sequence of actions designed to end the deadlock. To begin with, the group recommends a "last chance" private message to Premier Khrushchev, warning that further actions could be taken shortly. If the message fails to produce the desired outcome, the group suggests tightening the blockade, arranging for other countries in Latin America and elsewhere to apply diplomatic pressure on Fidel Castro, and using intense low-altitude reconnaissance as a form of psychological warfare. The ExComm also notes that one other option exists but recommends that it only be used as a last-ditch measure: "provoking" an attack on U.S. reconnaissance planes and responding by striking a variety of Cuban targets, including the IL-28 bombers. (*Cuban Contingency Paper: Next Steps on the IL-28's*, 11/14/62)

November 14, 1962: Premier Khrushchev sends another message to President Kennedy on the IL-28 issue. Khrushchev hedges on when the Soviet Union will remove the bombers, but states that "it can be done in 2–3 months." He also complains that the United States is "not carrying out its commitments" to end overflights and quarantine, nor has it agreed to "register" the noninvasion pledge. (Document 71, *Premier Khrushchev's Letter to President Kennedy, Regarding Removal of the IL-28 Aircraft*, 11/14/62)

President Kennedy discusses the Cuban situation with Harold MacMillan over the telephone. Kennedy admits that no firm strategy for ironing out the remaining issues has been decided upon: "We do not want to crank up the quarantine again over the bombers. The only question is whether we should do that or take some other action. For example, we might say the whole deal is off and withdraw our no invasion pledge and harass them generally." (MacMillan, p. 215)

November 15, 1962—7:00 P.M.: In a five-page letter to U Thant, Fidel Castro warns that Cuba will fire on U.S. reconnaissance planes: any aircraft flying over Cuban airspace, he says, do so "at the risk of being destroyed." Noting that the United States has already inspected Soviet ships at sea, he also declares that Cuba will continue to reject "unilateral inspection by any body, national or international, on Cuban territory." U.S. intelligence has reported during the day that Soviet control of the Cuban air defense system has tightened sharply. Cuban fighter aircraft are detected practicing low-level flight tactics in the Havana area. (*Summary of Items of Significant Interest Period 160701–170700 November 1962*, 11/17/62)

November 15, 1962: President Kennedy writes to Premier Khrushchev on the continuing IL-28 issue. His letter complains that the "three major parts of the undertakings on your side—the removal of the IL-28's, the arrangements for verification, and safeguards against introduction—have not yet been carried out." During the day, Anatoly Dobrynin is informed that

the IL-28 issue has "reached a turning point," and that unless the matter is resolved, the United States and Soviet Union will "soon find ourselves back in a position of increasing tension." (Document 72, *President Kennedy's Letter to Premier Krushchev*, 11/15/62; *Status of the Negotiations on Removal of IL-28's*, 11/16/62)

November 16, 1962—7:00 A.M.: The largest amphibious landing since World War II begins as part of an exercise at Onslow Beach, North Carolina. The two-day exercise, a full-scale rehearsal for an invasion of Cuba, includes six marine battalion landing teams, four by assault boats and two by helicopter assault carriers. (*CINCLANT Historical Account of Cuban Crisis*, 4/29/63, p. 151; *Summary of Items of Significant Interest Period 090701–100700 November 1962*, 11/10/62)

November 16, 1962—4:05 P.M.: The JCS meets with President Kennedy to report on the readiness status of forces that would be involved in any military action against Cuba. U.S. forces massed for a Cuban invasion have reached their peak strength, the JCS reports: some 100,000 Army troops, 40,000 Marines and 14,500 paratroopers stand ready, with 550 combat aircraft and over 180 ships available to support an invasion. Kennedy is advised that this advanced state of readiness can be maintained for about thirty days. The talking paper prepared for Maxwell Taylor for this meeting spells out the JCS position on the IL-28 deadlock: they recommend that the United States continue to press the Soviet Union to remove the bombers, suggesting that the quarantine be extended to POL (petroleum, oil, and lubricants) if no progress is made. If the quarantine does not succeed in having the aircraft removed, the Joint Chiefs warn that the United States "should be prepared to take them out by air attack." (Document 73, *General Maxwell Taylor, "Talking Paper for Meeting with the President,"* 11/16/62; *Department of Defense Operations during the Cuban Missile Crisis*, 2/12/63, pp. 8, 12–14; *Summary of Items of Significant Interest Period 180701–190700 November 1962*, 11/19/62)

November 18, 1962: John McCloy and Adlai Stevenson have a long meeting with Vasily Kuznetsov and Valerian Zorin to try to force the dispute over the IL-28s to a head. McCloy repeatedly warns Kuznetsov that President Kennedy is scheduling a press conference for 6:00 P.M. on November 20, and that the United States must have a pledge that the bombers will be removed by that time. McCloy also continues to raise U.S. concerns over the lack of on-site verification, the possibility that new "offensive weapons" might be introduced into Cuba and the continued presence of four reinforced Soviet troop regiments in Cuba. Stevenson reports to the ExComm that the negotiations ended with "no indication from Kuznetsov that they would give way in regard to [the] IL-28's." (*Cuba-Meeting between McCloy and Kuznetsov, Sunday, November 18, 1962,* 11/19/62)

November 19, 1962—10:00 A.M.: At a morning ExComm session, President Kennedy authorizes high-level reconnaissance flights but again suspends low-level sorties. Robert Kennedy scrawls notes on the back of an envelope during the meeting: "President reluctant to send in low-level flights...How far can we push K[hrushchev?]." During the day, the attorney general meets with Georgi Bolshakov and warns him that low-level reconnaissance will begin again unless the Soviet Union promises to remove the bombers. Robert Kennedy states that he needs a response to the IL-28 issue before the president's press conference the next day. (*NSC Executive Committee Record of Action, November 19, 1962, 10:00 A.M., Meeting No. 27,* 11/19/62; Schlesinger, p. 526)

November 19, 1962—8:25 P.M.: Letters from President Kennedy to Charles de Gaulle, Konrad Adenauer, and Harold Macmillan are transmitted by the State Department. Kennedy warns the European leaders that if the IL-28s are not withdrawn, further U.S. action might result, including the extension of the quarantine to include POL and the possibility of an air attack against Cuba in response to attacks on U.S. reconnaissance planes. Although the overall situation is said to be "somewhat less dangerous than it was in October," Kennedy warns that getting Premier Khrushchev to back down again in some ways might be more difficult than it was during the missile crisis. Similar messages for Latin American heads of state are also sent during the evening. (*Text of Personal Message from President Kennedy to Charles de Gaulle, Konrad Adenauer and Harold Macmillan on the IL-28 Situation,* 11/19/62)

November 19, 1962: Fidel Castro informs U Thant that the Cuban government will not object if the Soviet Union removes the IL-28s from Cuba, thereby ending the crisis over the Soviet bombers. In a letter announcing his new position, Castro renounces any claim to the aircraft, stating that the IL-28 aircraft are "the property of the Soviet Government." However, the letter warns again that any "warplane invading Cuban airspace could do so only at the risk of being destroyed" and again rejects any unilateral inspection of Cuban territory. The Cuban government apparently had been persuaded to allow the bombers to be removed by the signing of a new Cuban-Soviet agreement under which the Soviet Union would leave an instruction center on the island where Cuban troops could be trained in the use of Soviet military equipment. (Document 75, *Prime Minister Castro's Letter to Secretary General U Thant, Withdrawing Opposition to Removal of IL-28 Aircraft,* 11/19/62; Alekseyev, p. 26)

November 20, 1962: President Kennedy directs an oral message through the Soviet ambassador for Chairman Khrushchev stating that he will announce a lower state of alert for U.S. forces at his press conference. (*Kennedy Message,* 11/20/62)

Premier Khrushchev formally agrees to remove the IL-28s from Cuba in a fourteen-page letter to President Kennedy. In his letter, Khrushchev complains that during their exchange of correspondence in October, Kennedy had not made "a single mention of bomber planes.... I informed you that the IL-28 planes are twelve years old and by their combat characteristics they at present cannot be classified as offensive types of weapons." Nonetheless, he added that "we intend to remove them within a month." In a separate transmission, Khrushchev urges that

Kennedy refrain from "hurting the national feelings of the Cubans" during his upcoming press conference. (Document 76, *Premier Khrushchev's Letter to President Kennedy, Announcing Withdrawl of IL-28 Aircraft from Cuba*, 11/20/62; Khrushchev Transmission, 11/20/62)

November 20, 1962—3:30 P.M.: After discussing Premier Khrushchev's letter agreeing to remove the IL-28s, the ExComm agrees to lift the quarantine. In addition, the SAC alert is ordered canceled and no low-altitude flights are authorized for November 21. U-2 missions are scheduled to verify the dismantling and withdrawal of the bomber aircraft. (Document 77, *Summary Record of NSC Executive Committee, November 20, 1962, 3:30 P.M., Meeting No. 28*, 11/20/62)

November 20, 1962—6:00 P.M.: President Kennedy announces at a press conference, "I have today been informed by Chairman Khrushchev that all of the IL-28 bombers in Cuba will be withdrawn in thirty days.... I have this afternoon instructed the Secretary of Defense to lift our naval quarantine." Kennedy suggests that because no on-site inspection has occurred, the preconditions for a U.S. noninvasion guarantee has not been met. Nonetheless, he states, "If all offensive weapons are removed from Cuba and kept out of the hemisphere in the future...and if Cuba is not used for the export of aggressive Communist purposes, there will be peace in the Caribbean." (*The President's News Conference of November 20, 1962*, 11/20/62)

November 20, 1962—11:21 P.M.: The JCS orders SAC to return to its normal airborne alert status, effective immediately. During the day, SAC forces lower their alert status from DEFCON 2, and other U.S. military commands reduced their alert status from DEFCON 3 to DEFCON 4. (*Summary of Items of Significant Interest Period 200701–210700 November 1962*, 11/21/62; Sagan, p. 101)

November 21, 1962—9:49 P.M.: In a cable to Adlai Stevenson and John McCloy, Dean Rusk summarizes the status of crisis following the IL-28 agreement:

The loose ends still remaining unfulfilled...are these: On [the] Soviet side, on-site U.N.-supervised verification of removal of offensive weapons, and longer-term safeguards against their reintroduction. On our side, formal assurances against invasion of Cuba.

Rusk notes that the United States favors settling the issue by having the U.S. and Soviet Union issue parallel declarations before the U.N. Security Council. The U.S. declaration, he writes, will state "our noninvasion assurances, contingent on Cuban behavior." (*Next Steps in New York Negotiations*, 11/21/62)

November 21, 1962: President Kennedy sends a brief letter to Premier Khrushchev welcoming the Soviet leader's decision to remove the IL-28s. Kennedy writes, "I have been glad to get your letter of November 20, which arrived in good time yesterday. As you will have seen, I was able to announce the lifting of our quarantine promptly at my press conference, on the basis of your welcome assurance that the IL-28 bombers will be removed within a month." Kennedy also reassures Khrushchev that "there need be no fear of any invasion of Cuba while matters take their present favorable course." (*Message for Chairman Khrushchev*, 11/21/62)

The president officially lifts the naval quarantine of Cuba, and measures are taken promptly by the U.S. Navy to return to a normal readiness posture. Secretary McNamara authorizes the secretary of the air force to release 14,200 air reservists, and the Defense Department removes involuntary extensions for the U.S. Navy and Marine Corps personnel. Almost simultaneously, the Soviet Union and other Warsaw Pact nations announce the cancellation of the special military preparedness measures that had been put into effect on October 23. (*Khrushchev's Cuban Venture in Retrospect*, 12/7/62; *Department of Defense Operations during the Cuban Missile Crisis*, 2/12/63, pp. 14, 19; Garthoff 1, p. 114)

November 22, 1962: Premier Khrushchev sends a five-page letter to Kennedy regarding the Soviet leader's views on Cuba and opinions on Fidel Castro.

Cuban leaders, he observes, are "young, expansive people—Spaniards in a word, to use it far from the pejorative sense." Given nationalist sensitivities in Cuba, Khrushchev asks Kennedy to avoid steps "capable of causing scratches to national pride and prestige" of the Cuban leadership. (*Premier Khrushchev's Letter to President Kennedy*, 11/22/62)

November 29, 1962—10:00 A.M.: The ExComm meets with President Kennedy to discuss intelligence and diplomatic reports on Cuba, U.S. declaratory policy on the IL-28 issue, the future of OPERATION MONGOOSE and "post mortems of Oct. 15–28." Kennedy directs the State Department to prepare a long-range plan to "keep pressure on Castro." (*NSC Executive Committee Record of Action, November 29, 1962, 10:00 A.M., Meeting No. 31*, 11/29/62; *Executive Committee Meeting, November 29, 1962, 10 A.M. Agenda*, 11/28/62)

November 29, 1962—4:30 P.M.: In a three-hour meeting with President Kennedy and Secretary of State Rusk, Anastas Mikoyan repeatedly presses for a clarification and a confirmation of a U.S. guarantee not to invade Cuba. Kennedy reassures Mikoyan that the United States has no intention of invading Cuba, but he backs away from the idea of issuing further formal guarantees, stressing that other conditions set out in his exchange of letters with Nikita Khrushchev have not been met (in particular, international on-site verification and safeguards on the reintroduction of strategic weapons into Cuba). However, Kennedy does state that if the Soviet Union abides by the exchange of correspondence, the United States will as well. (*U.S. Policy toward Cuba and Related Events 1 November 1961 – 15 March 1963*, ca. 3/16/63, pt. 3, p. 11; Garthoff 1, pp. 126–27)

December 3, 1962—11:00 A.M.: John McCloy meets with Soviet negotiators at the Waldorf Suite in New York City. Earlier, in one of the final sessions between the U.S. and Soviet negotiators, Vasily Kuznetsov met with McCloy at the McCloy's home in Connecticut. As their talk ended, Kuznetsov reportedly said, "all right, Mr. McCloy, we will get the IL-28's out as we

have taken the missiles out. But I want to tell you something, Mr. McCloy. The Soviet Union is not going to find itself in a position like this ever again." (*Chronology of Negotiations Re: Cuban Crisis*, 12/6/62; Bohlen, pp. 495-96)

December 4, 1962—5:30 P.M.: ExComm members discuss future policy toward Cuba at a working meeting held without President Kennedy. The group reviews U.S. planning for future overflights of Cuba, apparently agreeing that continued aerial reconnaissance is necessary to verify the removal of the IL-28s and to ensure offensive weapons are not reintroduced into Cuba. When John McCone raises the possibility that another U-2 might be shot down, the ExComm decides that the United States should respond by attacking one or more SAM sites. Troubled by the potential for a new crisis arising over another attack on U.S. reconnaissance, McCone writes to McGeorge Bundy the following morning to recommend that "diplomatic measures be taken" to assure that the United States does not find itself in the position of having to attack Soviet-controlled bases in Cuba. (*Warning That the United States May Soon Face the Contingency of Responding to a Shootdown of Another U-2*, 12/5/62; *Guidelines for Planning of Cuban Overflights*, 11/30/62)

December 5, 1962: Stevenson and McCloy send an eyes-only cable to Secretary Rusk and the president protesting their instructions to achieve and agreement on on-site verification even though all the missiles and planes have already been removed from Cuba. The cable states that they

> have the growing impression that effects of victory in public mind are being gradually effaced by prolonged and inconclusive negotiation which gives impression we are still seeking vital objective we have not achieved. If public presumes this objective is on-site verification, more and more importance will be attached to such inspection as negotiation continues. If and when we emerge from negotiation without achieving that objective, even though it may have been otherwise suc-

cessful, we will risk seeming to have failed rather than to have succeeded.(Bird, p. 538)

December 10, 1962: Khrushchev sends a nine-page letter to Kennedy on the situation in both Cuba and Berlin. He indicates that the United States and the Soviet Union have come to the final stage of the Cuban affair. The Soviet premier then raises the issue of Berlin and attempts to drive a wedge between the United States and German leader Konrad Adenauer. "Should really you and we—two great states—submit, willingly or unwillingly, to the old-aged man who both morally and physically is with one foot in [the] grave? Should we really become toys in his hands?" (*Premier Khrushchev's Letter to President Kennedy*, 12/10/62)

December 12, 1962: In a major 2 1/2–hour speech to the Supreme Soviet—his first major address since the Cuban crisis—Premier Khrushchev asserts that a U.S. "pledge" not to invade Cuba exists. He warns, however, that if the United States carries out an invasion, Cuba would not be left "defenseless." (*The Soviet Bloc Armed Forces and the Cuban Crisis: A Chronology*, 6/18/63, pp. 115, 121–22)

At a press conference, President Kennedy tells reporters that, in the best judgment of the United States, all strategic missiles and IL-28 bombers have been removed from Cuba. (*The President's News Conference of December 12, 1962*, 12/12/62)

December 14, 1962: President Kennedy writes to Premier Khrushchev in response to Khrushchev's December 11 message. The letter thanks Khrushchev "for [his] expression of appreciation of the understanding and flexibility we have tried to display" and expresses hope that a final settlement to the "Cuban question" could be found quickly. Kennedy also discusses communications between the two leaders during the missile crisis: he suggests that the use of reporters such as John Scali is not a satisfactory method of transmitting messages and expresses disappointment that Georgi Bolshakov, the channel for many exchanges between Kennedy and Khrushchev, is being called back to the Soviet Union. (*President Kennedy's Response to Khrushchev's December 11 Letter*, 12/14/62)

December 17, 1962: In a television and radio interview, President Kennedy offers some of his thoughts on the crisis. He observes that "if we had to act on Wednesday [October 17] in the first twenty-four hours, I don't think we would have chosen as prudently as we finally did." He characterizes the Soviet attempt to install missiles in Cuba as "an effort to materially change the balance of power.... It would have appeared to, and appearances contribute to reality." Kennedy compares the miscalculations leading to the Cuban missile crisis with those misjudgments that had led to World Wars I and II. When "you see the Soviet Union and the United States, so far separated in their beliefs...and you put the nuclear equation into that struggle; that is what makes this...such a dangerous time.... One mistake can make this whole thing blow up." (*Television and Radio Interview: "After Two Years—A Conversation with the President,"* 12/17/62)

December 19, 1962: Premier Khrushchev sends a letter to President Kennedy suggesting that the "time has come now to put an end once and for all to nuclear tests." He writes, "with the elimination of the Cuban crisis we relieved mankind of the direct menace of combat use of lethal nuclear weapons that impended over the world. Can't we solve a far simpler question—that of cessation of experimental explosions of nuclear weapons in the peaceful conditions?" Kennedy responds to Khrushchev's letter on December 28. Continued negotiations subsequently lead to the eventual signing of a limited test-ban treaty on August 5, 1963. (*Khrushchev's Letter*, 12/19/62; Garthoff 1, pp. 131, 134)

January 1963: Italy and Turkey announce that the IRBMs stationed in their countries will be phased out. In addition to the fifteen Turkish Jupiter missiles, thirty Jupiters deployed in Italy are affected by the decisions. (*Annual Report of the Secretary of the Army, July 1, 1962 to June 30, 1962*, 5/20/64, p. 248)

January 4, 1963: The Standing Group, an NSC group that eventually replaces the ExComm in reviewing U.S. policy toward Cuba, discusses McGeorge Bundy's proposal of opening communications with

Fidel Castro. Bundy later notes that the "gradual development of some form of accommodation with Castro" became a standard item in lists of policy alternatives considered by the Kennedy administration. Nonetheless, U.S. policy toward Castro vacillates considerably in the months after the missile crisis. Even as secret approaches to Castro are being weighed, the Kennedy administration also contemplates Pentagon proposals for military action against Castro, as well as a wide range of economic and covert programs to weaken the Castro government. (*Alleged Assassination Plots Involving Foreign Leaders*, 11/20/75, p. 173; Schlesinger, p. 538)

January 7, 1963: The United States and the Soviet Union agree to terminate U.N. consideration of the missile crisis. In a joint letter to U Thant, Adlai Stevenson and Vasily Kuznetsov note that while the two governments have not been able to "resolve all the problems" resulting from the crisis, sufficient progress has been made in implementing the Kennedy-Khrushchev understanding to warrant the end of negotiations at the United Nations. Carlos Lechuga, the Cuban ambassador to the United Nations, sends a letter to U Thant two hours prior to the delivery of the U.S.-Soviet letter. Lechuga objects to the settlement, insisting that Cuba cannot regard any agreement ending crisis negotiations as "effective" unless it meets the "five points" Castro had articulated on October 28, 1962. (*Reiteration of Castro's "Five Points" and Cuban Perspective on United Nations Negotiations*, 1/7/63; Document 79, *Adlai Stevenson and Vasily Kuznetov, Letter to the United Nations*, 1/7/63)

January 11, 1963: Dean Rusk, testifying at a closed hearing before the Senate foreign relations committee, clarifies the U.S. noninvasion assurance. The United States "never made an unadorned commitment not to invade Cuba in the first place," Rusk declared. In any case, Rusk adds that "a crucial element" in the Kennedy-Khrushchev understandings—onsite inspection and assurances against the reintroduction of strategic weapons into Cuba—was not fulfilled by the Cuban and Soviet governments. "If Castro were to do the kind of things which would from our point of view justify invasion," Rusk stresses, the United States would not consider any non-invasion assurance binding. (*Briefing of the World Situation*, 1/11/63)

January 15, 1963: The Soviet Union makes a final attempt to obtain a firm U.S. noninvasion pledge during a meeting between Vasily Kuznetsov and President Kennedy just prior to Kuznetsov's departure for Moscow. The president declines to extend any further assurances. (Garthoff 1, p. 128)

January 15, 1963: In a lengthy televised speech, Fidel Castro declares, "for us, the Caribbean crisis has not been resolved. A war was avoided but the peace was not won." Regarding a U.S. non-invasion guarantee, Castro says, "we don't believe in Kennedy's words. But Kennedy has given no pledge and if he did give it he has already withdrawn it." (*CR*, 3/12/63)

January 25, 1963: At its first meeting in over a month and during subsequent sessions, the ExComm considers various long-range plans to pressure Fidel Castro. The United States wants Castro removed from power but it recognizes that if this proves impossible, then it wants him to be independent of the Soviet Union. Policy papers suggest that the ultimate objective is replacement of the government by "one fully compatible with the goals of the United States." (*Participation in Cuban Missile Crisis Meetings, October 1962*, 10/5/68; Garthoff 1, p. 139)

Late January 1963: OPERATION MONGOOSE begins to be phased out. The Special Group Augmented is replaced by a different oversight organization, the Special Group, chaired by McGeorge Bundy. Although Mongoose is abolished, the CIA arm, Task Force W, continues to exist as the Special Affairs Staff, located at the CIA's Miami station. William Harvey, the head of Task Force W, is replaced by Desmond FitzGerald as head of the Special Affairs Staff. Covert operations against Fidel Castro continue during 1963 under FitzGerald. In addition to continuing attempts on Castro's life over the course of the year, CIA teams carry out at least six major operations in Cuba aimed at disrupting the Cuban government and economy. (*Cuba, operation mongoose*, 1/28/63; *Alleged Assassination Plots Involving Foreign Leaders*, 11/20/75, p. 170; Ranelagh, p. 388)

February 18, 1963: At Premier Khrushchev's direction, Anatoly Dobrynin delivers an aide-memoire to president Kennedy informing the president that "several thousand" Soviet troops still in Cuba would be withdrawn by March 15. No commitment to withdraw all Soviet military personnel is given, however. Unknown to the United States at the time, Khrushchev had agreed to Cuban demands to keep one of the four Soviet combat regiments in Cuba to act as a "tripwire" against a U.S. invasion. (*Informal Translation of Soviet Aide Memoire on the Soviet Decision to Withdraw Military Personnel From Cuba*, 2/18/63; Garthoff 1, p. 120)

February 21, 1963: The JCS are asked to undertake a comprehensive study of actions that might be taken in the event of a revolt in Cuba. The JCS in turn requests CINCLANT's view on several questions:

1) Possible military and para-military responses by the United States to a Cuban revolt...

3) How could we get arms and equipment to the rebels?

4) Under which circumstances should we consider invasion?

5) If the revolt were widespread and apparently successful, might we decide on a curtailed, rapid execution of CINCLANT Oplan 316 [the invasion plan of Cuba] in order to exploit in time the effects of the revolt on the Castro force? (*Addendum #1 Summary of Items of Significant Interest Period 200701–210700 February 1963*, 2/21/63)

March 21, 1963: President Kennedy criticizes recent attacks on Cuba by Cuban "exiles," saying that the raids only "strengthened the Russian position in Cuba." (*NYT*, 3/22/63)

March 26, 1963: The anti-Castro group L-66 attacks and sinks the Soviet ship *Baku* as it loads Cuban sugar at the harbor of Caibarien, Cuba. The assault on the *Baku*, as well as the one on the *L'Gov* a week earlier, are among the most serious attacks that have taken place during the year, and both incidents were strenuously protested by the Soviet Union and Cuba. (*Summary of Major Raids Carried Out by Anti-Castro Groups*, ca. 4/63; NYT, 3/28/63)

April 3, 1963: Sabotage operations against Cuba have been discontinued, McGeorge Bundy tells participants in a high-level administration meeting on Cuba, because the Special Group "had decided...that such activity is not worth the effort expended on it." This cessation of sabotage operations is short-lived however; President Kennedy approves a new set of operations on June 19 (see entry for June 19, 1963). (*Alleged Assassination Plots Involving Foreign Leaders*, 11/20/75, p. 173; Schlesinger 1, p. 544)

April 21, 1963: McGeorge Bundy submits to the NSC's Standing Group a memo on "Cuba Alternatives" discussing "possible new directions" for U.S. policy toward Cuba. Three possible alternatives are identified: forcing "a non-Communist solution in Cuba by all necessary means," insisting on "major but limited ends," or moving "in the direction of a gradual development of some form of accommodation with Castro." (*Alleged Assassination Plots Involving Foreign Leaders*, 11/20/75, p. 171)

April 25, 1963: Robert McNamara sends a handwritten note to President Kennedy informing him that "The last Jupiter missile in Turkey came down yesterday. The last Jupiter warhead will be flown out of Turkey on Saturday." On April 1, before the Jupiters are withdrawn, the first Polaris submarine is deployed in the Mediterranean Sea. No public announcement accompanied the withdrawal of the missiles, but reports that the missiles are to be dismantled are confirmed by the State Department on March 25. (*Interview with Raymond Hare by Dennis O'Brien: Jupiter Missiles in Turkey and the Missile Crisis*, 9/19/69; *Transcript of Press and Radio News Briefing*, 3/25/63;

Handwritten Note Informing President Kennedy That the Last Jupiter Missile in Turkey Was Dismantled, 4/25/63)

April 27–May 23, 1963: Fidel Castro and a large entourage begin a five-week, fourteen-city visit to the Soviet Union. Castro negotiates renewed pledges of Soviet aid in the event of a U.S. attack as well as changes in Soviet-Cuban sugar agreements. During the visit, Castro and Premier Khrushchev review all of the documents that have been exchanged between the Soviet Union and the United States as a result of the missile crisis. Castro later reveals that it is only at this time that he learned that the withdrawal of nuclear missiles from Turkey had been part of the agreement settling the crisis. (Szulc, p. 650; Sobel, pp. 124–25)

June 19, 1963: Following a Special Group meeting, President Kennedy approves a new sabotage program against Cuba. Whereas OPERATION MONGOOSE was aimed at eventually sparking an internal revolt, the new program seeks a more limited objective: "to nourish a spirit of resistance and disaffection which could lead to significant defections and other by-products of unrest." Numerous sabotage efforts against important economic targets are authorized by the Special Group during the autumn of 1963, and U.S.-assisted raids and assassination plots are not completely terminated until 1965 (see entries for October 3 and 24, 1963). (*Alleged Assassination Plots Involving Foreign Leaders*, 11/20/75)

June 20, 1963: A memorandum of understanding between the United States and the Soviet Union establishing a "hot line" between Washington and Moscow is signed. The agreement establishes a direct teletype communication link to be used "in time of emergency" in order to clarify intentions and prevent accident, miscalculation, or misunderstanding from leading to unintentional war. (*ACDA*, pp. 28–33)

October 13, 1964: Nikita Khrushchev is ousted from power. Former KGB chief Alexander Shelpin and his protégé, Vladamir Semichastny, reportedly instigate the action against Khrushchev. Although the Cuban missile crisis is not a major cause of Khrushchev's fall—the majority of the formal charges leveled against Krushchev reportedly deal with domestic affairs—his handling of the Cuban crisis may have contributed indirectly to his loss of support among the other high-level Soviet officials. (*WP*, 9/15/88; *Time*, 11/14/88)

August 4, 1970: Apparently prompted by Cuban fears of an invasion by the United States, Soviet Chargé Yuli M. Vorontsov meets with National Security Advisor Henry Kissinger some eight years after the Cuban missile crisis in an attempt to reconfirm the Kennedy-Khrushchev understanding on Cuba. Without consulting others within the administration, President Nixon and Henry Kissinger decide to "reaffirm" the understanding. On August 7, Kissinger meets with Vorontsov, and both give their word that the understanding is "still in full force." This is the first time that U.S. leaders have unequivocally accepted the mutual commitments proposed in 1962. (Garthoff 1, pp. 141–42; Nixon, p. 486)

September 9, 1970: A Soviet flotilla, including special vessels used to support the operations of Soviet nuclear submarines, arrives at the port of Cienfuegos, Cuba. (Garthoff 1, pp. 145–48)

October 6, 1970: In an attempt to defuse increasing diplomatic tensions over the Cienfiegos "submarine port," Anatoly Dobrynin meets with Henry Kissinger. The Soviet ambassador hands Kissinger a note reaffirming the Kennedy-Khrushchev understanding; it states that "in the Cuban question, the Soviet government continues to proceed from the understanding reached on this question in 1962." Dobrynin also states that "he was prepared on behalf of his government to affirm that ballistic missile submarines would never call there [Cuba] in an operational capacity." (*United States–Soviet Understanding on Offensive Weapons in Cuba*, 11/22/78; Hersh, p. 255; Nixon, p. 489)

October 9, 1970: Henry Kissinger gives Anatoly Dobrynin a formal message from President Nixon welcoming the Soviet assurances but offering the U.S. interpretation of the 1962 understanding that settled the Cuban missile crisis:

> The U.S. government understands that the U.S.S.R. will not establish, utilize, or permit the establishment of any facility in Cuba that can be employed to support or repair Soviet naval ships capable of carrying offensive weapons, i.e. submarines or surface ships armed with nuclear capable, surface-to-surface missiles.

The note lists five specific actions that the U.S. government would consider violations of the 1962 agreement. Dobrynin reportedly objects to the bluntness of the language but hints that the issue will soon be resolved. (*United States–Soviet Understanding on Offensive Weapons in Cuba*, 11/22/78; Hersh, p. 255; Nixon, p. 489)

October 23, 1970: Anatoly Dobrynin reassures Henry Kissinger that the Soviet Union does not have a military facility in Cuba and confirms that it will continue to abide by the 1962 Kennedy-Khrushchev agreement. Dobrynin also states that the Soviet Union will from August onward make diplomatic exchanges a part of the U.S.-Soviet understanding on Cuba. (*Declassification of David Newsom's Testimony on the U.S.–Soviet Understandings on Cuba*, 9/6/79)

November 30, 1978: President Jimmy Carter holds a news conference to quell the political controversy that erupts after the publication of a column by Rowland Evans and Robert Novak reporting the deployment of Soviet MiG-23 fighter-bombers in Cuba. Carter told reporters that the Soviet government has given him assurances that no shipments of arms to Cuba had or would violate the terms of the 1962 agreement. (Garthoff 1, pp. 149–50)

January 17, 1979: After reviewing the deployment of Soviet MiG-23 aircraft to Cuba, the State Department announces it has concluded that the aircraft are not configured for delivering nuclear weapons and thus do not constitute a violation of 1962 Kennedy-Khrushchev agreement. (Garthoff 3, p. 438)

August 1979: A crisis that develops in the Carter administration over the "discovery" of a 2,600-man Soviet military "brigade" ended abruptly when it was realized that the brigade has probably been stationed in Cuba since 1962, a vestige of the Cuban missile crisis. The Soviet Union had agreed in November 1962 that the brigade would be left behind to compensate Fidel Castro for the withdrawal of Soviet strategic missiles and a large number of Soviet forces (see entry for November 2, 1962). (Garthoff 1, p. 151)

September 14, 1983: President Reagan said of the 1962 Kennedy-Khrushchev understanding: "As far as I'm concerned, that agreement has been abrogated many times by the Soviet Union and Cuba in the bringing in of what can only be considered offensive weapons." (*The Kennedy-Khrushchev Agreement Has Been Abrogated Many Times*, 9/14/83)

September 18, 1983: In response to a reporter's question, President Reagan states that his administration is actively reviewing the Kennedy-Khrushchev understanding and the question of whether the continued transfer of MiG-23 aircraft to Cuba constitutes a violation of the agreement. The Reagan administration, like the Carter administration in 1978, ultimately decides that the MiGs should not be considered "offensive weapons." (Garthoff 1, p. 152)

March 5–8, 1987: Harvard University's Nuclear Crisis Project at the Center for Science and International Affairs hosts a major conference on the Cuban Missile Crisis in Hawks Cay, Florida. The first of five such conferences organized by Professor James G. Blight, the Hawks Cay meeting brings together many of the surviving members of the ExComm, including Robert McNamara, C. Douglas Dillon, George Ball, McGeorge Bundy, Theodore Sorensen, and Arthur Schlesinger, Jr., as well as the most prominent crisis scholars, among them Graham T. Allison, Ernest May, Joseph Nye, Richard Neustadt, and Thomas Schelling. The National Security Archive provides the documents for the conference, from which emerges a number of significant revelations—most notably that President Kennedy had secretly asked Secretary of State Dean Rusk to initiate a U.N. proposal on trading missiles in Turkey for Soviet missiles in Cuba if negotiations broke down between the superpowers. Proceedings from the conference, as well as those from a second conference held in October 1987, are later published in James G. Blight and David A. Welch's book, *On the Brink: Americans and Soviets Reexamine the Cuban Missile Crisis* (New York: Hill and Wang, 1989).

April 1987: The National Security Archive files twenty-seven Freedom of Information Act requests for thousands of pages of documentation on the Cuban missile crisis which the State Department has gathered and stored since 1965. The requests specify the file folders contained in five boxes of materials. The FOIAs are filed in the name of Professor Philip Brenner, a Cuba specialist and board member of the Archive.

October 11–13, 1987: A second conference on the Cuban missile crisis, organized by James G. Blight, takes place in Cambridge, Massachusetts. Former members of the ExComm and scholars are joined by three prominent Soviets: Fyodor Burlatsky, Khrushchev's former speechwriter and adviser; Sergo Mikoyan, son of former First Deputy Premier Anastas Mikoyan; and Georgi Shaknazarov, a personal aide to General Secretary Ghorbachev. The information provided by the Soviet participants fills a major gap in the one-sided history of the crisis; the conference results in compelling new analysis of the critical question of why Premier Khrushchev decided to deploy the missiles in Cuba. (Blight, pp. 225–90)

January 26, 1989: The National Security Archive releases substantive documentation on OPERATION MONGOOSE, the covert program authorized by President Kennedy to overthrow the Castro government. The documents, declassified for the first time as a result of a FOIA lawsuit filed against the State Department, offer a better understanding of events leading up to the missile crisis. According to the memoranda, CIA covert sabotage operations, combined with punitive economic measures and psychological operations, were intended to result in a popular uprising against Castro, the success of which would "require decisive military intervention" by the United States. The timetable established for Mongoose foresaw the revolt, and a U.S. invasion to support it, coming to fruition in October 1962—the month the missile crisis began. The new documentation lends credence to the argument that the Soviets and Cubans, whose agents had infiltrated MONGOOSE, believed a U.S. invasion was being planned and that the Soviet missiles were then deployed for defensive reasons. (Documents 5–9; "Papers Show 1962 U.S. Plan Against Castro," *NYT*, 1/27/89)

January 27–29, 1989: An unprecedented retrospective conference is held in Moscow. The third in a series organized by James G. Blight, the conference brings together the U.S., Soviet, and Cuban sides of the missile crisis for the first time. Besides lengthy discussion of the revelations in the OPERATION MONGOOSE documents, significant new facts about the crisis are disclosed:

- U.S. intelligence estimates of ten thousand to twelve thousand Soviet troops in Cuba during the crisis were far off, according to the Soviets. The real figure was over forty thousand.
- The Cubans expected the United States to invade and predicted up to eight hundred thousand casualties.
- At least twenty nuclear warheads were actually in Cuba but were never mounted on the rockets, according to General Dmitry Volkogonov, this is the first confirmation that the Soviets had managed to deploy warheads as well as missiles before the blockade was implemented.
- The U.S. withdrawal of missiles in Turkey was an explicit part of the U.S.-Soviet settlement of the missile crisis, according to Theodore Sorensen, who edited Robert Kennedy's memoir of the cri-

sis, *Thirteen Days*.

· Some of Soviet Ambassador Dobrynin's cables to Moscow were transmitted via a Western Union office in Washington, D.C.

The Moscow conference proceedings were subsequently published in Bruce J. Allyn, James G. Blight, and David A. Welch's book, *Back to the Brink: The Moscow Conference on the Cuban Missile Crisis*. (*WSJ*, 2/30/89)

January 3–7, 1991: A fourth conference on the missile crisis, "Cuba between the Superpowers," is held on the island of Antigua. Organized by James Blight, who is now at Brown University's Center for Foreign Policy Development, the conference is once again attended by American, Soviet, and Cuban officials. For the first time, the focus is on the U.S.-Cuban and Soviet-Cuban dynamic and Cuba's role in the crisis. (James G. Blight, David Lewis, and David Welch, "Cuba Between the Superpowers: Antigua, 3–7 January 1991," Transcript of the Meetings.)

January 6, 1992: Pursuant to a FOIA lawsuit filed by the National Security Archive, the Department of State releases the remaining correspondence between Kennedy and Khrushchev. The eleven letters, dating from October 30–December 19, 1962, shed new light on the continuing tension between the superpowers in the weeks following the climax of the crisis on October 28, 1962. They reveal, among other facts, that there was no secret deal between Kennedy and Khrushchev that would have constrained the United States from future overt intervention in Cuba. The release of the letters generates numerous newspaper articles, including front-page stories in *USA Today* and the *Miami Herald*. (Documents 64, 69–72, 76; "The Cuba Missile Crisis: Kennedy Left a Loophole," *NYT*, 1/7/92)

January 9–12, 1992: The last of five meetings, "The Tripartite Conference over the Crisis of October, 1962," organized by James Blight, Janet Lang, and Brown University's Center for Foreign Policy Development, is held in Havana, Cuba. Attended all four days by Fidel Castro, the last surviving world leader involved in the episode, as well as by former high-level officials from the United States, Cuba, and the former Soviet Union, the conference marks the apex of historical exploration of the crisis. Castro provides unparalleled accounts of his personal role in the events, as well as that of Cuba as a nation. Among the more astounding revelations that emerge from the delegation from the former Soviet Union is confirmation that the Soviets had installed short-range tactical nuclear weapons in Cuba, and that the local Soviet commander had the authority to fire those weapons without further direction from the Kremlin in the event of a U.S. invasion. (See Arthur Schlesinger, Jr., "Four Days with Fidel: A Havana Diary," *New York Review of Books*, 3/26/92; the proceedings will be published in James G. Blight, Bruce J. Allyn, and David A. Welch, with David Lewis, *Cuba On the Brink: Fidel Castro, the Missile Crisis and the Collapse of Communism* [New York: Pantheon Books, 1993])

ABBREVIATIONS

Abel = Abel, Elie. *The Missile Crisis*. Philadelphia: Lippincott, 1966.

ACDA = United States Arms Control and Disarmament Agency. *Arms Control and Disarmament Agreements*. Washington, D.C.: G.P.O., 1982.

Alekseyev = Alekseyev, Aleksandr. "*Karibskii Krizis: Kak Eto Bylo*." ("The Caribbean Crisis: As It Really Was.") *Ekho Planety* (Soviet Union) 33 (Nov. 1988): 27–37.

Allyn = Allyn, Bruce J., James Blight, and David A. Welch. "Essence of Revision: Moscow, Havana, and the Cuban Missile Crisis." *International Security* 14, no. 3 (Winter 1989/1990).

Ball = Ball, George. *The Past Has Another Pattern*. New York: W. W. Norton, 1982.

Betts = Betts, Richard. *Nuclear Blackmail and Nuclear Balance*. Washington, DC: Brookings Institution, 1978.

Blight = Blight, James, and David Welch. *On the Brink: Americans and Soviets Reexamine the Cuban Missile Crisis*. New York: Hill and Wang, 1989.

Bohlen = Bohlen, Charles. *Witness to History, 1929–1969*. New York: W. W. Norton, 1973.

Bourne = Bourne, Peter G. *Fidel: A Biography of Fidel Castro*. New York: Dodd, Mead, 1986.

Brenner = Brenner, Philip, William LeoGrande, Donna Rich, and Daniel Siegel, eds. *The Cuba Reader: The Making of a Revolutionary Society*. New York: Grove Press, 1988.

Bundy = Bundy, McGeorge. *Danger and Survival: Choices about the Bomb in the First Fifty Years*. New York: Random House, 1988.

CINCLANTFLT = *CINCLANTFLT Command History, May 21, 1963* (available at the National Security Archive).

Cline = Cline, Ray. "A CIA Reminiscence." *Washington Quarterly* 5 (Autumn 1982).

Cooper = *Oral History with Chester Cooper*, May 6, 1966 (available at the National Security Archive).

CR = *Congressional Record*.

Detzer = Detzer, David. *The Brink: Cuban Missile Crisis, 1962*. New York: Thomas Y. Crowell, 1979.

Draper = Draper, Theodore. "Castro and Communism: A Detailed Account of the Background and Consequences of the Missile Crisis in Cuba." Reporter 28 (Jan. 17, 1963): 35–48.

Garthoff 1 = Garthoff, Raymond L. *Reflections on the Cuban Missile Crisis*. 2nd ed. Washington, D.C.: Brookings Institution, 1989.

Garthoff 2 = Garthoff, Raymond L. "Cuban Missile Crisis: The Soviet Story." *Foreign Policy* 72 (Fall 1988).

Garthoff 3 = Garthoff, Raymond L. "American Reaction to Soviet Aircraft in Cuba, 1962 and 1978." *Political Science Quarterly* 95, no. 3 (Fall 1980).

Hersh = Hersh, Seymour M. *The Price of Power: Kissinger in the White House*. New York: Summit Books, 1983.

Hilsman = Hilsman, Roger. *To Move a Nation*. New York: Doubleday, 1967.

Hurwitch = Hurwitch, Robert A. "The Cuban Missile Crisis." *Foreign Service Journal* 48, no. 7 (1971): 17–20.

Issacson = Issacson, Walter, and Evan Thomas. *The Wise Men*. New York: Simon and Schuster, 1986.

Johns = Johns, Forrest R. *The Naval Quarantine of Cuba, 1962*. Master's Thesis, University of California, San Diego, 1984.

Johnson = Johnson, U. Alexis, with Jef O. McAllister. *The Right Hand of Power*. Englewood Cliffs, N.J.: Prentice Hall, 1984.

Kennedy = Kennedy, Robert. *Thirteen Days: A Memoir of the Cuban Missile Crisis*. New York: W. W. Norton, 1969.

Khrushchev = Khrushchev, Nikita. *Khrushchev Remembers: The Last Testament*. Translated and edited by Strobe Talbott. Boston: Little Brown, 1974.

MacMillan = MacMillan, Harold. *At the End of the Day, 1961–1963*. New York: Harper and Row, 1973.

Medvedev = Medvedev, Roy. *All Stalin's Men*. New York: Anchor Press, 1984.

Nixon = Nixon, Richard. *RN: The Memoirs of Richard Nixon*. New York: Grosset and Dunlap, 1978.

NYT = *The New York Times*.

OR = *Obras Revolucionarias* (Cuba).

Paterson 1 = Paterson, Thomas G. "The Historian as Detective: Senator Kenneth Keating, the Missiles in Cuba, and His Mysterious Sources." *Diplomatic History* 11, no. 1 (Winter 1987): 67–70.

Paterson 2 = Paterson, Thomas G., and William J. Brophy. "October Missiles and November Elections: The Cuban Missile Crisis and American Politics, 1962." *The Journal of American History* 73, no. 1 (June 1986).

Penkovsky = Penkovskiy, Oleg. *The Penkovskiy Papers*. Translated by Peter Deriabin. Garden City, N.Y.: Doubleday, 1965.

Prados = Prados, John. *The Soviet Estimate*. Princeton: Princeton University Press, 1986.

Ranelagh = Ranelagh, John. *The Agency: The Rise and Decline of the CIA*. New York: Simon and Schuster, 1987.

RN = Revolución (Cuba).

Sagan = Sagan, Scott. "Nuclear Alerts and Crisis Management." *International Security* (Spring 1985).

Salinger = Salinger, Pierre. *With Kennedy*. Garden City, N.Y.: Doubleday, 1966.

Schlesinger = Schlesinger, Arthur M., Jr. *Robert Kennedy and His Times*. Boston: Houghton Mifflin, 1978.

Sobel = Sobel, Lester A., ed. *Cuba, the U.S., and Russia 1960–63*. New York: Facts on File, 1964.

Sorensen = Sorensen, Theodore C. *Kennedy*. New York: Harper and Row, 1965.

Szulc = Szulc, Tad. *Fidel: A Critical Portrait*. New York: Avon Books, 1986.

Tatu = Tatu, Michel. *Power in the Kremlin*. New York: Viking, 1969.

Taylor = Taylor, Maxwell. *Swords and Plowshares*. New York: W. W. Norton, 1972.

Time = *Time Magazine*.

U Thant = Thant, U. *View from the UN*. Garden City, N.Y.: Doubleday, 1978.

WP = *The Washington Post*.

WSJ = *The Wall Street Journal*.

Wyden = Wyden, Peter. *The Bay of Pigs: The Untold Story*. New York: Simon and Schuster, 1980.

BIBLIOGRAPHY

SELECTED WORKS

Abel, Elie. *The Missile Crisis*. Philadelphia: Lippincott, 1966.

Allison, Graham T. *Essence of Decision*. Boston: Little, Brown, 1971.

Allyn, Bruce, James Blight, and David Welch. "Essence of Revision: Moscow, Havana and the Cuban Missile Crisis." *International Security* 14, no. 3 (Winter 1989/1990).

Ball, George. *The Past Has Another Pattern*. New York: W. W. Norton, 1982.

Beschloss, R. Michael. *The Crisis Years: Kennedy and Khrushchev 1960–1963*. New York: HarperCollins, 1991.

Bird, Kai. *The Chairman: John McCloy and the Making of the American Establishment*. New York: Simon and Schuster, 1992.

Blight, James G., and David A. Welch. *On the Brink: Americans and Soviets Reexamine the Cuban Missile Crisis*. New York: Hill and Wang, 1989.

Blight, James G., Bruce J. Allyn, David A. Welch, with David Lewis. *Cuba on the Brink: Fidel Castro, the Missile Crisis and the Collapse of Communism*. New York: Pantheon Books, 1993.

Bundy, McGeorge. *Danger and Survival: Choices about the Bomb in the First Fifty Years*. New York: Random House, 1988.

Garthoff, Raymond L. *Reflections on the Cuban Missile Crisis*. 2 ed., Washington, D.C.: Brookings Institution, 1989.

Hershberg, James. "Before 'The Missiles of October': Did Kennedy Plan a Military Strike Against Cuba?" *Diplomatic History* 14, no. 12 (Spring 1990): 163–199.

Hilsman, Roger. *To Move a Nation*. New York: Doubleday, 1967.

Kennedy, Robert. *Thirteen Days: A Memoir of the Cuban Missile Crisis*. New York: W. W. Norton, 1969.

MacMillan, Harold. *At the End of the Day, 1961–1963*. New York: Harper and Row, 1973.

Newhouse, John. *War and Peace in the Nuclear Age*. New York: Alfred A. Knopf, 1989.

Paterson, Thomas G. "Fixation with Cuba: The Bay of Pigs, Missile Crisis, and Covert War against Castro." *In Kennedy's Quest For Victory: American Foreign Policy, 1961–1963*, edited by Thomas G. Paterson. New York: Oxford University Press, 1989.

Pope, Ronald R. *Soviet Views on the Cuban Missile Crisis: Myth and Reality in Foreign Policy Analysis*. Lanham, Md.: University Press of America, 1982.

Schlesinger, Arthur M., Jr. *A Thousand Days: JFK in the White House*. Boston: Houghton Mifflin, 1965.

———. "Four Days with Fidel: A Havana Diary," *The New York Review of Books*, March 26, 1992.

———. *Robert Kennedy and His Times*. Boston: Houghton Mifflin, 1978.

Sorensen, Theodore C. *Kennedy*. New York: Harper and Row, 1965.

Wyden, Peter. *The Bay of Pigs*. New York: Simon and Schuster, 1979.

BOOKS, ARTICLES AND DISSERTATIONS

Books

Aliano, Richard A. *American Defense Policy from Eisenhower to Kennedy: The Politics of Changing Military Requirements, 1957–1961*. Athens: Ohio University Press, 1975.

Alsop, Stewart. *The Center*. New York: Popular Library, 1968.

Armacost, Michael. *The Politics of Weapons Innovation: The Thor-Jupiter Controversy*. New York: Columbia University Press, 1969.

Ayers, Bradley Ear. *The War That Never Was: An Insider's Account of CIA*

Covert Operations against Cuba. Indianapolis: Bobbs-Merrill, 1976.

Ball, Desmond. *Politics and Force Levels: The Strategic Missile Program of the Kennedy Administration.* Berkeley: University of California Press, 1981.

Ball, Desmond, and Jeffrey Richelson, eds. *Strategic Nuclear Targeting.* Ithaca: Cornell University Press, 1986.

Barnet, Richard J. *The Alliance.* New York: Simon and Schuster, 1983.

Barton, John H., and Lawrence D. Weiler, eds. *International Arms Control: Issues and Agreements.* Palo Alto, Calif.: Stanford University Press, 1976.

Bayard, James. *The Real Story on Cuba.* Derby, Conn.: Arlington House, 1969.

Beggs, Robert. *The Cuban Missile Crisis.* London: Longman, 1971.

Bender, Lynn-Darrell. *Cuba v. United States: The Politics of Hostility.* San Juan, P.R.: Inter-American University Press, 1981.

Berman Robert P., and John C. Baker. *Soviet Strategic Forces: Requirements and Responses.* Washington, D.C.: Brookings Institution, 1982.

Betts, Richard K. *Nuclear Blackmail and Nuclear Balance.* Washington, D.C.: Brookings Institution, 1987.

Blaiser, Cole. *The Giant's Rival: The U.S.S.R. in Latin America.* Pittsburgh: University of Pittsburgh Press, 1983.

Blechman, Barry M., and Stephen S. Kaplan. *Force without War: U.S. Armed Forces As a Political Instrument.* Washington, D.C.: Brookings Institution, 1978.

Blight, James G. *The Shattered Crystal Ball: Fear and Learning in the Cuban Missile Crisis.* Totowa, N.J.: Rowan and Littlefield, 1989.

Bohlen, Charles. *Witness to History, 1929–1969.* New York: W. W. Norton, 1973.

Bonsal, Philip W. Cuba, *Castro, and the United States.* Pittsburgh: University of Pittsburgh Press, 1971.

Bottome, Edgar M. *The Missile Gap.* Cranbury, N.J.: Fairleigh Dickinson University Press, 1970.

Bourne, Peter G. *Fidel: A Biography of Fidel Castro.* New York: Dodd, Mead, 1986.

Bowles, Chester. *Promises to Keep: My Years in Public Life, 1941–1969.* New York: Harper and Row, 1971.

Bradlee, Benjamin C. *Conversations with Kennedy.* New York: W. W. Norton, 1975.

Brenner, Philip, William LeoGrande, Donna Rich, and Daniel Siegel, eds. *The Cuba Reader: The Making of a Revolutionary Society.* New York: Grove Press, 1988.

Brown, Neville. *Nuclear War.* New York: Praeger, 1981.

Brune, Lester H. *The Missile Crisis of October 1962: A Review of Issues and References.* Claremont, Calif.: Regina Books, 1985.

Burks, David. *Soviet Policy for Castro's Cuba.* Columbus: Ohio State University Press, 1964.

Burner, David, and Thomas R. West. *The Torch Is Passed: The Kennedy Brothers and American Liberalism.* New York: Atheneum, 1984.

Burrows, William E. *Deep Black: Space Espionage and National Security.* New York: Random House, 1986.

Caldwell, Dan. *American-Soviet Relations from 1947 to the Nixon Kissinger Grand Design.* Westport, Conn.: Greenwood Press, 1981.

Chayes, Abram. *The Cuban Missile Crisis: International Crises and the Role of Law.* New York: Oxford University Press, 1974.

Chilcote, Ronald H. *Cuba, 1953–1978: A Bibliographical Guide to the Literature.* New York: Kraus International Publications, 1986.

Cochran, Bert. *Adlai Stevenson.* New York: Funk and Wagnalls, 1969.

Cohen, Warren J. *Dean Rusk.* Totowa, N.J.: Cooper Square, 1980.

Collier, Peter, and David Horowitz. *The Kennedys: An American Drama.* New York: Warner Books, 1985.

Crane, Robert D. *Soviet Motives and Miscalculations Leading to the Cuban Missile Crisis: A Lesson for the Future.* Hudson Institute Discussion Paper HI-777-DP. Croton-on-Hudson, N.Y.: 1966.

Crassweller, Robert D. *Cuba and the U.S.: The Tangled Relationship.* New York: McGraw-Hill, 1980.

Daniel, James, and John G. Hubbell. *Strike in the West.* New York: Holt, Reinhart and Winston, 1963.

Davis, Kenneth S. *The Politics of Honor.* New York: Putman, 1967.

de Gaulle, Charles. *Memoirs of Hope: Renewal and Endeavor.* New York: Simon and Schuster, 1971.

Desnoes, Edmundo. *Inconsolable Memories.* New York: New American Library, 1967.

Destler, I. M. *Presidents, Bureaucrats, and Foreign Policy.* Princeton, N.J.: Princeton University Press, 1972.

Detzer, David. *The Brink: Cuban Missile Crisis, 1962.* New York: Thomas Y. Crowell, 1979.

Didion, Joan. *Miami.* New York: Simon and Schuster, 1987.

Dinerstein, Herbert. *The Making of a Missile Crisis.* Baltimore: Johns Hopkins University Press, 1976.

Divine, Robert A., ed. *The Cuban Missile Crisis: The Continuing Debate.* Chicago: Quadrangle, 1971.

Dominguez, Jorge I. *Cuba: Order and Revolution*. Cambridge, Mass.: Belknap Press, 1978.

Donovan, John C. *The Cold Warriors: A Policymaking Elite*. Lexington, Mass.: D.C. Heath, 1974.

Draper, Theodore. *Castroism: Theory and Practice*. New York: Praeger, 1965.

Etheredge, Lloyd S. *Can Governments Learn?: American Foreign Policy and Central American Revolutions*. New York: Pergamon Press, 1985.

Fagan, Richard R., et al. *Cubans in Exile*. Palo Alto, Calif.: Stanford University Press, 1968.

Fairlie, Henry. *The Kennedy Promise: The Politics of Expectation*. London: Eyre Methuen, 1973.

Falk, Pamela S. *Cuban Foreign Policy*. Lexington, Mass.: Lexington Books, 1984.

Fay, Paul B., Jr. *The Pleasure of His Company*. New York: Dell Books, 1966.

Fermoselle, Rafael. *The Evolution of the Cuban Military: 1492–1986*. Miami: Ediciones Universal, 1987.

Fitzsimons, Louise. *The Kennedy Doctrine*. New York: Random House, 1972.

Frankland, Mark. *Khrushchev*. New York: Stein and Day, 1967.

Franqui, Carlos. *Family Portrait with Fidel*. Translated by Alfred MacAdam. New York: Vintage, 1984.

Frei, Daniel. *Managing International Crises*. Beverly Hills, Calif.: Sage, 1982.

Gaddis, John Lewis. *Russia, the Soviet Union, and the United States: An Interpretive History*. New York: John Wiley and Sons, 1978.

Garthoff, Raymond L. *Intelligence Assessment and Policymaking:*

A Decision Point in the Kennedy Administration. Washington, D.C.: Brookings Institution, 1984.

George, Alexander L. *Presidential Control of Force: The Cuban Missile Crisis*. Santa Monica, Calif.: Rand, July 1967.

George, Alexander L., and Richard Smoke. *Deterrence in American Foreign Policy*. New York: Columbia University Press, 1974.

George, Alexander L., David K. Hall, and William R. Simons. *The Limits of Coercive Diplomacy*. Boston: Little, Brown, 1971.

Gillingham, Arthur. *The Cuban Missile Crisis: A Selected Bibliography*. Los Angeles: California State University Press, 1976.

Gottfried, Kurt, and Bruce Blair. *Crisis Stability and Nuclear War*. New York: Oxford University Press, 1985.

Griffith, William. *Cold War and Coexistence: Russia, China, and the United States*. Englewood Cliffs, N.J.: Prentice Hall, 1971.

Gromyko, Anatoly. *Through Russian Eyes: President Kennedy's 1036 Days*. Translated by Philip A. Garon. Washington, D.C.: International Library, 1973.

———. *Memoirs*. Translated by Harold Shukman; foreword by Henry A. Kissinger. New York: Doubleday, 1990.

Gromyko, Anatoly, and Andrei Kokoshin. *Bratya Kennedi (The Kennedy Brothers)*. Moscow: Mysl', 1985.

Grosser, Alfred. *The Western Alliance*. Translated by Michael Shaw. New York: Continuum, 1980.

Halperin, Maurice. *The Rise and Decline of Fidel Castro: An Essay in Contemporary History*. Berkeley: University of California Press, 1972.

Hammarskjold Forum. *The Inter-American Security System and the Cuban Crisis*. Dobbs Ferry, N.Y.:

Association of the Bar of the City of New York, 1962.

Hargrove, Erwin C. *The Power of the Modern Presidency*. New York: Alfred A. Knopf, 1974.

Harriman, W. Averell. *America and Russia in a Changing World: A Half Century of Personal Observations*. Garden City, N.Y.: Doubleday, 1967.

Harris, George. *Troubled Alliance: Turkish-American Problems in Historical Perspective 1945–1971*. Washington, D.C.: Brookings Institution, 1972.

Harris, Patricia. *Adlai: The Stevenson Years*. Nashville: Aurora Publishers, 1975.

Harvey, Mose L. *Soviet Combat Troops in Cuba: Implications of the Carter Solution for the U.S.S.R.* Miami: Advanced International Studies Institute, 1979.

Herken, Gregg. *Counsels of War*. New York: Alfred A. Knopf, 1985.

Hersh, Seymour M. *The Price of Power: Kissinger in the White House*. New York: Summit Books, 1983.

Hinckle, Warren, and William Turner. *The Fish Is Red: The Story of the Secret War against Castro*. New York: Harper and Row, 1981.

Hirsch, Phil, ed. *The Kennedy War Heroes*. New York: Pyramid Books, 1962.

Holsti, Ole R. *Crisis, Escalation, War*. Montreal: McGill-Queen's University Press, 1972.

Horelick, Arnold D., and Myron Rush. *Strategic Power and Soviet Foreign Policy*. Chicago: University of Chicago Press, 1965.

Hunt, E. Howard. *Give Us This Day*. New York: Popular Library, 1973.

Hyland, W., and R. W. Shyrock. *The Fall of Khrushchev*. New York: Funk and Wagnalls, 1968.

Issacson, Walter, and Evan Thomas. *The Wise Men*. New York: Simon and Schuster, 1986.

Jackson, Bruce. *Castro, the Kremlin, and Communism in Latin America*. Baltimore: Johns Hopkins University Press, 1969.

Janis, Irving L. *Victims of Groupthink: A Psychological Study of Foreign Policy Decisions and Fiascos*. Boston: Houghton Mifflin, 1972.

Jervis, Robert. *The Logic of Images in International Relations*. Princeton, N.J.: Princeton University Press, 1970.

———. *Perception and Misperception in International Politics*. Princeton, N.J.: Princeton University Press, 1976.

Johnson, U. Alexis, with Jef O. McAllister. *The Right Hand of Power*. Englewood Cliffs, N.J.: Prentice Hall, 1984.

Jones, Kirby, and Frank Mankiewicz. *With Fidel: A Portrait of Castro and Cuba*. New York: Playboy Press, 1975.

Kalb, Marvin, and Bernard Kalb. *Kissinger*. Boston: Little, Brown, 1978.

Kaplan, Fred. *The Wizards of Armageddon*. New York: Simon and Schuster, 1984.

Kaplan, Stephen S. *Diplomacy of Power: Soviet Armed Forces and Political Instrument*. Washington, D.C.: Brookings Institution, 1981.

Kern, Montague, Patricia W. Levering, and Ralph Levering. *The Kennedy Crises: The Press, the Presidency, and Foreign Policy*. Chapel Hill: University of North Carolina Press, 1983.

Kesaris, Paul L. *Operation Zapata: The "Ultrasensitive" Report and Testimony of the Board of Inquiry on the Bay of Pigs*. Classified Studies in Twentieth-Century Diplomatic and Military History. Frederick, Md.: Aletheia Books, 1981.

Khrushchev, Nikita. *Khrushchev Remembers*. Translated and edited by Strobe Talbott. Boston: Little, Brown, 1970.

———. *Khrushchev Remembers: The Last Testament*. Translated and edited by Strobe Talbott. Boston: Little, Brown and Co., 1974.

Kirkpatrick, Jeane J. *The Kennedy-Khrushchev Pact and the Sandinistas*. Washington, D.C.: Cuban American National Foundation.

Kolkowicz, Roman. *Conflicts in Soviet Party-Military Relations: 1962–1963*. Santa Monica, Calif.: Rand, 1963.

Kraft, Joseph. *Profiles in Power*. New York: New American Library, 1966.

Krock, Arthur. *Memoirs: Sixty Years on the Firing Line*. New York: Funk and Wagnalls, 1968.

Kurland, Gerald. *Cuban Missile Crisis*. Charlotteville, N.Y.: Sam Har Press, 1973.

Laqueur, Walter. *A World of Secrets: The Uses and Limits of Intelligence*. New York: Basic Books, 1985.

Larson, David L. *The Cuban Crisis of 1962: Selected Documents, Chronology and Bibiliography*. Landham, Md.: University Press of America, 1986.

Lazo, Mario. *Dagger in the Heart*. New York: Funk and Wagnalls, 1968.

Lebow, Richard Ned. *Between Peace and War: The Nature of International Crisis*. Baltimore: Johns Hopkins University Press, 1981.

LeMay, Curtis E. *America Is in Danger*. New York: Funk and Wagnalls, 1968.

Levesque, Jacques. *The U.S.S.R. and the Cuban Revolution: Soviet Ideological and Strategic Perspectives, 1959–1977*. New York: Praeger, 1978.

Lincoln, Evelyn. *My Twelve Years with John F. Kennedy*. New York: McKay, 1965.

Linden, Carl A. *Khrushchev and the Soviet Leadership, 1957–1964*. Baltimore: Johns Hopkins University Press, 1966.

Lockwood, Lee. *Castro's Cuba, Cuba's Fidel*. New York: Macmillan, 1973.

Lyon, Peyton V. *Canada in World Affairs*. Toronto: Oxford University Press, 1968.

Madariaga, Salvador de. *Latin America between the Eagle and the Bear*. New York: Prager, 1962.

Mankiewicz, Frank, and Kirby Jones. *With Fidel*. New York: Playboy Press, 1975.

Manrara, Luis V. *Betrayal Opened the Door to Russian Missiles in Red Cuba*. Miami: Truth About Cuba Committee, 1968.

Marchetti, Victor, and John D. Marks. *The CIA and the Cult of Intelligence*. New York: Dell, 1980.

Martin, John Bartlow. *Adlai Stevenson and the World*. Garden City, N.Y.: Doubleday, 1977.

Matthews, Herbert L. *Fidel Castro*. New York: Simon and Schuster, 1969.

McClintock, Michael. *Instruments of Statecraft: U.S. Guerilla Warfare, Counterinsurgency, and Counterterrorism, 1940–1990*. New York: Pnatheon Books, 1992.

McGovern, George. *Cuban Realities: May 1975. Report to the Committee on Foreign Relations, United States Senate*. Washington, D.C.: U.S Government Printing Office, 1975.

McNamara, Robert S. *Blundering into Disaster*. New York: Pantheon Books, 1986.

Medvedev, Roy. *Khrushchev*. Translated by Brian Pearce. Garden City, N.Y.: Anchor Press, Doubleday, 1983.

———. *All Stalin's Men*. New York: Anchor Press, 1984.

Morrison, de Lesseps S. *Latin American Mission: An Adventure in Hemisphere Diplomacy*. Edited by Gerold Frank. New York: Simon and Schuster, 1965.

Navarro, M. *An Analysis of Soviet Reasons for the Military Buildup in Cuba*. Maxwell Air Force Base, Ala.: Air University Library, 1964.

Newhouse, John. *War and Peace in the Nuclear Age*. New York: Alfred A. Knopf, 1989.

Nixon, Richard M. *Six Crises*. Garden City, N.Y.: Doubleday, 1962.

———. *RN: The Memoirs of Richard Nixon*. New York: Grosset and Dunlap, 1978.

Nunnerly, David. *President Kennedy and Britain*. New York: St. Martin's Press, 1972.

O'Donnell, Kenneth, and David Powers with Joe McCarthy. *Johnny We Hardly Knew Ye*. Boston: Little, Brown, 1972.

Oliver, Covey. *The Inter-American Security System and the Cuban Crisis*. Dobbs Ferry, N.Y.: Oceana Publications, 1964.

Pachter, Henry. *Collision Course: The Cuban Missile Crisis and Coexistence*. New York: Praeger, 1963.

Paper, Lewis J. *John F. Kennedy: The Promise and the Performance*. New York: DeCapo Press, 1975.

Parmet, Herbert S. *Jack: The Struggles of John F. Kennedy*. New York: Dial Press, 1980.

———. *JFK: The Presidency of John F. Kennedy*. New York: Dial Press, 1983.

Penkovskiy, Oleg. *The Penkovskiy Papers*. Translated by Peter Deriabin. Garden City, N.Y.: Doubleday, 1965.

Plank, John, ed. *Cuba and the United States*. Washington, D.C.: Brookings Institution, 1967.

Prados, John. *Presidents' Secret Wars*. New York: Quill, 1986.

———. *The Soviet Estimate*. Princeton, N.J.: Princeton University Press, 1986.

Quester, George H. *Nuclear Diplomacy: The First Twenty-five Years*. New York: Viking, 1970.

Rádványi, János. *Hungary and the Superpowers: The 1956 Revolution and Realpolitik*. Palo Alto, Calif.: Hoover Institution Press, 1972.

Ranelagh, John. *The Agency: The Rise and Decline of the CIA*. New York: Simon and Schuster, 1987.

Rapoport, Anatol. *The Big Two: Soviet-American Perceptions of Foreign Policy*. New York: Pegasus, 1971.

Redford, Robert. *Canada and Three Crises*. Lindsey, Ontario: John Deyell, 1968.

Richelson, Jeffrey. *American Espionage and the Soviet Target*. New York: Quill, 1987.

Robbins, Carla Anne. *The Cuban Threat*. New York: McGraw-Hill, 1982.

Rostow, W. W. *View from the Seventh Floor*. New York: Harper and Row, 1964.

Rusk, Dean. *Winds of Freedom*. Boston: Beacon, 1963.

Russell, Bertrand. *Unarmed Victory*. New York: Simon and Schuster, 1963.

Salinger, Pierre. *With Kennedy*. Garden City, N.Y.: Doubleday, 1966.

Schelling, Thomas C. *Arms and Influence*. New Haven, Conn.: Yale University Press, 1966.

Schwartz, David N. *NATO's Nuclear Dilemmas*. Washington, D.C.: Brookings Institution, 1983.

Shevchenko, Arkady N. *Breaking with Moscow*. New York: Ballantine Books, 1986.

Sidey, Hugh. *John F. Kennedy, President*. Greenwich, Conn.: Crest Books, 1963.

Slater, Jerome. *The OAS and U.S. Foreign Policy*. Columbus: Ohio State University Press, 1967.

Smith, Joseph B. *Portrait of a Cold Warrior*. New York: Ballantine Books, 1976.

Smith, Robert F. *What Happened in Cuba? A Documentary History*. New York: Twayne Publishers, 1963.

Smith, Wayne S. *The Closest of Enemies: A Personal and Diplomatic Account of U.S.-Cuban Relations since 1957*. New York: W. W. Norton, 1987.

Sobel, Lester A., ed. *Cuba, the U.S., and Russia 1960–63*. New York: Facts on File, 1964.

Sorensen, Theodore C. *Decision Making in the White House*. New York: Columbia University Press, 1963.

———. *Kennedy*. New York: Harper and Row, 1965.

Steel, Ronald. *Walter Lippman and the American Century*. New York: Vintage Books, Random House, 1980.

Stevenson, Adlai E. *Looking Outward*. New York: Harper and Row, 1963.

Stone, I. F. *Time of Torment*. New York: Random House, 1967.

Suarez, Andres. *Cuba: Castroism and Communism, 1959–1966*. Cambridge, Mass.: MIT Press, 1967.

Sulzberger, C. L. *The Last of the Giants*. New York: Macmillan, 1970.

Szulc, Tad. *Fidel: A Critical Portrait*. New York: Avon Books, 1986.

Tatu, Michel. *Power in the Kremlin*. New York: Viking, 1969.

Taylor, Maxwell D. *Responsibility and Response*. New York: Harper and Row, 1967.

———. *Swords and Plowshares*. New York: W. W. Norton, 1972.

Tetlow, Edwin. *Eye on Cuba*. New York: Harcourt, Brace and World, 1966.

Thant, U. *View from the UN*. Garden City, N.Y.: Doubleday, 1978.

Theberge, James D. *Soviet Seapower in the Caribbean: Political and Strategic Implications*. New York: Praeger, 1972.

Thomas, Hugh. *Cuban Revolution*. New York: Harper and Row, 1963.

———. *Cuba: The Pursuit of Freedom*. New York: Harper and Row, 1971.

Trewhitt, Henry L. *McNamara*. New York: Harper and Row, 1971.

Trivers, Robert. *Three Crises in American Foreign Affairs and a Continuing Revolution*. Carbondale: Southern Illinois University Press, 1972.

U.S. Central Intelligence Agency. *Cuban Chronology 1959–79: A Reference Aid*. Washington, D.C.: National Foreign Assessment Center, 1982.

U.S. Department of State. *Events in United States-Cuban Relations, A Chronology*. Washington, D.C.: G.P.O., 1963.

Ulam, Adam. *Expansion and Coexistence*. New York: Praeger, 1968.

———. *The Rivals: America and Russia since World War II*. New York: Viking, 1971.

Ury, William Langer, and Richard Smoke. *Beyond the Hotline: Controlling a Nuclear Crisis: A Report to the United States Arms Control and Disarmament Agency*. Cambridge, Mass.: Nuclear Negotiation Project, Harvard Law School, 1984.

Valdes, Nelson P., and Edwin Lieuwen. *The Cuban Revolution: A Research-Study Guide 1959–1969*. Albuquerque: University of New Mexico Press, 1971.

Varney, Harold L. *Cuba: The Truth— We Shout Victory, but Khrushchev Still Has Cuba*. New York: Committee on Pan-American Policy, 1963.

Vosjoli, P. L. Thyraude de. *Lamia*. Boston: Little, Brown, 1970.

Walton, Richard J. *Cold War and Counterrevolution: The Foreign Policy of John F. Kennedy*. New York: Viking, 1972.

Weintal, Edward, and Charles Bartlett. *Facing the Brink*. New York: Charles Scribner's Sons, 1967.

West, J. B. *Upstairs at the White House*. New York: Coward, McCann and Geoghegan, 1973.

White, Tom. *Missiles over Cuba*. Brea, Calif.: Uplift Books, 1981.

Williams, Phil. *Crisis Management: Confrontation and Diplomacy in the Nuclear Age*. New York: John Wiley, 1976.

Wills, Garry. *The Kennedy Imprisonment*. New York: Pocket Books, 1982.

Wise, David, and Thomas B. Ross. *The Invisible Government*. New York: Bantam Books, 1964.

Wolfe, Thomas W. *Soviet Strategy at the Crossroads*. Cambridge, Mass.: Harvard University Press, 1964.

Wright, Peter. *Spycatcher*. New York: Viking, 1987.

Wyden, Peter. *The Bay of Pigs: The Untold Story*. New York: Simon and Schuster, 1980.

Yarmolinsky, Adam. *The Military Establishment*. New York: Harper and Row, 1971.

Young, Oran. *The Politics of Force: Bargaining during International Crises*. Princeton, N.J.: Princeton University Press, 1968.

Zeitlin, Maurice, and Robert Scheer. *Cuba: Tragedy in Our Hemisphere*. New York: Grove Press, 1963.

Zhurkin, V. V., and Ye. Primakov. *International Conflicts*. Arlington, Va.: Joint Publications Research Service, 1973.

Articles

"A Record for History." *Army Navy Air Force Journal and Register* 100 (Dec. 8, 1962): 11.

"Action Report: Cuban Crisis." *All Hands* 552 (Jan. 1963): 16–19.

"Aerospace Power in the Cuban Crisis." *Air Force Information Policy Letter Supplement for Commanders* 117 (March 1963): 12.

"After Cuba: Who Stood for What?" *U.S. News and World Report* (Dec. 12, 1962).

"Air Force and Naval Outfits Deployed to Bolster Coastal Defense Set Up." *Air Force Times* 23 (Oct. 27, 1962): 4.

"All Out Support for Cuba." *Peking Review* 5 (Nov. 9, 1962): 11.

"Another Cuban Missile Crisis?" *Foreign Report* (U.K.) (Feb. 19, 1981): 1–3.

"Background on Cuban Policy." *Air Force Information Policy Letter Supplement for Commanders* 112 (Oct. 1962): 12.

"Changed Plans." *Army Navy Air Force Journal and Register* 100 (Oct. 27, 1962): 1ff.

"Checkmate." *Interceptor* 5 (Feb. 1962): 22–23.

"CNO Tells Why Reserves Were Not Called up in the Cuban Crisis." *Officer* 39 (Feb. 1963): 21.

"Conversation with Castro." *Oui* (Jan. 1975): 113ff.

"Cuba: From Protests to the Removal of Soviet Missiles." *Current Digest of the Soviet Press* 14 (Nov. 21, 1962): 3–15.

"Cuba and Berlin." *The New Republic* (Nov. 3, 1962): 1–5.

"Cuba and Sea Power." *Navy* 5 (Nov. 1962): 6.

"Cuba and Vietnam Provide Valuable Training, 'Laboratory' Experience." *Army Navy Air Force Journal and Register* 100 (April 6, 1963): 2ff.

"Cuba Will Impact Budget." *Army Navy Air Force Journal and Register* 100 (Oct. 27, 1962): 1ff.

"Cuban Crisis Diary: An Account of the Washington Meetings and Decision-Making during October's Dangerous Days." *Navy: The Magazine of Sea Power* 6 (Feb. 1963): 18–21.

"Deterrence Credited with Cuban Backdown." *Air Force Times* 23 (Dec. 15, 1962): 41.

"DOD Tells Troops Reason behind U.S. Actions in Cuba Emergency." *Air Force Times* 23 (Nov. 10, 1962): 24.

"Efforts to Negotiate a Peaceful Settlement." *U.N. Review* 9 (Nov. 1962): 14–15.

"Forces Put on Alert in Cuba Emergency." *Air Force Times* 23 (Oct. 27, 1962): 1ff.

"Guantánamo Evacuees Get Special Allowance." *Air Force Times* 23 (Nov. 4, 1962): 2.

"I Spied on Castro's Cuba." *Ebony* (April 1963): 16ff.

"Major Rudolf Anderson, Jr. USAF." *Air Force and Space Digest* (Dec. 1962): 21.

"MATS Airlift to Guantánamo Praised by Navy." *Air Force Times* 23 (Nov. 10, 1962): 4.

"MILSTRIP: How Did It Work in the Cuban Crisis?" *National Defense Transportation Journal* 19 (Sept.–Oct. 1963): 36–37.

"More GI Bill Time Sought for Cuba Crisis Recall." *Air Force Times* 23 (Nov. 3, 1962): 22.

"Our Cuban Policy." *Airpower Historian* 9 (Oct. 1962): 254.

"Recalled Depart in Crisis Thaw." *Air Force Times* 23 (Dec. 1, 1962): 1ff.

"SAC's Power Is Lesson of Cuba." *Army Navy Air Force Journal and Register* 100 (Dec. 15, 1962): 19ff.

"Son's Defense: Kremlin Issues Official Version." *Newsweek* 78 (Aug. 9, 1971): 111–12.

"The Air National Guard in the Cuban Crisis." *National Guardsman* 17 (Jan. 1963): 10–11.

"The Cienfuegos Caper." *Navy* 12 (Dec. 1970): 36–37.

"The Credible Deterrent." *Army Navy Air Force Journal and Register* 100 (Nov. 3, 1962): 1–3.

"The Cuba Crisis: Ready and Steady." *Marine Corps Gazette* 47 (Jan. 1963): 1.

"The Strategic Bargain." *Foreign Report* (U.K.) (Nov. 8, 1962).

"The Varying Fortunes of Incremental Commitment: An Inquiry into the Cuban and Southeast Asian Cases." *International Studies* 1, no. 3 (1974): 14–21.

"Tighter Rules Govern Rules for Recall." *Air Force Times* 23 (Nov. 10, 1962): 1ff.

"Transportation in the Cuban Crisis." *National Defense Transportation Journal* 19 (March–April 1963): 23–24.

Acheson, Dean. "Dean Acheson's Version of Robert Kennedy's Version of the Cuban Missile Affair." *Esquire* (Feb. 1969): 76–77.

Allison, Graham T. "Conceptual Models and the Cuban Crisis." *American Political Science Review* 63 (Sept. 1969): 689–718.

———. "Cuban Missiles and Kennedy Macho: New Evidence To Dispel the Myth." *Washington Monthly* 4 (Oct. 1975): 14–19.

Alsop, Joseph. "Kennedy's Grand Strategy." *Saturday Evening Post* (March 31, 1962): 11–17.

Alsop, Stewart. "Our New Strategy: The Alternative to Total War." *Saturday Evening Post* 235 (Dec. 1, 1962): 13–18.

Alsop, Stewart, and Charles Bartlett. "In Time of Crisis." *Saturday Evening Post* 235 (Dec. 8, 1962): 16–20.

Anderson, George W., Jr. "The Navy and the Decision-making Process in Diplomatic Crisis." In *Proceedings of a U.S. Naval History Symposium*. Annapolis: U.S. Naval Academy, 1973.

———. "The Cuban Blockade: An Admiral's Memoir." *Washington Quarterly* (Autumn 1982): 83–87.

———. "As I Recall…the Cuban Missile Crisis." *U.S. Naval Institute Proceedings* 113 (Sept. 1987): 44–45.

Anderson, Jack. "Cuba Stronger Today Than in '62 Crisis Year." *Washington Post* (Nov. 2, 1983): B15.

Anderson, Paul A. "Justifications and Precedents As Constraints in Foreign Policy Decision-making." *American Journal of Political Science* 25 (Nov. 1981): 738–61.

———. "Decision Making by Objections and the Cuban Missile Crisis." *Administrative Science Quarterly* 28, no. 2 (June 1983): 201–22.

Armstrong, Scott, and Philip Brenner. "Putting Cuba and Crisis Back in the Cuban Missile Crisis." In *The Cuba Reader: The Making of a Revolutionary Society*, edited by Philip Brenner, William Leogrande, Donna Rich and Daniel Siegel. New York: Grove Press, 1988.

Arnold, Joseph C. "Omens and Oracles." *United States Naval Institute Proceedings* 106 (August 1980): 47–53.

Ascoli, Max. "Escalation from the Bay of Pigs." *Reporter* 27 (Nov. 8, 1962): 24–25.

Asprey, Robert B. "FMLANT: Profile of Readiness." *Marine Corps Gazette* 47 (Jan. 1963): 260–76.

Aynesworth, Hugh. "LBJ Leaked to Dallas Paper Cuba Missile Crisis Options." *Washington Times* (Oct. 26, 1987): A1.

Ball, Desmond. "U.S. Strategic Forces: How Would They Be Used?" *International Security* 7, no. 3 (Winter 1982/1983).

Barclay, C.N. "Cuba—1962." *Army Quarterly* 86 (April 1963): 28–32.

Bernstein, Barton J. "Their Finest Hour?" *Correspondent* 32 (Aug. 1964): 119–21.

——. "The Cuban Missile Crisis." In *Reflections on the Cold War*, edited by Lynn Miller and Ronald Prussen, pp. 11–142. Philadelphia: Temple University, 1974.

——. "Courage and Commitment: The Missiles of October." *Foreign Service Journal* 52 (Oct. 1975): 9–11, 24–27.

——. "Kennedy Brinkmanship." *Inquiry* 2 (April 1979): 19–22.

——. "Kennedy and Ending the Missile Crisis: Bombers, Inspection, and the No Invasion Pledge." *Foreign Service Journal* 56 (July 1979): 8–12.

——. "The Cuban Missile Crisis: Trading the Jupiters in Turkey?" *Political Science Quarterly* 95, no. 1 (Spring 1980): 97–125.

——. "The Week We Almost Went to War." *Bulletin of the Atomic Scientists* 32 (Feb. 1986): 13–21.

Bernstein, Barton J., and Roger Hagan. "Military Value of Missiles in Cuba."

Bulletin of Atomic Scientists 19 (Feb. 1963): 8–13.

Blake, Charles. "The Cuban Missile Crisis of 1962." In *A Quarter Century of Air Power: Studies in the Employment of Air Power 1947–1972*, edited by John H. Scrivner, Jr. Maxwell Air Force Base, Ala.: Air University, 1973.

Blight, James G. "Toward a Policy-relevant Psychology of Avoiding Nuclear War: Lessons for Psychologists from the Cuban Missile Crisis." *American Psychology* 42 (Jan. 1987): 12–19.

Blight, James G., Joseph Nye, and David Welch. "The Cuban Missile Crisis Revisited." *Foreign Affairs* (Fall 1987): 170–88.

Booda, Larry. "U.S. Watches for Possible Cuban IRBMs." *Aviation Week and Space Technology* (Oct. 1, 1962): 20–21.

Branch, Taylor, and Crile, George III. "The Kennedy Vendetta: How the CIA Waged a Silent War against Castro." *Harpers* 251 (Aug. 1975): 49–63.

Brandon, Henry. "An Untold Story of the Cuban Crisis." *Saturday Review* (March 9, 1963): 56–57.

Brenner, Philip. "Cuba and the Missile Crisis." *Journal of Latin American Studies* 22 (Feb. 1990): 115–42.

Brodie, Bernard. "What Price Conventional Capabilities in Europe?" In *Problems of National Strategy*, edited by Henry A. Kissinger. New York: Praeger, 1965.

Brzezinski, Zbigniew. "Cuba in Soviet Strategy." *The New Republic* (Nov. 3, 1962): 7–8.

Bundy, McGeorge. "The Presidency and the Peace." *Foreign Affairs* 42 (April 1964): 353–65.

Bundy, McGeorge, transcriber, and James G. Blight, ed. "October 27, 1962: Transcripts of the ExComm."

International Security 12, no. 3 (Winter 1987/1988).

Burlatsky, Feodor. "Black Saturday." *Literaturnaya Gazeta* (Nov. 12, 1983).

——. "The Caribbean Crisis and Its Lessons." *Literaturnaya Gazeta* (Nov. 11, 1987): 14. In FBIS, *Daily Report: Soviet Union* (Nov. 17, 1987).

Burlatsky, Feodor, Sergo Mikoyan, and Georgi Shaknazarov. "New Thinking about an Old Crisis: Cuba, 1962." In *Windows of Opportunity: From Cold War to Peaceful Competition in U.S.-Soviet Relations*, edited by Graham T. Allison and William L. Ury. Cambridge, Mass.: Ballinger, 1989.

Burnham, James. "Intelligence on Cuba." *The National Review* 13 (Nov. 20, 1962): 587.

Caldwell, Dan. "A Research Note on the Cuban Quarantine." *International Studies Quarterly* 22, no. 4 (Dec. 1978): 625–33.

Callander, Bruce. "Crisis Spurs Cockpit Duty for Excused." *Air Force Times* 23 (Nov. 10, 1962): 1ff.

Chase, Stuart. "Political Missiles in Cuba." *War/Peace Report* 3 (Feb. 1963): 9–10.

Chayes, Abram. "Law and the Quarantine of Cuba." *Foreign Affairs* 41 (April 1963): 550–57.

Chesler, Mark, and Richard Schmuck. "Student Reactions to the Cuban Crisis and Public Dissent." *Public Opinion Quarterly* 28 (Fall 1964): 467–82.

Cline, Ray. "A CIA Reminiscence." *Washington Quarterly* 5 (Autumn 1982).

Clizbe, R. J. "MATS and the Cuban Crisis." *National Defense Transportation Journal* 19 (Nov.–Dec. 1963): 52ff.

Cohen, Eliot A. "Why We Should Stop Studying the Cuban Missile Crisis." *National Interest* (Winter 1986): 3–13.

Cottrell, Alvin J. "Soviet Views of U.S. Overseas Bases." *Orbis* 7 (Spring 1963): 77–95.

Cousins, Norman. "The Cuban Missile Crisis: An Anniversary." *Saturday Review* 5 (Oct. 15, 1977): 5.

Cowhey, Peter F., and David D. Laitin. "Bearing the Burden: A Model of Presidential Responsibility." *International Studies Quarterly* 22 (June 1978): 267–96.

Crane, Robert D. "The Sino-Soviet Dispute on War and the Cuban Crisis." *Orbis* 8 (Fall 1964): 537–49.

Crane, Robert D. "The Cuban Crisis: A Strategic Analysis of American and Soviet Policy." *Orbis* 6 (Winter 1965): 528–63.

Crosby, Ralph. "The Cuban Missile Crisis—the Soviet View." *Military Review* 56 (Sept. 1976): 58–70.

Daniel, Jean. "Why Moscow Sent Us the Missiles." *The Observer* (U.K.) (Dec. 8, 1963): 21–22.

Daniel, Jean. "Further Clarification." *The New Republic* (Dec. 21, 1963): 6–7.

Dewart, Leslie. "The Cuban Crisis Revisted." *Studies on the Left* 5 (Spring 1965): 15–40.

DeWeerd, H.A. "British Attitudes in the Cuban Crisis." *RAND Memorandum* P-2709 (Feb. 1963).

Dick, James C. "The Strategic Arms Race, 1957–1961: Who Opened a Missile Gap?" *Journal of Politics* 34 (Nov. 1972): 1062–1110.

Draper, Theodore. "Castro and Communism: A Detailed Account of the Background and Consequences of the Missile Crisis in Cuba." *Reporter* 28 (Jan. 17, 1963): 35–48.

Ekman, Paul, et al. "Coping with Cuba: Divergent Policy Preferences of State Political Leaders." *Journal of Conflict Resolution* 10 (June 1966): 180–97.

Eleson, P. "Underwater Ordnance." *Ordnance* 47 (Jan.–Feb. 1963): 384ff.

Ellsberg, Daniel. "The Day Castro Almost Started World War III." *New York Times* (Oct. 31, 1987).

Fagan, Richard R. "Cuba and the Soviet Union." *Western Quarterly* 2, no. 1 (Winter 1978): 69–81.

Francis, Michael J. "The U.S. Press and Castro: A Study in Declining Relations." *Journalism Quarterly* 44 (Summer 1967): 257–66.

Frankel, Max. "A Washington Education." *Columbia Forum* (Winter 1973): 9–14.

Fraser, Niall M., and Keith W. Hipel. "Dynamic Modeling of the Cuban Missile Crisis." *Conflict Management and Peace Science* 6, no. 2 (Spring 1983): 1–18.

Freedman, Lawrence. "Crisis Management." *NATO's Fifteen Nations* 24 (Oct.–Nov. 1979): 16–17.

Fulbright, J. William. "Fulbright's Role in the Cuban Missile Crisis." *Inter-American Economic Affairs* 27 (Spring 1975): 86–94.

Galbraith, John Kenneth. "Storm Over Havana: Who Were the Real Heroes?" (Jan. 19, 1969): 16.

Gardner, R.N. "The U.N. in Crisis: Cuba and the Congo." *Department of State Bulletin* 48 (April 1, 1963): 477–81.

Garthoff, Raymond L. "Soviet Views on the Interrelation of Diplomacy and Military Strategy." *Political Science Quarterly* 94, no. 3 (Fall 1979): 391–405.

____. "American Reaction to Soviet Aircraft in Cuba, 1962 and 1978." *Political Science Quarterly* 95, no. 3 (Fall 1980).

———. "The Meaning of the Missiles." *Washington Quarterly* 5 (Autumn 1982): 76–82.

———. "Handling the Cienfuegos Crisis." *International Security* 8, no. 1 (Summer 1983).

———. "The Cuban 'Contras' Caper: Did CIA Squads Threaten JFK Handling of the Missile Crisis?" *Washington Post* (Oct. 25, 1987): C3.

———. "Cuban Missile Crisis: The Soviet Story." *Foreign Policy* 72 (Fall 1988).

Gates, Ed. "Recalls Swell Force to 885,000: 14,215 Men in Eight Wings Ordered Up." *Air Force Times* 23 (Nov. 3, 1962): 1.

———. "Crisis Lifts 666 from AU Classes." *Air Force Times* 23 (Nov. 10, 1962): 1ff.

George, Alexander L. "The Operational Code: A Neglected Approach to the Study of Political Leaders and Decision-making." *International Studies Quarterly* 13 (June 1969): 190–222.

———. "The Case for Multiple Advocacy in Making Foreign Policy." Includes comments by I. M. Destler and Alexander George. *American Political Science Review* 66 (Sept. 1972): 751–95.

———. "Crisis Management: The Interaction of Political and Military Considerations." *Survival* 26, no. 5 (Sept.–Oct. 1984): 223–34.

Gerberding, William P. "International Law and the Cuban Missile Crisis." In *International Law and Political Crisis: An Analytical Casebook*, edited by Lawrence Scheinman and David K. Wilkinson, pp. 175–211. Boston: Little, Brown, 1968.

Ghent, Jocelyn Maynard. "Canada and the United States, and the Cuban Missile Crisis." *Pacific Historical Review* 48 (May 1979): 159–84.

Gleichauf, Justin F. "Red Presence in Cuba: The Genesis of a Crisis." *Army* 29 (Nov. 1979): 34–38.

Gonzales, Edward. "Castro's Revolution: Cuban Communist Appeals and the Soviet Response." *World Politics* 21 (Oct. 1968): 29–68.

Grady, John. "Twenty-fifth Anniversary of Missile Crisis Marked." *Air Force Times* 48 (Nov. 2, 1987): 45ff.

Gray, Colin S. "Gap Prediction and America's Defense: Arms Race Behavior in the Eisenhower Years." *Orbis* 16 (Spring 1972): 257–74.

Green, Fred. "The Intelligence Arm: The Cuban Missile Crisis." In *Foreign Policy in the Sixties: The Issues and the Instruments*, edited by Roger Hilsman and Robert C. Good, pp. 127–40. Baltimore: Johns Hopkins University Press, 1965.

Guran, M. Elizabeth. "Arms Interdiction and the U.S. Navy: Prospects in Central America." *Naval War College Review* 39 (Aug. 1986): 73–87.

Haffner, Donald L. "Those Frigging Missiles: JFK, Cuba, and U.S. Missiles in Turkey." *Orbis* 21 (Summer 1977): 307–34.

Hagan, Roger. "Triumph or Tragedy?" *Dissent* 10 (Winter 1963): 13–26.

Hampson, Fen Osler. "The Divided Decision-Maker: American Domestic Politics and the Cuban Crises." *International Security* 9 (Winter 1984–85): 130–65.

Hargrove, Erwin C. "Presidential Personality and Revisionist Views of the Presidency." *American Journal of Political Science* 17 (Nov. 1973): 819–35.

Hayward, John T., and Paul J. Keaney. "Command and Control in the Nuclear Age." *U.S. Naval Institute Proceedings* 89 (Nov. 1963): 38–43.

Hersh, Seymour. "Was Castro Out of Control in 1962? New Evidence Shows the Soviets Weren't Calling All the Shots in the Cuban Missile Crisis." *Washington Post* (Oct. 11, 1987): H1.

Hilsman, Roger. "The Cuban Crisis: How Close We Were to War." *Look* 28, no. 17 (Aug. 25, 1964).

Hilsman, Roger, and Ronald Steel. "An Exchange of Views." *New York Review of Books* 12 (May 8, 1969): 17–21.

Hilton, Ronald. "Cuba: Invitation to Disaster." *Nation* 195 (Sept. 28, 1962): 171–74.

———. "A Note on Latin America." *Council for Correspondence Newsletter* no. 21 (Oct. 1962): 42–44.

Hodgson, John H. "Soviet Foreign Policy: Mental Alienation or Universal Revolution." *Western Political Quarterly* 24 (Dec. 1971): 653–65.

Holsti, Ole R. "Theories of Crisis Decision Making." In *Diplomacy*, edited by Paul Gordon Lauren, pp. 99–136. New York: Free Press, 1979.

Holsti, Ole R., Richard A. Brody, and Robert C. North. "Measuring Effect and Action in International Reaction Models: Empirical Materials from the 1962 Cuban Crisis." *Journal of Peace Research* 1 (1964): 170–89.

Holz, Robert. Editorial. *Aviation Week and Space Technology* (Nov. 12, 1962): 21.

Home, Lord. "We Need Be Neither Red nor Dead." *Air Force and Space Digest* 46 (Jan. 1963): 6.

Horelick, Arnold D. "The Cuban Missile Crisis: An Analysis of Soviet Calculations and Behavior." *World Politics* 16 (April 1964): 363–89.

Horowitz, Irving Louis. "Deterrence Games: From Academic Casebook to Military Codebook." In *The Structure of Conflict*, edited by Paul Swingle. New York: Academic Press, 1970.

Howard, Anthony. "Lurching into the Cannon's Mouth." *New Statesman* 77 (Jan. 31, 1969): 144–45.

Hurwitch, Robert A. "The Cuban Missile Crisis." *Foreign Service Journal* 48, no. 7 (1971): 17–20.

Jackson, William D. "The Soviets and Strategic Arms: Toward an Evaluation of the Record." *Political Science Quarterly* 94 (Summer 1979): 243–61.

Jenkins, Ray. "How Close Did We Come to War Over Cuba?" *War/Peace Report* 3 (Dec. 1963): 3–6.

John, Forrest R. "United We Stood." *U.S. Naval Institute Proceedings* 111 (Jan. 1985): 73–87.

Jones, Mel. "Crisis Report." *Leatherneck* 16 (April 1963): 18–27, 63.

Julien, Claude. "Kennedy-Castro." *Le Monde* (March 22, 1963).

Kahan, Jerome H., and Anne K. Lang. "The Cuban Missile Crisis: A Study of Its Strategic Context." *Political Science Quarterly* 87 (Dec. 1972): 564–90.

Kaplan H. R. "The Coast Guard's Cuban Patrol." *Navy* 8 (March 1965): 30–36.

Kateb, George. "Kennedy As Statesman." *Commentary* 41 (June 1966): 54–60.

Katz, Amon H. "The Soviets and the U-2 Photos." *RAND Memorandum* RM-384-PR (March 1963).

Keating, Kenneth. "My Advance View of the Cuban Crisis." *Look* 28 (Nov. 3, 1964): 96–106.

Kelly, Joe W. "MATS Looks at the Cuban Crisis." *Air University Review* 14 (Sept.-Oct. 1963): 2–20.

Kennedy, Robert F. "Lessons of the Cuban Crisis." *Saturday Review* 51 (Oct. 26, 1968): 24.

———. *In His Own Words: The Unpublished Recollections of the Kennedy Years.* Edited by Edwin O. Guthman and Jeffrey Shulman. New York: Bantam Books, 1988.

Kenworthy, E. W., Anthony Lewis, and Max Frankel. "Cuban Crisis: A Step by Step Review." *New York Times* (Nov. 3, 1962): 1, 6–7.

Kester, Charles. "Guantánamo Bay." *Leatherneck* 46 (Feb. 1963): 19–25.

Kestner, Jack. "The Navy and Cuba: Operational Report." *Navy* 6 (Jan. 1963): 5–11ff.

Kirkpatrick, Jeane J. "Our Cuban Misadventures." Atlantic Community *Quarterly* 24 (Summer 1986): 155–56.

Kirkpatrick, L. "Cold War Operations: The Politics of Communist Confrontation, Part V—The Cuban Case History." *Naval War College Review* 20, no. 8 (1968): 40–41.

Kissinger, Henry. "Reflections on Cuba." *Reporter* 27 (Nov. 22, 1962): 21–24.

Knebel, Fletcher. "In Crisis: 154 Hours on the Brink." *Look* (Dec. 18, 1962).

Knorr, Klaus. "Failure in National Intelligence Estimates: The Cast of the Cuban Crisis." *World Politics* 16 (April 1964): 455–67.

Knox, William E. "Close-up of Khrushchev during a Crisis." *New York Times Magazine* (Nov. 18, 1962): 32ff.

Kohn, Richard H., and Joseph P. Harahan, eds. "U.S. Strategic Air Power, 1948–1962: Excerpts from an Interview with Generals Curtis E. LeMay, Leon W. Johnson, David A. Burchinal, and Jack J. Catton." *International Security* 12, no. 4 (Spring 1988): 932–93.

Kolkowicz, Roman. "The Red Hawks on the Rationality of Nuclear War." *RAND Memorandum* RM-4899-PR (1963).

Kranish, Arthur. "The Cuban Crisis: Peace in Our Time or a Battleground between the Truth and the Lie?" *Western Aerospace* 43 (Jan. 1963): 6.

Kristi, Jim. "Missiles of October." *Combat Crew* 37 (Oct. 1987): 16–17.

Kruls, H.J. "The Significance of Khrushchev's Retreat from Cuba." *NATO's Fifteen Nations* 7 (Dec. 1962–Jan. 1963): 14.

Laird, Melvin. "Why We Need Spies." *Reader's Digest* 144 (March 1979): 87–92.

Leavitt, William. "Cuba and Counterspace." *Air Force and Space Digest* 45 (Dec. 1962): 62–63.

Lebow, Richard Ned. "The Cuban Missile Crisis: Reading the Lessons Correctly." *Political Science Quarterly* 98 (Fall 1982): 431–58.

———. "Deterrence Failure Revisted." *International Security* 12, no. 1 (Summer 1987): 197–213.

———. "Was Khrushchev Bluffing in Cuba?" *Bulletin of the Atomic Scientists* (April 1988).

———. "Provocative Deterrence: A New Look at the Cuban Missile Crisis." Arms Control Today (July–Aug. 1988): 15–16.

LeFeber, Walter. "Kennedy, Johnson and the Revisionists." *Foreign Service Journal* 50 (May 1973): 31–33, 39.

LeMay, Curtis E. "The Cuban Experience: Responses and Lessons." *Air Force Information Policy Letter Supplement for Commanders* 114 (Dec. 1962): 2–7.

LeMay, Curtis E. "Deterrence in Action." *Ordnance* 47 (March–April 1963): 526–28.

Leng, R.J. "Reason and the Russians: Crisis Bargaining Beliefs and the Historical Record." *American Political Science Review* 78 (June 1984): 338–55.

LeoGrande, William. "Uneasy Allies: The Press and Government during the Cuban Missile Crisis." Center for War, Peace, and the News Media Occasional Paper no. 3. New York: New York University, 1987.

Licklider, Roy E. "The Missile Gap Controversy." *Political Science Quarterly* 85 (Dec. 1970): 600–15.

Lippman, Walter. "Cuba: Watchful Waiting." *New York Herald Tribune* (Sept. 15, 1962).

———. "Cuba and the Nuclear Risk." *Atlantic* 211 (Feb. 1963): 55–58.

Lockhart, Charles. "Problem in the Management and Resolution of International Conflicts." *World Politics* 29 (April 1977): 370–403.

Lowenthal, David. "U.S. Cuban Policy: Illusion and Reality." *The National Review* 14 (Jan. 29, 1963): 61–63.

Lukas, J. Anthony. "Class Reunion: Kennedy's Men Relive the Cuban Missile Crisis." *New York Times Magazine* (Aug. 30, 1987): 22–27, 51, 58, 61.

Mackintosh, Malcolm. "Soviet Motives in Cuba." *Survival* 5 (Jan.–Feb. 1963): 16–18.

McConnell, Jerry. "Incident in History— Intercept of Marcula." All Hands 551 (Dec. 1962): 2–5.

McGwire, Michael. "Soviet Naval Interests and Intentions in the Caribbean." *Soviet Naval Developments: Capability and Context*, edited by Michael MccGwire. New York: Praeger, 1973.

McDonough, Joseph A. "Crisis Diplomacy: Cuba 1962." *Naval War College Review* 19 (Summer 1966): 1–35.

McDougal, Myles S. "The Soviet-Cuban Quarantine and Self Defense." *American Journal of International Law* 57 (July 1963): 597–604.

McGovern, George. "A Talk with Castro." *New York Times Magazine* (March 13, 1977): 20ff.

McNamara, Robert. "Red Missiles in Cuba: An Inside Story from Secretary McNamara." *U.S. News and World Report* 53 (Nov. 1962): 44–50.

———. "U.S. Military Might and Those Who Man It." *Air Force Information Policy Letter Supplement for Commanders* 13 (Dec. 1964): 12–18.

————. "The Military Role of Nuclear Weapons: Perceptions and Misperceptions." *Foreign Affairs* 62, no. 1 (Fall 1983): 59–80.

Meyer, Frank S. "The 1962 Elections: The Turning of the Tide." *The National Review* (Dec. 4, 1962).

Millett, Allen R. "Crisis in Cuba." Marine Corps *Gazette* 71 (Nov. 1987): 55–57.

Moisi, Dominique. "Analogy As Temptation: Understanding the Present International Crisis." *Social Research* 48 (Winter 1981): 739–48.

Monger, Thomas M. "Personality and Decision Making: John F. Kennedy in Four Crisis Decisions." *Canadian Journal of Political Science* 2 (June 1969): 200–25.

Montoro, Adrian G. "Moscow Was Caught between Cuba and U.S." *New York Times* (Nov. 17, 1987).

Morgenthau, Hans J. "Cuba: The Wake of Isolation." *Commentary* 34 (Nov. 1962): 427–30.

Moser, Con. "The Time of the Angel: The U-2, Cuba, and the CIA." *American Heritage* 28 (Oct. 1977): 4–15.

Murphy, Charles S. V. "Khrushchev's Paper Bear." *Fortune* 70 (Dec. 1964): 115, 224–30.

Nathan, James A. "The Missile Crisis: His Finest Hour Now." *World Politics* 27 (Jan. 1976): 256–81.

Neustadt, Richard. "Kennedy and the Presidency: A Premature Appraisal." *Political Science Quarterly* 79 (Sept. 1964): 321–34.

Neustadt, Richard, and Graham T. Allison. "Afterword." In *Thirteen Days: A Memoir of the Cuban Missile Crisis*, by Robert F. Kennedy. New York: W. W. Norton, 1969.

Nitze, Paul. "Foreword." In *Arms Treaties with Moscow: Unequal Terms Unevenly Applied?*, by Donald G. Brennan. New York: National Strategy Information Center, 1975.

Nixon, Richard. "Cuba, Castro, and John F. Kennedy." *Reader's Digest* 85 (Nov. 1964): 283–300.

Norris, John G. "Call up of Air Force Reservists Helped Convince Kremlin United States Meant Business." *Officer* 38 (Dec. 1962): 8.

Olcheski, Bill. "Reserves Filling Need in Crisis, Deeds Show." *Air Force Times* 23 (Nov. 10, 1962): 4.

Orme, John. "Deterrence Failures: A Second Look." *International Security* 2, no. 4 (Spring 1987): 96–125.

Oulahan, Richard Jr. "The Decision." *Life* (Nov. 2, 1962).

Paige, G. D. "Comparative Case Analysis of Crisis Decisions: Korea and Cuba." In *International Crisis: Insights from Behavioral Research*, edited by Charles F. Hermann, pp. 41–55. New York: Free Press, 1972.

Paper, Lewis J. "The Moral Implications of the Cuban Missile Crisis." *American Scholar* 41 (Spring 1979): 276–83.

Paterson, Thomas G. "Bearing the Burden: A Critical Look at JFK's Foreign Policy." *Virginia Quarterly Review* 54 (Spring 1978): 193–212.

————. "The Historian as Detective: Senator Kenneth Keating, the Missiles in Cuba, and His Mysterious Sources." *Diplomatic History* 11, no. 1 (Winter 1987): 67–70.

————. "Fixation with Cuba: The Bay of Pigs, Missile Crisis, and Covert War against Castro." In *Kennedy's Quest For Victory: American Foreign Policy, 1961–1963*, edited by Thomas G. Paterson. New York: Oxford University Press, 1989.

Paterson, Thomas G., and William J. Brophy. "October Missiles and November Elections: The Cuban Missile Crisis and American Politics, 1962." *Journal of American History* 73, no. 1 (June 1986).

Pederson, John C. "Soviet Reporting of the Cuban Crisis." *U.S. Naval Institute Proceedings* 91 (Oct. 1965): 54–63.

Perez, Louis A., Jr. "Army Politics in Socialist Cuba." *Journal of Latin American Studies* 8, no. 2 (Nov. 1966): 251–57.

Pincus, Walter. "Standing at the Brink of Nuclear War: U.S. Planned to Attack Soviet Targets In Cuba, Then To Invade." *Washington Post* (July 25, 1985): A1.

Piper, Don C. "The Cuban Missile Crisis and International Law: Precipitous Decline of Unilateral Development." *World Affairs* 138 (Summer 1975): 26–31.

Pocalyko, Michael N. "25 Years after the Blink." *U.S. Naval Institute Proceedings* (Sept. 1987): 41–47.

Pollard, Robert A. "The Cuban Missile Crisis: Legacies and Lessons." *Wilson Quarterly* 5 (Autumn 1982): 148–58.

Pomerance, Josephine W. "The Cuban Missile Crisis and the Test Ban Negotiations." *Journal of Conflict Resolution* 7, no. 3 (1963): 553–59.

Price, Thomas J. "Constraints on Foreign Policy Making: Stability and Flexibility in Three Crises." *International Studies Quarterly* 22, no. 3 (Sept. 1978).

Quester, George. "Missiles in Cuba, 1970." *Foreign Affairs* 49 (April 1971): 494–506.

Rabinowich, Eugene. "After Cuba: Two Lessons." *Bulletin of the Atomic Scientists* 19 (Feb. 1963): 2–8.

Rabkin, Rhoda P. "U.S.-Soviet Rivalry in Central America and the Caribbean." *Journal of International Affairs* 34, no. 2 (Fall/Winter 1980–1981): 329–51.

Reilly, Henry J. "Cuban Crisis Brings Home Lessons of Preparedness." *Officer* 38 (Dec. 1962): 18.

Rodman, Peter W. "The Missiles of October: Twenty Years Later." *Commentary* 74 (Oct. 1982): 39–45.

Rogers, Warren, Jr. "Reflections on the Bob and John Show." *The New Republic* (Feb. 23, 1963): 10–11.

Rood, Harold W. "Military Operations against Cuba." *Claremont Quarterly* 10 (Winter 1963): 5–18.

Rosenberg, David Alan. "The Origins of Overkill: Nuclear Weapons and American Strategy, 1945–1960." *International Security* 7, no. 4 (Spring 1983).

Rovere, Richard. "Letter from Washington." *New Yorker* 39 (March 2, 1963): 125–31.

Rusk, Dean, et al. "The Lessons of the Cuban Missile Crisis." *Time* 120 (Sept. 27, 1982): 85.

Sagan, Scott. "Nuclear Alerts and Crisis Management." *International Security* (Spring 1985).

———. "SIOP-62: The Nuclear War Plan Briefing to President Kennedy." *International Security* (Summer 1987): 22–51.

Scali, John. "I Was the Secret Go-between in the Cuban Crisis." *Family Weekly* (Oct. 25, 1964): 4–5, 12–14.

Scherer, John L. "Reinterpreting Soviet Behavior during the Cuban Missile Crisis." *World Affairs* 144 (Fall 1981): 110–25.

Schevechenko, A. "Bon Voyage, Cuban Friends." *Current Digest of the Soviet Press* 15 (Oct. 9, 1963): 21.

Schwartz, Morton. "The Cuban Missile Venture." In *Cases in Comparative Politics*, edited by James B. Christopher and Bernard E. Brown, pp. 268–301. 2d ed. Boston: Little, Brown, 1969.

Severeid, Eric. "The Final Troubled Hours of Adlai Stevenson." *Look* 29 (Nov. 30, 1965): 81–86.

Shalom, Stephen R. "International Lawyers and Other Apologists: The Case of the Cuban Missile Crisis." *Polity* 12, no. 1 (1979): 83–109.

Shershun, Carroll S. "A Sense of Urgency." *Airman* (Feb. 1963): 2–6.

Sherwin, Martin J., and Peter Winn. "The U.S. and Cuba." *Western Quarterly* 2, no. 1 (Winter 1978): 57–68.

Shuchman, Daniel. "Nuclear Strategy and the Problem of Command and Control." *Survival* 29 (July–Aug. 1987): 336–59.

Silber, John R. "The Kennedy Doctrine: Principles for a Settlement in Central America." *Strategic Review* 12 (Fall 1984): 13–21.

Smith, Steve. "Allison and the Cuban Missile Crisis: A Review of the Bureaucratic Politics Model of Foreign Policy Decision Making." *Millennium: The Journal of International Studies* 9, no. 1 (Spring 1980).

Smith, Wayne S. "Critical Junctures in U.S.-Cuban Relations: The Diplomatic Record." *Diplomatic History* 12, no. 4 (Fall 1988): 463–481.

Smolansky, Oles M. "Moscow and the Cuban Missile Crisis: Reflections on Khrushchev's Brinksmanship." *Politico* 33 (Sept. 1968): 509–26.

Sorensen, Theodore C. "Reflections on a Grim but Hopeful Anniversary." *Miami Herald* (Nov. 1, 1987): 1C, 5C.

Steel, Ronald. "Endgame, Thirteen Days." *New York Review of Books* 12 (March 13, 1969): 15–22.

Steel, Ronald. "The Kennedy Fantasy." *New York Review of Books* 15 (Nov. 19, 1970): 3–12.

Steel, Ronald. "Cooling It." *New York Review of Books* 19 (Oct. 1972): 43–46.

Steele, John L. "The Adlai Stevenson Affair." *Life* 24 (Dec. 14, 1962): 44–46.

Steinberg, Blema S. "Goals in Conflict: Escalation, Cuba 1961." *Canadian Journal of Political Science* (March 1981): 81–105.

Steinbruner, John. "An Assessment of Nuclear Crises." In *The Dangers of Nuclear War*, edited by Franklyn Griffiths and John C. Polanyi. Toronto: University of Toronto Press, 1979.

Stoessinger, John G. "Power and Elements of National Power." *Naval War College Review* 20 (March 1968): 11–27.

Stone, I. F. "The Brink." *New York Review of Books* 6 (April 14, 1966): 12–16.

Strauch, Ralph E. "Winners and Losers: A Conceptual Barrier in Our Strategic Thinking." *Air University Review* 23 (July–Aug. 1972): 33-44.

Sugden, G. Scott. "Public Diplomacy and the Missiles of October." *Naval War College Review* 24, no. 2 (1971): 28–43.

Sullivan, Michael P. "Commitment and the Escalation of Conflicts." *Western Political Quarterly* 25 (March 1972): 28–38.

Symington, Stuart. "Where the Missile Gap Went." *Reporter* 26 (Feb. 15, 1962).

Szulc, Tad. "Cuba on Our Mind." *Esquire* (Feb. 1974): 90ff.

———. "Kennedy's Cold War." *The New Republic* 177 (Dec. 24, 1977): 19–21.

———. "Castro on John Kennedy and the Missile Crisis." *Los Angeles Times* (April 15, 1985): pt. IV, 1 and 3.

Taubman, Philip. "Gromyko Says Mao Wanted Soviet A-Bomb Used on G.I.'s." *New York Times* (Feb. 22, 1988): A1.

Taylor, Maxwell D. "The Legitimate Claims of National Security." *Foreign Affairs* 52, no. 3 (April 1974).

———. "Reflections on a Grim October." *Washington Post* (Oct. 5, 1982).

Thant, U. "The Cuban Affair: Negotiation and Compromise the Only Course." *Vital Speeches* 29 (Nov. 15, 1962): 76–77.

Thomas, Hugh. "Paradoxes of Castro's Cuba." *New Statesman* 72 (Aug. 26, 1966): 283–85.

Toledano, R. "Cuba Story: Wraps Off." *National Review* 14 (Aug. 9, 1963): 288–89.

Trachtenberg, Marc. "The Influence of Nuclear Weapons in the Cuban Missile Crisis." *International Security* 10, no. 1 (Summer 1985): 137–63.

Trachtenberg, Marc. "White House Tapes and Minutes of the Cuban Missile Crisis: Introduction to Documents." *International Security* 10, no. 1 (Summer 1985): 164–202.

Trainor, James. "Cuba Missile Threat Detailed." *Missiles and Rockets* (Oct. 29, 1962): 12ff.

Ullman, Harlan. "The Cuban Missile Crisis and Soviet Naval Development: Myths and Realities." *Naval War College Review* 28 (Winter 1976): 45–56.

Valentine, Andrew J. "Rx: Quarantine." *U.S. Naval Institute Proceedings* 89 (May 1963): 38–50.

Volsky, George. "The Soviet-Cuban Connection." *Current History* 80 (Oct. 1981): 325–28.

Welch, David A., ed. "Proceedings of the Hawk's Cay Conference on the Cuban Missile Crisis, March 5–8, 1987." *Center for Science and International Affairs Working Paper* no. 89-1. Cambridge, Mass.: January 1989.

———. "Proceedings of the Cambridge Conference on the Cuban Missile Crisis." *Center for Science and International Affairs Working Paper* no. 89-2. Cambridge, Mass.: January 1989.

Welch, David A., and James G. Blight. "The Eleventh Hour of the Cuban Missile Crisis: An Introduction to the ExComm Transcripts." *International Security* 12, no. 3 (Winter 1978–1988).

Welch, Richard E., Jr. "Lippmann, Berle, and the U.S. Response to the Cuban Revolution." *Diplomatic History* 6 (Spring 1982): 125–43.

Will, George. "The Lessons of the Cuban Crisis." *Newsweek* (Oct. 11, 1982): 120.

Wilson, Desmond P. "Strategic Projections and Policy Options in the Soviet-Cuban Relationship." *Orbis* 7, no. 2 (Summer 1968).

Wilson, Larman C. "International Law and the U.S. Cuban Quarantine of 1962." *Journal of Inter-American Studies* 7 (Oct. 1965): 485–92.

Windass, G.S. "The Cuban Crisis and World Order." *International Relations* 3 (April 1966): 1–5.

Wisnack, Joseph P. "Old Ironsides [1st Armored Division] Response to the Cuban Crisis." *Army* 13 (April 1963): 26–30.

Witze, Claude. "SAC's Shadow Over Cuba." *Air Force and Space Digest* 45 (Dec. 1962): 8.

———. "Airpower in the News." *Air Force Magazine* (Jan. 1963): 13–17.

Wohlstetter, Albert, and Roberta Wohlstetter. "Controlling the Risks in Cuba." *Adelphi Paper* no. 17. London: Institute for Strategic Studies, April 1965.

Wohlstetter, Roberta. "Cuba and Pearl Harbor: Hindsight and Foresight." *Foreign Affairs* 43, no. 4 (June 1965).

Wright, Quincy. "The Cuban Quarantine of 1962." In *Power and Order*, edited by John Stoessinger and Alan F. Westin, pp. 179–213. New York: Harcourt, Brace and World, 1964.

Wrong, Dennis H. "After the Cuban Crisis." *Commentary* (Jan. 1963): 28–33.

Wuriu, Tom. "Details on Red Missiles in Cuba Spelled out at Defense Briefing." *Air Force Times* 23 (Nov. 10, 1962): 10.

Young, Leilyn M. "Win—Its Meaning in Crisis Resolution." *Military Review* 46 (Jan. 1966): 30–39.

Zuckert, Eugene M. "Today, Tomorrow, and the Day after Tomorrow." *Air Force Information Policy Letter Supplement for Commanders* 114 (Dec. 1962): 8–14.

Dissertations

Barlow, Jeffrey G. "President John F. Kennedy and His Joint Chiefs of Staff." Ph.D. dissertation, University of South Carolina, 1981.

Bernard, Ross. "American Government in Crisis: An Analysis of the Executive Branch of Government during the Cuban Missile Crisis." Ph.D. dissertation, New York University, 1971.

Hoagland, Steven William. "Operational Codes and International Crises: The Berlin Wall and the Cuban Missile Cases." Ph.D. dissertation, Arizona State University, 1978.

Johns, Forrest R. "The Naval Quarantine of Cuba, 1962." Master's thesis, University of California, San Diego, 1984.

Kozar, Paul M. "The Politics of Deterrence: A Comparative Assessment of American and Soviet Defense Policy, 1960-1964." Ph.D. dissertation, Georgetown University, 1984.

Layson, Walter Wells. "The Political and Strategic Aspects of the 1962 Cuban Crisis." Ph.D. dissertation, University of Virginia, 1969.

Medland, William James. "The American-Soviet Nuclear Confrontation of 1962: An Historiographical Account." Ph.D. dissertation, Ball State University, 1979.

Mendenhall, Warner DeWitt. "The Concept of United States Crisis Management in the Bi-Polar World." Ph.D. dissertation, Kent State University, 1982.

Pope, Ronald R. "Soviet Foreign Affairs Specialists: An Evaluation of Their Direct and Indirect Impact on Soviet Foreign Policy Decision Making Based on Their Analysis of Cuba, 1958-1961 and Chile, 1969-1973." Ph.D. dissertation, University of Pennsylvania, 1975.

Rogers, John Philip. "The Crisis Bargaining Code Model: The Influence of Cognitive Beliefs and Processes on U.S. Policy-Making during Crises." Ph.D. dissertation, University of Texas at Austin, 1986.

Runkus, Raymond Alston. "The Cuban Missile Crisis: A Decision Making Analysis of the Quarantine Policy with Special Emphasis upon the Implications for Decision Making Theory." Ph.D. dissertation, University of Oklahoma, 1972.

Sandman, Joshua Harry. "The Cuban Missile Crisis: Developing A Prescriptive Model for Handling Nuclear Age Crisis." Ph.D. dissertation, New York University, 1979.

Skillern, William Gustaf. "An Analysis of the Decision Making Process in the Cuban Missile Crisis." Ph.D. dissertation, University of Idaho, 1971.

Stuart, Douglas Thomas. "The Relative Potency of Leaders Beliefs As a Determinant of Foreign Policy: John F. Kennedy's Operational Code." Ph.D. dissertation, University of Southern California, 1979.

Tierney, Kevin Beirne. "American Cuban Relations, 1957-1963." Ph.D. dissertation, Syracuse University, 1975.

Travis, John Turner. "The Functions of Law in International Crisis." Ph.D. dissertation, University of Arizona, 1974.

Usowski, Peter Stanley. "John F. Kennedy and the Central Intelligence Agency: Policy and Intelligence." Ph.D. dissertation, George Washington University, 1987.

ABOUT THE EDITORS

Laurence Chang was an analyst at the National Security Archive from 1987 to 1990. He has authored and edited several works on the missile crisis, including the Archive's microfiche collection, *The Cuban Missile Crisis, 1962: The Making of U.S. Policy*. In January 1989 he attended the Harvard University Cuban missile crisis conference in Moscow. Chang is currently a doctoral student at Stanford University and resides in Menlo Park, California.

Peter Kornbluh is a senior analyst at the National Security Archive and Adjunct Assistant Professor of International and Public Affairs at Columbia University. He is the author of *Nicaragua: The Price of Intervention*, and co-editor of *Low-Intensity Warfare*. He has also edited two Archive microfiche collections: *The Iran-Contra Affair: The Making of a Scandal, 1983-1988* (with Malcolm Byrne), and *Nicaragua: The Making of U.S. Policy, 1978-1990*. Kornbluh attended the Tripartite Conference on the October Crisis of 1962, hosted by the Cuban government in Havana in January 1992. He lives in Washington, D.C.

ABOUT THE NATIONAL SECURITY ARCHIVE

The National Security Archive is a nonprofit, nonpartisan organization that combines the functions of a foreign policy research institute, a library of declassified U.S. government documents, an indexer and publisher, and a legal advocate of the Freedom of Information Act and the public's right to know. The mission of the Archive is to serve scholars, students, journalists, Congress, public interest organizations, and concerned citizens by obtaining and disseminating internal U.S. government documentation that is indispensable for informed public debate on important issues of foreign and national security policy. The Archive is supported by royalties from its publications and donations from foundations and individuals. It is located at 1755 Massachusetts Avenue, N.W., Washington, D.C., 20036. The Archive's microfiche collections of documents are available through Chadwyck-Healey, 1101 King St., Alexandria, VA, 22314.

Portrait of a President

President

REVISED EDITION

PORTRAIT BY ARNOLD NEWMAN COURTESY HOLIDAY MAGAZINE

Portrait of a President

JOHN F. KENNEDY IN PROFILE

Revised Edition with a New
Introduction and Epilogue

WILLIAM MANCHESTER

LITTLE, BROWN AND COMPANY · BOSTON · TORONTO

REVISED EDITION

Parts of this book first appeared in *Holiday.*

Published simultaneously in Canada
by Little, Brown & Company (Canada) Limited

PRINTED IN THE UNITED STATES OF AMERICA

To
John Kennerly Manchester
and
to his future

———

To Don Congdon
And our eighteen years of friendship
With gratitude for his firmness
When he stood by my side
Battling for the integrity
Of another manuscript

Contents

Introduction to the First Edition

Inaugural day dawned bleak and cold, and as the morning wore on it grew glum. The preliminary ceremonies were lagging. Outside the Capitol, impatient spectators shivered, while inside, the President-Elect, sharing their mood, fingered his speech in the Military Affairs Committee Room. Ten minutes before noon he moved restlessly into the corridor, but he didn't get far; the Secretary of the Senate barred the way, explaining that the Upper House wasn't ready to receive him. "All right," the President-to-be said cheerfully. "We'll go back and wait some more."

That was almost three decades ago. The following morning — March 5, 1933 — a brief version of the episode was published on an inside page of the *New York Times*. Eight days later it appeared in *Time,* and there it was discovered in the 1950's by a Harvard professor preparing a multi-volume chronicle of the Roosevelt era. In itself the story is trivial, merely suggestive of Franklin Roosevelt's resilience. History, however, is a gossamer spun of such incidents, and the pilgrimage of this one, from a brittle page of newsprint to Arthur M. Schlesinger, Jr.'s *The Crisis of the Old Order*, tells a great deal about the spinner's trade. Reporters and scholars are inclined to think of themselves as antithetical. Call a newspaperman's copy recondite and he reaches for a pica ruler; tell a professor his paper is just journalism and he invites you to join him in the gym. The feud is an old one. It is time to stop it. The only difference between the two is a difference of time; today's journalism is tomorrow's history.

Portrait of a President is journalism. The writer has labored on the other side of the barricade, but this monograph has been written while moving along the advancing edge of the present. It is not definitive in any sense, nor does it pretend to be an assessment of the Kennedy Administration. Proximity to great events distorts our vision, and the few tentative judgments I have set down may be quickly outdated. The political tide has a way of washing away those who would predict its course. I freely concede, for example, that on the morning after the off-year elections I may devoutly wish that I could run a few pages through the typewriter once more, and in that context it may be useful to point out that the period of my study has been from April 1961 to April 1962 — roughly, from Cuba to Big Steel. Some may conclude from this that the text is a narrative, beginning with failure and ending in triumph. For them one more warning flag must be hoisted. This is not a chronological account. It is, rather, an attempt to understand and explain a highly complex individual playing a unique role. Thus its material is not confined to the year of investigation. I have, as it were, revved the film of John Kennedy's life through a series of projectors, stopping it whenever I found a relevant frame. The sum of these superimposed frames is, or is meant to be, something resembling a portrait.

Bibliognosts will note that there are few footnotes. Work of this sort cannot be annotated. Because so much of the material could only be attributed to what academics call "personal information," the writer would be constantly referring himself to himself — a pedagogic absurdity. Moreover, if every fact were subject to direct citation, the manuscript could not have been written. Readers will find that I revere the Presidency and admire this President; nevertheless, those who are close to a Chief Executive in office are not likely to deal with any writer, however sympathetic, who cannot shield them from embarrassment. Thus from time to time the text refers to "an aide," "an ex-roommate," "an adviser," etc. At present you have only my word that these people exist, although I have arranged to deposit my files in the Olin Library, Wesleyan University, Middletown, Connecticut.

My chief sources are personal observations of the President in 1961 and 1962 and some forty other interviews with members of his Administration, his family, his present friends, and those who have known him in the past. Whenever possible I have used my legs to track down data, but journalism, like history, is a ceaseless flow. Much that follows is a synthesis of my own findings and those of others. My debt to my colleagues is great and is gratefully acknowledged. Occasionally I encountered different versions of the facts; in those cases I settled for the account which seemed to me to be correct. Among the books which were especially helpful were *John Kennedy: A Political Profile*, by James MacGregor Burns (New York: Harcourt, Brace, 1960); *PT 109: John F. Kennedy in World War II*, by Robert J. Donovan (New York: McGraw-Hill, 1961); *Let Us Begin: The First 100 Days of the Kennedy Administration*, comprising contributions from Eric F. Goldman, Barbara Ward, Wallace Westfeldt, Jr., Ira Wolfert, Sidney Hyman, and Martin Agronsky (New York: Simon and Schuster, 1961); *The American President*, by Sidney Hyman (New York: Harper, 1954); *Why England Slept*, by John F. Kennedy (New York: Funk, 1940); *Profiles in Courage*, by John F. Kennedy (New York: Harper, 1936); *To Turn the Tide: A Selection from President Kennedy's Public Statements from His Election Through the 1961 Adjournment of Congress, Setting Forth the Goals of His First Legislative Year*, edited by John W. Gardner, with a foreword by Carl Sandburg and an introduction by President Kennedy (New York: Harper, 1962); *I'm for Roosevelt*, by Joseph P. Kennedy (New York: Reynal and Hitchcock, 1936); *The American Presidency: An Interpre-*

tation, by Harold J. Laski (New York: Harper, 1940); *The Remarkable Kennedys,* by Joseph P. McCarthy (New York: Dial, 1960); *Presidential Power: The Politics of Leadership,* by Richard Neustadt (New York: John Wiley, 1960); *Six Crises,* by Richard M. Nixon (New York: Doubleday, 1962); *The Kennedy Government,* by Stan Opotowsky (New York: E. P. Dutton, 1961); *Abraham Lincoln: The War Years,* Volume Four, by Carl Sandburg (New York: Harcourt, Brace, 1939); *The Crisis of the Old Order, 1919-1933,* by Arthur M. Schlesinger, Jr. (Boston: Houghton Mifflin, 1957); *The Coming of the New Deal,* also by Mr. Schlesinger (Boston: Houghton Mifflin, 1958); and *The Making of the President 1960,* by Theodore H. White (New York: Atheneum, 1961).

The number of newspaper and magazine sources on any Administration approaches infinity. During this inquiry I drew on the files of the *New York Times* — a very special debt — and on the Associated Press, the *Chicago Daily News,* the *Greensboro Daily News,* the *Hartford Courant,* the *Harvard Alumni Bulletin,* the *New York Herald Tribune,* the *New York Times Magazine, The Times* of London, United Press International, the *Wall Street Journal,* the *Washington Post and Times-Herald,* the *Department of State Bulletin, Esquire, Harper's Magazine, Holiday, Life, Look, Nation's Business,* the *New Republic, Newsweek,* the *New Yorker,* the *Reporter,* the *Saturday Evening Post,* the *Saturday Review, Time,* and *U.S.*

News and World Report. Signed articles that were particularly valuable include Stewart Alsop's "The White House Insiders," *Saturday Evening Post* (June 10, 1961); Russell Baker's "Why Kennedy Has Trouble on the Hill," *New York Times Magazine* (April 16, 1961); David Butler's "An Englishman's Reflections on the Change of Administration," *American Scholar* (Autumn, 1961); Douglass Cater's "The Kennedy Look in the Arts," *Horizon* (September, 1961); Frederic W. Collins's "The Mind of John F. Kennedy," *New Republic* (May 8, 1961); Rowland Evans, Jr.'s "That Wit in the White House," *Saturday Evening Post* (September 2, 1961); Arthur N. Holcombe's "John F. Kennedy '40 as Presidential Cabinet-Maker," *Harvard Alumni Bulletin* (May 27, 1961); Alfred Kazin's "The President and Other Intellectuals," *American Scholar* (Autumn, 1961); Fletcher Knebel's "Kennedy and His Pals," *Look* (April 25, 1961); Raymond Moley's "FDR — JFK: A Brain Truster Compares Two Presidents," *Newsweek* (April 17, 1961); Hans J. Morganthau's " 'Alone with Himself and History,' " *New York Times Magazine* (November 13, 1960); Richard H. Rovere's "Notes on the Establishment in America," *American Scholar* (Autumn, 1961); William V. Shannon's "The Kennedy Administration: The Early Months," *American Scholar* (Autumn, 1961), and the Washington dispatches of Joseph Alsop, Marquis Childs, Henry Gemill, Arthur Krock, Walter Lippmann, Allan L. Otten, James Reston, and Merriman Smith.

The writer offers deepest thanks to those individuals who gave generously of their time, provided advice, loaned material, and furnished their recollections of the past and their reflections on the present. Inevitably some names must be omitted, but special gratitude is extended to:

John F. Kennedy, President of the United States of America;

Mr. K. LeMoyne Billings; Professor and Mrs. James M. Burns; Miss Christine Camp; Mr. Douglass Cater; Mrs. Russell G. D'Oench; Mr. Paul B. Fay, Jr., Undersecretary of the Navy; Mr. Richard N. Goodwin, Assistant Secretary of State for Inter-American Affairs; Mr. Andrew T. Hatcher, Associate Press Secretary to the President; Mr. Cornelius W. Heine; Mr. Fred Holborn, Special Assistant to the President; Mr. Edward M. Kennedy; Mr. Joseph P. Kennedy; Mr. Robert F. Kennedy, Attorney General of the United States; Mr. Joseph P. Kirby; Mr. Arthur Krock; Mrs. Evelyn Lincoln, personal secretary to the President; Mr. Lawrence F. O'Brien, Special Assistant to the President; Mr. P. Kenneth O'Donnell, Special Assistant to the President; Mr. David Powers, Special Assistant to the President; Mr. James A. Reed, Assistant Secretary of the Treasury; Mr. George Ross; Mr. Pierre Salinger, Press Secretary to the President; Mr. Arthur M. Schlesinger, Jr., Special Assistant to the President; Mr. Harry Sions, Editorial Director of *Holiday Magazine;* Mr. Theodore C. Sorensen, Special Counsel to the President; Miss Pamela Turnure,

Press Secretary to Mrs. John F. Kennedy; and Mr. Gore Vidal.

The views in the text are not always their views, and certainly the responsibility for any sins of omission or commission is mine alone, but without their cooperation this study would have been impossible, and without the insight they have given me it would be a bloodless audit. Whatever its other faults, I hope that it is more than that.

W.M.

Middletown, Connecticut
May, 1962

Introduction to
This Edition

"To REWRITE years after," Sean O'Faolain once told me, "is a form of forgery." I didn't know what he meant then. Now I do. It had been my thought, in taking up these pages again, to recast everything in the past, changing tenses and adding perspective. But books are mysterious, even to their authors; they have secret sources of vitality, and whatever vigor this one has lies in its immediacy. It was written when John Kennedy was President of the United States, when there was every reason to believe that he would finish his first term, win reelection in the landslide that had been denied him in 1960, and go on to a triumphant second term. *Portrait of a President* was never meant to be definitive. It is less a biography than a photograph — hence the title — and no scrupulous artist retouches his work.

Though less than five years old, this volume is really a period piece. The memory which his fellow countrymen would retain of President Kennedy was forever transformed in the crucible of November

1963, and so were the countrymen. During the year of mourning we came to realize that more than the Presidency had changed. We were different men, living in a different land. Kennedy's emphasis on reform, innovation and idealism had been succeeded by a resolve to make yesterday's system work. And yesterday, for the new President, was the capital of Franklin Roosevelt's 1930's. The shift in values was discernible in thousands of little ways, all of them trivial if taken alone, yet significant in the aggregate. Before Dallas it was fashionable in some circles to deprecate Kennedy "style," as though he had achieved popularity through some trick. But as the Comte de Buffon pointed out, *"Le style est l'homme même"* — the style is the man himself — and that is as true in politics as in literature. Once Kennedy had gone we realized that, for we knew what we had lost.

We knew because after Arlington the tone in the White House changed dramatically. That brief golden hour when American culture had enjoyed the patronage of the Chief Executive was over. Milton Berle, not Robert Frost, was the mansion's honored guest now. The New Christy Minstrels, not Pablo Casals, played in the East Room. Lucy (or Luci, as she began to spell her name) celebrated her Catholic christening by doing the frug and chose for her wedding the Shrine of the Immaculate Conception, which Jacqueline Kennedy disliked and which she had rejected, over the protests of the Church hierarchy, as the scene of her husband's funeral Mass.

Because Washingtonians are servile players of follow-the-leader, Johnsonian taste became their taste. This writer recalls an afternoon with Mrs. Johnson in the White House's family sitting room, which is described in the opening pages of this book and which was where Mrs. Kennedy had planned her husband's state funeral. The new First Lady, a charming hostess, asked her guest to join her for a drink. The author asked for a daiquiri. The waiter apologized. Daiquiris, which had been President Kennedy's only cocktail, were no longer served in the executive mansion. It was then, looking around the once familiar room, that I sensed how much it had altered, and how much of a stranger I was.

Even the few survivors of the enchanted past had been transformed. Bob McNamara, replacing Bob Kennedy as the second most powerful man in the government, was no longer known as the genius of peace who had reasserted civilian control of the military. He had become a war lord. Once he had been a symbol of John Kennedy's passion for excellence. Now one examined his hair-part and old-fashioned spectacles and realized, for the first time, that he had a prewar look. The fashion transition was smooth. That year my office was next to that of Evelyn Lincoln, who had been President Kennedy's private secretary, and we used to marvel at the ease with

which the hostesses of Georgetown and Cleveland
Park had switched gears. They bought Him and Her
beagles, fawned on male guests who wore cowboy
boots and on wives with sugary nicknames, and became accustomed to public displays of affection between spouses which would have brought a frosty
stare from President Kennedy. Some even learned to
digest jalapeño peppers, deermeat sausage, and Dallas jailhouse chili, though the Kennedys' White House
chef didn't. He quit.

Over lunches in the Federal City Club I would ask
Arthur Schlesinger how he was doing. "I'm plodding
gloomily along," he would say, and I would nod
glumly. There was nothing wrong with the new
Washington; the flaw lay in us. We simply didn't belong in the capital any more. We were anchored there
by the zeal of historians. He was writing his book
about the thousand days when the President we had
known had reigned over this city; I was writing my
account of that reign's catastrophic climax, when the
most spectacular crime of this century brought an entire nation to its knees. The following year we fled
northward. At one time I had thought of the District
of Columbia as the most beautiful, exciting and challenging community in the world. These days I go
there infrequently and secretly, like a burglar.

Portrait of a President was limned when the sun
stood high and the light was dazzling. This is how
the thirty-fifth Chief Executive looked to one observer then, before the drifting mists of legend ob-

scured the man. It is the work of an admirer. I did not apologize for my enthusiasm then, nor shall I now. I have been a student of politics all my life, and I have known some able politicians: three Presidents, the greatest of England's twentieth-century Prime Ministers, the revolutionary President of Egypt, a gaggle of Communist and Nazi bosses, India's Nehru and Burma's U Nu. Kennedy stood alone. He had more vision than any of them, more courage, and, to my ear, more eloquence. In him Aristotle's memorable definition of man — that he is a political being, and a being endowed with speech — was brilliantly realized. Not everyone grasped that at the time. The first reception of this book was mixed. Some of my colleagues thought me too ardent. Tom Wicker was disappointed. Arthur Krock sternly reminded me that I was Mencken's biographer, and that Mencken had insisted that a writer, confronted by a man in public office, should always look down on him. James Mac-Gregor Burns is quoted on page 217 of this book on its subject: "I wonder how much he will be loved by the people, in the Lincoln sense. Liked — yes. But loved?"

That was in the penultimate year of the Kennedy Presidency. In November 1963 the question was answered more fervently, perhaps, than any other question in history — and fresh responses come every day. If you doubt that, go to Washington. Cross Memorial Bridge to Arlington. Walk up the slope beneath Custis Lee Mansion. Stand by the endless line of anonymous Americans circling the grave, and watch their faces.

W. M.

Middletown, Connecticut
September, 1966

ONE

You Must Never Forget

THE WHITE HOUSE is very white. Under a roving moon its freshly painted sandstone walls gleam through Andrew Jackson's beloved magnolias with a haunting, ghostcandle glow, and the barbered lawn lies quiet as a park, and sometimes, when the light shifts, the mansion seems to recede. Partly this is a trick of landscaping, partly it is us. So much intrudes. Americans take their Presidency personally. In retrospect you recall pledges of allegiance in chalkdusty classrooms, and blue eagles, and Hoover's medicine ball, and Raymond Massey in that odd hat, and Carl Sandburg writing of the day the calendar said Good Friday —

The oaks and chestnuts stood grave and thoughtful.

From any window of the honorable Executive Mansion they were above reproach. . . .

Did any clairvoyant foreteller write a forecast that today, this April the Fourteenth, one man must hear a deep sea bell and a farewell gong and take a ride skyward swifter than Elijah in the chariot of fire?

Thus mythbound, you lurk behind the old black iron fence on Pennsylvania Avenue, squinting at the floodlit north façade. The haze of tribal sentiment grows denser. You can scarcely believe that the shrine is inhabited.

It is, because the White House is also a house. The lower rooms lack domesticity — each year over a million tourists file through them under the illusion that they are seeing the President's lodgings, when all they are in is a museum — but when a concealed elevator rises to the second floor above ground level you emerge in the First Family's residential apartment, and there the tone is quite different. This suite is closed to the public; no part of it was shown on CBS's Jacqueline Kennedy Show. It is very much a home, though not all the public would recognize it as such, because it is so precisely upper-class. The last tenants

were comfortably middle-class. Their tastes ran to
the music of Fred Waring and Lawrence Welk; to
color television sets, red leather chairs, war trophies.
Today the only martial note among the furnishings
is the photograph of the First Lady's father wearing
a World War I second lieutenant's uniform, and
even he gazes out from his frame with genteel, East
Egg urbanity.

The new look is subdued elegance. Achieving it
was no mean accomplishment. The mansion has
changed enormously since the days when John G.
Nicolay called it "a dirty, rickety concern," yet it can
scarcely be called a triumph of design. Ceilings are
lofty dustcatchers, rooms are chopped up, doors open
inconveniently. Stepping from the elevator you find
yourself in a small vestibule which debouches into a
huge hall. This passage runs east and west, bisecting
the entire floor like a concourse and creating something of a traffic problem. The President's oval study
opens on it from the south, and so — directly across
from the elevator — does his bedroom. The children
sleep along the north side. The western extremity of
the corridor has been converted into a family sitting
room, which leads to the First Lady's bedroom and
the dining room. This arrangement is successful, but
eastward the yawning hall ends in splendid anticli-
max. The state bedrooms are down there. In them,
theoretically, eminent guests from other nations may
retire to enjoy an enticing view of the Treasury next

door. Actually celebrities board in Blair House, and the state rooms, always vacant, somehow evoke memories of a resort hotel out of season.

The effect could easily be that of a refurbished New York elevator flat. It's not, because the great, barnlike corridor has been toned down by an ingenious use of color, *objets d'art,* and graceful furniture. Slipcovered French chairs are grouped invitingly on off-white rugs. Lovely chandeliers sparkle overhead. American paintings by George Catlin, Maurice Prendergast, Winslow Homer, and John Singer Sargent hang on tinted walls, and below them are handsomely mounted vases and sculptures, a Louis Quinze desk, and a spinet. The most vivid hues, however, come from book jackets. Altogether there are several thousand volumes, rising in endless tiers: graceful books on art, squat histories, multi-volume encyclopedias, Churchill's memoirs, a few modern novels — Nevil Shute's *On the Beach,* Giuseppe di Lampedusa's *The Leopard,* Harper Lee's *To Kill a Mockingbird* — and many biographies, including a battered, jacketless copy of *Profiles in Courage,* which seems a shabby orphan here, because everything else is tidy and quietly expensive. The hi-fi-FM-TV in the west sitting room is long, low, masked. The portable bar there is stocked with Beefeater gin and Ballantine's Scotch ("She hath done what she could," read the fatalistic banner which the W.C.T.U. gave the mansion in memory of Mrs. Rutherford B. "Lemonade Lucy" Hayes). White matchbooks bear the gold inscription *The President's House*, and the spine of a buckram scrapbook the simple legend *Caroline*.

Caroline's father approaches with celerity, shoulders hunched and burnished black shoes gliding in a Boston social gait. His dress conforms to the décor: a tailored two-button navy blue suit, a white shirt with a spread collar, a narrow Ivy tie held by a gold alligator-grip clasp shaped like a tiny PT boat. Like many public men he seems shorter than his photographs, and startlingly older. On television he looks younger than his age, but forty million screens are wrong. The figure tapers like a boxer's; the glossy hair is chestnut, with only a suggestion of gray at the temples. The face, however, is deeply lined, especially around the mouth, and the eyes give an even stronger impression of maturity. They are opaque, gray, and often hooded by long lashes. There is about them an air of being withdrawn, as John Hay wrote of Lincoln, into "an inner sanctuary of thought, sitting in judgment on the scene and feeling its far reach into the future." It is impossible to read John Fitzgerald Francis Kennedy's mind, but obviously there is much on it. Upon the evening of this visit he has been President of the United States nearly a year.

"Let's go in here." (The familiar, starchy *he-ah*.) He moves past his bedroom door, toward the formal, yellow-walled oval study which looks out on the Washington Monument, and opening the door he precedes his visitor. This is protocol. Over four hundred indignant letters have inquired of the White House why the President always seems to be a few steps ahead of his wife. "Jackie," he once replied lightly, "will just have to walk faster." Actually she's not allowed to. The President outranks everyone, including ladies. On Cape Cod, or in Virginia or Florida, Jacqueline goes first at his insistence, but in the capital that's out. Early in his administration he tried to hold a door for Eleanor Roosevelt. She hung back.

"No, you go first," she said. "You are the President."

He laughed. "I keep forgetting."

"But you must never forget," Mrs. Roosevelt said gently.

He remembers now. We sit in the study — he in his upholstered Northern Porch rocker, a duplicate of the one downstairs in his West Wing office — and he reflects on the changes which the Presidency has wrought in his life.

"In eleven weeks I went from senator to President, and in that short space of time I inherited Laos, Cuba, Berlin, the nuclear threat, and all the rest. It was a terrific adjustment to make. I've made it now, but naturally there have been some changes. It's certainly true that I'm more isolated socially. In the beginning I tried to carry on the life I had led, going out, seeing people; but I soon realized that was impossible. Apart from state dinners I suppose I see only three or four people socially. But I have no feeling of withdrawing. After all, everyone's life is circumscribed. And in many ways I see and hear more than anyone else."

His right hand, which is never still — it almost seems to have a life of its own — drums on a matchbook, on the rocker arm, on a shaving scar, on his teeth. His eyes are hooded. For a long moment the only sounds are the rhythmic rock of the chair and the muted tick of a gold mantel clock behind him.

Then:

"So much depends on my actions. So I am seeing fewer people, simplifying my life, organizing it so that I am not always on the edge of irritability."

The hand makes a sudden, spastic fist.

Talking with writers is one of the President's relaxations, and presently he does relax, speaking with clarity and wit about his early life, his family, the war years, the years in Congress, and his rise to the most powerful office in the world. It is a pleasant evening. Yet beneath us the oaks and chestnuts stand grave and thoughtful. Every hour in the Executive Mansion is an hour in history. In South Vietnam tonight Communist guerrillas are attacking in battalion strength. In Algeria one O.A.S. threatens a putsch, while in South America another O.A.S. quibbles over Cuban sanctions. Andrei Gromyko is insisting that East Germans be given full control over Berlin access routes. London feels bullish about a new summit, Paris is grimly bearish, and Syria is seething. At home Jimmy Hoffa is celebrating his fourth anniversary as Teamster president, while the Senate Armed Services

Committee has announced that it will hold hearings on Administration censorship of Pentagon brass. Housing, unemployment, and gold — each a code word for a knotty problem — have a brighter sound these days, thanks to vigorous executive action. There is still a ten per cent gap between the nation's productive capacity and its actual performance, however, and even the educators seem uninterested in education. The country as a whole feels sanguine, but there are many dissidents. Alfred Kazin is uneasy. Dwight Eisenhower is unhappy; so, even at this early date, is Roger M. Blough. The Americans for Democratic Action are most unhappy, and Margaret Chase Smith wonders aloud whether the author of *Profiles* lacks the courage to blow up the world.

Instinctively all these — and Gromyko, Macmillan, de Gaulle, and even Hoffa — turn to 1600 Pennsylvania Avenue. It is the one place to which every buck is passed and where, as Harry Truman observed, the buck stops. Early in his tenure Kennedy had an imperfect understanding of this. At meetings of the National Security Council he would inquire of issues, "Let's see — did we inherit these, or are they our own?" It was Douglas MacArthur, of all people, who reminded him that the Presidency is a continuum. "The chickens are coming home to roost," the fading old soldier told him, "and you live in the chicken house." Ultimately every American problem becomes the President's. At the same time, the number of issues has multiplied. Because the world is more complex, and because this nation plays a larger role in it, the Chief Executive is empowered to make command decisions that were inconceivable twenty years ago, which means that Senator Smith's speech — whatever one thinks of her discretion — was directed to the right address.

To this address, to this home, and to its householder. The President must never forget, nor can he. More and more the discussion with his evening visitor turns to Germany, South America, domestic legislation, and the Soviet position on arms control, a problem so renitent that young John Kennedy analyzed it in his undergraduate thesis two decades ago. These quarters are *en famille,* but public life is never truly private once an ivory Princess telephone across the room rings. If a matter is urgent, any one of several aides or Cabinet ministers may call him at any hour. And once, as we stand by the blue and gold presidential flag, looking out at the winking red lights of the bone-white Monument, the President speaks of his Hairbreadth Harry mandate. "I've gone over the election hurdle," he says, his hand exploring in his hair. "Now I have the necessary support at home. This — this *base* is all-important. A chief of state cannot deal abroad effectively unless he has it. I'm over the hump now, but the first four months were delicate."

The early days of any Administration are vital, in the opinion of Columbia Professor Richard E. Neustadt, whose scholarly volume *Presidential Power* John Kennedy read during the 1960 campaign. Neustadt wrote that a Chief Executive's public image "takes shape for most constituents no later than the first time they see him being President (a different thing from seeing him as a candidate)." The first time Kennedy's constituents saw him as President he was at the post and pulling away. Noticing that there were no Negroes among the Coast Guard cadets in the inaugural parade, he started an official inquiry on the spot. The next morning he was in his bare office, witnessing the swearing in of his Cabinet, pumping Harry Truman's hand, and firing off Executive Order No. 1, to double the food rations of four million needy Americans. In the weeks which followed he continued to vibrate with energy. He would pace corridors, read on his feet, dictate rapidly, dart out for brisk constitutionals around the monument, and return in a sprint, snapping his restless fingers. "I never heard of a President who wanted to know so much," said Charles Bohlen. Some members of the government were so hard-pressed by the President that routine work suffered. A committee chairman from the Hill complained, "*He* may have two hours to spend, but *I* don't"; and Llewellyn Thompson, Ambassador to Russia, who was seldom alone with Eisenhower for more than ten minutes, had four two-hour sessions with Kennedy. The talk wasn't small talk. "When you see the President," a senator remarked, "you have to get in your car and drive like blazes back to the Capitol to beat his memo commenting on what you told him."

One day a hundred people were counted entering the West Wing office. One powwow there produced seventeen separate directives, and two months after taking the oath the new Chief Magistrate had issued thirty-two official messages and legislative recommendations — Eisenhower had issued five in his first two months — while delivering twelve speeches, promulgating twenty-two Executive Orders and proclamations, sending twenty-eight communications to foreign chiefs of state, and holding seven press conferences. A Washington wag observed that the new President seemed determined to be not only his own Secretary of State, but his own Mrs. Roosevelt, too. No detail seemed too small for him. Noting that Army guerrillas had been deprived of their green berets, he ordered that they be returned. Conferring with generals about Southeast Asian strategy, he tested the carbines being shipped to Saigon, and as his first presidential spring approached he even detected crab grass on the greening White House lawn and told the gardeners to get rid of it.

Some of his early activity was an extension of the inaugural binge: being President was fun. Some of it was a carryover from three years of incessant barnstorming: he was still behaving like a nominee. And some was a natural consequence of his appetite for work. Both John and Bobby Kennedy had spent most of their Washington years toiling at the other end of

Pennsylvania Avenue; they were genuinely amazed to learn that all executive offices shut down Saturdays. The Attorney General sent a note of appreciation to everyone who had worked in the Justice Building on the Administration's first Washington's Birthday, and the President ordered Saturday office hours for his staff to set a good (if vain) example for the rest of the government.

But the hatless, coatless, on-the-ball vigor also had a shrewd political motive. Kennedy was out to expand that all-important base. The people he needed were watching him, and he wanted to be sure they liked what they saw. Americans approve of self-starters. Thus it was helpful for reporters to report that the new President was very much in charge and was encumbered by piles of documents and swarms of advisers; useful for the word to be passed that Dean Acheson had been given just four days to hammer out a detailed NATO report. The first, televised press conferences were, of course, crucial. One of them — the third — was watched by some sixty-five million people in twenty-one and a half million homes. These performances were live. Kennedy had to be not only his own Mrs. Roosevelt, but also his own Robert Montgomery. Bearing down in his best IBM manner, he became something of his own Mnemosyne as well; reporters learned that the President knew all about the sale of a surplus Navy building in West Virginia and could quote from memory a statistic about Cuban molasses which had appeared four days earlier near the end of a government report.

The wisdom of the Neustadt approach was presently reflected in studies by opinion samplers. Kennedy's racing start had converted a quarter of the American electorate. His base was as big as Ike's. And in the quiet of his study he concedes that this effect was calculated: "I've always believed that a first impression is important. In press conferences I gave the impression of knowing what I was doing, and my general activity, in my judgment, stimulated confidence. Cuba could have been difficult if I hadn't done that."

"Presidents, like great French restaurants, have an *ambiance* all their own," Douglass Cater has observed. The Kennedy image was forming, an amalgam of Jacqueline's camellia beauty, Caroline's Kate Greenaway charm, the Ciceronian rhetoric of the President's speeches, the football on the Attorney General's desk, the generous gestures toward the defeated party, and the new idealism. Gone were the Mad Avenue slogans ("bigger bang for a buck," "rolling readjustment," "brinksmanship," "agonizing reappraisal"); instead there was to be a policy of action, typified by the new Secretary of Labor, who settled a strike during his first twenty-four hours in office and announced that in the new Washington the deadline for everything would be "the day before yesterday." Like the harassed senator, everyone in the new Cabinet appeared to be driving like blazes, working fourteen-hour days and displaying symptoms of Kennedy hypomania. One was observed simultaneously signing his mail, carrying on a telephone conversation, and relaying instructions to his secretary by crude semaphore; a second barely found time to take his own oath of office; and a third, Robert McNamara, startled Pentagon guards by his habit of showing up at 7:30 each morning, his ballpoint at the ready.

Today the Administration looks back wistfully on its first flush of enthusiasm. There was a freshness then, a boundless vitality; and perhaps there was also some naïveté. "We had the feeling that there was a plasticity to events, that they could be molded, that this guy was unlimited," Special Assistant Arthur M. Schlesinger, Jr., recalls. John Kennedy seemed to share that feeling. After the inaugural parade he had reached the White House in a state of euphoria. "He was exalted," says Ted Sorensen, Special Counsel to the President. "It was no secret that he wanted the Presidency. He had won it in a bitter contest. Like most men he was ambitious in his profession, and now he was at the pinnacle."

Any man who reaches that pinnacle brings a gang with him. Schlesinger and Sorensen were typical of Kennedy's. The capital was enchanted by the invasion of a witty, bespectacled delegation of ideologues, most of them with advanced degrees, all of which seemed to have been granted in Cambridge, Massachusetts. "If you think Republicans are lonely in

Washington," said Senator Thruston B. Morton, "you
ought to be a Yale Republican." "The definition of a
failure," one of the arrivals' bright flashes went, "is a
Yale man driving an Edsel with a Nixon sticker on
it." They might have said an *old* Yale man. For the
incomers were much younger than the outgoers, and
it is significant that their first inspiration, the Peace
Corps, was an appeal to young bloods.

"The torch," the President had said on the Capitol
steps, "has been passed to a new generation of Americans." Walter Lippmann reckoned the difference between the Eisenhower and Kennedy Administrations
at about thirty years, and to venerable Washingtonians the junior members of the new team seem very
junior indeed. During Eisenhower's first inauguration
Sorensen was an angry young man of the A.D.A.
Jacqueline Bouvier was a giddy girl interviewing inaugural celebrities; as Madame de Gaulle's guest in
1961 she still looked rather like a *jeune fille* traveling
under the eagle eye of her chaperone. Bobby Kennedy's wife Ethel refers to politicos as "goodies" and
"baddies." It is startling to recall that when John
Kennedy first ran against the baddies in 1946, Ethel's
husband was too young to do more than work the
streets of Cambridge under the supervision of Le-
Moyne Billings, who had roomed with the candidate
at Choate School. At the time of the Berlin airlift the
present Attorney General was a cub reporter for the
now defunct Boston *Post*, and five years later, when
working for Senator Joseph McCarthy, he was able to

slip undetected into a football game between Harvard and Yale dormitory teams. Senator John L. McClellan continues to treat him with a paternalistic air, even as, in the first days of the New Frontier, the United States Ambassador to the United Nations was fatherly toward the President of the United States. Twice in the Administration's first year — during the Cuban episode and the Freedom Rides — Yale graduates ran afoul of Harvard men. Each clash had overtones of The Game. In the first, Richard Bissell of the CIA and the Blue seemed to some to be a scapegoat for the Crimson. In the second, the Attorney General argued with a group of Riders from New Haven, one of whom alleges that the President's brother called them "a bunch of Yalies."

This collegiate theme is both entertaining and deceptive. John Kennedy may be "the boy" to Eisenhower, but at forty-five he has his full growth. His is the youngest Cabinet since McKinley's, but George Washington's was younger than either. Despite G.O.P wheezes about the children's crusade, most of the Administration's movers and shakers are middle-aged, and they have the diversity of mature men. Niccolò Machiavelli, who preceded Neustadt, believed that "the first impression that one gets of a ruler and of his brains is from seeing the men he has around him." Anyone who takes a sharp look at the men around Kennedy discovers that the genus falls into three distinct species: the professors (Rooseveltians); the politicians (chiefly Irish); and such old friends as Lem Billings and Charles F. Spalding, a New York investment banker. Each group has its own traits. The old friends have known the President longest. Unlike Eisenhower, whose presidential friendships were formed late in life, Kennedy has been close to most of these men for at least twenty years. Collectively they are trustworthy, loyal, helpful, friendly mesomorphs. They are well-heeled and often Republicans, though it would be wrong to underscore that, because they never argue about politics. The professors, on the other hand, argue about politics all the time, while the Irish politicians listen to your arguments and then agree warmly, because they are empathic, flexible, and lacking in the self-consciousness of the intellectuals. When Secretary of Commerce Luther Hodges was Governor of North Carolina, he posed for a national magazine in shorts stamped *Made in N.C.* Professor Schlesinger and Dean McGeorge Bundy never appear publicly in their underwear.

Hodges is over sixty. In a government whose average minister is in his forties, this places him, chronologically at least, beyond the New Frontier. It also puts him outside the circle of presidential intimates, the most prominent members of which are the Attorney General, thirty-five, Robert McNamara, forty-five, Douglas Dillon, fifty-two, and Arthur Goldberg, fifty-three, of the Cabinet; Appointments Secretary Ken O'Donnell, thirty-eight, in whom the President places great trust; Schlesinger, forty-four, to whom he likes to talk; and Bundy, forty-three, and Sorensen, thirty-three, the two advisers who exert the greatest influence on him. Thus, while this is not an Administration of yearlings, some grasp of the generational factor is essential to an understanding of the Kennedy Presidency. The fact that the Chief Executive has surrounded himself with contemporaries suggests its importance to him, and it has loomed large in his career. The anybody-but-Jack coalition which formed before his nomination was really a bloc of older men fighting younger men. Behind the charge of Kennedy "inexperience" lay the resentment of old stagers who were being shoved into the wings, and behind the urbane manners of the Frontiersmen today there is a similar awareness of age.

This is the veteran generation. They were young in the early 1940's, and most of them were very much in the war. Men Eisenhower's age were in charge of the maps, but men Kennedy's age did the actual fighting. The President himself was a PT commander in the Solomon Islands. A fellow officer — who laid his hand open while operating one of the boat's machine guns — was Lieutenant (j.g.) Byron R. White, now Mr. Justice White. On nearby Bougainville, Orville Freeman, the present Secretary of Agriculture, was a Marine officer; his face still bears scars of a Japanese bullet. Ken O'Donnell was a fighter pilot, Schlesinger was in the OSS, Press Secretary Pierre Salinger was a teen-age minesweeper captain. Even Robert Kennedy enlisted in the Navy at the age of seventeen, though he missed combat, which annoyed him no end. Afterward he went to South America with Lem Billings. "The war was still fresh in people's minds down there," Billings recalls, "and they'd ask where we had been, what we'd done. Bobby didn't have anything to say. I used to kid him about it. He didn't think it especially funny."

The thought of Bobby at war is diverting — he is warlike enough in peacetime — but his intuition was correct. He had missed the central, formative episode of his time. The style of the Frontier was shaped in those years. When John Kennedy was asked about his reaction to F.D.R.'s death in 1945 he replied calmly, "I had no deeply traumatic experience." This may puzzle those who remember the grief among civilians. It is less surprising to men who spent the early Forties on the red, ragged fringe of the war; they had learned to keep themselves to themselves, to avoid getting hurt. Today the President, speaking in the idiom of his time, scorns soul-searching as "couch talk," and nearly all those who are close to him hold the world at arm's length. There is no Adlai Stevenson among them; eloquence is not their forte. Their strong points are manipulation, expertise, and efficiency, even to the sacrifice of individuality. "We're developing a new policy community here," one of the Harvard men says. "Most of the men around Kennedy are not only of the same generation; they're alike in other ways, too. They all went to college, they're political creatures — though none are

stridently political — and they have pretty much
the same gifts. The fact that they have different titles
is just accident, and they know it. People like Bohlen,
Nitze, Bundy, and Rostow could easily have one another's jobs. You might say they're interchangeable
parts."

Since age seems to attract the President more than
party labels — Bundy, Dillon, and McNamara are
Republicans — this writer suggested that he is a generational chauvinist. "I don't think that's the right
word," he said reflectively. "I suppose that if you
went through my Administration you'd find that most
of my advisers are my age, give or take eight years.
But I think most people are more comfortable with
people their own age." They are, though few are as
devoted to their peer group as he is. His partiality is
clearly a factor in his personal diplomacy; he is proud
of his relationships with Konrad Adenauer and Harold Macmillan, yet he has seemed more at ease with
Hugh Gaitskell and Willy Brandt. Charles de Gaulle
is an exception to this rule. De Gaulle appears to belong not merely to a different generation, but to another century; he won't even have a telephone in his
office. The President admires him, however, and he
made elaborate preparations for their first meeting.
"It went off beautifully," one of the men who was
present says trenchantly. "De Gaulle was like a professor. Our man was the student who had boned up.
We got A."

The old guard does die, of course. Observing Bobby's whirlwind activity in Tokyo, a septuagenarian Japanese politician sighed, "The days are here for the younger generation to take over." Lippmann once noted that about fifteen years after every major war (*e.g.*, 1933) the wartime leaders reach senescence and political upheaval follows. John Kennedy feels that 1960 was an omen — that his generation is rising to power in other countries — and he has remarked more than once that by the time he leaves office he will probably be the senior statesman of the West. The change may brighten chances of understanding abroad, though it doesn't promise much on the Hill, where seniority assures a superannuated leadership. Roosevelt was thwarted by nine old men. Kennedy must deal with a Congress full of them.

The President's youthful informality is one of the sources of his political charm. In the Senate he had kept his office door open at all times, and it was after the inaugural, when his instincts were still those of the candidate, that he attempted "to carry on the life I had led." It was a plucky try, if soon abandoned. Unlike Bobby, he didn't work in his shirtsleeves. Away from his desk, however, he thought he needn't stand on ceremony. One evening he slipped into a neighborhood movie with a friend, Paul B. "Red" Fay, Jr., to see *Spartacus*, and one Saturday he picked up his golf clubs and completely vanished for three hours while the White House press corps seethed. He and Jacqueline also decided to go visiting like any other Washington couple. Here informality collided with the formality of the Presidency. Where a Chief Executive breaks bread, and who breaks it with him, is a matter of more than passing interest to the capital. Mainly it is the professional concern of twenty-four men in the Office of Protocol. Among other things there is a tradition that the occupant of the White House must remain socially aloof. As Herbert Hoover put it, "the President of the United States never calls on anyone." Precedent requires that the man who has solemnly sworn to execute the office of Chief Magistrate not only preserve, protect, and defend the Constitution, but that he do it, whenever possible, in his own home.

The First Family's hosts were to include Rowland Evans, Jr., of the New York *Herald Tribune*. Evans had told no one about it, not even his bureau chief. But in Washington there is a rather large number of people whose business it is to know the little preferences of a President — as, for example, the fact that John Kennedy's only cocktail is a daiquiri. Thus when the hostess phoned a Georgetown liquor dealer and emphatically ordered "one of your best bottles of rum," she told him more than she intended. "Why, Mrs. *Evans!*" he gasped. The secret was out. The morning of the party an Evans neighbor opened his front door and found his sidewalk encased in ice. Ice, however, was rapidly disappearing from the Evans walk; a small army of District employees was chipping away the last slivers. The neighbor asked huffily why the special treatment. He was told and since he, like Evans, was a member of the working press, the dream of a quiet evening out was destroyed. The workmen might as well have stuck around to render "Hail to the Chief."

The Chief hasn't retreated behind his seal. In many ways he is as informal as ever. Since the anniversary of his first year in office he has, some think, returned to his inaugural mood. Several friendships which had been interrupted have been renewed. In press conferences he is more relaxed, more buoyant — and, unfortunately, more likely to lapse into the spongy chaos of Eisenhower syntax. With an interviewer he continues to be as frank as Saint Augustine, and he still worries the Secret Service by falling into crowds and confounds Press Secretary Pierre Salinger by permitting him to distribute advance texts of presidential speeches which are then scrapped at the point of declamation. In Palm Beach or on Cape Cod, where, Bobby says, "he can really relax," he slips away now and then. A letter arrived from a Hyannis Port neighbor thanking him so much for calling; the billet created an anxious stir in the White House because, it developed, no one there had heard of the signer.

He has even made a few social sallies near the capital. Sargent Shriver, Director of the Peace Corps and his brother-in-law, was entertaining some eighty people late in Kennedy's second presidential winter when the door opened, admitting both the President *and* the Vice President. The guests, stunned, fell si-

lent. Kennedy, prepared for this, moved about skill-
fully, chatting until the party resumed its momentum.
"It's a gift," observes Arthur Krock of the New York
Times. "He doesn't know how to be stuffy." Occasionally his lack of stuffiness can result in wild incongruity. Once this writer was leaving the oval office in the
West Wing. As he prepared to thread his way out
through the maze of check points, Secret Service men,
and White House police, the President said lightly,
"Any time you're coming by, drop in."

Despite this casual air, his way of life has changed
perceptibly since his investiture. He sees his films in a
private theater under the mansion's East Terrace,
where he laughed at *Make Mine Mink*, or in his
father's projection room at the family compound on
the Cape, where he tensely watched the demolition
of *The Guns of Navarone*. He has always been an ardent movie-goer. Theaters have been his favorite
form of election night relaxation; he took his grandfather to one when returns were being counted in his
first primary, and went to another with two friends
during the tense West Virginia primary of 1960. His
all-time favorite is *Casablanca,* which he has seen at
least four times, though while squiring Jacqueline
Bouvier about he often took her to Westerns and Civil
War pictures. During his first months in office he continued to watch one or two films a week. Later the
number dwindled; during a two-month period at
the end of his first year in office he saw just five (*Paris
Blues, Lover Come Back, Purple Hills, Carry on Con-*

stable, and *Loss of Innocence*). He has also become less patient with the screen. Before the inaugural he would sit through almost any flop. No more: if he becomes bored he may order that the last reel be shown, so he can see how everything turned out, or leave without a word. Since his election he has walked out on Elizabeth Taylor (*Butterfield* 8) and Marilyn Monroe (*The Misfits*), and he gave up on Billy Wilder's comedy *One, Two, Three,* perhaps because he can't see anything funny about Berlin.

So many topics are grave to a Chief Executive, and even if he tried to forget, he couldn't. Everyone he meets or knows is conscious of his office. The day after he defeated Richard Nixon in the wards of South Chicago a bunch of Kennedys were horsing around on the playing fields of Hyannis Port, watched by their peppery, seventy-two-year-old father, former Ambassador to Britain Joseph P. Kennedy, who is still known as "the ambassador." The President-Elect lunged at a long pass and missed, and the future Attorney General, on the other team, delivered an opinion. "All guts and no brains," he muttered lugubriously. Those present remember that, because they all knew it was the end of something. In the future such a razz would be disrespectful. The great days of touch were over; the new game was follow-the-leader. The same day several Kennedy friends were sitting in Bobby's Cape home when the leader entered, and they rose instinctively.

They didn't decide this, nor did he. Like his social

life, it was a matter of precedent. Something about
the Presidency discourages familiarity; Schlesinger
was once observed slipping into his suit coat before
taking a telephone call from the oval office. That was
a tribute, not to a man, but to an institution. The incumbent and the office reign together, which is why
a Chief Executive speaks of himself, on formal occasions, as "we." Each inaugural brings renewed appreciation of this dualism. In 1932 the ambassador
was traveling on Franklin Roosevelt's campaign train.
After one of the candidate's speeches he accosted him
with a blistering critique. "The stupidest thing I ever
heard," he called it, adding a string of bitter epithets.
Calling on President Roosevelt a few months later at
the White House, he remembered that philippic. "I
was appalled," he recalled recently. "It had been per-
missible then. But in the presence of the power and
majesty of the Presidency it seemed unforgivable."
George "Barney" Ross was similarly appalled when,
upon being shown into President Kennedy's office, he
blurted out, "Hi, Jack!" "I was mortified," Ross says.
"I still brood over it. I'm not the kind that's disrespectful normally; it just popped out." Yet if anyone
is entitled to be familiar with John Kennedy, it is
Ross; as fellow officers they were shipwrecked together for five days during the war.

John Kennedy's age makes him a striking example
of the power of custom. One afternoon in the White
House this writer heard the bark of his voice approaching and heard, almost simultaneously, the rus-

tle of expensive tweed. A few feet away Averell Harriman, a party power when John Kennedy was gyrating through the Big Apple in Harvard's Winthrop House, was coming to attention. Until his inaugural oath the President was still a junior senator. Yet men like Byrd, Keating, Eastland, and Dirksen defer to him now. "I haven't forfeited my faith in John Fitzgerald Kennedy!" the Republican Senate leader cried during the U.N. bond debate, while Carl Hayden, in his eighties, says simply, "I'm just anxious to be as helpful as I can to the President." Lyndon Johnson, who was Senator Kennedy's congressional leader and his chief rival for the 1960 nomination, has become almost unctuous. The President has described their new relationship as "a real love affair." "Lyndon has undergone a real metamorphosis," says a man who knows him well. "He used to be brisk, incisive. Now he dotes on Kennedy. He has become a rather sweet old man."

Today none of the Hyannis Port scrimmagers publicly use the President's first name in his presence. Bobby (to his chagrin) has remained Bobby — even in Cabinet meetings the Chief Executive so addresses him. Jack, however, has gone forever — in the same meetings, Bobby calls his brother "Mr. President." Only in private does the Attorney General revert to the diminutive, which in his case is "Johnny." Occasionally a show-off Boston pal writes a letter beginning "Dear Jack," but nearly everyone else is scrupulously correct. "I'm certainly not going to call my son 'Mr. President' when we're alone together," the ambassador remarked shortly before his stroke in December 1961, "but if there are people around we don't know very well I do, and it doesn't seem at all strange." "Jacqueline always calls him 'the President,'" says Arthur Krock, a friend of both since they were children. "She even calls him 'the President' to me." "I used to kid him all the time," says Red Fay, who, like Ross, served in the Navy with him, "but not any more. You just don't kid the President of the United States."

Once you did. Reportedly John Quincy Adams was subjected to a humiliating interview when a newspaperwoman discovered him swimming naked in the Potomac, sat on his clothes, and declined to leave until he had replied to her inquiries. Washingtonians of a century ago saw nothing remarkable in a Chief Executive insisting, "Call me Mr. Lincoln; 'Mr. President' is entirely too formal for us." Lincoln put up with extraordinary incivilities from strangers, but that was before the evolution of what Senator Eugene J. McCarthy has called the "cult of the Presidency." The cult has arisen because the President has become so much more sovereign. With the historic drift of power from Capitol Hill, more and more power has been vested in him. A few years ago the Hoover Commission found that among other things he was accountable for nine major departments, 104 bureaus, twelve sections, 108 services, fifty-one branches, 631 divisions, nineteen administrations, six agencies, four boards, six commands, twenty commissions, nineteen corporations, ten headquarters, three authorities, and 263 miscellaneous organizations. Since that survey his responsibilities have continued to multiply. No wonder we sir him, rise for him, and stand aside for him.

Thus the President is honored — and isolated. There is nothing teamy about the institution. It is no place for Groupthink. As a historian Kennedy knew that, but reality was still something of a blow. He had regarded political campaigning — "the treadmill," he calls it — as the most exhausting drudgery conceivable, and he has been startled to find that the Presidency is as demanding as it is. Those closest to him agree that it has affected him. Always introspective, he has, some feel, become readier to reveal his thoughts. During the worst of the Berlin crisis he phoned Fay. "Have you built your bomb shelter?" he inquired. "No, I built a swimming pool instead," Fay replied. "You made a mistake," the President commented. "And," Fay adds, "he was dead serious." The Attorney General thinks the fact that his brother has always been pensive means that he is less alone than most Chief Executives, though Bobby adds, "It's obvious that the possibilities of nuclear war are never far from his mind." In one of those bursts of frankness which startle writers the President told one of them, "If you could think only of yourself it would be easy to say you'd press the button, and easy to press it, too." That was after his somber Vienna meeting with

Khrushchev, when he asked his aides for an estimate of how many Americans might die in a nuclear holocaust. The answer was seventy million. It took a while to sink in. "He campaigned as a Democrat, and I don't think he fully understood what it meant to be President of all the people until after Vienna," a Republican friend observes. "Then he grasped, *really* grasped that the life of every man, woman, and child in this country — not to mention lives abroad — depended upon him." The President estimates that eighty per cent of his first year in office was spent mulling over foreign policy. In the 1960's foreign policy thoughts are long thoughts. "Of course he's preoccupied," a member of the Kennedy family remarks. "It would be a miracle if he weren't. Saigon, Germany, fifty-megaton bombs — that's why he can't get to sleep until two or three in the morning."

One worry which vexes him less is his image; he wears his political hat a bit more blithely. His skin is still thinner than that of most politicians, as witness his testy cancellation of all White House subscriptions to the New York *Herald Tribune*. Washington bureau chiefs have grown accustomed to phone calls from the President, and occasionally he boils over. Doris Fleeson, the liberal columnist, can make him growl; a *Fortune* harpoon drew presidential blood, and when Pauline Frederick appeared on NBC's Huntley-Brinkley Report to dispraise one of his U.N. decisions, he thundered right back at his television screen. Yet on the whole he seems quicker to shrug off press criticism than he was during his first weeks in the mansion. He is less vulnerable to such gadflies as David Lawrence, and as a rule he doesn't darken unless he thinks a critic has his facts balled up. A man can respond to just so many stimuli. A President has to be selective; he is likelier to survive if he remains in good spirits. Kennedy has become quicker to see, or even make, a joke at his own expense. In the Big Steel row he displayed a glint of humor, and during one of the councils of war over Cuba he listened quietly as speaker after speaker commented on the scope of the disaster; then, observing that the politicians looked desolate, he turned to Schlesinger and said dryly, "Arthur, when you write the history of my first term — *The Only Years* . . ."

Of course, he doesn't want them to be the only years. When eight-year-old Eric Sorensen wrote him that he liked the White House, the President wrote back, "So do I," and when Eric commented that he would enjoy living there some day, the presidential reply was, "Sorry, Eric, you'll have to wait your turn." The inaugural thrill has gone; each day he must make some thirty major decisions, and each decision leaves him with an endless agenda of unfinished business, but he seems to look forward confidently, and with relish, to a second term. Janio Quadros's resignation from the presidency of Brazil appalled him. "He doesn't have the right to resign!" he protested to a friend of the family who was with him at the time. "Sure, there are times when I'd like to go off to the

South of France and take in the sun, but no man can just quit his responsibilities and walk away." Even the desire to walk away is unlike him. His whole life has been a hunt for challenges. When he decided to stalk the Presidency, his father was dubious. "I said, 'What do you want that job for?'" Joe Kennedy recalled after the election. "I told him, 'It's the worst job in the world.' And he said, 'We've had problems for the past two thousand years, and they've been solved by humans, and today's can be, too.'" The ambassador's son had confidence in a specific human, himself. He retains it, though the first big rumble of his first term did inspire an agonizing reappraisal of some other bipeds across the river and under the trees of the Pentagon.

The Bay of Pigs was for him an hour of bitter truth. Its lessons are never far from his mind. In his first reaction to Quadros's charge that the Brazilian government had been undermined by foreign influences the President snapped, "If there was one place where we played it —" and he paused, "*straight* — it was in Brazil." In that pause he may have been thinking of Cuba. Cuba was not so straight. It was more of a sort of a three-cushion shot. Its failure to drop into the bag staggered the new President. "This is the first time he lost anything," an aide said. That fall he himself remarked that "If a man stays in hot politics long enough, he acquires an albatross," and Pig Bay, he added, was his. The implications of the tragedy were vast — they are still being discussed in the White

House, where Cuba is called "the bone in Kennedy's throat" — and among them was the realization that men thought to be infallible had proved to be highly fallible. "He had expected to rely on certain experts one hundred per cent," a presidential assistant explained, "and in this Cuban thing they let him down two hundred per cent." One Kennedy adviser stopped referring to the CIA at all. Instead he spoke scornfully of "the spies." "I know that outfit," said the ambassador, who was one of Eisenhower's intelligence advisers, "and I wouldn't pay them a hundred bucks a week. It's a lucky thing they were found out early; the best thing that could've happened, in fact. Cuba gave this Administration a chance to be great."

Certainly Washington's mood changed sharply. The football disappeared from Bobby's desk; his brother became more difficult to see. Their first-stage rocket had burned out. It was time a new guidance system took over. "We were like a gambler whose winning streak has been broken," says one of the young Cantabs. "Laos came at the same time, and then Berlin. The world appeared more intractable." The Bay of Pigs adventure had been so disastrous that a repetition was unthinkable. Immediate solutions were elusive, yet all problems were urgent, and growing more so. "Every incoming American Administration plunges at once into international crisis," Barbara Ward has written, but here was a phalanx of crises. As a veteran Washington correspondent had predicted, the emergencies were building up like a coral reef. By late summer Berlin was on the brink, the Southeast Asian dominoes were tottering, and the President, whose back was more painful than the public knew, was both ill and anxious. After his Vienna meeting with Khrushchev his trust in the power of rationalism — a faith which had reached its peak the year before, after his victory in West Virginia, which he believes he won by reasoning — had been replaced by faith in the big battalions. One battalion worked. The President ordered an armed convoy to Berlin, and it traveled the *Autobahn* unmolested. Then Laos was removed, at least for the moment, from the critical list. The Chinese Reds began tarring the Russian Reds, who reciprocated; the drums of the Congo were muffled, and NATO had a stronger look. By November temperatures everywhere were normal. The world, having passed through a minor convulsion, had emerged unchanged.

But the President of the United States had changed. During the first seismic jolts his friends and aides had begun to detect subtle changes in his manner. It was Billings's impression that "Suddenly he was hard to get close to. He was thinking all the time." After a 3 A.M. meeting with the Joint Chiefs over Cuba he walked out through the French windows of his office, through the rose garden, and paced the south grounds alone for half an hour. He had always been a gregarious man. No one could remember his doing anything like that before. Again, when he finished his Berlin speech on July 25, 1961, he turned away from the television cameras, left his office without speaking to anyone, and strode back to the mansion by himself. Jacqueline and the children were on the Cape. Only solitude awaited him, but that was what he needed just then. "He had less time for trivia," says Assistant Secretary of the Navy James A. Reed, another friend from PT days, "and he was more restless." His hand became increasingly active; he was forever pulling up his socks, toying absently with his telephone, arranging papers on his desk and then rearranging them. Fred Holborn, a special presidential assistant, believes that he became more philosophical, and another aide thinks he detected signs of humility. This is not a Kennedy trait — he was a cocky President-Elect — but it is a presidential trait. "There are a great many people, I expect a million in the country, who could have done the job better than I could, but I had the job and I had to do it," Harry Truman said, and while Kennedy didn't go that far, his manner did suggest a tempering.

All his life he had shunned routine. During his senatorial days his aides had been little more than aides-de-camp; he would decide that something needed doing and then, like as not, he would wind up doing it himself. These habits had persisted through his early White House months, when more than one minor figure in the State Department was aghast to find himself dealing directly with the President via telephone. They began to change that summer. In most departments he now deals with the top of the ladder: secretaries and undersecretaries. State has been an exception, but even there he goes no lower than the assistant secretary rung. For the first time he has some sense of the delegation of power and is reasonably comfortable with a staff. The web of system has appeared; briefings of the Chief Executive follow a more orderly pattern. Scheduled conferences have emerged — the Cabinet and the reorganized National Security Council meet twice a month, and each week a Tuesday luncheon group plans security moves, to be followed by a Thursday luncheon group which acts on the plans. He will never be methodical. Every week or so he misplaces his reading spectacles — he's slightly farsighted — and has to acquire new ones, and although he reads rapidly, he's not a good paper mover; the end of each afternoon brings a frantic rescue operation as aides rush in to retrieve memoranda they've left on his desk. He still hates to be told what to do, still dislikes contrived conferences, and still keeps his talks with the Cabinet as brief as possible. But the hectic half-hour appointments of the first year are no more. In middle age his life has finally begun to move in patterns.

The President's work day starts in bed. Each morning a White House butler hands a stack of newspapers to the President's bespectacled Negro valet, who brings them into the bedroom at 7:30 A.M. As James Reston of the New York *Times* noted, Kennedy takes printer's ink for breakfast. While still in his pajamas — or lying in his bathtub, under a board which supports the papers — he examines staff memos, scans every inch of the *Times,* and then riffles through the *Wall Street Journal,* the Baltimore *Sun,* and the Washington *Post,* concentrating on columnists. A line of type may echo around the world. When he read that under Defense policy it was impossible for American soldiers wounded in Vietnam to receive the Purple Heart, he issued an Executive Order reversing the policy. He appears to have total recall; nothing ever seems to be erased from his mind. The results of his morning perusals must be seen to be believed. Once the attitude of American business was being discussed at a Cabinet meeting, and the President, in support of a point, casually cited a quarter-page advertisement which, he said, had been published the previous week in the financial pages of the *Times.* He named the date, the page number, and the ad's position on the page. His ministers were skeptical — none of them had noticed it, not even Secretary of the Treasury Dillon — so the President called for the edition, and there it was, just as he had said. Again, an editorial viewed with alarm his proposal to increase the number of regular Army divisions, and he told Salinger indignantly, "They said just the opposite in another editorial six months ago. Find it." Unlucky Pierre couldn't. He was plowing through a blizzard of newsprint when his phone rang. "I don't know why it takes you so long to put your finger on something," the President complained. "It was in the upper right hand editorial column, and it had some data about battleships." He cited some of the data. Then Pierre discovered it and confirmed him.

By 9 A.M. Kennedy is in his oval office, meeting appointments, after which he takes a fifteen-minute dip in his ninety-degree White House pool. Presidential exertion is sharply limited by Dr. Janet Travell, his physician; since his back injury during an Ottawa tree-planting ceremony in May 1961, his only exercise has been swimming and workouts with dumbbells under the supervision of a Navy chief petty officer, and his freestyle stroke is hampered by a light medical corset which he must wear at all times. After lunch he follows Eisenhower's example and takes a brief siesta. Awakening, he hits his best stride of the day. In the first months he returned to the West Wing and worked there until 7:30, but with the family in Hyannis Port during his first presidential summer, he began spending afternoons in the private apartment. He liked it. Opportunities for reflection were greater; between appointments he could read and think. For a time he was rarely seen in the West Wing after his noon meal. Toward the end of his first year the pendulum began to swing back — with the return of Congress there were more formal meetings — though he still prefers the quiet mansion, and stays there when he can.

At the end of the day bills and correspondence are brought to him for signature. He dines at 8 P.M., while

Sorensen and Mrs. Evelyn Lincoln, the President's personal secretary, assemble his evening reading in a file which is usually delivered by Brigadier General Chester V. Clifton, his military aide. Presidential homework is heavy, and is faithfully done; once an inch-thick report reached him at 10:30 P.M., and the next morning he had finished it and was ready to talk about it. He reads, not in the oval study, but in the west sitting room, which is informal and comfortable and which, since most of its furniture came from the Kennedys' Georgetown house, stirs memories of other days. The only desk is a frail antique. Kennedy doesn't use it. Instead he sprawls on a slip-covered couch, distributing papers on the floor. He writes here, too, scribbling on yellow, ruled, legal-length pads. If the manuscript is a speech, he has help. First drafts are written by Sorensen, and the two men bounce subsequent drafts back and forth, though the speaker naturally has the last word. He uses it, too. He edits phrases up to the moment of delivery and beyond — in the middle of his second State of the Union address he departed from the text, polishing prose from the rostrum.

In the sitting room this writer once watched another guest, a foreign policy adviser, admiring the walls of books. "You know, they put a fine library in my office," he murmured wistfully, "and I haven't had time to turn a page." The President makes time, which, considering his burden of official reading, is something of a feat. Books are saved for weekends, but even then he is accompanied by a heavy black alligator briefcase containing weekly agency reports, background synopses, and — by presidential direction — anything which any ranking member of the Administration feels is important.

This is a sharp change from the Eisenhower chain-of-command concept. As a senator, Kennedy scouted the notion of an administrative Vice President,.and as Chief Executive he has abolished Sherman Adams's old job. Ever since a clique of Andrew Jackson's cronies tried to elude public attention by using the White House kitchen door, most Presidents have had a kitchen cabinet — administrative assistants, aides, and advisers who are, in fact, closer to the Chief Executive than full-fledged ministers. Under Eisenhower everyone in both cabinets was assigned a slot in a tidy table of organization. In theory differences anywhere in the government were to be settled down below, by the numbers. In practice a number of feuds worsened; *e.g.*, the Secretary of the Treasury is said to have refused to talk to the Budget Director on the telephone. Senator Kennedy watched this sort of thing with distaste. The State and Defense Departments, he said, were dealing with one another like "so many Venetian envoys." Even if the chain worked perfectly, he was against it; like Winston Churchill he was wary of staffs that can dictate command decisions, and one of his first executive acts was to eliminate Eisenhower's Operations Coordinating

Board and seventeen interdepartmental agencies. His Administration is much more of a one-man show. No one tells him what he will read or whom he will see. Any member of the official family can check with Mrs. Lincoln in the morning and receive a hearing.

The idea is to keep the President posted, to provide him with choices — to give him, as one aide put it, "binocular vision." Seeing the big picture is an old presidential problem. Minutiae keep cluttering up the lenses. "Now go away!" Lincoln told a visitor. "Go away! I cannot attend to all these details. I could as easily bail out the Potomac with a teaspoon!" The Presidency was less than a year old when George Washington confided to a French diplomat that he couldn't even keep up with his correspondence, although, as Sidney Hyman has pointed out, the first President could prepare his budget on a single sheet of paper; one year he appointed only sixty-five officials. A modern budget is a million-and-a-half words long, and Kennedy, who directed a staff of twenty-one men in his senatorial days, is answerable for 2,350,000 employees. Big government is, by its very size, a labyrinth. Henry S. Rowan, a Harvard professor who is serving as Kennedy's Deputy Assistant Secretary of Defense, says the Pentagon alone is like "a log going down the river with twenty-five thousand ants on it, each thinking he's steering." Harry Truman called the whole thing "oppressive." Accurately predicting Eisenhower's difficulties with it, Truman said in 1952, "He'll sit here and he'll say, 'Do this! Do that!' *And nothing will happen.* Poor Ike. It won't be a bit like the Army. He'll find it very frustrating."

A Chief Executive's major problem, said Washington, is "seclusion from information." If it was a crux then, it has since become an enigma, and Kennedy, hoping to profit from the lessons of his predecessors, carefully built competition into his Administration. Each department, for example, has liaison men in it who may report two or three times a day, telling the White House how things are shaping up. Some old-timers in the government look upon these expediters as meddlers, and call them *Kennedystas*. Their resentment is resented by the President. It is his nature to take a hand in all things, and he feels he must stir up Washington's Bumbledom.

School texts still teach that there are three branches to American government: executive, legislative, and judicial. They err. There are four. The executive is split into the President and the bureaucracy, a sprawling, diffuse collection of organisms which has become, in Schlesinger's vivid phrase, "this exasperating Jello." By far the most gelatinous department is State. The President's failure to turn over State's goo depresses him, as it depressed his predecessors, and his determination to do something about it led to a shakeup of Foggy Bottom ten months after his inaugural. The appointment of George W. Ball as undersecretary has given him some sense of

anchorage there. He is sanguine about his ambassadors and McNamara's strong role in Defense, and he
has no sense of sabotage in the Treasury. State, Defense, and the Treasury — the big three — are familiar to the President now. The same cannot be said for
lesser departments. Because of his concentration
on foreign affairs and the economy he has had to
watch some domestic issues out of the corner of his
eye. Secretary of the Interior Stewart L. Udall's attempts to catch his full attention have left Udall
frustrated, and despite Secretary of Agriculture Orville Freeman's new program, most of the President's
knowledge of farms seems to have been acquired in
the Wisconsin primary of 1960. At this writing he
finds Agriculture and Interior rather mysterious,
meaning that data about them goes into the evening
file, into the weekend briefcase.

"I *need* information," he says, "and I get a lot." It
comes to him diversely — from an eighteen-button
telephone console in his office, from radiophones in
presidential cars and planes, from a Signal Corps con-
traption a few feet from his desk which can tape
sounds on almost any wave length in the world and
rebroadcast them at his convenience, and via powerful new generators which have been installed on the
Kennedy yacht *Marlin* to relay coded messages when
he is aboard. Much of the material he receives is solicited. Newspaper editors invited to lunch with the
President are asked to bring memos on problems in
their areas. When he asks private citizens to send him

proposals, as he did in the Berlin speech, he is in dead earnest. "Roosevelt got most of his ideas from talking to people," he told Professor James M. Burns of Williams College. "I get most of mine from reading." But he gets many ideas from people, too. Indeed, he is extremely effective during meetings *à deux*. In Washington — "the City of Conversation," Henry James called it — Kennedy has become the conversationalist-in-chief. On a platform he lacks Churchill's pulpit touch; he is at his best in dialogue. Gore Vidal, a friend of the Kennedys, remarks that "Those who like him tend to tell him everything. You feel he ought to know, and he's terrifically interested. He's really a great gossip." Mention an acquaintance, an ally, or a potential antagonist in 1964, and John Kennedy is instantly alert. Have you seen him lately? he wants to know. How is he? What's he doing? Is such-and-such true? His curiosity ranges beyond official Washington — when *Advise and Consent* was being filmed, he phoned the set one night for a progress report — though it is felt most keenly, of course, in the government. "This morning he called me at eight-fifteen and asked me for advice," Larry O'Brien, his master politician, said during a day of intricate congressional maneuvering. "That doesn't mean he'll follow it. Later I found he was calling a lot of other people, too." Dean Rusk and Douglas Dillon are summoned to the West Wing two or three times a week for interrogations, and Edward R. Murrow, director of the United

States Information Agency, calls his White House telephone "the blowtorch."

The President has been called the best reporter in Washington. In 1945, as a correspondent, he covered the birth of the U.N. and wrote analyses of European politics. Arthur Krock recalls that although Kennedy was merely a green cub, he was virtually the only unbiased writer to predict Churchill's defeat in Britain's general election that year. Merriman Smith, the senior White House correspondent, believes that his news skill is one reason that few biting questions are asked of him now in press conferences. The questioners are wary, Smith reasons, because "a reporter who tackles him poorly prepared is liable to be shown up before a nation-wide audience." Certainly Kennedy has the journalist's gift for seizing conversational initiative; a visiting writer is very likely to emerge from the Executive Mansion with the disquieting realization that the President has been interviewing *him*.

"What do they want me to do?" he says of his critics. "Why don't they put it down on paper?" One criticism which has been put down is that he is getting too *much* information, that he has veered from the red tape of the Eisenhower staff system to the opposite extreme. The President "did not want a Cabinet of the traditional kind," according to his old government teacher at Harvard, emeritus Professor Arthur N. Holcombe. "What he wanted was energetic and efficient department management." But the objectors insist that true efficiency can only be found in even more frequent Cabinet meetings, and more important, in the correct use of channels. Too many presidential task forces are swimming around Washington, the argument runs; the White House staff has become an undisciplined herd. The new Administration has "done a good job of confusing me and all my friends," Eisenhower complained, during a speech in which he went on to predict an inflation that would curl your hair.

Of course, what confuses Gettysburg needn't baffle the rest of the country — Eisenhower was sometimes bewildered by the Administration that preceded Kennedy's — and whether the government should be run like the Army or a PT squadron is an open-end question anyhow. Every President has his own system; Lincoln (as William H. Seward scornfully noted) kept his files in the sweatband of his stovepipe hat. Actually Kennedy's part of the operation, the bridge of the flagship, is neat as a bandbox. As a World War II naval officer the CO once received a low rating in military bearing and neatness; and when he took off for his most memorable sea action, the PT base lacked a record of the men aboard because he had neglected to see to it that a muster sheet was turned in to headquarters. That couldn't happen now. In his forties he is all spit and polish, and he expects his subordinates to be competent executives. The public sawing-in-half of Chester Bowles during the

New Frontier's first year had nothing to do with Bowles's ideas. Someone had told the President that Bowles was a good administrator, and someone had been dead wrong. Adlai Stevenson, on the other hand, has won presidential admiration because he turned the United States U.N. operation, which was jerry, into America's best-run embassy. Kennedy and Stevenson will never be a perfect fit, but their relationship is far better than anyone had expected it to be. There is candor between them, and respect, and the President is impressed by Stevenson's intellectual depth and sinew.

"If a democracy cannot produce able leaders its chance for survival is slight," John Kennedy wrote during his last year with Professor Holcombe. A Roosevelt or a Lincoln wouldn't correlate leadership with managerial ability. A Kennedy does, and he has developed remarkable gifts for personal command. He knows precisely when to lose his temper with an underling — flushing and sharpening his New England vowels — and when to recover it so the scar will heal quickly. His assumption of responsibility is total. There have been no private recriminations over bad advice, not even after Cuba; indeed, his restraint then served to weld the new Administration together. He's not blindly loyal. He just waits. Bowles was carted off eventually, and Allen Dulles became a retired spy — after the heat was off. When one of his men is in the soup, he tries to extricate him; G. Mennen Williams inflamed Europe by announcing that Africa should be for the Africans, and the President wondered aloud who else Africa should be for. It was no answer, but it did shift the spotlight away from Soapy's embarrassment.

Perhaps Kennedy's most effective administrative tool is his memory. "He can still drive down an avenue in Boston," one of his political lieutenants has said, "and remember which stores put up his campaign posters ten years ago." There is some sleight of hand here. No one could recall as much as he seems to. He has a way of recollecting a fragment of an incident — the circumstances under which he met someone, say — and revealing this in such a way that the man leaves with the impression that his name, rank, and serial number are indelibly fixed in the President's mind. Yet even when the most skeptical reservations are made, examples of his retention are astonishing. During the Los Angeles convention he needed no notes; he knew every delegate's preference, down to the half-vote. The whole country watched his extemporaneous performance in the campaign debates, and since then he has displayed familiarity with Geneva conferences which were reported in the *Times* when he was at Choate. After a 1962 press conference Reston wrote: "How he knew the precise drop in milk consumption in 1960, the percentage rise in textile imports from 1957 to 1960, and the number of speeches cleared by the Defense Department last year — 1,200 — is not quite clear, but anyway, he did."

One evening the President was discussing a judicial appointment with four friends, among them James A. Reed and a writer. "I'm not so sure lawyers are as infallible as you think," Kennedy said to the writer. "I remember some trouble Jim here had in a firm." He then proceeded to retell a story Reed had told him ten years before. "*I* had forgotten all about it," Jim said afterward. "Suddenly I realized that he was practically quoting me verbatim — that his account was almost word-for-word the one I'd given him then. It was uncanny." These tape recorder performances are so extraordinary that people who don't know the President often refuse to credit them. Shortly after his second State of the Union speech Kennedy received a brief visit from Floyd Patterson. Feeling the heavyweight champion's muscles, the President chatted with him about past Patterson bouts, episodes in the fighter's career, and possible challengers. Bystanders assumed he had been briefed. "He not only hadn't been briefed," Salinger said afterward. "I didn't even know he followed the fights."

Genius for detail is not genius. It won't raze Berlin's wall or reduce Castro, and were it compulsive it could become a big waste of what is, after all, the most valuable time in the nation. Kept in check, though, it is a handy device. The boss may not remember everything, but if his staff thinks he does, the effect is the same. Kennedy is careful to cultivate that impression. He has a disturbing way of giving orders so casually ("Do this for me, will you?") that newcomers aren't

sure he's serious. Six weeks later, in the middle of another discussion, he will turn to the man responsible
and inquire — as though opening a book at a book-
mark — "Did you make that call?" In consequence
the White House has learned that *no* task may be
treated lightly. He has been known to take an interest
in individual expense accounts, and even typists have
been disciplined. Signing nearly half a ream of routine letters daily, he can still pick out errors. Passing
one girl's desk he inquired, "What was the idea of
waiting a month to answer a letter?" A typical display
of Kennedy mnemonics followed: a recitation of the
date of the original letter, the name of the correspondent, the date of the reply. "To spot that one,"
the girl's supervisor points out, "he had to read the
answer *and* the original underneath. And that was
one of a batch of two hundred that day."

Compared to the incoming mail that day, Kennedy's
two hundred replies were only a mite. Stenographers
may believe that an omniscient President is meeting all the demands on his office. The White House
postman knows better, and the weight of his bag gives
some inkling of the gap between what is asked of a
Chief Executive and what can be done. Each week
Kennedy himself receives some seventeen thousand
letters — even Caroline gets four hundred — offering
blessings, giving advice, making requests. Many follow familiar patterns. The bag usually contains some
mimeographed stuff, inspired by lobbies. Since this

represents no individual effort, it gets no individual attention. It is simply dumped. During the school year a thousand letters arrive weekly from classrooms. These are handled more gently. Another thousand ask for pictures of the President (they get them) and copies of his autograph (they get facsimiles). Other correspondents believe it is more blessed to give. Among the letters there are always some bundles and crates. The custom of sending presents to the potentate goes back to the days of myrrh, and democracy hasn't altered it. Thomas Jefferson received a 1235-pound cheese from a Massachusetts town. John Quincy Adams acquired floral specimens; Andrew Jackson, clay pipes; Franklin Roosevelt, stamps. Lemonade Lucy Hayes got a lot of lemons. John Kennedy's packages contain handicrafts, curios, and Indian headdresses, which are turned over to the National Archives; rocking chairs, rugs, clothing, and jewelry, which are returned with thanks; and books, which are kept.

When all the routine mail has been set aside, however, the balance of correspondence is still heavily in the public's favor, and the best Kennedy can do is make sure that his evening file includes samples from the lot, with every fiftieth or hundredth epistle — depending on the pressure of other business — marked for his attention. Some of them make curious reading. People complain about inflation, taxes, social security, unemployment, *apartheid,* Krishna Menon, television commercials. A Pennsylvania woman wondered why he said "I shall" instead of "I will." She knew her grammar, but felt there wasn't sufficient determination in the expression of "mere futurity." A Marine's wife denounced "that Hiss brainchild, the United Nations charter." A Minneapolis constituent wanted him to investigate foreign aid, start testing bombs, quit talking about disarmament, listen more attentively to the Senate Internal Security Subcommittee, do something about Outer Mongolia, invade Cuba — and cut the budget.

Individual missives are absurd, but in sum they are touching. They represent an instinctive turning to leadership which transcends the sophistications of American politics. In Washington it is hard to see this. The capital thinks in terms of Administrations, but out where the postmarks are affixed these distinctions become blurred. There Americans have a tendency to lump Presidents together — since the 1960 inaugural the White House has received mail addressed to every occupant from Coolidge to Eisenhower. To most of his constituents John Kennedy is one of a line of men, and because he stands where Jefferson and Lincoln stood, their light falls on his shoulders. The typical American, Clinton Rossiter wrote, thinks of his Chief Executive "as a combination scoutmaster, Delphic oracle, hero of the silver screen, and father of the multitudes." He is, said Sidney Hyman, "the guide and interpreter of public opinion, the keeper of the conscience, the ceremonial head, the disciplinarian and the source of clemency," and Theodore H. White called him "the nation's chief educator, the nation's chief persuader." As every taxpayer knows, he is also the chief public servant. The house at 1600 Pennsylvania Avenue is the public's property, and in time of stress its owners eye it anxiously. It is always watched these days. On the sidewalks the silent men press against the fence, peering up. From above the view is startling — it dismayed Jacqueline Kennedy at first — but the watchers mean well. Their stares, like the letters and the bundled tributes, are mute offerings. The people want to do something. They want to give their President direct, immediate help.

And they can't. "So many of the banalities are correct," a member of Kennedy's kitchen cabinet says. "It *is* the loneliest job in the world." Part of "the extraordinary isolation imposed upon the President," as Woodrow Wilson called it, is inherent in the system. Congressmen work with other congressmen; Supreme Court justices with other justices; but there are only two superpower chieftains in the world, and to talk shop the President must go to the summit, which has proved to be not only profitless but disagreeable. If he is to fill his office properly he cannot even lean on men of his own party. To meet vital issues he must be prepared to break away from party and appeal to the entire nation. Lincoln felt the strain of this solitude when he moved to make the Emancipation Proclamation; so did Wilson when, for ten days in 1917, he wrestled with his war message.

But Wilson could share that decision. In those days Congress still declared war. No more; since the Formosa Resolution making war is a presidential matter. The atom has given the Chief Executive what Dean Rusk describes as an "almost unbearable responsibility." It is a cruel fact of our time that the graver the choice, the fewer the men who may make it. Nuclear tests were resumed by decree; no other way was open. In most matters of foreign policy John Kennedy confers with Rusk, McNamara, the Attorney General, Mac Bundy, Lyndon Johnson, John McCone, General Maxwell Taylor, and the Joint Chiefs, but if he must act quickly, he may consult only the first three, and should the big question arise — the need for a retaliatory attack after absorbing an enemy blow — he would have only his own counsel. He alone can launch a Minuteman capable of destroying a fourth of Moscow after a twenty-minute run. Among the obligations which he must never forget, this is the first, and among the reasons why he cannot forget is that visible evidence of it is never far from him. The code which would launch total thermonuclear attack is kept in a slender black case bearing a double lock. This case is constantly in possession of one of a team of five Army warrant officers. The warrant officer on duty goes wherever the President goes. They spell each other, but no one can spell John Kennedy. In Hyannis Port, Palm Beach, or Middleburg, Virginia, that burden follows the President of the United States. It is the most harrowing game of solitaire in the world, and there is only that other player, co-existing on the other side of the globe.

The President glides through the lovely apartment, moving slowly, escorting his guest to the elevator. Two floors below, a crew-cut Secret Service man awaits the descent; near him an inconspicuously dressed warrant officer keeps the vigil; but here there is only a host and his guest, chatting about mutual acquaintances. The suite is still as still. Flowered drapes have been drawn across the broad west window, masking the rose garden; eastward, moonbeams freckle the old green roof of the Treasury; within, tiny points of light twinkle on a hall spinet, on a picture of Princess Stanislas Radziwill, on a framed snapshot of young Jacqueline Bouvier with her father and on another of Caroline romping with hers. The President's hand reaches for the elevator button and is withdrawn. He wants to say something else. He says it, and the hand rises and falls again. And again. And then again.

The conversation is idle. The guest, a person of no consequence, senses that he is merely someone who will listen, that this is the end of the day, and that when he leaves there will be no one. He wants to help, and he can't, and abruptly he understands all the earnest letter-writers and donors of useless gifts and simple starers — all those who reach so far and still cannot touch, because none can reach here.

Now everything has been said. The fisting hand

opens and brushes the button. The black wrought-steel door slides open.

"Just press G — ground floor," says the flat New England voice. "Goodnight." And John Kennedy walks back toward the oval study by himself: alone.

TWO

The Establishmentarian

Two DAYS after his U.N. disarmament speech in the fall of 1961 the President of the United States boarded his ninety-two-foot cabin cruiser for a twenty-minute run on Narragansett Bay. It was a gaudy autumn day. *Honey Fitz* wore a bustle of sparkling foam. The man who had cruised these waters as a World War II lieutenant (j.g.) was in a blithe mood, and as he passed Newport Naval Station sailors greeted his little flagship with a twenty-one-gun salute.

"This isn't so bad, Mr. President," an appreciative guest observed.

John Kennedy grinned. "It's a lot better than having your ears beaten in by Goodie Knight in California," he said.

Richard Nixon, beached on the West Coast, would have winced at that. That week he was pinned down by the political artillery of Goodwin Knight, then his chief Republican gubernatorial rival, and the President's remark underscored the fact that Nixon's plight was a direct consequence of his loss to Kennedy the previous fall. In 1960 the two men whose lives are now so far apart were separated by some 120,000 votes, less than one-fifth of one per cent of the popular vote. The winner had won a photo-finish — "a miracle," he himself called it. He had just managed to resolder the old Roosevelt coalition of labor, northern minority groups, and the South, and it had taken some doing, not all of which had been visible on the television debates. He attracted a big Negro vote by expressing sympathy for Martin Luther King, but he also found it expedient to confer with a Southern governor and the head of the state's White Citizens' Council, who endorsed him the moment the conference was over. A writer inquired of this peculiar coincidence, "How did that happen?" Kennedy shrugged and replied, "Just lucky, I guess."

There was that, too. There has always been that. His father once called him a "lucky mush," and others have noted chance's uncanny habit of backstopping him. By some strange process he even wins when he loses. Shortly after the Cuban caper his Gallup rating reached a new high, and he himself remarked wryly,

"It seems as though the more mistakes I make, the more popular I become." Big Steel's rhubarb was called "a domestic Cuba" by one pundit, but three days later Steel collapsed, and there stood Jack the giant-killer — "almost making you believe," Lem Billings said at the time, "that he has the touch of the supernatural on his shoulder." The steel Donnybrook reminded Billings of 1956. Chosen that summer to put Adlai Stevenson's name in nomination, Senator Kennedy found that he had a chance for second place on the Democrat ticket, and he went for it. In far-off France there was a muffled explosion. Joe Kennedy, vacationing there, felt that he was making a hideous mistake. "I was sure Adlai would lose," the ambassador recalled shortly after the Narragansett Bay outing, "and that his defeat would be blamed on Jack's Catholicism." Jack came within an eyelash of becoming the vice-presidential choice; his defeat was variously blamed on his backing of the Benson farm policy, the dismantling of the convention's totalizer score board, and some peculiar behavior by Delegate John W. McCormack of Massachusetts. Yet none of these offered much consolation. The blunt truth was that he had been beaten. Next day the New York *Herald Tribune* commented, "The famous Kennedy luck ran out today." It hadn't, though. Things were just the other way round. Stevenson went down anyhow, but the sacrificial lamb was Estes Kefauver, while the nation remembered young Kennedy smiling cheerfully at his Chicago rebuff. He himself was among the first to grasp the significance of this. Told that he would be a cinch for the number two spot after Eisenhower's second term, he replied, "I'm not running for the Vice Presidency any more. I'm running for the Presidency." During the next four years he barnstormed the country, and sure enough, by the summer of 1960 he had become his party's front runner.

Before his nomination he was relaxing on the Cypress Point, California, golf course with Red Fay. On the 150-yard fifteenth hole, Fay recalls, the candidate-to-be teed off with a seven iron and almost got a hole-in-one. As the ball rolled across the green Kennedy leaped up and down, shouting at it, "Get out of there!" "What's the matter?" Fay cried. "You crazy?" Kennedy wasn't crazy. He was just thinking ahead. "If it drops in," he explained rapidly, "everybody in the country will know about it in five minutes, and they'll think another golfer is trying to get into the White House. Get *out* of there!" The ball then stopped, inches from the cup.

His luck has held so often that long ago it generated an enviable optimism. Even in the buggy, virescent trough of the Solomons his favorite song was "Blue Skies." Somehow, despite his vitality and his nervous mannerisms, he conveys an impression of quiet confidence. "If it were not so calm, if it were more strident and pushful, it would be plain arrogance," Stewart Alsop once commented. Occasionally it has come close to arrogance. Proposing to Jacqueline Bouvier, he informed her that he had actually decided to marry her a year before. He hadn't been ready then; now he was. "How *big* of you!" she cried. But while this suggests that he was sure of himself, he wasn't too sure, since after all, she did accept him. Things have had a way of working out that way — his way. Asked before his presidential campaign how he proposed to win the election, he replied easily, "In the debates." After he had done precisely that, he chose Ben Smith, a former Harvard roommate, to fill out his Senate term, and Mrs. Smith, riffling through an old diary of her husband's, found this 1941 note: *Saw Jack again today and we settled the affairs of the world.* Jack himself had first won the title of senator by challenging Henry Cabot Lodge, the incumbent, in 1952. That was the year of the first Eisenhower avalanche. Late in election night the challenger took a walk in the Boston Public Garden with another ex-roommate, Torbert Macdonald. Eisenhower was sweeping the state, Lodge was in the lead. But John Kennedy not only assumed victory; he had gone beyond it. To Macdonald he said thoughtfully, "I wonder what job Eisenhower's going to give Lodge?" Six hours later Lodge conceded, and a blizzard of good wishes descended upon the new champ. He always seems to get more than his share of good wishes — his presidential mail is twice as large as Eisenhower's — perhaps because he has a curious way of involving people, including opponents, in his struggles. After a trying convalescence in 1955 he found a huge basket of fruit in his senatorial office. The card read, *Welcome home — Dick Nixon.*

This is the stuff of legend: the luck of the Irish, Roscommon arisen. Boston Irishmen love legends. In Somerville and Charlestown many a man regarded the verdict of 1960 as the final vindication of the Ould Sod. Strolling around the Massachusetts State House with the President's younger brother Ted, this writer encountered an elderly Curley satellite. "Well, the Yankees are finally whipped!" trumpeted the man, whose first name is actually Patsy. The writer ventured that Beacon Hill's power had been broken at least a generation ago, but Patsy rambled on with the wild inconsistency of an Edwin O'Connor character. "Now," he said darkly, "we got to watch out for the Guineas. Ever notice how a Guinea cries in jail? No spirit, no spirit at all. I'd rather work with a Jew than a Guinea. The only people that are happy in jail are the niggers. Niggers have a grand time in the can, because they can sleep all the time," Patsy reflected. "But the worst of the lot are the Yankees. They're *prejudiced.*"

Clearly there is something bogus here. Boston's ethnic loyalties are a carryover from the days when, as John Kennedy has observed, each wave of immigrants "disliked and distrusted the next." The Irish, probably because they spoke English, became the leaders of the downtrodden. But the notion that they have always been a deprived proletarian race doesn't hold up. From Ireland came the Duke of Wellington, Lord Kitchener, and Montgomery of Alamein; even St. Patrick's name was Patricius Magnus, which indicates that he was gently born. American Paddies have also done rather well, and not only recently. Among the Presidents of Irish descent are Andrew Jackson and Chester A. Arthur. Well before the potato famine, which ended some time ago, there were Irish aristocrats in this country, and while it's not generally known in Somerville, the White House itself was designed by a native of Ireland. Its classic façade was inspired by a house in Dublin.

Of course, bigotry was a nuisance. Yet Boston's Hibernians have given as good as they got. If it was impossible for a pre-Kennedy Catholic to be President, it was, and continues to be, almost impossible for anyone else to hold local office. And it is notable that southern Europeans, although fully qualified members of the Church, are excluded from the religious martyrdom. As Kenneth Galbraith commented sardonically in a review of an O'Connor novel, there is a feeling "that the Irish soul is an exceptionally sensitive and friable organ that provides unlimited opportunities for study." Larry O'Brien may confess that "these days it's hard to tell the difference between the Irish and the Yankee Irish," but to the O'Briens of an older generation this is cultural miscegenation. For them the President is a magnificent symbol. In their minds his presence at 1600 Pennsylvania Avenue represents absolution from outrageous

fortune and three-decker tenements. Pat and Mike
have finally put the Cabots and Lowells in their
places — or rather, Himself has done it, which is the
same thing, since he is one of them.

It's a grand myth, and if you reach far enough into
the past you can find a cast. Himself is a descendant of
one Pat Kennedy, who left an Erin hamlet with the
fine emerald name of New Ross, Wexford County, a
century ago and landed on East Boston's Noodle Island during that eight-year period when the British
lack of interest in parity was driving over a million
Irishmen to the United States. Pat's son Patrick J.,
for whom another presidential cabin cruiser is now
named, grew black handle-bar mustaches, ran a sa-
loon, and became a local Democratic leader, at various times holding office as fire commissioner, street
commissioner, election commissioner, and state representative; and Patrick J.'s son Joseph P. Kennedy
married the daughter of a pol celebrated for his public renditions of "Sweet Adeline."

This gifted tenor was John F. "Honey Fitz" Fitzgerald, or *"El Dulce Adelino,"* as he was hailed by
Franklin Roosevelt, who never missed an ethnic bet.
With Honey Fitz the tale grows richer. He had been
brought up in an authentic eight-family tenement not
far from the old North Church. In his teens he had
been a clerk under Leverett Saltonstall, grandfather
of the present senator. He went on to become Boston's
first mayor of Irish parentage, only to have his own
senatorial ambitions foiled in 1916 by another emi-

nent modern Republican's grandfather, Henry Cabot
Lodge, Sr., the bugbear of Woodrow Wilson and a
silkstocking who is remembered for his fight to stifle
immigration. Add the fact that Honey's own five-
year-old grandson, Jack Kennedy, tagged along on
one of his campaigns and functioned as an audience
of one while the old man rehearsed his speeches, and
the fable seems complete.* It is more leprechaunish
than *The Last Hurrah*, if less plausible.

The trouble with it is that it omits a key character
— Jack's father — and the ambassador is not the sort
of man you ignore. Irish-Americans are supposed to
be fun-loving but indigent. As a boy of eight Joe Kennedy had revealed an entrepreneural mutation, ped-
dling candy and peanuts on Boston excursion boats,
and he had gone on to shatter the cultural pattern by
graduating from Harvard ('12). In college he had
been a poor economics student, which is like pointing
out that Einstein flunked math, because when Joe
entered banking he became a wizard of such tricky
stock dodges as market rigging, matched orders, margin manipulation, and washed and short sales. In one
of President Kennedy's favorite suspense novels a
character remarks that "to become very rich you have
to be helped by a combination of remarkable circum-

---

* An illusion. At this writing Ted Kennedy has taken dead aim
on the United States Senate. The Republican marksman is George
Cabot Lodge, thirty-four, the son of the President's 1952 victim
and the grandson of Honey's 1916 nemesis. In senatorial years
Boston may become the city where the Lodges speak only to de-
nounce the Kennedys, and vice versa.

stances and an unbroken run of luck. . . . At the beginning, getting together the first ten thousand, or the first hundred thousand, things have to go damn right." Things never went wrong for Joe. He never gave them a chance. By the skillful use of sheer money he multiplied his fortune again and again, amassing the astounding sum of two hundred and fifty million dollars.

Wealth can't change a man's background. During a political strategy conference a few years ago, one of Jack's advisers hinted that the ambassador wouldn't appreciate the average man's point of view. "What do you mean?" Joe flared. "I happen to be the most average guy in this whole damned outfit." Like many tycoons he has sometimes tended to exaggerate his humble origins — as Abe Martin observed, the older a man gets, the farther he had to walk to school as a boy — yet he had a point. His earthy, on-the-make manner has reached men baffled by the sophistication of his son's Administration. Though a financier, Joe was a maverick during his money-making years. According to Arthur Krock, he didn't acquire status until Franklin Roosevelt, anxious to stamp out the practices which had made men like him rich, appointed him to the Securities and Exchange Commission. Roosevelt decided that only an insider could do the job and asked Krock to write a flattering story about Joe, paving the way for his confirmation. The appointee served 431 days as chairman and became respectable, but under his veneer he was still the improper Bostonian. Once two of his new associates protested his habit of playing classical records after every session. "You dumb bastards don't appreciate culture," he replied.

Money can, however, provide a new background for the next generation. Joe's did. With his first roll he left Boston for the suburb of Brookline, and he has kept going ever since. His children don't share his heritage. Their mother didn't hang out wash in the back yard. They were raised in villas, with the merry chatter of ticker tape on the front porch in the summer, and their shirts have not only white collars, but monograms. They don't fit the legend at all. The President isn't parochial; he doesn't speak with a brogue; he never dances a jig or sings "Danny Boy." In fact, there is little sentiment in him. "I once asked him if he'd ever fallen desperately, hopelessly in love," James M. Burns recalls, "and he just shrugged and said, 'I'm not the heavy lover type.'" He's not the pal type, either. After the inaugural one of his oldest and most devoted Boston supporters let it be known that he was interested in a federal judgeship. It would have been a safe appointment — Massachusetts is, after all, John Kennedy's political fief. The aspirant was close to the ambassador, and after Joe's stroke the nomination would have been accepted as a tender gesture. Honey Fitz would have rushed it through. Honey's grandson didn't. "The President seems determined to get as far as possible from the Al Smith stereotype," Burns says, and a member of the White

House staff suggests that "Kennedy's appreciation of Ireland is merely a literary appreciation." The green label just won't stick to him. When Robert Frost advised him to "be more Irish than Harvard," he could scarcely respond. The President knew Robert Frost, he knew Harvard. But Irish? He hasn't a single mannerism of the shanty Irish, the lace-curtain Irish, or even what Jim Curley leeringly called "the cut-glass Irish." Try to imagine him in a cocked derby and all visions of shamrocks vanish.

Paul Dever, former Governor of Massachusetts, once remarked that "Jack is the first Irish Brahmin." If by Brahmin he meant Yankee blueblood, even this is doubtful. The President's ties with New England are surprisingly slight. He used his state as a springboard to national leadership and then decimated the local party. About all he has in common with Boston now are his affection for the Red Sox, some paintings his wife borrowed from the Boston Museum of Fine Arts, and his accent, which is chiefly evocative of Harvard Yard (although Joe Kennedy calls McCarthy "McCardy," his son sounds the dental). Jack was born in the Brookline house, which was recently repainted light gray by public-spirited volunteers, but he remembers little of those years. His father, a titan at thirty, was acquiring homes in Palm Beach and Bronxville, New York, to which he moved his growing family when the future President was nine years old. Jack didn't live in the Hub again until he prepared to run for Congress after World War II. At that time virtually the only constituent he knew was his aging grandfather. To establish a legal residence he rented a living room and bedroom suite at the hotel where Honey was living, the Bellevue, directly across the street from the Massachusetts State House. Later he moved a few doors away, to 122 Bowdoin Street, apartment 36. His mother installed wall-to-wall carpeting — it is still there — and when he voted for himself in 1960, that was the address he signed to the register. Yet he has rarely been there. Apartment 36 has served a number of valuable functions. For a time it was a way station for legislators from outlying districts. Once Jacqueline went there to be interviewed, with her husband, on Murrow's *Person-to-Person* program. And in the second year of the New Frontier its rather shabby furniture was being used by supporters of Ted Kennedy's Senate candidacy. At no time, however, has it been a genuine home, and long before Richard Nixon offended California Democrats by referring to the President as a "carpetbagger" some disgruntled Bostonians were calling their most famous citizen just that.

William V. Shannon of the New York *Post* compared John Kennedy to an Oxonian who leaves London to stand for Commons in a provincial town where he is known but his family isn't. Charles Spalding, a Kennedy friend, has likened the family to English Whigs of a century ago, and another observer believes that the ambassador resembles the old school British nob who expects his sons to excel in various professions. To the professional Irishman all these parallels are odious, but they are valid. The very rich are, after all, the aristocracy of capitalism. The size of Joe's bank account had made his name familiar in a number of households both in and out of Boston — as an undergraduate Jack saw his family lampooned by Sophie Tucker and Victor Moore in *Leave It to Me* — and before the war his eldest son was being groomed for public office.

In photographs Joseph P. Kennedy, Jr., is his father to the life. They were similar in other ways: hearty, brilliant, outgoing. In 1940 young Joe was elected as a delegate (anti-Roosevelt) to the Democratic National Convention. He was about to set course for Washington, and no one who ever met him doubted he would make it. Then the war intervened. The hope of the clan went down heroically on a volunteer attempt to bomb the Nazis' key V-2 base, leaving Jack as the oldest surviving son. A few weeks after Japan's surrender Jim Curley hurrahed his way back into the mayoralty of Boston, and a former naval person found himself on the streets of the Eleventh Massachusetts Congressional District, running for Curley's empty seat. The candidate was gaunt and awkward. "He was meant to be a writer and a thinker," says Krock. "He made himself over. When Joe died I thought the political genius of the family was gone, but this one has just as much charm as his brother." In 1946, however, Jack lacked his brother's confidence. Before the war he had tried for his Harvard class presidency and failed. Now he painfully wrote out his fifteen-minute speeches in longhand and memorized them verbatim. The business manager of that campaign still has some of the manuscripts. "If Joe were alive I wouldn't be in this," Jack told the voters diffidently. "I'm only trying to fill his shoes."

He filled them — and Honey climbed on a table and sang *"El Dulce Adelino* — after a madcap primary battle in which he outbarnstormed nine other candidates, including an ex-WAC major who wore her uniform and two Italians who were both named Joseph Russo. Along the way he acquired political style and revealed the first flashes of the wit which is now famous. (At one picnic each of his opponents was introduced as a Bostonian who had come up "the hard way." For obvious reasons, that was dropped from Jack's introduction, so he began by explaining, "I'm the one who didn't come up the hard way.") His spectacular career since then tends to obscure the fact that if Joe were alive, he probably wouldn't be in this. Still, it remains a fact, and a tantalizing one. Where would he be if his brother had lived?

So adroit a politician has he become that some of his acquaintances insist he would be precisely where he is. "Politics was in his blood, waiting to come out," says O'Brien. "He'd have found his way to it," Lem Billings says. Because the war changed everything, there is no way of telling. Certainly he showed no political bent before then. At Harvard he did major in government, but he was chiefly interested in foreign affairs — when he did write a paper on domestic politics, he chose to study an unknown Republican. In the brief hiatus between his graduation and wartime service, he vacillated. He thought of Yale Law School, decided he preferred Stanford Business School, changed his mind after six months there and took off for a trip through South America. Jim Reed believes he would have become an attorney, if only for a time. The President himself is among those who wonder what would have become of him, and he says today, "I'm sure I would have gone to law school after the war. Beyond that, I can't say. I was at loose ends. I was interested in ideas, and I might have gone into journalism. The exchange of ideas that goes with teaching attracted me, but" — he shakes his head — "scholarship requires a special kind of discipline; it wouldn't be my strength."

Yet once he felt otherwise about faculty life. Six years after he succeeded Curley he was campaigning for the Senate in Amherst, the site of the University of Massachusetts and small, heavily endowed Amherst College. His appearance in the university's Old Chapel was a great success. Student questions were good; he was in top form, and afterward he felt exhilarated. Leaving town, his car passed through the handsome Amherst College campus. He turned to O'Brien, commented on the class differences between the two schools, and nodded in the direction of the less ivied state institution. "If it hadn't been for the

death of my brother," he said, "I'd probably be teaching in some place like that."

His preference for the red-brick university was revealing. It was an expression of the helping hand
ideal, which in turn arises from the political faith of a
small, influential elite: the patricians of the Democratic party. The creed of this elite seems to be far
closer to the core of John Kennedy than Erin, the
Hub, or the Pope. Its roots may be traced to Thomas
Jefferson, and it has played a vital, if controversial,
role in our national life. Sidney Hyman wrote admir-
ingly that "if there is any recurrent political pattern"
in the Presidency, "it is that the troubled conscience
of men who inherit wealth often makes them far more
generous and resilient in their social attitudes than
the self-made man with his purse-proud 'good conscience.'" George Humphrey, contrarily, made the
caustic observation that Democrats were led by men
who succeeded to their fortunes and Republicans by
those who had made their own, and any American of
the veteran generation can remember how bitterly
Franklin Roosevelt was denounced as a traitor to his
class.

Theodore Roosevelt was similarly regarded; so, in
many quarters, is the present Governor of New York,
for the tradition still has an enclave in the G.O.P.
Nevertheless, rich Democrats are the most enthusiastic sharers of the wealth, and in or out of office Ken-

nedy would have been one of them. Reared with what used to be called the advantages, he is, as Lippmann has said, a "thoroughbred." And there was never a chance that he might turn Republican. His father, for one, would have been shocked. People recall the ambassador's isolationism and call him a reactionary; they overlook his stanch support of New Deal legislation. In the crucial year of 1936 he published a book, *I'm For Roosevelt,* sharply rebuking fellow financiers who opposed F.D.R. Until his recent stroke he was decrying Republican dominance over the American press, and his scathing language — scathing even for him — was especially striking because some of his targets were among his oldest personal friends. His continuing loyalty to his party may be puzzling, but it is as real as his millions, and John Kennedy, receiving massive transfusions of both, was fated to follow that line of *noblesse oblige* whose leaders, until his inaugural, were Adlai Stevenson, Averell Harriman, and Thomas Finletter.

Like any caste, this one has its quirks, tabus, and high signs. Some are complex, even inexplicable. No member in good standing, for example, would dream of surrendering dignity to political expedience. In 1960 Kennedy gave the voters restrained Harvard prose (he felt his opponent talked down to the people), and it was some time before he could bring himself to allude publicly to his wife's election-year pregnancy, despite its appeal. Nor do individuals in the patriciate see any conflict between their sympathy for other ranks and their own elegant tastes. The President smokes H. Uppman's cigars — long, thin, and expensive, the brand of Edward VII — and he patronizes Harriman's and Finletter's New York tailor, H. Harris & Co., whose other clients include Nelson Aldrich Rockefeller.

Because so many men of means are Republicans, there is a great deal of interfaith mingling. After Jacqueline Kennedy had appointed a fine arts advisory committee for the White House it turned out that three out of four members were members of the other party. The President's Palm Beach neighbors are overwhelmingly Republican, and so are the citizens of Hyannis Port, who gave over sixty per cent of their vote to Richard Nixon in 1960, just as Hyde Park went for Hoover, Landon, Willkie, and Dewey in the Roosevelt years. Chance meetings aren't awkward, however, because civility is the first law of gentility. When Kennedy ran against Henry Cabot Lodge their debates were almost courtly; they avoided such embarrassing proper nouns as Korea and McCarthy. Having confiscated Lodge's seat, Kennedy hit it off splendidly with his senatorial colleague from Massachusetts, Leverett Saltonstall, another fellow Cantab, and a Yale Democrat who ran against Saltonstall did so without the junior senator's support. Breeding rises above party. People with a great deal in common understand each other instantly, and can talk in shorthand. The President rarely makes friends quickly, yet he and McGeorge Bundy, his soft-spoken national security aide, were immediately congenial. "He and Mac come from the same background," a mutual friend explains. "*They* didn't know each other, but their *families* did."

Cultivated families admire elegance, and John Kennedy sets great store by good form. His circle doesn't include men who wear clocks on their socks, or call Shakespeare the Bard, or say budgetwise. "You know, most of my friends have certain traits in common," he told Red Fay. "They don't smoke, they don't drink, and they don't play poker. I didn't find these things out until I knew them; I just seem to be attracted by men like that. Maybe it's chemical." More likely it's social instinct. "He just doesn't like big fat guys or grouches," one of these friends observes. Neither does he like photographers who suggest that he pose in church, nor reporters who ask intimate questions, nor name-droppers. At a Hyannis Port party in the summer of 1961 a stranger kept referring familiarly to "Dick" Russell. The President left vexed. Afterward he explained, with some heat, "In the many years I've known him I've never called him anything but *Senator* Russell." Although he and Harold Macmillan chat frequently on the transatlantic telephone, they still address one another as "Mr. Prime Minister" and "Mr. President," and during Cabinet meetings Kennedy misters everyone except his brother. Toward the end of his Administration's first year an editor who was in his office heard him engage in three informal phone conversations with the Secretary of State. The tone of each was informal, but at the end of the third talk the President said quietly, "Thank you, Mr. Rusk."

The clarity of Mr. Rusk's prose was a major factor in his appointment. Like all patricians, John Kennedy likes men of grace; someone who writes felicitously is halfway home with him. At the height of the Berlin crisis of 1961 he received a letter from Charles de Gaulle urging him not to negotiate. De Gaulle, himself a Nichomachean gentleman, had put his case exquisitely. His coda began, "Upon what field shall we meet?" An eloquent march of metaphors followed, demonstrating that in the writer's judgment there was no proper field. The addressee, visibly excited, read it aloud to three friends. "Isn't that beautiful?" he said at the end. "You agree with it?" asked one of the listeners. "Oh, no!" the President said instantly. "But what a marvelous style!"

Among the other requisites of Democratic Forsytes seems to be the display of a few symptoms of Anglophilia. They all have a West End air, but none of them is a patch on the President. He has more than symptoms; he has a chronic case. Shipwrecked during the war, he was found in the jungle by a native boy who handed him a note from an allied agent. The message opened ceremoniously, *On His Majesty's Service*. Lieutenant Kennedy grinned. "You've got to hand it to the British," he said to Ensign Barney Ross, and afterward the lieutenant and the agent enjoyed a cup of tea together in the boondocks. Today

Kennedy's affection for that happy breed abides. It is conspicuous in his reserve, the cut of his clothes, his fondness for understatement, his daughter's nurse — Maude Shaw, a British nanny — and especially in his reading habits. His favourite biographies are Cecil's *Melbourne*, Churchill's *Marlborough*, and Duff-Cooper's *Talleyrand*, all by Britons. In the White House he reads the English press as thoroughly as American newspapers, poring over the *Spectator*, *Times*, *New Statesman*, *Economist*, and *Manchester Guardian Weekly*, and if one of them says something beastly about him he will be stung, even though it may have only a handful of subscribers in the United States.

The President's menus aren't British, but they're not American, either. Harry Truman once called himself a meat-and-potatoes man. His Democratic legatee is more of an oeufs-en-gelée-and-filet-mignon-with-sauce-Béarnaise-and-stuffed-artichokes man. In this we see the fine Gallic hand of Jacqueline Bouvier. Jacqueline honors a different prescript — theirs was a sort of hands across the English Channel marriage — and she is partial to French food, French furniture, and French wine; during her husband's senatorial days she used to tuck a bottle of wine in his lunch hamper and send him packing off to the Hill like a Hemingway hero.

Their tastes differ in other ways, because their backgrounds are different. The Kennedys are unique. Jacqueline, on the other hand, comes from a milieu which is familiar to any reader of the novels of F. Scott Fitzgerald, whose daughter is among the First Lady's friends. It is a world of estates with swimming pools, badminton courts, and stables, where little girls play under the eye of French governesses, are taught to dance with little boys in Eton jackets, and frequently learn to accept the fact that their parents are divorced. The charms of this environment are exaggerated. Since there is a felt need to be terribly chic, society tends to degenerate into café society, which is dreary, sterile, inbred. President Kennedy visited a Palm Beach New Year's Eve party, but the terribly chic newspaper there didn't mention it. The social idols of the hour were Porfirio Rubirosa, the Dominican playboy, and his wife Odile, so the paper ran a front-page picture of Odile doing the twist. Its editor explained, "We feel there are a lot of people just as important as the President."

The Gibbon of this twisting culture is Cholly Knickerbocker, alias Igor Cassini. The brother of the First Lady's dress designer, Cholly writes a Hearst column, and when Jacqueline Kennedy came out he named her the year's top debutante. She was an outstanding choice. As Cholly said archly, "You don't have to read a batch of press clippings to be aware of her qualities." Even so, society page editors riffled through her clippings with professional respect. Her father, John Vernon Bouvier III, was a stockbroker and a descendant of a Revolutionary War officer. There is a Bouvier Street in Philadelphia; there were Drexels in the fam-

ily background. Jacqueline had attended Miss Cha-
pin's School for the haughty in New York and had
gone on to Miss Porter's School in Farmington, Connecticut, and to Vassar. She was a horsewoman, she
wrote poetry on the side; *Vogue* became aware of her,
and so did *Life*.

Yet she is more than an ex-deb now. Jacqueline is
no Eleanor Roosevelt, but she's not an Odile Rubirosa, either. Because she has a strong artistic bent,
she has moved from the trivial to the aesthetic, and
is, in her *comme il faut* way, just as U as her husband.
It was the impeccable Arthur Krock — Krock appears and reappears in the Kennedy saga, like a benign linking character in a Henry James novel — who
persuaded the Washington *Times-Herald* to hire her
as an Inquiring Camera Girl, and her fastidiousness
has been endorsed by Russell Lynes.

Its quality is reflected in her redecoration of the
Executive Mansion. "Of course I'm voting for Nixon,"
read a 1960 caption in the *New Yorker,* "but I can't
help wishing I could see what Jackie would do with
the White House." She was bound to do something;
as the late Ike Hoover, a veteran White House usher,
once observed, every First Family does everything as
differently as possible from the one before. Still, there
have been few changes of the guard so striking as
1961's. After the election the First Lady-Elect was
itching to redecorate the house. If there is one thing
a bluestocking hates it is fake antiques, and the public rooms of the White House were full of reproduc-

tions. The moment Mamie left, Jacqueline started heaving them out — along with the potted palms — and replacing them with the genuine article. Windows were opened, fireplaces were lighted for the first time in eight years, and McKinley's portrait was moved to a ground floor corridor.

Joe Kennedy, remembering the White House as it was in Roosevelt's time ("very cold"), remarked with his usual flinty detachment that his daughter-in-law had done a sensational job. Her television tour of the state rooms impressed a lot of dumb bastards who don't appreciate culture, though they might take exception to some of her ancillary activities. For she has done more than redecorate; the mansion has become a national home to creative Americans. Dwight Eisenhower, the painter, declared that he wasn't too certain what was art, but he knew what he liked, and Harry Truman, the pianist, said of something he didn't like that if it was art, he was a Hottentot. Jacqueline Kennedy, the connoisseur, makes both look like Hottentots, if not outright clods. She has a rare visual eye and is enthusiastic about all the fine arts, including the performing arts. As First Lady she encourages the Washington and New York ballets, the National Symphony, and the Washington Opera Society; the National Theater has a presidential box for the first time in forty years. She has introduced a series of concerts for children, and the mansion's East Room, which Abigail Adams used as a laundry and in which Theodore Roosevelt held a jujitsu exhibition, has under the Kennedys heard the anguish of *Macbeth,* the strains of Pablo Casals, and the thumps of Jerome Robbins's ballet troupe. If anyone mutters that these goings on are Frenchy, the hostess is insouciant. Where excellence is at stake, she won't give an inch to mass taste. She wants the best entertainment, the best appointments, the best personal appearance. Kenneth of Lilly Daché does her hair, and when she spoke to a group of farmers in a Venezuelan barnyard she wore an apricot dress and a coat of silk and linen sewed by Oleg Cassini.

Jacqueline is an eclectic blend of traditionalism and *ton.* In repose she evokes memories of young Edwardian ladies briefing themselves before a party by writing conversation topics on the sticks of a fan. In action she resembles a woman athlete. Really she is both. Most children of this century shed the past easily; they have little of it to shed. She comes from a class that has been bred to remember. At the same time, she has an exceptional sense of personal security and is, therefore, unafraid of innovation. Where Mary Lincoln wept because a gown was ruined, Jacqueline wears pedal pushers. But she has that uniformed nanny for Caroline. But she doesn't always use the nanny. She herself wheels a baby carriage, and round her neck she wears a classic, triple strand of pearls. The impression is of anomaly, as of a lovely mansion wired for sound. In her White House this is literally true. Moving to 1600 Pennsylvania Avenue, she surrounded herself with her own antiques and retainers

—meantime installing an intercom on the south porch to relay the cadence of John F. Kennedy, Jr.'s naptime breathing.

Since the inaugural Jacqueline's poetry has been appearing in fragments, like Emily Dickinson's. Recently a classmate unearthed a comic ode written for the classmate's wedding. It began by prophesying that the bride:

> *. . . in wedded bliss soon will be*
> *Vassar will miss her & so will we*
> *But watch yo' step honey on that path*
> *   of roses*
> *There's mo' thorns 'neath them thar*
> *   leaves than you Knowses . . .*

In her clear script Jacqueline drew a stark picture of six o'clock feedings and burnt toast, of the young wife envying "Jackie drinkin' Borbon at the Sorbon." Then the poetess peered into the far future, and prophecy ran amok:

> *Jackie skinny & underpaid*
> *Is earning her living as the French*
> *   maid . . .*

Her Farmington yearbook noted that Jacqueline's ambition was "Not to be a housewife." She averted that, and without becoming a French maid, though she has encountered some rather prickly thorns of her own. While her role as cultural leader is agreeable, she is far less responsive to the nation's interest in her private life. In fact, she is probably the least enthusiastic company wife in the country. Her diffidence is so genuine that it is doubtful she grasped what lay ahead when she became engaged to the most eligible bachelor in Washington. The timing of every event seemed to be determined by the requirements of her husband's career — after a two-year courtship, their marriage had to await the adjournment of Congress in 1953 — and personal moments were observed by riptides of gaping mobs. She was aghast at the uninvited horde that showed up for the wedding, alarmed by the fingers that were forever plucking at her clothes. Most cruel was the summer of 1956, when Jack lost the Vice Presidential nomination. They had bought a $125,000 home in Virginia; she was expecting a child. Exhausted after the convention, Jack left to join his father abroad — and in his absence she lost her baby. The tragedy was duly noted in print, and the whole experience became such a nightmare that they sold the house, to Bobby and Ethel.

Glen Ora, the John Kennedys' house in Middleburg, Virginia, is a recent acquisition. To avoid the Pennsylvania Avenue showcase the First Lady spends much of her time there. Yet each time she goes, it is a news story. Her goldfish bowl grows more translucent all the time. No First Lady has been exposed to so blinding a glare of publicity since Frances Cleveland's picture was used, without authorization, to advertise a liver medicine. High school girls copy Jacqueline shamelessly; the length of her skirts, the dimensions of her form-fitting slacks, her preference for pink (sometimes called "hot pink") receive as much attention as all Katanga. And now she has a new worry. Caroline is a cynosure; people shout at her when she passes in a car, and she has begun to wonder why. Most mothers look forward to the day their first child will be able to read. This mother dreads it, for hers will be reading about herself. It's disconcerting enough to have small fry ogling the White House tennis courts and yelping, "You goofed, Jackie!" To find your little daughter a cover girl is far worse. Jacqueline's disapproval is good-humored — she calls herself Salinger's "greatest cross" — but it is also loud and clear. Recently a friend asked her how she liked an article about Caroline. She made a face. "Too cute," she said. "It made her sound like a spoiled brat." "Pierre liked it," the friend remarked, "and so did the President." She made another face and said tartly, "They're not very good judges, if you don't mind my saying so."

Curiosity about the First Family is inescapable. They entertain on the grand scale — Washington, in the President's words, is a much jazzier town these days. They are comely — a national campus poll in the spring of 1962 disclosed that American coeds feel their Chief Executive has more sex appeal than anybody, including Rock Hudson, and to men Jacqueline is a poster of beauty. Lastly, they have small children.

Wives gloat over bulletins describing Caroline's four-poster bed, the baby's white wicker bassinet, and the conversion of the White House solarium (where Eisenhower charcoal-broiled sirloin steaks) into a playroom. "You could see it was a great satisfaction to the people," Huckleberry Finn said of a piece of small news, "because naturally they wanted to know." They still do. No one should understand better than a former Inquiring Camera Girl, and women reporters, forced to rely on pre-inaugural photographs — which are dated by Caroline's baby fat — grumble about the "velvet curtain." But turnabout is not fair play. Jacqueline wasn't raised to be a newspaperwoman. She was brought up to be a lady, which isn't even the same thing as a First Lady. A lady is expected to be protective of the private I, like a scholar — like, say, young Jack Kennedy, whose shyness, though ruthlessly suppressed, may still be limned in President John Kennedy.

The President and his wife complement one another. Courting Jacqueline, he gave her biographies. She riposted with books she had illustrated. After their wedding she studied American history in Georgetown, the better to understand him, and since entering the mansion he has begun to share her regard for the fine arts. He is not conspicuously comfortable at White House soirées; frequently he turns the conversation to politics or slips away to run through his mail. All the same, he has come a long way. In his bedroom he has had high fidelity equipment installed, permitting him to hear classical records on Washington FM stations and revealing a preference unknown in his years of ascent, when, as someone said, his hunger for good music was satisfied by the swinging measures of "Hail to the Chief."

Jacqueline's mind is appreciative, his is inquiring. They meet in literature, for there is no author whose work is so remote that he cannot extract something from it. Among the writers who have been their guests at 1600 Pennsylvania Avenue are e. e. cummings as well as Barbara Ward, Robert Frost as well as Sir Charles Snow. Gore Vidal, another caller, suggested that the President examine *Coriolanus* for an earlier playwright's views of democracy, and the President and his wife read it aloud one foggy day at the Cape, although later, as Vidal remembers it, "He made the point with some charm that Shakespeare's knowledge of the democratic process was, to say the least, limited."

The anti-Shakespeare vote is rather large in parts of this country. Many a two-fisted American would be startled to learn what his chief had been up to. Those who know him merely wonder how he missed *Coriolanus* before. It's not like him to be so ill-read. He is the most literate President since Woodrow Wilson — F.D.R. talked to authors, he didn't read them — and when not writing his own books he has generally had his nose in somebody else's. "I've known him thirty years," says Lem Billings. "There has never been a moment when he didn't have something to read, and usually he has been working on at least two books at the same time." As a very young boy he was deep in James Fenimore Cooper. Bound for the South Pacific on a Navy transport he was either urging fellow officers to read his current favorites, Franz Werfel's *The Forty Days of Musa Dagh* and John Buchan's *Pilgrim's Way*, or poring over new finds; on Tulagi he read *War and Peace*, which is now among the volumes in the west sitting room. He was the chief senatorial patron of the Library of Congress, and after his presidential nomination he relaxed with Anthony Trollope. Today he complains that his literary diet is curtailed, yet recent examples of his general reading include George Kennan's *Russia and the West Under Lenin and Stalin*, Alan Moorehead's *The White Nile*, Henry A. Kissinger's *Necessity for Choice*, A. J. P. Taylor's *Origins of the Second World War*, Barbara W. Tuchman's *The Guns of August*, the historical novels of Mary Renault, and the thrillers of Ian Fleming.

There is such a thing as an intellectual profile. John Kennedy is too versatile to fit any palimpsested image, but this is one of the shadows he casts. He has always been attracted by ideas — during the war he kept a looseleaf notebook to record thoughts — and by the stimulus of debate. Red Fay remembers that in the Solomons Lieutenant Kennedy's Tulagi tent became "a world affairs forum, with the occupant as the moderator." He would cross foils with anyone, on almost any topic. He was silenced just once, and under the circumstances there wasn't much he could have said; a visiting Republican officer, not realizing who his antagonist was, bitterly denounced Roosevelt's appointment of wealthy ambassadors. Jim Reed, meeting Kennedy, instantly found himself in a verbal duel over Munich. Ensign Reed blamed Chamberlain; the lieutenant, Britain's marshmallow mood of the Thirties. "I came out second best," Reed recalls. "I didn't know he'd written a *book* about it."

As Richard Nixon discovered, Kennedy can quote other authors than himself. His bookishness is one of his debating strengths; he can bury an opponent in a cascade of facts. Even his conversation is studded with allusions, and he may be the only Hearst reporter ever to have cited Richard Brinsley Sheridan in a news story. In a single address he has quoted Wilson, Goethe, Faulkner, Artemus Ward, Finley Peter Dunne, Swift, Emerson, Lord Asquith, Tennyson, and Queen Victoria. His maiden speech in the Senate was so heavy it didn't make the New York *Times*. Since then he has learned the value of the offhand reference — reminding de Gaulle of Jefferson's and Franklin's affection for France, say, or twitting a convention of newspaper publishers by reminding them that Karl Marx was a correspondent for the New York *Tribune,* or casually revealing his familiarity with contemporary literature, as in his remarks after Hemingway's death.

Inevitably the induction of his Administration

brought a dramatic change in the official status of the literati. Under the old regime they had been outcasts. The Republicans did issue a cacophonous edict declaring that the party should "facilitate the utilization of friendly academicians in party affairs at all levels," but they didn't follow through practicewise. An Eisenhower Cabinet member inquired of *The Old Man and the Sea,* "Who would want to read a book about an old man who was a failure?" and Eisenhower himself declined to step into Sherman Adams's office and shake Robert Frost's hand. Kennedy's inaugural, on the other hand, was attended by some eighty invited artists, including W. H. Auden, Lewis Mumford, Allen Tate, and John Steinbeck, who in a hyperbolic mood expressed satisfaction that "literacy is no longer prima-facie evidence of treason."

If anything, scholarly achievement has become a requisite for appointees. A Mauldin cartoon depicted the new key to the capital — a Phi Beta Kappa key. As Truman admired generals and Eisenhower tycoons, Kennedy leans on fellow students. Among his advisers are some fifteen Rhodes scholars, led by the Secretary of State, and four professional historians. The Secretary of Defense, the Commissioner of Internal Revenue, the Chairman of the Civil Service Commission, and the ambassadors to India, Yugoslavia, and Japan are former college teachers. The President's expert on gold is a professor; so is the chief lieutenant of the Secretary of Agriculture, who is himself a member of Phi Beta Kappa. Even the President's military adviser, General Maxwell D. Taylor, came to him from the Lincoln Center for the Performing Arts, and for the first time in history the White House has a cultural coordinator, albeit a Yale man. The list of authors on the New Frontier is endless — it includes eight diplomats, four White House aides, the Solicitor General, the Assistant Secretary of State for International Affairs, the Deputy Assistant of State for Public Affairs, the Chief of the Disarmament Administration, the Chairman of the Council of Economic Advisers, the Postmaster General, and the Attorney General. Those who don't write read widely; Secretary Udall's private dining room is a haven for such Washington visitors as Arnold Toynbee. Udall's first act upon assuming office was to study Harold Ickes's autobiography, and while in the office of the Secretary of the Treasury one may browse through a library which, during a recent call, included volumes by Churchill, Neustadt, Schlesinger, Galbraith, and, of course, a copy of *Profiles in Courage*.

If their leader weren't captain of the West, doubtless he would be a member of the West's literary elite. His qualifications are gilt-edged: a Pulitzer Prize and original work which has been translated into Arabic, Japanese, Turkish, Vietnamese, Telegu, and Indonesian. He wouldn't be an intellectual giant — his scholarship is more persevering than illustrious — but he would be accepted, and he would find the company congenial, for he has more than a touch of artistic temperament. Like most writers, he is an insomniac.

His sleeplessness is not confined to periods of crisis. Sometimes he conducts routine business of the Federal Government at odd hours; Lyndon Johnson and Pierre Salinger are among those who have received presidential calls after midnight. When he does drop off, he's easily disturbed. One of his former roommates found that Kennedy disliked the bed near the window, so the roommate took it, which meant that when he rose to use the bathroom at night he had to tiptoe around Jack. No matter how softly he crept, a lanky figure would heave up and snap, "God, can't you stop the racket?"

Intellectuals are often nonconformists. Their early school records may be unimpressive because as children they were indifferent to curricula — this was true of Jack at Choate — though in the freer environment of college they are likely to improve, as he did in Cambridge. They are inclined to be impatient of details; *e.g.,* orthography. Kennedy, like Fitzgerald, became a popular author without mastering this elementary skill. Despite his expensive boarding schools he long wrote literary "litary," and as a Harvard graduate he was capable of spelling peculiar "peciliar." In the White House his handwritten memoranda are usually correct, but occasionally he will glance up from the paper and ask for help, and his calligraphy has deteriorated. Handwriting specimens from his youth are quite legible, while presidential communications have been returned to the mansion with the baffled inquiry, "Who signed my letter?"

Details are unimportant because the litary man is preoccupied. At Choate, a classmate remembers, "the biggest complaints about him were that his room was never neat and he was always late to classes." Before his marriage and his subsequent conversion into a fashion plate he would appear on Capitol Hill in khaki trousers and mismated socks. For a time he carried candy to nibble between meals; Reed remembers the shocked look on the face of a hostess when Kennedy, engrossed in a dinner conversation, ignored the steak in front of him and absent-mindedly began popping caramels in his mouth. He is always leaving things behind, and though he should have learned how to handle money years ago — he had a checking account in prep school and dabbled in stocks at Harvard — he never seems to have any with him. His wartime crew, knowing that his family had plenty of moolah, thought it odd that he would put the bite on them until payday. After the war one veteran came to Boston to help him politick. "I couldn't afford to be bouncing for different expenses," he recalls, "but I found I was catching the tabs. It was the old story. His pockets were empty. Then he flew West to see me. I was watching every penny — making three hundred a month and a child on the way. Well, he didn't have a cent. I had to give him twenty dollars to get on the plane. I said, listen, I want this back, I need it. Of course, I got it." Senator George Smathers, a Southern Democrat who is one of the President's social friends, got his back on a European trip by picking up *all* the tabs and later sending his amnesic companion a bill for half.

Bobby Kennedy attributes this trait to their parents' deliberate de-emphasizing of the family fortune. "Mother impressed on us the value of nickels, dimes, and quarters," he says, "but we were never conscious of wealth. The opposite was preached constantly, so we forget about money. For example, I didn't bring any with me today. I just didn't think about it. He's the same way." Yet Bobby isn't distracted in other ways. The President is. The Attorney General's comb is always within reach, but during the 1960 campaign his older brother borrowed combs, and even pencils, from the press.

Theodore H. White, the historian of that election, wrote that at times "following him was like attending a peripatetic and anecdotal course in American history." The candidate was campaigning and lecturing at the same time. He was also studying; his preparation for the first debate with Nixon resembled nothing so much as a pre-exam cram session. Like all scholars he enjoys the learning process, and his old school tie holds him fast. The library housing his presidential papers will be in Cambridge. When he defended the electoral college, Professor Holcombe marshaled his arguments for him. Asked by the Senate to chair the committee which would pick America's five greatest deceased senators (they were to be Clay, Webster, Calhoun, La Follette, and Taft), he turned to his old faculty for advice. And it is significant that two of the

President's three favorite pundits — Walter Lippmann, Joseph Alsop, and James Reston — are Harvard men. (The odd man is Reston, who went to some school out West.)

In the fall of 1961 John F. Kennedy, Jr., could be observed wriggling in the back of a Hyannis Port station wagon, wearing a crimson sweater with a tiny H on it. "Of all the boys Jack likes Harvard best," Joe Kennedy said then. "Bobby and Teddy don't care for it much, and I guess I have the old Boston prejudice against it. But it means a lot to him." How much it meant had been revealed earlier that year, when approximately one-third of all first-rank appointments, including four Cabinet posts, went to old wearers of the Crimson. His *Alumni Bulletin* depicted the White House with an enormous Harvard banner draped across the front. "Harvard men," the President's former government teacher observed cheerfully, "are clearly entitled to have faith in the new Cabinet."

There is irony here. Harvard, like Shakespeare and ballet troupes, provokes uneasy stirrings among the electorate. A Saltonstall or a Lodge couldn't indulge himself so. Kennedy can, because it is so hard to credit highbrow bias in a Boston Irish Catholic. "Jack's Catholicism is the very thing that has brought him into prominence," Schlesinger told Joe McCarthy, biographer of the Kennedy family, before the election. "Looking as Jack does and talking as he does, a liberal minded senator from New England who went to Choate School and comes from a wealthy family —

if he were just another Protestant, nobody would pay much attention to him." Having passed the religious test, the President is now free to embrace institutions considered antithetical to the Irish. Thus the Roscommon myth is an asset; John Kennedy can elevate men who, under Adlai Stevenson, would have been scored as "eggheads," and his wife can blithely follow her class instincts, even to presenting him with a pink hunting jacket, which won hardly any votes in East Boston.

Honey Fitz never rode to hounds, read the *Economist,* or hung around violoncellists. "Sweet Adeline" and popcorn in Fenway Park were good enough for Honey, which may be the reason Lodge, Sr., licked him. For a democratic country the United States is highly susceptible to well-heeled candidates. Shortly after Harriman's election to the governorship of New York he was asked whether America should be run by a wellborn elite, and he instantly replied, "Yes, if they can get elected." Nowadays they get elected often. Kennedy beat Nixon, the man who had come up the hard way, and many people believe Nelson Rockefeller, with Mrs. Rockefeller, could have taken them both. In a stable, competitive society, the discreet patrician has total status. He is acceptable everywhere — as, in a revolutionary society, he would be acceptable nowhere. During the 1950's, a Massachusetts politician told Joe McCarthy, "If you had a Kennedy sticker on your car it meant that you were mixing with the right people." In the 1960's smart fashion models remake themselves to look like Jacqueline, because that is what their clients want. "The President and his wife," Edwin A. Roberts wrote in the *Wall Street Journal*, "are regarded somewhat like Hollywood heroes, a golden couple with absolutely everything a world can offer and loved because of it."

Honey, who died in 1950, would have enjoyed his grandson's success, though he might have flinched at some of the implications. John Kennedy's career bears a striking resemblance to that of a member of the Establishment. The word is rarely heard in this country. It means the ruling class to educated Englishmen, whom young Jack first encountered in large numbers during his late, impressionable adolescence. The ambassador was a real ambassador then, and while he was cutting a swath in the Court of St. James (by typically refusing to wear satin knee pants), his children mixed with the pukka London gentry. Jack's favorite sister Kathleen ("Kick") joined it permanently, marrying the Marquess of Hartington. The marquess died in France fighting with the Coldstream Guards, and later Kick was killed in a plane crash while en route to the Riviera, but the ties remain, relating the President by marriage to David Ormsby-Gore, the British ambassador in Washington and, more distantly, to Harold Macmillan. Ormsby-Gore is in addition an old acquaintance of John Kennedy's. During the late 1930's the future President was commuting between Harvard and the

United Kingdom, and he made lasting friendships among the toffs. It is a sardonic footnote to Sinn Feinism that when he visited Patrick Kennedy's Wexford County birthplace, he was accompanied by an English lady. Afterward she remarked — to her escort's dismay — "That was just like Tobacco Road."

The American Establishment is more elusive than Britain's. Here it is a concept rather than a club, and no two sociologists are in accord on its membership list. Writing in the *American Scholar*, Richard H. Rovere concludes that while John Kennedy belongs, he is not of the "Inner Circle" — as, for example, Dean Rusk is. Kennedy himself takes the position that every President is an ex-officio Establishmentarian. The office excepted, however, he doubts his eligibility. Rocking thoughtfully he says, "I'm of the Establishment in the sense of where I've lived, and my schools, but in the sense of the Anglo-Saxon Establishment — no. When I go into the N.A.M. I get a pretty cold reception; they're not very sympathetic. You really have to be a Republican to be a member. Of course, Nixon doesn't belong, but Rockefeller is the epitome of it. In my case, my politics and my religion are against it. If the Democratic party had an Establishment candidate, it was Stevenson."

Yet Catholicism apart — and it was set apart on November 8, 1960 — the President's social values are indistinguishable from Stevenson's. Every cultural anthropologist who has scrutinized the Establishment agrees that the New York *Times* is at the core of it.

"The *Times*," Rovere writes, "has no close rival as an Establishment voice." It is a voice to which Kennedy continually harks. "I've seen him leaf through that paper looking for criticism," says a friend who visits him weekends. "Ninety per cent will be favorable, but he tortures himself, seeking out the rest." This, as a *Times* leader would say, is not without significance. The President doesn't feel that way about the Chicago *Tribune*, despite its circulation. He is as devoted to New York's Old Gray Lady as the late George Apley was to the late Boston *Transcript*, and his fidelity is of long standing. Lem Billings recalls that when they met at Choate in 1931, fourteen-year-old Jack Kennedy was a *Times* subscriber — "the only subscriber that age I knew, and he read every word of it." The President feels that the Lady's editorial page sermons are as weighty as *Times* news is thorough, an attitude explicable only on Establishmentarian grounds. Salinger keeps telling him that the paper reaches a limited audience. A political scientist reports, "I've said to him, 'Look. The *Times* has one following, the *Courier-Journal* a second, the San Francisco *Chronicle* a third. You have to get this thing in perspective.'" It doesn't matter. What counts is that the subscription list of the *Times* includes John F. Kennedy, Choate '35, and an old boy wants the good opinion of his compeers.

The rules of traditional aristocracy are very firm on one point: the great leap to acceptance may not be made in one generation. Certain privileges and to-

kens of recognition are withheld from the self-made
man, but are available to his scions. Joe's public service under three Presidents notwithstanding, he was
never granted an honorary degree by Harvard. His
son the senator was so invested in 1956, and is an
overseer of the university. The way had been paved
by the father, first with a generous crust of precious
metals. The ambassador resolved all conceivable
financial problems while his children were still children. He gave each an initial trust fund of over a
million dollars, putting them in a position where they
"could spit in my eye." As John Jacob Astor III used
to say, a man who has a million dollars is as well off
as if he were rich. With the maturing of subsequent
trust funds, the assets of the young Kennedys have
multiplied, and today the President is rich even by
Astor standards. At the time he took office he was
worth about ten million dollars, all of it in government bonds. Sixteen months later, when he passed
his forty-fifth birthday, he received half again as
much, and still more will come to him when he is
fifty. His present trust income, after taxes, is in the
neighborhood of a hundred thousand dollars a year.

In his school days the family wealth permitted him
to see the world before he joined the Navy, and, more
important, it paid for a lot of Back Jack handbills
later. One of the untaught facts of political life is that
running for President costs lots of money. Any man
infected with Potomac Fever must somehow lay his
hands on a large supply of cash. He can inherit it —

in *Six Crises* Richard Nixon predicts that soon only heirs of wealthy men may be candidates — or he can make himself attractive to the well-heeled, as Nixon himself did. There is no third way. Post-convention bills are enormous, and for a man who is compelled to fight his way to the convention through primaries, as Kennedy was, the total bill is staggering. Long before his nomination he was spending seventy thousand dollars a year out of his pocket for his Washington office; the budget for a single banquet was two thousand dollars. Barnstorming the nation, he bought his own plane — with his mileage it was cheaper than commercial flights — and on Election Day 1960 Hyannis Port was outfitted with four teletypes and thirty new phones, many of them direct lines. The long distance tab that night was estimated at ten thousand dollars. In the G.O.P. these disagreeable details are handled by assorted Maecenases; the predicament of the Democrats explains their affection for candidates with private troves. Someone must pay the ransoms of ambition, and in Jack Kennedy's case the someone worked diligently in New York, at 230 Park Avenue, behind a ninth floor door which bears in bold letters the name of Joseph P. Kennedy.

The father gave his son much more than cash, however. Long ago he created a soil — some would say a hothouse — in which exotic shoots could flourish. This setting has determined the direction of John Kennedy's life at countless little junctures. If it had been less plush, for instance, he would never have

gone into PT's. In the early months of World War II
the Motor Torpedo Boat command was looking for
youths with yachting experience — a select class.
The cadre they recruited was bound to be atypical.
There was Ensign Paul G. Pennoyer, Jr., for example,
a grandson of J. P. Morgan. And there was Kennedy,
who had sailed on a championship crew at Harvard,
and who spied his first PT while in Martha's Vineyard
at the helm of his own sloop.

Later the politician was to find his patriciate friends
immensely useful. Intelligent, educated, and independent, they could leave their paneled offices and
cotillions and pitch in when he needed able campaign
executives. From the Bellevue Hotel to the White
House, he has been surrounded by men who have
given his career an elegant, mandarin tone. "In 1960
we all took leaves of absences from our offices and
started out in Wisconsin," Billings says. "There were
ten districts in that first state, and we took over four
of them. I had the third, Lacrosse. Then there was
Ben Smith — he had the tenth — and Ted Reardon
and Chuck Spalding. We picked up momentum in
West Virginia, and when we reached Nebraska, Rip
Horton joined us." Reardon and Smith went to Harvard, Spalding to Yale; Ralph Horton, like Billings
himself, is a Princetonian. Year after year they and a
dozen others have given Kennedy the old Ivy college
try. The fact that several hold vital offices in his Washington is unsurprising. His loyalty to them is as strong
as ethnic bonds were to his grandfather. No one calls

them cronies — though that is what they really **are** — because it is generally felt that their service is a bargain for the government. In Sargent Shriver's phrase they are "blue-chip men," the very kind of public servants that Administrations attempt, usually with small success, to lure to the capital.

Their role tends to overshadow the part which older men of power have played in Kennedy's life. For years patroons of the ambassador's generation were patrons of his son. The ambassador never hesitated to make this claim on his friends; at every turning point in Jack's early life some member of the U.S. Establishment was waiting to greet him and, if necessary, to help him. Based in Florida as a junior naval officer, he discussed public affairs with James Cox, the Democratic presidential candidate of 1920. Discharged from the Navy, he was appointed special correspondent by William Randolph Hearst. Arriving in the lower house of Congress, he inherited Arthur Krock's Negro valet, and when he moved into the upper house he became Herbert Hoover's "favorite Democratic Senator."

The political advantage of these contacts is questionable. They brought no new support to the candidate or his party. Their educative value, on the other hand, is incalculable. Wherever Jack went, he saw the seats of authority at close range. On one prewar trip his hosts were Bill Bullitt in Paris, Tony Biddle in Warsaw, and Chip Bohlen in Moscow. And while still an undergraduate he himself knew the solemnity of responsibility. The Nazis sank a British liner, and his father sent him to Glasgow to handle the problem of American survivors. Thus Jack became a cosmopolite — though scarcely a socialite — and turned out a best seller about the gathering storm, for which one of Joe's friends suggested a title and an agent, while another, Henry Luce, wrote the foreword. Declared Luce: "If John Kennedy is characteristic of the younger generation — and I believe he is — many of us would be happy to have the destinies of the Republic turned over to his generation at once."

But the author of *Why England Slept* wasn't characteristic. The representative American of twenty-three hadn't watched a bullfight or climbed Mt. Vesuvius, hadn't met Cardinal Eugenio Pacelli, hadn't chatted with Franklin Roosevelt and Winston Churchill and couldn't, for that matter, have coaxed the publisher of *Time* into writing an introduction to his first manuscript. All these came to pass because the ambassador had passed the word along. That he should have done so is not strange. Nor is it odd that the beneficiary of so extensive a preparation should become a polished leader. The remarkable thing is that he should ever have become identified with an oppressed minority, and that this, indeed, should have been the key issue in his bid for national power. Somehow our electoral system works, but the American voter moves in a mysterious way, his wonders to perform.

THREE

Sort of Sideways

IN A QUIET office at 1701 K Street, far from the madding press club, is Arthur Krock. Courtly, courteous, surrounded by classics and honorary degrees, he contemplates Washington with a lofty eye. Here in the capital Krock's position is quasi-judicial. If his manner these days is also a trifle paternal, it should be remembered that he was a Washington correspondent seven years before John Kennedy was born, and that his perspective on the Kennedy Presidency is unique.

"I've known him since he was a little boy. I titled his first book" — he displays his copy, with a worshipful inscription signed *Jack Kennedy*. "When he was broken up during the war I sent him out to J. G. F. Speiden's Arizona ranch to recuperate, and when he came down here as freshman congressman and was invited to the White House, I asked him to give me accounts of what happened. I've still got those reports — long, detailed, typed — very good. Then I was on the Pulitzer board, and I worked as hard as I could to get him that prize. He is intelligent. And he certainly has courage; there's no doubt of that. But —"

But Krock is saturnine. The New Frontier does not enchant him. His ties to the First Family — he wistfully recalls escorting Jacqueline Bouvier to her first Gridiron tea — merely make his gloom harder to bear. The whole business reminds him of the Thirties, when he felt obliged to return dire verdicts against another old friend, from Hyde Park. There was no helping it then, there is none now. Krock calls presidential shots as he sees them, and his is a conservative eye.

"As a candidate he hit Eisenhower for indecisiveness, for lack of candor, for failure to use the full powers of his office," he says of Kennedy. "Well, he has repeated every one of the errors of weaknesses he attributed to Eisenhower. Take Cuba. He was indecisive there. You can't blame his advisers; the ultimate responsibility was his." Krock lights a cigar and draws deeply. "I'm doubtful that we did the best we could in selecting this President. I have grave reservations, although really neither he nor Nixon was big enough for the job. No one could be. The difficulties that Kennedy saw in 1960 are inherent in the office."

If any Washingtonian is immune to panoply, it is Arthur Krock. Yet there is more to the Presidency than the incumbent. Like the New York *Times*, it is an institution. And when it is seen in its institutional light, even a Krock is dazzled. A few nights earlier he watched the John Kennedys on television. "I had to pinch myself," he says. "They've been transformed. They're exalted, they have a presence. *That's* the office, too."

The office does more for some than for others. There is no clear relationship between the degree of exaltation and the judgment of history — the Roosevelts had immense presence and are still regarded highly, but Warren Harding, our worst Chief Executive, was one of the most popular. All the same, it is clear that the Presidency brought Kennedy far more new support than anyone had anticipated. For almost a decade opinion samplers had reported that Dwight Eisenhower was the man most Americans admired. On the first anniversary of the Kennedy inaugural they found that Ike's successor had succeeded him here, too. To his uncritical admirers the young President has an irresistible charisma. "I believe in anything he believes in!" a woman gasped after one of his public appearances, and once when he went for a stroll on the south grounds of the White House two passing motorists, each cheering him, collided.

At times the First Family seems to dominate the newspapers. During his campaign Kennedy had repeatedly declared that he was tired of getting up every morning and reading what Khrushchev and Castro were doing; he wanted to know what the President of the United States was doing. Several months after moving into the new mansion he remarked dryly to Sorensen that "Some people are tired of getting up every morning and reading what Kennedy is doing. They want to read what Khrushchev and Castro are doing." They didn't really. Watching the President had become an opiate of the masses, and it was accompanied by a kind of Nell Gwyn crush — a Kennedy barber, swamped with requests for tufts of his hair, was asked didn't he think it all ridiculous; his shy reply was that he had taken some home to his wife. Only the Capitol, Washington's high ground, was inaccessible to the tide. John Kennedy was too familiar a figure on the Hill; one senator said tartly, "He is just someone who used to sit beside me — when he happened to be here." Nevertheless, even there Representative Hale Boggs was overheard early in 1962 advertising the fact that he had received a letter from the President "in his own handwriting."

There is nothing novel about this enthusiasm. It is the very stuff of leadership. A man must kindle it to win high office, and the qualities that put him there tend to increase the public's affection. Let a new tenant move into the White House and his followers exaggerate his every virtue. Grant's distaste for red tape was the talk of the Seventies; Coolidge's laconism, the marvel of the Twenties. The public resolves that a Chief Executive shall gain in stature, so he does. Those who have known him before regard him as a stranger. Waiting outside Franklin Roosevelt's office Norman Thomas said to Raymond Fosdick, "Ray, that fellow in there is not the fellow we used to know. There's been a miracle here." Similarly, Barney Ross says of John Kennedy, "The big difference in him is, he's grown while the rest of us have stood still. He's deeper, more mature, more intellectual. Out there in the Pacific we were equal. Now all of us, all his old friends, hold him in awe." Ross grins. "Of course, how much of that is the Presidency, I don't know. It *does* have an aura."

A new President's former colleagues begin to dote on him, and some of them go so far as to ape him. Bess Furman noticed that everyone around Roosevelt laughed the same way he did — "a little toss-back of the head, then all-out, tooth-displaying mirth." Kennedy's first mimic was Ted Sorensen. Even before the election Sorensen was being called the boss's alter ego: "When Jack is wounded," reporters said, "Ted bleeds." He had picked up his chief's mannerisms, his writing style, his thought processes. A friend of the Kennedys' watched him and blurted out, "Say, you're more like Jack than Jack himself." Sorensen looked disturbed — as would any man whose identity is threatened. The blurter remembers that Jack drew him aside. "Don't," he ordered. "He gets that from all sides." Today Sorensen has lots of company. Recently Red Fay was addressing an audience. "In the middle of the speech," he says, "I realized I had the old head cocked to the right; the left hand going, stabbing the air, making a point; and the other hand level, sawing air." A few weeks later Pierre Salinger did precisely the same thing over a Kansas City television station. The instant he left the studio someone taunted him about it, though he had been unaware of imitating anyone. Some people think Caroline has begun to hunch her shoulders like her father, and certainly there are scores of men in Washington who have unconsciously adopted the Kennedy pause, the Kennedy walk, and the Kennedy habit of disciplining a shock of unruly hair — even when they haven't got unruly hair or, for that matter, hair.

What is extraordinary about all this is the President's reaction to it. He observes the tributes paid to him almost as though they were meant for someone else. His self-possession isn't as majestic as that of the dying Webster — "Wife, children, doctor, I trust on this occasion I have said nothing unworthy of Daniel Webster" — but without using the third person he does convey a third-person air. This objectivity gives him a certain tactical edge with people. It permits him to edit his professional friendships dispassionately — some say ruthlessly. Few politicians have been able to rise so rapidly without incurring massive political debts. Apart from the Attorney General and the Secretary of Health, Education, and Welfare, his strongest campaign backers are absent from his Cabinet, which includes two former governors of small political caliber, an ex-congressman, two Republicans, and — as Secretary of State — an inactive Democrat whose pre-convention choice was Adlai Stevenson. In choosing his ministers the President's only traditional standard was geographic distribution. Appointments weren't made to meet any election commitment. He didn't even think about them until he had become President-Elect. He assumes most men support him out of conviction, not for payola. Their faith in him neither surprises nor elates. It is simply there, like the Washington Monument. Discovering an incompetent appointee on a lower level he demanded, "What's he doing in the government?" "He admired you so much," he was told. "His imagination was fired by your eloquence in the campaign, your dedication, your vision." Most leaders would have been warmed, if only momentarily, by this intimation of magnetic appeal. This one nodded shortly. "Yes, that happens," he said flatly, "but now would you please explain what he's doing in the government?"

Obviously such an attitude is instinctive. If he had not had it, it would not have been possible to invent it. And indeed, detachment has run through his forty-five years like a lonely thread. Motoring through Europe with Lem Billings the summer after his freshman year at Harvard, he was intent upon taking each nation's pulse. The car was his, and he would give a lift

to any hitchhiker to quiz him in pidgin about attitudes toward aggression, hopes for peace, faith in the
Maginot Line. What impressed Billings most was that
Kennedy was seldom offended by anyone, even when
offense was intended. At Vesuvius two German soldiers they had picked up secretly decided to beat
them to the top. The Americans, opting for the gentler
of the two slopes, were greeted at the summit by their
crowing guests. Billings thought this rude. Kennedy
merely made a note about the Teutonic will to win.
Again, in Munich, they learned that the great tourist
stunt was to drink a stein of beer outside the Hofbrau
House and then slip away with the stein. It was all
good fun, and a Nazi there told them how to do it.
They were quite taken by the man. Despite his brown
shirt he was well educated, spoke English with an Oxford accent, and seemed to be going out of his way to
be genial. They followed his plan — and were instantly caught. As a waiter stopped Billings and retrieved the stein from under his coat, they turned
and beheld their brown-shirted planner laughing de-
risively. He had deliberately trapped them. Billings
was enraged, but Kennedy, unruffled, merely made
another quiet note, this time about Nazi treachery.

"Emotions move people far more strongly than
facts," he observed unemotionally, chronicling the
collapse of the prewar West, and to his father he
wrote — during the agony of the German blitz — "I
of course don't want to take sides too much." His personal destiny has been treated as impersonally.

"What do you want to do?" he asked his PT crew as they swam around the sinking hulk of their boat. "I have nothing to lose." Eleven years later, when he lay critically ill after an operation, his father was struck by his fatalistic attitude. Either he would die or he wouldn't, he said; there wasn't much he could do about it. At one point during the hectic vice-presidential nomination of 1956, he appeared to have won. The whole country was in a sweat. Sorensen held out his hand to congratulate him, but Kennedy, calmly dressing in front of a television screen like an Ingmar Bergman character, replied, "No, not yet." On election night four years later, in front of another television set, Jacqueline Kennedy said, "Oh, Bunny, you're President now!" With the objectivity of a commentator he reported to her that it was too early to tell. Antagonists are judged by the same unbiased eye. In that 1956 convention his rebuff was widely attributed to the floor strategy of the present Speaker of the House, a Massachusetts Democrat but no friend. "If McCormack wanted to put the knife in me, he had every right to do so," Kennedy said neutrally. "That's politics." And in that 1960 triumph, when his staff fumed because Richard Nixon postponed his admission of defeat, he told them, "Why should he concede? I wouldn't."

Deep in the man is a sense of autonomy, a capacity to view all society extrinsically. Kennedy enthusiasts attribute his presidential victory to political genius; with chilly realism he observes that a switch here, a switch there, and the genius would be named Nixon. One of his favorite phrases is "in my judgment." His judgment is unlike anyone else's. He ignores people whom the world esteems, values people the world ignores, and sorts them out according to their talents. To a remarkable degree his friendships are compartmentalized. They include a number of men who would like to shoot one another on sight. In Congress he was on pleasant terms with Vito Marcantonio, John Rankin, Paul Douglas, and Barry Goldwater. In the White House his personal, political, and social allies rarely mix. Sorensen continues to be very close to him. Their relationship is almost telepathic. In the West Wing they anticipate one another and need scarcely speak as they work together, disposing of administrivia. But this is an office association; after hours they rarely see each other. At the same time, Kennedy's social acquaintances tend to be apolitical, and his literary acquaintances to be apolitical and asocial. If a man's convictions conflict with his role, he checks them at the door. John Sherman Cooper is a Republican senator. He comes to 1600 Pennsylvania Avenue not as a Republican, however, but as a friend.

"Don't take down a fence until you know why it was put up," Robert Frost wrote. John Kennedy likes that line. For him good fences make a good Presidency. He erects them between people, and between problems. The day the Russians announced that they would resume nuclear testing he was talking to a

Washington correspondent. Mac Bundy entered the room with the news. The Chief Executive listened intently — and went on with the interview. Again, this writer was in the oval study when word of Sam Rayburn's fatal illness reached the President. He crossed his study to take the call. Clearly he was moved, and he said so. Then he replaced the receiver in its cradle, returned to his rocker, and, after rocking in silence for a moment, resumed the conversation.

We were discussing *Why England Slept,* his description of how England slept through appeasement, which sold eighty thousand copies twenty-two years ago and was reissued last fall. Reappraising it he displayed the same aloofness: "I dipped into it recently. Parts of it were heavy going. I don't know whether people would be interested in it now." He was reminded of a prescient passage in the book, describing Russian disarmament proposals of the Thirties as propaganda devices, and he nodded thoughtfully, as though acknowledging a point in behalf of an absent author. "Yes, parts of it are relevant today," he conceded. "Of course, they could take nuclear disarmament now, because they have conventional weapons." He reflected again and made a counter point: the study was dated. "You know, the League experience is not encouraging," he concluded. "They had the best chance we've had, because there was no bitterness; Hitler wasn't strong yet."

The absent writer — gangling young Jack Ken-

nedy, snub-nosed and tense — sounded several notes
in 1940 which are familiar in the 1960's: the need to
sacrifice during crises, to avoid public scapegoats,
and to keep isms out of Latin America; and the importance of voluntary restraint in an independent
press. His book drew another conclusion which is
important in understanding the man he was to become. It dealt with one of the most vexing dilemmas
in contemporary politics, the short-run advantages of
totalitarian governments over republics. Although
"freedom from centralized authoritarianism" is one of
democracy's great cornerstones, he wrote, that very
liberty can threaten national security. Regimented
people can be told what to do; free people must be
won over, and the winning takes time. Quoting Sir
Stanley Baldwin, who estimated the lag between a
democracy and a dictatorship at two years, Kennedy
blamed the inertia of that era on the British public.
Then, broadening his indictment, he charged that the
United States had also been "asleep at the switch."
Later this concept grew on him, and he was reminded
of, and discomforted by, the contest between Sparta
and Athens. In the Tulagi tent debates, Fay recalls,
"he had a strong feeling that we were fighting in that
God-forsaken place because we, the voters, had failed
to see the issues clearly. He said that as citizens we
all held office, and that we hadn't done a very good
job of meeting our responsibilities."

That, really, is the theme of *Profiles in Courage*.
Kennedy's political heroes had to be heroic because

their constituents weren't as farsighted as they were; each leader had to choose between a surrender of principle and disregard for what Thomas Hart Benton called "the bubble of popularity that is won without merit and lost without crime." When *Profiles* was published the author told a Harvard audience that elected representatives are forever "dragging the anchor of public opinion." He didn't despise the anchor. It was there, it had to be moved. He simply observed that as long as a politician is attached to it he cannot "with dexterity slip from position to position," as, he added pointedly, the scholar can.

Today Kennedy the politician-scholar compares the Nazi threat of twenty-five years ago with the Soviet menace today. He has called America's 1950's "the years the locust have eaten," the very phrase Sir Stanley used to describe Britain's 1930's. Completing the figure, Dwight Eisenhower would be our Neville Chamberlain and John Kennedy our Winston Churchill — unless Eisenhower were Baldwin, in which case the umbrella would go to Kennedy. Really the comparison of eras is little more than a historian's game. It has some validity; America now, like England then, has been indolent, complacent, unaware. The difficulty is that cold war, unlike war, doesn't generate much heat at home. Although the President has sounded calls to action, the alarm bell seems muted. As Joe Kennedy wrote four years before the publication of *Why England Slept*, "Americans are not easily stirred to action. The spectacle must be dramatic. The movie is worthless unless it is at least colossal." A Chief Executive's command is worthless unless it is at least Churchillian. If the presidential trumpet gives an uncertain sound, only Ted Sorensen will prepare himself to the battle.

John Kennedy hasn't changed course. The twentieth-century challenge to democratic resourcefulness is still very much on his mind. "He mentions it all the time," says Salinger. "That," says Sorensen, "is one of the reasons he sought the Presidency. He felt that people needed to grasp the nettle." Presidents, however, can be just so forceful. A free society exercises continual restraints upon them. Musing over the problem of meeting Russian thrusts he says, "There *are* advantages to centralized power." He casually cites a luncheon at which he tried to induce network executives to release material for the United States Information Agency. "In Russia that would be no problem," he says wryly. "It wouldn't even be a matter for thought." Reminded that Harry Truman called presidential power the power to persuade, he nods vigorously and comments, "Yes, that's it."

Since Baldwin's day — even since Truman's — the problem has acquired a new shape. A President may issue bold executive orders, which makes things easier. But he must act in concert with other chiefs of state, which makes them much harder. "Everything is different now," Bobby Kennedy remarks. "The lag isn't two years any more. We can move more quickly.

Yet democracy is still more cumbersome than dictatorship. If this were a dictatorship the President could
grind out stuff day after day, as Khrushchev can.
Even answering Khrushchev is a problem; England
thinks we should talk, France not. The President must
consult his allies — and Fulbright and Dirksen —
and at the same time keep his own house in order.
One of our chief allies may agree to a proposal only
if Country X approves of it. Another will agree only if
Country X isn't even informed of it. This requires a
mastery of politics not even contemplated twenty
years ago."

A nineteenth-century Frenchman had his suspicions, though. "It is chiefly in foreign relations,"
Alexis de Tocqueville wrote a hundred and twenty-five
years before Kennedy's election, "that the executive
power of a nation finds occasion to exert its skill and
strength. If the existence of the Union were perpetu-
ally threatened, if its chief interests were in daily connection with those or other powerful nations, the
executive department would assume increased importance in proportion to the measures expected of it and
to those which it would execute." In the Sixties that
waxing importance is felt everywhere. Asked at the
inaugural what Europe expected of America's new
President, a man fresh from there replied, "Too
much." The President himself sums up his diplomatic
position in those first weeks: "I was new to the world
scene. I succeeded Eisenhower, who was known and

whose position was clear. Naturally there was some curiosity about me. Also, I was young, and most of the men I would be dealing with were older."

He satisfied their curiosity with a technique de Tocqueville couldn't have foreseen: the personal confrontation. Kennedy summitry began almost at once; in the first ten months of his Administration he held seventy-five meetings with other chiefs of state, and despite the commotions of his second presidential spring he turned aside to entertain such obscure visiting firemen as Cameroun's Ahmadou Ahidjo, Togo's Sylvanus Olympio, and His Beatitude Makarios III, President of Cyprus. On the whole, these confrontations have been a success. Though they later found bones to pick with him, even Charles de Gaulle and Konrad Adenauer were impressed. De Gaulle remarked that in his entire life he had encountered only two genuine statesmen, and one of them was Kennedy; Adenauer, de Gaulle's other choice, announced as he departed the Executive Mansion, "I've never left this house feeling better." Communists felt worse, because the President's footwork was so much faster than theirs. To the proverb-quoting Russians he was proverbial — "You have offered to trade us an apple for an orchard. We don't do that in this country." — and he pointedly told Nikita Khrushchev that he hoped Khrushchev would be able to keep his Lenin Peace Prize. Even when Kennedy skidded he seemed to keep his footing. His Canadian visit disclosed that his French hadn't improved a bit since his 1937 trip with Billings, so he turned it to his advantage — by comparing it with Prime Minister John Diefenbaker's.

"He was so much better prepared than Diefenbaker and Macmillan that it was embarrassing," a witness to those conferences observes. His youth, it had been predicted, would put him at a strategic disadvantage in conclaves. Yet foreign secretaries are as struck by his talent for the specific as office secretaries, and so are their chiefs. Among those who have taken his measure and then commented upon this circumstantial gift are Macmillan, David Ben-Gurion, Willy Brandt, Hayato Ideka of Japan, Modibo Keita of Mali, Mohammed Ayub Khan of Pakistan, and Achmed Sukarno of Indonesia and the Greater East Asia Co-Prosperity Sphere. "Your President," Britain's Prime Minister murmured, "catches on to ideas very fast." Ben-Gurion had expected oratory. Instead the President led him into a room, closed the door, and regaled him with statistics about Israel. Ideka wondered where all the aides and *aides mémoire* were. He seemed to be alone with this one man, this rocking encyclopedia on the Far East. But the widest eyes were those of Willy Brandt. Most Americans are familiar with Willy's office, mayor of West Berlin. Few are aware that there is also a mayor of *East* Berlin, whose father, Friedrich Ebert, was the first president of the Weimar Republic. Their own President not only knew it; he knew more than his guest about the man. "I couldn't answer some of his questions," Willy confessed at lunch immediately after his baptism of facts. "He asked me whether Ebert's other son was also a Communist. Ebert's other son! I didn't even know he *had* another son!"

The success of these Information Please blitzes demonstrates that political and diplomatic arts really aren't so far apart. Larry O'Brien, a Massachusetts Hibernian who did not grow up on the Kennedy side of the tracks, believes attention to detail is the key to the President's success at the polls. "It's a kind of toughness," he says, "though not many people recognize it as that. He just works harder and longer than anyone else. When he got to L.A., it was all done. The others were only hoping." Actually the cultivated memory has always been a tool of American politicians. Reportedly George Washington could remember the name of anyone he had met once. As Adlai Stevenson said to James M. Farley at a national convention, "Hi, Jim. You know, I never forget a face." Honey Fitz, the East Boston boy who became mayor of all Boston, liked to talk about the "Irish Switch" — shaking hands with one voter while gossiping with a second — but Abraham Lincoln was practicing this technique a hundred years ago, following a precept which had been set forth in the Boston *Atlas* of 1836: "Those who would have votes must descend into the forum and take the voters by the hand."

What sets the mayor's grandson apart is his application of the principle. With him it has reached corporate proportions. Faces are not only remembered; every warm and willing body is enlisted as a volunteer. Operating under Larry O'Brien's First Law of Politics (the more campaigners, the better) Kennedy recruited two hundred and eighty-six secretaries and twenty-one thousand workers for one Massachusetts election. Long before his presidential nomination, lists of names were being broken down state by state, entered into card files, and coded. Intricate wall maps were also prepared, though the candidate never seemed to need any. He carried them in his mind. "When he launched the big primary drive in Hyannis Port he lectured us on the entire country," O'Brien says. "Some of the people there, even though they had worked with him before, were amazed at his knowledge of political nuances. He could discuss Cuyahoga County in Ohio then. He knew who the powers there were, who to see, what to say. He could do this coast-to-coast, and he did — for three hours."

The President is proud of his political skills. Although he vigorously denies it, one member of his staff has the impression that he received an ironic pleasure from Adenauer's loss in last year's election. "*Der Alte* had played the virtuoso," the aide observes, "insisting that he had an instinctive feeling for the Germanic character, and he stirred a little professional jealousy in our man." Our man didn't acquire his knowledge of the American character from his readings in history, from Harvard's Professor Holcombe, or from any of the political scientists around him. He won it, as he won elections, in the forum, where his memory was harnessed to his staying power. Kennedy's fidgeting hand has never been too tired for one more Switch. On the eve of his re-election to the Senate in 1958, with landslide victory over a Hobson's choice Republican already conceded to him, he was riding back to his headquarters in a stupor of exhaustion. Suddenly he spied a woman crossing the street. His hand was blooded — literally — with the ferocious amiability of campaigning, but he mumbled, "Stop the car," wobbled out, and gave her a final, tremulous, I'd-appreciate-your-vote hand-shake.

Today O'Brien keeps a different kind of card file, containing entries for every congressman. Each bears helpful notations: names of friends, relatives, lodge affiliations, etc. He uses this information effectively, and so does his employer, during coffee hours and meals with men from Capitol Hill. The President makes it a point to remember legislators' birthdays; sometimes he telephones them to gabble about the days when they were members of the same cheery club, and once he swooped down by helicopter to attend a luncheon on Harry Byrd's country estate. These aren't casual social gestures. He is courting them, as they, and he, court constituents. The first President since Andrew Johnson to have served in both House and Senate, Kennedy makes a wily suitor, and he doesn't rely entirely on his endearing young charms. Sometimes he tries logic, promoting his trade program by showing tariff charts to congressional guests. Other times O'Brien, his Cyrano, lets them peep at his popularity polls. Kennedy's hidden persuaders are highly diverse — he used Ayub Khan as a foreign aid lobbyist — and they include the knuckle-duster. When O'Brien isn't busy with Hill liaison he turns to patronage, a subject of vast interest at the other end of Pennsylvania Avenue.

In this game the President's great stake is his prestige. Any Chief Executive's prestige is in constant flux. It grows when he takes a stand and wins, shrinks when he loses, wastes away if he is inert. Wastage is unlikely in this Administration. Some people think Kennedy tries too hard, but that is his nature. He keeps looking for winning combinations — urging policy changes on the Federal Reserve Board, say, or directing Secretary Goldberg to referee labor negotiations — and to the exasperation of Ken O'Donnell, who arranges his appointments, he persists in receiving an astonishing number of individuals. "It's hard not to get invited to the White House these days," he remarked during his first year. Invitations are scarcer now, though many are still welcomed, including titans of the press. Kennedy confers regularly with Salinger, meets publishers, and is interviewed by such alien Krocks as Alex Adzhubei of *Izvestia.* "A lot of his visits are pure public relations," one of his professorial assistants concedes. "Let's face it," says O'Brien. "He sells himself."

His self-sell reduces the dangers of open ruptures

at home. National leaders everywhere crave unified support — Kennedy, perhaps, more than most. "Naturally," he says. "There is a desire to maintain basic agreement." Yet in a democracy attempts at a solid front can be hazardous. Joe Cannon claimed that McKinley kept his ear so close to the ground it was full of grasshoppers. "I can't talk to you now," says the premier in an old European story; "there go my followers." Faith that political guile can win major issues without a fight may lead to jeopardy of an entire program, and the President is being watched carefully in that light. James M. Burns, in his pre-election biography of Kennedy, suggested that he "might have difficulty" doing more than "responding to political pressures and gusts of opinion." Today Burns comments, "He said he would be a party President, and he's not. He said he wouldn't be above the battle, and he is." The President, says Gore Vidal, "is reluctant to spend any of his popularity." Vidal remembers telling Kennedy how difficult it was to cast Frank Lovejoy's part in *The Best Man*. The President asked why, and "I explained that actors don't like to play unpopular roles; they become actors because they want to be admired. He smiled and nodded at once. Most people would have trouble understanding, but he saw it immediately."

This may be figmental. Like all great politicians, Kennedy has a knack for putting himself in someone else's shoes. During the war he took a gunboat from Tulagi to Rendova on a routine run. Jim Reed was aboard; so was a green ensign. After they reached the base Reed remarked to the skipper that he had seen the new officer in his tent, crying. "Jack didn't say anything," Reed recalls, "but shortly after that I looked for him, and he was gone. I looked everywhere, for two and a half hours. Finally I found him. He'd been with that ensign all that time, talking to him, calming him down." Those who charge Kennedy with a lack of warmth have in mind his inability, or reluctance, to arouse ideological fervor; none doubt this instinctive tact, which recurs in his life with the persistence of a sonata theme. Burns tells how he asked for the President-Elect's vacant Senate seat. "I guess I'm about a hundred and fiftieth on the list," he said to him, "but I want to put my name in." "No, Jim, you're not a hundred and fiftieth," Kennedy replied. "As a matter of fact, you're fourth or fifth." "I was so elated at this promotion," Burns says with a grin, "that it was a week before I realized he'd said no." During a White House reception for Secretary Dillon the line got stuck, and the most junior guest found himself vis-à-vis the President; they talked for about five minutes, and as the line moved on the young man, who is in the Treasury, realized that they had spent the entire time discussing the problems of a young Treasury man. Learning in Paris that de Gaulle is distracted by visitors who smoke in his office, Kennedy quietly put his cigars away. And when he visited Rayburn's Dallas hospital, and the mother of a child in braces asked whether he would have time to talk to her son, he made the time. Next day a reporter asked the mother if she was a Republican. "I *was*," she replied.

Nevertheless it is true that the President is sustained by confidence in what one member of his Cabinet has called "the integrity of compromise." And somehow the phrase does lack razzle-dazzle. Although every politician is a compromiser, most attempt to dress the product attractively. The chief ribbon for the Kennedy package was picked up at a party before his acceptance of the 1960 nomination, when Walt Rostow, now Counsellor of the State Department, told the candidate, "I know what the first sentence of your speech ought to be. You ought to say, 'This country is ready to get moving again, and I'm prepared to lead it.'" Since the inaugural there have been periodic assurances of movement, but political shellbacks expect something more. They want an embattled chieftain, a Horatius; a leader who will give the world a kick in the old kazzazza.

Because they measure Kennedy by their yardsticks, they fail. He baffles them, and they blame him. Blaming the President is an American custom almost as old as bundling. He is, after all, the biggest target in the land, and the formation of every presidential cult is followed by the congealment of an anti-cult. "Remember," Woodrow Wilson warned his daughter when his first Administration was sailing along smoothly, "the pack is always waiting to tear one to pieces."

Andrew Jackson was portrayed as an adulterer, Lincoln as a baboon, Harry Truman as a haberdasher. Thomas Jefferson was "Mad Tom," and even Washington was scarred. "I am accused of being the enemy of America, and subject to the influence of a foreign country," he wrote Mad Tom, ". . . and every act of my Administration is tortured, in such exaggerated and indecent terms as could scarcely be applied to Nero, to a notorious defaulter, or even to a common pickpocket." That passage was once quoted by John Kennedy, who added: "But he stood firm." Kennedy's own posture is illumined by a glance at the devices which, enriched by the family treasury, won him the office. There isn't a firework in the lot. They were selected on the theory that the United States has changed as its face has changed, that fresh approaches are required in a country which is no longer a land of cracker barrels, front porches, woodsheds, or, until recently, of rocking chairs.

His methods are very like those of the Establishment — of the transferred Oxonian — and they were introduced in the most inauspicious of environments. He made his debut in the burlesque house of American politics. "We have a fine party," a Massachusetts Democrat once said. "The only trouble with it is that we have ten thousand leaders." He might have added that they all wore baggy pants. Anything went in Boston, provided it was vaudevillian. The ambassador can recall two lackeys telling his father, "Pat, we voted a hundred and twenty-eight times today," and

Ted Kennedy recounts the story of Honey Fitz going to a prize fight, climbing into the ring, and making a speech. "Everybody tried to stop him, and no one could. He went on for fifteen minutes, with fights breaking out all over the place. You can't imagine Jack doing that. Those days are dead."

They are also mourned. Ted's own entourage includes men who speak reverently of "the master," by whom they do not mean the President. They are thinking of fun-loving Jim Curley, the Purple Shamrock. Curley always left them laughing. He called Saltonstall "Pinocchio" and the crowd guffawed and stamped its feet, and old-timers treasure his comment on the appointment, to a minor post, of Endicott Peabody Saltonstall. "All three of them?" the Shamrock asked. In the postwar years such mummery still dominated Boston politics, and Jack Kennedy's ambitions were the target of a couple of choice custard pies. One buffoon passed the word that Kick Kennedy had married a descendant of Oliver Cromwell, that evil man; another predicted that thanks to Jack, the St. Lawrence Seaway would start "right at the front door of the Merchandise Mart in Chicago, which is owned by old Joe Kennedy."

This is a game any number can play. If old Joe's son had opted for slapstick, he could have engaged a troupe of stipendiary churls to spread the classic counter rumors — that his opponents had been excommunicated, jailed on morals charges, and endorsed by the Planned Parenthood Federation — or to pound on doors in the middle of the night, demanding that the enraged inhabitants vote for the opposition. There would have been plenty of volunteers. His name brought a mob of them to the Hotel Bellevue. "Kennedy was wonderful with those *Last Hurrah* characters," says Jim Reed. "He never promised them anything, but they all had the impression that something would be coming to them, because that was what they wanted to believe." "They crowded around him like moths around a flame," Billings remembers. "His two rooms were jam-packed every day from 6 A.M. on."

In the beginning the candidate welcomed everyone; he was glad to have any support at all. Then, slowly, he began separating the men from the boys — and keeping the boys. Kennedy's patrician vote-cadgers were making their bow. The aging mountebanks were sent out to the street, where they may still be found, chuckling over old Curley stories. Inside, Billings and Reed became typical members of what Kennedy called his "junior brain trust." Both were doing graduate work at Harvard, and that fitted: the junior trust was a potpourri of eager intellectuals, veterans, gray-flanneled ex-roommates, out-of-state Protestant Republicans, and one Harvard valet named Taylor. In Boston this was incredible; it was like enlisting the Houston Jaycees to mastermind a Bombay campaign against Krishna Menon. Honey Fitz tried to be helpful. He sent over some seasoned precinct workers, who stared at what one leathery pol called "all those crew-cut college boys in the silk suits" and boggled. This was politics? They departed for a quick belt in the Bellevue bar and left their old friend's grandson to his fate. It is highly improbable that any of them suspected what that fate would be.

The young man's first triumph seemed to be a freak. It could only be attributed to his father's money, and that continued to be the accepted explanation, even after he had won a third congressional term without spending a penny. He knew nothing about traditional political stagecraft, nor would he learn. No wakes for him, no paupers on the payroll; in office he retained his aversion to corn and went back to the same new drawing board. "The way to get along," Sam Rayburn told him, "is to go along." Kennedy wouldn't go along. As his father once said, "Nobody tells Jack what to do unless he wants to be told." The callow congressman refused to sign a pardon petition for Curley when that grand old man, through some misunderstanding, was imprisoned for fraud, and he continued to consult witless youths. Stalking his Senate seat, he chose as chief scout a lawyer who had played JV football with him at Harvard. If anything, the age of his advisers was growing more tender; Bobby's generation had left college now, and from it he recruited O'Donnell and Richard K. Donahue. By now Kennedy had become openly contemptuous of political hacks, while they, in turn, could only marvel that he had the effrontery to be a candidate for anything. His personal organization — it was entirely personal — was so ignorant that its members didn't know who the big wheels of the party were; at a national convention they snubbed Mayor Richard J. Daley of Chicago and Carmine De Sapio, who in those bygone days was a power to reckon with. Meanwhile Himself was seen reading John Buchan's biography of Cromwell and — worse and worse — Paul Blanshard's *American Freedom and Catholic Power*. Retribution, both divine and secular, seemed certain.

Powerful secular forces in his own party affixed him with the evil eye. Curley, out of stir, swore vengeance and was delighted when the chump volunteered to commit hara-kiri by running against Lodge, a task nobody else wanted. To make certain everything went ill for Kennedy, the Shamrock turned his coat and quietly slipped across the party line to help Lodge, who had defeated him in another Senate race sixteen years before. The returns came in: strike one against the bosses. Four years later the greenhorn tangled with John McCormack, the state's senior Democrat, and the scavengers waited to pick up the pieces. The result was strike two. Then, as the Eisenhower years waned, two of the mightiest figures in the national leadership — Rayburn and Truman — held a Washington tête-à-tête in the back seat of a Cadillac and decided that whoever the next President was, his name wouldn't be Kennedy. That was followed by strike three. Every Indian sign had failed. Jack had not only foiled the bullies; he had thrashed them soundly. Running for reelection to the Senate in

1958, he received approximately three of every four votes cast, the largest margin in the history of Massachusetts elections. After the McCormack joust the pieces the scavengers found were McCormack's; the tyro had officially replaced him as state leader. And in 1960, Rayburn and Truman never got off the ground.

Meanwhile his Republican opponents, one by one, were entering the shadow of eclipse. There are few signs that they will emerge soon. As President he has occupied stage center, and the G.O.P. has been obliged to move over. When the Republican National Committee met early in 1962, Chairman William Miller compared the President to Hitler and asked for funds to investigate the men around him. Kennedy didn't rise to the bait. He felt the charges were self-defeating, and some of Miller's colleagues seemed to agree. ("Who ever heard of Schlesinger back where I came from?" complained a man from the West. "We're in a vacuum at the moment," a comitteeman confessed.) Rockefeller excepted, the party's leadership sounds rather daunted, which may puzzle some, for Nixon came very close in 1960. But the gracile Democratic plurality that autumn had encouraged hopes of a G.O.P. dawn in 1961, and the dawn had proved false. Richard J. Hughes was supposed to lose the governorship of New Jersey by eighty thousand votes. All the polls said so. Then the President's road show, still shunning ballyhoo, entered the state and pulled Hughes across.

One upset is a freak. A string of them is a trend, and clearly this trend says something about the motion of the United States which is far more significant than Rostow's slogan. The country isn't ready to get moving again; it has been moving for some time, and its political locus is away from bossism, sectionalism, and partisanship. American mothers, Gallup found, often think of their sons as future Presidents; rarely as future politicians. The electorate doesn't fancy bowlers and smelly cigars. The new breed smokes less, and the voters enjoy it more. From his beginnings in Curley's old congressional district, Kennedy sensed that this was to be the era of what Leo Egan calls "the coffee-filled room." In Massachusetts shillelaghs had become vulgar. Catholics yearned for respectability, so the candidate carefully fostered the impression that he was an office-seeker of another stripe, reserved and unpretentious. "The young Irish had settled in places like Belmont, Winchester, Brookline, and Lexington," O'Brien says. "These are Republican towns, and they didn't want to be a minority, so they switched their registrations. Then in '52 the President broke through and they had a new leader. The significant thing about that vote was the breakdown. In the cities he ran abreast of the Democratic ticket, but outside the cities he ran way ahead of it. That's where he won."

Kennedy's shunning of kingmakers naturally made them uneasy, and his presidential behavior has justified their suspicions. In New York he supported the

rebel challenge to Tammany Hall; he even denounced the awarding of choice ambassadorships to
big party contributors, a blow which struck some venerable Democrats as being sharper than a serpent's
tooth. Yet it would be naïve to suppose that he is
prompted by idealism. No politician can afford to be
any better than he ought to be — until he retires —
and Kennedy isn't hostile to classic politics. His inno-
vations are technological. An age of wide screens demands mannerly candidates and open covenants. The
President has decided to accept television debates
with his 1964 opponent (and to demand similar debates for lesser offices) because his audience will accept nothing less. Connivance and evasiveness are
trademarks of the old pols; the new style is an inversion of them. The people liked Ike because he seemed
above the ward scramble, and they like his successor
because, as he once said, he returned from the war
"not as a Democratic wheelhorse who came up from
the ranks — I came in sort of sideways."

He might have added that after slithering in, he
found himself right in the middle of the road. That
is where most Americans see themselves; their national purpose is to avoid the ruts on either side. The
President is farther down the road than they are. He
knows, as they do not, that big government is here to
stay, and he recognizes that the frustrations of coexistence are permanent. Their lag accounts for the
gap between their regard for him and their disregard
for much of his program; it is hard for them to see the

implications of the Common Market, which may become the greatest issue of this Administration. But
they can see him and they trust him. Every Chief
Executive mirrors his time. When the Union was
riven, Lincoln was a figure of anguish. The nation
was boisterous sixty years ago; so was Theodore
Roosevelt. Coolidge slept a lot, and Eisenhower made
folks happy. Kennedy is bland, wary, polite. The
qualities he doesn't have are the qualities the young
marrieds in the suburban developments don't want.
He lacks emotional fire, and they distrust fire; they
associate oratory with hams. The message of his career is clear: the new strength is a muted strength.
The new leader must be restrained, and aloof from
alien corn.

The older generation seldom got that message. Between it and him lay a deep and often unbridgeable
chasm. Basic communication became difficult; in
1960 the junior brain trusters used older recruits —
men like John Bailey of Connecticut and Hyman
Raskin of Chicago — as interpreters. On the eve of
the election Dick Donahue watched a group of elder
Democrats who were eying the nominee enviously.
"You know," Donahue said to Theodore H. White,
"they can't understand this. They think he has a
trick. They're listening to him because they think if
they learn the trick they can be President, too." Today a White House aide believes that in the capital,
where so many men of power are the ambassador's
age, "this generational thing is more wrenching than

144 ~ *Portrait of a President*

any bill, any issue, any program." Another aide, Larry O'Brien, observes that "Through the years he has been consistently underestimated by the pols. Back in '52 he surprised Lodge, and in '60 he astonished Johnson. They just can't get it."

Their children get it, though. All the talk of surging Goldwater youth is eyewash. Opinion samplers have observed that the younger the voters, the stronger their preference for Kennedy. If everyone over thirty had stayed away from the polls, he would have been swept into the White House. His peers have never underrated him. Indeed, some of them have anticipated him. In 1941 the Navy ordered him to lecture to some Charleston, South Carolina, factory workers on sabotage. Lem Billings, in town for his brother's wedding, went over to listen. "He didn't know much about the subject," Billings says, "but he'd done his homework, and he gave them a good, impressive speech about the two types of incinerator bombs. Then he made the mistake of asking for questions. The first one was, 'How do you tell the difference when they hit?' He didn't hesitate. He said, 'I'm glad you asked that question. Next week we'll have a specialist in that field give a demonstration.' Right then I picked him as a political comer." Later Billings found his political arguments so persuasive that he changed his own registration from Republican to Democratic. All the officers who were with Kennedy in PT's, says Jim Reed, "came back from the war talking about him, sold on him." Red Fay was more specific; his San Francisco neighbors remember that he returned from the Pacific predicting that a naval lieutenant named Kennedy would be President some day. The following spring Red went East to help crush the congressional aspirations of the ex-WAC major and the Joseph Russos. Late in the summer of 1961 he was visiting his home, and while going through some old papers he found a note he had written home from the Bellevue, where he joined the roommate legion.

I am living here with Jack Kennedy, who is really out on a big scale, he had scribbled on April 5, 1946. *If by chance the West Coast papers carry a story about me running for Secretary of the Navy, kill it. It's the Undersecretary of the Navy I get.*

The scribbler's present address is the Pentagon. Three days after scaling the biggest hurdle of all, Jack Kennedy — who never saw this letter — appointed his old shipmate Undersecretary of the Navy.

Undersecretary Fay's prescience startles him now, though it shouldn't. He had seen the future before. In the first week of August, 1943, he was executive officer of PT-167, and on Florida Island, off Guadalcanal, he encountered the commander of a second PT boat, who told him how a third had been rammed and sunk by a Jap destroyer.

"There was a tremendous explosion — then everybody was gone," said the eyewitness.

Red bluntly called him a liar. "I don't believe it," he said. "Not everybody. It couldn't happen."

At the time this was a minority report. The official

opinion was that the crew of the rammed craft had gone down in enemy waters, and that her skipper, Lieutenant (j.g.) John F. Kennedy, aged twenty-six, had been killed in action.

FOUR

Flat Out, All Out

ONE MONDAY MORNING in the late summer of 1961 a glittering 707 jet bearing the official seal of the President of the United States landed in Washington, and its chief passenger prepared to debark. Leaving his compartment amidships, he found two other men awaiting the ramp — a Secret Service man and a friend who, like John Kennedy, is a veteran of the Solomon Islands campaign.

The President turned to the Secret Service agent. "Man, do you realize you're standing next to one of of the great heroes of the last war?" he asked him gravely. His friend began to redden. The famous voice continued reverently: "Yes, in those years" (*yee-ahs*) "he put in more time on coral reefs, tied up more Japanese troops, won more victories single-handed against-all-odds with his back-against-the . . ."

By now the guest was scarlet, the agent grinning broadly. Both were aware that an authentic hero stood there, and that it wasn't either of them. John Kennedy's wartime valor has become as much a part of American lore as Theodore Roosevelt's ride up Kettle Hill. John Hersey described it at the time in a *New Yorker* dispatch. A U. S. Navy oil painting in the White House shows the Japanese destroyer *Amagiri* ramming Kennedy's PT-109 on the tar-black night of August 2, 1943. Jack Warner, who voted for Dick Nixon, contracted to film a big-budget production depicting the time the lieutenant — to be played by Cliff Robertson — put in on coral reefs after the crash. Robert J. Donovan has written a book about PT-109, and on Kolombangara Island Donovan found that for nearly twenty years the natives have been singing a folk song about "Captain" Kennedy's bravery in Blacklett Strait. The singers were gratified to learn that the captain had been picked headman of his tribe back home.

Actually he hadn't any business being in the islands twenty years ago. He wasn't fit. After he had been reported killed, a fellow officer wrote home, "The man that said the cream of a nation is lost in war can never be accused of making an overstatement of a very cruel fact"; but the headman-to-be certainly wasn't the physical cream. To many Americans today he seems the eternal youth — wiry and agile, with the profile of a Lindbergh and the glowing health of a Merriwell. This image is a triumph of will. His life has been dogged by illness. There have been interludes, of course. During the Los Angeles convention he could elude reporters by jumping a fence; he was once a Burning Tree member, and before the Ottawa tree-planting he liked to practice chip shots on the White House lawn. But disability has always returned in one form or another. Although his spine improved in the winter of 1961-1962, lusty exercise is out. His big executive chair is of corrective design, and to minimize strain he must constantly wear both his corset and corrective quarter-inch lift in his left heel.

No single calamity is responsible for his medical history. He has had a series of physical mishaps — so many, indeed, that some of his friends wonder whether he may be accident-prone. As boys he and his older brother collided on bikes; young Joe was unhurt, but Jack required twenty-eight stitches. Aged fourteen, he had to drop out of school for a convalescence, the first in a series of interruptions which were to check his formal education again and again. When Westbrook Pegler advised Nixon to demand that Kennedy "quit talking the lace-curtain geechee and speak Americanese if he knows the American language after his years of dear old London school," he wrote with characteristic Peglerian exorbitance. Jack didn't even spend one year, or even one term in the London School of Economics; jaundice forced him to withdraw. Three months after entering Princeton he had to quit again, bedridden. The following autumn he switched to Harvard. Playing football as a sophomore, he sprained his back. As war approached he tried to enlist. The Army wouldn't take him. There was that back, and he was thin as a shad. After building up his body he made the Navy — which then decided he would be more useful at a desk.

In an early letter listing sisterly complaints against him Jean Kennedy had written, "He had a temperature of 102° one night, too, and Miss Cahill couldn't make him mind." Jack never was very good at minding, especially when sick. Once, when ordered to the Harvard infirmary with grippe, he sneaked over to the pool an hour each day to practice his backstroke, hoping the coach would send him in there against Yale. Instead his grippe had worsened, and the coach had picked another backstroker named Richard Tregaskis. Afterward Tregaskis went out to the islands and wrote *Guadalcanal Diary*. Jack also reached Guadalcanal waters, because he wouldn't mind the Navy any better than he had Miss Cahill. Objecting to the home front, he enlisted the aid of one of the most determined men in the world, his father. Joe Kennedy put heat on what he called "the brass who had been on my London staff," and the fleet changed its mind.

In the Pacific the ambassador's son was assigned

to a series of makeshift bases, all of them dreadful holes. Americans had thought of the South Seas as an exotic land where lazy winds whispered in palm fronds, and Sadie Thompson seduced missionaries, and native girls dived for pearls in fitted sarongs, like Dorothy Lamour. The charms of the women had been badly oversold; they were closer to Big Daddy Lipscomb than Lamour. If possible, the terrain was even less attractive. On Bougainville, bulldozers vanished in spongy bottomless swamps, and at Cape Gloucester — where sixteen inches of rain fell in a single day — twenty-five Marines were killed by huge falling trees. Jungles crawled with snakes, crocodiles, headhunters. As an officer Kennedy was entitled to a houseboy, but that wasn't much comfort; his boy turned out to be a cannibal whose culinary triumphs had included a missionary.

This was the heyday of the great gripe, and Jack didn't suffer in silence. To his brother Bobby he wrote that at a physical examination "I coughed hollowly, rolled my eyes, croaked a couple of times, but all to no avail." He was also addicted to the wartime lament "I've been shafted" — which, since it came out of his Harvard euphonium as "shahfted," earned him the sobriquet "Shafty." Yet when he had a chance to return stateside, he declined, although his aching back had grown worse. The nightly combat missions didn't help it. His boat was about as long as the presidential cabin cruiser *Honey Fitz,* which is where the comparison stops. The cabin cruiser has carpets, curtains, armchairs, beds. Aboard 109 the skipper slept on a plywood board.

Years later a Midwestern youth asked him how he happened to become a war hero. "It was involuntary," he replied. "They sank my boat." The explanation omits a lot. The ramming left eleven seamen (the seating capacity of *Honey Fitz* today) floundering in seas that were shark-infested and swarming with Japanese. One survivor was badly burned, and the impact of the enemy destroyer had dealt Jack's sprained spine a cruel blow; as he ricocheted against his cockpit he had thought, "This is how it feels to be killed." Nevertheless it was he who towed the injured sailor for four hours, using the man's life jacket strap as a towrope and leading the crew to an island over three miles away. Because the strap was in his teeth he swallowed a great deal of brine; he threw up on the beach. His condition notwithstanding, next evening he breaststroked into the middle of the strait with a .38 pistol and a battle lantern and treaded water through the night, hoping to attract the attention of friendly craft. There were none.

Kennedys are strong swimmers — as a boy the President could freestyle fifty yards in thirty seconds; Caroline learned to swim in the summer of 1961, at the age of three — but when the hot sun rose the next morning he had been in the water for the better part of a day and a half. The return to the island took him five hours; he barely made it. Again he retched on

the shore, again he resolved to go on. Once more haul-
ing the helpless casualty, who survived the war to
become a California postman, he moved his men to a
second island, and then went on to a third with Ensign Barney Ross. Encountering friendly Melanesians,
he chiseled a message on a fragment of a coconut:
*Native knows posit he can pilot 11 alive need small
boat Kennedy.* The crude appeal reached an Australian coastwatcher named Arthur Reginald Evans.
Seven natives hid Jack under palm fronds in the bottom of a dugout and paddled him to Evans, after
which the coastwatcher's radio brought three liberating PT's from Rendova, thirty miles away.

To the rescuers the rescue seemed miraculous.
Two sister PT's had seen the crash, and it was assumed that all hands had been lost. Searches had
been perfunctory; the lost men had been mourned.
Not all their relatives were aware of it, however. On
Cape Cod, half a world away, eleven-year-old Ted
Kennedy was buying newspapers for his grandfather.
He glanced at the Boston *Herald* and jumped — four
drawings on the front page depicted the ramming
and the crew's deliverance. "I was dumfounded," he
says. "I hadn't been told anything about it." Only
one person on the Cape had known, and he hadn't
talked. Joe Kennedy had been informed that his son
was gone. He had lived with that report for four days,
saying nothing. Eighteen years later he could still remember coming in from his Hyannis Port stables and
seeing his wife rushing toward him. "I just turned on a

news broadcast," she was crying. "They say Jack's been saved. Saved from what?" The ambassador turned away. "Oh —" He shrugged deeply. "Nothing. It was nothing."

Since his first week as President the coconut fragment, encased in plastic, has been a fixture on John Kennedy's desk. His ordeal didn't diminish his love of the sea, acquired on the Cape as a child. Among his White House trophies are maps of the Solomons, the harpoon section of a dart gun, a well-thumbed copy of *Fishing Boats of the World,* and, mounted on the wall of a waiting room across from Ken O'Donnell's office, a huge sailfish he caught on September 16, 1953, while honeymooning at Acapulco, Mexico. As a bachelor congressman he sailed in Washington's tidal basin with Ted Reardon. Jacqueline Bouvier was courted aboard his twenty-four-foot sailboat off Hyannis Port, and when the sea is right he likes to take off for hour-and-a-half cruises aboard *Honey Fitz* or *Marlin,* his fifty-two-foot motor cruiser, reading newspapers in the stern or watching the First Lady zoom by on water skis. Mention the island war and his eyes light up, although, curiously, it wasn't until after his inaugural that he learned his chief benefactor's identity. The coastwatcher had been the object of a search far more elaborate than that for 109's castaways. It ended when Evans, now a Sydney accountant, called an Australian newspaper. He was invited to Washington, where the President apologized for forgetting to return his Japanese rifle eighteen years before.

In that setting the reunion struck a mellow note. The marooning, in the words of a wartime hit tune, was long ago and far away. There seemed to be no connection between then and now. Yet the lieutenant of those distant days was very like the President of today. He has matured, of course. A 1945 photograph shows him being decorated for heroism by Captain Frederick L. Conklin, USN. In it the reserve lieutenant looks as unstarched as a beer jacket. The Commander in Chief of the 1960's is suaver. Nevertheless, during a similar ceremony he did drop Alan B. Shepard's medal, and despite his awesome office he suggests the mobility and unorthodoxy of youth. "You know, I still find it hard to believe that fellow is President of the United States," says a veteran Washington correspondent, shaking his head. People Kennedy's age often share this attitude. "For some reason, Mr. President, your living in the same house with Lincoln's bed impresses the hell out of me," one of his former roommates told him. Sometimes he himself appears to feel that way, and defers to older men when all men, regardless of age, should defer to him. After leading John Diefenbaker to a battery of television cameras outside the White House he told him, "Now you make your statement while I go back to the office and get your coat."

As a young man he was exceptionally boyish. When Red Fay reported to a PT training center at Melville, Rhode Island, in 1942, he found a group of men playing touch. Among them was a stripling who, he thought, was "a high school kid horning in on the game." Next day he learned the urchin was Jack Kennedy, his instructor. After his rescue of 109's crew the skipper was ordered to brief a new batch of sailors on the Solomons. Meeting them on Tulagi, he told them to stand around him in a wide circle. But they couldn't take this beanpole with bars seriously. The instant he started talking the boots crowded in, yammering questions until he gave up and said if there was ever anything he could do for them, just let him know. ("The worst mistake I ever made. They've been letting me know ever since.") Later, during his first years in the capital, he was joined by the Kennedy family cook, who tried to put some flesh on him. She failed; he became weedier and weedier, reminding some colleagues of Jimmy Stewart playing *Mr. Smith Goes to Washington*. Jack's habits didn't help. His brush-cut carelessly combed with a little Wildroot, he would slip into a sweatshirt, pick up a baseball glove or a football, and sally out looking for a game. One November day in 1949 his Melville comedy with Fay was reenacted. Representative Kennedy was watching a squad of real high school kids practicing. He borrowed a uniform and joined them, and none of the players noticed anything unusual. The coach asked one, "How's the congressman doing?" "Is that what they call him?" asked the boy. "He needs a lot of work, Coach. What year's he in?"

On the Hill a seasoned lobbyist continually addressed him as "laddie." Tourists mistook him for a college student with a patronage appointment, and one morning in an elevator a stranger murmured to him, "Fourth floor, please." These awkward incidents persisted during his first days in the Senate. According to a page boy, the new member of the upper house was waved away from a special phone. "Sorry, mister," a guard told him. "These are reserved for the senators." And when he tried to board a presidential train in Springfield, Massachusetts, he was thrown off by James J. Rowley — who is now chief of his Secret Service. The ejected young pol wasn't offended, though there were times when he thought he and the congressional page boys should swap jobs, he wryly confessed to the Washington *Times-Herald*'s Miss Bouvier.

The President tells these stories about himself. His wit is cool, merciless, and surprisingly impartial. Of course, he enjoys taunting adversaries most. To a group of businessmen he said, "It would be premature to ask your support in the next election, and inaccurate to thank you for it in the past," and on another occasion he compared his election to a Notre Dame-Syracuse football game which had been won with a disputed penalty, adding that "I'm like Notre Dame. We just take it as it comes along. We're not giving it back." But neither allies nor relatives are exempt. If

one is maladroit, heavy on his feet, or just heavy —
Salinger has a tendency toward what posture charts
call stocky — he is not allowed to forget it. A friend,
comparing their common backgrounds, suggested
that he and the President were pretty much alike.
Kennedy peered at him a moment. "You're not at all
like me," he said. "You walk like a duck." A lawyer
wrote him that his racket-busting brother would make
a better Chief Executive. He replied, "I have consulted Bobby about it, and, to my dismay, the idea
appeals to him." When Bobby hesitated to enter the
Cabinet, the President-Elect reassured him that "We'll
announce it in a whisper at midnight so no one will
notice it." Critics, noticing it and disapproving of it,
protested that the future Attorney General had never
tried a case in court. "I can't see that it's wrong to give
him a little legal experience before he goes out to
practice law," John Kennedy told Washington's Al-
falfa Club. Afterward the appointee came up and
told him that he didn't think that was very funny.
His older brother commented that he would have to
kid himself; people liked it. Nobody can handle a
Kennedy like a Kennedy. "Yes, but you weren't kidding yourself," Bobby pointed out. "You were kidding
me."

Like Lincoln, the President is a mild practical
joker — before his voice became renowned he liked
to call people up and pretend he was someone else —
with an instinctive gift for drollery. During a discussion of office-seekers with a Southerner, he came to

the name of another Southerner. The man had applied for the governorship of the Virgin Islands. "That
job usually goes to a Negro," he pointed out, "and he
isn't a Negro." He paused. "Is he?" It was the President who first said of Ted Kennedy's senatorial primary race against Eddie McCormack, the Speaker's
nephew, that "We'd rather be Ted than Ed." That was
during his 1962 Gridiron Club speech, when he also
remarked, "I know my Republican friends were glad
to see my wife feeding an elephant in India. She gave
him sugar and nuts. But of course the elephant wasn't
satisfied." The same evening he plunged a long
needle into both Arthur Krock and the capital's all-
white Metropolitan Club — "Krock criticized me for
not letting President Tshombe of Katanga come here,
so I told him we would work out a deal. I'll give
Tshombe a visa and Arthur can give him a dinner at
the Metropolitan Club."

Fred Holborn of the White House staff thinks the
Presidency has improved Kennedy's wit: "It used to
be rehearsed. Now it's sharper, more spontaneous,
less derivative. And ceremonies bring it out at its
best, because he likes to poke fun at rituals." Unable
to attend a testimonial luncheon for the Postmaster
General, the President sent a graceful apology and
added the postscript, "I am sending this message by
wire, since I want to be certain that this message
reaches you in the right place and at the right time."
In Wisconsin he was made honorary chieftain of an
Indian tribe. Donning his headdress he said, "Next

time I go to the movies to see cowboys and Indians, I'll be with us." Paying tribute to Clark Clifford for his services during the transitional period between the election and the inauguration, he announced that Clifford hadn't requested any reward — "all he asked in return was that we advertise his firm on the backs of the one-dollar bills."

His eye for the ridiculous also sharpens during crises. As the returns seesawed on election night 1960, he received a long distance call from Lyndon Johnson in Texas. His anxious staff awaited his version of the vice-presidential nominee's words. It was: " 'I hear *you*'re losing Ohio, but *we*'re doing fine in Pennsylvania.' " At the climax of the Cuban misadventure, Kennedy bipartisanship was embarrassed when Stewart Udall appeared on an ABC panel show and attributed the landing to Eisenhower planners. Afterward he was summoned to a phone. The White House was calling. Reportedly the President's first words were, "Which of us does not make mistakes?" The trouble with the status quo in Berlin, Kennedy has complained, is that there is too much quo and not enough status. And at the crucial moment of his Solomons feat — his deliverance from starvation — he was in top form. PT-157 raced in to meet him, recognition shots were exchanged, and a voice called, "Hey, Jack!" "Where the hell have you been?" he answered. "We've got some food for you," he was told. "No thanks," said Shafty. "I just had a coconut."

Those who assume that banter means indifference should reflect on his circumstances that night. He was emaciated, exhausted, and lacerated by coral wounds. If he had lacked pluck there would have been no rendezvous with PT-157. "The big thing that came out in Kennedy that week was his drive," Barney Ross says. "I knew it was useless for him to swim out in the water that first night. You couldn't stop him, though. He didn't make a federal case out of it, but there it was. He just had to find a way back. And then, when we were picked up, he couldn't wait to get another boat. Everything was go, go, go with him. If it had been up to the rest of us, we would've been content to sit there and wait to be rescued." Unaware that they had been written off, the crew thought Navy PBY's must be scouting the area, and with enemy troops all around — a barge of Japs passed within a few hundred yards of their first beach — Kennedy's island-hopping seemed an invitation to trouble. Eventually they realized that his go, go, go had saved them. Abandoned in hostile waters, he had driven himself as though the destiny of the United States were his personal responsibility. Today it is: and there is a connection.

The most humdrum wartime chore was a big one for him. "Very willing and conscientious," the Navy described him in his first promotion report, and he never gave cause for retraction. In training an ensign missed the boat one day, and the laggard has a vivid recollection of how "the future President gave me the worst chewing out of my life — demanding to know where I'd been, asking me where the country would be if everybody in the Navy doped off that way, practically telling me I'd lost the war." On routine cruises in the Solomons Kennedy kept telling his crew, "Let's get more speed." The hull couldn't move fast enough for him. He couldn't bear the thought that 171, say, or 162 might outrev 109. Once he decided to beat another boat home at all costs. There was a rule about running down docks, but Jack the nimble — still not minding — took a chance his engines would reverse, lost the chance, and shahfted the pier. He had to be first. That was his style, that is his style. Through the years the same note of urgency has recurred. On his way to nominate Stevenson in 1956 he kept clenching his right fist and whispering to himself, "Go!" Campaigning in the 1960 West Virginia primary, he would snap his fingers at red lights, muttering, "Let's go." After Nixon's concession that fall his first words were, "All right, let's go," and when the First Lady publicly embraced the President after a trip abroad he blushed and then growled at his chauffeur, "Let's *go!*"

Each time he was going somewhere different. The important thing was to get there, to have a goal and reach it. There has been hardly a moment when he wasn't drawing a bead on a target — on Yale, on Tojo, on a domestic or foreign competitor. An exception was the morning of November 9, 1960. He was probably President-Elect, but it wasn't official. After breakfast he took a stroll along the Cape Cod beach, and to Ted, who walked with him, he remarked that for a few days there would be nothing to do, no decisions to make — no place, in short, to go. Taking a break was an odd experience for him. His sense of purpose dates back to his childhood, when he named his first sailboat *Victura,* explaining vaguely that it meant "something about winning." In prep school he was voted most likely to succeed, not because Joe Kennedy was rich — that cut no ice at Choate — and certainly not for his dead C scholarship, which, as his father has pointed out, probably wouldn't admit him to Harvard today. He was most likely because he was most eager; because, in Joe's words, "He's always been a fighter." Unable to win a letter in anything, Jack was nevertheless active in hockey, baseball, and football. "He was much too light for the big teams," his Choate roommate remembers, "yet he was always out there." Kennedy's own verdict on those featherweight years gives some inkling of their stubborn sweat: "I wasn't a terribly good athlete, but I participated."

His love of participation for its own sake has been noted even by those who aren't convinced that he is a terribly good President. "He did everything around here today but shinny up the Washington Monument," James Reston wrote from Washington in the late winter of 1962, "and it was obviously too cold and icy for that." If something is happening, Kennedy wants it to happen to him: "I can't hold back the stops. I have to go flat out, all out." In the 1950's one of his friends was working for the Emerson Drug Company in Baltimore. The company wanted to give its executives a speed reading course, but was two short of the number needed for a special class. The friend called Washington, and the quorum was filled by Jack and Bobby, who also likes to be in on things. "The fact that one was a United States Senator and the other was busy with the McClellan Committee didn't matter," the friend says. "They couldn't pass up a chance for self-improvement." The Kennedys commuted regularly from Washington, and Jack was not only active; this time he won his letter, with twelve hundred words a minute.

For him the Baltimore course was a natural. It was emulous, it was cerebral and, most important, it increased his velocity. As Ross noted, the word for him is Go. In the White House his appurtenances include the two cabin cruisers, a helicopter, a fleet of high-powered automobiles, and four private jets, all of which he uses. From his first days as a freshman congressman he was known as "the young man in a hurry." If there wasn't an office available, he campaigned just the same, driving through the night to address lodge meetings and subsisting on cheeseburgers and malted milk. Representative Kennedy was stumping western Massachusetts three years before he stood for the Senate; Senator Kennedy was barnstorming the nation three years before his election to the Presidency, and to hie him forth he acquired his forty-passenger Convair — the new *Victura*. Although he admired Jacqueline Bouvier the first time he met her, there was a period of six months in their courtship when he didn't even have time to see her. Now and then he would call her from some pay phone, "with," as she has put it, "a great clinking of coins," but there were no love letters, unless you count the postcard she showed their wedding party. It was the only message she had ever received from her intended, and the total text read, *Wish you were here. Jack.* Friends have observed that after Caroline identified her mother, the first words she learned — "Daddy," "airplane," "car," "shoe," "hat," and "thank you" — included at least three denoting motion. The senator's vim fascinated and bemused his bride. Playing Monopoly in Hyannis Port, she sometimes grew drowsy and deliberately blundered to get the thing over with. "Does Jack mind?" she was asked. She smiled. "Not if I'm on the other side."

He tired of Monopoly, as he later tired of bridge, Chinese checkers, backgammon, and The Game. They weren't getting him anywhere, and he can't bear to waste time. The President, a friend says, "thinks of words as the shortest distance between two points." A man who puts things in a nutshell wins his respect. A rambler loses. In private Kennedy will talk for hours, "but only," as a Harvard adviser puts it, "if there is real Ping-pong in the conversation." One Administration appointee brought a big reputation to Washington. He had intellect, insight, and experience, yet his stock kept falling because he lacked concision. He talked on and on until he found himself transferred to a new job, with the White House out of earshot.

Kennedy doesn't like to be held up by a windbag, a red light, or, for that matter, by his own body. Life among the Melanesian savages didn't reduce his impatience with his own infirmities. It merely made him frailer — and more intolerant of his frailty. In Blacklett Strait the disc between his fifth vertebra and his sacrum was ruptured. Navy surgeons had patched up his back with a metal plate, but the hole over it didn't close. V-J Day found him no better. When the lights went on again all over the world he was hollow-cheeked, sciatic, malarial, and Atabrine-yellow, and his weight had fallen to one hundred and twenty-five pounds. He wasn't really in shape for sailing, let alone a political scrimmage. So he entered, and won, that first wide-open congressional race.

Despite hot baths, couches, and rocking chairs, his spine grew worse, and at his wedding there was real doubt over whether he would be able to kneel at the altar. He knelt. Somehow he was always able to make that extra effort, suppress the pain, and carry things off. In his senatorial campaign against Lodge he was feverish, scarcely able to move without crutches. Not many voters knew it, because when the time came to enter a hall he would thrust his props aside and manage without them — "how," a friend who was with him later remarked, "I'll never know." Jim Reed was then living in Longmeadow, Springfield's blue-chip suburb, and they would meet on Kennedy's western swings. Reed remembers that "he'd stand through endless receptions, and give a speech afterward, and after the speech we'd have a bull session in Springfield till midnight, and *then* he'd drive back to the Cape. I couldn't have done it — and I didn't have a bad back." Yet this couldn't go on forever. Something had to give, the senator or his health. Two years later physicians gave him a choice: either invalidism or spinal fusion surgery with, at best, a narrow chance of survival. He punched his crutches. "I'd rather die than spend my life on these things," he said. He received the last rites, went through two operations, hovered on the dark edge, and then recovered at his father's Palm Beach house.

Jack the quick couldn't just lie there. He had to climb back on the ball somehow. During an earlier illness he had taken advantage of the occasion by quizzing the staff about medical aspects of legislation — "a doctor told me F.D.R. shouldn't have run for that fourth term," he recalls, explaining his vote for the constitutional amendment which limits his own White House tenure to eight years. In Florida his throbbing vertebrae wouldn't permit him to doze for more than an hour or so. He tried painting landscapes, but that wasn't really getting him anywhere, so he began using the sleepless nights to improve his mind. Sometimes he studied. A PT shipmate who visited him during his convalescence remembers that he would read two hours at a time, making notes on a clipboard and spending fifteen or twenty minutes at the end of a session memorizing what he had written. "I saw him again two or three months later," the shipmate says, "and I asked him about some of those notes. They came out in a torrent." Other times the patient used his clipboard as a crude desk. Arthur Krock, another bedside visitor, watched him, "strapped to a board, with another board on top of him, writing *Profiles in Courage*." Most sick men would have been content to wait — as 109's crew had wanted to wait — for external forces to deliver them. Few would have attempted to produce a book, and fewer would have brought it off. Pulitzer judges notwithstanding, *Profiles* is not brilliant history. The really singular thing about the book is that it was written at all.

Not everyone finds Kennedy's grit engaging. Some think it relentless, inhuman. His ambition is so very naked; they wish he'd camouflage it a little. After he picked his 1960 running mate he was asked by Adlai Stevenson, whose intentions are not nearly as conspicuous, why he had chosen Johnson. The candidate laid it on the line in five crisp words: "Because I want to win." To win he will go any distance. During a campaign telethon a rural woman called and asked him to do something about her roads. A travesty of diction followed. Kennedy couldn't understand her; he thought she was saying "rugs." "I really don't know what the President of the United States could do about your rugs," he said in exasperation. After the program, when someone solved her dialect, he wanted to call back and explain. It was a small stake, one vote, but the small stakes added up. In Reston's opinion, "The man is a calculating machine, with springs. He seems wound up and full of controlled nervous energy."

Early in his Administration Kennedy remarked that he had only four years in which to make good — an odd observation, and a revealing one. He is fighting the clock as well as the Russians, which explains his long hours, his gibes at pomp, and his repeated murmuring, at pointless functions, "Let me out of here." Once he feels he has extracted the last measure from a White House interview, he swings out of his rocking chair and lands on his feet. It is an effective gesture. The President is standing, so his visitor must stand, too, and one senses that the motion, in itself, gives him a sense of exhilaration. His wardrobe reflects this passion for activity. In cut and color it is appropriate for a chief of state, but in weight it is almost collegiate. Kennedy rejects apparel which would slow him down. He has few vests or hats, only one topcoat, and no overcoat at all. "The President," his tailor explains, "has steam heat instead of blood."

At year's end, as the Chief Executive darted about wintry Washington in light kit — there were just three years left to make good now — an elderly patient lay in room 355 of Palm Beach's St. Mary's Hospital, not far from the home in which *Profiles in Courage* was conceived. Richard Cardinal Cushing called and told him he would get well. The ambassador's stroke had affected his speech, but he made himself reply, "I . . . know . . . I . . . will." It was a promise. Within a month he was walking, reading, and watching television, and by April he could greet the President at the airport. The swiftness of that partial recovery shows that John Kennedy hasn't the only strong constitution in the country. Indeed, there is a clear relationship between the older man's vigor and his son's. Because Joe had spirit, he raised a spirited family. "Everything begins in childhood," he said in 1961. "If a boy runs off to play in a jazz band" — his expression revealed how horrible an example he thought that was — "there's something in that family that's wrong, and it goes way back." Way back in the early 1930's he was goading his sons. If young Joe and Jack lost a sailboat race, his rage was a caution; the only way to avoid it was to win. And victory was tangible, it was secular. In many large Catholic families a son goes into the priesthood and a daughter becomes a nun. Bobby and one of his sisters considered devoting their lives to their religion, but their father was intent on things of this world. "Joe had a dynastic impulse," according to Arthur Krock. "He had to be the first Irish ambassador to Britain. He had to have a son become President of the United States. And, by God, he did it."

There can be little doubt that he meant to do it. In

the opening pages of *I'm for Roosevelt* he declared that "I have no political ambitions for myself or my children." The disclaimer is hard to credit. Questioned about it after his son's inauguration, he offered a curious annotation: "I wasn't thinking of the Presidency then. I just wanted them to be useful civic servants. If they'd become sheriffs or selectmen, that would've been O.K. with me." Sequiturwise, this was non. The idea of a Kennedy even starting on so low a level is preposterous. Nor could Joe have settled for that. Clearly he was a father of great expectations; Jack's schools were hardly those of an apprentice bailiff. The 1959 Gridiron Club show probably came closer to the truth when a character playing the ambassador sang:

All of us, why not take all of us?
Fabulous — you can't live without us
My son Jack heads the procession
Then comes Bob, groomed for succession. . . .

Since the procession reached the Executive Mansion, repeating jokes about it has become a national pastime. One wit predicted that "We'll have Jack for eight years, Bobby for eight, and Teddy for eight. Then it'll be 1984." In an apocryphal story the President pins a medal on John Glenn and says, "You're doing pretty well for someone who isn't in the family." Joe's proprietary attitude has encouraged this sort of thing; so many of his comments about the Kennedys have been laced with *I-my-me*. Of Ted's impending Senate candidacy he said, "We aren't ready to announce that yet," and he confided to this writer that he found the President's first State of the Union address evocative of *I'm for Roosevelt*, though a comparison of the two texts was unrewarding. Later that day, strolling across Manhattan, he declared, "Bobby's the best Attorney General since Stone," and then paused, nodding significantly. Only later did his visitor recall that Attorney General Harlan Fiske Stone went on to become Chief Justice of the Supreme Court, and that conceivably the ambassador may have envisaged family leadership in all three branches of the government. Asked whether this was farfetched, an acquaintance of the Kennedys' said slowly, "I don't know. He *is* greedy."

Joe has never thought of himself as greedy. His attitude has been that America made him rich, and that he has been repaying the debt by contributing his children's gifts to the country. The ambassador-to-be began instilling a Samaritan sense in the civic-servants-to-be while they were babes and he was still battling in the market place. Money wasn't considered a fit topic for familial dinner conversations. "Big businessmen are the most overrated men in the country," he told them. "Here I am, a boy from East Boston, and *I* took 'em. So don't be impressed." Instead they argued about current events. "I raised them to be active in public service," he said proudly when the procession was fanning out across Washington, "and every one of them is. Every one of my sons-in-law, too. All except Peter Lawford." (Mr. Lawford, who married the President's sister Pat, is an actor.)

Lem Billings has vivid childhood memories of the Kennedy's family table. "It wasn't like any other dinner table," he recalls. The children had to be in their places five minutes early, and "the father kept the conversation on a high level. If you didn't talk about world affairs, you just didn't talk." Billings's conclusions would have surprised the ambassador, however. "Joe Kennedy likes to project a hardheaded image," he says. "Actually he's one of the most emotional people I've ever known. I think he didn't want his love for his children to overwhelm them, and talking about impersonal matters was one way to avoid it." Whatever the reason — dynastic impulse, patriotism, a surfeit of affection — a gauntlet was flung on the table, and each child lunged for it. Jack Kennedy's youthful devotion to the New York *Times* was one answer to the challenge. Virtually all of them became highly articulate in their teens; young Joe argued confidently with Harold Laski, and Kick Kennedy could logomachize with Winston Churchill. An exception was Bobby. His youth kept him seated down among the girls, outclassed, subdued. But little brother was down there watching, and in manhood, after a score of public speaking courses and countless evenings in front of mirrors, he untied his tongue. Bobby paid a price for this unleashing. In a glib family his delivery seems harsh, almost metallic. Teddy didn't face the forensic obstacle, because when he reached adolescence the big debaters had graduated. "By the time I was old enough to join in, there wasn't even a ban on talking business at the table," he says. "It wasn't necessary any more. These other things just seemed more important." Ted had another problem, though. As a Harvard freshman he found himself falling behind the standards set there by his three brothers, so he cheated. His subsequent suspension caused, as he delicately calls it, paternal "unhappiness." Two years later Ted entered Harvard again, and this time he went the distance. Joe's family script had made no provision for failure.

The ardor with which the Kennedys followed their father's lead has impressed even him. On the eve of his illness, before son-in-law Stephen Smith left the State Department to handle family affairs in New York, he wondered aloud whether he had gone too far. "I wish I'd saved *one* boy for the business," he said. "Here I am, seventy-three and I could drop dead any minute, and I have to keep working because they're in these other things." At the same time, he speculated about the parental role in shaping children. Perhaps, he reflected, it had been exaggerated. Barring business absences, he had been as attentive as a father could be, and certainly his wife was a devoted mother. Yet he wasn't at all certain that was the explanation: "Don't ask me what we did to make them this way. I don't know. Sure, I could give you some pat answers, but I've thought about it a lot, and I can't think of a single thing we tried that some of my friends haven't tried with very different results. If I knew what it was, I'd bottle it and sell it." He kept returning to one notion, though. "Competition — that's what makes them go. They're all competitive, including the girls. In fact, Eunice has more drive than Jack or even Bobby."

His daughter Eunice is the wife of R. Sargent Shriver, director of the Peace Corps. One Saturday she, Jean Smith, and Ethel Kennedy stopped by the White House for a swim in the pool. Afterward they decided to poke around the residential apartment, looking at new paintings. They thought the first family was in Virginia, so they went through the bedrooms, too, and in the last of them they discovered (and awakened) the President of the United States. The visitors can't be blamed. Presidents must nap, but it's something new for this calisthenic family. The Kennedys are what is known as vigorous stock. They will compete with anybody, in any field. Some of the in-laws have just as much moxie as the charter members — when Ethel picked up Marian Anderson for a concert, she entertained her by singing to her in the car — and the sisters, like their brothers, are fierce contenders in the tribal gymkhanas of touch, tag, and kick-the-can. Sex is not recognized as a handicap, nor is age. No holds are barred for women and children; everybody plays for keeps. Jacqueline made a ladylike retirement from lawn sport only after she had hurt an ankle, and Red Fay, returning to the Pentagon after a joy-through-strength weekend on the Cape, said grimly, "Of course, I know what they were really trying to do. They were trying to kill the old redhead." Hyannis Port games can be rougher than anything, including McCarthyism. The late Senator McCarthy wasn't even in their softball league. Once when he was visiting the ambassador they tried him at shortstop and then benched him. He had made four errors.

Fratricidal touch, as the world knows, is their specialty. They even have family-league touch trophies. There always seems to be an inflated football around somewhere — the day the country voted their top player into the White House he was flipping one around with Bobby and Teddy. As Harvard freshmen all the boys played end, a position requiring stout hearts. Jacqueline excepted, all hale members of the family are either passers or pass receivers today. John Kennedy and John Unitas are probably the two most famous quarterbacks in the country, and Kennedy, like Unitas, has thrown the long gainer on many memorable occasions, including Pearl Harbor Day. One published account has it that he spent the afternoon of December 7, 1941, in Griffith Stadium, watching the Redskins upend the Philadelphia Eagles, but according to Billings, who was with him, they were playing touch. Donning old clothes, they had driven downtown looking for a pickup game. After a fierce scrimmage with strangers around the Washington Monument, they headed home and heard the Pearl

Harbor bulletin on the car radio. Kennedy's first reaction was "to get into something." Though he was already in naval intelligence, that didn't count. It was
too much like being a spectator, he said. He might
not make a terribly good combat officer, but he still
wanted to participate.

The day of his wedding photographers were agog
to see deep scratches on his face. It wasn't anything
serious. He had merely toppled out of bounds and
into a bed of roses the day before. Secret Servicemen
were similarly startled when the new President-Elect
celebrated his election by joining an internecine family fray, calling signals for one squad while Bobby
(who won) led the other. In the months that followed
John Kennedy kept this up, and nobody knew quite
so well how to frighten Dr. Travell. Since then she
has sidelined him, but he was a great star. Playing
golf one day he learned that the country club's assistant pro had been a gridiron flash. Fishing the
ubiquitous football from a car trunk, he offered to
take him on. The pro teamed up with a rangy caddie,
Kennedy with a friend. The first side with three
touchdowns was to be the winner. "He threw three
perfect strikes to me," says the friend, who spent most
of his time in the makeshift end zone. "That gives you
some idea what kind of a touch football player the
President is. What's more, I dropped one, so he
pitched me a fourth." The final score was J.F.K., 18;
Pro, 0.

Woodrow Wilson, brooding over the strains of office, reflected that future generations would be obliged to pick their Presidents from the ranks of "wise and prudent athletes." Several athletes had preceded him; Teddy Roosevelt wasn't himself unless he'd had a brisk workout, and John Adams liked his swims in the buff. President Kennedy, however, has recruited a whole string of athletes. Sorensen's adoption of Kennedyisms includes a fondness for touch; McNamara plays squash Saturdays; Udall climbs mountains and, now and then, trespasses on private property and gets bawled out. Edward R. Murrow, who detests the strenuous life himself, calls it the "new zeal" Administration. It is a better team, in the literal sense, than anything Eisenhower could have put into the field. Among the inaugural starters were Udall (Arizona basketball ace), Secretary of Agriculture Orville Freeman (Minnesota varsity quarterback), Ken O'Donnell (Harvard football captain), former Deputy Attorney General — now Associate Justice — Byron "Whizzer" White (Colorado All-American), and, of course, the Attorney General, who played for the Cantabs and still keeps in shape despite the outrage of Jimmy Hoffa, who protested that Bobby's sporty manner of dress was undignified and was ruining this country's reputation abroad.

The President himself, though sedentary now, isn't quiescent. His key is still C major. In his own restless way he is exercising all the time. A reporter observed that he "never sits in a chair; he bivouacs in it." Two White House chairs have collapsed under the stress.

Once he capsized a swivel job — dumping himself on the floor — and on another occasion an antique blew up under him. It happened spectacularly, in the middle of a conference with congressional leaders. One moment he was fidgeting away, and the next moment there was an explosion, a hail of ancient splinters, and a loud thump as the Chief Executive sprawled at the feet of his astonished Vice President.

Perpetual motion has become a Kennedy signature, like Bourbon hemophilia or Borgia toxcity. Gore Vidal knew the ambassador's nine children when they were young. "I couldn't keep them straight," he remembers. "They were always running around like so many wirehaired terriers." "Whenever Teddy poked his head out the door," another friend of the family has remarked, "Jack would hit him with a pillow." With their father often away on deals and nine of them battling for the mother's attention, confusion was inevitable. Occasionally the family itself became muddled. To keep her children's medical and dental histories straight, Rose Fitzgerald Kennedy had to maintain a card index, and when she took them to the beach they had to wear identical bathing caps so she could keep track of them by counting heads. "The first time I remember meeting Bobby," the President has said in all seriousness, "was when he was three-and-a-half, one summer at the Cape."

When old Joe wasn't there, young Joe would act as a sort of deputy father. Being Kennedys, his brothers and sisters naturally vied with him, and intramurally his greatest rival was Jack, the next oldest. Over the years they fought the fiercest series of duels in the Kennedy record books; Bobby can still recall quailing with the girls while his big brothers slugged it out. "He had a pugnacious personality," the President has said of young Joe. "Later on it smoothed out, but it was quite a problem in my boyhood." In his late teens he still hadn't forgotten it. He picked Princeton partly because his brother had followed their father to Harvard, and though Jack changed his mind the next year, when the ambassador offered them trips abroad they went in opposite directions.

Yet while Jack defied young Joe, he also revered him. After the elder brother's death, those who knew him best — classmates, fellow officers, the family, and such friends of the family as Arthur Krock — contributed to a memoir, *As We Remember Joe.* Jack planned the book and selected as the envoi the lines from Maurice Baring: ". . . Our grief shall grow. For what can Spring renew/More fiercely for us than the need of you." The Kennedys instinctively compare scores in every activity; Bobby and Teddy followed Jack into the International News Service, and the ambassador has observed with a chuckle that "They even got married about the same time." But their sibling rivalry is only one side of the coin. The other face is a fierce tribal loyalty. Let one of them be threatened and the others hulk up, knuckles whitening. In pass patterns Bobby has no friends, he is all knees and elbows. Nevertheless he is the second man in the government today because, as one member of the kitchen cabinet explains it, "The President just naturally turns to him when he wants someone he can trust absolutely. This cuts across all lines; he will consult Bobby, not only on Justice affairs, but on any matter of importance." Joe's speculations notwithstanding, that feeling of kinship seems to be the natural outgrowth of continual parental supervision. That supervision did not stop when the brood achieved full growth. To the older Kennedys, the President's generation continued to be "the children"; Teddy, while an Assistant District Attorney and the father of two children of his own, remained "the baby." In the 1960's Rose and Joe persisted in vigil over what they still regarded as their nest. Perhaps Ted appeared on a Boston television channel and looked plump. In Hyannis Port they broke out the calorie charts and fired one off. Or perhaps the Attorney General of the United States was working too hard. He looked drawn. Georgetown began to gossip about it. Meanwhile, back at the ranch, his parents were already plotting to lure him away for a long weekend.

None of the boys has been watched more closely than young Joe's former sparring partner. Jack's arrival in postwar Washington was closely followed by the arrival of his mother, who wanted to check his rooms, and despite the separations from his father during his youth, Joe wrote him regularly, giving him pep talks via mail, lecturing him, and prodding him to improve his marks. When Jack was turning his Harvard thesis into a publishable manuscript — which he dedicated to his mother and father — the ambassador served as a second editor. From London he bombarded him with critiques,* and one of his passages appeared, almost intact, in the final version. In 1952 he was still exhorting him, this time egging him on against Henry Cabot Lodge, Jr.: "When you've beaten him, you've beaten the best. Why settle for something less?" Appointing Bobby as his campaign manager, Jack said wryly, "If I need somebody older there's no need to go outside the family. I can always get my father."

The ambassador would have been delighted. Unfortunately the appointment was out of the question. As the procession came out of the backstretch and approached the White House, Joe was obliged to withdraw into the background. For him this was an extremely difficult maneuver, but it was politic. Too many people remembered the years when he seemed to be an American Firster. He couldn't shut up entirely. Now and then he could be heard rumbling behind the scenes like a dormant volcano — "Not for chalk, money, or marbles will we take second place,"

* "You would be surprised how a book that really makes the grade with high-class people stands you in good stead for years to come," he wrote his son that summer. In April, 1961, Richard Nixon called on President Kennedy, who told him, in Nixon's words, that every public man should write a book "both for the mental discipline and because it tends to elevate him in popular esteem to the respected status of an 'intellectual.'" The visitor went off to write *Six Crises,* which shows how far Joe Kennedy's arm can reach.

he growled when it was suggested that his son settle
for the Vice Presidency in 1960 — but most of the
time he stayed put. His attitude toward entangle-
ments abroad hasn't changed much. As the father of
the Chief Executive he continued to be against foreign aid, and he confided that he thought trying to
hold Berlin was "a bloody mistake." Long ago he and
his most distinguished son agreed to disagree privately; there was little point in headlining their differences. After Jack's election to the Senate the ambassador would visit Washington just six hours a year,
stopping off on his way north from Palm Beach to
lunch with Krock, and between the installation of the
new Administration and his disability nearly a year
later he spent just one afternoon in the White House.

That doesn't mean he and his son aren't close. They
are, very. Joe played a quiet but valuable campaign
role in New York, New Jersey, and in Cook County,
Illinois, where he has heavy holdings. During the
Los Angeles convention he lurked nearby in Marion
Davies's Beverly Hills mansion; only after the issue
had been decided did he fly East, to watch, with
Henry Luce, Jack's acceptance on television. After
the election, father-son conversations eventually led
to the President-Elect's two most important Cabinet
choices, Dean Rusk and Robert McNamara, and the
emotional bond remained strong. When Bobby
phoned that the ambassador had been stricken, John
Kennedy was visibly affected. Hanging up, he told
an aide in a heavy voice, "Dad's gotten sick." The

stroke interrupted an extraordinary presidential relationship. Until then the two had kept in almost
constant touch by long-distance telephone. Joe had
made a good sounding board, perhaps because the
echo was so loud, and the President had called him as
many as a half-dozen times a day, to argue, as they
once did across the dinner table, about current events.

Under the unwritten rules of American politics it's
not sporting to have an influential father. All relatives
of officeholders are eyed dubiously. Blood lines are
supposed to stop at the White House door. The ideal
candidate is born in a Lincoln hut and orphaned as a
child, after which he makes his way upward through
snow and ice bearing a banner with the strange device *Ad astra per aspera,* or just *Per se.* In reality,
these are the men who become sheriffs and selectmen. Most Presidents have families. Even Lincoln
had one—*Dear Abe, I Received your Little check
for 50.00 I shoed it to Mother She cried like a child,*
read a letter which Dennis Hanks sent to 1600 Pennsylvania Avenue — and two Lincoln kin requested,
and were granted, presidential patronage. No Kennedy needs a Little check for 50.00. This President's
connections are better fixed than that one's were,
which would have been bad had he abused his
position on the way up. He didn't, unless campaign
financing is admissible evidence, in which case a
great many public men must stand in the dock. The
only time he openly curried favor was when he de-

cided to exchange stateside Navy duty for the sea, the Solomons, and the grimy cockpit of PT-109.

The father, in turn, might be indicted if he had tried to use his patriarchal power to dominate his son. Here the verdict is Scotch: not proven. Joe is undoubtedly a patriarch, but he himself took steps to counteract his own influence. He is an easy man to oversimplify, because he oversimplifies himself. His friendships with Hearst and Herbert Hoover suggest a stereotype, and then the stereotype disintegrates in the light of simultaneous ties with Jim Landis, Ben Cohen, William O. Douglas, and Tom Corcoran. He seems hidebound. Yet when his two oldest boys were still callow, he sent them to London to study under Harold Laski. Laski was a Socialist and an agnostic. In the ambassador's opinion he was also "a nut and a crank. I disagreed with everything he wrote. We were black and white. But I never taught the boys to disapprove of someone just because I didn't like him. They had heard enough from me, and I decided they should be exposed to someone of intelligence and vitality on the other side."

The exposure didn't take. Jack didn't turn pink, or even warm apricot. Defining his political hue has always been an exasperating task. The record reads any way you want it to read, depending on the tint of your own glasses. In one youthful letter he admired Italian fascism; in another he was critical of the Jesuits' role in Franco Spain. On Tulagi he argued that coconut plantation owners were entitled to compensation for trees damaged in the wear and tear of combat, a minority view at the time. Later, as a congressman, he became an enthusiastic supporter of Truman's domestic legislation — debating Taft-Hartley with young Nixon, and housing legislation with a still obscure Senator McCarthy — while he followed the G.O.P. line abroad on Yalta, Red China, and Owen Lattimore. He opposed Point Four, then circled the world in 1951 and decided to support it. He denounced the leaders of the American Legion as mossbacks and fought loyalty oaths, yet his record on anti-Communist witch-hunting was murky. His dedication to the Hoover Commission was so obvious, and his demands for economy in government so vehement, that many Massachusetts Republicans left their party to back him against Lodge. Later, as a presidential candidate, he sounded more like a Keynesian. Now, as President, he yearns, however vainly, for a balanced budget and has appointed Republicans to some forty sensitive posts in his Administration — meanwhile displaying rare courage in approaching the tariff nettle.

The Presidency subjects a man's past to dazzling light. "All the words he ever spoke or wrote, whether half asleep or wide awake, are exhumed and examined under circumstances to which they may no longer apply," Sidney Hyman wrote. Kennedy's critics have noted his public zigzags, and since he is not the only pungent politician, they have delivered some tart verdicts. One compared him to an elusive, light-weight, harum-scarum torpedo boat. A second suggested he show less profile and more courage. A third was reminded of Lord Bryce's opinion — cited in Allan Nevins's foreword to *Profiles* — that the American statesman "is apt to be timid in advocacy as well as infantile in suggestion." Kennedy himself has said of his early switch-hitting, "I'd just come out of my father's house at the time, and these were the things I knew." Unquestionably he was then aware of the ambassador's owlish eyes peering over his shoulder. Indeed, it can be argued that Joe felt quite safe in sending him to Laski, because he had already formed him. On the other hand, it may be held that sooner or later the cumulative effect of Harvard and European travel was bound to overwhelm the man who had made it all possible, and that, the President's academic friends are inclined to believe, is precisely what happened. According to them, the first stage of his career was a seesaw battle to free himself from his father's doctrines. In the mid-1950's, they contend, he severed the golden cord and became a liberal.

But he didn't become a Hubert Humphrey liberal. His brother Ted says that "He's a true liberal, approaching every problem with an open mind. How can you call a man a liberal if you can toss up a balloon and tell which way the wind's going to blow it for him?" It is true that the President seems quite free of prejudice. Unlike his father, he doesn't think of Jews as Jews, or call American Negroes "Lumumbas," or slight labor leaders. "Walter Reuther's wonderful," he told this writer when he discovered a common friendship there; "he's the last of the labor leaders with the old evangelical spirit." Nevertheless he can still sound the tory tocsin. Running across a magazine article critical of his Administration, he hurled it down and snapped, "What do these liberals want? Of course, I know. They want a deficit of seven billion dollars. Well, they should be happy. Berlin's going to cost us three and a half billion. That should bring enough pump-priming to satisfy them."

Harpoons from the left may hurt because he feels close to the harpooners. There is another explanation, however. Like many contemporaries, John Kennedy is impatient with all political gospels. Walter Lippmann, who seems to grow younger each year, spoke for the rising generation of Washington when he told the National Press Club that today "every truly civilized and enlightened man is conservative and liberal and progressive." Hardly anyone in the capital sounds the sectarian klaxons any more. They sound so flat, so meaningless. When the A.D.A. gives Thomas Dodd an eighty per cent liberal rating and barely passes William Fulbright with sixty per cent — these incredible scores were posted at the end of the first Kennedy year — A.D.A. shibboleths can no longer be treated seriously. Liberalism seems to belong to another time; perhaps in Spain of the early 1800's, when it first emerged under a party banner, as conservatism appeared in England thirty years later. "Liberal?

Conservative? I don't know what those labels mean," says Bobby Kennedy, shaking his head. The President himself hates to be pigeonholed. He prefers to quote Lincoln: "There are few things wholly evil or wholly good. Almost everything, especially of Government policy, is an inseparable compound of the two, so that our best judgment of the preponderance between them is continually demanded."

Asked what presidential label he expected to wear, Kennedy replied, "I hope to be responsible." He is an artist of the possible, an advocate of whatever will do the job. In his twenties he wrote that the British plan for Palestine seemed fair, and then added that justice wasn't enough; the need was for "a solution that will work." Searching for his own solutions in his forties, he follows no dogma, no dialectic, no theosophy. Carl Vinson once described him approvingly as "a practical young man," and one of the President's advisers says, "Actually he's always been a cautious politician." Yet he does like to get things done. To his wife he is an "idealist without illusions," which may be one way of calling him a pragmatist. The term isn't distasteful to him. "At least," he says, "we do things that work."

Like Jacqueline's historic curios, the belief that truth is tested by consequences finds its proper home in the White House. Despite its debt to British empiricism, pragmatism is an all-American philosophy. The word was coined by one Harvard man, C. S. Peirce, while another, William James, became the leader of the movement. William James would have enjoyed John Kennedy. They have more than ideas in common. James's health frequently failed him in his school years. During his youth his father's travels took the family to Europe, and that father — rich, ebullient, candid — had strong dynastic ambitions. It is of passing interest that the elder James fostered his paternal hopes by scorning business talk and encouraging lofty discussions at mealtimes, when he acted as moderator, teaching William, young Henry, and their fellow siblings how to debate. One family friend reported dinner arguments which grew so heated that the James boys brandished cutlery, but that sort of thing was unknown in the President's childhood. The Kennedys never used knives on each other. Joe would have thought it crude.

FIVE

Himself

THE PRESIDENT of the United States strides into the outer office, deftly skirts a spare rocker, and greets his visitor. It is now five months since the evening meeting which opened this book. John Kennedy is dressed as he was then, but his manner is much jauntier. The Administration's second winter is waning, and many of the burdens which seemed oppressive late in 1961 appear to be more tolerable. The Viet Cong are on the defensive, the American economy is strong, and censuring of military censorship has been discredited. At the moment the presidential mood is further boosted by a homely stimulant. It is a Saturday morning; at one o'clock he will join Jacqueline and the children for the weekend.

Yet as long as a Chief Executive remains here in the West Wing, it is the cockpit of action. Yesterday afternoon as the President talked with this writer his oval office was crisscrossed by aides. A door opened; Mac Bundy appeared with a dispatch. The knob turned again; Ted Sorensen was reporting. Saturdays should be quieter, but even now Evelyn Lincoln approaches.

"Yes, what's this?"

It is a document, it begs attention. He pauses to scan it and is, in that instant, framed against a background of framed photographs. The east wall, behind him, is a gallery of the great. There is one incongruity there. Among inscriptions from Harold Macmillan, Jawaharlal Nehru, and Douglas MacArthur — "with respect and admiration" — is a shelf bearing a gay piggy bank, a token of Caroline Kennedy's respect and admiration for Evelyn Lincoln. In a niche opposite are several snapshots of the donor. Like American bosses everywhere, the boss here enjoys displaying family memorabilia, and since he can't hang these prints in his own office he uses his secretary's.

The document read, the decision made, he leads the way into the oval office and closes the door.

The change is breathtaking. To an American no room in the world is so awesome. Partly this is a response to the Presidency — there can be no doubt where you are; the seal of the office is sculptured in the ceiling and repeated in the pattern of the gray rug below — and partly it is a submission to the spell of sheer beauty. The dimensions of the chamber are superb, appointments are exquisite, and the two wainscoted doors, when shut, blend into the wall, heightening the feeling of sanctum. Silence is absolute here; one thinks of a country estate, an illusion which is supported by the landscaping of the grounds outside. Looking out through the six French windows, each nearly twice as tall as a man, you see a vast reach of greenery and sky, and it takes a sharp eye to detect the unobtrusive White House policeman on the path beyond the rose garden. Today's sunlight is pale, lemon-colored. In another room it would be sickly, but filtered through the expanse of flawless glass it is almost streaming. Every detail of the office is clear: the naval paintings on the gently curving wall, the framed union jack, Commodore John Barry's sword, the ship model on the mantel, the intricate carving of the Victorian desk. Because of this light, and because all other tones are muted, the strong primary colors of the American and presidential flags are extraordinarily vivid, like those in an illuminated manuscript.

Flags and desk are at one end, the mantel at the other. On either side of the firescreen are facing sofas, slipcovered with a coarse beige fabric. Between them is a coffee table and the rocking chair. The President motions his visitor to the sofa on his right and sits in the rocker, facing the fireplace and cocking a foot on a slipcover. As though on signal his right hand begins to pluck absently at his tie. Then, as he talks, the hand drops to his knee, rises to stress a point, drops and rises again. His thoughts seem to come in rushes. He will comment; reflect briefly, as though weighing his own remarks; and then develop the comment. Very seldom does he avoid a topic, unless it involves security or — for the shield of reserve is always there — his privacy.

His conversation is versatile and, because of his penchant for detail, somewhat annotated. In a single meeting he deals with kinks in the balance of power, the Western Alliance, Asia, Africa, atomic testing, the Kremlin, the Eighty-seventh Congress. Domestic issues are broken down into automation, agriculture, medical care for the aged, the importance of being first in space, the difficulties of attracting gifted men to civil service, and, in an aside, the pleasant predicament of the bookies. Again and again he introduces the historical analogy, the Kennedy cachet: Vietnam is compared to postwar Greece, Berlin to postwar Austria, Korea to post-Punic War Rome, whose citizens were more sympathetic to police actions than twentieth-century Americans are.

It is an encyclopedic performance, and any writer who has condescended to climbers on the political ladder (while he himself has remained in journalism, which is more of a trampoline) is likely to feel a bit contrite. Occasionally the President's replies are vague, but he cannot be outfenced or outfoxed. Asked what he plans to do after his second term, he answers with a cagey grin that he doesn't yet know what he'll do after his *first* term. Then he concedes that "I was talking to Truman about this the other day," and — an example of the interviewee becoming the interviewer — he asks in turn, "What *do* ex-Presidents do?" Ex-President John Quincy Adams's return to the House of Representatives is mentioned, and his twenty-eighth successor swiftly points out, "Yes, but he made conditions. I doubt they'd be acceptable today."

Although a member of no party, Adams was appointed chairman of congressional committees, a practice which would be unthinkable now. Actually it is hard to say what would be acceptable in today's House. Thus far it has been a slough for John Kennedy. At times his legislative program has seemed to be an example of how to try in Congress without really succeeding. The President feels sanguine about the eventual fate of his big 1962 bills, and there are signs that the summer ahead may prove him right, but on the morning of this meeting the vote gap down the street is far more troubling than the missile gap he advertised in his campaign. Although he did secure housing, minimum wage, and foreign aid bills during the first session, he took more lumps than a honeymooning President should, and the second session opened with a barrage of rolling pins. Republicans claim that he is too clever. The real culprit seems to be the gerrymander, a pet of entrenched legislators and a monster to national leaders. Kennedy began his political career with faith in classical checks and balances, he being an entrenched congressman at the time. His yearning for a strong President came later, coincident with his yearning for the Presidency. In 1960 he called for strength, but the fickle public, while choosing him, decided at the same time to reject a score of representatives who would have seen things his way. He is a progressive President working with a Congress more conservative than Ike's. The early Sixties may, of course, mark the beginning of the end of diehard representation. With the Supreme Court ruling that urban citizens are entitled to appeal to federal courts if they aren't getting a fair shake from rural G.O.P. state legislatures, the character of those legislatures is expected to change. Since legislatures draw congressional districting lines, the House should change, too. But that lies far ahead. We are still in the season of the rotten borough. "Washington," John Kennedy once said lightly, "is a city of Southern efficiency and Northern charm." Rarely have the efficient Southern Democrats and the charming Northern Republicans dallied more successfully than in the first year of the Kennedy Administration. The spawn of the House womb was by Halleck out of Howard Smith, a union which proved to be exceedingly barren. The reactionaries, Reuther once charged, were "in bed together, hand in glove."

The President doesn't call it the do-nothing, good-for-nothing Eighty-seventh. He is, rather, unruffled. Joe Kennedy used to keep a sign on his desk reading,

After you've done your best, the hell with it. That, the ambassador maintained, "is the only sane point of view for any executive — including a Chief Executive." His son observes the legislative-executive tug-of-war with almost a bystander's curiosity. He ticks off the biases of individual congressmen and concludes, "There's nothing that can be done about a man from a safe district. He'll vote the way he wants to." The number of men straddling the fence at any given time is likely to be quite small. Of the five hundred and thirty-seven senators and representatives, less than a tenth are subject to persuasion on a vital bill. So the branches duel: "You've always had tension between the White House and the Hill," he says quietly, "and you always will."

What was, is; what is, will be. That is the Kennedy acceptance, the line of departure. He does not stop there, of course, but none of the changes he proposes would raze the frame we know. As he tots up world events since his inaugural, one is struck by his sense of historical continuity. The path he follows is illumed by familiar beacons at his back. His context is the world in being, which, to the jaundiced, means negativism, "no-win." If you pick your issues, you can build a case for that. On many fronts he is frankly defending the status quo. Thus the absence of a Laotian collapse is cause for cheer. The Congo chess game is going well, for there is a chance of stability and no American troops have been committed. The fact that the U.N. did not fall apart after Dag Hammar-

skjold's death inspires optimism, the Berlin wall is a
point for our side since it was a confession of Red
failure, and the Cuban carcinoma is less unsightly
now that more and more Latin Americans realize
Castro is a bad lot. No-win, in sum, is no-lose; they
also serve who only stand and wait.

To leave the President there, however, would be to
foul him. Every leader, even an insurgent, must fight
some holding actions. John Kennedy does not see
success in the absence of failure. He sees it where
Fourth of July orators used to say they saw it — in
the export of the American Revolution. For Kennedy there are no lesser breeds without the law; to
him our eighteenth-century seeds are still viable, and
sowable in almost any soil. He believes, as John Foster
Dulles did not believe, that newly free nations have
the right to true independence. Krishna Menon's manners are annoying but irrelevant; when neutral governments are rude the President doesn't go off and
sulk. He prefers to dwell on a conversation with
Nehru, who told him that while in prison during
World War II he received a message of encouragement from Franklin Roosevelt. Nehru treasures that
memory, John Kennedy thinks it a good thing he
does, and his program is designed to spread the same
encouraging light to other lands. He means to be-
friend them and help them, which, in a nutshell, is
the argument for long-term economic loans.

"We have this foreign aid fight every year," he says.
In the wan sunlight of this Saturday forenoon, the

Capitol again looms large; money bills must come out of the lower House, which the Constitution entrusted with the national cash register. And once more his tone is matter-of-fact, accepting. America's heritage is the American President's trust, though the modifications of nearly two centuries are as important to him as the words of the founding fathers. Reminded that James Madison favored congressional control over foreign policy, he shakes his head vigorously. "That would be unthinkable today. You couldn't have divided authority and still be free. Time has changed a great many things. The executive has grown so; the legislative branch looks to the executive for leadership. But there are also congressional institutions which were not anticipated by the founding fathers. For example, the seniority system was not foreseen." He rubs his knee. "The system does seem to work this way, and there seems to be an inevitability about it." Of his own Administration he holds that "My relations with Congress are satisfactory. They will continue to be satisfactory if I'm strong in the country."

Yet what kind of strength does the country want? President Kennedy is reminded of Senator Kennedy's concern about American flaccidity. He and the men around him pointed out that prosperous societies tend to sink into apathy. Those to whom much is given rarely feel the obligation to give anything in return; a nation glued to Huckleberry Hound cannot hear the audio of clarion calls. Machiavelli pointed out that it

was "necessary that Moses should find the people of
Israel slaves in Egypt and oppressed by the Egyp-
tians, so that they were disposed to follow him in
order to escape from their servitude." Machiavelli's
stark logic is unanswerable: no discontent, no Moses.
If a people lack any sense of oppression, what value
can a pragmatist find in their esteem?

Kennedy smiles. "Naturally a President must be
willing to lose some of his popularity. Far better that
than do as Coolidge did — go out in a blaze of glory
and leave a time bomb."

The President motions his visitor to remain. Opening a French window he stands by it a moment, enjoying the dank air; then, abruptly, he throws his shoulders back, revealing the blue *JFK* on his shirt. It is an
exuberant gesture, and as he returns to his rocker the
writer remarks that the Kennedy glory has never
blazed more brightly; the latest Gallup poll has given
him a favorable rating of eighty-two per cent. Does
he feel any sense of compassion for the plight of the
Republican party?

The President's reply is negative, and somewhat
salty. Indeed, he feels so little compassion that his
visitor feels obliged to explain. It can be argued that
the Republicans may eventually join such political
ghosts as the Know-Nothings, the Anti-Masons, the
Barnburners, and the Locofocos. This morning the
G.O.P. holds just sixteen of fifty governorships,
thirty-six of one hundred senatorial seats, 174 of 437

House seats. The voters are heavily Democratic; at last count fewer than two of every five preferred the minority party. Over the past three decades Republicans have controlled Congress for just four years — despite Eisenhower's appeal, three of his four congresses were led by the opposition — and the general was elected as a war hero, not as a party man. Omitting him, there hasn't been a Republican Chief Executive since 1933. For most of the last thirty years the history of the G.O.P. has been gloom and doom.

"I'll give *you* the history of the last *hundred* years." The right hand darts up. "Except for Roosevelt, the century has been dominated by Republicans. Who were the other Democrats? There was Cleveland. There was Wilson — who was reelected to his second term by one of the narrowest of margins. Truman's margin was tiny, too, and so was mine. A shift of a few votes in 1960 and they'd be in here. They can take any issue — Laos, South Vietnam — and try to ride it to the top. What throws the congressional figures off, and those of the state houses, is the Democratic South."

Still, there is that Galluping eighty-two per cent. The figure is both imposing and perplexing. Truman's margin dwindled sharply after his slender victory, but Kennedy is outscoring the idols, Roosevelt and Eisenhower; he even gets Pulliam fan letters from intransigent Republican Indiana. The President has pondered this, and pinching fingers he counts off what he believes to be the reasons for his prestige. "First there is the national respect for the Presidency. Formerly I was seen as a partisan figure and a Catholic. Now they see me as President. Second, my desires are those of most of the American people. Third, people sense that we face terribly difficult problems — the fact that after Cuba I took full responsibility, and that we haven't gotten into serious trouble, are factors here. Finally, I don't attempt to run the office on a partisan basis. Truman did; he could. I can't. I need support for the Common Market, for example, and in the Congo. That's more important than a partisan exchange. I have to have the Congress behind me. I can't alienate them."

Kennedy seldom alienates anyone deliberately, and that, the poll takers have found, is one reason for his appeal. At home he tries to avoid what he calls "a highly charged political position"; abroad he is correct and attentive, a sort of one-man listening post. Of the inscribed photographs in the next room he says, "Contacts with other chiefs of state don't alter the basic structure; they can't change a culture. They *do* make relationships easier. And they help you determine how events are going to go. A talk may not settle anything. Often it appears fruitless. But later you can make a more realistic judgment of reactions. In that sense even the Vienna meeting was useful, although it eased no tensions, because it permitted, at least on my part, a more precise estimate of Mr. Khrushchev's intentions."

Other Presidents could be swashbucklers, but "that

is no guide. There is no valid comparison with the past. Our era is even different from Truman's. In Truman's time we had the bomb, we were supreme. During the decade from '45 to '55 our relative power was so much greater. It wasn't until the last two years of Eisenhower's second term that the balance really shifted. This is something that every President from now on must face. Because the balance has changed, we're challenged in so many areas — in Laos, in Vietnam, in Haiti . . ." His hand opens slowly, suggesting a world of challenges. "We simply must reconcile ourselves to the fact that a total solution is impossible in a nuclear age."

Americans have been bred to think otherwise. Our history fosters the belief that we can do anything, and quickly, too. De Tocqueville found us the least philosophical of creatures. A few moral saws served us well enough. Our driving force has been an impatient energy — "We are," wrote Henry Wallace, "a people given to excesses." That ginger conquered the old frontier, and John Kennedy's let's-go version of it brought his own frontier to the Potomac. But the atom, Albert Einstein warned, requires a new way of thinking. Our ancestors' maxims already seem rather quaint. Davy Crockett's, about making sure you're right and then going ahead, is as useless as modern thrift plans are thriftless. The philosopher Glenn Gray suggests that we have abandoned pioneer morality and are groping toward something else, that Puritan notions of right and wrong are being replaced by a Hellenic sense of the fitness of things. And indeed, we do appear to be less interested in rectitude than in suitability; Panmunjom taught us that in war there really is a substitute for victory. The Air Force watchword — "The difficult we do immediately, the impossible takes a little longer" — is a relic of the pre-air age. The impossible is literally impossible now. More temperate slogans are suggested for the Sixties: Talleyrand's "Above all, no zeal," or Thucydides' "Men do what they can, and suffer what they must."

The John Birch Society doesn't intend to take this lying down. It has no relevance to Americanism as hundred per cent Americans know it. Birchers believe in standing tall and thinking big; they remember Valley Forge and the Alamo, and red blood courses through their veins. Lately they and their fellow rightists — Christian Crusaders, Circuit Riders, Liberty Lobbyists, National Indignation Rallies — have been enjoying a marginal vogue. The Cuban folly, like Britain's Suez fiasco, aroused votaries of good old-time patriotism. The clearer the new way of thinking becomes, the more the lunatic fringe frays; Pierre Salinger, who is as American as pizza, has actually been accused of being "the head of the Communist conspiracy in the United States." Each month new species of Americanists debouch from the woodwork with combat-ready tape recorders and advance grimly, denouncing the United Nations, the continent of Africa, and one another.

The President's response to these angry Americans

is typically rational. He merely observes that the world is complex and dangerous, that rightists yearn for simplicity and safety, and that they err. "Radical solutions won't work," he says, shifting in his chair, "but there is a gradual, evolutionary process. Events are moving all the time, whether or not we are aware of them. Take this dissension in the Communist system — the China split, Albania. We couldn't have predicted it, and here it is. In my judgment we should guide the right processes in a variety of ways. We are doing that by binding ourselves more closely to the Atlantic community in economic matters, by helping the United Nations build a world of free states that can maintain their freedom, and, in South America, through the *Alianza*. The *Alianza* is evolutionary, but in the long run it will add up to the same thing as a revolution." He rocks a moment. "There isn't any magic in it. Our purpose is to prevent the balance of power from swinging to the Communist bloc. You maintain your position and hope that eventually there will be enough fission in their society."

Really the Pro-Blues are a Republican problem — as Wallace, fourteen years ago, was a threat to Democrats. The money the ultras aren't contributing to G.O.P. campaigns is money they wouldn't have contributed to the New Frontier anyhow. Yet Kennedy's waiting game is also repugnant to enthusiasts in his own camp; the *Reporter* has been as glum as the *National Review*. There is this difference: Democratic idealists counted on more. Except for the Custer's

Last Stand Stevensonians, most Northern Democrats backed Jack in 1960. The intelligentsia, which is as vital to the Democratic party as industrialists are to Republicans, was jubilant at his triumph. Their expectations were at least as great as the Old Guard's had been in 1953. Kennedy, they noted approvingly, solicited the opinions of certified experts and listened attentively. Those who were close to him should have realized that meant nothing. In campaigns he often asked reporters' advice and rarely took it. But the intellectuals — including a number of newspapermen — soared above facts. Their man was in the White House, and they weren't going to let anything spoil the party.

Then came Cuba, the soggy blanket. Pig Bay shocked them. The rightists denounced the President for failing to provide air cover. The scholastics couldn't understand how he could have bought such a vulgar plan; Chet Bowles wouldn't have touched it. By summer they were rushing Cassandra assessments of the Kennedy Presidency to the printer. "Why?" Ted Kennedy asked in December. "The time to judge this Administration is three years from now." Ted was prejudiced, but he had a point. It seemed a trifle early to write his brother off. The crux of power is timing. For a politician, wrote the author of *Profiles in Courage*, "to decide at which point and on what issue he will risk his career is a difficult and soul-searching decision." Able leaders know how to wait, and when to strike. The greatest American Presidents have been better at landings than take-offs. Theodore Roosevelt and Woodrow Wilson didn't make their marks until their second terms, and at the end of Lincoln's first year his major accomplishments were the passage of the first Legal Tender Act and the total disruption of the Union.

Nevertheless, after Cuba the flak of criticism thickened. Joseph Rauh of the A.D.A. summed up the liberal position: "Compared to the high hopes we had, he's a bitter disappointment." The more Kennedy's Gallup percentage waxed, the more insistent were the demands that he convert it into achievement. How could he do it? He certainly couldn't convert it all. Apart from Franklin Roosevelt's first three months in the mansion, few Presidents have been able to bring the full weight of their prestige to bear upon events. Harry Truman snorted, "I sit here all day trying to persuade people to do the things they ought to have sense enough to do without my persuading them." Still, Truman managed to do a lot of persuading when, according to Gallup, only twenty-three per cent of the American people approved of him. As Kennedy entered his second year he wore the aura of a matinee idol, yet progress along his Frontier was spotty. "Certainly he's got the country going again," one presidential aide said defensively. "Look what Minow's done to TV programing." Examinations of the economy and the Atlantic alliance suggested a more favorable verdict than that, but the political scientists and the capital pros were unconsoled. At cocktail parties you heard worn jokes about "the third Eisenhower Administration," caustic digs at the President's brothers and brothers-in-law, complaints about lack of vision. Obviously Georgetown was disillusioned.

Georgetown was disillusioned, the public content. There was irony here. No one had understood the difference between general approbation and the sanction of experts better than candidate Kennedy; none had seen more clearly the justice in the professionals' laments. His own offices were peopled with men who had wrung their hands over Eisenhower apathy and craved leadership. Privately some of them have shared the disappointment of the cocktail circuit. This one blamed the legacy of events. That one thought the President's concept of national leadership was limited by his senatorial experience, that in press conferences he appeared to be unaware of the vast, unsophisticated audience of television eavesdroppers. A third brooded over America's mood, her sullen refusal to recognize her peril. "It was the best of times, it was the worst of times," wrote a parliamentary reporter named Dickens. "It was the spring of hope, it was the winter of despair, we had everything before us, we had nothing before us. . . ."

The President's liberal scolds were demanding unremitting boldness — as though boldness would convert Wilbur Mills, Jim Delaney, or Howard Smith — and they wanted plenty of gunsmoke. Many of them felt that he should have staked everything on thwarting John McCormack's yearning for the Speakership. He would have gained respect, they contended, even if he had failed. "That," a presidential adviser agrees, "was one time Kennedy would have fought if he'd thought he had a gambler's chance of winning." But there was no chance. Every congressional barometer indicated that he would have been certain to fail. The President's only achievement would have been a loss of face, and in politics there is no solace in defeat. So divorced from reality was the McCormack-shall-not-pass argument that its explanation must lie elsewhere. "The fact is, of course, that no successful President could satisfy the intellectual's longing for logical, uncompromising purity," a contributor to the *American Scholar* conceded. "In the White House, as in baseball, 'nice guys finish last.'"

Perhaps the key to the purists' disenchantment lies in their political weaning. Most of the reigning ideologues left their teens in the heyday of the New Deal. For them the name Roosevelt has a special magic; it lures them toward a sentimental journey into the past. We are accustomed to conservative necromancy. Both Eisenhower and Robert A. Taft, in different ways, attracted those who pined for a vanished America — for long shirttails, celluloid collars, flypaper, whalebone corsets, harvest home suppers, and the benevolent paternalism of the Cleveland Business Men's Marching Club. Today that longing has been matched by a liberal nostalgia, which winds its mournful horn in the breasts of those who look back with sad affection to the Great Depression, when they were children, and liberalism was a viable crusade, and Fala was alive, wagging his little tail.

"Of course there is a yearning for the Thirties," says the President, nodding vehemently. "It's only natural. Every generation remembers its youth." He cites an elderly Washington columnist who still laments the departure of Wilsonian idealism, and adds, "Perhaps in another ten years we'll have another period we hark back to. But nostalgia is particularly characteristic of the New Deal liberals right now."

He bears some responsibility for their hangovers. The all-out enthusiasm of J.F.K.'s first weeks — the late nights, the manic mood — and the influx of professors inevitably evoked memories of F.D.R., and at the outset the President encouraged reminiscence. He had announced that his first months would be patterned after the Hundred Days of 1933. Like Roosevelt he decorated his office with maritime mementos. Schlesinger, the New Deal historian, was brought into the government. The organization (or disorganization) of the White House took the press corps back a quarter-century; some of the older correspondents thought even Kennedy's mannerisms were like Roosevelt's. Washington took its cue accordingly. Vice President Johnson of Texas was compared to Vice President Garner of Texas, and it was duly noted that Benjamin Cohen, Thomas Corcoran, James H. Rowe, Jr., Abe Fortas, and Mrs. Anna Rosenberg, all old New Dealers, were advising Johnson. Carl Sandburg announced that Kennedy was "a little more like F.D.R. than any other President." The new Chief Executive's breakfasts in bed and his skimming of the morning papers were quickly tagged as Rooseveltian. Raymond Moley dwelt on the "likeness in self-confidence, activism, and personal charm"; in Kennedy, as in Roosevelt, he wrote, "there is love of power and authority and intense ambition." Even Arthur Krock reverted to the crabby old Krock of yesteryear, and when Sorensen, who works on presidential speeches, became known as "the Sam Rosenman of the staff," and the President's pleasantries with Dirksen and Halleck were compared to Roosevelt's friendships with Charlie McNary and Joe Martin, the reincarnation seemed complete. All that was lacking was word that spectral Bourbons had gone to the Trans-Lux to hiss Kennedy.

The word never came. The parallel had been badly drawn. Temperamentally President Kennedy has far less in common with President Roosevelt than has, say, Nelson Rockefeller, and as he himself belatedly points out, "The two eras are entirely different. Roosevelt's problems were wholly domestic; mine are largely foreign. There is no validity to the comparison." Nevertheless, those for whom the F.D.R. image was explicit have clung to it, and in their fervor some of them have created a Roosevelt who never existed. "They forget that he was such a showoff and dissembler," says James M. Burns, who has published studies of both Presidents. "They remember the Hundred Days, the second Hundred Days, the 1936 election, the court pack — to show that the hero stumbled — and then the coming of the war. But they skip over the second term, when F.D.R. had a very tough time. In 1936, 1937, and 1938 he was overcome by obstacles. This was the time of the recession; everything was going badly for him. They don't remember that in those years he was evasive, noncommittal, exasperatingly cautious — and the despair of the intellectuals." That despair had, in fact, become manifest even before the end of the first term, when the father of a Harvard freshman denounced the Administration's denouncers. After excoriating the Birchers of the time, Joseph P. Kennedy observed that "On the opposite front, the New Deal is assailed by melancholy radicals who want so many things, and want them done overnight."

As a realist John Kennedy shares his father's distrust of political romantics, and as an historian he is equipped to ambush those who distort the past. Toward the end of one White House meeting a New York editor accosted him. "Let me tell you what I think you should do," he said waspishly. "You should go on the radio every week, like F.D.R., and tell the people —"

The President interrupted him. "Roosevelt went on the radio every week?"

"That's right," said the editor, "for his weekly fireside chat."

In cool riposte Kennedy informed him that during

twelve years in office Franklin D. Roosevelt delivered just twenty-seven fireside chats, an average of less than one every five months, and that the maximum in any year was four.

To ardent admirers the master of such minutiae naturally appears to be a mastermind. "Back in '46 we knew that if we exposed him for a ten-minute coffee session we'd pick up a high percentage of volunteer workers," says Lem Billings, who works on Madison Avenue. "I've often thought that if we had a product to advertise on television with that kind of a return, we'd get fantastic results." Yet the question of the President's intellect does have another side. "Intellectually he's committed," Burns says; "emotional commitment is a different matter, though. The people who want a fighting President do have an argument. Think of Harry Truman in 1948. He just plugged away down the line for what he believed in, and he happened to win. Kennedy has been wonderful at communicating ideas, but he hasn't communicated anything like the Truman image of '48. I wonder how much he will be loved by the people, in the Lincoln sense. Liked — yes. But loved?"

Certainly John Kennedy is not as lovable as Abe. He has a weaker grip on the nation's heartstrings, and the reason isn't that he hasn't been shot. One explanation is posited in the area; the lonely crowd is shy of affection. Another, however, is inherent in the man himself. The President's response to his public is that of an intrigued window-shopper, or an inquisitive reporter. His mind is so literal that at times he seems to lack the capacity to generalize — to kindle all the facts and set them ablaze. It is a remarkable fact that he approved the censure of Joe McCarthy, not because McCarthyism offended him, but because he merely thought the senator had been out of order. Campaigning in Little Rock, he was asked what he would do if he became President, and he astounded his audience by giving them a specific, point-by-point account of the steps a Chief Executive could take. No visionary flights; just a cold blueprint. Again, this writer inquired of him whether one of his public remarks ("I feel that the Adams family intimidates us all. . . .") meant that a President with a sense of history is inclined to judge himself against Presidents of the past. The reply was a cogent analysis of the strengths of the Adams family.

Some see this trait as a weakness. It need not be. Caesar and Napoleon shared it. The reluctance to enter into meditative penumbrae means the absence of dogma, which in turn means calm, good-humored relations with men all along the political spectrum. It need not even fault him intellectually. "Remember, Toynbee is not the only philosopher of history," an old Kennedy acquaintance observes. "The President doesn't resemble him much, but he has a lot in common with Sir Lewis Namier — and, for that matter, with Tacitus."

Anxius et intentus agere. "Always active, never impulsive." As the first anniversary of Kennedy's inauguration came and went Tacitus (55?–after 117 A.D.) seemed to be the real Schlesinger of his Administration. He struck closer to the bone than Machiavelli, de Tocqueville, Thucydides, or Joe Alsop. The President remained in perpetual motion, prodding Washington drones, poring over diplomatic cables, accosting his staff Monday mornings with sheafs of cables hacked from Sunday papers. He moved swiftly, yet it was all deliberate speed. Privately he seethed over Republican sniping at his foreign policy, but he rarely mounted a counterattack; he called, rather, for nonpartisan solidarity. Abroad he navigated an extremely narrow channel, and Everett McKinley Dirksen was his co-pilot. In a jam, he reached for the flag. After Cuba he consulted Eisenhower, Hoover, MacArthur, Nixon, Rockefeller, and Goldwater, a spectacle which displeased Democratic partisans but pleased the country. The words he entered into the record were carefully weighed; you couldn't imagine him dashing off a savage note to a critic of Caroline's voice. He cherished Bulwer-Lytton's maxim, "When it is not necessary to change it is necessary not to change," and the moves he did make were preceded by elaborate card-file preparation and a realistic appreciation of the limits of government. *Omnia scire, non omnia exsequi.* "He knew all, though he did not always act upon all he knew."

Aging liberals were unreconciled — the capital still buzzed with talk of fireside chats, take-it-to-the-people campaigns, "appeals to the nation." None of it came from 1600 Pennsylvania Avenue. The right also thundered on — "We need a man on horseback," a rootin tootin Texan told the President, "and many people think you are riding Caroline's tricycle." John Kennedy wouldn't sit that sort of horse well. Robert Frost advised him that "Poetry and power is the formula for an Augustan age," and in reply he received a scrawled, "Power all the way." Yet the President didn't mean the tub-thumping power of a Castro. He is just not that kind of man. "Regardless of the identities of those who will occupy the White House in the years to come," his father wrote in *I'm for Roosevelt*, the problems would require "self-restraint." That quality was inconspicuous in both the bombastic ambassador and the bantam cock he was then championing. John Kennedy, on the other hand, is anti-histrionic by nature. He hates to be a bore. He hasn't the egomania of those who never doubt that the masses are panting to hear them. And at his age he's not likely to become a flamboyant, happy warrior.

But he is a warrior: a man whose life reveals great physical valor and fierce, inscrutable drives. To the blustering Texan he replied frostily, "Wars are easier to talk about than they are to fight. I'm just as tough as you are, and I didn't get elected President by arriving at soft judgments." While a large part of his success may be put down to prudent calculation, he has made the tough choice too often to be dismissed as a trimmer. In his first campaign he was the only

candidate to back Truman's British loan, and his support of the St. Lawrence Seaway led New England
newspapers to the conclusion that he was committing
senatorial suicide. As a presidential aspirant he raised
the religious issue despite protests from his staff; as
President-Elect he ignored State Department advice
and responded warmly to Khrushchev's congratula-
tory message; as President he made the politically in-
expedient decision to close some seventy military installations and raised the banner of free trade, which
an opportunist, remembering Cleveland, would have
kept tightly furled. He honors the heroic tradition;
one of his Republican friends believes that Richard
Nixon's irresolute behavior during their race destroyed him in Kennedy's eyes. "I remember him saying in 1956 that if anything happened to Ike, the
country would be in good hands," Jim Reed says. "But
he admires courage, and he feels that Nixon was pusil-
lanimous in 1960 — especially in the first debate,
where he kept saying, 'I agree with you.' He had expected Nixon to stand up to him, and was contemptuous of him when he didn't."

Sometimes a single chain of events discloses the
character of a leader with chain-lightning clarity.
Andrew Jackson's flashing response to South Carolin-
ian tariff defiance, Andrew Johnson's tactless blunders after the Tenure of Office Act, Theodore Roosevelt's swift support of Panamanian secession, Harding's Alaskan panic — each sequence has left a vivid

impression of a man caught in the lens of time. For John Kennedy such an illumination came in the fifteenth month of his Presidency, when, for seventy-two hours, he was tested in the Bessemer heat of the Big Steel challenge.

The test began with a bland question at four o'clock on the afternoon of Tuesday, April 10, 1962. Ken O'Donnell's West Wing telephone rang, and on the other end was a spokesman for Roger M. Blough, chairman of the board of the United States Steel Corporation. The chairman was flying to Washington; could he see the President? O'Donnell had no idea what was up, but he was cordial. Blough was a familiar figure in the mansion. Two weeks before, the steel industry and the steelworkers' union had signed a contract which had been heralded as a dike against inflation, and the Chief Executive, whose prestige had become deeply committed during the negotiations, had praised it as "industrial statesmanship of the highest order." O'Donnell set the appointment for 5:45 P.M.

In the oval office it was an exceptionally quiet afternoon. Kennedy thought he might even have time for a book. Double-checking, he asked Mrs. Lincoln whether he was in the clear.

"You have Mr. Blough at a quarter to six," she told him.

"Mr. Blough?"

"Yes."

The President was puzzled. "Get me Kenny O'Donnell."

O'Donnell confirmed it, and shortly before six the steel chairman entered the oval office. Kennedy waved him to the right-hand sofa, sat in the rocker, and waited.

"Perhaps the easiest way to explain why I am here is to give you this and let you read it," Blough said, handing him a four-page press release.

The mimeographed handout — it was already on its way to the newspapers — announced that his firm was boosting the price of steel six dollars a ton. The action itself was shocking, and the manner in which the President was informed suggested a deliberate, sandbagging snub. "I think you have made a terrible mistake," he told Blough stonily. He instructed Mrs. Lincoln to fetch Secretary Goldberg. The three of them talked for fifty minutes, and after Blough departed five aides were summoned. Pacing the floor, the President tautly recalled a row between Joe Kennedy and steel executives in 1937. At the time he had believed that his father's denunciations of them were exaggerated.* Now he understood. For now his blood

---

* In a version published by the New York *Times* on April 23, 1962, the President was quoted as having said, "My father always told me that all businessmen were sons-of-bitches but I never believed him till now!" Although Orvil E. Dryfoos, publisher of the *Times*, wrote a letter to the President apologizing for this, the rendering was widely circulated. It inspired a great deal of indignation in the business community and, in some quarters, a show of hypocritical dismay. For example, an Oklahoma City news-

was up. His urbane mask was off; he was on collision course. "U. S. Steel picked the wrong President to double-cross," one aide said afterward. "Six o'clock, six o'clock," Kennedy muttered to himself as that evening's guests entered the White House at 9:45. They were in black tie; the occasion was his annual reception for members of Congress. Just a year before, he had been drawn aside and told of the Pig Bay disaster, and tonight he remarked dryly, "I think we're going to call off congressional receptions. Last year it was Cuba, now this."

Wednesday at breakfast he heard reports from economists and statisticians who had worked almost all night, gathering data. Then he told Sorensen to begin drafting a statement. His hope was to head off U. S. Steel's competitors. It seemed vain. By afternoon, when he mounted his press conference rostrum, five of them, led by Bethlehem Steel, had matched Blough's increase. A thoroughly aroused President faced the reporters. While the members of Blough's high command glowered at a television set twenty stories above Manhattan's Broadway, he gibbeted them with language which made "economic royalists" sound almost benign. Citing particulars to show the new prices were unjustified, he warned of antitrust investigations, the cancellation of proposed tax benefits for industry, and the loss of defense orders.

---

paper piously headed a story, "JFK Used Bad Words in Steel Crisis," and described the operative phrase as "gutter language." Yet this language enjoyed a splendid vogue in the same newspaper's city room when this writer inhabited it.

This was onstage. Backstage, New Frontiersmen with steel friends were telephoning them, trying to persuade the companies which hadn't raised rates to stay put. As a member of the staff said later, "Anybody who knew anybody else got on the horn." Switchboards were ablaze, for a lot of people knew people — the vice chairman of Inland Steel received an early morning greeting from the Undersecretary of Commerce, a fellow old boy of Chicago's Harvard School for Boys ('23), and one steel man was proselytized by four members of the Administration. Secretary McNamara sat at his desk, personally dialing number after number; the President himself made innumerable calls, notably one to Edgar Kaiser, chairman of Kaiser Steel, in California. Meanwhile Bobby had a posse of FBI agents prowling the night, routing out reporters to verify a quotation from Bethlehem's president opposing a price hike.

"Gestapo tactics!" cried the chairman of the Republican National Committee, and the pro-steelie *Wall Street Journal*, discovering that one of its men had been awakened by Bobby's dawn patrol, was fit to be tied. Beyond doubt the President was using the full powers of his office. And beyond doubt they were working. Thursday Roger Blough conceded that if his competitors didn't follow his lead he would be in a fix. Already five of them were wavering, two seriously. Friday morning the U. S. Steel chairman called Secretary Goldberg. Roger was doing a twist. His people were going to have a quiet little talk in New

York, he said; would the Secretary like to sit in? Goldberg accepted and then phoned the President for advice. Kennedy's terms were simple: unconditional surrender. The conclave was held secretly in uptown New York's Carlyle Hotel, with Goldberg and Clark Clifford present, but even as Clifford was lecturing the company men their hopes for a united industry were fading. First Blough was called to the phone, then Goldberg. Inland Steel and Kaiser had broken ranks — in Washington the President said, "Good! Good! Very good!" — and their abstention had forced Bethlehem to recant. At a quarter after five that same afternoon Blough tossed in the towel. This time there was no handout. The news of Kennedy's victory came over an AP teletype in the West Wing and was relayed by Sorensen to Norfolk, Virginia, where the President was watching naval maneuvers. Hearing it as he debarked from a nuclear submarine, he announced that the people were "most gratified," and that Big Steel was now "serving the public interest." The three-day blitz was over.

Fascinated by Kennedy's display of presidential pyrotechnics, most Americans missed the revealing display of Himself. It was all there. U. S. Steel's unexpected flaunting of the Jolly Roger brought out the President's competitive drive, his wit in adversity, his reliance on Bobby, and his instinctive turning, in tense moments, to thoughts of his father. The Wednesday statement, edited by him moments before its presentation, confirmed his affinity for detail and his sense of history — certain passages evoked rhythms of T.R., F.D.R., and Woodrow Wilson. The phone calls to Establishment magnates demonstrated the recherché tone of his government. Finally, in choosing to counterattack he had remained the canny politician. Big Steel has little appeal in the nation; the Republicans, who defended the tycoons, were following their fatal instinct for the impolitic.*

Undeniably the crisis changed him. Crises do shape a President, and may, in time, completely transform him — at the end of their Administrations Herbert Hoover and Harry Truman were very different men. At this writing it would be hazardous, even presumptuous, to predict the ultimate effect of the office on John Kennedy. In the rumbles ahead, each of his qualities will be tempered, smashed, or recast. Clearly the second week of April, 1962, fortified the President's sense of confidence; it strengthened his feeling of the country, and the country's feeling for him. It further fused his political faith; until then, no one had realized how deeply he believed in economic planning. This was the most conspicuous harvest of Blough's seed, and it incited extravagant reactions. The steelsymps promptly developed delusions of persecution; within two months they had raised such a

---

* The fact that the President's popularity dropped four points after the steel fight merely demonstrates that when a leader strikes out in *any* direction he always leaves a few stragglers. Those who follow this numbers game noted that Kennedy was still nearly ten points above Eisenhower's average rating, and nearly thirty above Truman's. Actually he should shed more popularity fat. Inevitably he will.

convincing bogy that the stock market threw a major convulsion. For them the discovery that Kennedy meant business with business overrode everything else — a financial writer charged that he had thrown an "anti-business tantrum." Humbler men were thrilled — "Oh, didn't he do a good one!" exclaimed a delighted Robert Frost, adding that "Somebody's got to get angry."

Actually both had missed the essence of him. A show of strength is not wrath. It was true, as one White House aide put it, that his Tuesday mood was "controlled fury." Certainly he was indignant. In the face of such provocation no man could have remained serene. What was remarkable, however, was the control. During that first session in the oval office Goldberg flew at Blough, but Kennedy, though arctic, was civil. There was no Truman stridor in his press conference thrust; it was delivered with the hard, measured cadence of a judge pronouncing sentence on the perpetrators of a particularly inexcusable crime. He gnawed no carpets, he didn't foam, he avoided the "highly charged political position." Even before U. S. Steel struck its colors he was warning his staff that "it is very important that we not take any action that could be interpreted as vindictive"; and when the firm's chairman requested another appointment four days later ("This," said the voice on the other end of the horn, "is Roger Blough, the man you've been reading about"), he was received graciously, the guest of a Chief Executive still anxious for his cooperation. Like Goethe, John Kennedy believes that genius lies in knowing where to stop. He had shown the mailed fist, and then he had sheathed it in deepest velvet. Once more he was himself, the quiet American.

In every emergency, so the democratic faith goes, the United States finds a President capable of taking arms against her sea of troubles. The Georgetown quarterbacks, despite their momentary elation over the steel triumph, continue to distrust Kennedy's tranquillity. They want him to adopt the iron tone every day, everywhere. Like the Circuit Riders and the Liberty Lobbyists, they may know their history too well. This is not the Augustan Age. It is the nuclear age, and the country's real enemies are rocket-rattlers, not robber barons. A national leader who tackled today's problems with the all-or-nothing gusto of a Roosevelt could wind up with literally nothing — no life, no nation. Kennedy must speak softly, for he carries the biggest stick of all time. In Blacklett Strait after the crash of PT-109 he told his drenched crew, "There's nothing in the book about a situation like this." Nor is there now. His generation is writing its own primer, the first lesson of which is patience. Icy antagonists must be dealt with icily. "Khrushchev," Larry O'Brien observes wryly, "has some unusual advantages as a politician." Countering these advantages requires exceptional qualities, and one of them may be the President's poise. Perhaps this is the new courage, and his the first profile in it. A sedulous poise can be deceptive. That 3 A.M. mote of light in the mansion's third-floor rear is there because his involvement is total. Only do not expect him to mount a rostrum the next day and break out a crying towel. It is highly improbable that he will talk to you about it if you ask. Inquire about his insomnia and he changes the subject. Mention the burdens of office and he turns aside with a light understatement: "I have a nice home, the office is close by, and the pay is good."

The home — his and America's fifty million others — is, of course, the point of the thing; certainly there is no other excuse for the arms insanity. In the White House bromides about the wife and kids sound less absurd. "Let's do this for Jack, for Jackie, and for Caroline," was the rallying cry of O'Brien's Hill scouts in the Eighty-seventh's first session. It became a joke. The notion that Jack and Jackie needed anything was entertaining, and the political possibilities of baby-kissing had been exhausted some time ago. Yet aversion for corn obscures the patent fact that without the Carolines, nuclear age tension would be not only unbearable, but somewhat pointless. "It doesn't really matter as far as you and I are concerned," John Kennedy confided to an intimate after his futile attempt to stare Khrushchev down in Vienna. "What really matters is the children." Obviously the whole works, if it does work, is working for them, and their ignorance of the hows and whys merely makes the task more poignant.

The First Family's first child treats the panoply of office with innocent irreverence. Without understanding what the Presidency is, she is for it. One autumn day when hurricane warnings were posted the Kennedys evacuated Hyannis Port for a nearby camp, and Caroline raced around asking whether anyone wanted to ride "in a *White House* car," knowing that, for some strange reason, the phrase would impress adults. It would be stretching to call her a typical little girl — the typical child does not remark, as Caroline did when she spotted a costumed figure on a liquor label, "Oh, there's Louis Quatorze!" — but that was a sign of her mother's membership in the Quality, not of her father's job. Swank aside, she seems normal enough to most people. There is an exception. "Caroline," Joe Kennedy told me earnestly, "is a genius," and his judgment was not, he insisted, influenced by the fact that she happened to be his granddaughter. After the hurricane blew out to sea he took her and her Welsh terrier Charley for a two-and-a-half-hour boat ride. They talked all the time, and the ambassador regarded it as an extremely interesting conversation, a real exchange of views. At one point they discussed Charley's character. She spoke at some length about the ways of dogs, and Joe listened, rapt, as though she were Albert Payson Terhune.

The President is answerable for much of the public interest in his daughter. At 6:45 P.M. on Hyannis Port Saturdays, for example, he hoists her and her peers aboard his motorized golf cart and convoys his squealing passengers to a candy store four blocks away. Being in the driver's seat, he could discourage press coverage of the ritual. He doesn't. He has a hunch his daughter enjoys the attention, and he knows he does. Such diversions were impossible for Senator Kennedy, because he wasn't around. Being Chief Executive has brought him an unexpected bonus: he is much closer to his family. Caroline's mother likes that part. "Jackie thought the Presidency would hurt their marriage," one of the couple's oldest friends says, "and she has been surprised and pleased to find that it's the other way around." From her sitting room window in the mansion proper she can and occasionally does look down on the rose garden and the French windows of his office. Jacqueline rarely intrudes in the West Wing, though after watching the successful retrieval of John Glenn over the sitting room's television set she did dart downstairs, race along the outdoor portico, and burst in on her husband, quivering with excitement.

Caroline makes the trip more often. Frequently she wanders over just to say hello. If he is busy she can chat with Mrs. Lincoln, and she doesn't mind. She sees so much of him elsewhere these days. Mornings she watches him shave with his safety razor and talks to him while he bathes. Her mother has always read to her; now he does, too, explaining the adventure of Goldilocks, the forgetfulness of Bo-peep, and the London Bridge disaster, together with assorted animal tales. As a scholar he prefers a child's version of the *Iliad* and the *Odyssey,* and as an author he likes to spin tales of his own, although, like many another father, he sometimes buckles under the demand for new material and resorts to literary piracy. One of Caroline's favorites is a sea story. He has embroidered it a great deal, and by now it would make a pretty fair novel. The chief character is a one-legged sea captain who pursues a white whale.

Looking around him the President says, "I was away every weekend for three years." He smiles slightly and adds, with the air of the sailor home from the sea and the hunter home from the Hill, "Now I've settled down." Caroline literally believes this — certain politicians will be startled to learn that she thinks of the Executive Mansion as a permanent Kennedy acquisition — and certainly her father's new routine suggests that of a man striking root. He habitually smokes one or two cigars every day, eats lunch regularly for the first time since childhood, and has put on ten pounds. The weight is largely a tribute to a superb chef his wife hired in New York. It is also something of a problem, because it all goes to his jowls. On television the effect would be singular, so four days before a major speech he goes on a crash diet. That ascetic expression on your screen is partly illusion. The man is simply starved.

He doesn't diet for vanity's sake. The sudden appearance of a puffy Chief Executive might unsettle the nation, and today a President must think of such things. The time has passed when a William Howard Taft could regularly get himself wedged in a White House bathtub and howl to be extricated. Embassies would howl back if there were such incidents now. Cartoons would be drawn in Amsterdam and Bombay; editorials would be written, prestige reevaluated. Most of the people for whom the President is responsible have never seen him — entire nations are ineligible to vote for him — yet they feel his impact all the same. "When he creaks they groan," wrote Sidney Hyman. "When he wobbles they feel unhinged." The many cables Jacqueline Kennedy has received from French towns laying claim to her Bouvier ancestry are not a tribute to her Gallic charm; de Gaulle *gloire* notwithstanding, Frenchmen know that Jacqueline's husband has almost as much to say about the future of their country as Marianne's guardian. "The President of the United States," writes David Butler, of Oxford, "is the President of Britain. However closely the British guard their independence, however scrupulously the President respects it, he still makes decisions that are more important to their fate than any made by the Prime Minister."

His every act is significant to someone. In the era of the Zoomar lens, even the details of his personal life assume ludicrous importance. Let him decline a Homburg, and a segment of the economy shudders. Let him reach for a cigar, a glass of milk, a rocking chair — or the *Iliad* — and other segments feel braced. If he signs documents with Estabrook pens,

Parker pens must be presented to visiting children. The very temperature on his thermometer can influence stock exchanges; whenever he appears in bad weather without a hat his tailor gets complaining letters. The President is being watched all the time. If he grew fat, developed a tic, or began to speak with a stammer, there would be repercussions.

For while the world has changed, the Presidency is essentially unchanged. It is stfll a very personal office. Only one man can hold it. From a distance it tends to merge with the entire executive branch; its powers seem to be divided among the faceless members of a team. In crises this comforts those to whom facelessness and anonymity suggest impersonal precision. They delude themselves. Sitting with the President, one's most vivid perception is of the man's solitude, followed by a realization of why, for most voters, the White House hasn't much to do with conventional politics. Politics puts a man there, and helps him get the job done, but he cannot be a true chief unless we, and he, know when to forget party loyalties. He and his understudy are the sole men for whom we all vote. Without a President there could be no United States.

President Kennedy gives his various publics varied impressions. Diverse observers see him playing left field, right field, center field, all fields — carrying a red flag, a black flag, or no flag at all. This variety may arise from the complexity of the man. Really he is many men. He is a patrician and a politician;

he is both a field commander and a scholar. He shuns emotional displays. Yet he is moved by poverty, and when he is crossed he is a Tartar. He is jocose, but under the façade there is, though scarcely suspected, a dark vein of sadness. Although he is astonishingly candid, no one can keep a secret better. Despite his intellectualism, he is disdainful of academics. Despite his disdain for reformers, he has a vision of, and a plan for, global freedom. Statesmen who have spurned the mob stimulate him, but no President has cultivated the crowd so assiduously, and in him introversion and extroversion coexist.

He is not all things to all men. Among the labels which do not fit him are hotspur, demagogue, zealot. Dramatic breaks with tradition do not tempt him. He lives in a nation of bland change, of hueless progress, of silent, automated engines that move society almost without society's knowledge. His loyalty to his generation may be stronger than his loyalty to any other group. In America this is an age without passion for political novelty, and he acts his age. Nevertheless, he himself is not phlegmatic. Indeed, his most striking trait is his stamina. It has borne him through sickness and catastrophe. It won him the great prize, and with it he will be driven to close the Russian gap. He is the second son of a proud father, he survived to be first, and under certain circumstances survival itself can set a man apart.

That father is among the President's publics now, observing him with the rest of us. Unlike the haberdasher's correspondents, he doesn't fret about the weather. "I see him on TV, in rain and cold, bare-headed — and I don't worry," Joe Kennedy said as the opening year of the new Administration drew to a close. "I know nothing can happen to him. I tell you, something's watching out for him. I've stood by his deathbed four times. Each time I said good-by to him, and he always came back. In that respect he *is* like F.D.R. Because F.D.R. went to the edge, and he came back, too. And afterward he was unique. It's the same thing with Jack. You can't put your finger on it, but there's that difference. When you've been through something like that back, and the Pacific, what can hurt you? Who's going to scare you?"

Visiting Ted Kennedy's Senate campaign head-quarters at 122 Bowdoin Street, Boston, this writer was shown certain wartime relics which had been overlooked by the President. The setting was anoma-lous: a dark, third-floor closet. The contents of the closet were a hodgepodge thrust aside to make space for the youngest Kennedy's politicking. Most of the odds and ends were trivia, but some were historic. Piled on a shelf were the late Joseph P. Kennedy, Jr.'s lawbooks, later used by Bobby and Ted. Below them, on another shelf, lay John Kennedy's Navy sword. And on a wire hanger in the back was the President's World War II dress blue uniform. The two rows of ribbons were upside down, the tailoring lacked H. Harris & Co.'s touch. Yet the nap was still stiff from the cleaner's iron, and the distinctive boxer's silhouette was familiar. The jacket had been hanging there a long time, its braid tarnishing, its ribbons begging readjustment. But Ted's pols, toiling away in the next room to the accompaniment of piped music, left it undisturbed. No one tried it on, of course. Somehow that would have been improper.

Besides, it wouldn't have fitted any of them.

Wake

In 1963 this writer was living in the Ruhr valley, replowing the rich soil of Germany's past for a study of the Krupp dynasty's dark influence on four centuries of Teuton history. On the evening of June 23 my telephone rang. The caller, a presidential aide, explained that the Chief Executive was staying in Bad Godesberg and wondered whether I would like to come down for a reception. Regretfully I declined, pointing out that my opinions of the convicted Nazi war criminal who had become the Common Market's greatest industrialist were unlikely to be popular with Bonn's leaders, and that if the President became identified with me now it might be held against him later. Thus I went off on a Rhine cruise, missing my chance for a final talk with the leader of my generation. Five months later he was slain in Dallas. It was then, at the request of his widow, that I set aside the writing of the Krupp book and began an exhaustive, two-year inquiry into the assassination.

Back in Washington I encountered Captain Cecil Stoughton, the presidential photographer, in the corridor outside what was now Lyndon Johnson's office. I asked him, "What did you do in Parkland Hospital?" His eyes filled. He said quietly, "I died." He might have been speaking for all of us. No matter where we had been on November 22, millions of us had suffered an irreparable loss when word came that John Kennedy had been killed. We would never again be completely whole; when we went to Arlington, we knelt by the grave of the selves we had been. Pat Moynihan had put it superbly the evening after the tragedy. "We'll never laugh again," Mary Mc-Grory had told him. "Oh, we'll laugh again," Pat had said. "But we'll never be young again."

> *Let the word go forth from this time and place, to friend and foe alike, that the torch has been passed to a new generation of Americans — born in this century, tempered by war, disciplined by a hard and bitter peace, proud of our ancient heritage. . . .*

He had been given less than three years to hold
that torch aloft, and we were crushed, for we knew
the splendid lightning wouldn't strike the same place
twice. His election had been a freak. Until 1960 Cal-
vin Coolidge had been thought of as the last Massachusetts President. Candidates these days had to be
from the big states. Kennedy, moreover, was a Harvard man and a Roman Catholic, which, though the
nation has forgotten it, was regarded as a fatal handicap until he surmounted it. He had not exaggerated
in calling his victory over Nixon a miracle. It had been
a prodigy, and prodigies do not repeat themselves.
Besides, there was only one John Kennedy. Many,
craving the impossible, tried to find his genius repeated in his brothers. Their yearning was understandable. It was also doomed. A man — any man —
is unique; in his prime he is the honed product of a
million events and forces which have been brought
to bear upon him. This man, for example, had been
in the Solomons. No one who knew him could doubt
that the Islands had helped shape him. Bob and
Ted hadn't been in combat; they hadn't been tried
on that anvil. To be sure, they were like him in other
ways. Bob had his tough fiber, Ted his charm. But
neither had both. In 1962 there was a Washington
mot: "Bobby plus Teddy equals the President." It is
as true now as it was then, and a billion tears cannot
alter it.

This is not the place to tell the story of *The Death*

of a President. Instead I should like to set down a brief account of what life was like for the President's survivors. Despite long absences in Texas and elsewhere, I saw the Kennedys and the men and women who had been members of the Kennedy team from time to time, and because of my peculiar task I became a repository for confidences, the more sensitive of which shall remain under seal until another generation has risen and gone. Still, it is possible to suggest the character of the aftermath of the great funeral. Defining mood is always difficult, because it is evanescent, and the challenge is best met by a variation on the method which surveyors call triangulation, determining elusive dimensions by taking bearings from various fixed positions.

The first two points are the fawn-colored, three-story house at 3017 N Street where Mrs. Kennedy lived with her two children that ghastly spring after the burial, and Hickory Hill, Bob Kennedy's brick mansion on the other side of the Potomac. In early 1964 both had an air of utter unreality. For the first six months of the Johnson administration the homes of the Attorney General and his widowed sister-in-law displayed all the outward trappings of power. Each was tied into the executive mansion's switchboard — the distinctive white phones were in nearly every room — and Kennedy people came and left in chauffeur-driven black White House Mercuries. On N Street there were even Secret Service agents. Bob McNamara sometimes called with presents for Caroline and John; occasionally the President himself stopped by. Thoughtful and concerned, Lyndon Johnson did everything he could think of to soften the blow. Yet the agony remained. Every reminder of White House privilege recalled the staggering loss. Once it had been possible to ignore the Secret Service. Not now, not after Dallas; you could see Mrs. Kennedy stiffen when an agent passed. She would nap afternoons and lie awake through the night in terrible anguish. Sometimes this writer attempted to change the conversation with her, mentioning mutual friends, books, *anything* except the dreadful fact that lay between us. Once she flared, "Do you think I can talk about girls I used to know, or other people's happiness, or best sellers? Do you think I can *think* about them?" She couldn't; it was absurd to expect her even to try. To add to the impossibility of N Street, there was always a dense mass of spectators standing across the street when you left. They would search your face expectantly, as though expecting stupendous news. If their gaping was hard on others, it was intolerable for her, and when she asked whether she should move to New York, the only possible answer was, "Yes."

In the weeks before she left she spent much of her time at Hickory Hill with Bob and Ethel. Ethel had barely held herself together during the funeral, while Jackie and Bob had rallied to face the world with unforgettable gallantry. Now the roles were reversed. They were deep in the umbra of depression, while

Ethel (and, to an increasing extent, Jean Kennedy Smith) attempted to divert them. Days there would be frantic touch-football exhibitions, with Ethel throwing looping passes to her flock; after dark the hostess arranged informal parties. I remember one social occasion when, not feeling especially festive myself, I strolled out to the portico. Suddenly Jackie loomed out of the night. Presumably agents were about, but they were concealed; all one could see was this incredibly lovely woman, dressed completely in white, looking about with an ineffably lost look. At that moment there were perhaps at least a hundred million men who would have leaped to help her, but they weren't there. Then, recognizing a familiar face, she smiled faintly and held out her hand. It was a gesture as graceful as a pirouette, and with that poignant smile it was heartbreaking.

Another fixed point in this triangulation is the compound. Over two years later, in the Indian summer of 1966, she sent the *Caroline* to pick me up at La Guardia. As I descended the ramp at Hyannis airport I saw her behind the fence, wearing dark glasses and waving. She has always been affected by the weather — in April and May of 1964 it seemed that the rain would never stop — and now the morning was golden and so was she. Yet even without the sun she would have been vivacious. She had learned to live with what, in that first season of mourning, appeared to be insupportable. She looked younger, stronger, more self-assured. After changing clothes (and tiptoeing around the house of the Ambassador, whose paralysis

continued cruelly year after year) we took young
John out in the Kennedys' Boston Whaler. John, con-
valescing from a tonsillectomy, wasn't allowed in the
water. He stayed in the boat beside the driver, peering out with a brooding expression evocative of his
father, while his mother water-skiied. Her performance on a water ski — she only uses one — is astonishing. It is an acrobatic feat. Slaloming, with the tow
rope between the toes of her other foot, she swept
back and forth in giddy arcs, leaping high at the
turns in a shimmer of spray. Afterward the driver took
John in and I joined her for a long swim, which became a painful reminder that the President's widow
was still a child when he swam that remote strait with
a .38 and a battle lantern. In the Islands the author
had been a strong swimmer, too, but today he creaked
and lagged behind while Jackie, with her youth,
flashed ahead. Awkward for the laggard; yet good to
see.

Bobby, characteristically, had recovered by plung-
ing into work. That is the next fixed point: politics.
Politics isn't a place. You can find it anywhere. I first
encountered Bob's '64 campaign in the shallow end
of the Hickory Hill swimming pool. It was the year's
first warm Saturday, and he, his wife, and I were
languidly peering down at our feet in the water.

"What do you think Bobby should do?" Ethel
asked suddenly.

The Kennedys have always had a way of involving
you in their decisions — the President would solicit
a visitor's opinions on the most momentous affairs of

state — and sometimes it is a little hard to know how to respond. I glanced over at Bob cautiously. He was examining his toes with exceptional interest. Finally I said, "*I* don't know, Ethel. I haven't any special qualifications. Whatever he's going to do, he'll do it, no matter what I say."

She and I talked briefly about Justice. Clearly there could be no question of his staying on there. Even before the assassination he had started to refer to his years as Attorney General in the past tense; during what would have been his brother's second term he had planned to serve in some other capacity, probably at State. But now what? At the time the papers were full of stories about how hard he was trying to get the vice presidential nomination. I hadn't seen any sign of it. It was, in fact, a preposterous idea, both for LBJ and RFK. They would never have meshed then.

"Of course, there's the governorship of Massachusetts," I hazarded. That sounds presumptuous, but I meant it; the state needed a good administration, and I was convinced that Chub Peabody wouldn't survive the primary.

"What about this Senate thing in New York?" Ethel inquired.

Again I sneaked a glance at Bob. He had just raised his right foot from the pool and was staring at the big toe. He seemed to find it fascinating.

"That's a terrible idea. Keating would take him," I said incisively.

At 2:30 P.M. September 1, Barney Ross, Jim Reed, Jim McShane and I rode up on the *Caroline* for Bob's nomination. We watched him dress at the Carlyle (like his brother eight years before in the Stock Yard Inn, he calmly watched the balloting on a television screen) and then, hurrying to the Seventh Regiment Armory, we formed a human shield for Ethel and the children in a corner. The pressure from the crowd was unbelievable — an auspicious sign, though some missed it. In October Arthur Schlesinger told me that the polls were alarming, and Ed Guthman said, "If you can think of something to do, *do* it." There followed a frantic period in which a great many Kennedy friends — including Arthur and Ted Sorensen, who were confronting urgent book deadlines — set everything else aside and pitched in. And then, after the results were in, one realized that the volunteers hadn't been needed. The campaign of the third Kennedy brother to be elected to the U.S. Senate would have succeeded without them. All their speech writing and stumping had demonstrated was that the family name continued to command remarkable allegiance among gifted men.

The big political question in Bob's career, then as now, was Lyndon Baines Johnson. In those first months the New Frontiersmen who were staying on in the White House (e.g., O'Brien, O'Donnell) provided useful liaison. It was needed, because the Kennedys were anxious to help the new Chief Executive. Thus the triangulation is incomplete unless the White

House is included as a fixed position. Unfortunately this writer can't contribute much about that. I had my own problems there, and the biggest one was my identification with Johnson's predecessor. However, I recall one incident which offers some insight into the misunderstandings which spring up between the President and Kennedy men. On the evening of June 14, 1965, I attended a dinner party in Georgetown. Bob Kennedy came late — he had been on the Senate floor — and he was still attacking his dessert when the ladies went off and left the rest of us to our brandy and cigars. Seated around the table were Bob, Arthur, Averell Harriman, John Bartlow Martin, a diplomat, a New Frontiersman who had hung on in the West Wing, and me. The conversation opened with a discussion of Latin America. Bob had been critical of State's policy in Santo Domingo, and Averell was gently chiding him through Arthur.

"Someone like you, John," he said, gesturing at Martin, "should write a book" — John, who had just finished a 5,000-page manuscript, looked stunned — "about these bleeding hearts like Arthur. They're against all benevolent despotism. You have to have it. I remember that when I was a young man there was a magnificent benevolent despot in Mexico. He was handsome, charming, honest; a shrewd, farsighted administrator."

He paused for breath, and Bob looked up from his pie.

"Maximilian?" he asked.

The next course was the mayoralty of New York. Arthur thought the only Democrat who could take Lindsay was Pat Moynihan. Bob said it was too late; just getting a name known to New Yorkers took time and great bales of cash. Nevertheless everyone there, with one exception, agreed that Pat would make a splendid mayor.

That was a Monday. The following Saturday morning I met Mary Bundy on the street in Cleveland Park. "Have you seen this morning's *Times?*" she asked excitedly. "There's a long page-one story about Pat Moynihan for mayor."

She led me into her kitchen and handed me the paper. I never did find out who was responsible for it, but clearly the source was one of the men at Monday's dinner; everything in the story had been said there. Certainly Pat had nothing to do with it. He was in a remote Yugoslavian town, where the *Times* had reached him by telephone. He was, he said, bewildered.

Lyndon Johnson didn't believe him. The President was convinced Pat had managed the whole thing, and while he expressed a grudging admiration for the expertise that could produce a front-page *Times* story from a Balkan hamlet, he resented such free-lancing. Thenceforth Pat's job as Assistant Secretary of Labor became impossible, and shortly thereafter he resigned, thus joining the great exodus of those who had come to the capital with great dreams in January 1961 and now found that they were misfits.

It would be pleasant to report that the bond among those who had been unified by President Kennedy's leadership, and who had drawn even closer together in the hour of national grief, continued undiminished. It didn't always. As Dave Powers once told me, "He made everybody around him look ten feet tall. Now he's gone and they're shrinking." Inevitably there were misunderstandings between those who left and the few who stayed. Some couldn't see why Larry O'Brien would accept a post in Lyndon Johnson's Cabinet. One even heard of resentment of Dr. George Burkley, the gentle presidential physician, who remained at his post and accepted promotion from Rear Admiral to Vice Admiral. This was unfair and unrealistic, of course, and so was the pique directed at the Kennedy people who published their memoirs. The only safe course was to stay out of print. But Schlesinger, Sorensen, Salinger, Red Fay, and Evelyn Lincoln felt compelled to publish, and I have joined them. Ironically Jacqueline Kennedy, who had captured the imagination of the world, didn't want its admiration. During one afternoon late in 1966 she referred me to pages 88 and 89 of this book and said, "I still feel that way." The only possible explanation to her was that she had become a historical figure. While one may sympathize with her wishes — one can scarcely do otherwise — the responsibility to history seems clear, as she herself had recognized in asking me to write my account of late November 1963.

Yet the dominant memories of the Kennedy after-

glow are not the sadness of N Street, the convalescence in Hyannis, the resurgence of Robert Kennedy,
the delicate problem of relations with the new Administration, or the disagreements among the survivors. They are, rather, a series of impressions that
float by and recur and recur again, like a continuous
performance movie. One recalls standing in St. Matthew's Cathedral behind the family on May 29, 1964,
toward the end of the Mass commemorating what
would have been the President's forty-seventh birthday. The choir sang "The Star-Spangled Banner" and
"The Navy Hymn," and then the young widow left
the front pew and walked down the long aisle, a child
in either hand, her face a pale mask, the eyes sight-
less, the chin brave and high.

One remembers an entirely different atmosphere in
the Federal City Club on the evening of September
3, when friends gathered to say farewell to the man
who had just resigned as Attorney General and was
about to open his New York senatorial campaign.
("Do you know any good advance men?" he asked
me as I came in. I asked back, "Do they have to be
New Yorkers?" He looked anxious and said, "I'm
afraid they do.") Everyone was trying to be funny.
David Brinkley made a droll speech, Ethel presented
her husband with his own Cabinet chair, and Jim Mc-
Shane demonstrated how he would teach Bob to talk
like a New Yorker. But the funniest people were the
musicians, who meant to be dead serious. Over and
over they played "The Sidewalks of New York" and

"When Irish Eyes Are Smiling." Bob glanced at the band and winced, as though he had bitten down on a bad tooth. He murmured dryly, "Really grabs you, doesn't it?"

The farewells were coming rapidly now. Nearly every week someone left the White House — a Presidential assistant, a staff aide, a key secretary, a Secret Service agent, a chauffeur — and on November 22, when we assembled in St. Matthew's once more and then crossed to Arlington with the new Senator-Elect, the number of familiar faces had dwindled. Mrs. Kennedy was in New York, which was a good thing, for the scene at the graveside was unfortunate. We lined up behind Bob and approached the eternal flame individually. Douglas Dillon was directly in front of me, screening my view, and it wasn't until he reached the front and knelt that I saw what was happening. Packed around the white picket fence were perhaps two score amateur cameramen, photographing the President's friends on their knees. Under such circumstances prayer was impossible; one departed hastily.

The impact of John Kennedy is still felt in the capital and the country, but by that autumn we were well into the Lyndon Johnson era. The last good-bye party I attended was given by Senator Robert Kennedy for two of his most devoted and talented lieutenants, Burke Marshall and Ed Guthman, and it was here that a friend said to me, "You know, we're too young to be holding reunions." The affair *was* like a reunion.

Ken O'Donnell was reminiscing with Teddy White, Mary McGrory was brooding, Nick Katzenbach and the host were talking earnestly in a corner, and only Art Buchwald, with his incomparable thrusts at the new Administration, seemed to belong to today. Some longed for a vague, dazzling tomorrow, but most were looking back to yesterday, and one remembers the pang when a speaker quoted Shakespeare's King Harry —

This story shall the good man teach his son;
And Crispin Crispian shall ne'er go by,
From this day to the ending of the world,
But we in it shall be remembered:
We few, we happy few, we band of brothers;
For he to-day that sheds his blood with me
Shall be my brother; be he ne'er so vile,
This day shall gentle his condition:
And gentlemen in England now a-bed
Shall think themselves accursed they were not here,
And hold their manhoods cheap whiles any speaks
That fought with us upon Saint Crispin's day.

The President had often recited those lines. And had anyone reminded the men who had fought with him that since the third century the Feast of Crispian has been celebrated at the end of October, they would have disagreed; for them it came just a month later.

In his inaugural he said,

*All this will not be finished in the first 100
days. Nor will it be finished in the first 1,000
days, nor even perhaps in our lifetime on
this planet. But let us begin.*

The world has turned over many times since he
flung out his challenge on the Capitol steps, but truth
does not change. Bedrock remains bedrock, and the
trustees of his legacy may begin anew by noting
that the dread and hope of the twentieth century continue to hang in suspended tension, and that within
green memory the lessons of honor have been etched
upon the national conscience by the life and passion
of the thirty-fifth Chief Executive of the United
States.

The lessons of honor — and of dishonor.

On the evening of November 24, 1963, a member
of the Kennedy administration received a long-distance call from one of America's most eminent
women. Lee Oswald was dead, and she was dis-
tressed. This was the greatest of crimes, she said; the
most outrageous of acts; the worst that could have
happened. When she had finished he replied icily
that the worst had happened on Friday. Confused,
she commenced to weep, and her tears and her be-
wilderment were symptoms of an illness which has
afflicted society for a half-century. In that late autumn of 1963 the conditioned reflexes of the American intellectual were prepared for the murder of an
assassin — not for the murder of the nation's First

Magistrate; and the situation is even more singular among certain Europeans, who, by a fantastic feat of mental gymnastics, have made Oswald the martyr of Dallas.

This is madness. But there is a system to the fugue. It is a measure of mid-century *Angst* that while the ignoble are treated with instinctive compassion, nobility is discounted, and even discredited. John Kennedy was a scholar. Yet many of the very men who should have identified themselves with his Presidency were uncomfortable with it. Somehow they couldn't believe in him. Such leaders, they thought, belonged to the past — to the legends of Siegfried, Balder, Attis, and Arthur — if indeed they had ever existed outside of balladry, which was doubtful. In any event the leonine mold had been broken. It therefore followed that this young President who seemed to have been cast from it must be an impostor. Modern greatness was a mirage. The apotheosis who had entered the White House in January of 1961 was a new Quixote, splendidly armored in an era which had become convinced that all armor was tin.

The victim, or antihero — their own word — was very different. *He* was entirely credible. The puerile, Chaplinesque patsy was familiar to them; his sufferings had been celebrated in a thousand contemporary novels and volumes of tragic verse. Of course, there were some dissenters. Robert Frost protested what he called his "tenderer-than-thou" colleagues. Man, he said, was becoming "a diminished thing." And Lord

Russell mocked what he described as "the superior virtue of the oppressed." They were treated as Luddites. Every intellectual had vicariously shared the sufferings of the misfit, the nonconformist, the antiauthoritarian, the picaresque rebel at war with society. Alienation, as it was known among the neosophists, had become a cultural vogue.

Kennedy was very much aware of this mode; unlike most politicians he was acquainted with both the fashion setters and their work. He had realized from the outset that the knee-jerk absolutists among them would regard him as a counterrevolutionary. He had written vividly of the gallantry they deprecated, and he spoke eloquently of the need for a new idealism. In Houston, the night before his death, he quoted the Scriptures: *"Where there is no vision, the people perish."*

His words did not reach the pedants. Their hearts were too small to receive a President. But there was hardly an academic cloister — hardly a single coldbed of antihero nonworship — which wasn't primed to sympathize with the wretched waif who was to become his murderer. For every serious fictive work of the past thirty years whose chief character resembled John Kennedy, there have been a hundred whose protagonist was Lee Oswald. "Alas," wrote Thomas Carlyle, "the hero of old has had to cramp himself into strange places; the world knows not well at any time what to do with him, so foreign is his aspect in the world!"

Benjamin Disraeli once told the House of Commons that "a university should be a place of light, of liberty, and of learning." He didn't find it necessary to follow through and define learning. In 1873 everyone knew. Today the world spins on a wobblier axis. In an eclectic age, in an age of flux and elusive shadow — in this age of the darkling plain we are less certain. Society looks at itself and beholds an image like a carnival mirror. With the ardor of a medieval dance craze men from places "of light, of liberty, and of learning" stampede toward the new shibboleths. The highest of all, the glittering prize at the top of the pole, is unconventionality. Some time ago I encountered a singular advertisement in a magazine which enjoys a large circulation among undergraduates. In large letters the headline read, "JOIN THE BEAT GENERATION!" Underneath were instructions on how to join. You merely had to buy one or more items from a list which included "Beat Generation" rings, "Beat Generation" lapel insignia, "Beat Generation" sweatshirts — each with an antic coat of arms on which, among other things, there was a rampant glass of spirits. The implication was clear: Be a nonconformist with the rest of us.

Clearly logic has nothing to do with such fetishes. What is going on here is a highly emotional revolt against all tradition. It has been in progress for quite some time — Dadaism is nearly fifty years old — and now it has reached the Reign of Terror stage; now the revolution is devouring its own. The explanation lies in the shape of twentieth-century history which has, on the whole, been rather depressing. Two great wars, an enervating Depression, and the constant threat that civilization may at any moment be hammered into the earth like a white-hot saucer have weakened faith in traditional authority. Thus many intellectuals — who as a group are far more comfortable with inflexible doctrine than they will concede — have embraced neosophism as revealed religion.

Before the revolt we lived according to an intricate pyramid of values. On the whole it was an unsatisfactory structure: unsound, rigid, and, within, stifling. A novel, for example, had to tell a story; painting and statuary had to be representational, music had to be tuneful. The theater was sterile. In life, deviations from the ideal were ignored; in art they were likely to be suppressed.

Today that pyramid has been inverted. Everything which was, is not; everything which was not, is. A novel which displays any semblance of form is dubious. The photographs which are most admired are taken from odd angles with the lens deliberately out of focus. One of the best ways to study the inversion is to watch the films acclaimed in Cannes. In some of them protest is total. They appear to be about drab people to whom nothing seems to happen — but then, one cannot be certain, because the camera is usually turned in some other direction.

As incoherent as a superstition, the notion that inversion will solve the macerating problems of our time also has a superstition's power. It would be hard to find an American institution free of its spell. Certainly the American home isn't. The dictatorial father of Freud's time is extinct. Once he roamed the land in vast herds, snorting virile snorts and refreshing himself in austere men's clubs walled with fumed oak before thundering home to preside over his cave. In the 1960's he survives as a flaccid parody of his grandfather, a comic figure on televised situation comedies whose cretin blunders are deftly corrected by his amused family. He is cheap household help.

Above all — or perhaps I should say beneath all — lies an implacable enmity toward the concept of excellence which John Kennedy exalted. We are confronted by a gray tide of mediocrity. The myth is current that we are all children of the same gravid earth bitch, that every homo sap is like every other homo sap, that any suggestion otherwise is pretentious, and that every authority is a bugbear. If you acquire a light you must cast about quickly for a bushel. If you receive a Phi Beta Kappa key, or an honorary degree, or a Legion of Honor riband, or any of the bijoux in which people once took pride, you are expected to stow it away in a murky backstair corner. Pride is regarded as primping; as preening.

It naturally follows that the distinctions which separated men from men have become suspect. Instead of leadership we have problem-solving teams. Instead of judges we have referees. Instead of a General-in-Chief (once a venerable title in the American military establishment) we have a Chairman of the Joint Chiefs, and in lieu of grace and style we have the cult of informality, which in some obscure way is regarded as democratic virtue — as though Mirabeau and Tom Paine would have endorsed come-as-you-are barbecues and the aggressive use of nicknames.

Without vision the people perish.

But there is a pendulum, and it swings.

It is a torsion that lies deep in the silent engine of history. It is never at rest, and when it has reached the end of a cycle, when the systolic is ready to replace the diastolic — when the moment of climax has arrived — its own weight reverses it. Then it becomes irresistible, and all the incantations of all the druids in all the Hercynian groves of neosophistry can neither arrest it nor deter it for an instant. The change does not announce itself, but certain individuals can hold the mirror up to the future, and in 1961 such a prescient statesman assumed the Presidency of the United States.

To grasp what he meant, one must first comprehend what he seemed to mean. The two are not at all alike. There is a montage, and we know it well, for in each picture he is the central figure. We see him first as the boy in the splayed-out football helmet, and the athlete in the black silk swimsuit. Next there is a snapshot of the debonair officer posing in the Solomons with a cane and an easy smile, followed by another wartime photograph in which he is being decorated for valor. We watch the young congressman, the young senator, the gay groom; and after his inaugural the images flash by with bewildering speed. In the album of our memory there are thousands of frames of him, striding bareheaded and confident through our lives and into history, and together they create an overwhelming impression of a strapping physique, of boundless health and untapped reservoirs of energy.

But though a man may seem to be larger than life, he's not really. Each of us has his dark star. Even the brightest of us — which he was — is shadowed by another self, the negative that complements the positive print. Throughout life we are in constant dialogue with this other self, sometimes battling it, sometimes losing. It is a measure of this man's stature that he fought these private struggles so successfully that most of his countrymen were unaware there had been any conflict. That victory was a triumph of one man's will. And, indeed, it was a remarkable triumph.

In his lifetime this was poorly understood. Much else about him was misunderstood. For all the millions of words which had been written about him, few saw what he was, and this became startlingly clear in the weekend after his death. Those whose job it is to study Presidents had written that he was too remote from the people, too lacking in folksy charm. Then he was dead, and a million lined the streets of Washington to watch the gun carriage bearing his body pass. The entire world went through a convulsion of grief. And why? Because of his elegance, his self-deprecating wit, his sophistication? That was largely camouflage. He never really admired the irrationalism and mechanism of his time. He remained apart from the ideological style-setters; he declined to join the bland who led the bland. The one illness which never afflicted him was the cloying narcissism which clots the modern idiom. *He* never felt victimized. *He* never felt alienated. That was left to his assassin.

And this is why John Kennedy meant and continues to mean so much to so many. He wrote of valor, believed in heroes, and made his life a monument to that faith. Duty, dedication, and devotion lay at the core of him, and if those words sound quaint the fault lies with us and not with them. "Unless democracy can produce able leaders," he had written at Harvard, "its chances of survival are slight." That thought became his keel, and that was the kind of democracy Paine and Mirabeau would have understood. Ultimately he seemed as the Winged Lion in the Book of Revelations, with six pairs of wings about him and eyes before, behind, and within. It was illusion. He wasn't even especially tall. But he appeared taller because he was reaching, and because he would never stop reaching his grasp became quite extraordinary.

After the agony of November 1963, after the nightmare; after the great coffin had been lowered into the numb Virginia soil and the wound in the earth had been closed and the perpetual light had been left to shine upon the unmending scar; after the public grief (the private grief went on and on, for those whose love has been boundless must endure a boundless anguish); throughout that iron winter and the greening spring some of us were, for a time, literally disabled. All we could do then was mourn and offer his memory our sprig of lilac, hearing in the sleepless night the stutter of the drums on Pennsylvania Avenue, realizing that victory could never ride at his stirrups now, because those stirrups held the reversed boots of the fallen chieftain.

But now, I think, we should recall the vivid hour when he was our champion; pondering what he was, what he meant, what he said — and what he left unsaid, for much of his message was implicit in the staves of his life, and much more was written between the lines. When he told the Germans in Rudolf Wilde Platz, *"Ich bin ein Berliner,"* and *"Lass' sie nach Berlin kommen,"* for example, what he was really saying was, *"Ich bin Bürger der Stadt der Vernunft. Schliesst euch an — und Zahlt euere Steurn"* ("I am a citizen of the city of thought. Follow my lead — and pay your taxes").

The taxes in the city of thought are not coin. They are the act of judgment, the calculated risk, the free assumption of responsibility. They are heavy, they are strenuous — no one knew that better than he did — and they are paid in vain unless they lead to vision. But since the alternative to vision is to perish, since the choice is between payment and extinction, there is no option. We must see that horse recaparisoned and remounted by another champion of thought. We must perceive that no weapon can destroy the gift he gave us, unless we let it. He was stronger than flesh in life, and that strength is still among us, waiting to be invoked. The gift is still here, waiting to be taken. In taking it we can do more than grieve, remembering how much more he would have done — and remembering that the first man to answer the tocsin would have been John Kennedy.

It is the least we can do for him. It is the least we can do for ourselves. And we shall do it, provided we do not for a moment forget the Biblical warning he never lived to deliver to the audience that awaited him in that stricken city of Dallas, Texas:

"Except the Lord keep the city, the watchman waketh but in vain."